A Variorum Commentary on

the Poems of John Milton

MERRITT Y. HUGHES
General Editor

THE COMPLETE SERIES

Volume I

The Latin and Greek Poems
  Douglas Bush

The Italian Poems
  J. E. Shaw and A. Bartlett Giamatti

Volume II

The Minor English Poems
  A. S. P. Woodhouse and Douglas Bush

Volume III

Paradise Lost
  Merritt Y. Hughes

Volume IV

Paradise Regained
  Walter MacKellar

Volume V

Samson Agonistes
  William R. Parker and John M. Steadman

Volume VI

The Prosody of the English Poems
  Edward R. Weismiller

A Variorum Commentary on
The Poems of
John Milton

Volume Two

THE MINOR ENGLISH POEMS

A. S. P. WOODHOUSE *and* DOUGLAS BUSH

Part Two

New York

COLUMBIA UNIVERSITY PRESS

1972

First published 1972 by
Columbia University Press, New York
Copyright © 1972 Columbia University Press
International Standard Book Number: 0 231 08881 7
Library of Congress Catalog Card Number: 70 129962
Printed in Great Britain

Publication of this VARIORUM COMMENTARY
ON THE POEMS OF JOHN MILTON was made possible by funds granted by the Carnegie Corporation
of New York. That Corporation is not, however,
the author, owner, publisher, or proprietor of this
publication, and is not to be understood as
approving by virtue of its grant any of the statements made or views expressed therein.

The Varsity Fund of the University of Toronto
has generously provided, in honor of the late
A. S. P. Woodhouse, additional funds which have
helped to make possible publication of this volume.

Contents

Contents

ABBREVIATIONS FOR THE TITLES
OF MILTON'S WRITINGS

Variorum Commentary		Columbia *Works*
Acced	Accedence Commenc't Grammar	G
AddCM	Additional Correspondence and Marginalia	ACM
AddCorr	Additional Correspondence	AC
Animad	Animadversions upon the Remonstrants Defence	A
Apol	An Apology against a Pamphlet	AP
Arc	Arcades	ARC
Areop	Areopagitica	AR
Asclep	'Asclepiads' (called 'Choriambics,' *Works* 1, 327)	
BrNotes	Brief Notes upon a late Sermon	BN or N
Bucer	The Judgement of Martin Bucer, concerning Divorce	M
CarEl	Carmina Elegiaca	CE
Carrier 1, 2	On the University Carrier; Another on the same	UC
CharLP	Milton's Character of the Long Parliament	TC
Circum	Upon the Circumcision	CI
CivP	A Treatise of Civil power	CP
Colas	Colasterion	C
ComBk	Commonplace Book	CB
Comus	Comus	CO
DDD	The Doctrine and Discipline of Divorce	D. and D.

Abbreviations: Titles of Milton's Writings

Variorum Commentary		Columbia Works
DecDut	Declaration against the Dutch	DEC
Def 1	Pro Populo Anglicano Defensio (First Defence of the English People)	1D
Def 2	Pro Populo Anglicano Defensio Secunda (Second Defence)	2D
Defpro Se	Pro Se Defensio	SD
DocCh	De Doctrina Christiana	CD
EC	English Correspondence	EC
Educ	Of Education	E
EffSc	In Effigiei Eius Sculptorem	IEE
Eikon	Eikonoklastes	K
El 1, &c.	Elegia 1, &c.	EL
Eli	In obitum Praesulis Eliensis	PE
EpDam	Epitaphium Damonis	ED
Epistol	Familiar Letters of Milton	FE
EProl	Early Prolusion by Milton	EP
EpWin	Epitaph on the Marchioness of Winchester	EM
FInf	On the Death of a fair Infant	I
Hirelings	Considerations touching The likeliest means to remove Hirelings out of the church	H
HistBr	History of Britain	B
HistMosc	Brief History of Moscovia	HM
Hor	Fifth Ode of Horace	HOR
Idea	De Idea Platonica	IPA
IlPen	Il Penseroso	IP

Abbreviations: Titles of Milton's Writings

Variorum Commentary		Columbia Works
InvBom	In inventorem Bombardae	IB
L'All	L'Allegro	L'A
Leon 1, &c.	Ad Leonoram Romae canentem	LR
LetFr	Letter to a Friend	LF
LetMonk	Letter to General Monk	LM
LetPat	A Declaration or Letters Patents of the Election of this Present King of Poland	LP
Log	Art of Logic	LO
Lyc	Lycidas	L
Mansus	Mansus	MA
Mar	Marginalia	MAR
May	Song. On May Morning	MM
MC	Miscellaneous Correspondence	MC
Nat	On the Morning of Christ's Nativity	N
Naturam	Naturam non pati senium	NS
NewF	On the new forcers of Conscience	FC
OAP	Observations on the Articles of Peace	O
Passion	The Passion	PA
Patrem	Ad Patrem	ADP
PE	Of Prelatical Episcopacy	P
PhilReg	Philosophus ad Regem	PAR
PL	Paradise Lost	PL
PR	Paradise Regain'd	PR
Procan	In obitum Procancellarii medici	PM
ProdBom 1, &c.	In Proditionem Bombardicam 1, &c.	PB

Abbreviations: Titles of Milton's Writings

Variorum Commentary		Columbia Works
Prol 1, &c.	Prolusions 1, &c.	PO
Propos	Proposalls of Certaine Expedients for the Preventing of a Civill War Now Feard	PRO
Ps 1, &c.	Psalms 1, &c.	PS
QNov	In quintum Novembris	QN
RCG	The Reason of Church-governement Urg'd against Prelaty	CG
Ref	Of Reformation Touching Church-Discipline in England	R
REW	The Readie & Easie Way to Establish a Free Commonwealth	W
Rous	Ad Joannem Rousium	JR
RH	Apologus de Rustico et Hero	RH
SA	Samson Agonistes	SA
Salmas 1, &c.	On Salmasius 1, &c.	
Sals	Ad Salsillum poetam Romanum	AS
Shak	On Shakespear. 1630	SH
SolMus	At a solemn Musick	SM
Sonn 1, &c.	Sonnet 1, &c.	S
Tetr	Tetrachordon	T
Time	On Time	TI
TKM	The Tenure of Kings and Magistrates	TE
TR	Of True Religion, Haeresie, Schism, Toleration	TR
Vac	At a Vacation Exercise in the Colledge	V

ABBREVIATIONS FOR TITLES OF PERIODICALS, ETC.

AJP   *American Journal of Philology*
AN&Q   *American Notes and Queries*
CL   *Comparative Literature*
ELH   *Journal of English Literary History*
ELN   *English Language Notes*
ES   *English Studies*
Essays and Studies   *Essays and Studies by Members of the English Association*
Explic.   *The Explicator*
Facs.   Vol. 1 of H. F. Fletcher's facsimile ed. (see Index, under Milton)
HLQ   *Huntington Library Quarterly*
JEGP   *Journal of English and Germanic Philology*
JHI   *Journal of the History of Ideas*
JWCI   *Journal of the Warburg and Courtauld Institutes*
MiltonN   *Milton Newsletter* (1970 f., *Milton Quarterly*)
MLN   *Modern Language Notes*
MLQ   *Modern Language Quarterly*
MLR   *Modern Language Review*
MP   *Modern Philology*
N&Q   *Notes and Queries*
PBSA   *Papers of the Bibliographical Society of America*
PMLA   *Publications of the Modern Language Association of America*
PQ   *Philological Quarterly*
RES   *Review of English Studies*
SCN   *Seventeenth-Century News*
SEL   *Studies in English Literature*
SB   *Studies in Bibliography*
SP   *Studies in Philology*
TLS   [London] *Times Literary Supplement*
TSLL   *Texas Studies in Literature and Language*
UTQ   *University of Toronto Quarterly*
V.C.   *Variorum Commentary*

Sonnets

I. TEXTS AND CHRONOLOGY

Milton's twenty-four sonnets were written over a period of 28 or 30 years. 'O Nightingale' and the five Italian sonnets (with the *Canzone*) have been assigned to 1628–30 [Honigmann's recent dissent is recorded at the end of this section], and *Sonnet* 7 ('How soon hath time') to Milton's twenty-fourth birthday, 1632. The other sonnets were spread over the years 1642–58 (if we accept 1658 for 'Methought I saw'). Some of these Milton dated himself; most others can be conjecturally dated within fairly close limits that have been generally agreed upon. 'O Nightingale,' the Italian sonnets, and the English sonnets 7–10 ('How soon hath time'; 'Captain or Colonel'; 'Lady that in the prime'; and 'Daughter to that good Earl') were included in the *Poems* of 1645 and reprinted in the second edition of 1673. This second edition added ten sonnets (in the numbering of the Columbia *Works*: 11–14, 18–21, 23, and the unnumbered *On the new forcers of Conscience*). Four others (*Works*: 15, to Fairfax; 16, to Cromwell; 17, to Vane; 22, 'Cyriack, this three years day') were excluded, presumably for political reasons. Particulars about dates and circumstances of all the sonnets are given in the individual headnotes. [A compendious summary of such material is given, along with much annotation, in E. S. Le Comte, *A Milton Dictionary* (New York, 1961), 299–312.]

[Of these 24 sonnets 13 appear, in one or more versions, in the Cambridge MS. It may be convenient to have these listed, with their page numbers in vol. 1 (1943) of H. F. Fletcher's Facsimile edition of Milton's complete poetical works, in the numbering of the Columbia edition:

7. 'How soon hath Time,' as quoted in Milton's Letter to a Friend (388).   8. 'Captain or Colonel' (396).   9. 'Lady that in the prime' (396).

10. 'Daughter to that good Earl' (396).   11. 'A Book was writ of late' (two texts, 450, 452).   12. 'I did but prompt the age' (2 texts, 444, 450). 13. *To Mr. H. Lawes, on his Aires* (3 texts, 444, 448).   14. 'When Faith and Love' (3 texts, 446, 448).   15. 'Fairfax, whose name in armes' (452). 16. 'Cromwell, our cheif of men' (452).   17. 'Vane, young in yeares' (454).   23. 'Methought I saw' (388). *On the new forcers of Conscience* (454).

A number of the sonnets in the MS. have titles which were not used in the printed editions and these give useful clues to persons or circumstances. The general value of the MS. is, as usual, that it shows the author in the process of composition and revision and supplies a check on the printed versions.]

D. H. Stevens ('The Order of Milton's Sonnets,' *MP* 17, 1919–20, 25–33) concluded that the numbering of the sonnets in the Cambridge MS., with the direction for printing *On the new forcers*, gives us the order in which Milton intended them to be printed, that whenever it can be tested by other evidence this order is seen to be strictly chronological, and that whenever the 1673 edition deviates (as in reversing the order of 11 and 12 and isolating *On the new forcers*), it is due to the evident carelessness and confusion of that edition. J. H. Hanford ('The Arrangement and Dates of Milton's Sonnets,' *MP* 18, 1920–1, 475–83) put more confidence in the 1673 order and examined both the MS. itself and internal evidence in supporting or opposing Stevens' conclusions regarding particular dates. J. S. Smart (*Sonnets of Milton*, Glasgow, 1921; repr., Oxford, 1966) was little concerned with the MS. but gave his attention to internal and external evidence in regard to individual sonnets, a majority of which can be satisfactorily dated on such evidence. We may, then, accept the assumption that the order indicated in the MS. is chronological in its general intention and is strictly chronological in all cases where no cogent evidence can be adduced against its being so.

[M. Kelley ('Milton's Later Sonnets and the Cambridge Manuscript,' *MP* 54, 1956–7, 20–5), starting from the sonnets that were or can be certainly dated, sees clear evidence 'that in the Cambridge Manuscript Milton's numbers indicate the order in which he composed his later sonnets.' Three sonnets which do not now appear in the MS.—*On the late Massacher*, 'When I consider,' and 'Lawrence'—were printed in 1673 under the numbers 15, 16, and 17. That edition omitted, for political reasons, the sonnets to Fairfax, Cromwell, and Vane. 'If we allow for this omission by adding 3 to the three 1673 numbers and take the 1673 order as the order of composition, then we may conclude that Milton originally numbered "On the late Massacher" 18, "When I consider" 19, and "Lawrence of vertuous Father" 20.' Kelley argues that the MS. once contained transcripts of all the later sonnets. The argument is too complex for summary. Kelley's conclusions about the disputed dates of *Sonnets* 19 and 23—his special concern—are given in the headnotes to those poems.

In his *Milton's Sonnets* (London and New York, 1966), the first elaborate edition since Smart's, E. A. J. Honigmann (59-75) opposes Kelley's argument for strict chronological sequence; like most scholars, he accepts chronology as the general principle of arrangement, but one modified on occasion by other considerations, especially theme or atmosphere (see Honigmann in 11 below, and introductions, below, to *Sonnets* 1, 8, 19, 20, 22). On one point, the dating of the Italian poems (which does not directly concern us), Honigmann questions the modern consensus, beginning with Smart, which puts these pieces somewhere in 1628-30; he returns to the old view that they were written in 1638, during Milton's sojourn in Italy, but his arguments may be thought unconvincing. In spite of this dating, he sees (67) Milton's first English sonnet (which he dates in 1629) 'as an introduction to the Italian poems,' and the last Italian sonnet as linked 'quite naturally with the second English sonnet' ('How soon hath time') of 1632.

Parker (746-8) says that, 'since the sonnets form a distinct group' in 1645 and 1673, 'they almost certainly have a chronology of their own.... Nearly every sonnet which can be dated with confidence is in correct chronological order, and so we may reasonably assume that Milton *attempted* thus to arrange them. A possible exception or two need not disturb this inference, because a poet's memory may occasionally be less certain than his intentions.' Parker's views on the dating of some later sonnets are given below in the respective headnotes. He would conjecturally assign *Sonnet* 1 to April or May, 1629, soon after *Elegy* 5, and the Italian poems to 1630.]

II. CRITICISM [D.B.]

Milton's sonnets fall into two main groups, public and private (a few might be called both), and within each group sonnets may, in keeping with decorum, display kinship or wide variations in style as in theme. The public sonnets range from the mainly journalistic colloquialism of the two on the reception of the tracts on divorce to the sublime imprecation, 'Avenge O Lord thy slaughter'd Saints.' The private sonnets range from invitations to young friends for lunch and talk to Milton's vision of his dead wife. In his first English sonnet and the five Italian ones the young poet paid his tribute to the amatory tradition which since Petrarch had largely dominated European sonneteering and had inspired the Elizabethan sequences. 'How soon hath time' was the first of Milton's personal stocktakings, an earnest dedication of his talents to God's service; later renewals of that pledge were the two sonnets on his blindness. Other personal sonnets, on the middle level of sobriety or geniality, were admiring or hospitable addresses to friends. If such sonnets, at once informal and dignified, recall the Horace of the Sabine farm, the fervent and exalted sonnets on public men and events recall the spirit, though not of course the form, of Horace's prophetic and admonitory odes on the state of Rome and Italy. Both strains in Milton have been fully explored by John Finley ('Milton and Horace: A Study of Milton's Sonnets,' *Harvard Studies in Classical Philology* 48, 1937, 29–73), who is often quoted in the notes below.

While the successive editors of Milton's poems, notably Masson, and Pattison in his edition of the sonnets (1883) brought together considerable material, J. S. Smart's edition of the sonnets (1921) added a great deal, especially in regard to some of the persons addressed and the occasion and circumstances of both private and public sonnets. On the critical side, Smart also placed Milton's sonnets more accurately in the

European tradition. As everyone knows, the Elizabethans had used variations of the English pattern introduced by Wyatt and Surrey (three quatrains and a couplet), which invited a development of the theme quite different from that of the Italian pattern (an octave of two quatrains and a sestet of two tercets). It was natural that Milton, whose attachment to things Italian his Italian sonnets early demonstrated, should adopt the Italian scheme. But he was charged by Pattison and others with rough disregard of the correct Italian technique. These charges, said Smart (26), lie 'not in the arrangement of the rimes, but in the relation of the lines to the sentences. In a typical Italian sonnet... the statement of ideas harmonises with the division of the poem into quatrains and tercets.... The pauses required by the sense occur with almost perfect regularity at the ends of lines, a complete break anywhere inside a line being avoided.' This method 'is irreproachably observed' in 'How soon hath time,' 'Captain or Colonel,' the sonnets addressed to Lady Margaret Ley and Fairfax, and the first one addressed to Cyriack Skinner. But in the sonnets to Vane, Cromwell, and Lawrence, on the Piedmont massacre, on his blindness, and his dead wife, Milton's divisions of sense do not conform to lines, quatrains, or tercets, and pauses or full stops occur within the lines. Such evidently deliberate violations of the supposed rules may, in spite of the formal divisions and the patterns of rhymes, convert sonnets into solid units, in effect almost paragraphs of blank verse akin to those of *Paradise Lost*.

Whereas a number of nineteenth-century English critics formulated a code of rules which had no real basis in Italian practice, Smart found ample historical support for Milton's procedure in a mass of sonnets written by Italians after Petrarch. One conspicuous rebel was Giovanni della Casa (1503–56), who 'deliberately broke with the Petrarchian tradition of regularity and smoothness,' and whose sonnets display the licences Milton exploited. The resemblance, Smart notes, was observed in 1846 by James Glassford, but was not followed up, he seems to imply, because of the prejudice in favour of strict and even quite factitious rules. Smart recorded the fact that in December 1629 Milton acquired a copy of Della Casa's *Rime et Prose*; the volume containing this, along with

Dante's *Amoroso Convivio* and Benedetto Varchi's *Sonetti*, is now in the New York Public Library (Parker, 749, n. 14).

Smart also corrected the conventional view of Milton's subject matter, the notion that it was he who 'emancipated the sonnet' from the bondage of the single theme of love. One famous emancipator was Tasso, whose three bodies of sonnets comprise 419 on love, 486 on heroical themes, and 87 sacred and moral pieces; and Tasso was one of Milton's favourite poets. Even in England the sonnet had not been entirely confined to love, either in the sixteenth century or in the likewise copious output of the early seventeenth. 'Milton's position among the writers of the sonnet is not due to any sudden breaking away from an outworn convention. It is due to his greatness as a poet, the wide compass of his powers, the extent of his reading, his many-sided character, and his interest in life, literature, society, politics and religion' (Smart, 42). Further, Milton 'was free from the two marked failings of earlier English sonneteers—indiscriminate borrowing and self-repetition.' And, in spite of his learning, he was not a bookish imitator; his inspiration always comes from 'the immediately real event.' Dr. Johnson was wrong about the sonnets as about most things Miltonic: 'Milton...was a genius that could cut a Colossus from a rock; but could not carve heads upon cherry-stones' (*Boswell's Life of Johnson*, ed. G. B. Hill and L. F. Powell, Oxford, 1934, 4, 305). No one else has connected Milton's sonnets with cherry-stones; even those in which he is most relaxed are massive.

A few general comments, old and modern, may be included here.

Samuel Johnson (*Lives*, ed. Hill, 1, 169–70): 'The *Sonnets* were written in different parts of his life upon different occasions. They deserve not any particular criticism; for of the best it can only be said that they are not bad, and perhaps only the eighth and the twenty-first are truly entitled to this slender commendation. The fabrick of a sonnet, however adapted to the Italian language, has never succeeded in ours, which, having greater variety of termination, requires the rhymes to be often changed.'

William Wordsworth, to an unknown correspondent, November 1802 (*The Early Letters of William and Dorothy Wordsworth (1787–1805)*, ed. Ernest de Selincourt, Oxford, 1935, 312):

'Milton's Sonnets...I think manly and dignified compositions, distinguished by simplicity and unity of object and aim, and undisfigured by false or vicious ornaments. They are in several places incorrect, and sometimes uncouth in language, and, perhaps, in some, inharmonious; yet, upon the whole, I think the music exceedingly well suited to its end, that is, it has an energetic and varied flow of sound crowding into narrow room more of the combined effect of rhyme and blank verse than can be done by any other kind of verse I know of. The Sonnets of Milton which I like best are that to *Cyriack Skinner*; on his *Blindness*; *Captain or Colonel*; *Massacre of Piedmont*; *Cromwell*, except two last lines; *Fairfax*, &c.'

Wordsworth, letter to A. Dyce ('? spring, 1833'), *Letters of William and Dorothy Wordsworth: The Later Years*, ed. E. de Selincourt (3 v., Oxford, 1939), 2, 653:

'Milton, however, has not submitted to this [the Italian pattern of octave and sestet]. In the better half of his sonnets the sense does not close with the rhyme at the eighth line, but overflows into the second portion of the metre. Now it has struck me, that this is not done merely to gratify the ear by variety and freedom of sound, but also to aid in giving that pervading sense of intense Unity in which the excellence of the Sonnet has always seemed to me mainly to consist. Instead of looking at this composition as a piece of architecture, making a whole out of three parts, I have been much in the habit of preferring the image of an orbicular body,—a sphere—or a dew-drop. All this will appear to you a little fanciful. . . .'

There is no need of quoting Wordsworth's 'Milton! thou shouldst be living at this hour,' or his tribute in 'Scorn not the Sonnet.' His account of being stirred to emulation is given in his *Poetical Works*, ed. E. de Selincourt and H. Darbishire (5 v., Oxford, 1940–9), 3, 417.

Hazlitt ('On Milton's Sonnets,' *New Monthly Magazine*, March 1822; *Table-Talk*, 18; *Works*, ed. Howe, 8, 174–81)—whose notoriously low opinion of Shakespeare's sonnets is avowed here—prized Milton's because 'they have more...personal and internal character than any others'; they may perhaps 'be said to be almost the first effusions of this sort of natural and personal sentiment in the language.' 'The Sonnets are a kind of pensive record of past achievements, loves, and friendships, and a noble exhortation to himself to bear up with cheerful hope and confidence to the last.' 'The beauty of Milton's Sonnets is their sincerity, the spirit of poetical patriotism which they breathe'; Wordsworth has not Milton's 'high and various imagination, nor his deep and fixed principle.' Milton 'had taken his part boldly and stood to it manfully, and submitted to the change of times with pious fortitude, building his consolations on the resources of his own mind and the recollection of the past, instead of endeavouring to make himself a retreat for the time to come.' The sonnets to Cromwell, Fairfax, and Vane 'are full of exalted praise and dignified advice,' 'neither familiar nor servile.' 'He pays the full tribute of admiration for great acts atchieved, and suggests becoming occasion to deserve higher praise.' 'The most spirited and impassioned of them all, and the most inspired with a sort of prophetic fury,' is the one on the massacre in Piedmont. In *Sonnet* 19 'we see the jealous watchfulness of his mind over the use of his high gifts, and the beautiful manner in which he satisfies himself that virtuous thoughts and intentions are not the least acceptable offering to the Almighty.' The sonnets to Lawes and Lawrence 'breathe the very soul of music and friendship.' In the last sonnet 'the rare union' of classical allusion and personal experience gives 'voluptuous dignity and touching purity to Milton's delineation of the female character.' The whole tenor of Milton's smaller compositions contradicts the notion that he 'only shone on great subjects' and could not adorn the ordinary occasions of familiar life and harmless pleasure.

Robert Bridges (*Poems of John Keats*, ed. G. Thorn Drury, London, 1896, lxx–lxxi) observed that 'Horace elaborated a form of ode which is easier to recognise than in few words describe; and a number of Milton's sonnets may be referred to this ode form. If we compare, for example, his *Cyriack, whose grandsire*, with *Martiis coelebs* [3. 8] or *Æli vetusto* [3. 17], there can be no doubt that Milton was here deliberately using the sonnet form to do the work of Horace's tight stanzas; and not the whole of Shakespeare's or Petrarch's sonnets set alongside will show enough kinship with these sonnets of Milton to draw them away from their affinity with Horace. Such sonnets, too, as his addresses to Vane, Fairfax, and Cromwell are properly odes, and should be called odes, or at least odic sonnets.'

In a 'Note on the Sonnets of Milton' (*Life and Letters*, 64, 1950, 165–9), Peter Hellings remarks that the sonnets reflect Milton's habit of writing poetry 'only on subjects which implied the themes his whole spiritual being was constructed around. The themes of the sonnets re-echo or foreshadow those dominant elsewhere: nature, the dedicated life, the power of poetry, virtue, wisdom before freedom, music, conviviality, blindness, marriage, and the state of the nation.' In them he is also working toward the grand style of the projected epic. Even as early as the *Vacation Exercise* he had shown his '*choice* of a grand manner for a specific purpose, the importance he attached to sound, and the pressure of sense.' Everywhere his concern is 'that the sound should be appropriate to the general matter.' Thus

in the sonnets the complexity of his 'grand' manner is applied only to those subjects where it seems fitting: those on *Cromwell, Vane, the Massacre*, and the first sonnet on his blindness (the second, it is worth noting, has affinities with the tone and imagery of *Samson*). In *Vane* there is in the structure a deliberate reflection of the bewildering complexity Vane has mastered. In *Cromwell* the relentless verse movement finds its climax in 'Worster's laureat wreath', to be followed by a pause and the quietly impressive statement 'yet much remains To conquer still'. But this is not allowed to remain generalized statement, and by the introduction of a particular example with its attendant emotion the generalization grows into the plea of the final couplet....

Milton's greatness as a sonneteer lies in his breaking through the Petrarchan rules. In contrast to most sonneteers, he 'knew as exactly as any poet can know, what he wanted to say, or more precisely, the effect he wished to create, and...anticipating modern practice, he deliberately distorted the syntactical aspect of language for the sake of emotional and imaginative power.'

As for the complaint of Eliot and others that Milton deserted the tradition of conversational language, 'even the tone and rhythm of conversation...are present in a number of those sonnets not constructed in the "grand" manner. These give them their restraint and sincerity.' Milton's sentences come to a natural end, they are not forced into a Petrarchan straitjacket. Indeed, his 'inversions, ellipses, involutions, delayed verbs, are elaborations of precisely the things we do in speech under certain compulsions—excitement, passion, or for dramatic effect.' The quiet sonnet to Lady Margaret Ley, which opens and closes 'on a conversational note,...is yet beautifully divided into half by the employment in the second quatrain of the "grand" manner, and the whole is welded into one continuous sentence.' Here 'not only is the verse movement of the middle section a climax of great power, but the use of Chaeronea, for sound and association, is one of the most effective "placings" of a name in the whole of Milton's work.' In general, 'Milton, more consciously perhaps than anyone else, exploited not so much speech rhythms as speech *habits* in the sonnets; and it may be from these that the later variety and richness of the "grand" manner originates.'

In his valuable *Italian Element in Milton's Verse* (1954), F. T. Prince, like Smart, sees the style of Milton's sonnets as a large step toward his epic manner, and, accepting the general validity of Smart's short account, he gives a much fuller and more precise analysis of the more or less classicist theory and practice of Bembo, Della Casa, and Tasso, and of the effects of Italian influence on Milton. 'Della Casa's contribution to the formation of the Italian idea of the "magnificent" style was of fundamental importance; and this was the style that, described and applied by Tasso, was recreated in his own language by Milton....Milton is indebted to Della Casa not only indirectly, through his greater successor, but directly: Milton's sonnets show that he took as his prime models the sonnets of Della Casa and not the less polished imitations of them produced by Tasso in his *Heroic Sonnets*' (3). The 'magnificent' style was to be achieved, not through clarity, regularity, and smoothness, but through complexity and difficulty: some main devices used to that end were distortion of the natural order of words, Latinate diction, the employment of long phrases and clauses that suspended the sense, the placing of strong pauses within the line, and the deliberate accumulation of elisions (14, 21–8). Such aims required a new conception of 'decorum.'

'The "Petrarchian stanza", as Milton calls it, is the only fixed form from Italian poetry which he continued to use after the early experiment of the lines *Upon the Circumcision*....He was able to remain faithful to the fixed pattern of the sonnet only because the particular tradition of Italian sonnet-writing he followed allowed a deliberate modification of its stanzaic character' (89). Prince's comments on *Sonnets* 1 and 7 are excerpted in the critical headnotes to those pieces. On the main body of sonnets of 1642–58 he makes general and specific comments. In these 'the complexity of the word-order and the development of the rhythm ...for the first time approach the diction and rhythm of the epics; and it seems clear that for Milton these occasional poems were closely related to the conception of style which he was holding in reserve for his great work.

'The sonnets are therefore essays, on a small scale, in the "magnificent" style; and Milton confines his topics to such as could appropriately be presented in this stately garb. Certainly, if the majority of his sonnets are on religious or political themes, the proper field of heroic verse, a few may be distinguished as verging upon the mock-heroic: the more intimate, and particularly the convivial invitations to his young pupils, have the Horatian quality of something approaching self-parody. The controversial sonnets also turn the stiff difficulty of the verse, the *asprezza* of the "magnificent" style, to a mocking purpose.

'All this is sufficiently personal, and indeed the force of Milton's sonnets consists essentially in their springing (like *Lycidas*) out of immediate and intense circumstances. Yet enough has been said of the Renaissance tradition which they follow to make it clear how closely they adhere to that formal heritage. Milton thinks only of himself and of his subject; but his poetry follows Della Casa, in so far as it is based upon a complete identity of principles. It is scarcely worth the trouble to single out small tricks of style, detailed verbal resemblances, or resemblances of movement, when these affinities are due to the deeper kinship of mood and manner' (103–4). Prince would emphasize more than Smart did 'the complexity of the word-order: not only for its own predominant function in the beauty of the poems, but for its derivation from the Italian tradition.' 'It is the artificiality of the word-order' that 'alone makes possible the continuous interplay of the expected and the unexpected, the transformation of occasional verse into singular and vivid poetry' (104). Thus 'if we "normalize" the word-order in a sonnet by Milton (or suspend our response to the music and movement of the language) there seems little left to admire. Yet the underlying prose-quality often to be detected in the sonnets is as much a source of strength as of weakness; it is just the way in which this rational plainness, this solidity, become poetic, that may excite most admiration' (104–5).

Taylor Stoehr ('Syntax and Poetic Form in Milton's Sonnets,' *English Studies* 45, 1964, 289–301) is quoted below, in regard to *Sonnets* 7, 16, 18, 19, 23.

David V. Harrington ('Feeling and Form in Milton's Sonnets,' *Western Humanities Review* 20, 1966, 317–28) thinks that autobiographical and topical interest has blurred the usual estimate of the sonnets; he would apply objective aesthetic criteria, especially concreteness of imagery and prosodic mastery. He finds *Sonnet* 1 a conventional demonstration of skill; *Sonnet* 7 dependent mainly on 'the force of the poet's personality'; *Sonnet* 11 ('A book was writ') a decided success in its own vein of decorum; *Sonnet* 14 (on Mrs Thomason) a made-to-order tissue of pieties and personifications; the sonnet to Cromwell alive largely in its topicality and that to Fairfax a piece of 'rhyming, metrical prose'; *Sonnet* 18 (Piedmont) a forceful burst of deep and impersonal feeling; and *Sonnet* 23 ('Methought I saw') a concrete and imaginative expression of loneliness. The more famous sonnet on Milton's blindness is more universal and objective than the one addressed to Skinner. The critic's concern with feeling controlled by form results, more often than not, in agreement with general opinion, but his brief appraisals are hardly adequate.

Going on from Smart, Prince, and others, Honigmann (*Milton's Sonnets*, 1966, 31–53) emphasizes, with detailed illustration, the topicality of the sonnets and thematic parallels and contrasts which help to unify a single sonnet or to link sonnets with one another. We may notice first his more general remarks on structure and classification (41–3). 'Whereas Petrarch and his early imitators divided the sonnet into four parts, two quatrains (the octave) and two tercets (the sestet), and made the syntax dependent on these divisions, with a pause after each one, Della Casa dissociated syntax and metrics by means of *enjambement*.

'Milton copied both Italian types, not infrequently tending towards the Petrarchan, or something very like it, when the subject demanded gracefulness (e.g. X, XIII and XIV), but preferring the method of Della Casa when he strove for the sublime (e.g. XVI, XVIII and XIX). Both gave play to characteristic Miltonic styles, practised by him in other poems over a large span of years.' Whichever mode he uses, Milton's 'sentences are always so perfectly articulated' that, with all 'their finely chiselled effects,' they do flow; e.g. 'When I consider' 'differs in its fluency from the typical Elizabethan sonnet, which moves forward from point to point, in that it possesses a controlling centre' (41).

Honigmann (42–3) would somewhat modify Smart's 'demolition' of the supposed Italian principle of a pause or turn after the second quatrain. This was employed by Italian sonneteers often enough to amount to a principle, and Milton understood and followed it strictly in *Sonnets* 7, 10, 13, 15, and 20; in 11, 16, 17, 19, and 23 he also made a sharp turn, but in the eighth, ninth, or tenth line.

Another structural device is 'the thought that turns back upon itself in the concluding lines,' either openly or subtly (43–5). Honigmann's comments on this feature are recorded in notes on 7. 14, 9. 13, 11. 12–14, 18. 11, 19. 14, 20. 13–14, 21. 9–14, 23. 14. [Cf. also 17. 13–14.]

Within the general division of public and private sonnets there are subdivisions, some of them related to other genres (45 f.). Three public sonnets of praise (15–17: Fairfax, Cromwell, Vane) go with such more or less private sonnets of praise as 9, 10, 13 ('Lady that in the prime'; Lady Margaret Ley; Henry Lawes). Three (14, 18, 23: Mrs Thomason; Piedmont; Mrs Milton) commemorate the dead. 'The *execration* or *vituperation* could follow the pattern of the praise, pouring scorn on the subject's ancestors, listing his follies or vices...' (50), and for these decorum prescribed a colloquial style: 'In these three poems [11, 12, *New forcers*] we come close to the classical epigram, from which the sonnet is sometimes said to originate.'

Among Milton's very diverse themes, the most conspicuous one is freedom of conscience, which links together *Sonnets* 11–12, 15–18, and *New forcers* (Honigmann, 34–8). In regard to the various thematic links he has some more or less new observations (65–74), sometimes suggestive and convincing, sometimes rather strained. Some groupings of sonnets have long been obvious: 9 and 10; 11 and 12; 15–17; 20–2; but there are links also between 1 and 2; 6 and 7; 12 and 13; 13 and 14; and others. Some of these discussions may be more usefully noticed in connection with individual sonnets, but one representative and compendious paragraph may be quoted here (69):

'Sonnet VIII follows on from VII in presenting a poet more assured of his powers but still very much preoccupied with this subject. In both VIII and IX the poet applauds *pity and ruth* and deprecates *anger*: and no doubt *deed of honour* and *gentle acts* (VIII. 3, 6) are to be compared with the virtuous young lady's more admirable *deeds of light* (IX. 10). Liberty, the cardinal theme in XI, makes a preliminary appearance in X, and in both poems love of liberty implies love of goodness. Sonnets XIV and XV immortalise *firm unshak'n vertue*, in a woman meekly living a private life, and in a soldier very much in the public eye. Fairfax's *name in armes through Europe rings*: Mrs Thomason's good works *spake the truth of thee in glorious Theams | Before the Judge*. The generosity of the one is rewarded with *azure wings*, the other has to combat *serpent wings*, *Fraud*, *Avarice* and *Rapine*—a contrast, surely, of two kinds of Christian warrior.'

Honigmann concludes (70) that, while of course Milton never thought of a sonnet sequence, there are so many general and particular parallels in idea and detail that these occasional sonnets do cohere far more closely than critics have realized. This coherence is due chiefly to the strong presence of Milton everywhere. The sonnets 'as a series reflect his personality more vividly than any other single work—comparing in this, on a slightly reduced scale, with Horace's *Odes*. Praising or dispraising,

Milton usually makes us conscious of two ways of life, one of them his own. . . . Indeed, Milton seems obsessed by the struggles of virtue towards self-fulfilment. . . . In short, we are made to feel that the poet cannot escape certain all-important ideas, because he identifies himself with them so completely. And, of course, Milton's very style reinforces this impression of his self-concentration and of his personal and continuous presence, just as it does in *Paradise Lost*, where it acted similarly as a unifying device.' Further, the omission of the manuscript titles, with 'three understandable exceptions' (12, 13, 18) 'plays down the occasional nature of the poems' and 'the numbers strengthen the impression of continuity. Read through as a numbered series the sonnets chronicle one man's reactions to the events and individuals of his time, one man's self-exploration and exploration of values, he, the poet, remaining the common factor and a rival centre of interest even when the ostensible subject is a nightingale or Oliver Cromwell.' (72)

Sonnet 1 *(O Nightingale)*

꿎

I. DATE

In the *Poems* the English *Sonnet* 1 is followed by *Sonnets* 2–6 and a *Canzone*, in Italian. It is generally agreed that these pieces are associated in theme and in date, but the date is a matter of inference and depends partly on a reading of Milton's early development. Tillyard (*Milton*, 1930, 43 f.) placed the whole group after *The Passion* in 1630, and found in *Sonnet* 3. 13–14 an allusion to the failure of that poem (372). Hanford ('Youth,' 1925, 119–21) associated *Sonnet* 1 (and *May Morning*) with *Elegy* 5 in May 1629, and had the Italian poems follow immediately, the whole Petrarchan phase being closed by 'the winter of 1629–30.' Hanford's desire was to make the chronology conform to the development suggested by Milton's retrospective account in the *Apology* (*Works* 3, 302–6) of his changing interests and attitudes; these he read as the abandonment of amatory Ovidianism for the more idealized treatment of love and beauty practised by Dante and Petrarch, and this in turn for a wholehearted dedication to religious poetry. The difficulty of this injecting of the Petrarchan phase between *Elegy* 5 and the *Nativity* (with *Elegy* 6) is attested by awkward overlapping at the beginning and at the end. It is of course possible that to *Elegy* 5 and *May Morning* Milton added a third May-time poem, *Sonnet* 1, which is Petrarchan in form, but there is an extreme disparity between the buoyant and affirmative tone of *Elegy* 5 and *May Morning* and that of the *Sonnet*. *Sonnets* 1–6 have the appearance of a temporary retreat to secular and erotic verse and associate themselves more readily with the failure of *The Passion* than with the success of the *Nativity*. Accordingly they are here tentatively assigned to 1630. *Sonnet* 1, as the last of Milton's May-time poems, was written, not unnaturally, with the earlier *Elegy* 5 in mind; though

354

utterly different in mood, the *Elegy* indicates a mind receptive to thoughts of love and is thus a fitting prelude to the Italian poems and to whatever experience, real or imaginary, lay behind them.

[In his edition (1953) Hanford dated *Sonnets* 1–6 in '1628?'. Hughes assigns the group to 1630. J. Carey (*RES* 14, 1963, 383–6) takes the much discussed last lines of *Elegy* 6, in particular the phrase *patriis...cicutis*, to refer to poems Milton had written, not in his own, but in Diodati's, native language, Italian. This interpretation would place the Italian poems not long before the *Nativity* of Christmas 1629 (see the note on Milton's *Elegy* 6. 89). According to the general principle of chronological order, *Sonnet* 1 presumably preceded the Italian poems, with which it is commonly linked because of its theme and tone; it is of course a spring-time poem. Thus opinions range within the years 1628–30. Honigmann dates *Sonnet* 1 in 1629, although (as we observed in the general introduction above) he puts the Italian poems in 1638 and sees *Sonnet* 1 as an introduction to them (see the end of II below). As we have noted, Parker (746–8) would put *Sonnet* 1 in the spring of 1629, soon after *Elegy* 5, the Italian poems in 1630 (755, n. 36, where he cites Carey's article). Seeing in *cicutis* (*El* 6. 89: see Carey above) a pastoral implication, Parker (747) asks if we should move *Arcades* or *L'Allegro* and *Il Penseroso* back to 1629; 'Or was Milton thinking of the nightingale sonnet...?' Carey (*Poems*, 88) asserts without question that *Sonnets* 1–6 'were written in 1629'; he is more cautious in the headnote to *Sonnet* 2 and in *Elegy* 6. 89–90. The dating of the Italian poems is discussed in the commentary on them by J. E. Shaw and A. B. Giamatti in *V.C.* 1 and touched on above in the Chronological Survey.]

II. CRITICISM [D.B.]

Hanford ('Youth,' 119) notes that the first lines of the sonnet are a direct translation from the Latin of Milton's *Elegy* 5 (lines 25–6); 'and the conclusion embodies a declaration of the rôle which Milton has consciously adopted in accordance with his own feelings and his devotion to his Roman models....The sonnet is not, however, itself Ovidian in tone. Neither is it, like the song [*May Morning*], Elizabethan. It suggests rather the direct influence of Italian models and represents a transition on Milton's part to a new set of foreign poetic allegiances, responding to and helping to determine an important change in literary mood.'

Tillyard (*Milton*, 1930, 46–50): 'The sonnet...must be considered along with the six Italian poems, a conjunction by which it gains greatly in significance. Allowing all we can for the conventional extravagance of the sonneteer, we must admit that these poems tell of an actual experience and that Milton, towards the end of his college career, and probably at the age of twenty-one, was paying some kind of court to a lady' (46).

'The sonnet *O Nightingale* is the first and *Il Penseroso* the last of what I should call Milton's poems of early maturity. With the exception of the Italian experiments and the Hobson epitaphs the poems in the group are all marked by a new sureness of touch, a knowledge of what can be achieved, and a resolve not to go beyond the clearly achievable. A serenity pervades them that doubtless had its counterpart in Milton's life at the time....The sonnet..., though so close probably in time to the *Nativity Ode*, marks a new stage in Milton's poetical growth....The inspiration that created the *Ode* was not recoverable, was a sudden fire-up: but the sonnet springs from a mind that has won a certain degree of force as its permanent possession....There is in it the sense of deliberateness, of the exercise of the conscious will, united with the primary inspiration, that marks all Milton's mature poetry but which is not so conspicuous in the *Nativity Ode*. He has already imposed his peculiar Latinised arrangement of words on the English poetical sentence and with no hesitating hand' [lines 5–7].

'The poem is not, of course, one of Milton's greatest, but it is faultless in structure and has much verbal felicity. The climax, coming in line 9 with the words, "Now timely sing," is led up to with cunningly delayed expectation; and the epithet "shallow" applied to the cuckoo in line 6, criticising at once the song and the manners of that irresponsible bird, is rich in meaning. The poem reflects a mind exquisitely alert, eager for experience, but gravely master of itself. And the eagerness and mastery do not conflict: they are balanced or even help each other.' Tillyard goes on to object to Raleigh's and Pattison's prejudiced disparagement of the sonnet.

F. T. Prince (*Italian Element*, 1954): 'Sonnet 1...is not only in mood and tone the least Miltonic of the English sonnets: it is also alone in not using those devices of phrasing which are characteristic of all Italian sonnets, and of which Milton shows such a complete grasp in the rest of his sonnets in English' (91). It 'is indeed Italian in its form and manner. It recalls Bembo in its slightly solemn trifling, its very literary tone, and even in the epigrammatic turn of its conclusion. It achieves the total effect of balance and unity demanded by the form. But in the details of its diction it shows none of the minutely applied parallelism found in Milton's Italian poems' and in *Sonnet 7* and later sonnets (96).

J. L. Lievsay ('Milton Among the Nightingales,' *Renaissance Papers 1958, 1959, 1960,* 1961, 36–45) discusses the special and lasting significance the nightingale's song had for Milton, and comments thus on this early example: 'The most striking addition [to traditional associations] is, of course, the folklore contrast of cuckoo and nightingale. The cuckoo, "rude Bird of Hate", is not merely inimical to the nightingale as bringer of "fresh hope" to "the Lover's heart"; it is also the traditional scornful symbol of cuckoldry and unchastity. The opposition thus helps to establish (or indicates as already established) in the poet's mind the symbolic identification of Philomel and chastity which is to receive an almost explicit reiteration in *Comus*. We may note, too, the ambiguity of allegiance common to bird and poet in the last three lines, a deliberate intimation of their essential kinship. The nightingale and I, Milton is saying, ought not to be at odds: our function is the same. Less striking, perhaps, but indicative of what is to remain his lifelong verbal pattern is Milton's choice of words to describe the mode of the nightingale's song —"warbl'st", "liquid notes", "soft lay". The *warbled* song of the nightingale is a constant in the Miltonic vocabulary.'

(This sonnet, and Lievsay's general topic, were discussed by Alden Sampson, *Studies in Milton* (New York, 1913), 4–15.)

Honigmann (*Milton's Sonnets*, 1966, 87) remarks that this, 'One of

Milton's most sensuous and delightful poems, itself not without *liquid notes*, . . . may be classed as a straightforward "complaint,"' yet it is playful as well as courtly. After suggesting that 'an allusion to the vulgar idea of "mating"' is 'smuggled' into the poem in the word 'mate,' he concludes, more happily: 'But perhaps one should say no more than that the *cuckoo*, the slight verbal extravagance of *the rude Bird of Hate* and *my hopeles doom*, the emphatic placing of *mate*, and the general situation, which has gone on *from yeer to yeer*, have potentially comic implications which are nevertheless kept in check: the poet expresses two moods, corresponding to the two birds, and tries to defeat the cuckoo and the mood it typifies.'

Speaking of *Sonnet* I 'as an introduction to the Italian poems', Honigmann says (67): 'The nightingale, the mate of both the Muse and Love (I. 13), melts into the Italian lady who sings so sweetly and compels the poet's love. The imagery of I and II reinforces the symbol: the nightingale's *bloomy Spray* leads into *l' herbosa val* (the flowery vale) and *Là, onde l' alta tua virtù s' infiora* (there, where *blooms* thy lofty might); the bird's *soft lay* prepares for the lady's *spirto gentil* (gentle spirit), and the *amorous power* of its song for the *disio amoroso* (amorous longing) induced by the lady.'

III. NOTES

Newton (reported by Todd) noted that the sonnet was founded upon the same notion or tradition as Chaucer's *The Cuckoo and the Nightingale*—that is, the poem of that title now attributed to Sir Thomas Clanvowe but formerly printed among Chaucer's works (*Chaucerian and Other Pieces*, ed. W. W. Skeat, Oxford, 1897, lvii f., 347–58). It recounts 'how lovers had a tokeninge, / And among hem it was a comune tale, / That it were good to here the nightingale / Rather than the lewde cukkow singe': how the poet, on 'the thridde night of May,' not having yet heard the nightingale, goes forth in quest of it, but, falling asleep, dreams that he hears the cuckoo first, and thereafter the nightingale; whereupon the two birds fall into debate, the nightingale championing love and its service and the cuckoo opposing, till the poet starts up and drives the cuckoo away, thus earning the gratitude of the nightingale, which promises him better fortune next May. Smart extends his account of the theme to early examples in French, but the supposedly Chaucerian poem was Milton's source or is the appropriate analogue [Skeat, lxi, gives parallels]. But the main idea was a commonplace when Milton wrote; Verity (*Milton's Sonnets*, Cambridge, 1895 f.) quoted Burton: 'He is then too confident and rapt beyond himself, as if he had heard the nightingale in the spring before the cuckoo' (*Anat.* 3. 2. 3; 3, 144).

1–2 *O Nightingale...Woods are still.* 'The nightingale often appears in Italian sonnets and canzoni, and sometimes with a conventional opening on which Milton's first line is closely modelled; cf. "O rosignuol, che'n queste verdi fronde / Sovra'l fugace rio fermar ti suoli,"—*Bembo*; "Bel rosignuol, che'n su le fronde vaghe / D'una fiorita e ricca valle assiso / Apri a' tuo' accenti intorno il Paradiso, / E fai ch'indi ogni duol tra noi s'appaghe,"—*Giacomo Cenci*' (Smart). Todd noted three sonnets to the nightingale in Marino, *Rime Boscherecce* (*La Lira*, Venice, 1602, 70, 100), and remarked, as others have, on Milton's own evident fondness for the nightingale: cf. *El* 5. 25–6, *IlPen* 56–64, *Comus* 233–4, 565–6, *PL* 3. 38–40, 4. 602–4, 648, 655, 771, 5. 39–41, 7. 435–6, 8. 518–20, *PR* 4. 245–6, and *Prol* 2 and 7 (*Works* 12, 153, 283); [cf. some classical precedents in the note on *IlPen* 61–2]. Verity compared especially *El* 5. 25–36, but the sober invocation of the sonnet differs markedly in tone from the joyous invitation of *El* 5, and, as Smart observed, in theme and tone it more resembles *El* 7. It is idle to discuss the accuracy of Milton's knowledge of nightingales in connection with the highly stylized bird singing on its *bloomy Spray*. The woods are *still*, silent, since no other bird sings at night (Verity).

4 *jolly hours lead on propitious May.* In classic myth the Hours (Lat. *Horae*) were associated with the seasons and months (cf. Ovid, *M.* 2. 25–30; Spenser, *F.Q.* 7. 7. 28–45; *Comus* 983–6 and 985 n.), and the course of the year was described as the dance of the Hours (cf. *PL* 4. 266–8: 'Pan / Knit with the Graces and the Hours in dance / Led on th' Eternal Spring'); hence *lead on*, itself suggestive of the dance. The epithet *jolly* seems to refer to the gay apparel (*OED* 8) of the Hours in spring. Todd noted that the epithet is applied by Spenser to Summer and June (*F.Q.* 7. 7. 29, 35). Browne remarks that '*jolly* has here not quite lost its primary meaning of "handsome," "comely" (Fr. *jolif*).' Pattison (*Milton's Sonnets*, London and New York, 1883) regarded this as the usual sense in Chaucer and Spenser, and still predominant in Milton's day, citing 'Full jolly knight he seemd' (*F.Q.* 1. 1. 1) of the far from jovial Red Cross knight, and 'With jolly plumes their crests adorn'd' (Fairfax, *Jerusalem* 1. 35); he lamented the subsequent vulgarizing of the word, as illustrating the hazards of poetry in a living language. Hughes (1937) notes the happiness and floral associations of the Hours in the Orphic Hymn to them [no. 43: *Orphei Hymni*, ed. G. Quandt, p. 33]. The meaning 'joyous, gladsome' (*OED* 1) might be supported from the description of the Hours in connection with spring in *Comus* and *PL* (cited above) [and from the Homeric epithet (*Il.* 21. 450) cited by Keightley]. Pattison observed that Shakespeare placed the nightingale's song 'in summer's front' (*Sonn.* 102). [On classical and Elizabethan treatment of the Hours see P. Elmen, 'Shakespeare's Gentle Hours,' *Shakespeare Quarterly* 4, 1953, 301–9.]

5–7 *Thy liquid notes...success in love.* See above, on Clanvowe's poem. For the image of the day's eye, cf. *Comus* 977 and the note on *IlPen* 141.

6 *shallow*: thin, harsh. *OED* 4 gives only one example: 'it must needs make the sound perfecter, and not so shallow and jarring' (Bacon, *Sylva Sylvarum* 3. 223, *Works* 2, 420), but this is no doubt the correct interpretation rather than Verity's 'stupid,' referring to the bird's monotonous cry. [Brooks and Hardy seem to take a meaning akin to Verity's, since they call the word 'a brilliant touch,' which 'helps keep the tone light and charming: that is, it emphasizes the quality of the cuckoo's song rather than the "hate" which it is said to represent, and warns us not to take the poet's fear of "hopeles doom" entirely seriously.' Besides 'thin,' Honigmann cites other 'appropriate' meanings given in *OED*: 'lacking depth; superficial'; he quotes and apparently endorses Brooks and Hardy.] The Columbia Index ('Sappho,' 2, 1725) is in error in reporting an influence on this line (S. Elledge, *MLN* 58, 1943, 551).

9 *timely.* Since 'early' (*OED* 1) is also 'at a fitting or suitable time' (ibid. 2), the word here combines the two meanings.

rude. [Honigmann explains as 'uncivilized; unmusical (of sounds)'; but the word surely applies also to the unpleasant significance of the bird's song for both the lover and the married (Shakespeare, *L.L.L.* 5. 2. 908–12, 917–21).]

10 *ny.* ['The spelling is clearly dictated by the liking for eye-rhyme' (H. Darbishire).]

12 [In spite of the semicolon (also in 1645), *yet...why* evidently goes with the preceding clause, leaving the last two lines as a general conclusion. Editors since Newton have commonly put a colon or period after *why*.]

13 [Woodhouse saw a difficulty in Milton's appearing 'to treat the *Muse* as masculine,' although the word cannot mean poet as in *Lyc* 19, and should mean poetry or song. Presumably it has the latter and logical meaning, since *his* takes its gender from the second and nearer subject, *Love*, i.e. Cupid; 'her' may be understood for *Muse*. Honigmann explains similarly, but remarks: 'Perhaps *his* = its, though this use of the word was now old-fashioned'—but it was Milton's normal use throughout his life (see *Nat* 106 n.).]

14 *serve*. Verity quotes from Clanvowe the nightingale's retort to the cuckoo's sneers: 'who that wol the god of love not serve, / I dar wel say, is worthy for to sterve' (133–4: Skeat, 352). On *train*, see *IlPen* 10 n.

Sonnet 7 *(How soon hath time)*

I. DATE AND CIRCUMSTANCES

This sonnet, published without title in 1645 and 1673, was until recent times assigned to Milton's twenty-third birthday, 9 December 1631, on the supposed evidence of 'my three and twentieth year' (line 2). [Titles in various editions which include 'Twenty-third' or 'Twenty-three' are editorial additions and have no authority.] But W. R. Parker (*RES* 11, 1935, 276–83) showed that Milton's use of the Latin phrase *Anno aetatis*, with which he dated nine early poems [a tenth, *Elegy* 7, has an ambiguous variation], would almost inevitably extend to use of the analogous phrase in English: hence 'my three and twentieth year' does not mean the year between the twenty-second and twenty-third birthdays, but that between the twenty-third and twenty-fourth. [See above, the beginning of section 1 of the Chronological Survey, and Parker, *Milton*, 784–6.] So the sonnet is to be dated on Milton's twenty-fourth birthday, 9 December 1632.

This partly clears up a problem presented by the two drafts of a letter to an unidentified friend which appear in the Cambridge MS. (*Works* 12, 320–5; *C.P.W.* 1, 1953, 318–21). [Parker formerly proposed Milton's boyhood tutor, Thomas Young, as the friend (*TLS*, 16 May 1936, 420); but he now (*Milton*, 783, n. 13) thinks that, if Milton had been addressing Young, he would have written, as he had before, in Latin.] The letter refers to the sonnet as 'some of my nightward thoughts some while since' [for the substance of the letter see Hanford and Woodhouse under Criticism below]. In view of their contents the drafts cannot have been written till a considerable time after Milton's retirement from Cambridge (July 1632) and his taking up private studies, and 'some while' (clearly a shorter period) after the writing of *Sonnet* 7, i.e. after 9 December 1632; thus the letter was presumably written early in 1633 (Parker, *RES* 11; *Milton*, 786–7).

[The altered date for the sonnet fits much better with what we know of Milton's outward circumstances and state of mind. In December 1631 he was in the middle of his last year at Cambridge; he had attained something like popularity among fellow students and dons and a distinctive reputation as a poet; and he was looking forward to taking his M.A. and beginning an independent life. He had therefore no visible reason for being dissatisfied with himself and his career. In December 1632, on the other hand, while his Cambridge contemporaries were forging ahead in their various occupations, Milton was a recluse in his father's house, pursuing solitary study with no acclaim except that of his intellectual and religious conscience, and he might well feel uncertain and depressed by the thought of what might seem at times unprofitable labour directed toward an unknown end.]

II. CRITICISM [D.B.]

Hanford ('Youth,' 1925, 128–30), assuming the traditional date, Milton's twenty-third birthday, sees his 'sense of a lack of inward ripeness... primarily with reference to his own ideals,' a sense which 'could have been dissipated only by a successful beginning at epic poetry' or by other poems on the level of the *Nativity*. 'The result of his dissatisfaction appears to have been the resolution to wait patiently for his time, withdrawing his energies for the present from serious composition and devoting himself to intellectual, moral, and aesthetic self-cultivation.' The letter to an unknown friend gives further evidence of the moral earnestness already recorded in *Elegy* 6 and *Sonnet* 7. The friend's plea that the young man leave his bookish self-indulgence for active service, presumably as a clergyman, evokes a very sober examination of his own motives [*Works* 12, 320–5; *C.P.W.* 1, 318–21]. Probably Milton 'had not yet altogether abandoned the plan of entering the church.' Whatever his lifework is to be, he feels the need of fuller preparation, though he copies the sonnet as evidence of 'a certain belatedness' he is aware of in himself.

'It is odd but characteristic that Milton should, in this statement, say nothing whatever regarding his literary purposes and ambitions,' with which no doubt the friend would have small sympathy.

In *Poems* (1953) Hanford accepts Parker's dating of the sonnet on Milton's twenty-fourth birthday. The young poet's 'trouble at the slow development of his powers is characteristic. Beneath his confidence in the ultimate attaining of his goal there was a deep distrust. As he here expresses doubt of his maturity so in *Paradise Lost* [9. 25-6, 41-7] he fears that he is too old to fulfil his task. In both cases his resort is to prayer and acquiescence.'

Woodhouse ('Notes,' 1943-4, 66-101), agreeing in the main with the pattern traced by Hanford ('Youth'), thinks that 'the decision which Milton finally reached in respect of his poetry, and the religious experience from which the decision sprang, turned on a larger axis than the rejection of the elegiac and erotic. This becomes clear if *Sonnet* 7 . . . (which the critics have either virtually ignored or misinterpreted) is given its proper place as the record of an experience just as definite and far more decisive than that of the *Nativity Ode* and *Elegy* 6. For it is impossible to escape the conclusion that there is some fading of the experience recorded in the latter poems and some relapse from the position which they attain—it is not a question of *Sonnets* 1-6 only [which Woodhouse (80) places in the spring and summer of 1630], but of the other secular verse as well. On the threshold of the Horton period Milton's act of self-dedication required to be renewed, as it was in *Sonnet* 7. From the determination there taken, to live and write hereafter "As ever in my great Taskmaster's eye," there is no retreat: it leaves its mark on the whole of Milton's subsequent career. And this time the decision subsumes in silence the rejection of erotic in favour of religious themes. Moreover, the recognition that if the December of 1629 sees a first decision and resolve, that of 1632 sees its final and irrevocable confirmation, removes the difficulty of *Sonnets* 1-6 and the other secular verse of 1630-32.' (67)

'Taken together, the *Nativity Ode* and *How soon hath Time* give evidence of an experience which stands to Milton in place of what the Puritans called conversion. It differs in being closely connected with his poetry, in which it finds its chief expression. And it appears to differ in its gradual character and the absence of any marked self-abasement.' But such writers as Richard Baxter recognized 'that the process of regeneration is often gentle and gradual, the maturing of the seeds sown by a Christian education,' and in Milton's case this would mean 'simply an intensified aspiration after spiritual things and a more conscious act of self-dedication.' (73–4)

After some five months [July–November 1632] of living at home, Milton broke his apparent silence in this sonnet. 'Its meaning has been somewhat obscured by taking it in too close conjunction with the prose Letter to a Friend [*Works* 12, 320–5], in which a copy of the sonnet was included. Grierson describes the poem as, with the letter, an apology for waiting and learning. It is nothing of the kind. It is, first, a consideration of Milton's little achievement to date, which can be assigned no satisfactory meaning unless we read it in the light of his large ambitions for the future in poetry, and secondly, a renewed and more decisive dedication of himself to God's service, which not only has the effect of resolving his doubts and fears, but leaves its mark on nearly all his subsequent poetry. The letter obscures the issue because (to speak quite frankly) it is a somewhat disingenuous document. The decision as between the pulpit and poetry has, it seems almost certain, been already taken, at least in Milton's mind. This, clearly, is unknown to the possibly too officious friend, and the letter does not undeceive him. Nor can he be let into the full meaning of the sonnet. It is included simply because it says quite unequivocally that Milton holds himself to be in God's hand. This the friend requires to be told, and this Milton lets the sonnet tell him. By us, however, it must be read not as part of the letter but for itself.

'It opens on the uncharacteristic note of self-distrust: How little he has so far accomplished; how immature he seems; how dubious the promise of future achievement, on which he has staked everything! Yes, but he is in God's hand. Much or little, soon or late, it will be as God has determined. All that is in the poet's power, and all that matters, is that by grace he may use his talent in God's service and with submission to his will. . . . Thus Milton renews his self-dedication and with it the clouds roll away. The thoughts in the octave are brought to a head by the approach of his twenty-fourth birthday, with its sense of the flying years. But the whole poem is the outcome of the period of silent self-examination, and records the final and decisive phase of Milton's early religious experience. The mark of a genuine religious experience is its power to change one's view of things, and of the relation of the self thereto. In the sestet Milton marshals the resources of his faith to meet the doubts and fears formulated in the octave, and the result is not strictly speaking to dispel them, but to resolve the problem by raising it to a religious level where self-regarding thoughts are simply irrelevant. This is the more remarkable when we remember Milton's unpliant egoism and his intense desire to excel.

'The poem is more than a record of Milton's experience. As in *Elegy* 5, and the *Nativity Ode*, the experience is realized in the very act of recording it. The imposition of aesthetic pattern upon the extra-aesthetic materials of experience makes the experience of the poem, which in this case is at once religious and aesthetic. In *Elegy* 5, and in large measure in the *Nativity Ode*, there is nothing problematical; the attitude and effect are those of simple acceptance; no "resolution" of conflicting elements occurs. Here, in *How soon hath Time*, one encounters at last, though in a simple and rudimentary form, the full Miltonic pattern and function (the resolution of conflict by the imposition of aesthetic pattern).' The same process and result appear in 'When I consider,' in *Comus, Lycidas*, and *Epitaphium Damonis*. 'In some ways—not in all—*How soon hath Time* is more characteristic than the *Nativity Ode*. It builds upon the experience in that poem, but is in itself more decisive. The effect of Milton's renewed dedication of himself and his life-work to God's service can be traced immediately and through years.' (95–7)

Brooks and Hardy (1951: 153–5), though unaware of Parker's dating of the sonnet, see its 'primary interest' as autobiographical. They observe that 'The shift in line 4 from the image of the thief to that of the late spring would hardly have satisfied one of the metaphysical poets; but it might well have pleased an Elizabethan dramatist. At any rate it was characteristically Miltonic. And equally characteristic is the way in which, with the second quatrain, the play of imagery is apparently abandoned for a rather sober, even prosaic statement, although the "spring" metaphor is carried on in the phrase "inward ripenes."' The sestet 'indicates a kind of paradoxical reliance upon time in spite of' Milton's distrust of it. 'For time is not a blind and capricious force but the instrument of the "will of Heav'n."' 'The young poet's confidence in Providence, far from mitigating his own responsibility, doubles it.'

F. T. Prince (*Italian Element*, 1954) remarks that, whereas *Sonnet* 1 ('O Nightingale') uses no Italian devices, *Sonnet* 7 'shows a noticeable number' of them. 'It seems certain that Milton had learnt their use and importance from the experiment of writing the six poems in Italian which his own arrangement places between Sonnet 1 and Sonnet VII' (91). One comprehensive device, first illustrated in Milton's Italian sonnets, is parallelism of structure, especially the pairing of adjectives and substantives and especially at the end of a line (94). In *Sonnet* 7, which has a confident grasp not felt in *Sonnet* 1, 'The quatrains are more carefully distinguished and internally balanced..., and in the tercets the poem makes its assertions with a striking outburst of those parallelisms which we have seen Milton practising in Italian' (96).

M. Cheek ('Of Two Sonnets of Milton,' *Renaissance Papers 1956*, University of South Carolina, 1956; repr. in Barker, *Milton*, 1965) begins a comparative analysis of *Sonnets* 7 and 19 by noting the fundamental consistency and unity of Milton's general outlook and of the body of his poetry. Both of these sonnets came at critical moments in his life. The imagery and contents of the sonnet of 1652 on his blindness are in some respects closer than the early sonnet to the Letter to a Friend in which the latter was copied. That Letter refers to three scriptural passages on which Milton's argument rests: John 9. 4, on the need to work while it is day; Matt. 25. 14–30, the parable of the talents; and Matt. 20. 1–16, the parable of the early and late workers in the vineyard. *Sonnet* 7— apart from the quite general 'great Task-master'—does not refer directly to any one of the three biblical passages, though lines 9–12 may echo the parable of the vineyard in a reversed way, the idea being, not the reward of the late-comer, but the labourer's own assurance that, however delayed, he will come and work in accordance with God's will. But the imagery of the octave is that of time as a thief and the garden of youth, and the texture of the sestet is abstract. The sonnet combines the Renaissance theme of *tempus fugit* with religious self-dedication.

In the sonnet of 1652 the imagery 'is almost wholly scriptural' and, moreover, 'drawn largely from the several gospel passages cited' in Milton's early Letter. The whole passage from John 9 provides 'the outer frame of the octave, extending through its first two lines, interrupted through its next four, and then picked up and carried through its last two; the reference to the parable of the buried talent being inserted in between and constituting lines three through six.... Here light is used in several senses, in all the three perhaps that John associated with it, and in addition certainly in that which Milton in his letter gave it': physical vision, the light of day in which man works, and service of humanity (since the poet brings light into the world). Further, embedded within the image of light is the parable of the buried talent, which Milton had echoed in his Letter when he was looking forward to using his talent; now it is buried alive. Milton had other talents, but they were insignificant in comparison with the power to serve God and man through poetry. Thus two of the scriptural passages of the early Letter form the framework and matter of the octave; and the sestet, like that of *Sonnet* 7, 'though it does not in detail employ the imagery of the third scriptural passage..., that of the later-comers into the vineyard, yet breathes the spirit of it, going even farther than the earlier poem, to say "They also serve who only stand and wait."'

P. M. Withim ('A Prosodic Analysis of Milton's Seventh Sonnet,' *Bucknell Review*, 6, 4, 1956–7, 29–34) shows that Milton here accepts the full discipline of the form, with only minor irregularities. Complexity of emotion determines the complexity of versification: 'the thought of the entire poem is built up on a system of reversals and contradictions.' Each of the quatrains presents a paradox, and the two contradict each other, though the second preserves continuity in that it issues from and explains the first. The sestet is a flat contradiction [or should one rather say resolution?] of the octave; and its bare statement is in contrast with the imagery used in the octave.

Taylor Stoehr ('Syntax and Poetic Form in Milton's Sonnets,' *English Studies*, 45, 1964, 289–301) observes that *Sonnet 7* 'displays a perfectly regular Petrarchan pattern, with a strong break at the turn. There are, in fact, falling terminal junctures (the strongest kind) at the ends of lines 2, 4, 8, 12, and 14, while none occur within the lines. Even more striking, every line ends with a terminal juncture of some kind, rising, falling, or sustained. In the octave the caesuras are all sustained terminal junctures, with no significant changes in pitch or stress; thus the rhymes, already emphasized in the Petrarchan scheme by their very frequency, are further intensified by distinctive intonation, since they come at points of terminal juncture marked by differences in pitch, stress, and duration of pause. This is indeed "in strictest measure", and its effect, of course, is to draw attention to the formal structure of the sonnet.' Stoehr finds that 'the excessive formality of the sonnet has a double function. The dangerous—or even impious, because it aspires too high—ambition of the young poet is at once contained and displayed in the same strict elegance. The careful conforming to convention keeps the tone moderate, reverent; the brilliance of execution satisfies the ambition. Yet the result, one must admit, is a rather cold perfection.'

[Perhaps it may be said that one admits no such thing, nor the application of 'even impious' to a humble vow of obedience to God's will.]

L. L. Martz (Summers, *Lyric Milton*, 1965, 14–15) notes the startling effect of this sonnet, following the amatory sonnets 1–6, and stresses a strict Calvinist sense of grace: 'the speaker's future lies completely in the hands of God. Though Time has stolen away his youth, all his hopes remain as valid as they ever were; nothing has really changed, for the use of his life depends upon the timeless will and eye and grace of God.' In contrast with the preceding sonnets, 'the sternness of the doctrine itself may suggest a veering from one youthful extreme to another— especially since the movement of the sonnet still maintains a conventional, end-stopped, balanced manner.'

III. NOTES

1 *suttle*: subtle, 'cunning, insidiously sly' (*OED* 10), but the emphasis is less on the cunning of the thief than on the imperceptibility of the theft (ibid. 5). [Warton quoted Juvenal 9. 128–9: *dum serta‿unguenta puellas | poscimus, obrepit non intellecta senectus.*]

2 *on his wing*: by the very act of flight. ['For the traditional image of Time's *wings*' Honigmann cites Shakespeare, *W. Tale* 4. 1. 3–4: 'Now take upon me, in the name of Time, | To use my wings'; and compares also *R. III* 3. 7. 168 ('the stealing hours of time') and 5. 3. 86.] *three and twentieth yeer*: [MS. and *Poems* of 1645 read *twentith* (*Facs.* 388, 181).] In Milton's usage the phrase almost certainly means what would now be called his twenty-fourth year; see headnote.

3 *career*. See note on *IlPen* 121. This word, and *hasting dayes* and *late spring* carry an implied reference to the sun. [Honigmann cites Job 9. 25: 'my days... flee away, they see no good.']

4–8 *But my late spring...timely-happy spirits indu'th.* Only in a mood of depression could Milton dismiss the evidence of his own genius, *El* 5, *Nat*, probably *EpWin*, *L'All*, and *IlPen*, and possibly *Arc*, clearly blossoms of achievement as well as buds of promise. In his youthful appearance (which later became a matter of pride: *Def* 2, *Works* 8, 61), Smart sees evidence of Milton's late maturing but misses the unconscious testimony of his curious assumption that at twenty-four he is merely *to manhood...arriv'd so near.* [In the Letter to a Friend probably of early 1633 (see I and II above) Milton said: 'I am something suspicious of my selfe, & doe take notice of a certaine belatednesse in me' (*Works* 12, 322, 325), and, as proof, copied the sonnet.]

Various attempts have been made to particularize the *more timely-happy spirits* with whom Milton contrasts himself, though he did not need to have any actual persons in mind. Smart suggested his Cambridge contemporary, Thomas Randolph (1605–35), whose *Aristippus* 'had been performed at the University and published in 1630' and whose *Jealous Lovers*, in 1632, 'was acted at Trinity before the King and Queen, and received with great applause.' His poems 'were published posthumously in 1638' but, thinks Smart, Milton's familiarity with them in MS. 'may be inferred from some curious similarities of expression in *Comus* and *L'Allegro*' [see below, *Comus* III. 9 and III n., and *L'All* 24 n.]; there is also the probable accidental linking of *Comus* and Randolph's poems (*Comus* III. 9 below). [Hanford ('Youth,' 128) dismisses the suggestion of

Randolph as 'patently absurd, for there was nothing in the work of Randolph or any contemporary poet that Milton could have envied'; he adds that 'Lucan or even Sir Philip Sidney would be a more plausible suggestion, if we must assume that Milton had any particular person in mind.'] A. H. Nethercot (*MLN* 49, 1934, 158–62) suggested the precocious Cowley, who was born in 1618 and whose *Poetical Blossoms*, dated 1633, had been known in MS. in some circles a couple of years earlier and may have been published in 1632. Spenser was suggested by R. M. Smith (*MLN* 60, 1945, 394–8), who tacitly assumed that the sonnet is a defence of delay and saw an analogy with Spenser's verses to Harvey in his letter of 5 October 1579 (*Namque sinu pudet...Frugibus et vacuas speratis cernere spicas*). [D. C. Dorian (*The English Diodatis*, New Brunswick, 1950, 143–4), more plausibly, nominated Diodati, who, though some months younger than Milton, had made more rapid academic progress.] Hughes mentions Sidney's 'somewhat similar defense of himself' in *Astrophel* 23. It is worth noting that Milton later deprecated precociousness: 'To me it always appeared best to grow slowly, and as it were, by imperceptible advances. You ⟨More⟩ are that mushroom, who, when only just out of your boyhood, went to Geneva, and all at once popped up professor of Greek; and, as you tell, ...bore away "the palm from so many men who were" your elders...by favour of that genius, which was then only beginning to blossom' (*Defpro Se, Works* 9, 281).

5 *deceive the truth*: prove false to the truth (*OED*: deceive 3). The construction seems to be modelled on 'deceive, i.e. betray, one's trust.'

8 *timely-happy*: *timely*, in addition to meaning seasonable (*OED* 2 quotes Sidney, Ps. 1. 9, 'timely fruite to nourish'), might also carry the suggestion of 'early'; *OED* 1 quotes E. Sandys, *Sermons*, ed. J. Ayre (Parker Society, 1842, 301): 'the timeliest fruit often cometh to least proof.' Cf. *Sonn* 1. 9 n. [*indu'th*: endueth, is inherent in (*OED*: endue 9 b).]

9 Verity et al. find the antecedent for *it* in *inward ripenes* (7). See below on 13–14.

10–12 *still in strictest measure eev'n,* | *...the will of Heav'n.* Lewis Campbell ('Milton and Pindar,' *Classical Review* 8, 1894, 349) compared Pindar, *Nem.* 4. 41–3: 'But, whatsoever excellence Lord Destiny assigned me, well I know that the lapse of time will bring it to its appointed perfection' (L.C.L.). [W. T. Lendrum (ibid. 9, 1895, 10–11) objected to the parallel on the ground that the contexts are quite different, that Milton is humbly accepting God's will and

Pindar is sublimely confident of his destiny. R. Y. Tyrrell (ibid. 11–12) endorsed Campbell and added *euthupompos aion* ('time guiding aright') from *Nem.* 2. 7–8. There are doubtless many more or less similar utterances, pagan and Christian, e.g. Epictetus, *Encheiridion* 53 (quoting the famous Hymn of Cleanthes): 'Lead thou me on, O Zeus, and Destiny, / To that goal long ago to me assigned. / I'll follow and not falter; if my will / Prove weak and craven, still I'll follow on' (L.C.L., 2, 537).] For Milton's substitution of *the will of Heav'n* for Destiny, cf. God's 'what I will is Fate' (*PL* 7. 173). [*still*: 'in future no less than formerly' (Lockwood).] *eev'n, / To*: equal to, neither more nor less than is required for.

13–14 *All is, if I have grace to use it so, / As ever in my great task Masters eye.* Editors have been generally silent on these lines, which are not easy to interpret with certainty. Browne proposed: '*All is*, i.e. "in strictest measure even," &c. He had said, "It shall be;" now he corrects himself—"nay, all my life is so already, if I have grace to use it as in God's sight." ' Verity follows Browne. Other suggestions have been made. K. Svendsen (*Explic.* 7, 1948–9, Item 53) sees three possible meanings, but, taking *ripenes* (7) as the antecedent of *it* in 13 (as in 9 and 10), gives as his preferred paraphrase: 'All that matters is whether I have grace to use my ripeness in accordance with the will of God as one ever in His sight.' Dorian (ibid. 8, 1949–50, Item 10) attempts a more radical solution by making *ever* (14) stand for eternity and paraphrasing: 'All time [cf. 12] is, if I have grace to use it so, as eternity in God's sight.' These explanations have the merit of retaining the punctuation of 1645 and 1673; but there is difficulty (partly evaded by Browne) in taking *if I...use it so* as a conditional clause, since it makes the statement of fact (God's apportionment of talent to destiny, or God's view of time) depend on Milton's attitude, whereas the whole point is that fact is fact and Milton's attitude must conform to it. And as to the punctuation, can we, in the light of MS. and 1645-73, be sure that a comma did not intrude itself after *so* in 1645 and escape detection? The MS. copies the sonnet with no punctuation whatever; the punctuation of 1645 and 1673, as given above, is followed by Todd and later editors, except Smart, who (without comment) omits the comma after *so*. A colon would clarify the probable meaning: 'All ⟨that matters⟩ is: whether I have grace to use it so, as ever ⟨conscious of being⟩ in my great Taskmaster's ⟨enjoining⟩ eye' (Woodhouse, 'Notes,' 96, n. 45); [this paraphrase would seem to agree pretty much with Svendsen's above]. *If* (earlier *that if*) was a common synonym for *whether*, though usually with such verbs as *see, ask, learn* (*OED* II. 9). Wright notes that *grace* is here used 'in the theological sense of the favour of God, giving inspiration and strength.' Milton is thinking primarily, however, not of God's gift (save as it is equal to what God will demand of him) but of his own response to it. Taken in its simple meaning, *task Master*, one who assigns the task to be done, is unobjectionable, but Milton here risks the associations of harshness and injustice conveyed by the word in scripture (e.g. Exod. 1. 11; 3. 7; 5. 6, 10: Verity). 'The reference to God as a "task Master" implies that God's overseeing requires his work to be of the best—not merely that a good outcome is certain because of God's supervision' (Brooks and Hardy). [Bell cited the parable of the labourers in the vineyard (Matt. 20. 1–16) and Milton's Letter to a Friend; see Hanford and M. Cheek in II above. Honigmann quotes 2 Chron. 16. 9: 'For the eyes of the Lord run to and fro throughout the whole earth, to shew himself strong in the behalf of them whose heart is perfect toward him'; Ps. 33. 18: 'Behold, the eye of the Lord is upon them that fear him...,' and 34. 15; and Milton's later declaration that when travelling he lived with the consciousness that he 'certainly could not escape the eyes of God' (*Def* 2, *Works* 8, 127). Honigmann also (44) notes the unifying effect of 'the backward glance': 'the poet's uneasiness about false appearances, in the octave, is cancelled by the reflection that the *great task-Masters eye* sees *the truth*, so that no mere *semblance* can *deceive*.']

Sonnet 8 *(Captain or Colonel, or Knight in Arms)*

⚜

I. DATE AND CIRCUMSTANCES

Without title in 1645 and 1673, the sonnet in the MS. has two titles: *On his dore when ye Citty expected an assault*, deleted, and below it, *When the assault was intended to ye Citty* (*Facs.* 396). [The first title is in the hand of the copyist who wrote out the sonnet, the second in Milton's: the use of a copyist in 1642 is unexplained (Parker, 874, n. 24).] After the battle of Edgehill (23 October 1642) the retreat of the parliamentary army under the Earl of Essex left open the road to London, and Charles advanced as far as Turnham Green; but he then withdrew (13 November). 'While suspense and anxiety prevailed around him..., Milton... remained calm and detached, and converted the moment of peril into a theme for slightly playful verse. But the suggestion that the sonnet was actually placed on the door of his dwelling, to placate some Royalist commander, need not be taken seriously: we are in the presence of a poetical situation, not of a practical expedient' (Smart). [Parker (loc. cit.) thinks the light tone suggests composition after the crisis; but there are the two titles, and, after the event, would the sonnet be cast in such a dramatic form?] The form, as Finley (36–7) points out, is that of the inscription, initially a set of verses carved on some public edifice or monument, but later practised by Greek and Roman writers as a minor poetic genre. In addition to examples from the *Greek Anthology*, Finley cites Horace (*C.* 1. 28), Propertius (4. 2), and Catullus (4).

[Honigmann dissents from the accepted view of the date and circumstances: (i) whereas 'Royalist atrocities against Parliamentarians were widely publicised in the autumn of 1642,' 'Milton writes detachedly,

374

playfully, as if for a less serious situation,' yet (ii) 'Milton, of all people, could scarcely think of himself as detached, being already notorious as the author of some of the most bitter anti-Royalist pamphlets of his day.' The facts are that Milton did not become notorious until after his first tract on divorce (i.e. after the second edition of February 1644, which had his name), and that he had written no anti-Royalist tracts; he had written five tracts (four of them anonymous) against the bishops, and in the first he had shown himself a good monarchist. Honigmann's third point is that Milton ('a marked man and a declared enemy') 'was not the man to ask for special favours in a situation like that of 1642.' But to say this is to misread the poem, which uses the occasion for general reflections on the place and power of poetry in war-time. Finally, Honigmann notes that Milton deleted one of two titles and also the date 1642 in the MS. (*Facs.* 396): 'We must suppose, therefore, that he came to recognise that the date was wrong.' But he might, looking back, have been mistaken in deleting the date (as his memory was sometimes at fault), or he might have deleted it because he did not date, or retain the dates of, the fair copies of other sonnets. For these reasons, which may appear tenuous, Honigmann would associate the sonnet with 'another intended assault' of May 1641, when it was feared that the army, with the king's connivance, was to have the looting of London.]

II. CRITICISM [D.B.]

Brooks and Hardy (1951: 156–7): 'If the appeal to the officer is not serious, yet the confidence which Milton reposes in the power of poetry is genuine. Of that we need have no doubt.' The poem's seriousness is the seriousness 'of wry humor, of an ironic little joke in which the poet contemplates, a little ruefully but still with a fine inner confidence, the place of the poet in a jostling world of men at arms and forays and sallies.'

Daiches (*Milton*, 1957, 132): 'We begin...face to face with the anticipated Royalist officer; we end far away in time and place, listening to "the repeated air of sad *Electra's* Poet". That phrase itself...with its quiet retrospective melancholy, helps the withdrawal from seventeenth-century London to ancient Athens, and the withdrawal is part of the design and intention of the poem.'

Prince (*Comus*, 1968, 162): 'The movement of the sonnet widens out from the grim possibilities of defeat in war—the armed men, the helpless private house—to remote lands and times, and echoes of the magnanimity of conquerors. The poet's quiet suburban house becomes the bower of the Muses, the walls of London are seen as the walls of ancient Athens; though they were saved "from ruin bare" in the past, they represent greatness ruined by time. Yet the two far-off historic incidents evoke what cannot be destroyed by time—poetry.'

III. NOTES

1 *Colonel.* Milton adopted the spelling that was coming into greater favour (as compared with *Coronel*), the three-syllable pronunciation which was universal when he wrote, and the accent on the final syllable which was common in verse (*OED*). Warton noted the phrase *Knight in Arms* in Shakespeare, *R. II* 1. 3. 26.

2 *Whose chance...may sease*: whose fortune it may be to seize.

3 *deed of honour*: ⟨act of⟩ chivalry (Wright), with possibly the secondary suggestion of a deed showing respect. MS. and 1645 have *If ever deed of honour...please* instead of *If deed of honour...ever please* (*Facs.* 396, 181).

5–8 *He can requite...circle warms.* 'It was Pindar's formal task to give fame through verse, and Horace...increasingly felt the gift of fame to be his own function and that of poetry'; this is 'one of his dominant themes in the fourth book ⟨of odes⟩' (Finley, 37). Pattison cited many examples of the poet's claim to confer immortal fame: Propertius (2. 34); Petrarch, Ronsard, Malherbe; Drayton, *Idea* 6 (Drayton, 2, 313); Shakespeare, *Sonn.* 55, 81. Cf. Spenser, *S.C.*, *October* 65–6: 'For ever, who in derring doe were dreade, / The loftie verse of hem was loved aye'; and the long Gloss on these lines cited below in 10–12 n. Spenser gave the convention a new turn by dedicating the *Faerie Queene* to Elizabeth to live with the eternity of her fame.

5 Keightley noticed that *charms* here has precisely the force of Lat. *carmina*, poems with magical powers, as in Virgil, *E.* 8. 69–71. [See *IlPen* 81–4 n.]

6 *gentle acts.* The adjective suggests both mild (*OED* 8) and noble, generous (ibid. 3), as becomes a knight in arms. Cf. Chaucer, *C.T., Prol.* 72.

8 *Suns bright circle*: [the body or orb of the sun (*OED*: circle, *sb.* 5; Lockwood, Verity), with probably a suggestion of its orbit also. Cf. the same phrase in *PL* 4. 578. Finley (38) quotes Horace, *C.* 4. 14. 5–6: *qua sol habitabiles | inlustrat oras.*]

10–14 Finley (38) observes that the concluding with examples and thus achieving a quiet ending is Horatian; cf. *C.* 4. 8.

10–12 The Gloss on Spenser's *October* 65 (above, 5–8 n.) comments: 'He sheweth the cause, why Poetes were wont be had in such honor of noble men; that is, that by them their worthines and valor shold through theyr famous Posies be commended to al posterities.…And that such account hath bene always made of Poetes, aswell sheweth this…that Alexander destroying Thebes, when he was enformed that the famous Lyrick Poet Pindarus was borne in that citie, not onely commaunded streightly, that no man should upon payne of death do any violence to that house by fire or otherwise: but also specially spared most, and some highly rewarded, that were of hys kinne. So favoured he the only name of a Poete.' The story is from Pliny, *N.H.* 7. 29. 109.

10 *The great Emathian Conqueror. Emathian*: Macedonian (as in *PR* 3. 290), Emathia being a district of Alexander's native Macedonia: [a kind of synecdoche common in Latin poetry. The periphrasis—one of the elements of the 'grand style' that develop in the sonnets—is functional: it heightens the contrast between the all-powerful man of action and the Theban poet. Honigmann sees in 9 f. a sardonic contrast implied between the heroic past and the present and between Alexander and 'a petty commander' in London.]

11 Warton remarked that *Temple and Towre* was a frequent combination 'in the old metrical romances' and that it recurs in *PR* 3. 268, 4. 34. MS. has *temple' and towre*, as if to indicate partial elision of the second syllable.

12–14 *And the repeated air…from ruine bare.* The second instance of clemency (as Warton noted) is from Plutarch (*Lysander* 15): after it was proposed that Athens be razed, the city was saved because, when 'a certain Phocian sang the first chorus in the "Electra" of Euripides [168 f.], which begins with "O thou daughter of Agamemnon, / I am come, Electra, to thy rustic court," all were moved to compassion, and felt it to be a cruel deed to abolish and destroy a city which was so famous, and produced such poets' (*Lives*, L.C.L., 4, 273). This explains *repeated*, recited (*OED*: *v.* 2), but here applied to something (in the play) sung by the chorus, which is hence called an *air*.

Sonnet 9 *(Lady that in the prime of earliest youth)*

I. SUBJECT AND DATE

The sonnet has no title in MS., 1645, or 1673. The poem itself supplies all the knowledge we have or need about the situation. A young girl of Milton's acquaintance has given herself to religious study and contemplation; she has been rebuked or derided for her devotion, but has borne it without anger, feeling only pity for her critics. Milton writes the sonnet to console and encourage her; [throughout he 'carefully eschews giving any advice...He pays her the compliment of merely describing with satisfaction what she has done' (Brooks and Hardy)]. Unless or until new evidence appears it is idle to speculate on her identity. Masson mentions as the merest conjecture that she may be the Miss Davis whom (according to Edward Phillips) Milton thought of marrying when he was deserted by Mary Powell, but Smart observes that this is in no sense a love sonnet, and that the poet, as an elder friend, is addressing a girl still very young (line 1). Smart himself conjectured that she might have been the daughter of the pious, studious, and beloved Mrs Catharine Thomason in whose memory Milton was to write *Sonnet* 14. Milton was of course a friend of the Thomasons, but the suggestion rests on the idea 'like mother like daughter'; and the implication of criticism from other members of the home circle runs counter to what we know of the Thomason family. Further, Smart may be wrong in thinking that 'prime of youth' is compatible with the age of 'ten or twelve, and perhaps...less' (see below, 1 n.). In a word, there is no case for Miss Davis or Miss Thomason. [Honigmann would identify the young woman as Mary Powell. Even if we grant, as some passages in the first

378

divorce tract suggest, that Milton 'deceived himself' as to her 'Puritan inclinations' during their brief courtship, it is difficult to agree that Mary 'very neatly fits the situation.' Parker (875, n. 26) rules out Miss Davis, Miss Thomason, and Lady Margaret Ley, and thinks either Mary Powell or Lady Alice Egerton (of *Comus*) more likely, especially the last. We may be unable to see either one as a real or apparent martyr, and Lady Alice (aged 23 in 1642) seems out of the question: as Parker himself says (792, n. 42), 'the Egertons were a religious family, and there is some evidence of Puritan leanings.']

The sonnet can be dated only loosely as of 1642–5: the evidence is that it was printed in the *Poems* of 1645 and was placed after *Sonnet* 8, written in November 1642. [Parker (876, n. 26) assigns *Sonnet* 9 and also 10 to 1642 or early 1643, mainly because Milton 'wrote his sonnets in chronological "bunches" and rarely mixed prose with original composition in poetry.' This may be a reason, but an accomplished poet—witness Keats—may write a sonnet, even a good sonnet, in an hour or less, in the midst of other activities.]

Pattison remarked on the very different attitude towards women displayed by this and the following sonnet in comparison with the conventional Petrarchan kind.

II. CRITICISM

[F. T. Prince (*Italian Element*, 1954, 105–6), dealing with a poem usually disparaged, continues his exposition of Italian devices, especially the distortion of natural word-order and its result, 'the continuous interplay of the expected and the unexpected.' 'The poem contains no thought which could be considered ingenious or profound or, in its context, unusual. The special quality of the statements made is rather that they are appropriate, and recognizably so at a first rehearsal. In this respect it shows, like Della Casa's compliments, the value, for serious poetry, of the critical idea of decorum. As for the poetic "realization" of the thoughts: the images...are all more or less allegorical in nature, and remain so, for all the freshness or force he imparts to them. We have thus "the broad way and the green" deriving from the New Testament; "the Hill of heav'nly Truth", a moral and poetic commonplace; the "lamp" and the "Bridegroom" come, of course, from the parable of the Wise and the Foolish Virgins, and retain their simple picturesque beauty, heightened by the mildly rich language and metaphor: "odorous", "deeds of light", "Hope that reaps not shame", "feastful friends", and "the mid hour of night".

'The beauty of the poem resides only partially in these elements of image and metaphor, which are all spiritualized and allegorical. It is to be found far more in the sound of the words in relation to the movement of the thought. Both thought and words are carefully arranged, or disarranged. Incomplete phrases and clauses are inverted and inter-polated, then completed, in a way absolutely new in English poetry, and which heightens the reader's attention and brings out the value of every syllable. There is thus an impression of rigour and tension, even when the thought is not in itself difficult. Milton emphasizes equally the end of his lines and the end of his sentences, both when they coincide and when they part company; thus he takes advantage both of the rigid complex rhyme-scheme and of the freedom of his periods, and gains an effect of weight by increasing the number of strong pauses he can make in what remains a short poem. In his choice of rhymes and other words he is influenced by the *asprezza* of his Italian models: that is, he likes strong and contrasting and slightly unusual sounds. The parallelistic phrasing which comes from the Italian sonnets is very evident and carefully placed in relation to the line-endings.']

III. NOTES

1 *prime of earliest youth*: 'The "springtime" of human life...from about 21 to 28 years of age' (*OED*: prime, *sb.*[1] 8). Though *prime* admitted of other suggestions—the 'first age of anything' (ibid. 6), or 'the lunar cycle of 19 years' (ibid. 4b), in which case the phrase would mean less than nineteen—what seems conclusively to establish *OED*'s interpretation is that *prime of youth* was re-peatedly used to distinguish this period from *prime* as the period of greatest perfection or vigour (ibid. 9).

2–4 *the broad way and the green...the Hill of heav'nly Truth.* Browne compared 'the primrose path of dalliance' (Shakespeare, *Ham.* 1. 3. 50), of some value for idea though not for phrasing. More relevant are two other comparisons: 'broad is the way, that leadeth to destruction,' but 'narrow is the way, which leadeth unto life, and few there be that find it' (Matt. 7. 13–14: Keightley); and '...Chauser doth saye verie well in the Parsons tale, the greene path waye to hel...' (Ascham, *Toxophilus*, *English Works*, ed. W. A. Wright, Cambridge, 1904, 23: Smart). The phrase is not in the *Parson's Tale* and Ascham's memory was at fault, as Smart observes. [Honigmann quotes Daniel, *Delia* 6 ('Faire is my love'), 5–6: 'A modest maide, deckt with a blush of honour, / Whose feete doe treade greene pathes of youth and love' (*Poems and A Defence of Ryme*, ed. A. C. Sprague, London, 1950.] For the image of the toilsome upward path to virtue in contrast with the easy way of vice, Keightley compared Hesiod's hill of virtue (*Works and Days* 287–92). Finley (69) adds Plato, *Rep.* 2. 364 C, *Laws* 4. 718E; Horace, *C.* 3. 24. 44. Hughes suggests that the whole is influenced by Holbein's illustrations of the *Table of Cebes*, 'which show young people trifling at the foot of the rugged mountain of *Truth* while men and women struggle up a steep path to the citadel of true felicity....' [Perhaps the most familiar example nowadays is that in Donne's *Satyre* 3. 79 f. Le Comte (*Yet Once More*, 120–1) adds phrases from Milton's prose and verse: *Works* 3, 239, 261, and 12, 112; *PR* 2. 217, 'on the top of Vertues hill'; and *Patrem* 69, *Qua via lata patet.*]

5–6 *The better part...Chosen thou hast.* Editors cite Luke 10. 38–42 and Ruth 1. 14. Hughes explains: '*Mary*, whom Jesus praised for choosing "that good part, which shall not be taken away from her" (Luke x, 42), and *Ruth*, who gave up her home in Moab to live with her Hebrew mother-in-law, Naomi (Ruth i, 14), traditionally exemplified Christian womanhood.'

6 *overween*: presume, as in 'Mowbray, you overween to take it so' (Shakespeare, *2 H. IV* 4. 1. 149: *OED* 1). Todd noticed Milton's repeated use of this word.

7 *growing vertues.* MS. first had *blooming*, then *prospering*, finally *growing*.
fret their spleen. The spleen was regarded as 'the seat of melancholy or morose feelings' (*OED* 1 b), and the word was used in the sense of 'ill-humour: irritable or peevish temper' (ibid. 6). To *fret* the *spleen* would be to irritate and increase ill-humour (*OED*: fret *v.*¹ 8), the opposite of curbing the spleen (cf. 'Let others learn by him to curb their spleens': Chapman, *Tragedy of Charles Duke of Byron* 5. 1. 136).

8 *pity and ruth*. Editors from Newton (reported by Todd) onward have remarked upon Milton's precedents for rhyming words with identical spelling but different meaning, both English (e.g. Spenser, *F.Q.* 1. 6. 39, 7. 6. 38) and Italian (Tasso, *G.L.* 1. 18, 15. 16); and, from Todd onward, upon the occurrence of *pity and ruth* together in earlier poets (e.g. *F.Q.* 1. 6. 12).

9–14 *Thy care is fixt...Virgin wise and pure*. The parable of the wise and foolish virgins (Matt. 25. 1–13: Keightley) supplies the basic motif of the sestet. The lady of the sonnet is addressed as *Virgin wise* (14); her life is like the replenished lamps of the wise virgins (10); and like them she is ready to greet *the Bridegroom* (12) and gain—indeed she may be sure she has already gained —the *entrance* (14) denied to the foolish ones. The reference, as in the parable, is to the Jewish marriage custom, which there as here is allegorized. With *Hope that reaps not shame* (11), Hurd (in Warton and Todd) compared Rom. 5. 5: 'And hope maketh not ashamed; because the love of God is shed abroad in our hearts by the Holy Ghost which is given unto us.' Browne adds Rom. 10. 11: 'Whosoever believeth on him shall not be ashamed.' Milton's phrase with its scriptural echoes is part of his effort to comfort and encourage the lady, shamed by the rebukes or ridicule of others.

10 *deeds of light*. [Honigmann cites John 3. 19–21: '...men loved darkness rather than light, because their deeds were evil. For every one that doeth evil hateth the light,...lest his deeds should be reproved. But he that doeth truth cometh to the light, that his deeds may be made manifest....'

11 *Hope...shame*. See 9–14 n.

12 *Thou*: ['emphatically placed, to contrast with *they* (l. 6)' (Honigmann).] The adjective *feastfull* (festive: *OED* 1) occurs in Spenser (Warton: see *F.Q.* 6. 10. 22) and in *SA* 1741 (Todd).

13 *Passes to bliss at the mid hour of night*. MS. first had *opens the dore of Bliss, that houre of night*, deleted, and the present text substituted, but first with *watch*, replaced by *howr* (*Facs.* 396). [Honigmann (44) notes the use of unifying contrast: 'the worldly pleasures implied by *the broad way and the green* yield at the end ...to the heavenly *bliss* of the *Bridegroom with his feastfull friends*, a contrast reinforced by *the prime of earliest youth* and *the mid hour of night*.'

14 *entrance*. [Honigmann quotes John 10. 9: 'I am the door: by me if any man enter in, he shall be saved....' See 9–14 n. above.]

Sonnet 10 *(Daughter to that good Earl)*

I. SUBJECT AND DATE

[The date, like that of *Sonnet* 9, can be given only as 1642–5; in position it was the last sonnet printed in the *Poems* of 1645 and presumably was the latest written.]

The sonnet has no title in the editions of 1645 and 1673. The MS. gives a title, in Milton's hand: *To yͤ Lady Margaret Ley (Facs.* 397). Smart brought together what is known of Lady Margaret and her family that throws light on the sonnet. She was the daughter of James Ley (1550–1629), who became Lord Chief Justice in January 1621, and in that capacity presided over the House of Lords at the trial of Lord Chancellor Bacon on the charge of corruption and pronounced sentence upon him. Ley was created Earl of Marlborough by Charles I, and held for brief periods the offices first of Lord High Treasurer, then of Lord President of the Council. He retired from office in December 1628 (Pattison noted Clarendon's statement [*History*, ed. Macray, 1888, 1, 59] that he 'was removed under pretence of his age and disability for the work'); he died in the following March. Lady Margaret (as also a younger sister) was unmarried and lived with him to the end of his life. It appears from the sonnet that her relations with him were peculiarly close and affectionate. On 30 December 1641, when she was over thirty, she married John Hobson, and they were for a time neighbours of Milton's in Aldersgate Street; Hobson was assessed for a dwelling there in March 1644 (Smart, 160). [Parker (876, n. 27) observes that the use of Lady Margaret's maiden name in the MS. title suggests composition before the date of her marriage, whereas the sonnet's number in the sequence 'argues for a date not long after 12 November 1642' (the time of *Sonnet* 8; it is not clear why it should follow soon, or why 1642–5 is not open). As for the first point, the maiden name, as Parker says, helps to identify the Earl; and it was not uncommon for persons to continue to be known by their more familiar title, whether higher or lower than their actual one, e.g. the Countess Dowager of Derby, or Bacon.] Edward Phillips records the Hobsons' intimacy with Milton: 'This Lady being a Woman of great Wit and Ingenuity, had a particular Honour for him, and took much delight in his Company, as likewise her husband Captain Hobson, a very Accomplish'd Gentleman' (Darbishire, *Early Lives*, 64). Though his wife's family were Royalists, Hobson served as lieutenant-colonel of the Parliament's Westminster Regiment in the early years of the Civil War.

[Some critical comments by P. Hellings (1950) are cited above in 'Sonnets: 11.'

A. Rudrum (*Comus*, 1967, 87–8) sees Milton facing 'a difficult technical problem: how to compress into a poem of fourteen lines both an adequate suggestion of her father's virtues and a sufficiently distinguished compliment to her. The problem is solved by a masterly handling of syntax. The first phrase is vocative:...The rest of the octet consists of a complex piling-up of phrases and clauses modifying "that good Earl", but all through the octet there is no main verb: whatever it was that Milton set out to say to the lady he has not said it yet.' This delaying of the main clause arouses suspense and adds force when it comes, in line 11: 'me thinks I see him living yet.' 'Thus the full force of the compliment paid to the Earl in the octet is transferred (by a great feat of compression, in a single line) to his daughter. All the energy of the poem up to this point is compressed into that eleventh line: it is because of this that one is not driven to protest that the sonnet is really a compliment to the Earl rather than to his daughter.']

II. NOTES

1–2 *Daughter to that good Earl...Treasury.* See the headnote. Verity observes that *that* (as also in 5, 6, 8) signifies 'the well-known' (cf. Lat. *ille*). On Milton's Horatian fondness for a reference to the descent of the person addressed, see below, *Sonn* 20. 1 n.

3 *Who liv'd...gold or fee*: a glancing allusion, by way of contrast, to Bacon, at whose trial the Earl had presided (see headnote)? MS. first had a phrase which would have made the allusion slightly more pointed: *left them*, deleted, and *liv'd in* substituted [but this single correction, as Parker suggests (876, n. 27), 'looks like a simple case of miscopying (the eye having skipped to the line below)']. The praise of the Earl's public career is, Finley notes (53), reminiscent of Horace on Pollio (*C.* 2. 1. 13–16) and Lollius (4. 9. 34–44).

4 *And left them...in himself content*. Since he is addressing the daughter and refers specifically to her account of her father's life (12), we may be sure that the details Milton refers to are authentic. This line suggests voluntary retirement (at a very advanced age), unclouded by disagreement with the policy of Charles or premonition of the political disaster to follow. [Honigmann explains as 'Either "more content with himself as a private person", or "more content with himself for not taking bribes." ' The context would seem to favour the first interpretation.] Finley (53) notes the characteristically Horatian themes of honesty and contentment (e.g. *S.* 1. 6. 96–7).

5–6 *Till the sad breaking... | Broke him*. Parliament was finally dissolved on 10 March 1629, after members had resorted to the violent expedient of holding the Speaker in the chair while the Commons passed their resolution against the King's policy. The Earl died four days later, on 14 March. No doubt Milton had Lady Margaret's authority for the belief that the news hastened his end.

6–8 *as that dishonest victory...man eloquent*. Milton refers to the tradition (traceable only as far back as Dionysius of Halicarnassus, and of dubious reliability, as Smart notes) that, shocked by Philip of Macedon's defeat of the Athenian and Theban forces at Chaeronea in 338 B.C., the aged rhetorician Isocrates died of voluntary starvation four days later. [Starnes–Talbert (259) observe that the story was told in C. Stephanus' *Dictionarium* and R. Stephanus' *Thesaurus Linguae Latinae*.] This victory Milton describes as *dishonest*, i.e. Lat. *inhonestus*, 'not glorious but shameful' (Smart). The allusion is presumably Milton's comment on the fact reported by Lady Margaret, and its full implication cannot be determined with certainty. Smart notes that the alliance of the Athenians and their ancient enemies, the Thebans, was in response to Philip's threat to the liberties of Greece, which actually perished with their defeat. The implication would then be that Milton regards Philip's destruction of liberty (a reading supported by *dishonest victory* and the *breaking of that Parlament*) as the cause of Isocrates' death and applies the analogy to Charles's dissolution of Parliament and the death of the Earl. Clarendon's view that the Earl's removal from office was enforced under a specious pretence (headnote, above) suggests some opposition to the royal policy but not its degree. Wright notes that Isocrates 'had appealed to Philip of Macedon to reconcile the differences of the Greek states in order to lead their united forces against the barbarian Persians,' a hope destroyed by the battle. If this aspect of the matter were present to Milton, the implication would be quite different, namely, that the Earl's policy was to reconcile King and Parliament (as his loyal and rewarded service of the crown would indeed suggest) and that his hopes, like those of Isocrates, were shattered. This seems better to fit the facts, while the condemnation of Charles by the implied comparison of him to Philip seems better to suit Milton's own principles (and prejudices). Is it possible that Milton wrote the lines in one sense and allowed Lady Margaret to read them in the other?

9–10 *Though later born...your Father flourisht*: though born too late to have taken note of the events of his career as they occurred. [Honigmann remarks, on *later born*: 'Not literally true, as Milton was born in 1608, unless *flourish* = "to be in one's bloom or prime" (*O.E.D.* 4).' *you.* 'In all his other sonnets Milton used the second person singular: he switched to the plural form here for the sake of the rhyme' (Honigmann).]

13 *all*: all that hear you.

14 *Honour'd Margaret.* Smart notes that 'At least three Italian sonnets close with a similar line,' and cites: *come vertú di stella margherita* (Dante, *Rime*, ed. G. Contini, 2nd ed., Torino, 1946, *Sonn.* 36 (lxxxix), p. 122); *preziosa e mirabil Margherita* (Tasso, *Poesie*, ed. Flora, p. 856); *Preziosa e celeste Margherita* (Claudio Tolomei).

Sonnet 11 *(A Book was writ of late call'd Tetrachordon)*

✺

I. DATE AND CIRCUMSTANCES

Tetrachordon was published on 4 March 1645 (the day George Thomason acquired it). By the time Milton wrote the sonnet, the tract had, he says, 'walk'd the Town a while,' but was 'now seldom por'd on.' Thus the sonnet can hardly have been composed before midsummer of 1645. Since the sonnets appear to have been printed mainly in chronological order, and since *Sonnet* 13 was written in February 1646, this last date gives a presumable *terminus ad quem* for *Sonnets* 11 and 12. All that we can say is that there is no evidence to suggest that *Sonnets* 12–11 did not follow 10 and precede 13, and none that compels us to infer that 12 did not precede 11 (as their original numbering in the MS. seems to imply).

This and the remaining sonnets were not in the 1645 volume. *Sonnet* 11 and *Sonnet* 12 ('I did but prompt the age') appear in MS. in reverse order and each sonnet in two copies. *Sonnet* 12, numbered 11, is at the foot of a sheet containing a draft and a fair copy of 13 (*Facs.* 444–5); this copy, in Milton's hand (designated in *Works* 1, 437, as MS. 1), has the title *On the detraction wch follow'd ᵘᵖon my writing certain treatises.* It appears again, numbered 12, on a small sheet, with the same title in slightly different spelling and the direction 'vid. ante'; this copy, in the hand of an amanuensis, is designated as MS. 2 (*Works* 1, 437; *Facs.* 450–1). Above the title (*Works* 1, 438) the MS. has a note: 'these sonnets follow yᵉ 10. in yᵉ printed booke' (i.e. they are, in 1673, to be added after the first ten sonnets as they appeared in 1645). On the lower half of this same small sheet is the amanuensis' copy (MS. 2) of *Sonnet* 11 (numbered 12); it is followed on the next sheet by a much-altered draft

387

(MS. 1) in Milton's hand (*Facs.* 450–3). The order in MS. (followed by Smart) seems the more suitable in relation to both subject and tone; 12 is general and more serious, 11 is particular and humorous, and deals only with one 'treatise.' It is not easy to see why the order was reversed in 1673, unless, intending the poems to be read together, Milton wished to end on a serious note [see Parker in the next paragraph].

[Honigmann, who follows the MS. order (11: 'I did but prompt'; 12: 'A Book was writ'), refers (117) to Masson's 1645–6 for both sonnets and thinks 1646 or 1647 'a more likely date, at least for XII, a rough draft of which follows in the Cambridge Manuscript after XIV, since XIV cannot be earlier than December 1646': see *Facs.* 450–3. Parker (897, n. 118) thinks that the reversal in 1673 of the MS. order offers no difficulty: 'it is rather obvious that the printed order was an effort to make the subject of *I did but prompt* (titled "On the same") clear to readers almost thirty years later.' Parker (300, 928, n. 32) also thinks that *Sonnet* 11 ('A Book was writ') was written probably soon after the publication of Milton's *Poems*, 'in late 1645 or January of 1646.' Hanford, Shawcross, and Carey date '1647?']

The certain treatises referred to in the MS. title are Milton's four pamphlets on divorce: *The Doctrine and Discipline of Divorce* (*c.* 1 August 1643; 2nd ed., much enlarged, *c.* 1 February 1644); *The Judgement of Martin Bucer, concerning Divorce* (early August, 1644), in which Milton found a predecessor and ally in a great Reformation divine; and *Tetrachordon* and *Colasterion* (both published 4 March 1645), the last a reply to an attack. These writings, notably the first and third, are central documents in Milton's campaign for liberty in the domestic field, one of the three areas (religious, domestic, and civil) into which, in retrospect, he divided that campaign (*Def* 2, *Works* 8, 131–3). This was one ground of his interest in divorce [an interest illustrated by entries in his Commonplace Book]. The other ground was personal: Mary Powell, whom he had married about 1 June [or in July?] 1642, had after a short time gone to visit her family and refused to return. It is the public aspects of the divorce question with which the sonnets deal. The *Doctrine and Discipline* sets forth Milton's general position on marriage and its annulment, with appeals to scripture and to the law of nature. It argues from the primary purpose for which marriage was instituted by God, namely, in Milton's view (based on Gen. 2. 18), for companionship, that when an insuperable obstacle to the realization of this purpose appears, the marriage (which is in effect no marriage) should be annulled, on what would today be called grounds of incompatibility of temper, and on the model of the Mosaic bill of divorcement. Evidently to Milton's surprise, the work was attacked by leaders of the Puritan party [as well as by some Anglicans]: Herbert Palmer, for example, condemned it in a sermon to Parliament as 'a wicked book...deserving to be burnt.' It is against this kind of reception, false to the principles of liberty for which the Civil War was, in his estimation, being fought, that Milton protests in *Sonnet* 12. Among opponents of Milton's views were some men who were to figure in the later sonnet, *On the new forcers of Conscience*: William Prynne (*Twelve Considerable Serious Questions*, September 1644), Herbert Palmer (*The Glasse of Gods Providence*, November 1644), the anonymous *Answer to...The Doctrine and Discipline of Divorce* (November 1644), Daniel Featley (*The Dippers Dipt*, February 1645), Ephraim Pagitt (*Heresiography*, May 1645; 2nd and later editions, with expanded reference), Robert Baillie (*Dissuasive from the Errours Of the Time*, November 1645), Thomas Edwards (*Gangraena*, February [January?] 1646; *Second Part*, May 1646). For the relevant extracts, see Parker, *Milton's Contemporary Reputation* (Columbus, 1940), 73 f.

Sonnet 11 complains with wry humour, not of the opposition to the tract, but of neglect, and of the ignorance which cannot be brought to understand even the title. Johnson regarded *Sonnet* 11 as 'contemptible' (*Lives*, I, 106); Todd, reporting the opinion, replied: 'But Milton wrote this Sonnet in sport.'

11. NOTES

1 *A Book...call'd Tetrachordon.* MS. 1 had *I writt a book*, deleted, and present reading substituted. The Greek *tetrachordon* meant a scale of four notes (*OED*: tetrachord 1, 2). Milton applied the term, as his title page indicated, to 'The four chief places in Scripture, which treat of Mariage, or nullities in Mariage,' namely, Gen. 1. 27–8, 'compar'd and explain'd' by Gen. 2. 18, 23–4; Deut. 24.

1–2; Matt. 5. 31–2, with Matt. 19. 3–11; 1 Cor. 7. 10–16. He was bound to explain more fully the scriptural grounds for his view of marriage and divorce and to remove the supposed scriptural objections to the latter.

2 *wov'n*. MS. 1 had *weav'd it*, deleted, *wov'n* substituted. By *matter* Milton means the substance of the argument (whose gathering was termed in rhetoric *inventio*); by *form* the ordering of the argument (*dispositio*); and by *stile* the clothing of it with appropriate expression (*elocutio*) [cf. Quintilian 3. 3. 1]. He had ample precedent for extending the application of *both* from two to more than two objects, the force of the expression then ceasing to be adjectival and the meaning approximating 'not only...but' (*OED*: B and B 1 b).

3 *The Subject new: it walk'd*. MS. 1 had *It went off well about*, deleted, and present reading substituted. Finley (71) notes classical precedents for treating a book as a living thing: Martial 3. 2, 10. 104, 11. 1; Horace, *Ep.* 1. 20; Ovid, *Tr.* 1. 1, *P.* 4. 5.

4 *Numbring good intellects* (MS. 1, *wits*, corrected to *intellects*, and *but now is* changed to *now*): including in the list of readers (Lockwood). The idea seems to be that, by applying a test of understanding, the book separated, and determined the number of, *good intellects* in the city (cf. Pattison). Smart quotes: '...I like better that entry of truth which cometh peaceably with chalk to mark up those minds which are capable to lodge and harbour it, than that which cometh with pugnacity and contention' (Bacon, *Adv.*, *Works* 3, 363). Todd suggests that in rhyming *por'd on* with *Tetrachordon* Milton 'intended to ridicule'—perhaps 'remembered with amusement' would be more accurate—a couplet in *Eleg.* 5 of Wither's *Prince Henries Obsequies* (1612); 'Who was himselfe, a booke for Kings to pore on: / And might have bin thy ΒΑΣΙΛΙΚΟΝ ΔΩΡΟΝ' (*Juvenilia*, Part 2, Spenser Society, 1871, 379).

5 *stall-reader*: one who pauses to read the books on the stall outside a book-seller's shop. The shops and stalls, then for the most part in St Paul's Church-yard, were clustered around the walls of the old cathedral (Smart). Such brows-ing is of course an age-old practice; Smart cites Martial's reference (11. 1) to idlers in Quirinus' Colonnade who glanced casually at the poet's verses.

6–7 *in file | Stand spelling fals*: stand in a row along the stall, misinterpreting what they read. There is in *spelling* a suggestion of reading letter by letter, with difficulty (*OED*: spell *v.*² 1), as well as mistaking the sense. *Mile-End* was a mile outside Aldgate and the eastern limit of London, so that the phrase means 'while one might walk to the town's end' (Smart, Wright).

8–11 *Why is it harder...Quintilian stare and gasp.* [*Why* 'could be an adverb
or an interjection' (Honigmann).] Smart (following Warton, Sir Walter Scott
[note to ch. 15, *A Legend of Montrose*], and Masson, in opposition to Newton)
is no doubt right in saying that Milton's attention is fixed on the *rugged* Scottish
names (*rugged*: harsh, *OED a.*[1] 5; MS. 1 (*Facs.* 452) first had *barbarous*, then
rough hewn, finally *rugged*), to which, during the Civil War, the English have
become so accustomed that they have grown *sleek* (smooth, *OED* 2) *to our like
mouths*, i.e. in our utterance, which has grown likewise *rugged* (*OED*: like 1 d;
Hughes, 1937). He selects his examples with this, and not the character of particular persons, in view: 'It is the scholar and stylist who speaks, not the politi-
cian.' At the same time we may remember that the incursion of Scots, which
began with the union of the crowns in 1603, was unpopular, and hostile feeling
was much aggravated by the dictatorial attitude of the Scottish allies in the
Parliamentary cause and the Westminster Assembly. Probably this feeling
counted in Milton's selecting a good subject of mockery, and that he shared it
is clear from *On the new forcers of Conscience*. The names, *Gordon*, *Colkitto*, and
Macdonnel (Macdonald)—if they refer to individuals—are those of Royalists,
followers of Montrose. '*Colkitto, i.e. Coll Ciotach*, or "left-handed Colin", was
a familiar title given to one of the Macdonalds, who acted as Montrose's
lieutenant' (Smart). Masson hints darkly at the likelihood that *Galasp* was yet
another name used by the one person called indifferently Macdonald or Colkitto. Quintilian discusses the choice of words, emphasizing the classical virtues
of clarity and simplicity and also the value of euphony (8. 3), [and, as Hughes
notes, he censures foreign barbarisms (1. 5. 8 f.)]. Smart observes that Martial,
himself a Spaniard, comments (4. 55) on the prejudice against uncouth foreign
names which were avoided by fastidious writers on account of their harsh
sound.

12–14 *Thy age, like ours,...King Edward Greek.* Sir John Cheke (1514–57),
Professor of Greek at Cambridge and tutor to Edward VI, was remembered by
Roger Ascham, in his *Toxophilus* [and *The Schoolmaster*, *passim*], for his
inspirational reading of the Greek classics with his students. Smart, who quotes
Toxophilus, adds phrases (in translation) from Cheke's *De Pronuntiatione
Graecae potissimum Linguae Disputationes* (Basle, 1555, 47), written in defence
of Erasmus' pronunciation against Bishop Gardiner: 'When the Latin language
was restored, it was not...without much commotion and indignation of mind.
The Greek language was hateful to many, and is so now; and there are those

who dissuade young men from its study.' Milton was evidently ignorant of that assertion [or, in view of abundant contrary evidence, did not take it seriously], if Masson (followed by Rolfe, Verity, Wright, and others) is correct in paraphrasing 'Thy age did not, like ours, hate learning,' etc. On the strength of Cheke's words, Smart [followed by Honigmann, Rudrum (*Comus*, 89), Prince] interprets the lines in an opposite sense, giving them a touch of irony: the two ages alike hated not learning worse than toad or asp, but quite as much as either (Warton and Todd cite earlier examples of toad and snake as objects of hatred). H. Schultz (*MLN* 69, 1954, 495–7) opposes Masson et al. on grounds of syntax and upholds Smart's view (without mention of him); he supports this reading by citing Bucer, Bernard Gilpin, Latimer, Thomas Lever, Thomas Starkey, and John Bale on the decay of learning in the 16th century, and especially Cheke's own *The True Subject to the Rebell* as reissued by the Royalist Gerard Langbaine the elder, with 'a preface that pointed Cheke's tract against the Puritan "sedition" of 1641,' which Milton may have half-consciously remembered as he wrote. [But other evidence, such as Ascham's exuberant testimony to Cheke's teaching and the flourishing of Greek, is much too strong to be brushed off. See, e.g., D. Bush, 'Tudor Humanism and Henry VIII,' *UTQ* 7, 1937–8, 162–77 (repr. in *Engaged & Disengaged*, Cambridge, Mass., 1966); F. Caspari, *Humanism & the Social Order in Tudor England* (Chicago, 1954), 130 f.; L. V. Ryan, *Roger Ascham* (Stanford, 1963), 14 f. Varying estimates of the state of learning are given by M. L. Clarke, *Classical Education in Britain 1500–1900* (Cambridge, 1959), M. H. Curtis, *Oxford and Cambridge in Transition, 1558–1642* (Oxford, 1959), K. Charlton, *Education in Renaissance England* (London, 1965), and Joan Simon, *Education and Society in Tudor England* (Cambridge, 1966), 204 f. and *passim*. J. M. French (*MLN* 70, 1955, 404–5) opposed Schultz and reaffirmed the opinion of Masson et al., citing *Tetr* (*Works* 4, 231) for Milton's view of the reign of Edward as the purest and sincerest age of the Reformation. Finally, the allusion to the famous Cheke and his age seems to be pointless unless it is brought in as a contrast to Milton's own time. Parker (928, n. 32) is inclined to agree with French, Masson, et al. Carey summarizes the opposed views without taking sides.

Honigmann (44), illustrating the way in which Milton's thought turns back upon itself, notes the Greek title in the first line and the last word, *Greek*.]

Sonnet 12: *On the same*
(*I did but prompt the age*)

I. DATE

See the headnote to *Sonnet* 11. The title *On the same*, if taken literally, would refer to the subject of 11, the reception of *Tetrachordon* alone. But probably it refers to the MS. title of 11, *On the detraction wch follow'd ^{upon} my writing certain treatises* (*Facs.* 444; cf. 450), which may have been intended for print but was omitted when the order of the sonnets was changed. On this assumption the reference of *Sonnet* 12 would not be confined to *Tetrachordon*; [see also 5–7 n. below. Shawcross (*N&Q* 8, 1961, 179–80) would put the sonnet about September 1645, a time when the material for the volume of Milton's poems would be in the printer's hands. Parker (896–7, n. 118) puts 'I did but prompt' 'a good many months earlier' than 'A Book was writ,' chiefly because of 'the considerable difference of tone; Milton is angry, not amused. In temper *I did but prompt* is a poetical counterpart of *Colasterion*.' Whereas the other sonnet, about neglect of *Tetrachordon*, must have been written some ('ten?') months after 4 March 1645, 'I did but prompt' 'is about a treatise or "treatises" actually read, and reviled,' presumably and chiefly the first tract on divorce, 'which had met with "detraction" from at least five writers by May 1645.' Carey dates in 1646.]

II. NOTES

1 *to quit their cloggs*: to give up, renounce (*OED* 5), with some suggestion of 'rid oneself of' (ibid. 1c) and 'leave, separate from' (ibid. 7) their encumbrances (Lockwood) or restraints (Verity). Literally, a clog was a heavy piece of wood attached to the leg or neck of man or beast to impede motion or prevent escape (*OED* 2).

2 *the known rules of antient libertie.* Hughes rightly notes that *the known rules* to which Milton appealed in the divorce tracts were drawn mainly from the Old Testament (the Mosaic bill of divorcement, etc.). But he also repeatedly invoked reason, nature, and the law of nature, as when he wrote of existing restrictions on divorce as 'crossing a Law not onely writt'n by Moses, but character'd in us by nature, of more antiquity...then marriage it selfe; which Law is to force nothing against the faultles proprieties of nature...' (*DDD*, *Works* 3, 383); and these principles he further related to the doctrine of Christian liberty (see below, 8–11 n.).

3–4 *a barbarous noise...Apes and Doggs.* For *Cuckoes* MS. 1 (*Facs.* 444) had *buzzards*. The primary suggestion is a chorus of appalling cacophony. But Smart thinks that Milton chose the components with a view to the qualities assigned to them by moralizers of natural history: the owl typifying ignorance and preference for darkness; the cuckoo, ingratitude and also conceit (as endlessly repeating its own name); and the dog, quarrelsomeness and detraction. Smart illustrates the last example from U. Aldrovandi, *De Quadrupedibus*: 'As dogs bark at a stranger, so detractors, when they read some new work, find fault with the author for what they do not understand, and so seem to be both Zoili and barking dogs.' MS. 1 has no punctuation after *dogs*; MS. 2 (*Facs.* 451) has what appears to be a semicolon, possibly deleted, followed by a period. The semicolon is obviously correct.

5–7 *As when those Hinds...Sun and Moon in fee.* The effect of a cacophonous chorus is continued by the reference to *Froggs*. The implied description of Milton's critics as *Hinds* (rustics, boors: *OED*: sb.² 3) may be compared with his likening of the author of the anonymous *Answer to the Doctrine and Discipline of Divorce* to 'a Country Hinde sometimes ambitious to shew his betters that hee is not so simple as you take him' (*Works* 4, 257). The allusion in the sonnet is to Ovid, *M.* 6. 317–81: Latona, fleeing from the wrath of Juno, and bearing with her Apollo and Diana, her twin offspring by Jove, destined to hold *in fee* (as their absolute and rightful possession—*OED*: sb.² 2b) *the Sun and Moon* respectively, came to a small lake where she encountered a group of rustics; she asked to be allowed to quench her thirst, for her own sake and that of the infants she nursed, asserting the natural right of all persons to sun, air, and water; when they prevented and reviled her and muddied the water,

Latona, roused to anger, transformed them to frogs. [The lines are a signal example of Milton's rising from a satirical snort to the grand style, and the sudden elevation is an integral part of the idea. The general application is clear enough, but Parker (*Explic.* 8, 1949–50, Item 3; *Milton*, 897, n. 118) sharpened the point by suggesting that the phrase *twin-born progenie* glances at the twin tracts on divorce, *Tetrachordon* and *Colasterion*, published on 4 March 1645. T. E. Maresca (*MLN* 76, 1961, 491–4) notes allegorical interpretations of Ovid's tale, particularly a medieval one as developed by Alexander Ross (*Mystagogus Poeticus*, 1653, 28–9, 99–100 [also in 1648 ed., 26, 97]: Apollo as the son 'of an obscure maid,' Diana as 'Gods Church': 'Thus, in likening himself to Latona, Milton is defending the truth of the *Tetrachordon*, his progeny, for which Apollo and Diana—Christ and his Church—have become the metaphors.' This seems very far-fetched, though it is adopted without question by Rudrum (*Comus*, 90–1).]

8 *But this is. . .Pearl to Hoggs.* Cf. 'Give not that which is holy unto the dogs, neither cast ye your pearls before swine' (Matt. 7. 6). The *Hoggs*, though metaphorical, complete the suggestion of a chorus of animal sounds. Verity notes that, warned by the reception of the *Doctrine and Discipline*, Milton had expressed a similar contempt for the ignorant on the title page of *Tetrachordon*, in a quotation from Euripides' *Medea* (298–301) which speaks of bringing strange wisdom to dullards.

8–12 *But this is. . .wise and good.* MS. 1 (though not MS. 2) has the period after *Fee* (7), thus commencing a new sentence with *But* as in the text. The only other significant change is at 10, where MS. 1 (*Facs.* 444) has *hate the truth wherby they should be free*, corrected to *still revolt when Truth would set them free*; *make* for *set* appears in MS. 2 (*Facs.* 450), but is corrected to *sett*; *make* brings the phrasing closer to John 8. 32 (quoted below), which Milton evidently had in mind. The lines are somewhat ambiguous. The hogs *That bawle for freedom in their senceless mood* (*mood* in the sense of emotional state, though often confused with *mode*, manner) appear to be the rabble, who kick against the restrictions of reason and Christian morals, comprehending nothing of Christ's words: 'And ye shall know the truth, and the truth shall make you free' (John 8. 32). Pattison quotes *DDD*: 'What though the brood of Belial, the draffe of men, to whom no liberty is pleasing, but unbridl'd and vagabond lust. . ., will laugh broad perhaps, to see so great a strength of Scripture mustering up in favour, as they suppose, of their debausheries; they will know better, when they shall hence learne, that honest liberty is the greatest foe to dishonest licence' (*Works* 3, 370). Consonant with this, the most obvious interpretation of *Licence they mean when they cry libertie* (11) would be that Milton is extending his attack from those who ignorantly rejected his doctrine to those who, with equal ignorance, accepted and misapplied it as a sanction of licence. It was probably such readers that Milton had in mind when he said he would rather hear of his treatises' being translated into Latin than into Dutch (and by implication that he wished they had been published in Latin in the first instance). 'For,' he continued, 'my experience in those books of mine has now been that the vulgar still receive according to their wont opinions not already common' (*Epistol* 16, *Works* 12, 72–3; cf. similar remarks in *Def* 2, *Works* 8, 115). Hurd (reported by Warton and Todd) avoided the addition of 'the vulgar' by taking the line in a different (though less obvious) sense, that is, as referring to those who hypocritically condemn Milton's doctrine as licentious because they know that in reality it would curb their own licentiousness. He quoted in illustration: '. . . nothing more licentious then some known to be, whose hypocrisie yet shames not to take offence at this doctrine for licence; when as indeed they feare it would remove licence, and leave them but few companions' (*Tetr*, *Works* 4, 218). This would mean that the *Hoggs* are some of the same persons referred to above in the list of animals, and that they rebel against *truth*, Milton's whole doctrine; this reading is certainly possible.

N. H. Henry ('Who Meant Licence When They Cried Liberty?' *MLN* 66, 1951, 509–13) avoids a change of reference in another way: he argues that the reference throughout the sonnet is to the ignorant enthusiasts who misapplied Milton's doctrine—the class of persons attacked by Thomas Edwards in *Gangraena* (1646) as a sect of 'divorcers' and illustrated by a woman preacher, Mrs Attaway, who, citing Milton, left her 'unsanctified' husband for another woman's husband (Part 1, 113–15, 11, 9, 83, 87, 111, 25–7). These are the *Owles . . . and Doggs* (4) and the *Hoggs* (8), not the Presbyterians who railed against Milton's tracts. Henry's argument seems unacceptable: it assumes that Milton did not know what he was trying to do or changed his mind in the process of composition (for, although *detraction* was crossed out in MS. 1, the repeated MS. title cannot be completely ignored); also, it is unjustifiable to assume that the only alternative is to make the whole apply to Presbyterian opponents. It is at least equally possible that in *Sonnets* 11 and 12 Milton is inveighing against the ignorant who cannot understand his writings, and whose misunderstanding issues for the most part in detraction, though sometimes in acceptance equally deplorable. Most editors, even Smart, are silent on this whole problem. [Honigmann also is not convinced by Henry's argument.]

The contrast between liberty and licence which is central in Milton's doctrine of liberty had (as Smart makes clear) a long history. It was invoked by Cicero, who denounced the statue of Liberty set up by Clodius on his confiscated property as *simulacrum non libertatis publicae, sed licentiae* (*De Domo Sua* 51. 131). Livy spoke of corrupted aristocratic youth who preferred their own licence to the liberty of all (3. 37), and of others who pleaded for liberty or rather for licence if the truth were told (34. 2). The tradition was continued or revived in the Renaissance, e.g. by Machiavelli in the beginning of the fourth book of his *History of Florence*. [Honigmann (32, n. 1) illustrates the traditional antithesis, put in religious terms, from pamphlets of 1645–6.]

Illustrating line 12, *For who loves that, must first be wise and good*, editors have noted Milton's repeated insistence on virtue as the foundation of true liberty, 'which is to be sought for not from without, but within, and is to be obtained principally not by fighting, but by the just regulation and by the proper conduct of life' (*Def* 2, *Works* 8, 131). Hurd (reported by Warton and Todd) quoted 'none can love freedom heartilie, but good men; the rest love not freedom, but licence' (*TKM, Works* 5, 1); Smart: 'libertie hath a sharp and double edge fitt onelie to be handl'd by just and vertuous men' (*HistBr, Works* 10, 324); Hughes: 'true Libertie / . . .alwayes with right Reason dwells / Twinn'd, and from her hath no dividual being' (*PL* 12. 83–5). We may add 'Love vertue, she alone is free' (*Comus* 1018); 'Well knows every wise Nation that their Liberty consists in manly and honest labours, in sobriety . . .; and when the people slacken, and fall to loosenes, and riot, then doe they as much as if they laid downe their necks for some wily Tyrant to get up and ride' (*Ref, Works* 3, 523); '. . .know, that as to be free is precisely the same thing as to be pious, wise, just and temperate, careful of one's own, abstinent from what is another's, and thence, in fine, magnanimous and brave—so, to be the opposite of these, is the same thing as to be a slave' (*Def* 2, *Works* 8, 249–51).

The general principles of liberty to which Milton refers in these lines are primarily neither of Old Testament nor of classical origin, but are essentially those of what was called 'Christian Liberty' or 'the Liberty of the Gospel' (cf. *DocCh* 1. 26–7; *CivP, Works* 6, 28–32), as these passages from *Tetrachordon* illustrate:

For nothing now adayes is more degenerately forgott'n, then the true dignity of man. . . . Although if we consider that just and naturall privileges men neither can rightly seek, nor dare fully claime, unlesse they be ally'd to inward goodnesse, and stedfast knowledge, and that the want of this quells them to a servile sense of their own conscious unworthinesse, it may save the wondring why in this age many are so opposite both to human and to Christian liberty, either while they understand not, or envy others that do.... (*Works* 4, 74.)

Man was created in God's image, and endowed with

Wisdom, Purity, Justice....All which being lost in Adam, was recover'd with gain by the merits of Christ....But Christ having cancell'd the hand writing of ordinances which was against us, Coloss. 2.14. and interpreted the fulfilling of all through charity, hath in that respect set us over law, in the free custody of his love, and left us victorious under the guidance of his living Spirit, not under the dead letter; to follow that which most edifies, most aides and furders a religious life, makes us holiest and likest to his immortall Image, not that which makes us most conformable and captive to civill and subordinat precepts....(ibid. 74–5.)

And 'indeed no ordinance human or from heav'n can binde against the good of man; so that to keep them strictly against that end, is all one with to breake them' (ibid. 75). This principle the very heathen could recognize; witness Cicero: '*All law*, saith he, *we ought referr to the common good, and interpret by that, not by the scrowl of letters. No man observes law for laws sake, but for the good of them for whom it was made*' (ibid. 75).

13–14 *But from that mark...loss of blood*: *they* (those who fail to understand these principles of true liberty) *roave*, shoot away from the *mark* (*OED*: rove v. 2); and this despite all the *wast of wealth* (expenditure that has proved useless by not attaining the end, true liberty) and *loss* of lives. It was to be a common complaint of soldiers in the Civil War that the ends for which they had fought were not achieved. [Milton's phrasing is somewhat condensed and elliptical but the sense, as just paraphrased, seems quite clear. L. S. Cox (*ELN* 3, 1965–6, 102–4) finds difficulties in the logic, especially of *For*, and she would —following one draft (*Facs.* 444)—put a comma after *roave*, paraphrasing: 'We see the extent of their missing their proposed target by the extent of their property destruction and carnage'—which surely distorts the meaning.]

Sonnet 13 *To Mr. H. Lawes, on his Aires*

❦

I. DATE AND SUBJECT

There are three copies of the sonnet in the Cambridge MS.: a rough draft in Milton's hand, deleted (MS. 1); a fair copy also in his hand (MS. 2); a fair copy in the hand of an amanuensis (MS. 3): so labelled in *Works* 1, 440; texts in *Facs.* 444, 448. The sonnet was first printed in *Choice Psalmes* (1648) by Henry and William Lawes (*Facs.* 368). The Columbia text is that of 1673.

MS. 1 has the title *To my freind Mr Hen. Laws Feb. 9. 1645* (i.e. 1646 N.S.). MS. 2 has—added by the amanuensis—*To M^r. Hen: Laws on the publishing of his Aires*; MS. 3, the same but with the name changed to *Lawes*. The 1648 title was 'To my Friend M^r. *Henry Lawes*'; the 1673 title, '*To Mr. H. Lawes, on his Aires.*' Lawes' *Ayres and Dialogues* did not appear till 1653; meanwhile the sonnet had been printed in the *Choice Psalmes* (1648). It has been plausibly suggested that there may have been a plan to publish the airs in 1646, a plan not carried out. [Parker (1026, n. 52) thinks that the amanuensis' transcripts of *Sonnets* 11–14 were made in 1653.] *167/43*

In his note on Henry Lawes (1595/6–1662) Smart had the benefit of Masson's researches, but not of Willa M. Evans' *Henry Lawes: Musician and Friend of Poets* (New York, 1941), from which his information is here supplemented. In addition to being a Gentleman of the Chapel Royal (from 1626), Lawes was a member (from 1630) of the 'King's Private Musicke' 'for the voices'; his duties included much besides the composition of songs, particularly a share in planning, composing, and directing court entertainments and performing in them. Thus in the year of

Comus Lawes had a part in Shirley's *Triumph of Peace* when it was performed at Whitehall, and he composed the settings at least of the songs in Carew's *Coelum Britannicum*. [This last point is questionable: see *Comus* III. 3.] It would appear that Lawes's connection with the Egerton family as music teacher continued after his appointment to the King's Music, though his duties at court and on royal progresses must have occupied most of his time. No doubt it was this connection, as well as his experience with court masques, that led to his commission to produce *Comus*. His performing therein in the guise of the Earl of Bridgewater's shepherd, skilled in music, has been thought to confirm the inference that he was still in the family's service as a teacher of Lady Alice and her brothers.

We do not know either the time or the circumstances of the beginning of Milton's friendship with Lawes. That it antedated *Arcades*—and that Lawes solicited Milton's aid in that work—is only the most probable hypothesis; indeed it is only probable hypothesis that Lawes produced the entertainment of which *Arcades* was a part or took the role of the Genius of the Wood. In the preparing of *Comus* at least the two were brought into close co-operation, and in that, if not earlier, their friendship matured; Milton entrusted to Lawes the revision of his text for presentation and the later printing of the full text. Nor was their friendship impaired by Lawes's ardent attachment to the Royalist cause; his and his brother's *Choice Psalmes put into Musick* (1648) carried not only a noble dedication to his defeated and imprisoned king but Milton's sonnet among the commendatory verses. Lawes set to music lyrics by many of the poets of the time, Jonson, Beaumont, Fletcher, Donne, Carew, Herrick, Lovelace, Suckling, Randolph, Townshend, Katherine Philips, Shirley, Davenant, and Waller; and he received enthusiastic tributes from more than one. Waller's *To Mr. Henry Lawes, who had then newly set a Song of mine in the Year, 1635* is of interest because it makes a point similar to Milton's—the composer's respect for the poet's words and sense:

> So others with Division hide
> The Light of Sense, the Poets Pride,

But you alone may truly boast
That not a syllable is lost;
The Writer's and the Setter's skill
At once the ravish't Eare do fill.

Miss Evans finds in Lawes' respect for the poem, and his careful skill in giving the words appropriate musical accompaniment, the special mark of his compositions, and an innovation welcome to poets. [Cf. Spaeth, *Music*, 124–8, and Eric Hart, 'Introduction to Henry Lawes,' *Music & Letters* 32 (1951), 217–25, 328–44). But, as Honigmann observes, Lawes in 1657 addressed verses to John Wilson in which he gave Wilson the place of pioneer that Milton had given to Lawes himself (quoted by Miss Evans, 219–20). Honigmann also cites M. Lefkowitz (*William Lawes*, London, 1960, 150–1), who denies the priority given by Milton to Henry Lawes and says that many other men 'were setting verse in precisely the same manner at precisely the same time.'] In an unpublished paper Miss Evans (who is working on a large study of the sonnet) suggests that Milton's musical father was a notable offender in subordinating sense to sound, which Milton could not fail to remember.

[G. L. Finney (*Musical Backgrounds*, 170) remarks that this sonnet 'gives the reader a sense of stepping into an entirely different musical environment from that of the earlier poems,' in which music had been more or less symbolic (as it was to be again in *PL*). In the sonnet '"Music"...means merely notes written for words.' Milton praises Lawes not for giving delight or elevating the soul 'but because (although one may rightly question the historical accuracy of the statement) it was he who "First taught...short and long." Not harmony, but setting of words, matters. Lawes is honored not for imaging divine harmony, but for serving the poet.'

Honigmann (67–8) observes parallels that link the apparently remote *Sonnet* 11 ('A Book was writ of late') with the sonnet to Lawes. Both are concerned with the art and the strict rules of composition, literary and musical. Milton deplores the forcing of the language required by outlandish names, and praises Lawes for not forcing it. 'Milton stands aloof from the *file* of stall-readers and Lawes is exempted *from the throng*.'

The one sonnet ends with King Edward being taught by Cheke and the other with Dante listening to Casella, and both Cheke and Lawes are praised as teachers of their respective ages. Moreover, Dante's Casella 'leads into the beginning of XIV in the same way, though perhaps not so patently,' and there are parallels between 13 and 14.

Sir Donald Tovey ('Words and Music,' *The Main Stream of Music and Other Essays*, London and New York, 1949, 210) thought that, in praising Lawes' adaptation of music to words, Milton forgot the work of the earlier generation of English composers; Tovey complained also that Lawes' aim led him 'to over-punctuate the words and interrupt the flow of his music.' E. Hart (331 n.: see above) suggested that Milton's terms were loosely complimentary, not technically precise. Questioning both these judgments, Audrey Davidson ('Milton on the Music of Henry Lawes,' *MiltonN* 2, 1968, 19–23) observes the *two* points in Milton's first line, 'tuneful and well measur'd,' and thinks that Milton is concerned with quantity in the classical sense. Lawes, with concern for the meaning and importance of words, was at pains to match 'spoken pitch levels to musical settings.' Lawes' 'setting the meaning of the words is most clearly seen in "Ariadne Deserted,"' the 'Story' Milton referred to. Miss Davidson also amplifies Milton's epithets, 'tuneful' and 'smooth,' and sees reminders of Lawes the singer in 'the Priest of Phoebus' Choir' and the allusion to Casella.

MacDonald Emslie ('Milton on Lawes: The Trinity MS Revisions,' *Music in English Renaissance Drama*, ed. John H. Long, Lexington, Kentucky, 1968, 96–102) sees revised phrases as pointing more clearly toward the mode of which Lawes was a special master, 'the declamatory ayre'—although Milton took the licence of an admirer in giving his friend a priority he could not have claimed in the adaptation of the music to the words. In lines 2–3 (see note below) revisions suggest that Milton 'wished to emphasize the declamatory quality of Lawes' ayres,' his recognition of 'Just accentuation, a voice-line that respects and is based on the speech movement of the words.' The revision of line 8 (see n. below) turns from general praise to the particular qualities of the declamatory ayre, tunefulness ('smoothe aire') and the accentuation of

Sonnet 13

English ('humor best our tongue'). Line 9, beginning 'Thou honour'st Verse,' is likewise in accordance with Lawes' concern for the prior importance of the words. The concluding reference to Dante's Casella and his compelling song implies that Lawes' declamatory song has similar rhetorical power to hold an audience. Thus 'Milton's remarks... about Lawes' songs are not...idle praise, but pertinent comment.']

II. NOTES

1   *measur'd*. See below, *Arc* 71 n.

2-3   *span | Words with just note and accent*: measure, as with the hand (*OED*: span 2), the words, giving to each its note of proper length and the stress that usage and the sense require. MS. 1 first had *words with just notes, wch till then us'd to scan*, deleted; then *when most were wont to scan*; finally as in text (*Facs.* 444).

3-4   *scan | With Midas Ears, committing short and long*. Since to *scan* is to determine the number and nature of the feet in a line of verse, often by counting on the fingers, the word carries on the suggestion of measurement by hand given in *span*. The whole phrase means: 'judge of metrical and musical effect with as little discrimination as Midas did, in other words like an ass.' When Pan dared to contend with Apollo in song, only Midas, king of Phrygia, who heard both, preferred Pan's performance, and Apollo punished him by changing his ears to those of an ass (Ovid, *M.* 11. 153–93). Finley (56) compares Persius 1. 121, and notes that 'the idea of a faulty ear causing mistakes in scansion is reminiscent of' Horace's *A.P.* 251–74, particularly *legitimumque sonum digitis callemus et aure*. Todd cited 'Mydas-eares relent not at my moane' (Nashe, *Pierce Penilesse, Works* 1, 158). Warton noted the Latinism of *committing*; *committo* means 'join, put together,' of two or more objects. Browne further notes that the verb was used of gladiators in combat. *OED: v.* 9b adopts Johnson's definition, 'place in a state of hostility or incongruity.' MS. 1 first had *committing*, then *misjoyning*, finally *committing*. In both cases the idea is 'offending against quantity and harmony' (Richardson, reported by Todd) by a disproportion between the length of syllable and note, and also in stress or beat (since the classical terms applied to quantity were in English prosody transferred to accent); cf. *just note and accent* (3). [Cf. Campion, *Observations*,

1602 (G. G. Smith, 2, 329): 'In joyning of words to harmony there is nothing more offensive to the eare then to place a long sillable with a short note, or a short sillable with a long note, though in the last the vowell often beares it out.'] Browne remarks that the offence Milton complains of was still derided in *The Spectator* (18), which commented on the long cadences assigned to such words as 'and' and 'from' in opera music.

5 For *worth* MS. 1 substitutes *wit*, then returns to *worth*. With *exempts thee from the throng* Richardson (reported by Todd) compared *me...secernunt populo* (Horace, *C.* 1. 1. 29–32).

6 *With praise...look wan*. MS. 1 (*Facs.* 444) had *and gives thee praise above the pipe of Pan* (carrying on the allusion of 3–4); the deletion of only the first five words may indicate the intention of preserving the allusion, later abandoned. [Honigmann quotes 'pale / With envy' (Shakespeare, *H. V* 5. 2. 378–9).]

7 *shalt be writ*: a Latinism. Newton (reported by Todd) compared *Scriberis Vario fortis et hostium | victor* (Horace, *C.* 1. 6. 1–2).

8 *That with smooth aire...our tongue*. MS. 1 (*Facs.* 444) has *that didst reform thy art, the cheif among. aire*: melody (Wright); cf. *OED* 19. The sense of the line is that *aire* (music) is fitted perfectly to the words (what the *tongue* utters) [and perhaps also 'our language' (*OED*: tongue 8)]. Browne compared 'smooth dittied Song' (*Comus* 86).

9 *send*. [This, the 1673 reading, is a manifest misprint for the *lend* of MSS. 1–3 and the 1648 text (*Works* 1, 441; *Facs.* 444, 448, 368).]

10 *Priest of Phoebus Quire*. Finley (55) cites *Musarum sacerdos* (Horace, *C.* 3. 1. 3). [Cf. the earlier tacit allusion to Apollo (3–4 n.).]

11 *Story*. The sonnet as first printed in 1648 has a marginal note: 'The story of Ariadne set by him in Music': i.e. Cartwright's *Ariadne Deserted*; Lawes' music for this poem was not printed until his *Ayres and Dialogues* (1653). [See *Plays and Poems of William Cartwright*, ed. G. B. Evans (Madison, 1951), 488–91, 717–22.]

12–14 *Dante shall give...milder shades of Purgatory*. MS. 1 had *Fame by the Tuscan's leav, shall*, deleted. The reference, as all editors note, is to *Purg.* 2, 76–117, which tells how Dante's friend, Casella the musician, came forward to greet him, how they talked affectionately together, and how, on Dante's asking him to sing, he sang Dante's *Amor che ne la mente mi ragiona.* The *shades* are *milder* because less horrible than those described in the *Inferno* (Warton, Masson, et al.); *shades* means darkness, as in 'the shades of night' (*OED* 2). Diekhoff (*MLN* 52, 1937, 409–10), noting the cancelled *mildest* in MS. 1, suggested that the comparison is not between the shades of purgatory and hell but between different degrees of shade in purgatory.

Sonnet 14 *(When Faith and Love which parted from thee never)*

※

I. DATE AND SUBJECT

There are three copies in MS.: a rough draft in Milton's hand (MS. 1), a fair copy also in his hand (MS. 2), and a third copy in the hand of an amanuensis (MS. 3) (*Works* 1, 442; *Facs.* 446–9). MS. 1 supplies a title, which identifies the person commemorated and gives the approximate date of the sonnet: *On yᵉ religious memorie of Mʳˢ Catharine Thomason my christian freind deceas'd 16 Decem. 1646* (this later deleted; see end of this headnote). Editors before Smart failed to identify the person because they misread the name in the deleted title as Thomson. Actually, she was the wife of George Thomason (d. 1666), a London bookseller and a man of considerable knowledge. Smart summed up whatever is known and relevant concerning the husband and wife. [Smart's researches have been much amplified—beyond the scope of this note—by Lois Spencer's articles on Thomason's 'Professional and Literary Connexions' (*Library*, Ser. 5, 13, 1958, 102–18) and his 'Politics' (ibid. 14, 1959, 11–27), and by J. J. McAleer ('The King's Pamphlets,' *Library Chronicle*, University of Pennsylvania, 27, 1961, 163–75).] Thomason's chief title to fame is that with extraordinary foresight he set himself, on the meeting of the Long Parliament, to collect whatever came from the press bearing on the issues of the day; the result was the great Thomason Collection, now in the British Museum, which numbers over 22,000 items printed during 1640–60. *Areopagitica* and some other tracts carry the words *Ex Dono Authoris*. Thomason travelled in Italy to collect books, of which he issued a catalogue in 1647. It was probably by him that Milton despatched a letter to Carlo Dati in Florence, in which he wrote:

Sonnet 14

'The charge of this I shall commit, rightly I hope, to Bookseller James, or to his master, my very familiar acquaintance' (*Works* 12, 53), that is, presumably, to Thomason's apprentice, James Allestree, or to Thomason himself. [Miss Spencer sees Thomason as one of the many Presbyterians whose sympathies, in the later 1640s, veered toward the King, the only safeguard, it seemed to them, against the growing power of the Army and the Independents.] In 1651 Thomason was implicated in a Presbyterian–Royalist plot to bring back Charles II (a fact Smart ignores), and was imprisoned for some weeks.

Milton's poem attests his affectionate admiration for the wife and for her piety and good works. She was the niece and ward of Henry Fetherston, the bookseller to whom Thomason had been apprenticed, and we may assume that her love of books and learning, shown by references in Thomason's will, was fostered first by her guardian, then by her husband. The will also shows the devotion of the latter, who left instructions that he should be buried by the side of his 'late dear and only wife' at St Dunstan's in the West. He further directed: '...my son George having received a large proportion of my...dear wife's library already I do... bequeath the remainder...to my ⟨other⟩...children...; that, looking upon them, they may remember to whom they did once belong; hoping that they will make the better use of them for their precious and dear mother's sake' (Smart, 81). Catharine Thomason was buried on 12 December 1646; [she left at least eight children]. Thus the date of her death is wrongly given in the cancelled title; it is perhaps significant that *16* appears to have been scored out before the whole was cancelled, though Smart prefers to think that the *16* was a misplaced start of *1646*. It may, however, be the date of the composition of the sonnet.

Smart noted the recognition by W. Davies (*Athenaeum*, 29 September 1888) of the sonnet's similarity to one by Domenico Mantova (1553), and printed it for comparison. [R. L. Ramsay ('Morality Themes in Milton's Poetry,' *SP* 15, 1918, 142) found in this sonnet Milton's 'most detailed use' of the medieval allegory of 'the Coming of Death.' 'This reads almost like a condenst version of the old morality *Everyman*. "Flesh" in line 4 (in the first draft, which is here followed) corresponds to the morality figures Beauty and Wits; we have Good Deeds in line 5, in "Works and Alms"; and the graces Faith and Love replace Knowledge and Confession.'

Saintsbury (*Cambridge Hist. Eng. Lit.* 7, 131) pronounced the sonnet 'the most commonplace thing that Milton ever wrote'; which may be true, though Saintsbury's gusto did not often extend to utterances of devout piety.]

II. NOTES

1 *Faith and Love.* [Honigmann quotes *DocCh* 1. 1 (*Works* 14, 23): 'Christian doctrine is comprehended under two divisions: Faith, or the knowledge of God; and Love, or the worship of God'; and *CivP* (ibid. 6, 21): 'What evangelic religion is, is told in two words, faith and charitie; or beleef and practise.']

2 *dwell with God.* [Honigmann cites Ps. 140. 13: 'the upright shall dwell in thy presence.']

3-4 *this earthy load | Of Death, call'd Life.* MS. 1 (*Facs.* 446) had *clod*, changed to *load*; and, for *Death, call'd Life, Flesh & sin*, deleted and changed to final reading. Pattison compared *questa morte, che si chiama vita* (Petrarch, *Sonn.* 216). Browne cited: 'who shall deliver me from the body of this death?' (Rom. 7. 24). [Honigmann illustrates the 'popular paradox' with John 12. 25: 'he that hateth his life in this world shall keep it unto life eternal.']

4 *us.* MS. 1 had *man*, deleted, replaced by *us*. For the second *Life*, MS. 1 had *heavn*, deleted, replaced by *life*; MS. 2, *life*; MS. 3, *blis*, deleted, replaced by *life* (*Facs.* 446, 448).

5-8 *Thy Works...Follow'd thee.* Keightley compared: 'Thy prayers and thine alms are come up for a memorial before God' (Acts 10. 4); and 'Blessed are the dead which die in the Lord...they may rest from their labours; and their works do follow them' (Rev. 14. 13).

6-8 *Staid not behind...bliss for ever.* In place of these lines MS. 1 had: *Strait follow'd thee the path that Saints have trod | Still when* (first *as*, changed to *when*) *they journey'd from this dark abode | Up to ye Realm of peace & Joy for ever*; deleted, and replaced by present text, but with *Truth* for *Faith* in line 7 (*Facs.* 446). Pattison runs the *golden rod* of *Faith* back to Athene's staff of office (Homer, *Od.* 16. 172), notes that Somnus had such a wand in the Latin poets, and illustrates its use from Drummond (1, 8 n. and 11). [Warton cited the 'golden reed' of Rev. 21. 15 (cf. ibid. 11. 1), which Milton mentioned twice in *RCG* (*Works* 3, 185, 194).]

8 [Honigmann notes that there is here no hint of the 'Mortalist' heresy expressed directly in *DocCh* 1. 13 (*Works* 15, 219 f.) and dramatically in *PL* 10. 782 f.: the doctrine that the soul dies with the body and remains dead till the Resurrection.]

9 *Love led them on, and Faith who knew them best.* MS. 1 had: *Faith shew'd* (replacing *who led on*, deleted)*ye way & shee who saw* (replacing *& knew*) *them best*. MS. 2: *Love led the(m) on* (replacing *Faith shew'd the way*), and *Faith who knew them* (replacing *she who saw them*) *best* (*Facs.* 446).

10-13 *Thy hand-maids, clad them...Before the Judge.* Pattison compared *Deux freres emplumés, qui d'une aile dorée | Peinte à lames d'azur* (Ronsard, *Hymne de Calaïs* 2, *Œuvres*, ed. P. Laumonier, Paris, 8, 1935, 255). Warton compared *PL* 11. 14–20: 'To Heav'n thir [Adam's and Eve's] prayers | Flew up,' 'clad | With incense,' 'Before the Fathers throne.' With *bid thee rest*, cf. Rev. 14. 13 (quoted above, 5–8 n.); also Heb. 4. 3, 11. [Cf. also Milton, *El* 3. 63–4.]

12 *speak...on glorious Theams.* MSS. 1, 2, and 3 all have *spake* (*Facs.* 446–8). The reason for the change to *speak* (1673) is clear: what has gone before has happened, is concluded, while the speaking, the fame in heaven, continues. MSS. 1 and 2 have *in glorious theames*; MS. 3 and 1673, *on glorious*. Grierson (*TLS*, 15 Jan. 1925, 40) noted *in* in the two copies in Milton's hand and suggested that this is the correct reading, *on* an undetected scribal error; further, that *Theam* is here used as a musical term, with the sense of the plainsong or *canto fermo* of a contrapuntal piece (*OED* 4). The line, then, means 'speak the truth of thee in glorious strains.'

14 *And drink...immortal streams.* Warton compared: 'thou shalt make them drink of the river of thy pleasures. For with thee is the fountain of life' (Ps. 36. 8–9); and *EpDam* 206–7: *Æthereos haurit latices & gaudia potat | Ore Sacro.* Verity and Smart added: 'And he shewed me a pure river of water of life, clear as crystal, proceeding out of the throne of God and of the Lamb'; and 'And whosoever will, let him take the water of life freely' (Rev. 22. 1, 17).

Sonnet 15 *(Fairfax, whose name in armes through Europe rings)*

❦

I. DATE AND CIRCUMSTANCES

This sonnet of 1648 exists in the MS. in Milton's hand (*Facs.* 453), from which it is printed. Its omission from the *Poems* of 1673 was presumably due less to the person addressed (since Fairfax, now dead, had long ago made his peace with the monarchy) than to the sentiments and expressions it contained. The sonnet was first printed in *Letters of State* edited by Edward Phillips (1694), p. xlvi (*Facs.* 372). Variants are recorded in *Works* 1, 444–5; only two of these have any critical interest (see 5 n., 6–8 n.).

Sir Thomas Fairfax (1612–71), who became Lord Fairfax (in the Scottish peerage) on the death of his father in the year of the sonnet, had long been inured to war. He matriculated at St John's College, Cambridge, in 1626, served on the continent in 1629, commanded during the first Scottish ('Bishops'') war, was a parliamentary general in the north (where his family's estate lay) from 1642, and played an important part in the victory of Marston Moor (1644). In 1645 he became commander-in-chief of the New Model Army, with Cromwell as his lieutenant-general. His skill, energy, and great personal courage did much to ensure its series of victories, Naseby in particular. But the political leadership of the New Model (which, owing to these victories, became a force in politics comparable to the King and the Parliament) passed into the hands of Cromwell. Fairfax presided over the deliberations of its Council, but the policy was devised and implemented by Cromwell and the Commissary-general, Ireton (as is evident from the documents assembled in *Puritanism and Liberty*, ed. Woodhouse, London, 1938, 2nd ed., 1950). If Milton expected decisive political action from Fairfax, he clearly mistook his man, who was in politics indecisive and ambiguous, and whose talents were all military. These came into play again in 1648, in suppressing the widespread Royalist outbreaks, seconded by a Scottish invasion, which are sometimes called the Second Civil War. To these events Milton refers (6–8 n.). Smart notes that the deleted title in MS., *On y* Lord Gen. Fairfax at y* seige of Colchester*, indicates that the sonnet was written some time between 14 June, when the siege began, and 27 August, when the town surrendered; and further, that the terms of Milton's reference to the 'fals North' (7) indicate that he had not yet heard the news of Cromwell's defeat of the Scots at Preston (17 August). [The reference also puts the sonnet, if Milton's present tense is to be taken literally, in the period between 8 July (the Scots' invasion) and 17 August. Parker, however, while recognizing this (940, n. 72), suggests that 'the sonnet was composed later in the year, as a tribute to Fairfax's latest victory.']

II. NOTES

1–4 *Fairfax...remotest kings.* Milton and the majority of his party, the Independents, had by now despaired of a firm agreement with Charles and become avowed republicans. It is by no means certain, however, that Fairfax was of their number.

Finley (48, 52) notes, as one form of Horatian address which Milton adopts, the name (stated or implied) accompanied by praise of representative exploits (cf. *C.* 4. 5 and 4. 14, and *Sonn* 16 and 17), though admittedly the elaboration in a clause running to several lines is more in the Italian manner; cf. Tasso: *Signor, ch'in picciol corpo animo chiudi | Immenso*...(*Rime Eroiche* 76, in *Rime* 3, 43, *Opere*, ed. G. Rosini, 5, 1822). With *rings* (is filled with talk or report of: *OED*: *v.*² 3c, whose earliest example is of 1608 and the next of 1675) Pattison compared 'Darius, of whose huge powre all Asia range' (Surrey, *Poems*, ed. Padelford, Seattle, 1928, 93) and 'Of whose great triumphs all the world shall ring' (Ariosto, *O.F.*, tr. Harington, 2nd ed., 1607, 7. 53).

5 *vertue.* Phillips (1694) has *Valour*, which retains at least part of the meaning of *vertue*, Lat. *virtus*, which means the sum of manly powers, including courage, but also capacity and moral worth. For the former Smart quotes: 'It is held |

That valour is the chiefest virtue' (Shakespeare, *Cor.* 2. 2. 87–8); for the latter, Hughes (1937) quotes: 'Virtue he had, deserving to command' (Shakespeare, *1 H. VI* 1. 1. 9).

6–8 *though new rebellions...their serpent wings.* For the Royalist risings of 1648 see the headnote. According to Apollodorus (2. 5. 2) the Lernean Hydra had eight heads which could be destroyed but only that two might grow in the place of each (this Hercules managed to prevent by having Iolaus sear the bleeding stumps), and a ninth head, reputed to be immortal, which Hercules lopped off, thus killing the monster. [The allusion, in various applications, was a commonplace: some editors cite Shakespeare, *1 H. IV* 5. 4. 25: 'Another king? They grow like Hydra's heads'; and *2 H. IV* 4. 2. 38, 'this Hydra son of war.'] Pattison noted the association of the Hydra with revolt in Malherbe: *Que l'hydre de la France en révoltes féconde* [*Œuvres*, ed. M. L. Lalanne, 5 v., Paris, 1862–9, 1, 262]. Finley (59) quoted Horace: *non hydra secto corpore firmior | vinci dolentem crevit in Herculem* (*C.* 4. 4. 61–2). [Marvell telescoped two Herculean feats for the sake of an hyperbole: 'And now the Hydra of seaven Provinces / Is strangled by our Infant Hercules' (*Character of Holland*, 1653, lines 137–8: *Poems*, ed. H. Macdonald, London and Cambridge, Mass., 1952).] The only known authority (noticed by Warton, reported by Todd) for making the Hydra a winged creature is the single word *ptanon* in Euripides' *Ion* 195, rejected by modern editors but perhaps accepted by Milton; [the word was in the edition he owned (*Works* 18, 304, 318), *Euripidis Tragoediæ*, Geneva, 1602, 2, 625]. Verity notes that several of the offspring of Echidna, mother of the Hydra, were indeed winged monsters. With the 1694 reading, *her Serpent Wings*, the reference would inevitably be to the Hydra; but with the MS. *their* it might well be to *new rebellions* (6) and not to the Hydra directly at all. The Scottish invasion was held by its opponents to be a violation of the Solemn League and Covenant; hence *the fals North displaies | Her brok'n league.* The verb *impe* means literally to graft new feathers in the wing of a hawk; hence to strengthen or improve the flight of (*OED* 4b, which also cites Sylvester, *Sonn.* 4: 'Imping his broken wings with better plumes,' Grosart, 2, 321). The image was common in poetry: examples are cited from Spenser, Shakespeare, Drayton, et al.

J. T. Shawcross (*N&Q* 2, 1955, 195–6) argues (i) that the march into England of Hamilton's Scottish army, which displayed, made evident, the treachery of Scotland in signing a treaty with Charles in violation of the Covenant, did not serve to *impe*, strengthen, the English rebellions; the rebellions were designed to distract the government while Hamilton's final blow was being prepared; (ii) that *their serpent wings* (8) should read *her* as in Phillips' text of 1694, that *their* is nowhere else used by Milton in MS., but always *thir* or *thire*, and that the MS. shows signs of having been altered (presumably by another hand) from *her* to *their*; (iii) that what Milton wrote was *& the fals North displaies | Her brok'n league, to impe her serpent wings*; (iv) that this avoids historical inaccuracy and disposes also of the problem of the winged Hydra (see above), since the image of Scotland is not that of a Hydra but of a winged serpent (or dragon). [Cf. D. C. Allen, 'Milton's Winged Serpents' (*MLN* 59, 1944, 537–8), a gloss on *PL* 7. 482–4.]

9 *O yet a nobler task.* Here as in *Sonn* 16 (Cromwell), it is tasks to come rather than past victories that engage Milton's chief interest. He expects Fairfax to assume political leadership and purge the government of corruption.

10–13 *For what can Warr... | Of Public Fraud.* There were bitter complaints of confusion and corruption in the financing of government and the war by the Long Parliament and its committees, and Milton abhorred such violations of the purity and good name of the cause he idealized. That he refers here to Parliament and its committees (with which the Army had been at odds) and not to the ambitious avarice of the Presbyterian clergy (as Pattison implies) is confirmed by the well-known digression in his *History of Britain*, a passage suppressed when the book was printed in 1670. He there complains that, 'after many labours, much blood-shed, & vast expence' (cf. lines 13–14), the cause was brought 'to ridiculous frustration' by the fact that 'once the superficial zeale and popular fumes that acted thir new magistracie were cool'd and spent,' each member

betooke himself, setting the commonwealth behinde and his private ends before, to doe as his owne profit or ambition led him. Then was justice delai'd & soone after deny'd.... Some who had bin call'd from shops & warehouses without other merit to sit in supreme councels & committies, as thir breeding was, fell to hucster the common-wealth; others did thereafter as men could sooth and humour them best: so that hee onely who could give most, or under covert of hypocritical zeal insinuate basest enjoy'd unworthylie the rewards of learning & fidelitie, or escap'd the punishment of his crimes and misdeeds. (*Works* 10, 319–20)

Nor was this the worst. The public funds were squandered and embezzled so that creditors could not receive the payments due them and 'that faith which ought to bee kept as sacred and inviolable as any thing holy, the public faith, after infinite summs receiv'd & all the wealth of the church, not better imploy'd, but swallow'd up into a private gulfe, was not ere long asham'd to confess bankrupt' (cf. lines 12–13). And 'besides the sweetness of briberie and other gaine,' 'the love of rule' and 'thir owne guiltiness and the dreaded name of just account' which made them determined to retain power, Milton suggests that to this end 'there were of thir owne number who secretly contriv'd and fomented those troubles and combustions in the land which openly they sate to remedy' (*Works* 10, 321; cf. lines 10–11). In the sonnet Milton is writing of the unpurged Parliament, but, in ejecting the members of the Rump on 20 April 1653, Cromwell was to complain that some were 'corrupt and unjust Men and scandalous to the Profession of the Gospel' (W. C. Abbott, *Writings and Speeches of Oliver Cromwell*, 2, Cambridge, Mass., 1939, 642).

10 *Warr*. Shawcross (*N&Q* 2, 1955, 196) would read *Warrs*, with, he argues, the support of the MS., in which he finds indication of a broken *s*, and as demanded by the sense and the historical fact of the series of outbreaks that Fairfax was engaged in suppressing. [Carey questions Shawcross's reading of the MS.]

11 *Truth*. ['Milton and other Independents had good reason to fear that *Truth* would suffer *Violence*. As recently as May, 1648, the Presbyterians in Parliament had passed a new law making it a capital offence to persist in heretical errors (Masson, *Life*, iii. 600–1). Milton naturally identified himself with *Truth*, and he and his beliefs were now seriously threatened. Compare also XI. 10, XVI. 4 and *New Forcers* 9–12.' (Honigmann).]

12 *Public Faith*. [This phrase, originally meaning 'simply "national honour," ' was, Honigmann shows, common in Parliamentary documents and 'was widely used to refer to a form of National Debt incurred by the Parliament: placed beside *Public Fraud*, *Avarice and Rapine*, this is clearly its significance in the sonnet.' He thinks that the anger of Milton's last lines 'reflects not only the woeful state of England but also a highly personal sense of wrong,' and he quotes the preface to the suppressed passage of *HistBr*, published in 1681 as *Mr John Miltons Character of the Long Parliament* (*Works* 18, 247): 'It is reported... that Mr. Milton had lent most of his Personal Estate upon the Publick Faith; which when he somewhat earnestly and warmly pressed to have restored... after a long and chargeable Attendance, met with very sharp Rebukes... And he had not probably mended his worldly condition in those days, but by performing such Service for them, as afterwards he did, for which scarce anything

would appear too great.' Honigmann associates this experience with the time
of the sonnet, but that seems very doubtful. Cf. Parker, 996, n. 165.]

13-14 *In vain doth Valour... | ...share the land.* Cf. *Sonn* 12. 8–14 and notes.
[Finley (59) quotes Horace, *C.* 3. 24. 25–9, 35–6, and 3. 4. 65–8. *share*:
'To receive, possess, occupy together with others' (*OED*: *v.*² 4b, citing this
line as illustrating a figurative sense).

Sonnet 16 *(Cromwell, our cheif of men)*

꧁

I. DATE AND CIRCUMSTANCES

The sonnet was first printed, with variations, by Edward Phillips in *Letters of State* (1694); his text is reproduced in *Facs.* 372. In the MS. (*Facs.* 452) the sonnet is given both a title and a date: *To the Lord Generall Cromwell May 1652 | On the proposalls of certaine ministers at y*ᵉ *Commtee for Propagation of the Gospell* (deleted). The octave, which runs over into line 9, contains Milton's unstinted praise of Cromwell, a matter Smart discusses at length [praise which was to be both amplified and qualified in the *Second Defence* of 1654]; but the pith of the sonnet is the championing of 'free Conscience' in the sestet, which requires somewhat fuller treatment than Smart gives it. [Honigmann is more specific than Smart.]

The Puritan triumph brought utter confusion to organized religion in England. From the overthrow of episcopal government in the English Church, we may recognize three positions: the Presbyterians (the party of the right in the Puritan coalition) demanded a national church on the Scottish model, with rigorous conformity enforced by the state; but their attempt to set up their system was wrecked by the opposition of the Independents (the party of the centre) and the Separatists (forming the parties of the left), and further by the disunion and discredit of the Presbyterian group in the later phases of the Civil War. In the ranks of the Independents there were varying shades of opinion and their position was rendered the more fluid and obscure by their uneasy alliance with the parties of the left; but their core was made up of what had been known as Non-separating Congregationalists. Conceding, indeed maintaining, the duty of a Christian state to ensure provision for pure public worship and instruction, they had, in the days of Presbyterian

416

ascendancy, sought merely an 'accommodation' for themselves, that is, permission for their gathered churches outside the national establishment. This was the position of the 'Dissenting Brethren' in the Westminster Assembly (see Milton, *C.P.W.* 2, ed. E. Sirluck, 1959, ch. 2, sect. 5); but with the shift in the centre of power, and their limited alliance with the left, the Independents advanced to a position of qualified toleration. The Separatist groups demanded (not always with entire consistency) the complete separation of church and state, and at least for themselves complete liberty of conscience. The differences between the importance attached to the question of the magistrate's power in religious matters, and the opposition of Independents and Separatists on this issue, are attested by the Whitehall Debates on the *Agreement of the People*, in which Philip Nye, one of the original Dissenting Brethren, joined Ireton in upholding the responsibility and the real though not unlimited power of the magistrate, against John Goodwin and others who maintained the Separatist view and paraphrased the arguments of Roger Williams' *Bloudy Tenent of Persecution* (see Woodhouse, *Puritanism and Liberty*, 125–69).

By 1652 the state of the Church was chaotic. The Presbyterian organization had failed to take root even in the few places where it had been put in force; there was no regular mode of appointing parochial ministers and no effective means of curbing unqualified or heretical preachers. In February 1652 the spread of heresy was illustrated by the publication in London of the Latin text of the Racovian Catechism, embodying the doctrine of the Socinian churches in Poland. [This work—which Milton was said to have licensed—was burned in April by order of the House of Commons (H. J. McLachlan, *Socinianism in Seventeenth-Century England*, Oxford, 1951, 187 f.; French, *L.R.* 3, 206, 212–13, 5, 421; Honigmann, 146.] A petition to Parliament by fifteen ministers contained the signature of Philip Nye, but the leader and chief spokesman for the Independent position of limited toleration was John Owen, now chaplain to Cromwell. Attached to the petition was a plan for settling outstanding ecclesiastical questions. In response to this plan Parliament (i.e. the Rump) appointed on 18 February a Committee for the Propagation of the Gospel, of which Cromwell was a member. The ministers' proposals included the setting up of two Commissions, partly lay and partly clerical, substantially identical in function, though not in name, with the Triers and Ejectors, adopted as part of Cromwell's reorganization of the Church in 1654. Those presenting themselves to the Commissioners for licences to preach should be required to produce testimonies of 'their piety and soundness in the faith' from six godly Christians, at least two of them ministers. There was to be no compulsion to attend the ministrations of the parochial clergy thus set up, but dissenting persons were required to give notice to the magistrate of their places of regular meeting (obviously a political as much as a religious safeguard) and, finally, opponents of those Christian doctrines plainly affirmed by Scripture to be necessary for salvation should not be allowed to preach or promulgate anything against them. In response to a demand for clarification on these doctrinal points the ministers drew up a list of fifteen fundamentals of Christianity: none were to be allowed to promulgate their beliefs if they questioned the Trinity, the Incarnation, the Resurrection, justification by Grace, the necessity of forsaking sin, or sought to discover the mind of God otherwise than by Scripture, or forsook and despised the duties of worship. Gardiner observes that Owen would have been unlikely to advance the proposals without Cromwell's general approval (and their evident influence in the settlement of 1654 strongly argues such approval), but that at the same time Cromwell strove in the Committee to prevent a further narrowing of the toleration proposed. Parliament did not consider the Committee's report until February 1653, almost a year after the ministers' original petition. Closely connected with the whole question of a national ministry was that of its being supported by tithes, to which there was much opposition among extremists; on 29 April Parliament instructed the Committee to examine the possibility of other means of support, but left tithes in force until other means were provided. (See S. R. Gardiner, *History of the Commonwealth and Protectorate*, rev. ed., 4 v., London, 1903, 2, 98–105.)

In the sonnet Milton presumably addresses Cromwell as a member of the committee and relies on the General's known efforts on behalf of toleration for those of tender conscience since the days of the New Model, though he probably misjudged the extent of agreement with himself on the unlawfulness of a supported ministry. Milton's uncharitable attack on the ministers' motives was perhaps sharpened by Parliament's action on 29 April, in continuing support by tithes until the Committee could recommend some other means [Abbott, *Cromwell*, 2, 1939, 537]. Masson, who did much to clear up the background of the sonnet, speaks of Roger Williams' presence in London at the time of these transactions and suggests that he inspired and guided the opposition to Owen's scheme, and that Milton agreed with Williams' demand for the complete separation of church and state and already shared his opinion on tithes expressed in *The Hireling Ministry None of Christs, or A Discourse touching the Propagating the Gospel of Christ Jesus* (London, 1652), an opinion Milton was later to set forth in his *Likeliest Means to Remove Hirelings* (1659); see Masson, *P.W.* 1, 222–9.

This sonnet completes, so far as his verse is concerned, the record of Milton's leftward movement in ecclesiastical questions. In *Il Penseroso* (1631–2?) he was responsive to the beauty of the Anglican service, though he had already, in *Elegy* 4 (1627) shown his disapproval of the exclusion of Puritan ministers. In *Lycidas* (1637) he attacked the Church on this same ground, among others, and condemned its clergy as greedy hirelings. After his alliance in 1641–2 with the Presbyterian party, the Smectymnuus group in particular, he reacted against the Presbyterians because they condemned his views on divorce (see *Sonn* 11 and 12) and, more largely, because they wanted to impose their own system with no toleration for dissenters; witness *On the new forcers of Conscience* (1646?), with its famous conclusion, 'New Presbyter is but Old Priest writ Large.' Now in 1652 Milton attacks, as violently as he ever attacked bishop or presbyter, the Independents who champion a public ministry, and combines the hirelings of *Lycidas* with the wolf from which they could not defend the flock into one deadly phrase, 'hireling wolves.' The rest of the record is in his prose works: the attack on episcopacy and defence of a modified Presbyterian settlement (the five pamphlets of 1641–2), the plea for toleration (*Areop*, 1644), to which is added the separation of church and state (*Def* 2, 1654; *CivP*, 1659), the attack on the political attitude of the Presbyterians (*TKM*, 1649), and, for his final position on the church, *DocCh* (1658–60). Milton's belief in toleration closely resembled Cromwell's and was less liberal than that of Roger Williams and perhaps the Levellers (who regarded freedom of conscience as a *natural* and not merely a *Christian* right), since it extended only to dissenters within the Puritan group. In one respect indeed the proposal of the ministers whom Milton here condemns was more liberal, since (like the *Agreement of the People*) it did not contain the usual proviso that toleration should not extend to Roman Catholics or Episcopalians [cf. Milton's *TR*, 1673].

In Milton's attitude toward Cromwell Smart finds some inconsistency or at least short-sightedness, but his varying pronouncements are not difficult to understand. In this sonnet he is praising the leader to whose character, policy, and exertions more than to anything else the defeat of the Royalists was owed and in whose actions up to this point Milton never found anything to criticize. Moreover, he is appealing to the consistent champion of toleration. He would go further later and defend Cromwell's ejection of the Rump (20 April 1653) and his assumption of power when the Nominated ('Barebones') Parliament failed and no other resort was open. 'To your invincible virtue we all give place, all but such . . . who know not, that there is nothing in human society more pleasing to God, or more agreeable to reason, . . . more just in a state, . . . more useful, than that the most worthy should possess the sovereign power' (*Def* 2, *Works* 8, 223). In this there was no radical departure from Milton's principles, which were never in the least democratic (nor could anything have been less representative of the nation than the Rump); he never regarded Parliament as other than a means. But what was held by Cromwell was a trust—namely liberty, as Milton conceived it (ibid. 224–5); and the rest was admonition and advice. Cromwell was to implement what remained Milton's fundamental concern, the liberty of the individual, which, he believed, required freedom of expression, separation of church and state, reduction in the number of laws, and adequate provision for education: anyone who sought more than that was moved, not by a just desire for liberty, but by the spirit of ambition and faction (ibid. 234–40). It is highly significant that, in 1654, Milton further exhorts Cromwell to associate with him 'accomplished men and chosen citizens' of tried fidelity to these principles—Fleetwood, Lambert, Desborough, Whalley, Overton (ibid. 233–5), some of whom were to oppose Cromwell's later courses; for this is Milton's basic ideal, liberty safeguarded by men of known integrity and ability. In the light of this ideal and of the course of events in the later years of the Protectorate we must read Milton's plans for the government of England in the *Readie & Easie Way to Establish A Free Commonwealth* (1660), with its trust in the rule of such a group and its emphatic opposition to 'a single person,' and even his welcome of the restored Rump as 'recoverers of our liberty' in *Hirelings* and the words on the title-page of the second edition of the *Readie & Easie Way*: *et nos / consilium dedimus Syllae, demus populo nunc*—if indeed Smart is right in identifying Sulla with Cromwell. [Others, e.g. Hughes, take 'Sulla' to be General Monk, to whom Milton sent a letter (*Works* 6, 107–9, 357–8).]

II. CRITICISM [D.B.]

T. Stoehr ('Syntax,' etc., *English Studies* 45, 1964, 296–9): The syntactic pattern 'is almost exactly paralleled in the sonnets to Sir Henry Vane and Lady Margaret Ley, all three possessing that orbicularity of structure which Wordsworth admired' [see Wordsworth, introduction to Sonnets, above]. The syntax set going by the initial apostrophe to Cromwell is not resolved until the final couplet, 'Helpe us....' 'Locked within this structure we find a long dependent clause stretching over the entire octave,...followed by a series of three structures of predication which are, again, syntactically ambiguous....The most striking feature of the octave is the proliferation of structures of coordination....This balance is reinforced by other devices, such as the syntactic chiasmus in line 6, the alliteration of "faith" and "Fortitude" in line 3, and the combination of alliteration and semantic similarity in "Darwen stream" and "*Dunbarr feild*" in lines 7 and 8. The speaker is choosing his words, weighing unit against unit, matching syntactic element to syntactic element; his thoughts are marked off with terminal junctures (three times as many as in the sestet), falling regularly at normal points of caesura and at the ends of the lines. Such stately symmetry reveals more than Milton's sense of high purpose; the movement is majestic, even processional, as is proper to the celebration of a great military hero's return from the field. "And Worsters laureat wreath", which overflows the octave boundary, embellishes the turn with a kind of flourish, both in meaning and position, and this too suits the confident martial tone, being both grand and gratuitous.'

'The epideictic quality of the octave is complicated, however, by the "orbicular" construction of the whole sonnet. So long an initial passage as eight lines, *without a main verb*, is syntactically tentative, uncommitted, and therefore in peculiar tension with the assertive inner structure already noted.' 'Syntactically speaking, there is nothing for the "yet" [of 9] to coordinate, since the structure it begins is not of the same order as anything which has gone before. To be sure, semantic parallelism—the octave celebrating Cromwell's military glory, the sestet warning him of the civil strife still to be settled—makes the use of "yet" logical, but the tension between form and content increases the "structural anxiety" for a resolving main verb. Given these formal conditions, it is not surprising to find the movement of the sestet strongly pressing forward, in contrast to the slow, balanced octave.... This forward movement is reinforced by a relatively regular flow of the meter, and by the "running over" of the intonation patterns around the boundaries of the line ends, in contrast to the octave, where the paired and weighed units are cut on the pattern of the line lengths.' The word 'yet' brings a 'sudden explosion into movement' with the shift from glorious past to difficult present. 'The sestet seems to begin with just another structure of coordination, but the thought of how "much remains / To conquer still" changes the poet's mood; present hopes and fears crowd out the less impassioned memories of the past, and the syntactic structure itself is transformed from continuing coordination to predication, active and urgently direct.'

III. NOTES

1–2 *Cromwell, our cheif of men.* Finley (48) recalls Horace's address to Augustus as *maxime principum* (*C.* 4. 14. 6), etc.; on the Horatian mode of address see further *Sonn* 15. 1–4 n. *a cloud | Not of warr onely.* Newton (reported by Todd) cited *Aeneas nubem belli . . . | sustinet* (Virgil, *A.* 10. 809–10).

2 *detractions rude.* In *Def 2* (*Works* 8, 203 f.) Milton specifies a number of the charges brought against Cromwell by Royalists and Presbyterians and seeks to defend him.

3 *Guided by faith . . . Fortitude.* In *Def 2* (*Works* 8, 212–15) Milton describes Cromwell as known only, before he entered the national arena, for his religious character and the integrity of his life. 'He had cherished his confidence in God, he had nursed his great spirit in silence, for some extraordinary times.' He 'was a soldier, above all others the most exercised in the knowledge of himself; he had either destroyed, or reduced to his own control, all enemies within his own breast—vain hopes, fears, desires' (215). [Cf. Marvell, *Horatian Ode.* Honigmann remarks on Cromwell's 'well-known habit of searching his conscience in times of uncertainty: *faith* thus prepares for the importance of liberty of *conscience* (l. 13).']

4 *To peace & truth . . . plough'd.* [Hughes notes that 'In 1651 *Truth and Peace* appeared on a coin issued by Parliament to express its confidence in the results of Cromwell's victories' of 1648–51 (see 7–9 n.). Honigmann shows that the phrase *peace and truth* 'was as much repeated in its day as "the good old cause" and "*salus populi suprema lex.*"' Some—among them Milton here, no doubt— 'did so in allusion to the Solemn League and Covenant (1643), the concluding words of which summarised its aim as the establishing of truth (i.e. "true" religion) and peace.' Honigmann also quotes: ' "For there shall be peace and truth in my days" (Isa. xxxix. 8; cf. Esther ix. 30, Zech. viii. 19).']

5–6 *And on the neck . . . Gods Trophies.* 'The idea is that the servant of the true God has triumphed over the pagan goddess of Fortune' (Wright). In *on the neck* Verity finds an allusion to Joshua 10. 24–5; the whole passage is suggestive: 'And . . . when they brought out those kings . . . Joshua called for all the men of Israel, and said unto the captains of the men of war which went with him, Come near, put your feet upon the necks of these kings. . . . And Joshua said unto them, Fear not, nor be dismayed, be strong and of good courage: for thus shall the Lord do to all your enemies....And afterward Joshua smote them, and slew them....' Milton's exultant allusion (*crowned*) to the beheading of Charles and Cromwell's part therein (so different in attitude from Marvell's) is palpable: 'His malignity to Kings aided his imagination in the expression of this sublime sentiment' (Hurd, reported by Warton and Todd). Phillips (*Letters of State*, 1694, xlv: *Facs.* 372) still felt it necessary to omit the offensive allusion.

[*reard*: 'Because a *trophy* was originally a structure erected or set up (on the field of battle or in a public place)' (Honigmann). *his work*. 'To do "the work of God" is a biblical commonplace, as in John vi. 28, 1 Cor. xvi. 10' (Honigmann).]

7–9 *While Darwen stream...And Worsters laureat wreath.* The references are to the battle of Preston (17 August 1648), fought near the river *Darwen* in Lancashire, where Cromwell defeated the Scottish army under the Duke of Hamilton, sent to support the Royalist (and Presbyterian) risings in England (see *Sonn* 15, headnote); the battle of *Dunbar* (3 September 1650), where Cromwell's defeat of the Scots led to the virtual subjugation of Scotland; and finally the defeat of Charles II at the battle of *Worcester* on the anniversary of Dunbar (3 September 1651). Of the last Cromwell said: 'The dimensions of this mercy are above my thoughts. It is, for aught I know, a crowning mercy' [Abbott, *Cromwell*, 2, 1939, 463]—which lends special point to what would otherwise be simply a reference to the laurel wreath accorded to Roman victors. Verity cites Shakespeare, *Caesar* 5. 3. 82: 'Put on my brows this wreath of victory.' [Honigmann remarks that it 'is surely no accident' that Milton 'cites three of Cromwell's victories against the Scots Presbyterians rather than his triumphs over English royalists or Irish rebels,' and he cites Marchamont Needham and Sir Thomas Urquhart to illustrate the strength of English feeling against the Scots in the early 1650s. Cf. 11 n. below.]

8 *Dunbarr feild* is deleted in MS. (*Facs.* 452) and *Worsters laureat wreath* written in above the line; but it is also written in above the next line (9) in place of *twentie battles more*; presumably the correction was made in the wrong place and the mistake was not rectified. Editors retain the original reading of 8. Finley (60–1) finds the passage reminiscent of Horace's praise of Augustus' victories: *cantemus Augusti tropaea* ⟨cf. 6⟩ | *Caesaris, et rigidum Niphatem* | *Medumque flumen* ⟨cf. 7⟩ *gentibus additum* | *victis minores volvere vertices* (*C.* 2. 9. 19 f.). Finley discerns other hints: for *with blood of Scotts imbru'd* in the account of Latin blood staining the waters in the Civil Wars (*C.* 2. 1. 29–36); for *resounds* *thy praises loud* in *ut paterni | fluminis ripae . . . | redderet laudes tibi* (*C.* 1. 20. 5–7); and for *Worsters laureat wreath* in *Pollio . . . | cui laurus aeternos honores | Delmatico peperit triumpho* (*C.* 2. 1. 14–16).

10–11 *peace hath her victories | . . . warr.* [Smart et al. quote Cicero, *Off.* 1. 22. 74: *multae res exstiterunt urbanae maiores clarioresque quam bellicae.* Honigmann cites a similar sentiment in *Def* 2 (*Works* 8, 241).]

11 *new foes aries.* [MS., *aries*; Phillips, *arise.*] Warton (reported by Todd) wrongly supposed that Milton referred to the Presbyterian clergy in England and the mistake was perpetuated by Keightley, Browne, Rolfe, and Verity. Masson understood that it was the organization of the Church proposed by Owen and the Congregationalists that Milton was attacking (see headnote above). It is significant, however, that the victories of Cromwell that Milton speaks of are over the Scots. He thinks of the *new foes* as threatening, like the Scottish Presbyterians, *to bind our soules with secular chaines,* that is, to call in the power of the state to establish, and enforce conformity to, a national church. Cf. 7–9 n. above.

13–14 Verity and Smart assembled texts that find an echo here: 'The hireling fleeth, because he is an hireling, and careth not for the sheep' (John 10. 13); 'Beware of false prophets, which come to you in sheep's clothing, but inwardly they are ravening wolves' (Matt. 7. 15); 'For I know this, that after my departing shall grievous wolves enter in among you, not sparing the flock' (Acts 20. 29); '. . . the enemies of the cross of Christ: Whose end is destruction, whose God is their belly' (Phil. 3. 18–19). Editors notice the echoes of *Lyc* 113–22. Verity compared *PL* 12. 508–14. See headnote.

Sonnet 17 *('Vane, young in yeares, but in sage counsell old)*

襟

In addition to the texts in the MS. and Phillips' *Letters of State* (1694), this sonnet appears in George Sikes's *The Life and Death of Sir Henry Vane* (1662), 93–4 (*Facs.* 368, 373, 454). It is there introduced by the words: 'The Character of this deceased Statesman...I shall exhibit to you in a paper of Verses, composed by a learned Gentleman, and sent him, July 3. 1652.' This text differs in no critical point from that of the MS.

Sir Henry Vane the Younger (1613–62), son of Sir Henry Vane the Elder (d. 1655; hence the son's appellation), early adopted extreme Puritan views, coupled with a mystical form of religion. He consistently championed the Puritan cause and was active—especially in matters relating to the navy, foreign affairs, and religious toleration—in the Long Parliament, the Rump, and the Council of State, until Cromwell put an end to them and assumed power in 1653, an event which threw him into opposition to Cromwell. A man of marked ability and undoubted constancy to his principles, Vane was nevertheless distrusted by many, although the oft-quoted words of his former collaborator, Cromwell—'O Sir Henry Vane, Sir Henry Vane, the Lord deliver me from Sir Henry Vane' (J. Willcock, *Life of Sir Henry Vane the Younger*, London, 1913, 240)—must be read in the context of that opposition. Vane was technically not one of the regicides, but his punishment was demanded by Parliament, and he met his death with dignity and fortitude on the scaffold.

The sonnet, written a few weeks after *Sonnet* 16, is in some sort a companion to it, emphasizing first the recipient's role in an era of war (in Vane's case the Commonwealth's relations with the Dutch), then turning to peace and Milton's chief preoccupation, religion. Before the decisive defeat at the battle of Worcester (see above, *Sonnet* 16, headnote), Vane had aimed at an alliance, indeed a union, of the Dutch Republic with the Commonwealth, a visionary aim which the Dutch, expecting the fall of the Commonwealth, rejected. After Worcester the Dutch proposed a commercial union, but relations had steadily deteriorated, and, while negotiations dragged on, open hostilities broke out. Shortly before Milton wrote his sonnet, war was declared. Although, like Cromwell, Vane regretted the event and urged a speedy termination of the war, he threw all his effort into preparing the navy for effective action, and with remarkable success.

By implication Milton looks forward to the restoration of peace, and the redirecting of Vane's energies to the religious issue still pending in the Committee for the Propagation of the Gospel. With Vane's general views on the separation of church and state Milton here expresses complete agreement, though Vane's idea of religious toleration seems to have been, like that of his friend Roger Williams and unlike those of Milton and Cromwell, subject to no reservations.

II. NOTES

1 *Vane...counsell old.* Dunster (reported by Todd) compared 'Isaac, in yeers yong, but in wisdom growen' (Sylvester, *D.W.W.* 2. 3. 2. 120, Grosart, 1, 179). The phrase *young in yeares* reflects Sir Henry's appellation (see headnote) rather than his age, which was approaching forty. On the Horatian mode of address see *Sonn* 15. 1–4 n. ['After *young in yeares* Milton probably plays on the derivation of *senator* from *senis* [rather from *senex*], old' (Honigmann).]

2–4 *Then whome a better...African bold.* [Verity notes that the objective case *whome*, after *Then* (than), is more traditional than grammatical; he compares *PL* 1. 490, 2. 299, 5. 805.] As editors record, Milton is recalling accounts of the courage and public spirit displayed in the Roman senate during the invasions of Pyrrhus, king of Epirus, and the African Hannibal in the third century B.C.

One famous example is the report of Pyrrhus' ambassador that the Roman senate was a council of many kings (Plutarch, *Pyrrhus* 19, L.C.L. 9, 407; North, 4, 241). Another is the speech of Titus Manlius Torquatus against the popular outcry for ransoming prisoners who had weakly surrendered to Hannibal's forces, and the senate's response (Livy 22. 60–1). The *gownes* are the togas of the Roman senators and here stand for civil power: Smart cites *parvi enim sunt foris arma, nisi est consilium domi* (Cicero, *Off.* 1. 22. 76), and *Cedant arma togae, concedat laurea laudi* (ibid. 1. 22. 77).

5–9 *Whether to settle...all her equipage.* Vane strove for peace with the Dutch, but suspected their design of war while their envoys, sent to England, were still negotiating with the officers of the Commonwealth; when hostilities broke out, he threw his energies into preparing the navy (see headnote). Editors from Warton and Todd (reporting Warburton) onward have recognized the secondary allusion in *hollow states* to the Dutch States General. Hughes's idea (1937, 1957) of 'a punning suggestion that they are as hollow, or false, in character as their territory is hollow, or low-lying' seems unacceptable because *hollow*, while it clearly means insincere, false (*OED* 5), is not a synonym for low-lying, and because it would necessitate sacrificing the palpable word-play. [However, a geographical as well as an ethical pun is seen not only by Hughes but by M. Nicolson (*John Milton*, 173), Shawcross, Bush, and Carey; it is not clear whether it is recognized by various other commentators, e.g. Smart, Hanford. Further, one may not see any sacrifice of word-play but an enrichment of it; and the idea of *hollow* as low-lying is well within the bounds of seventeenth-century wit. Is that idea not present in 'pale and hollow eyes' (Milton, *Ps* 88. 44) and 'the hollow Deep / Of Hell' (*PL* 1. 314–15)? Apropos of *settle*, Honigmann remarks on Vane's consistent efforts to avoid strife by negotiation, e.g. in his early and ill-fated governorship of Massachusetts and 'in rephrasing the Solemn League and Covenant (1643) to the satisfaction of both the Scots and the English.']

6 *spelld*: deciphered, comprehended (*OED*: *v.*² 2 b); [cf. *IlPen* 170, *Sonn* 11. 7, *PR* 4. 385]. Smart quoted Sikes's *Life and Death of Vane* (96): 'Yet that he could conjecture and spel out the most reserved consults and secret drifts of forreign Councils against us...the Hollander did experience to their cost.' Willcock (220) notes that Vane had been described by the French ambassador as the only man in the Commons who understood European politics.

8 *nerves*: sinews, here figurative, as in '(the nerves of war) mony' (Sir Thomas

Herbert, *Some Yeares Travels*, 1638, 86: *OED* 2). The idea was already pro-
verbial in antiquity: Pattison cited Thucydides (1. 83), Cicero (*Phil.* 5. 2. 5:
nervos belli, pecuniam infinitam), Tacitus (*Hist.* 4. 74: *neque quies gentium sine
armis neque arma sine stipendiis*). [*Bartlett's Familiar Quotations*, ed. Emily M.
Beck (Boston, 1968, 104b, 181a) adds examples in Plutarch (*Agis and Cleo-
menes* 27, L.C.L. 10, 111; North, 8, 58), Rabelais (1. 46), and Bacon (*Of the
True Greatness of Kingdoms*), who rejects the idea. Ruth Mohl connects the sonnet with Milton's repeated (and approving) citation of Machiavelli's argument
that 'riches are not the nerves of war as is generally believed' (*Discorsi* 2. 10;
Milton, *Works* 18, 160, 212; R. Mohl in *C.P.W.* 1, 1953, 414–15, 498, and in
her *John Milton and His Commonplace Book* (New York, 1969), 135). Miss Mohl
and Honigmann cite M. Kelley's opinion that Milton's notes on the *Discorsi*
were made in the period November 1651–February 1652 ('Milton and Machiavelli's *Discorsi*,' *SB* 4, 1951–2, 123–7). Machiavelli attributed the saying to
Quintus Curtius: the only phrase of that kind I have observed is one put in the
mouth of Darius: *ferro geri bella, non auro* (5. 1. 8).]

9 *equipage*: apparatus of war (*OED* 3). Todd compared 'The God of warre
with his fiers equipage' (Spenser, *F.Q.* 1. 11. 6). [Cf. Spenser, *S.C.*, *October*
114: 'queint Bellona in her equipage.']

10 *Both spirituall. . .meanes*. MS. first had *What powre the Church & what the
civille meanes*: deleted, replaced by the present text (*Facs.* 454).

11 *What severs each. . .have don*. MS. first had *Thou teachest best, which few
have ever don*; then *Thou hast learnt well, a praise which few have won*; then, in
margin, the final text. [The apostrophe before *hast* indicates a slurred syllable.]
   which few have don. [Honigmann notes that in February 1652 Milton confided
to Hermann Mylius his low opinion of the education and political sense of
members of the Council of State (French, *L.R.* 3, 164).]

12 *The bounds of either sword*: the limits (*OED* 4) of the jurisdiction of the
two swords, spiritual and civil, i.e. church and state (cf. *On the new forcers* 15–16).
Reference to the two swords was common in Puritan controversy, especially
by those who, like Roger Williams, insisted on the sharp separation of the two
jurisdictions. For Williams and by this time, doubtless, for Milton also, 'the
sword of the Spirit' was 'the word of God' (Eph. 6. 17), but it included the
preaching of the word and the exercise of discipline, *within the congregation*,
admonition and excommunication. Pattison suggested that the 'two swords
together make up the "two-handed engine at the door" in Lycidas.'

13-14 *on thy firme hand...eldest son.* On this point opinions differed. It was no enemy of Puritan religion but Richard Baxter who complained that 'he hath done the Papists so much service, and this poor Nation and Religion so much wrong, that we and our Posterity are like to have cause and time enough to Lament it' (*Reliquiae*, 1696, pt. 1, p. 76; Willcock, 214). [On *eldest son* Smart commented: 'The *firstborn* of Religion, another trace of Biblical language. Cf. "Reuben, thou art my firstborn, my might, and the beginning of my strength, the excellency of dignity, and the excellency of power."—Genesis xlix. 3.' Milton's last phrase returns to *young in yeares* (1) and thus gives the sonnet a half-paradoxical frame.]

Sonnet 18 *On the late Massacher in Piemont*

I. DATE AND CIRCUMSTANCES

The sonnet is lacking in the MS., and there is but one text, that of 1673, so that we know nothing of Milton's first or second thoughts as he composed it.

The massacre of the Waldensians occurred on 24 April 1655, and the days following. Milton's sonnet gives every indication of having been struck out in the heat of emotion soon after the news reached him. Cromwell's official protest to the Duke of Savoy, drafted by Milton, was written on 25 May (*State Papers* 51, *Works* 13, 156–61), and it is reasonable to infer that the poem came little, if at all, later. [Parker (1036, n. 110) puts it 'not long after late May.']

The massacre was perpetrated by the Duke of Savoy's forces on the Protestant sect known as Waldensians or Vaudois, some of whom (in violation of an earlier treaty) had come down from the adjacent mountain valley and were settled on the plain of Piedmont.

The history of the sect is obscure. It was thought by the Protestants of Milton's day to date back to patristic, perhaps even to apostolic, times, and actually to have preserved the primitive faith and practice which the Reformers sought, by their return to Scripture and the removal of current abuses, to restore. Milton later referred to the Vaudois as 'our first reformers' and to 'those ancientest reformed churches of the Waldenses, if they rather continu'd not pure since the apostles' (*Hirelings, Works* 6, 84, 64). [In this same tract (p. 81) he draws upon 'Peter Gilles in his historie of the Waldenses in Piemont,' a work published in Geneva in 1644, which he had cited in his Commonplace Book (*C.P.W.* 1, 379;

Ruth Mohl, *John Milton and His Commonplace Book*, 80).] Modern research, however, has succeeded in tracing the Vaudois no farther than to the followers of one Valdes (Lat. Valdesius, Valdenius, Gualdensis; Ital. Valdo), a French merchant of Lyons in the latter part of the twelfth century, who organized a group of mendicant preachers, 'the Poor Men of Lyons.' Their message was a literal reading of the Gospels as the rule of faith and conduct: Valdes himself had sold his goods and given the proceeds to the poor according to Christ's injunction (Matt. 19. 21), and the 'Poor Men' went forth two and two, and with no provision, like the seventy disciples (Luke 10. 1–4). There was no avowed intention of repudiating the church and its teachings, but there was defiance of its silencing orders. Scattered widely, some of the Poor Men reached the Alpine regions of the later Vaudois. They probably met with a simple people prepared to receive their message by the retreat there of yet earlier reformers from Italy and the papal power. The primitive faith and practice found among the Waldensians when Milton wrote, agreeing so remarkably with the 'orthodox faith' of the reformers, is sufficiently explained by the initial emphasis on the Gospels, to which contact with the Reformed Churches in the sixteenth century had added some element of Pauline theology and a species of Protestant ministry. The Reformation also resulted for the Waldensians in a period of intermittent but intense persecution by their Roman Catholic rulers, extending from 1540 to 1690, of which the episode recorded in Milton's sonnet is a particularly shocking example.

The Waldensians were no passive martyrs but fought back with courage and some measure of success, so that Savoy was glad to come to terms with them in 1561 and grant a toleration, which was confined, however, within strict territorial limits. During nine decades following there were some renewed persecutions, for the most part instigated by France. Then in 1655 the fatal decree was issued in the name of the young Duke of Savoy, but probably under the influence of his mother, a granddaughter of the notorious Catherine de' Medici. The Vaudois had indeed transgressed the territorial limits set by the old treaty, and the decree ordered the immediate withdrawal of all those who refused to give undertakings to renounce their Protestantism within twenty days. The Vaudois made some resistance but were forced to withdraw. Now, however, the real purpose behind the renewed persecution appeared: namely, in violation of the treaty, to eradicate the Vaudois altogether. Troops were quartered on them throughout the area of guaranteed toleration, and on 24 April 1655 they made a concerted attack upon the villages, from which the Vaudois, taken by surprise, fled without resistance. The troops pursued them into the mountains, slaying all who fell into their hands, or taking them prisoner to be reserved for later execution. The crags are still shown from which many of the victims were hurled (Smart, 103). Many who escaped the soldiers perished among the Alpine snows.

Protestant Europe was shocked by treachery and barbarity which recalled St Bartholomew. Cromwell addressed to the Duke of Savoy a strong protest, which was of course penned by Milton, and which significantly contains the assertion that God 'has bin pleas'd to reserve the Jurisdiction and Power over the Conscience to himself alone' (*State Papers* 51, *Works* 13, 159). Cromwell also sought the intervention of the French king in a letter which attributes 'those inhuman Butcheries' to his officers, and urges the king to convince 'all Foreign Princes' of his own freedom from all responsibility for 'this prodigious Violence' by punishing these officers and by protecting the persecuted Vaudois (ibid. 56: pp. 180–3). He urged the Protestant states to join him in stronger protest against the detestable cruelties practised against their 'Brethren' in Piedmont, fellow adherents of 'the Orthodox Religion,' whose dwellings have been turned into 'Slaughter-houses' (ibid. 52–5, 58: pp. 162–79, 186–9). Cromwell was deeply moved. He sent to Geneva £2,000 for the immediate relief of the sufferers, to be followed by the proceeds of a public collection on their behalf (ibid. 59: pp. 188–92). Moreover, to Charles X of Sweden he plainly indicated his sense that the cause of all Protestants was at stake, which, 'although they differ among themselves in some things of little Consequence, is nevertheless the same in general and united in one common Interest.' He suggested that, if protests failed, they should join their 'Reputation, Authority, Councels, Forces, and whatever else is needful' in defence of the Vaudois (ibid. 53: pp.

168–71). [W. A. Turner (*N&Q* 193, 1948, 135–6) quotes from J. Leger, representative of the Vaudois, a statement which suggests that Cromwell's indignation was tinged with diplomacy.]

The phrases quoted above are from the English translations of these letters. Further information is given in Smart's introduction, 99–106; Gardiner, *Commonwealth and Protectorate* (1903), 4, 177–93; and excellent articles on 'Waldenses' by Mandell Creighton (*Encyc. Brit.*, 11th ed., 28) and W. F. Adeney (Hastings' *Encyc. Rel. Eth.*, 12). [See also Honigmann, who shows 'how closely the description and attitudes of the sonnet reproduce...accounts' given in newsletters. He quotes some, running from 7–14 May to 14–21 June, which, along with descriptive details, contain such words as 'late Massacre,' 'avenge,' 'saints,' and allusions to the Waldensians' retaining the purity of apostolic faith 'without any mixture of Idolatry or Superstition,' to lamentations echoing among the mountains, and to 'the poor banished men, who like the faithful of old, are wandring in the Wildernesses,...that they might sing as those that returned from the Babylonian Captivity.']

II. CRITICISM [D. B.]

Pattison (*Sonnets*, 1883, 58–60): 'It would not be easy to find a sonnet in any language of equal power to vibrate through all the fibres of feeling ...Yet with what homely materials is the effect produced! Not only is there not a single purple patch in the wording, but of thought, or image, all that there is is a borrowed thought, and one repeatedly borrowed, viz., Tertullian's saying, "the blood of the martyrs is the seed of the Church." It would not be impossible, but it would be sacrilege, to point to distinct faults in this famous piece; yet we may say that with a familiar quotation for its only thought, and with diction almost below ordinary, its forceful flood of suppressed passion sweeps along the hackneyed biblical phrases of which it is composed, just as a swollen river rolls before it the worn pebbles long ago brought down from the mountain side. From this sonnet we may learn that the poetry of a poem is lodged somewhere else than in its matter, or its thoughts, or its imagery, or its words. Our heart is here taken by storm, but not by any of these things. The poet hath breathed on us, and we have received his inspiration.'

K. Svendsen ('Milton's Sonnet on the Massacre in Piedmont,' *Shakespeare Association Bulletin* 20, 1945, 147–55) gave the first minute critique the sonnet has had. Pattison (see above) had seen Milton's general break with Petrarchan form and, in this sonnet, the effect of great power in spite of its mosaic of 'hackneyed biblical phrases.' But those phrases 'create a tone of religious indignation quite in keeping with the dramatic intensity of the prayer and the Old Testament flavor of the opening lines,' a flavour especially appealing to contemporary readers. So too the reference to God as shepherd and sower, and the connotation of Babylonian, heighten the religious feeling. The language is predominantly that of the King James version, and 'the parallelism in sentence structure increases the scriptural effect.' The words are predominantly native English and predominantly monosyllabic. Svendsen divides the sonnet into three parts: (1) 1–8: *a*. Vengeance (Old Testament God); *b*. Scene on earth; *c*. Innocence of the Waldensians and the cruelty of their foes; (2) 8–10: *moans...To Heav'n* (transition from earth to heaven); (3) 10–14: *martyr'd blood...Babylonian wo*: *a*. New Testament God; *b*. Fruits of martyrdom in earth and heaven. Thus the sonnet develops in a series of contrasts and paradoxes. This pattern and effect are fortified by language, images, and metre. Evocative words juxtapose the innocence of saintly people, God's flock, slaughtered like animals by bloody enemies; there is the suggestion of the divine power that can bring good out of evil, and that is more concerned for the welfare of his own than for vengeance. The word *roll'd* suggests brutal indifference as *hurl'd* would not have done. The imagery shifts to sowing and harvest, the multiplication of the faithful and the destruction of idolatry and pagan luxury and abuse of power. Verbal effects are heightened by alliteration, assonance, and the 'technique of dissonance.' In lines 3, 7, 8, 14, the stress is on the first syllable. There is only one (partially) end-stopped line, 2; in other lines stops at various points give a sense of both impetus and of control. [This summary by Woodhouse].

M. Van Doren (*Introduction to Poetry*, New York, 1951, 121–5) discusses the functional structure and sound of this 'one long groan of anger.' It begins like an avalanche starting on its way. The word *bones* (1) delays us between the powerful *slaughter'd* and *scatter'd*, words which produce the effect of rhyme. The sestet is not strictly separated from the octave even in sound, since the long *o* heard throughout the octave is carried on into at least three of the last six lines. Nine of the fourteen lines are run-on, and in seven cases the rhyme-word with its long *o* is so suspended that it demands prolongation. The late caesura in 7 (after *Piemontese*) heightens curiosity about what will follow *that roll'd*; in *Mother with Infant down the Rocks* 'the first three words send mother and infant down, and the next three dash them to their death.' In the whole sonnet sense, sound, and pauses work together. The *grow* of 12 is immediately reinforced by *hunder'd-fold*, 'and both are abundantly answered by the two closing words of the poem,' which recall biblical prophecy and in sound recall 'the woe that every preceding word...has embodied. The word becomes the thing....' The sonnet is no medley of undifferentiated sounds; it is 'highly articulate.' Certain phrases, rapped out 'as if some object were being struck,' are 'as crisp and distinct as the prevailing music is deeply mouthed; Milton's rage is alternately hot and cold, and the sign of coldness is this precision in the syllables,' each 'falling like a lash on the enemy's head and shoulders.' 'But then the entire poem has its precision'; the chosen words, in their chosen order, 'never fail to do the work Milton set out to do.'

F. T. Prince's general and particular comments on the technique of Milton's sonnets (*Italian Element*, 1954, 89–107, etc.) are summarized above in the section of general criticism (Sonnets II) and in the critical sections under some individual sonnets (1, 7, 9); those comments bear on *Sonnet* 18. In contrast with the 'calm, transparent, restraint' of *Sonnet* 9, *On the late Massacher in Piemont* and 'When I consider' 'show that his tendency when more deeply moved was to handle the form with very great boldness. In the pauses multiplied within their lines, and the ab- ruptness and bareness of certain of their sentences, these sonnets carry Della Casa's innovations much farther than any poet had ever done in Italian' (106).

Sonnet 18

T. Stoehr ('Syntax,' *ES* 45, 1964, 299–300): 'Cast in the form of three request structures, the sonnet begins boldly... with the main verb.... Thus the syntax, although solidly weighted with dependent clauses, appositive modifications, and the like, is clear from the very start.' 'Forget not' (5), a phrase 'linguistically redundant but poetically deft' and forceful, 'serves to link the first quatrain, with its burden of history, to the second request structure.' 'This pattern of demand, plea, and prayer has little of the stately balance and coordination found in the Cromwell octave' [see under *Sonn* 16 above]. 'All of the rhymes have at least an open juncture following them, and there are several terminal junctures punctuating the thought and giving it the rise and fall of a determined forward movement, slowing toward the end where a series of non-essential dependent clauses piles up after the main verb.... The transition to prayer in the sestet is especially interesting.' In the octave the 'interweaving of pronouns... establishes a kind of holy bond, which is violated by "*the* bloody *Piemontese*", marked as outsiders by the impersonality of the definite article. The helplessness of the victims is suggested by the loss of the pronouns in "Mother with Infant", and something of the violence of the scene comes through the tumbling rhythm, sharply cut off in the middle of line 8.... This ends the octave and the second request structure. "Their moans", although firmly tied to the octave by position, sound, and meaning (rhyming to "their groanes"), begins a new direction of the thought. The movement now is strongly iambic and upward.... The upward swing is paralleled by an expansion of subject matter, from the sharply defined description of line 8 to the generalized "Heav'n" and the metaphorical sowing and harvest in the sestet. Similarly, there is progression in time.... With change to a higher, more generalized perspective, expansion through metaphor, and postulation of future time, the aggressiveness of the octave deepens into quiet resolve and earnest appeal.... The emotion is public, and ends not in restraint, but in ceremony and prayer.'

L. Hyman ('Milton's "On the Late Massacre in Piedmont,"' *ELN* 3, 1965–6, 26–9) sees *Sonnet* 18 as a later and shorter *Lycidas*, 'a record not so much of the groans of the Piedmontese as of the poet's own struggle to overcome his shock at the ways of God to those just men who follow His way.' The poem is addressed to God, not to the perpetrators. God *must* avenge the martyrs and overcome the papacy because He is responsible. Milton's assurance of that ultimate victory appears in the language and tone and the progression of images from a downward to an upward movement. The final effect of the poem is not an English Protestant's 'mournful cry for revenge' but 'a cry for assurance that the inward grace of the true believer will be rewarded by an outward sign of God's favor.' Milton's attitude toward the papacy and the Puritan revolution ceases to be relevant: 'We need only participate in the struggle of a man who tests the strength of his convictions against the ways of God.'

Dale Herron ('Poetic Vision in Two Sonnets of Milton,' *MiltonN* 2, 1968, 23–8) discusses the working in *Sonnets* 18 and 19 of the biblical echoes that commentators have cited (see notes below). The opening prayer of *Sonnet* 18 contrasts bloody violence with the helpless innocence of the Waldensian 'Saints' (Rev. 6. 9–10; with 'Forget not,' cf. Rev. 3. 5). On their freedom from idolatry Milton uses Jer. 2. 27, which had evoked from Calvin a catalogue of Roman Catholic idolatries (*Commentaries on the Book of the Prophet Jeremiah and the Lamentations*, tr. J. Owen, 5 v., Edinburgh, 1850–5, 1, 127–30). The Waldensians are further identified with 'the holy cause of Protestantism' through the allusions to the pope and the 'Whore of Babylon' (Rev. 17–18). Lines 10–13, using the parable of the sower, develop the idea of Protestant triumph growing out of persecution and the 'relationship of regeneration to true comprehension' of the Gospel; Herron cites comments on seed, growth, and unblinded comprehension from Calvin, *Commentary on a Harmony of the Evangelists*, tr. W. Pringle, 2, 100 f. The poet, as one of those who see the truth, can feel and express the 'visionary fervor' the public event inspires.

Sonnet 18

III. NOTES

1 *Avenge...Saints.* Smart quoted Rev. 6.9–10: '...the souls of them that were slain for the word of God, and for the testimony which they held...cried with a loud voice, saying, How long, O Lord, holy and true, dost thou not judge and avenge our blood on them that dwell on the earth?' [Honigmann adds Luke 18. 7: 'And shall not God avenge his own elect, which cry day and night unto him...?']

1–2 *bones | Lie scatter'd.* [Honigmann cites Ps. 141. 7: 'Our bones are scattered at the grave's mouth....']

2 *Alpine mountains cold.* Warton cited 'Distill'd from tops of Alpine mountaines cold' (Fairfax, *Jerusalem* 13. 60).

3–4 *Ev'n them...Stocks and Stones.* Milton does not positively commit himself to the existence of the Waldensian church from primitive times, though *kept thy truth* suggests retention of, rather than return to, primitive simplicity in the days of image-worship, as *their antient Fold* (6) does also. See headnote. The phrase *Stocks and Stones* was a commonplace (*OED*: stock, *sb.*¹ 1 d). [D. S. Berkeley (*Explic.* 15, 1956–7, Item 58) cites Jer. 2. 27. *OED* cited Jer. 3. 9. The phrase appears twice on one page in John Bradford, *Writings*, ed. A. Townsend (Parker Society, 1848), 1, 153.]

3 *thy truth.* [Honigmann cites Ps. 86. 11: 'Teach me thy way, O Lord; I will walk in thy truth....' Cf. Milton's translation of this Psalm.]

5 *thy book*: the book to be consulted at the Judgment Day. Verity cited Rev. 20. 12. [Cf. Ps. 56. 8 ('put thou my tears into thy bottle: are they not in thy book?': Bell); Exod. 32. 32–3, Ps. 69. 28, Phil. 4. 3, Rev. 3. 5, 5. 1 f., 20. 15, 21. 27.]

6 *thy Sheep*: [a common biblical image for the faithful. Honigmann quotes Ps. 44. 22: 'Yea, for thy sake are we killed all the day long; we are counted as sheep for the slaughter'; and Rom. 8. 36. *Fold*: obviously carrying on the image of sheep and, since it means 'an enclosed piece of ground,...an appropriate word for the Alpine valleys' (Honigmann).]

7–8 *Slayn by the bloody Piemontese...the Rocks.* Cromwell's agent, Sir Samuel Morland, who carried his protest to the Duke of Savoy (see headnote), brought back a full account of the atrocities practised on the Waldensians, which he incorporated in his *History of The Evangelical Churches Of the Valleys of Piemont* (1658), 268 f. There the particular act Milton refers to is illustrated in a plate (344; see also pp. 368, 374).

439

8–9 *Their moans | The Vales redoubl'd to the Hills.* *redoubl'd*: re-echoed (*OED* 4). [Cf. Virgil, *E.* 6. 84: *pulsae referunt ad sidera valles*; *A.* 5. 150: *pulsati colles clamore resultant.* Oras ('Notes,' 93–4) observes that *OED* 2 gives this as the earliest example of *moan* in the sense of 'a prolonged low inarticulate murmur indicative of physical and mental suffering'; it cites no other instance until 1708. Oras follows Lockwood in seeing the traditional sense of lamentation, citing *EpWin* 55 and *Nat* 191. Honigmann refers to Exod. 2. 23: 'their cry came up unto God,' and similar biblical expressions.]

10–14 *Their martyr'd blood...Babylonian wo.* The lines are a tissue of reminiscences which the ordinary reader is expected to recognize and perhaps one or two will escape him: (1) 'The blood of the martyrs is the seed of the Church,' Tertullian's famous apothegm, noted by Todd without ascription, and quoted by Pattison: *Plures efficimur, quoties metimur a vobis: semen est sanguis Christianorum* (*Apologeticus* 50, Migne, *Pat. Lat.* 1, 535); (2) The parable of the sower (Matt. 13. 3–9), whose best result, when the seed 'fell into good ground,' was that it 'brought forth fruit...an hundredfold'; (3) The Pope's mitre with its triple crown, a common symbol for the papacy, e.g. Spenser, *F.Q.* 1. 7. 16; P. Fletcher, *Apoll.* 3. 16: 'Three mitred crownes the proud Impostor weares, / For he in earth, in hell, in heav'n will raigne' (Hughes); Milton, *QNov* 55 and 94 and notes; (4) The prophetic fulminations of Isaiah (13, etc.) and the mystical Babylon of Rev. 14. 8, 16. 19, 17–18, commonly applied by Protestants to papal Rome, and even by earlier writers, e.g. Petrarch, *Sonn.* 138, where the Roman Babylon is 'a fountain of woe' [*Fontana di dolore*], a sonnet which Milton had partly translated in *Ref* (*Works* 3, 27) and which he may be remembering here (Hughes). Some of the biblical phrases are: 'and great Babylon came in remembrance before God, to give unto her the cup of the wine of the fierceness of his wrath' (Rev. 16. 19); she is 'drunken with the blood of the saints ⟨cf. line 1⟩, and with the blood of the martyrs of Jesus' ⟨cf. 10⟩ (ibid. 17. 6); 'Come out of her, my people, that ye be not partakers of her sins, and that ye receive not of her plagues. For her sins have reached unto heaven, and God hath remembered her iniquities. Reward her even as she rewarded you' (18. 4–6: cf. line 1). The word *wo* in the sense of dire calamity (inflicted as a punishment), which is obviously the sense here (though *OED*: B 1 defines it merely as a condition of misery, affliction, or distress) is met in Rev. 9. 12, 'One woe is past; and, behold, there come two woes more hereafter,' which is followed by the account of the slaying of 'the third part of men' (ibid. 18) and the reserving of the rest, who, nevertheless, 'repented not of the works of their hands, that they should not worship...idols of...stone, and of wood' (ibid. 20: cf. line 4). [A. J. Weitzman (*MiltonN* 3, 1969, 55–7) sees an implied contrast between Augustine's earthly and heavenly city, between Babylon as corrupt and tyrannous authority and spiritual freedom, the kind of bondage the faithful must flee from (*City of God* 18. 18, 22, etc.). K. Svendsen (see 11 above) suggested a fusion of the myth of Cadmus and the dragon's teeth with the parable of the sower (Matt. 13. 3–9).]

11 *Italian fields.* Verity notes Milton's fondness for the word and cites 'Roaving the Celtick, and Iberian fields' (*Comus* 60) and 'Fled over Adria to th' Hesperian Fields' (*PL* 1. 520). But here the word is doubly appropriate, first, in relation to the metaphor of sowing, and, second, as the persecution began with the driving of the Waldensians from the plain of Piedmont into the mountains, whence the seed is to be carried and cover all Italy. [Honigmann (43–4) notes the characteristic way in which the thought turns back upon itself in the last lines: 'the bones *scatter'd* on the Alpine mountains cold have an obvious relationship with the blood and ashes *sown* o'er all the Italian fields, as has *thy truth* with *thy way*.']

13–14 [See 10–14 n. above. For *thy way*, see 3 n.]

Sonnet 19 *(When I consider how my light is spent)*

❧

I. DATE AND CIRCUMSTANCES

The only text is that of 1673.

For the dating of *Sonnet* 19 the order and numbering of the Sonnets become crucial, since we have no other definite evidence to draw on. The massacre in Piedmont, the subject of *Sonnet* 18, occurred on 24 April 1655 and the days following. That sonnet, as we saw, gives every indication of having been struck out in the heat of indignation soon after the news reached England. Cromwell's official protest to the Duke of Savoy was written on 25 May (*State Papers*, No. 51: Milton, *Works* 13, 161); and it has been reasonably assumed that *Sonnet* 18 was little, if at all, later. 'When I consider' is numbered 16 in the 1673 edition, which would correspond to 19 in the Cambridge MS. (see Kelley, above, general introduction to the Sonnets). If we assume the order to be chronological (and there is almost conclusive evidence for so doing), this would place *Sonnet* 19 at some point in, or later than, June 1655. But since *Sonnet* 22 commemorates the third anniversary of Milton's realization of total and irrecoverable blindness, which is generally assumed to have come upon him in 1652, it seems necessary to place *Sonnet* 19 at the earliest possible date in 1655, to make room for the two intervening sonnets, 20 and 21, invitations to Lawrence and Skinner to spend a few hours in Milton's company; these may well refer to the same occasion. *Sonnet* 20, written when 'Fields are dank, and ways are mire,' suggests the early winter (of 1655); and this would still leave room for *Sonnet* 22 before the end of the year. The evidence is thus compatible with a chronological sequence; and 22, though its subject is Milton's great afflic-

tion, shares the buoyancy and cheerfulness of 20 and 21. The chronological sequence is further supported by what may well be a reference
back to *Sonnet* 19, in the last line of 22: 'Content though blind, had I no
better guide' (but I have, in the acquiescence in God's will). All that can
be urged against this order is that the starting point of *Sonnet* 19 may be
thought to represent a more immediate response to the overwhelming
handicap of blindness than one would expect three years after the event.
But in dealing with any poet's—even Milton's—utterances, or with any
person's for that matter, one should never overlook the fact of fluctuating
moods: surely the blind man, however much he has schooled himself to
accept his lot, whatever the compensations he has taught himself to
recognize and value, may be subject at times to a sense of helplessness and
impotence in a world which he had once felt that he could work freely in
and as it were control. [But we know that Milton became blind early in
1652, at the latest, and *Sonnet* 22, if it 'commemorates the third anniversary,' could not come at the end of 1655: see the full discussion
below.]

The sonnet is Milton's first allusion in poetry to his blindness. We
may compare and contrast it with later references: *Sonnet* 22, written on
the third anniversary of his recognition of complete blindness, in which
he finds support partly in having sacrificed his sight 'In libertyes defence, my noble task'; the invocation to light in *PL* 3. 1–55, where
spiritual light is contrasted with physical darkness and triumphs over it;
SA 80–109, which, while a dramatic utterance, presumably owes its
peculiar poignancy to Milton's own experience and, though fitted to
Samson's situation, must go back to Milton's initial response of despair,
almost of panic.

To these passages in verse may be added the Latin prose of *Def* 2
(*Works* 8, 63–77), the noble and on occasion Job-like rebuttal of his
enemies' assertion that blindness has fallen upon him as a punishment:
'To be blind is not miserable; not to be able to bear blindness, that is
miserable.' 'As for myself, I call thee, O God, to witness, the searcher of
the inmost spirit, and of every thought, that I am not conscious of any
offense...the heinousness of which...could have called down this

calamity upon me above others.' 'Let the slanderers, then, of the judgments of God...know, that I neither repine at, nor repent me of my lot;...that I neither believe, nor have found that God is angry; nay, that...I have experienced, and...acknowledge his mercy, and his paternal goodness towards me; that above all, in regard of this calamity, I acquiesce in his divine will, for it is he himself who comforts and upholds my spirit....' 'Neither am I concerned at being classed...with the blind, with the afflicted, with the sorrowful, with the weak....There is a way, and the Apostle is my authority, through weakness to the greatest strength [cf. Parker, below, for Milton's other uses of this phrase]. May I be one of the weakest, provided only in my weakness that immortal and better vigour be put forth with greater effect; provided only in my darkness the light of the divine countenance does but the more brightly shine: for then I shall at once be the weakest and the most mighty; shall be at once blind, and of the most piercing sight. Thus, through this infirmity should I be consummated, perfected; thus, through this darkness should I be enrobed in light' (pp. 63, 67, 71, 73).

[D. B.] The first part of the summary above (Woodhouse's) embodies what seems to be recent or current orthodoxy: the dating of *Sonnet* 19 in 1655 has been upheld by Hanford (*MP* 18, 1920–1, 475–83; *Poems*, 1953), H. Darbishire (2, 316), M. Kelley, H. F. Robins, and J. T. Shawcross; Hughes in his 1957 edition shifted from his earlier '1652?' to 1655; Parker in 1958 shifted from 1655 to late 1651 and in 1968 shifted back to 1655. The arguments may be outlined (questioning will follow).

Kelley (*SCN* 11, 1953, 29; much enlarged in 'Milton's Later Sonnets and the Cambridge Manuscript,' *MP* 54, 1956–7, 20–5) follows and amplifies Hanford in maintaining chronological order. *Sonnet* 19 must be later than 18 (Piedmont) and 18 cannot be earlier than late April 1655 [as Woodhouse observes above, it would presumably come in late May or early June]. In accordance with his distinguishing among leaves and hands in the MS., Kelley proceeds (*MP* 54, 23):

Similarly, Sonnet 19 stood entered in the small-leaf collection before the composition of Sonnet 22, which was composed, as the number and text combine to indicate, later that same year; otherwise, as we have seen from the purpose of the small-leaf collection, Hand 5 rather than Hand 6 would have entered it in the Cambridge Manuscript. Under these circumstances, mid- or late 1655 seems the proper date for Milton's composition of Sonnet 19.

H. F. Robins ('Milton's First Sonnet on his Blindness,' *RES* 7, 1956, 360–6), while concerned mainly with interpretation of the sestet (see below, line 14 n.), argues for 1655. He would take Milton's two sonnets on his blindness as parallel rather than 'complementary' (Hanford's word, *Poems*). He sees an objection to 1652 in the fact that Milton's blindness had not come upon him suddenly but over a number of years, so that his adjustment would be complete before his sight was wholly lost. Robins sees an even more serious objection to 1652 in the inference it forces the reader to draw from the sestet. The conventional interpretation of the sonnet leads to an impasse: Milton, remembering the fate of the man who hid his talent, finds consolation in the assurance that he may serve God by regarding his blindness as a bar to future endeavour, that he cannot be expected to work; but this would directly contravene the import of the parable and would have seemed ignoble to the poet.

J. T. Shawcross ('Milton's Sonnet 19: Its Date of Authorship and its Interpretation,' *N&Q* 4, 1957, 442–6) sees the date 1655 fixed by the position of the sonnet between 18 (*c.* June 1655) and 20 (October– November 1655). The 'only argument' against this date has been that 'E're half my days' would imply a life-expectancy beyond 92 (the date 1652 would imply beyond 86, which is equally absurd). Shawcross suggests that Milton is recalling Isa. 65. 20, where the span of life is thought of as 100 years: thus Milton, aged 46 in 1655, has, in biblical terms, lived less than half his days. [But, Carey remarks, this verse of Isaiah 'is taken from a prophecy about the new Jerusalem, and relates to a future, not an actual state of affairs.'] Shawcross rejects Robins' view that Milton is rededicating himself to poetry. Moreover, in 1652 Milton would not have felt that he was one of those who wait, since he knew that Salmasius was preparing another assault. His positive resolve to wait accords best with late 1655: the anonymous biographer, Wood, and Phillips all remark on the quietness of his life after *Pro Se Defensio* (published in

August 1655). So *Sonnet* 19 should be placed after that date and close to *Sonnets* 20 and 21, i.e. around October–November 1655. Shawcross also cites Milton's letter to Philaras (28 September 1654) about the onset and symptoms of his blindness.

Among the arguments for 1655 that have been summarized the only real one is the supposedly strict chronological sequence of the sonnets as printed and as entered (actually or conjecturally) in the MS. It has been clear all along that the sonnets in general, so far as we know their dates, are in chronological order; but if in a single instance that order can be shown to be violated, the argument loses its independent weight and becomes only a matter of general probability that must yield if there is better evidence in particular cases. One clear case of a change in the printed order is that of *Sonnets* 11 and 12. But before going into arguments against 1655 it is desirable to observe the date of Milton's first consciousness of complete loss of sight, as nearly as scholars have been able to fix it.

W. R. Parker provided a succinct analysis of facts and inferences ('The Dates of Milton's Sonnets on Blindness,' *PMLA* 73, 1958, 196–200): he started from the data of J. M. French, *L.R.* 3 (1954), 197 f. (French had discussed the date of Milton's blindness in *PQ* 15, 1936, 93–4.) By 8 January 1650, when Milton was assigned the task of answering Salmasius, he had nearly lost the sight of one eye (*Def* 2, *Works* 8, 69). Later data are these:

After complete blindness,...Milton was given an assistant in his work as Latin Secretary (...11 March 1652), was excused from attending Council meetings (he attended with some regularity until March 1652), and received Council instructions at his home (there were such orders of the Council on 8 March, 6 and 15 April 1652).

Also, Milton associated his blindness with the time of his wife's death, about 5 May 1652 (*Defpro Se, Works* 9, 13–15), and the anonymous biographer (whom Parker takes to be Cyriack Skinner) puts her death 'a while after his blindness seizd him' (Darbishire, *Early Lives*, 33). All this evidence, says Parker, points to early 1652, perhaps February or March—the time that has been usually accepted.

But while French had arrived at a date about 28 February, Parker, reviewing the Mylius–Milton documents, infers a somewhat earlier time. Mylius, the Count of Oldenburg's agent, first saw Milton on 20 October 1651, when Milton took down names as Mylius talked. On 7 November Milton informed Mylius of illness, on 24 November of sore eyes. 'On 1 December 1651 Mylius learned from Secretary Frost, and noted in his diary, that Milton was almost blind.' On 3 January 1652, Mylius found Milton suffering from 'suffusion' in the eyes and wished him a full recovery.

During January and February of 1652 Mylius visited Milton at least a dozen times, each occasion recorded in his diary, but he said no more about the 'suffusion.' On 8 January he noted, without special comment, that Milton made certain notations in the margin of a manuscript. On 13 January, in the second draft of a letter to Milton, he diplomatically deleted a comment in the first draft about people 'blinded like bats. . . .' However, recording his farewell visit on 6 March 1652, Mylius noted that Milton was completely blind. . .at the age of forty-two, and *yet had signed his name to documents* which he presented to Mylius.

Parker finds three objections to French's inferred date for Milton's blindness (about 28 February): (1) 'Mylius does not say or imply that Milton had just become, or had recently become, totally blind. Rather he mentions blindness to explain his admiration at finding his friend's signature on the documents despite the handicap.' And he says Milton had mentioned 'perpetual blindness' in an earlier conversation, not later than 24 February; (2) Whereas French assumed that Milton signed these documents on 17 February, and therefore had some sight then, 'the *copies* which Milton presented to Mylius on 6 March were evidently signed shortly before they were presented. That is why Mylius commented on the fact of blindness'; (3) At their final meeting Milton told Mylius that he had become blind *anno quadragesimo secundo*, which (according to the method he had used in dating a number of early poems) would mean, not 'in his forty-second year,' but 'at the age of 42'—that is, before 9 December 1651, when he became 43. Parker also notes that the seven letters Milton sent to Mylius between 7 November

1651 and 21 February 1652 were all, including the signatures, in the hand of an amanuensis. On 19 November 1651, he did sign his name in a person's album, after he had dictated an inscription which begins with a Greek phrase from 2 Cor. 12. 9 ('my strength is made perfect in weakness'); and he quoted the same Pauline phrase in dictating an inscription in another album in September 1656 (French, *L.R.* 3, 104–5; 4, 118–19). 'Does not this argue that three weeks before his forty-third birthday he had considered his light spent and had begun to make his peace with God?' Parker—who on p. 199, n. 10, offers particular objections to Kelley's view—concludes that *Sonnet* 19 'should be assigned to late 1651'; and that 22 ('Cyriack, this three years day') 'should accordingly be assigned to 1654, some time after May, when the young Skinner became an admiring neighbor of the blind man' (cf. Parker, *Milton*, 1044, nn. 143, 144). One might have expected Parker to assign 22 to *c.* November 1654, three years rather than two and a half from the month in which he thinks Milton became blind. Parker's latest view on the problem of *Sonnet* 19 is summarized below.

Thus, whether we accept French's February 1652 or Parker's November 1651 or a time between, the date of Milton's becoming totally blind is narrowed down to a few months; that is a fact. In his own experience and memory the realization of such a calamity must have been associated with a still shorter time, if not a particular day (which is possible), at any rate with a few days or weeks. *Sonnet* 22 was, according to its first line, composed three years after Milton had become blind, and his 'three years' cannot be so loose as to mean any time between two and four years (see headnote to 22 below); this sonnet, therefore, ought to have been composed not later than, say, February–March 1655. But *Sonnet* 18 (Piedmont) cannot be earlier than May–June 1655. If the sequence is correct, *Sonnet* 18 is followed in time by *Sonnets* 19, 20 (which belongs to a winter), 21, and 22 (which records victory over protracted blindness)— and all these, in this order, must be got into the last six or seven months of 1655.

F. Pyle ('Milton's First Sonnet on his Blindness,' *RES* 9, 1958, 376–87) opposed Hanford's dating and, though he cited no later scholar on this point, argued that the chronological sequence does not hold, that the five sonnets 18–22 cannot, as Hanford said, be a consecutive series, and all composed in 1655. That order would put 20 (Lawrence) in the late spring of 1655, although it is a winter poem (line 2); it belongs either to the winter of 1654–5, before 18 (Piedmont), or to the winter of 1655–6 (or 1656–7), after 22 ('Cyriack, this three years day'). On the other hand, if 19 was written, as Pyle thinks, in or about 1652, after 16 and 17 (Cromwell and Vane), why was it printed after 18 (of 1655)? Pyle conjectures that, having made a pair of 11 and 12, Milton made a pair of the two invitations (20 and 21); that he also wished to pair off the two sonnets on his blindness (19 and 22), and interchanged 19 and 18, 18 being the only sonnet that stood between them; and that then, when 22 was withdrawn, 19 remained in its new place, out of order. This reconstruction is ingenious and possible, but admittedly guesswork; it does not, however, affect the exposure of the chronological fallacy. As E. Sirluck said (*JEGP* 60, 1961, 771, n. 51), Pyle showed that the order is not chronological and strongly reinforced Smart's date for *Sonnet* 19 (1652).

C. J. Morse ('The Dating of Milton's Sonnet xix,' *TLS*, 15 Sept. 1961, 620) reviewed this problem, though without explicit reference to the discussions surveyed here. He noted the chronological difficulty posed by *Sonnets* 19 and 22. He suggested that, before it was decided to withhold *Sonnets* 15–17 and 22, *Sonnet* 18 was moved out of order by way of rounding off the series of public sonnets before the private series 19–23 [cf. Parker, *PMLA* 73, 200, end of n. 10]. Morse would put *Sonnet* 19 in 'the months immediately following Milton's total blindness' (which he assumes, mistakenly, to have come in the summer of 1652).

Apart from peripheral and debatable suggestions, it is clear that the bibliographical argument for putting *Sonnet* 19 in 1655 will not hold up against the difficulties and contradictions that involves. And the chief internal objection is a large one. The main argument for dating *Sonnet* 19 in 1652 has always been the state of mind it expresses, so utterly different from the heroic confidence of *Sonnet* 22 (a kind of argument that has no weight with bibliographers). In 1921 Smart (108) said simply: 'The present poem, composed when the calamity was fresh, and before he had become accustomed to a life in darkness, opens with a mood of discouragement and grief, and closes with quiet resignation.' Tillyard (*Milton*, 1930, 388) disagreed with Hanford and Grierson (who upheld 1655) and agreed with Smart: 'the whole tone' of the sonnet points to an early date: could Milton possibly have uttered 'that one Talent... lodg'd with me useless' after writing *Defensio Secunda* (1654) in spite of his blindness? And although, as we have noted, Parker was later re-converted to 1655, we may quote some remarks he made in 1958 (*PMLA* 73, 200), when he felt obliged to give up 1655 for 1652:

I could never quite explain away the *sense of immediacy* which the opening lines of the sonnet conveyed to me (and to most of my students). These lines neither say nor imply 'When I consider how my light *was* exhausted' or '*has been* spent.' The words 'is spent' mean to me only 'is (now) gone'—and they go with 'E're half my days.' The world is not simply dark but 'wide' to the newly frustrated traveler...; there is a sense of light newly 'deny'd.' Patience prevents a murmur that arises from privation—and not privation lived with for all of three years.

Parker's latest opinion of the date—December 1655, a year and a half after *Sonnet* 22 (*Milton*, 468–72, 1042–3, n. 140)—is bound up with his interpretation of the sonnet, which is summarized (and questioned) at the end of II below. While recognizing his special knowledge of the problems, we may think the sentiments quoted just above far more persuasive than the interpretation of 1968. In that final view he takes Milton's 'light' to refer primarily to his poetical faculty and sees the poet tracing its 'exhaustion' to the beginning of his pamphleteering in 1641.

One more theory must be recorded. Honigmann, who gives, with many references, a short outline of the modern debate, seems inclined to favour a suggestion of his own: that 'Milton wrote his sonnet shortly before his birthday on 9 December 1644, when he could not foresee to what extent he might adjust himself to failing eye-sight.' He starts from Milton's letter to Philaras of 28 September 1654, in which he said: 'It is ten years, I think, more or less, since I felt my sight getting weak and dull'; and described the growing symptoms (*Works* 12, 67 f.). This confessedly uncertain recollection could of course be quite accurate. If Milton wrote the sonnet at the age of 35, midway in the Psalmist's span, the words 'E're half my days' would have a literal and valid explanation. Honigmann grants that there are objections to his date as well as to 1651–2 and 1655, but he does not go very far to meet them. The first intimations of 'failing eye-sight,' however alarming, could not, we may think, occasion the statement that his light was 'spent,' or the utter despair of the octave. Also, how is 1644 to be reconciled with 'this three years day' of *Sonnet* 22, which is assigned to 1655? Further, while Honigmann does not accept the principle of chronological order (which does clearly hold in general, with a few exceptions), he does not try to explain how a sonnet written in 1644 came to be placed where it is, after one certainly of 1655 and before one probably of 1655; other exceptions involve nothing like this aberration. Honigmann thinks *Sonnet* 19 was left out of the 1645 *Poems* because (according to Masson, *P.W.* 1, 89 f.) that publication was intended to rehabilitate Milton's mud-bespattered name and because an avowal of impending blindness would have invited his enemies to say—as they did later—that it was God's judgment; but this is all speculative. Honigmann finds it a 'coincidence worth pondering' that Milton 'withdrew from the world for several years just at the time when he first grew conscious of his failing sight, late in 1644'—that is, that he published no tracts between March 1645 and February 1649. (Honigmann cites Sirluck, *JEGP* 60, 1961, 749–85, but Sirluck attributes Milton's *poetical* inactivity to the failure of his marriage [1642].) By March 1645 Milton had published a dozen pamphlets and may for the time being have said his say; also, we know that he was working on the *History of Britain*, of which he had finished four books by early 1649 (*Def* 2, *Works* 8, 137), and he was also, from 1645 or 1646, collecting materials for the *Christian Doctrine* (Parker, 293). Thus the theory that *Sonnet* 19 was written in 1644 and the reasons adduced in support of it seem nebulous.

To add two commentators of 1968, Prince sees no point in efforts at precise dating, and Carey dates '1652?'

This survey of facts and arguments leads to what may seem an

inescapable conclusion: since the external arguments for strictly chronological sequence do not hold, the clear internal evidence of the poem may
be allowed its rightful authority. *Sonnet* 19 should be dated in 1652
(or, just possibly, at the end of 1651).

II. CRITICISM [D.B.]

Tillyard (*Milton*, 1930, 190–1), considering this sonnet in relation to the
rest of Milton's works, found it 'an extremely difficult and strange poem.
There is in it a tone of self-abasement found but once again in Milton.
In a way the theme is that of *Lycidas*: the ranking of the state of mind
above the deed. But the conception of the deed is quite different. In
Lycidas the deed is personal, the exercise of Milton's creative faculty:
in the sonnet it is the passive yielding to God's command; Milton
crouches in humble expectation, like a beaten dog ready to wag its tail at
the smallest token of its master's attention.' Tillyard sees in the sonnet the
signs of Milton's 'having suffered an extraordinary exhaustion of vita-
lity. Yet for all this weakness the sonnet shows the nature of Milton's
greatness and the promise of recovery.' He 'is stating that his own deeds
and genius are of less value than personal integrity.' In this sonnet at
least he has overcome despair. 'He has compounded with his afflictions
and...has made his bargain with fate. In an unusual lowliness he has
found repose. That attained, it was but a question of time for recovery
to follow.'

  Hans-Oskar Wilde ('Miltons Sonett "On His Blindness,"' pp. 36–49
in his *Beiträge zur englischen Literaturgeschichte des 17. Jahrhunderts*,
Breslau, 1932) studied the sonnet in relation to what was then the new
Miltonic criticism. He looked closely at the phrases and ideas that make
up an organic whole, and at the same time placed the utterance in the
large perspective of Milton's development and the Puritan revolution.
He saw the sonnet as a profoundly significant turning-point for the poet,
the theologian and thinker, and the man. Whereas the earlier Milton had
been, in a broad sense, a classicist, this sonnet, the product of a shattering
personal experience, grew out of, and inaugurated, the inwardness

which was henceforth to dominate Milton's writings, the revolutionist's deepening sense of man's necessary subjugation of self and trustful faith in God. Thus the sonnet is a prelude to the conflict and resolution written at large in the epics and *Samson*.

Eleanor G. Brown (*Milton's Blindness*, New York, 1934, 52–5) rightly protested against Tillyard's description of Milton's religious humility and resignation as the attitude of a beaten dog, and, with the sympathetic understanding of a fellow-sufferer, read the sonnet as a 'marvellous epitome of personal defeat and ultimate triumph.'

Earl Daniels (*The Art of Reading Poetry*, New York, 1941, 34–6), dismissing the fact of the poet's blindness as 'of the smallest significance,' concentrates on his adaptation of the parable of the talents (Matt. 25. 14–30), the 'source' of the poem's 'organic unity.' 'In the parable the one-talent man was afraid and hid the money; in the sonnet the poet is afraid he will be obliged, because he cannot see, to hide his talent for writing,' and 'it is death for the mind and spirit of an artist if he cannot find expression through his art. With the man in the story, fear is the incentive to wrong but voluntary action; the poet is afraid for the consequences of inaction which he is also afraid he cannot help. In the story the man evidently has no intention to use what was given him; but the poet is all the more bent to serve because blindness seems to have made his one talent useless. Both men try to defend themselves in a bad situation (see lines 7 and 8), and if we remember the fate of the character in the parable, the final six lines of the poem are strengthened, and we discover sharp, ironic contrast in the two situations: the talent is taken from the one who acted but acted wrong, while the poet, afraid he cannot act and so will be wrong—really failing to act at all—is reassured, "They also serve who only stand and wait."'

L. Kemp ('On A Sonnet By Milton,' *Hopkins Review* 6, 1952–3, 80–3) takes 'E're half my days' literally as meaning 'sometime before his 35th birthday,' say 1642. His main concern is Milton's theme, which, he thinks, is not blindness but loss of poetic inspiration ('light'), attended perhaps by a guilty sense of having wasted his time on pamphlets instead of using his poetic talent. Kemp ends his very strained argument by suggesting that the sonnet was not included in the 1645 volume because such an expression of discouragement would have given comfort to his controversial opponents. His main idea is revived by Parker (1968) and E. J. Hinz (1969), below.

In a close analysis of ideas and technique Paul Goodman (*The Structure of Literature*, Chicago, 1954, 192–215, more strictly, 204–15) sees in the sonnet 'an argument on justification by works. In the octave (vss. 1–7⅖) there is a justification of the self before God; this is given in the profusion of first-person pronouns. . . . The transition is given in the alienating epithet "*That* murmur" rather than "this" or "my" murmur. The octave is divided to give a subordinate motion of thought: "these being the circumstances, I therefore say"; the sestet breaks in on this reasoning, indeed before the eighth line is complete, and contradicts it.' The sestet 'too is divided (at vs. 11⅘) into two tercets.' The first tercet 'presents the correct argument with regard to man's justification: "Who best / Bear His mild yoke, they serve Him best." This is the end of the normal argument.' 'But. . .now *God* is glorified (vss. 12–13).'

'But if we consider the feeling rising through the poem, however, we see at once that the passion in the octave is not merely the appropriate anxiety at not being justified, not being able to play one's role, but even more it is despair at the deprivation and inaction, mounting to almost anger and insolence, in verse 7.' [Goodman goes on to say that it is 'death to hide' his talent, his poetic gift, 'because such a talent feeds on action and fame and otherwise "I" dies'; this is surely an unwarranted substitution of the supposed Miltonic 'egoism' for Milton's earnest sense of religious responsibility.] Milton's feeling is not humble and cannot be resolved by 'the correct injunction of Patience, . . . for the "I" must be not only justified but *satisfied*. It is this satisfaction that is given by the joyous anthem, "*His* state / Is kingly." *God* is justified, and by identification "I" is satisfied. We may then come to a satisfactory Patience, the confidence of "wait." The feeling of the octave is not resolved until this ending. This is everywhere the Miltonic theme.'

Goodman's subtle analysis of the expressive and emotional variations in metre and rhythm (207–14) cannot be summarized. He deals with 'certain main motions that are beyond dispute: the difficulty and agitation of the octave, in thought, sound, and syntax; the easy thought and syntax of the sestet as a whole and the freedom of the choriambs and overflows of the first tercet; the climax at "His state is Kingly"; the speed and excitement of the twelfth and thirteenth lines; and the slower, resolving, conclusive epigram.'

M. Cheek's discussion of this sonnet (1956) appears above, in criticism of *Sonnet 7*.

R. L. Slakey ('Milton's Sonnet "On his Blindness,"' *ELH* 27, 1960, 122–30) recalls several interpretations of the sestet: Tillyard (see above), the resignation of utter defeat [though Tillyard does see a ray of hope in 'waite']; Smart (108), 'religious abandon'; E. G. Brown (above), triumph. Slakey stresses the literal seriousness with which Milton takes the parable of the talents, which presents the alternatives of heaven and hell, salvation and damnation (Matt. 25. 30), a parable he had already touched in the Letter to a Friend enclosing *Sonnet 7* and in *RCG* (*Works* 3, 229). But for Milton there is a dilemma not present in the parable: is he exempt from penalties because he wishes even more intensely to use his talent but cannot? His will to serve is established in the octave; the sestet adds the willingness to bear God's mild yoke. And, though the exercise of the one talent of poetry seems no longer possible, there is the implied determination not to abandon the idea of serving somehow. This is far from either despair or abandon. Patience can reject man's accomplishments ('God doth not need') because it is not works but intentions that are important, and bearing the yoke is a return of a sort; he serves so long as he waits on the Lord (Ps. 27. 14). 'That the mediate intentions are frustrated makes no difference, for the final intention is fulfilled' (126). 'Wait' here negates every thought of self; it means waiting on God's will, but it does not mean abandoning the readiness for active service when the way thereto is opened and the command comes. 'The speaker begins with a limited understanding and is enlightened. His talent is not simply the specific poetic gift he has received; it is his blindness, his poetic gift, his frustration, and whatever else makes up his situation or present life condition' (127). The sestet provides 'an answer to the octave by rearranging experience. It offers great spiritual discovery for one who is intent upon serving God and whose only concern is his inadequacy for such service. Thus the poem is an affirmation. It does not close upon a clear note of resignation at all' (127). The idea of renewed aspiration might be confirmed by a sentence in Milton's Commonplace Book (*Works* 18, 129): 'A good man in some measure seems to excel even the angels, for the reason that housed in a weak and perishable body and struggling forever with desires, he nevertheless aspires to lead a life that resembles that of the heavenly host.' [This abstract by Woodhouse.]

Ann Gossman and G. W. Whiting ('Milton's First Sonnet on his Blindness,' *RES* 12, 1961, 364–70) oppose Slakey's view of the sonnet as affirmation (see above) and reassert the idea of resignation. They agree with Pyle in rejecting Robins' interpretation based on two classes of angels (see note on line 14 below), but object to Pyle's taking the imagery of the octave as 'mercantile,' to his contrasting the old Law and the new Gospel, and to his seeing the final emergence of 'steady hope.' Miss Gossman and Whiting—who regard the sonnet as an immediate, not a later, reaction to blindness—think that Milton is trying to learn how to bear his affliction; he does not say or imply that he has a special inner light or that he has any hope of regaining his creative power. He must have thought that his poetic career was ended.

This article is followed (ibid. 370–2) by a rejoinder from Pyle (see 1 above and, below, note on line 14). He reasserts the mercantile nature of the imagery and notes that, far from ignoring the last line, he gave to it two pages, using Luke 12. 35–40. 'The sonnet is a record of impatience recollected in a state of patience.'

P. R. Baumgartner ('Milton and Patience,' *SP* 60, 1963, 203–13) places the sonnet in the whole sequence of Milton's writings and sees it as a distinct turning-point. Hitherto, especially in prose, Milton had been militant and heroically confident in the rightness of his causes, and he had not been very patient in regard to an uncomplying wife or controversial opponents and enemies of liberty. He learned to practise the Christian virtue through calamitous experience, which tried and deepened his religious faith. The Christian virtue differs from the Stoic in growing out of faith in Providence which requires willing submission to God's will. Milton's understanding of the virtue, as set forth in the *Christian Doctrine* 2. 3 (*Works* 17, 67 f.), is especially that of Augustine and Lactantius. 'The theme of Christian patience is introduced with Milton's sonnet on his blindness, and it continues in the tone and language of the later sonnets, especially the two addressed to Cyriack Skinner. The tone of self-sufficiency and impatience persists in the prose tracts—especially the *Defensio Secunda*, the *Defensio pro Se*, and *The Ready and Easy Way*—up to the time of the Restoration. With *Paradise Lost*, however, patience, dependence, and submission become important themes and continue so to the end.' Examination of his writings suggests 'that, as a result of his blindness and the Restoration, Milton experienced a change of heart concerning the virtue of patience.' (See also the end of 14 n. below.)

T. Stoehr ('Syntax,' *ES* 45, 1964, 293–4): 'Whether described in terms of form or meaning, the power of the sonnet plainly lies in the tension between energy and control, a tension only inferable in the highly regular' *Sonnet* 7. 'That the syntax of the octave here seems almost out of control, gives the poem a perilous suspense, which the straightforward structure of the sestet then disperses and transcends. From the final lines of these two sonnets one might think that Milton's characteristic attitude when dealing with religious material is simply one of humility. But Mr. Goodman [see above] suggests that the poet's resentment cannot so easily "be resolved by the correct injunction of Patience, 'Bear His mild yoke'", and is only assuaged by an impious identification with God. Perhaps we need not go quite so far, but Mr. Goodman is certainly right that we do not have any ordinary humility in this sonnet. The interruption at line $7\frac{1}{2}$, before the turn, is as if Milton suddenly reined in from going too far, becoming too resentful.' In the sestet numerous pauses within the lines 'make for controlled, almost syllogistic movement, calming the troubled rhythm of the octave, while the emotion is sublimated in duty and praise. This is not humility but restraint.' Stoehr contrasts George Herbert's *The Holdfast*. 'This *self*-assertiveness in

Milton, this deep strength of ego, furnishes the energy of these sonnets, and allows—even demands—that he be always in control of his poetic form, shaping it to the ends of full expression, and not merely to the dictates of a pious submission to God's will.' [In view of Herbert's exquisite control, one might ask about the strength of his ego.]

G. Monteiro (*Explic.* 24, 1965–6, Item 67), starting from recent critics' uncertainties about Milton's meaning in the sestet, and from Goodman (*q.v.*), stresses the number of dental consonants (76 in 113 words): 'The net effect of this preponderance of *t*'s, *th*'s, and *d*'s is that it substantiates the subtle tension of spirit expressed in the argument' [the logic seems unclear]. The poem as a whole is an echo of Matthew's verse (25. 30) on the fate of the unprofitable servant. 'This view supports the contention (in Goodman's terms) that "the conclusion of the argument on justification is an impasse, for the thought does not do poetic justice to the gratuitous suffering, nor is it a sufficient reward for the talent" (p. 206).'

J. F. Huntley ('The Ecology and Anatomy of Criticism: Milton's Sonnet 19 and the Bee Simile in "Paradise Lost," 1. 768–76,' *Journal of Aesthetics and Art Criticism* 24, 1965–6, 383–91) uses the sonnet to illustrate his argument for the necessity of grasping a poem's structural meaning rather than fixing on individual items. This approach eliminates some recent interpretations. Milton's subject is the right attitude to be taken toward the parable of the talents, which 'appears to threaten "the non-achiever."' He does not identify himself with the third servant or reject the parable as unjust; he is learning to understand God's ways. Milton identifies himself, not with the fearful third servant, but with the first two, who love and are beloved of God. 'In effect, the sonnet challenges the false appearance of similarity between the speaker and the third servant in order to establish a real and radical difference between them.

'Thus the sonnet expresses Milton's concern with the inwardness and individuality of religious experience and his refusal to credit any of the visible, public tokens of faith or heresy. The words of the sonnet, by representing the movement of the speaker's mind, represent the essential features of man's experience of God as Milton saw them. Left to his own meditations, the speaker broods over his "injured merit" and begins to murmur against God's justice. But prevenient grace anticipates the drift of his thoughts and, long before they harden in his heart, returns them to due subordination, humility, self-respect, and love. The reply of Patience guides the speaker to embrace a state of mind which may seem inert to the superficial observer, but is in fact the vital activity of a healthy spirit. An unhealthy spirit in the octave was impatient to perform magnificent tasks in order to render a "true" account of his worth. The speaker grew resentful when these dreams, which so exceeded his talents, proved impossible.' Thus the poem 'suggests a condition of all earthbound men who contemplate their spiritual responsibility. All are lost and blind who think that their own day-labor will add up to a true account in God's eyes....Similarly, the one talent may refer biographically to Milton's poetic, political, or theological prowess, but inside the poem it suggests the one capacity which the speaker shares with all other men, a capacity for salvation.' This 'one talent for spiritual growth...was the talent endangered by the speaker's murmur and restored by God's free, prevenient gift of wisdom. What Patience says to the speaker illuminates his dark world and maps its width. Henceforth the speaker will navigate more surely toward this salvation.'

Honigmann (1966: 50–2) pronounces *Sonnet* 19 'Perhaps the most fascinatingly "traditional" sonnet of all.' 'Its biblical allusions are well known: but the vast body of religious and meditative verse which transformed them into poetic clichés seems less familiar, for notes in the learned periodicals continue to call attention to stray Miltonic "sources" and "analogues" in English poetry—most of which could be multiplied a hundredfold by a diligent searcher.' From Henry Lok's religious sonnets of 1597 Honigmann quotes, as representative, half a dozen bits (*Miscellanies of the Fuller Worthies' Library*, ed. Grosart, 2, 1871, 99, 107, 140, 153, 186, 204) which include such words and ideas, some of them repeated, as 'account,' 'gifts,' 'talent,' 'Thy service,' 'the sea and land,' 'at His appointment,' 'yoke of law,' 'suffer patiently.' 'Lok also made much of the blindness-motif' (Grosart, 118, 146, 152); 'The commonplace that post-lapsarian man is spiritually blind may be touched on in Milton's second line.'

Honigmann goes beyond traditional criticism in finding relationships of resemblance or partial contrast between some sonnets (see also the summary in the general introduction to the sonnets). He sees a notable instance in 18 and 19, whether or not the numbers represent chronological order. 'Both XVIII and XIX celebrate God's terrible way with His chosen, the slaughtered saints and the talented poet deprived of his sight. And not only is there an important kinship of subject: we should grow conscious also of other resemblances. There is a similar sense of spaciousness in the sonnets. And at the same point in each (l. 12) Milton discusses the *triple Tyrant* and the *kingly* state of God, and at the same point again (l. 14) hopes that generations unborn *may fly* the one, and proposes to *stand and waite* to serve the other. The *yoak* imposed by Milton's God appears all the more *milde* if "the reader's mind is held in a certain receptive poise" from sonnet XVIII to XIX, and the poet's *murmur* sounds the more ungrateful if one still hears the *moans* of the unfortunate mountaineers. Reading XIX after XVIII one finds a new dimension in the self-criticism of the more personal poem.' (65)

J. Pequigney ('Milton's Sonnet XIX Reconsidered,' *TSLL* 8, 1967, 485–98), reviewing critical discussion (and taking Kelley's 1955 as the most probable date), thinks it better to approach the sonnet, at least provisionally, as fictional rather than autobiographical. The octave presents 'a good if not perfect man' and asks how such a man should react to affliction. The parable of the talents 'dominates the imagination and conscience of the speaker,' who is concerned with himself and a 'sense of personal waste.' The uncapitalized 'patience' that introduces the sestet 'is not a second character brought upon the stage but a new quality in the protagonist' (489). 'The relationship between God and creature changes from that of master and servant to that of king and subject, with a corresponding expansion of the imagination from the confines of a manor to the scope of a kingdom or empire.' There is a shift from self-absorption and self-pity 'to an impersonal contemplation of celestial beings,... from egocentric concern to theocentric awareness'

(490). 'The fear of divine rebuke and punishment is displaced...by trust in providential disposition'; external darkness 'is recompensed by internal enlightenment.' The speech undercuts the premise of the octave and the parable, which become 'theologically improper.' Divergent lines of interpretation have followed from two senses of 'waite' in line 14, 'readiness to receive orders or...respectful attendance'; but M. Mack (*Milton*, 1961, 77, n. 14) was partly right in seeing the 'two senses of *stay expectant* and *attend*,' a view supported by *PL* 3. 59–60 and 648–50. 'The basic idea of the poem changes radically according to the restricted impression a reader takes of..."waite"': the sonnet holds both thematic lines in intelligible suspension (493). The maturity the speaker attains 'consists of a toleration of uncertainty and of the emotional flexibility with which he confronts the range of possibilities in an unknown but providentially directed future..."Thy will be done."' Pequigney queries the usual identification of the speaker's one talent with poetic power. He concludes by comparing the religious experience here drama-tized with that of Samson and that of Job.

D. Herron (see above, *Sonnet* 18, ii, under 1968) finds important links between the public *Sonnet* 18 and the private *Sonnet* 19. In both a tragic visitation demands an answer, and receives one, from a poet whose spiritual vision is true, though temporarily dimmed in *Sonnet* 19; and each poem moves from consideration of causeless suffering to a renewal of faith in God's justice. The octave of *Sonnet* 19 poses two problems, that embedded in the parable of the talents and that of defining true service to God. In *Sonnet* 7 the parable of the talents (along with that of the vineyard) had been concerned only with delayed service; here it con-cerns total frustration. The parable is interwoven with imagery of light and darkness. The climactic question of line 7 recalls not merely John 9. 4 but the whole chapter, on Christ's restoration of the blind man's sight. Mrs Herron (italicizing two words) quotes Calvin's comment on John 9. 4 (*The Gospel According to St. John 1–10*, tr. T. H. L. Parker, London, 1959, 239–40; [cf. the same work, tr. W. Pringle, 2 v., Edinburgh, 1847, 1, 367–8]): 'He [Christ] now testifies that he has been sent to manifest the Grace of God in enlightening the blind...He therefore calls the time fixed by the Father *the day*, in which he must finish the work commanded by Him.' Mrs Herron remarks: 'In echoing Jesus's own words concerning His mission among men, Milton again demonstrates that unique concept of his poetic mission that so often confronts us. Identifying his own fervor with Christ's, Milton demonstrates his awareness that his blindness is not banishment into darkness, but an acceptance into true light, the light of God's grace and the light of prophetic inspiration.'

Parker (1968: 468–72, 1042–3, n. 140), starting from the argument of L. Kemp (see above, 1952–3), develops his unorthodox interpretation. Milton's 'subject is not primarily blindness. The sonnet is actually a dramatic rejection, or qualification, of the parable of the talents.... Milton complains, not of blindness, but of his own misuse of time, of his own failure to employ fully his God-given powers as a poet. He postponed his prime effort; he allowed himself to be diverted by patriotism.' 'The poet, having devoted his energies to prose for many years, fears that he had neglected his single true talent, and now dreads the day of reckoning.' '"That one talent" can hardly mean mere ability to write in prose or verse, nor can it mean ability to serve one's country. Milton had been doing both....''That one talent'' must have seemed to him his long-felt, God-given capacity for composing a truly great poem—a capacity which, in the analogy of the parable, might have been taken from him as a punishment for his failure to use it.' The 'primary meaning of the word "light" in this sonnet is not eyesight, but Milton's "inward light" or poetic faculty....' Apropos of the much debated 'E're half my days' (see 2 n. below), Parker says: 'It seems probable...that he traced the exhaustion of his poetic "light" to the beginning of his pamphleteering back in 1641.' 'Was the Maker's gift of verse still to be put to its intended use, now that his light was "spent"? The answer to this question...is a flat rejection of the whole point of the parable of the talents. There is, Milton now realized, one thing more important...than making good use of divine gifts,' that is, patient acceptance of God's will, whether for active service or not.

One wonders, among other things, how Parker can conjure up a sense of guilt in view of Milton's repeated expressions of infinite pride in his many defences of liberty, e.g. *Def* 2 (*Works* 8, 5, 9–23, 129–39), *Sonnet* 22, *REW* (*Works* 6, 116), or the less familiar letter to Henry Oldenburg of 1654, in which, responding to his friend's exhortation to prepare for 'other labours,' Milton says: 'whether nobler or more useful I know not, for what can be nobler or more useful in human affairs than the vindication of Liberty?' He says further that the defence of liberty had taken him away from 'far different and altogether pleasanter studies: not that in any way I repent of what I have done, since it was necessary; for I am far from thinking that I have spent my toil, as you seem to hint, on matters of inferior consequence' (*Works* 12, 65). Toland says that Milton 'us'd frequently to tell those about him the intire Satisfaction of his Mind, that he had constantly imploy'd his Strength and Faculties in the defence of Liberty, and in a direct opposition to Slavery' (Darbishire, *Early Lives*, 194). Cf. below, *Sonn* 22, 10–12n.

E. J. Hinz ('New Light "On His Blindness,"' *Massachusetts Studies in English*, 2, 1, 1969, 1–10) goes on from L. Kemp (above, 1952–3; she does not cite Parker's theory) to argue that Milton's theme is not loss of sight but loss of inspiration, and she analyses the sonnet as one of his 'many examinations of the Christian virtue of patience.' The argument against loss of sight may be thought no more persuasive than its predecessors.

Lyle H. Kendall (*MiltonN* 3, 1969, 57) suggests, with well-founded diffidence, that Milton may have recalled George Wither's Emblem 47 (*Emblemes*, 1635, bk. 3, sig. 2B4^r). 'There are close correspondences in content, explicit or implied: blindness, inactivity, writing poetry, hiding gifts. And verbal echoes—light(ed), spent(d), world, hide, talent(s), gifts—reinforce the impression of indebtedness.'

III. NOTES

1 *When I consider*. [Honigmann (51) quotes from Henry Lok (see Honigmann in II above, under 1966) 'the same opening formula, a well-worn one: "*When I consider* of the holy band"' (*Poems*, ed. A. B. Grosart, 1871, 277); and also Shakespeare, *Sonn*. 15: 'When I consider every thing that grows.']

light: power of vision (*OED* 4), to be taken along with *dark world*. A very faint susceptibility to light remained with Milton for some years (*Epistol* 15, 28 Sept. 1654: *Works* 12, 69). [M. Cheek finds light used in several senses in this sonnet; see *Sonn* 7, Criticism, under 1956.]

2 *E're half my days*. These words have puzzled commentators, since one would naturally expect Milton not to assume more than the scriptural span of three score years and ten, and he was about 47 (or at the very least 44) when he wrote the sonnet. [As we see from discussions in 1 above, the probable date of the sonnet was early 1652 (or possibly late 1651), when Milton was 43 (or 42).] L. Kemp [see Criticism above, 1952–3] resorts to the desperate expedient of placing the sonnet in 1642 [for a different reason Honigmann, in 1 above, gives 1644], which defies the evidence of order and entails a total change of reference from loss of sight to loss of inspiration [(see Parker above, under Criticism, 1968). D. C. Dorian (*Explic.* 10, 1951–2, Item 16) suggested that *days* means the working days of maturity; he cited *day-labour* (7) and parallels in the Letter to a Friend of 1633 and the biblical phrases there echoed (*Works* 12, 320–5); cf. 3 n. below.] Shawcross (*N&Q* 4, 1957, 442–6: cited in 1 above) suggested that Milton had in mind Isaiah's prophetic allusion to a life-span of 100 years (65. 20), as accompanying such a reformation on earth as Milton was working for but could no longer work for in total blindness. [Parker (*PMLA* 73, 1958, 196–200: cited in 1 above) suggests that Milton may have come to think of his life-expectancy from the case of his father, who lived to be at least 84: 'Half of eighty-four is the age that Milton reported to Mylius as the time of total blindness. The coincidence is surely significant—the ironic contrast obvious. Only our unwillingness to allow Milton a private allusion in an intensely personal poem has blinded us to his impelling reason for ignoring (as his father's life had ignored) the scriptural delimitation of life'; but cf. Parker's later comment quoted above. C. J. Morse (*TLS*, 15 September 1961: cited in 1 above), though he rejects the idea of an early date for the sonnet and places it in 1652, notes the literal and scriptural accuracy of Dante, who 'sets the opening of the *Inferno* on his thirty-fifth birthday with the words "Nel mezzo del cammin di nostra vita."' Saillens (ibid. 6 October 1961, 672), apropos of Morse's citation of Dante, says that 'According to an immemorial popular belief, a man should normally reach a hundred,' and quotes Plato, *Rep.* 615 A–B:

For all the wrongs they had ever done to anyone and all whom they had severally wronged they had paid the penalty in turn tenfold for each, and the measure of this was by periods of a hundred years each, so that on the assumption that this was the length of human life the punishment might be ten times the crime (L.C.L. 2, 495–7).

It may be that Milton was only speaking loosely; cf. the Elizabethan preacher, Henry Smith: 'If thou wert borne but to day, thy journey is not an hundred yeeres: if thou bee a man, halfe thy time is spent already....' ('The Godly Mans Request,' *Sermons*, 1618, 283; *Sermons*, London, 1866, 1, 269).]

2 *dark world and wide*. Shawcross (see 2 n. above) sees in the epithets a reference not only to Milton's blindness but to the darkness of ignorance, extending widely over the world, which Milton was using his talent to dispel when loss of sight prevented the completing of his *account* [so also M. Cheek, 1 n. above. For a literal comment on his situation one might quote *Epistol* 20, 8 Nov. 1656 (*Works* 12, 83): 'Since to me at least, on account of my blindness, painted maps can hardly be of use, vainly surveying as I do with blind eyes the actual globe of the earth....']

3 *that one Talent*. Newton (reported by Todd) noted the allusion to the parable of the talents (Matt. 25. 14–30), which runs through 3–6, and commented on Milton's modesty in speaking of himself 'as if he had not five, or two, but only one talent' (cf. Matt. 25. 15). There is of course a play on the word *Talent*: in scripture, a denomination of monetary weight and value in the ancient world (*OED* 1 and 2), and power or ability of mind divinely entrusted to a person for use and improvement (ibid. 5). Verity equates *that one Talent* with Milton's 'poetic faculty'; but, considering at once his immediate occupation of writing in prose in defence of liberty and the importance he set upon it (cf. *Sonn* 22. 9–12; *Def* 2, *Works* 8, 128–39) and his sense that his higher gift was for poetry (*RCG*, *Works* 3, 235), one might better think of the *Talent* as simply the gift of written expression [and intellectual and imaginative power?]. The play on the word readily suggests itself, and did so to Barnabe Barnes in his *Divine Centurie of Spirituall Sonnets* (1595), 26 and 28 (J. L. Potter, *N&Q* 4, 1957, 447). The phrase *death to hide* is explained by Matt. 25. 30: 'And cast ye the unprofitable servant into outer darkness'; *death* standing for the utmost of punishment, as there the outer darkness. Smart noted that in the Letter to a Friend of 1633 (*Works* 12, 321 and 324) 'Milton describes his own sense of responsibility for the use of his genius, quoting the command of Christ that all should labour while it is light, and the parable concerning *the terrible seizing of him that hid the talent*.'

4 *useless*: [Honigmann, citing P. Drew (without reference), sees a 'pun on *use* = usury, interest'; so also Prince.]

6 *account*. [Honigmann suggests that Milton perhaps associates the parable of the talents with that in Matt. 18. 23 f.: 'Therefore is the kingdom of heaven likened unto a certain king, which would take account of his servants.' He also quotes Milton's remark about 'guifts of Gods imparting, which I boast not, but thankfully acknowledge, and feare also lest at my certaine account they be reckon'd to me many rather then few....' (*Apol, Works* 3, 282).]

7 *Doth God...light deny'd.* Commenting on Milton's allusion to 'the doctrine in the gospel, that we are to work only while it is light, and in the night no man can work' ⟨John 9. 4⟩, Warton—in a modern vein—adds: 'There is an ambiguity between the natural light of the day, and the author's blindness.' [Apropos of *day-labour*, Honigmann cites also the parable of the labourers in the vineyard (Matt. 20. 1 f.).]

8 *fondly*: foolishly (*OED* 1 and *Lyc* 56). *patience*. [Honigmann remarks that 'Christian patience, or faith in Providence, could be a saintly virtue,' and quotes Rev. 14. 12, Ps. 37. 7 f. Cf. *PL* 9. 32, *SA* 1287–96. See Baumgartner in II above, under 1963.] *prevent*: preclude, check (*OED* 6).

9 *That murmur.* The phrase emphasizes that the preceding question is asked by way of complaint or repining. [Honigmann remarks that the word is biblical, citing Ps. 106. 25, 1 Cor. 10. 10; cf. Exod. 16. 7, Num. 14. 27, Phil. 2. 14.]

10 *man's work or his own gifts*: 'Free-will or grace' (Warburton, reported by Warton and Todd), i.e. what man does by his own will and effort, or what God's gift enables him to achieve.

10–11 *who best / Bear his milde yoak.* Cf. 'Take my yoke upon you....For my yoke is easy....' (Matt. 11. 29–30); and also (in relation further to 14 below): 'The Lord is good unto them that wait for him....It is good that a man should both hope and quietly wait for the salvation of the Lord. It is good for a man that he bear the yoke....' (Lam. 3. 25–7). [Honigmann quotes *PR* 3. 194–5: 'who best / Can suffer, best can do.']

11 *State*: mode of existence (*OED* 3), but with a reflection back from *Kingly* suggesting greatness, power (ibid. state 16b). [Rudrum (*Comus*, 101) remarks that ' "patience" has given an *adequate* answer by line eleven: "they serve him best". To discern what is superadded is to understand why the ending of the sonnet is triumphant rather than resigned. When one comes to the words "his State / Is Kingly", the pulse quickens with excitement: it is like that moment in an anthem when the trumpets ring out. It is as if Milton (and the reader) is *identifying* with the kingliness of God, enjoying, and sharing, His splendour.']

12–13 *Thousands at his bidding...without rest.* Warton quoted Spenser on the angels: 'There they in their trinall triplicities / About him wait, and on his will depend, / Either with nimble wings to cut the skies, / When he them on his messages doth send, / Or on his owne dread presence to attend....' (*Hymne of Heavenly Love* 64–8); [cf. *F.Q.* 2. 8. 1–2]. Smart notes that in medieval angelology the Seraphim and Cherubim, the highest orders, have the perfect vision of God and never leave his presence; (however, the third group in this higher order, the Thrones, execute God's judgments: see above, *IlPen* 51–4 n.). To indicate that Protestant divinity did not here follow the medieval 'but sought to found its conception of the angelic nature only upon the Bible,' Smart quoted Robert Gell's *Sermon Touching Gods government of the World by Angels* (1650), 19–20: 'The Angels of God being by nature so noble, so active, could not be imployed onely in contemplation.' Their 'business is about the world, and all the creatures in it....For the Nations also need their government, yea every person, to inflame them with the love of God; therefore the Seraphim are first, then the Cherubim, for illumination and admonition....The Old Testament is full of their administration, yea and the New Testament also.' But see below, 14 n.

14 *They also serve...waite.* Verity took the line to refer directly to those other angels who, in contrast with the thousands first mentioned, stand constantly in God's presence; he cited 'I am Gabriel, that stand in the presence of God' (Luke 1. 19—but the verse continues 'and am sent'), and 'ten thousand times ten thousand stood before him' (Dan. 7. 10). Smart saw a contrast between men who humbly wait upon the fulfilment of God's purposes and angels who serve by acting on his behest. [*They* appears to have angels as its logical meaning, but of course the point of the dictum is its application to men.] Among biblical references turning on *waite*, Smart cited Ps. 27. 14, 37. 7, 123. 2, and 2 Thess. 3. 5; Hughes added Lam. 3. 26. Various interpretations of the line, usually accompanied by a suggested biblical source, have been offered in support of varying views of the poet's final attitude as passive or active, resigned or hopeful. [See also critical summaries in II above.]

R. A. Haug (*N&Q* 183, 1942, 224–5) suggested David's sharing of the spoils with those who were too weak to join in battle (1 Sam. 30. 21–4); but this shifts the emphasis from service to reward.

H. F. Robins (*RES* 7, 1956, 360–6: cited in I above) sees the sonnet as issuing in a positive rededication to poetry. Hanford's, and the usual, view of it as a poem of religious resignation ignores or contradicts the assurance of divine illumination already reached in *Def* 2 in 1654 [Robins dates the sonnet in 1655]. The true meaning, Robins holds, depends on a correct interpretation of 12–14:

according to pseudo-Dionysius and Thomas Aquinas it is the five lower orders of angels who are sent abroad to execute God's commands, while the four higher orders stand ever in God's presence and receive from him directly the commands which they transmit to the lower orders to execute. Thus, the sonnet implies, Milton's affliction, with its attendant illumination, raises him to a status comparable with that of the higher orders; and this is the resolution of his doubt and fear, the assurance that his highest talent (for poetry) may be fully exercised, and the parable of the talents read not as threat but as encouragement. But it is very doubtful, in the light of the actions assigned in *PL* to Raphael, Gabriel, and Michael, whether Milton accepted the distinction in the roles of higher and lower angels; and Robins' reading of the sonnet seems altogether to ignore the force of *only* before *stand and waite* [to ignore, one might say, Milton's clear acceptance of a secondary kind of service].

A view partly similar to Robins' is taken by J. L. Jackson and W. E. Weese (*MLN* 72, 1957, 91–3), who would read line 14 in relation to Eph. 6 and *stand* in the sense of 'Put on the whole armour of God, that ye may be able to stand against the wiles of the devil' (6. 11). The emphasis is shifted from passive waiting to active serving, even perhaps to the writing of a great Christian work (suggested by St Paul's hope through inspired utterance 'to make known the mystery of the gospel': Eph. 6. 19).

[F. Pyle (*RES* 9, 1958, 376–87: cited in 1 above) opposes Robins for two main reasons. First, in *DocCh* and *PL* Milton showed his indifference to traditional distinctions in angelic orders and roles. [This is fully demonstrated by Robert H. West, *Milton and the Angels*, 1955, 132–43, etc., though he does not deal with this sonnet.] Secondly, Robins underestimates the extreme dejection of the octave of the sonnet, on which the significance of the sestet depends. Bitter complaint against God's exacting demands and harsh injustice gives place to recognition of his sovereignty and wisdom and to acquiescence in his will. The poet moves from the God of the Old Testament to the God of the New, from the doctrine of rewards and punishments to that of grace and faith: he has gained, or regained, a larger conception of God's ways and of the meaning of service. Pyle finds the spirit of the last line expressed in Luke 12. 35–40, where servants are ready and waiting expectantly (not in fear, as in the parable of the talents).

Baumgartner (see II above, under 1963) writes (208): 'For Milton, then, patience means neither inaction nor stoical indifference. The patient Christian, with faith in Divine Providence, seeks to know God's will and to act according to it, leaving the results to God. Thus when Milton writes "They also serve who only stand and waite," he is not renouncing action, but rather stating that, like the Angels in Revelation who serve before the throne and wait upon the command of God, man also serves by simply waiting upon the Divine Will.'

Honigmann cites 'Wait on the Lord' (Ps. 27. 14) as 'a phrase frequently found in the Bible. Milton may use *wait* = attend as a servant, to receive orders (*O.E.D.* 9), but its more common meaning, "stay in expectation", is surely present too: he reverts to the labourers in the vineyard, some of whom had to wait for work "standing idle in the marketplace." ' Honigmann also (44) notes the characteristic unifying device of contrast: 'the spaciousness of "this dark world and wide" as experienced by a single self-centred and restless man gives way to the vision of thousands of God-centred angels posting "o're Land and Ocean without rest "—a deliberate contrast, but not as logically established as that between "bent To *serve*" and "They also *serve* who only stand and waite." ']

[Woodhouse]. To sum up, it is evident that all interpretations recognize that the sonnet commences from a mood of depression, frustration, even impatience (since Patience has to intervene), and that the counsel of Patience is submission: 'who best / Bear his milde yoak, they serve him best.' The question is whether the remaining lines reinforce this counsel or add an entirely new conception. There is no mistaking the deliberate elaborating of 'God doth not need...' by 'his State / Is Kingly. Thousands at his bidding speed,' or the paralleling of 'serve who only stand and waite' with the statement that they *serve* best who merely *bear*. This on the face of it supports the idea of simple reinforcement. It is, of course, conceivable that the device might be used in order to insinuate, almost to cloak, a higher hope; but if this indeed were the case, one would expect a corresponding change of tone, a resolution issuing not in tranquillity, but in renewed energy. Paul Goodman [see II above] has contrasted the dominance of the first person in the octave and its giving place in the sestet to the glorification of God and the generalizing of the personal problem. This suggests that here, as in *Sonnet* 7, the problem posed is not so much resolved as lifted to a plane where self-regarding thoughts become irrelevant.

Sonnet 20 *(Lawrence of vertuous Father vertuous Son)*

❧

I. DATE AND CIRCUMSTANCES

[Although, as we have seen (*Sonnet* 19: 1), *Sonnets* 18–22 cannot be an unbroken consecutive series, chronological order must be accepted for all cases where contrary evidence does not prevail. Since *Sonnet* 18 belongs to May–June 1655, and 22 probably to early 1655 (Parker, 1044, n. 144, prefers June 1654), *Sonnets* 20 and 21, scholars have generally agreed, were presumably composed in 1655. Further, line 2 of *Sonnet* 20 —'Now that the Fields are dank, and ways are mire'—places it in late autumn or early winter, that is, of 1655–6. Honigmann, who discounts the principle of chronological arrangement, seems to have no warrant for stretching the implications of dank fields and miry ways and suggesting the possibility 'that the sonnet belongs to the period when Milton still walked for exercise, before 1652, and was addressed to a precocious youth of eighteen or nineteen.' Parker (1044, n. 142), while not disputing the usual 1655–6, suggests 1654–5 as quite possible. Carey, because of Milton's moving to Westminster in December 1651, dates 'during any winter from 1651–2 to 1656–7.']

The only text of the sonnet is that of 1673.

Smart showed that the Lawrence here addressed was Edward Lawrence (1633–57), the eldest son of Henry Lawrence, and not Henry, the second son, as Masson supposed. [Parker (loc. cit.) does 'not feel positive about this identification.'] The *vertuous Father*, Henry Lawrence (1600–64), was a native of St Ives, where his family was acquainted with Cromwell. He was educated at Emmanuel College, Cambridge, and was Puritan in his sympathies, but took no part in the Civil War, being abroad in the 1640s for the education of his young family. In 1648 he began to figure in public life and rose with the star of Cromwell, to whose interests he was firmly attached. He sat in successive parliaments, became Lord President of the Council of State, and in 1657 took his seat in Cromwell's second chamber. He had literary and especially theological avocations: he was Keeper of the Library at St James's House and wrote several theological treatises, one of them *Of our Communion and Warre with Angels* (1646). Milton refers to him as a man 'of the first capacity, and polished by liberal studies' (*Def* 2, *Works* 8, 235).

Among those who visited Milton in his garden-house in Petty France in the 1650s, Edward Phillips mentions 'young Lawrence,' together with Cyriack Skinner (see below, *Sonnets* 21, 22), as the recipients of sonnets (*Early Lives*, ed. H. Darbishire, 74). [Lawrence may have been, as Skinner was, a pupil of Milton's (Parker, 924, n. 19).] In one of Milton's letters to Henry Oldenburg, his friend (and a friend of Spinoza) and later the first secretary of the Royal Society, Milton says that to 'our Lawrence' he has given greetings as bidden (*Epistol* 24, 1 Aug. 1657: *Works* 12, 99). Smart printed drafts of four letters, found in the archives of the Royal Society, from Oldenburg to young Edward Lawrence, which serve to identify 'our Lawrence' of Milton's reference. Edward Lawrence died in 1657 (obviously after Milton's letter to Oldenburg cited above). The fleeting impression that we receive of him is of a precocious and studious boy and young man, who had some literary ambitions and gave promise of a bright future. Smart gathered the scanty records: Oldenburg's letters to him (two in French, and one each in Latin and Italian); his own Latin letter, written by him as his father's amanuensis at the age of thirteen; and poetic tributes by Davenant, together with a Royalist satire on Puritan leaders which refers to the eldest son of Henry Lawrence as the friend and admired patron of poets (Smart, 111–13, 166–73).

[For the necessity and rightness of occasional relaxation Milton had earlier cited the highest authority (*Tetr*, *Works* 4, 85–6):

No mortall nature can endure either in the actions of Religion, or study of wisdome, without somtime slackning the cords of intense thought and labour:

which lest we should think faulty, God himself conceals us not his own recreations before the world was built; *I was*, saith the eternall wisdome, *dayly his delight, playing alwayes before him* [cf. *PL* 7. 9–12]. And to him indeed wisdom is as a high towr of pleasure, but to us a steep hill, and we toyling ever about the bottom: he executes with ease the exploits of his omnipotence, as easie as with us it is to will: but no worthy enterprise can be don by us without continuall plodding and wearisomnes to our faint and sensitive abilities. We cannot therefore always be contemplative, or pragmaticall abroad, but have need of som delightfull intermissions, wherin the enlarg'd soul may leav off a while her severe schooling; and like a glad youth in wandring vacancy, may keep her hollidaies to joy and harmles pastime....]

J. Finley ('Milton and Horace,' 1937, 63–5) comments: 'It is impossible to overpraise the delicate and sure touch with which Milton in these sonnets makes Horace's lighter manner his own. The 20th sonnet is an invitation, like several in Horace, in which the poet, after contrasting the outer world of nature to the quiet scene of the meeting of friends, passes to some generalization concerning the conduct of life. The poem, as is perhaps natural in Milton's blindness, does not so much reproduce one ode as the spirit of many odes, and what is most masterly, does so in such a way as to lose nothing of Horace's charm while yet conveying perfectly Milton's more puritan and austere temperance....The phrase of address...is a most happy adaptation of *Od.* 1, 16, 1. The scene of a dark English winter sketched in the next lines is in the spirit of similar scenes in Horace's odes of invitation,...but Milton's description is as independently faithful to England as are Horace's to Italy. There follows a prophecy of a better season to come in Horace's manner....But the beautiful reference in line 8 to Christ's words conveys it would be hard to say what added sense of Christian joy in the spring.' For detailed references in Horace see the notes below.

[M. Van Doren (*Introduction to Poetry*, 1951, 123–5) contrasts this sonnet with *Sonnet* 18. The very gait of the opening syllables is gentle, unlike the mighty rush of the Piedmont sonnet. 'The rhyme sounds are tenor throughout,' or light and choice, like the promised entertainment. The phrase *a sullen day* 'already conquers the weather it creates, making it seem a good thing to have outdoors....The movement...is luxurious and relaxed, from phrase to phrase, from section to section; the octave and the sestet are properly separate, and within each of them the thought is developed with just enough complexity to tease the intellect of the listener but not with so much as to tax it.' 'But the sestet is the triumph of the poem.' Even the sound suggests the delicacy and grace of food, drink, music, and talk. 'As music is mentioned the sound of the words grows deeper and richer...; nothing...will ever disturb the clear, smiling calm, the knowing and cultivated courtesy that Milton has imagined' for the quiet medium of the poem.

Honigmann thinks that the sonnet glances in several ways at Puritan emphasis on work and concern with the kinds and degrees of relaxation permissible to Christians. He sees Milton framing his invitation 'very carefully' to avoid the charge of mere indulgence by appealing to the idea of gain, 'the "profit-motive,"' and striking 'at the very basis' of 'the whole rigorist edifice, its worship of industry,' by citing Christ's approval of 'the untoiling *Lillie.*' This seems needlessly strained; the terms and tone of the sonnet are in full accord with Milton's instincts and personality. See also Honigmann's comments on 20 and 21, quoted under the latter.]

II. NOTES

1 *Lawrence...Son.* Pattison compared *O matre pulchra filia pulchrior* (Horace, *C.* 1. 16. 1). Finley (48) notes that Horace is fond of commencing his address to persons with a reference to their descent (cf. *C.* 1. 1. 1, 1. 16. 1, 3. 17. 1, 3. 29. 1), and Milton follows suit (*Sonn* 10, 20, 21). The epithet *vertuous* 'is used in a Latin sense, and denotes the possession of mental power or capacity, eminence of character' (Smart); but the commoner meaning of virtue, moral and fundamental, is certainly (in the context) included.

2–5 *Now that...Season gaining.* Finley (64 [with misprints corrected]) notes descriptions of the seasons in Horace's odes of invitation: 1. 9 (winter), 1. 4 and 4. 12 (spring), 1. 17 and 3. 29 (summer). With *Fields are dank* he compares *imbres nubibus hispidos | manant in agros* (*C.* 2. 9. 1–2).

4 *wast*: spend, pass, occupy (*OED* 8). The word is perhaps chosen because it is to be implied that in reality this is not a waste of time, which *will run | On* *smoother* for the relaxation. With *wast a sullen day* Pattison compared *morantem saepe diem mero | fregi* (Horace, *C.* 2. 7. 6–7).

6 *Favonius*: Zephyrus, the west wind, which ushered in the spring and promoted growth; cf. Seneca, *Naturales Quaestiones* 5. 16; Pliny, *N.H.* 2. 46. 119, etc. Pattison cited *Solvitur acris hiems grata vice veris et Favoni* (Horace, *C.* 1. 4. 1). [Cf. Milton, *El* 3. 47: *Serpit odoriferas per opes levis aura Favoni.*]

re-inspire: 'breathe upon once more' (Verity), or perhaps 'into,' either meaning being possible (*OED*: inspire 1). Warton cited 'and milde Favonius breathes' (Sir John Beaumont, *Bosworth-field*, 1629, 12; *Poems*, ed. Grosart, 1869, 38).

8 *The Lillie…nor spun.* Newton (reported by Todd) cited Matt. 6. 28: 'Consider the lilies of the field, how they grow; they toil not, neither do they spin.' In the light of this allusion, Todd further suggested that *cloth in fresh attire* (7) may echo Matt. 6. 30, 'if God so clothe the grass of the field.' See Finley's remark (1, above) on the added suggestion of reference to Christ's words.

9 *neat*: elegant, tasteful (*OED* 8b), but perhaps with a secondary suggestion of simplicity, freedom from superfluity (ibid. 7), reinforced by *light and choice.*

10 *Attick tast.* The word *tast* carries here more of its metaphorical than of its literal sense, and suggests 'such as would have been appreciated or preferred' (*OED* 7) in Athens. [Cf. *Cecropiosque sales* (*EpDam* 56).] Milton is perhaps thinking of the banquets in Plato with their accompaniment of good conversation. He never ceases to admire 'the old and elegant humanity of Greece' (*Areop*, *Works* 4, 295); and Athens is 'the eye of Greece…native to famous wits | Or hospitable' (*PR* 4. 240–2).

12 *Tuskan Ayre*: Italian music. [Edward Phillips recorded that, just before leaving Italy, Milton had shipped home 'a Parcel of curious and rare Books…; particularly a Chest or two of choice Musick-books of the best Masters flourishing about that time in Italy….' (Darbishire, *Early Lives*, 59).] Italy—especially Florence, the capital of Tuscany—like Athens remains for him a cultural ideal.

13–14 *He who of those delights can judge, And spare | To interpose them oft, is not unwise.* The meaning of *spare* has been debated. Keightley would understand 'time' and interpret '*interpose*, i.e. place them in the intervals of his serious occupations,' which makes the concluding lines a reinforcement of the invitation with no precautionary reservation. Masson, rejecting this interpretation, recognized the parallel with Lat. *parcere* (refrain from) with the infinitive, and interpreted 'refrain from interposing them [diversions] oft.' Masson is supported by Pattison, Rolfe, Bell, Browne, Moody, Verity, Smart, Patterson, Hughes [1937: in 1957 Hughes accepted 'afford'], Wright, [Hanford, M. Nicolson, Prince]. There is English as well as Latin precedent for the construction (*OED* 6c), and it harmonizes with *interpose*, 'introduce...in the way of interference' (*OED* 3; *Lyc* 152). Despite this abundant support, some attempt has been made to revive Keightley's interpretation (F. Neiman, *PMLA* 64, 1949, 480–3; Elizabeth Jackson, ibid. 65, 1950, 328–9) on the following grounds: *spare* can mean 'save, or give (time)' to (*OED* 8c; but there is no example given where the object, time, is merely understood, and none followed by an infinitive), or 'supply (a person) with (something)' (*OED* 9a; but no example with direct and indirect objects understood, and none followed by an infinitive). The argument is equally worthless in the two cases: there is no known precedent to support Keightley's interpretation. Hence it is useless to urge: that *Sonnets* 20 and 21 are companion pieces and that the latter contains no such cautionary note as Masson finds in *Sonn* 20 (they are addressed to different persons requiring different counsel: see *Sonn* 21, notes); *or* that the delights Milton offers need no reservation in favour of temperance; *or* that Masson's interpretation would require not 'judge *and* spare' but 'judge *but* spare' (which assumes that *judge* means 'appreciate,' whereas it clearly means 'discriminate, set a proper value on things'); *or* that examples can be found in Horace where no such counsel is given. In a word, it is plain that all the honours rest with Masson, and (as Rolfe says) Keightley ought to have known better than to reverse a meaning so consonant with Milton's known attitude, and thus (as Smart puts it) to contradict the sentiment of moderation in so Horatian a poem and 'The rule of not too much, by temperance taught' (*PL* 11. 531). [Lascelles Abercrombie (*TLS*, 11 April 1936, 316) compared Benjamin Whichcote, Aphorism 348: 'He that would have the Perfection of Pleasure; must be Moderate in the Use of it.' Le Comte (*Yet Once More*, 146–8), opposing Neiman and E. Jackson, cites Milton's Latin and English in support of the meaning 'forbear.']

[D.B. In spite of the array of scholarly names, the case for 'forbear to' may be thought much weaker, and the case for 'spare time for' much stronger, than Woodhouse found them. The absence of any 'known precedent' is not fatal, since Milton's use of words and idioms is notoriously bold, and his usages cannot be limited by examples in *OED*—as this commentary often shows. The lack of any such reservation in the companion sonnet (21) is not quite negligible, at least for the reason given—unless we are to assume that the sober and virtuous Lawrence was in need of counsel that Skinner did not need. The Horatian argument seems strained: however much Horace is identified with the gospel of moderation, that is rarely the burden of his invitations to share wine (e.g. 1. 9, 17, 20, 2. 7, 3. 8, 17, 19, 21, 4. 11, 12). Further, the meaning 'forbear to' leaves the defensive *is not unwise* pointless and makes Milton guilty of a flat and feeble truism: 'a person who is wise in his judgment and enjoyment of diversions is not unwise.' There is also a concrete item. J. A. W. Bennett (*TLS*, 5 April 1963, 233) observed that Milton's last two lines echo the traditional elementary schoolbook, *Catonis Disticha* (ed. London, 1628, 3. 5; *Minor Latin Poets*, L.C.L., 3. 6, p. 610): *Interpone tuis interdum gaudia curis:* | *Ut possis animo quemvis sufferre laborem.* (One might add the dictum in the likewise familiar Mantuan, *E*. 9. 38 [*Eclogues*, ed. W. P. Mustard, Baltimore, 1911]: *Omne opus atque labor vult intervalla.*) Milton would of course expect the echo of *Cato* to be recognized, and *Interpone* does not carry the loaded meaning Masson and others have given to Milton's *interpose*. J.C. Maxwell (*TLS*, 26 April 1963, 314) remarked that 'One incidental result of Mr. Bennett's discovery... ought to be the final disappearance of the old belief that "spare to interpose" can mean "refrain from interposing."' V. Scholderer (ibid. 10 May, 341) objected that *interdum* in *Cato* 'can only mean "occasionally" or "now and then", so that if Milton...had the passage in mind he must have used "spare" restrictively in the sense of "refrain."' Maxwell (ibid. 17 May, 357) replied that 'Milton is more likely to have strengthened a familiar dictum than to have changed course so as to write "and spare to interpose them oft" in the sense of "and (yet) refrains from interposing them oft."' It may be observed that the quotation from *Tetrachordon* (1, above) in praise of diversion does not emphasize restraint. On the whole, we may think that 'spare time for' is at least as logical as 'forbear to,' and perhaps more so. Recent editors who accept the former sense are: N. Frye (1951), Hughes (1957), Shawcross (1963), Bush (1965), I. G. MacCaffrey (1966); also Rudrum (*Comus*, 102–4) and Parker (1044, n. 142). Honigmann notes that 'the more recent tendency is to relate sonnets XX and XXI, stressing that the drift of the two is the same,' i.e. that *spare* means 'spare time for.' Honigmann also remarks (44) that 'The question sent to Lawrence... ("Where shall we *sometimes* meet?"), is superseded when the poem concludes with "interpose them *oft*."' Carey, with brief recognition of debate, is non-committal.]

Sonnet 21 *(Cyriack, whose Grandsire on the Royal Bench)*

꧁

I. DATE AND CIRCUMSTANCES

The sonnet was presumably written in 1655 (see the headnote to *Sonnet* 20). [Honigmann, discounting as usual the principle of chronological order, says, apropos of line 8, that 'England was negotiating treaties with both Sweden and France a little earlier, in 1653–4, and both negotiations ran into difficulties (Masson, *Life*, 4, 553 f.). *The Swede* could refer to the Sweden of Queen Christina, and *the French* to the slippery France of Mazarin before or after 1654.' Apart from the question of order, Milton would hardly refer thus to the Sweden of the Christina whom he so elaborately eulogized in 1654 (*Def* 2, *Works* 8, 17, 103–9), and who abdicated in June of that year.]

The only complete text is that of 1673. Lines 5–14 appear in the MS. (*Facs.* 418) in the hand of an amanuensis, with no significant variants.

The maternal grandfather of Cyriack Skinner (1627–1700) was the famous Sir Edward Coke (1552–1634), Chief Justice of Common Pleas and later of the King's Bench, rival of Bacon, defender of the law and rights of Parliament against royal encroachments, and the greatest legal authority of his day through his *Reports* and his *Institutes of the Laws of England* (1628–44). With special emphasis Phillips mentions Skinner (with Lawrence) as a young admirer of Milton who visited him in the 1650s (see *Sonn* 20, headnote). Aubrey described him as 'an ingeniose young gentleman, scholar to John Milton' (*Brief Lives*, ed. A. Clark, 2 v., Oxford, 1898, 1, 290). Anthony Wood repeated Aubrey's phrase, with the further item 'a Merchants son of London' (*Athenae Oxon.* 2, 1692, 439). Hence Masson infers, and Smart [and Parker, 473, 881] state,

477

that Skinner had as a boy been placed under Milton's tuition. He was later admitted to Lincoln's Inn. His family was connected by friendship with that of Marvell, and Marvell wrote to Milton in 1654, congratulating him on Skinner's now being his neighbour. The young man was much interested in political speculation (and in foreign affairs, as the sonnet indicates), and sometimes took the chair at meetings of James Harrington's Rota (Aubrey and Wood, loc. cit.; French, *L.R.* 4, 275). To these interests Skinner evidently added a degree of enthusiasm for mathematics and science (sonnet, line 7); this is perhaps confirmed by his friendship with Milton's friend, Henry Oldenburg (*Epistol* 18, etc., *Works* 12, 79), later the first secretary of the Royal Society. Our sense of the intimacy of Milton's friendship with Skinner is much strengthened by the second sonnet to him (22). [The early anonymous biography of Milton, which Helen Darbishire attributed to Milton's nephew, John Phillips, has been more plausibly assigned to Skinner by W. R. Parker (*TLS*, 13 September 1957, 547; cf. R. W. Hunt, ibid. 11 October, 609; M. Kelley (who had suggested Skinner in *MP* 54, 1956–7, 25), ibid. 27 December, 787; Parker, *PMLA* 73, 1958, 197, n. 2, and *Milton*, 880–2). Honigmann agrees with Hunt that the hand-writing appealed to by Parker does not provide firm evidence for Skinner's authorship.]

Sonnets 20 and 21 are in some sort companion pieces, Horatian invitations to enjoy hospitality and diversion, and have something of a common pattern. The sonnets may even have accompanied invitations to the same gathering [so also Parker, 1044, n. 143].

[Honigmann (52) remarks that tradition may mislead as well as illuminate, and that Milton's 'Horatian invitations' 'were not necessarily invitations of the same sort.' The primary purpose of *Sonnet* 20 'is not to arrange a particular gaudy day but rather to suggest closer friendship, or at least to forestall the slackening of friendship.' If 21 concerned a party, 'the invitation was sent indecently late ("*To day* deep thoughts resolve with me to drench")'. I suspect that the sonnet is a *second* invitation to a young friend who had excused himself, an appeal for companionship much more pressing than that directed to Lawrence. Despite its superficial resemblances to Horace's bantering ode to

Quintius Hirpinus (II. xi) this is a sonnet of barely disguised rebuke, far removed from the spirit of the Horatian invitation.'

Honigmann (65–6) further remarks that *Sonnet* 19 ('When I consider') 'creates a new field of force within which the two next sonnets...lose some of their autonomy.' As in 19, so in the lighter situation of 20 and 21 Milton advises 'a similar submission to circumstances, the *hard Season* or the *cheerful hour* sent by God, and with it some relaxation from the pursuit of one's talent.' The poet 'passes on the lesson he had himself learnt....']

II. NOTES

1–3 *Cyriack...taught our Lawes.* The *Grandsire* is Sir Edward Coke (see headnote). *Themis*: goddess of Justice, who bore to Zeus Eunomia (Order), Dike (Justice), and Eirene (Peace) (Hesiod, *Theog.* 901–2). The *Royal Bench / Of Brittish Themis* means the Court of King's Bench. On the opening reference to the recipient's descent see *Sonn* 20. 1 n.

4 *at their Barr*: ['*i.e.* in administering the law' (Bell). 'The bar, or barrier, marked off the immediate precinct of the judge's seat. Milton therefore compared Coke not with barristers wrenching the law for their clients, but with other judges' (Honigmann). Milton had early expressed the sentiment of this line: *male custoditaque gentis / Jura* (*Patrem* 71–2).]

5–6 *drench / In mirth...no repenting drawes.* Finley (67) interprets *drench* (submerge, drown: *OED* 2) as alluding to wine (not specified here as it is in *Sonn* 20. 10), and this as reflecting the counsel of Horace (*C.* 3. 21. 9; 4. 12. 23). Warton remarked: 'This is the decent mirth of Martial, Nox non ebria, sed soluta curis' (10. 47). It is also the Mirth of *L'All*, with its 'unreproved pleasures' (38–40 and n.).

7 *Let Euclid...Archimedes pause* evidently refers to Skinner's interest in the mathematical and scientific studies now coming into greater prominence among intellectuals. In Milton's own humanistic program of 1644 these studies had received considerable stress (*Educ, Works* 4, 283–4) and he himself had earlier cultivated an amateur interest (*Def* 2, *Works* 8, 120–1). [Finley (66) cites *mitte civiles super urbe curas* (Horace, *C.* 3. 8. 17).]

8 *And what the Swede intend,...the French.* MS. had *intends*. International politics are represented by the military adventures of Charles X of Sweden and the diplomacy of Mazarin, the chief minister of France. Newton (reported by Todd) compared: *Quid bellicosus Cantaber et Scythes, | Hirpine Quincti, cogitet Hadria | divisus obiecto, remittas | quaerere* (Horace, *C.* 2. 11. 1–4). It is perhaps not fanciful to see in Skinner a prototype of Addison's Coffee House Politician, or, in Milton's invitation to him to quit for a day his scientific and political concerns, a smiling reference to a somewhat excessive enthusiasm, and even, in the next two lines, a gentle admonition.

9–14 *To measure life...cheerful hour, refrains.* The admonition seems to be twofold: to put first things first and concentrate on what is productive of *solid good* (9–10), then to give due welcome to *a cheerful hour* of relaxation. Pattison noted a similar sentiment in Montaigne, in the first sentences of *Upon Some Verses of Virgil* (3. 5: tr. Florio, Tudor Translations, 3 v., London, 1892–3, 3, 61):

Profitable thoughts, the more full and solide they are, the more combersome and heavy are they....We must have our minde instructed with meanes to sustaine and combate mischiefes, and furnished with rules how to live well and believe right: and often rouze and exercise it in this goodly study. But to a minde of the common stampe, it must be with intermission and moderation; it groweth weake, by being continually over-wrested.

[See Milton's own defence of occasional relaxation in the extract from *Tetrachordon* quoted above under *Sonn* 20, 1. Honigmann (44) comments on the thematic and structural unity: 'the praise of Cyriack Skinner's *Grandsire*...is not simply a bow to a famous ancestor, a traditional courtesy in this type of poem....It enables Milton to slip in the thought that the misguided *wrench our laws*, from which he proceeds to insinuate that Skinner wrenches life, overburdening it with cares: the contrast between Coke, who interpreted *our Lawes* correctly, and Skinner, who could not *measure life* correctly, is underlined with *applause* for the one (first quatrain) and *Heaven's disapproval* of the other (second tercet).' He remarks (185) on Milton's contrast between the mathematical measurers of line 7 and the measuring of life.]

9–10 *To measure life...the nearest way.* [Honigmann, citing the definition of a straight line, suggests a relation between *solid good* and solid geometry. More apt is his citing the same phrase from Raphael's comparison of earth and sun (*PL* 8. 93). See above, 9–14 n.]

14 *a cheerful hour.* [Honigmann suggests a quibble on 'good cheer.']

Sonnet 22 *(Cyriack, this three years day these eys)*

⁂

I. DATE AND CIRCUMSTANCES

[The idiom used in line 1 (see note below), taken by the older editors as indicating a precise anniversary day, may have had only the rough meaning 'for three years now' (Parker, 1044, n. 144); but, even so, the phrase, if it was to have any meaning at all, would be approximately accurate, say within a month or two. We must therefore place the sonnet in relation to the time when Milton became aware of complete blindness, i.e. February 1652 (French) or November 1651 (Parker) or some time between those dates (see *Sonnet* 19, 1). Thus, unless 'this three years day' is taken with unwarranted looseness, the sonnet would precede *Sonnet* 18 (Piedmont), which could not have been composed before May–June 1655. Parker (1044, n. 144) observes that for this reason 22 is usually assigned to the latter part of 1655. But, he goes on, the date of Milton's blindness puts the sonnet 'in the winter of 1654–5 or possibly the spring of 1655—surely not near the winter of 1655–6....' Parker strongly suspects that 22 was 'written in June 1654, after the publication' of *Def* 2, especially because 'From May 1654 onwards, Skinner was living near Milton in Petty France' (n. 143). It is not clear how Parker, dating Milton's blindness in late 1651, can put this sonnet in June 1654, which makes 'three years' loose indeed, and also makes *Sonnet* 19, if written in 1655 (as Parker now joins others in saying), an unaccountable relapse after the heroic confidence of *Sonnet* 22. Hanford and Hughes date *Sonnet* 22 in 1655, Shawcross in December 1655, Carey in '1655?']

Cyriack Skinner's relations with Milton are outlined in the headnote to *Sonnet* 21. It was no doubt on account of the reference to Milton's first *Defence* that *Sonnet* 22 was not included in the *Poems* of 1673. It was—with *Sonnets* 15, 16, and 17—printed by Edward Phillips in his edition of Milton's *Letters of State* (1694). The authoritative text is in the Cambridge MS. (*Facs.* 418). [Variants in Phillips' text (ibid. 373) are recorded below in notes on 3, 7, 8–9, 12, 14, and fully in *Works* 1, 449–50.] Phillips gave the sonnet the title *To Mr. Cyriac Skinner Upon his Blindness.*

II. NOTES

1 *this three years day.* [Newton, Warton, and Todd saw no need to explain this phrase. Warton (in 1785 only) mistakenly related it to the 'three years' of Milton's letter to Philaras, *Works* 12, 69. Keightley said: 'This would seem to mean, it is three years today since.' J. Dixon (*N & Q*, Ser. 4, 9, 1872, 445) proposed emending to 'Three years this day.' J. H. I. Oakley (ibid. Ser. 4, 10, 1872, 76–7; cf. Dixon, 153) said such exactness would be commonplace and was contradicted by Milton's account of the gradual worsening of his eyesight; the phrase hinted at the monotony of three years of darkness. For the use of *day* as 'space of time' Oakley cited Shakespeare, *2 H. VI* 2. 1. 2: 'I saw not better sport these seven years' day.' B. Nicholson (ibid. 11, 1873, 349) added 'this two years day' (Henry Chettle, *Kind-Hartes Dreame*, 1592: ed. G. B. Harrison, London, 1923, 39). Masson (*P.W.*, 1874, 2, 308; 1890, 1, 238) took the phrase to mean 'written on the third anniversary of the day from which he could date the completeness' of his blindness. Pattison evidently understood Milton to mean an anniversary (he looked back from March 1655 to March 1652, 'the date at which the blindness became total'), but, rather oddly, he cited Oakley and Shakespeare and Chettle as if they supported that view. Bell likewise explained as 'three years ago to-day' and cited Shakespeare. Verity said only: 'The time-reference...indicates that the Sonnet was written in 1655, the date of Milton's complete loss of sight being 1652.' *OED* does not seem to record Milton's phrase but gives some similar ones of 1451–1670 (day: IV. 11) in which 'day' means 'space of time.' Smart explained Milton's meaning as 'for three years,' citing the Shakespearian line in support of that general sense. Smart has been followed by Patterson, Hughes (1937), Wright, Honigmann, Parker (1 above), and Prince. To Shakespeare (as understood by Oakley and Smart) Honigmann adds a couplet from John Heywood's First Hundred Epigrams, no. 30 (*Works*, ed. B. A. Milligan, Urbana, 1956, 118; *Proverbs*, etc., ed. J. S. Farmer, London, 1906, 126): 'This twenty yeres daie in weather hot

or coole, / Thou handledst no caruyng nor woorkyng toole.' On the other side, the idea that Milton meant a precise day has been held by Keightley, Masson, Pattison, Bell, Hanford (apparently: 'The third anniversary of Milton's blindness fell in....1655': *Poems*), Woodhouse (headnote to *Sonnet* 19), M. Nicolson (*John Milton*, 155), Bush, and I. G. MacCaffrey.

The question is perhaps not entirely closed in favour of the general sense, 'for three years.' In Shakespeare and Heywood the idiom clearly means a long space of time, and that Milton meant only that might be supported by his saying *have forgot* rather than *forgot*. On the other hand, he had a bold way with words and was not always bound by common or older meanings. The strongest reason for a more specific interpretation is that the first line and indeed the whole sonnet imply an anniversary as the occasion of composition, the arrival of a particular and unforgettable day (or short space of time) associated with his realizing the fact of total blindness. If he was composing the sonnet at any time in late 1654 or during the year 1655, can we imagine him saying to himself: 'Since I have now been blind for somewhere between three and four years, it is fitting that today I should take stock of my feelings?' As for *have forgot*, his mind might easily slide from a definite opening into the oppressive thought of continuity of experience.]

1–2 *these eys, though clear...of spot.* In *Def* 2 Milton said that his eyes 'to external appearance...are as completely without injury, as clear and bright, without the semblance of a cloud, as the eyes of those whose sight is the most perfect' (*Works* 8, 61). [The anonymous biographer also says that, while 'his Eyes were none of the quickest,' 'his blindness, which proceeded from a Gutta Serena, added no further blemish to them' (Darbishire, *Early Lives*, 32).]

3 *Bereft of light*: [Phillips, *Bereft of Sight* (*Facs.* 373).]

4–6 *Nor to thir idle orbs...man or woman.* Cf. 'hath quencht thir Orbs' (*PL* 3. 25) and 'Thus with the Year / Seasons return, but not to me returns / Day, or the sweet approach of Ev'n or Morn, / Or sight of vernal bloom, or Summers Rose, / Or flocks, or heards, or human face divine' (ibid. 40–4). Verity noted Virgil's use of *orbs* in connection with eyes: *ardentis oculorum orbis* (*A.* 12. 670).

6 *argue*: dispute, contend against (*OED* 4b). Cf. *PR* 2. 94: 'I will not argue that, nor will repine.'

7 *heavns hand or will.* [MS. *Gods*, replaced by *heavns* (*Facs.* 418). 'God's *will* here = His purposes and commands (Matt. vii. 21), and God's *hand* = *either*

His executive power (as in Acts iv. 30: "By stretching forth thine hand to heal") *or* His chastisement (as in 1 Sam. v. 6: "But the hand of the Lord was heavy upon them").' (Honigmann). In speaking of his blindness Milton stresses his sense of God's ever-present mercy and care (*Def* 2, *Works* 8, 71–3; letter to Philaras, ibid. 12, 71). *bate a jot*: bate one *jot* (Phillips; *Facs.* 373). Honigmann cites Shakespeare, *Cor.* 2. 2. 144–5: 'neither will they bate / One jot of ceremony.']

8–9 *bear up...onward*: 'put the helm "up" so as to bring the vessel into the direction of the wind' (*OED* 37), a nautical image carried on in the next phrase, but also with a memory of the sense, 'keep up one's courage' (ibid. 21c).

steer | Right onward. [In the scribal MS. (*Facs.* 418) *bear up and* replaced *attend to*, and *Right onward* replaced *Uphillward*. This last word was 'Formed on the analogy of "to God-ward" (Exod. xviii. 19), "to thee-ward" (1 Sam. xix. 4), etc.' (Honigmann).] With *steer...onward* contrast 'only stand and waite' (*Sonn* 19. 14). [For Milton's resolute desire to go on working Honigmann cites his letter to Oldenburg of 6 July 1654 (*Works* 12, 65: partly quoted above under *Sonn* 19, end of section II); and Job 17. 9: 'The righteous also shall hold on his way'; Luke 9. 62: 'No man, having put his hand to the plough, and looking back, is fit for the kingdom of God.']

10 *conscience*: consciousness, inward knowledge (*OED* 1). [Honigmann quotes *Def* 2 (*Works* 8, 71): 'I would not exchange my own consciousness (*conscientiam*) of what I have done, for any act of theirs however well performed, or lose the recollection of it, which is always so calm and delightful to me'; and a statement from Toland. For this last, and other remarks by Milton, see the end of section II under *Sonn* 19.] *Friend*. The fact that Milton confides these intimate reflections to Skinner makes this no mere conventional form of address.

10–12 *to have lost...side to side*. In *Def* 2 Milton said that his physicians predicted complete blindness if he laboured on the task assigned him by the Council of State, an answer to Salmasius' *Defensio Regia* (he had nearly lost the sight of one eye before he began); but, knowing the cost, he fulfilled this imperative obligation and produced his *Pro Populo Anglicano Defensio* (1651): 'methought...that I must necessarily incur the loss of my eyes, or desert a sovereign duty,' 'that there were many who purchased a less good with a greater evil...glory, with death,' while 'I proposed to purchase a greater good with a less evil; namely, at the price of blindness only, to perform one of the noblest acts of duty' (*Works* 8, 69). Duty, not glory, was the motive; but the fame of the controversy and of his prowess in it helped to sustain his spirit after the

event. He speaks with pride of the great effect produced in Europe by the work
(*Def* 2, *Works* 8, 15–17, 191, 253). John Aubrey tells us: '...the only inducement
of severall foreigners that came over into England, was chiefly to see Oliver
Protector, and Mr. John Milton; and would see the house and chamber wher
he was borne. He was much more admired abrode then at home' (*Brief Lives*,
ed. A. Clark, 2, 72). It was no idle boast to write *Of which all Europe talks from
side to side*. [There has been some discounting of Milton's proud claim (e.g.
Parker, *Milton's Contemporary Reputation*, Columbus, 1940, 35–8; Milton,
C.P.W. 4, 1966, 554 f., 964 f.), but Parker in his biography of 1968 (379–91,
418 f., 975 f.: see also French, *L.R.* 2, 339–65, 3, 14 f.) makes a good deal of
Milton's Continental reputation. And, besides Aubrey, there are such other early
witnesses as Phillips and Toland (Darbishire, *Early Lives*, 74, 160–1). In any
case, if Milton exaggerated somewhat, it would be pardonable.]

10 *overply'd* [Hunter ('New Words,' 256) lists the word as a Miltonic coinage.
OED gives no other example before 1858.]

12 *talks*. Other editors besides Warton have preferred Phillips' *rings*, but the
MS. has Milton's authority (*Facs.* 373, 418). [Smart suggested that *rings* may
have been 'an unconscious transference' from line 1 of *Sonn* 15: 'Fairfax,
whose name in armes through Europe rings.' Cf. Masson and Todd.]

13 *mask*: [masque. The idea of life as a stage play is common in the Renaissance, e.g. in Shakespeare. For the particular significance of Milton's word
Honigmann quotes Bacon's reference, in the essay *Of Truth*, to 'the masks and
mummeries and triumphs of the world.' He adds: 'but Milton put more pressure on the word. We are reminded of the masks worn by masqueraders, by
which their sight was restricted.']

14 *Content...no better guide*. The nature of the *better guide* is suggested in
Sonn 19, in *PL* 1. 17–19, 3. 1–55, and many other passages of verse and prose.
[Phillips' text has *other* instead of the MS. *better* (*Facs.* 373, 418). Milton was
fond of *other* as an oblique understatement meaning 'heavenly' and the like
(cf. *Comus* 611, 631, *Lyc* 174, *PL* 3. 17), but here the sense needed more direct
expression. As Honigmann remarks, the word *guide* is in keeping with *blind*.
For Milton's contentment with his lot, see above, notes on 7, 10, and 10–12.]

Sonnet 23 (*Methought I saw my late espoused Saint*)

❦

I. DATE AND SUBJECT

The sonnet was printed in *Poems* (1673). The MS. version, in the hand of an amanuensis (see Dahlberg and Kelley below), has no significant variants (*Facs.* 388).

The sonnet has traditionally been assumed to refer to Milton's second wife, Katherine Woodcock (b. 1628), whom he married 12 November 1656, who gave birth to a daughter on 19 October 1657, and who died on 3 February 1658; the daughter died on 17 March. W. R. Parker, however, has sought to prove that the reference is to Milton's first wife, Mary Powell, who died in May 1652, three days after the birth of her fourth child. Parker ('Milton's Last Sonnet,' *RES* 21, 1945, 235–8) noted that the traditional view rests on the unsupported statement of Elijah Fenton in his far from authoritative life of Milton (1725); on the assumption that Milton entertained no love for Mary Powell and lived in discord with her throughout their marriage, though some of the early lives state specifically that the reconciliation lasted till her death; and on our complete ignorance regarding Katherine Woodcock ⟨which has not been complete since Smart's researches recorded below⟩. Parker goes on to argue that the reference to *Purification* (line 6), based on Lev. 12. 5, will not apply to Katherine, since the rite was completed after 66 days, and Katherine did not die in childbed, as Edward Phillips wrongly reported, but (according to the testimony of Milton's granddaughter, confirmed by the record of burial: Smart, 186; French, *L.R.* 4, 215) three and a half months after the child's birth, and 'of a Consumption.' Parker also argued that the words *once more I trust to have | Full sight of*

486

her in Heaven without restraint presuppose that he had thus seen her in earlier days, though he was now under the *restraint* of blindness, and apply perfectly to Mary but not at all to Katherine, whom he did not marry and, so far as we know, did not meet until after he was blind. Parker would date the sonnet in the latter part of 1655; he thereby preserves the chronological sequence of the numbered sonnets of 1673 but otherwise creates difficulties: e.g. explaining a sonnet written supposedly more than three years after Mary's death (cf. his interpretation of *late* in line 1).

[T. O. Mabbott (*N&Q* 189, 1945, 239) pointed to Milton's nuncupative will as giving no ground for such a fervent tribute to Mary.]

F. Pyle ('Milton's Sonnet on his "Late Espoused Saint,"' *RES* 25, 1949, 57–60) opposed Parker and defended the traditional view. Since Milton in his verse uses *late* as meaning 'recently' seventeen times and never in the special sense applied to the dead, the meaning of *late espoused Saint* is 'Saint but recently espoused,' not 'espoused Saint now dead.' Also, the reference in *Purification* implies a partial parallel with the rescue of Alcestis by Heracles (see below, 2–4 n.): Alcestis was restored to her husband but still had to undergo purification to release her from consecration to the nether gods (Euripides, *Alc.* 1144–6): Katherine seemed to have been restored as one who had (i.e. *because* she had) fulfilled the days of purification. *Her face was vail'd* (10) because, never having seen Katherine's face, Milton could not form an image of it. The words *once more...without restraint* are explained by the fact that the blind poet had seen her in his dream (but not freely, her face being veiled) and hopes *to have | Full sight of her in Heaven without* (this) *restraint.* Thus the significant details point to Milton's second wife.

R. M. Frye (*N&Q* 194, 1949, 321) supported Pyle's reading of 5–6 on syntactical grounds. There is no comma after *Mine* in MS. or 1673. We have 'an inverted unit,' with *Purification in the old Law* as subject, *did save* as verb, and *Mine* as object—which would not be applicable to Mary Powell, who died before the period of purification was completed.

The debate continued with Parker's reply to Pyle and Pyle's rejoinder (both in *RES* 2, 1951, 147–54), and a full note supporting Parker by J. T. Shawcross (*N&Q* 3, 1956, 202–4). Parker asserts that *late* was used in both senses in Milton's day and in his prose; that *Full sight* is ambiguous, and also *vail'd*, which is perhaps no more than a reference back to the Alcestis story; and finally that generations of critics have seen Parker's, not Pyle's, significance in the reference to *Purification* (though mistakenly supposing it applicable to Katherine because they assumed her to have died in childbed, instead of months later from a cause unconnected with it).

In reply Pyle said that we have no ground for asserting that Katherine's death had no connection with the birth of her child. Further, 2 February, the day before her death, was the Feast of the Purification of the Virgin Mary, which may account for the emphasis on purification and serve to suggest a comparison of Katherine and the Virgin; and the reaching of the religious level makes unthinkable a mere return to the pagan pattern of wifely excellence (Alcestis).

Shawcross (who summarized the controversy of 1945–54) found support for purification's not having been yet effected from *pure as her mind* (9) in contrast to the impurity of her body: she appears as (5) one purified, but is not; while *And such* (7) signifies 'because of what has just been said.' 'Only Mary would be considered impure of body, not Katherine.' [This idea Carey finds less convincing than Le Comte's etymological argument (see 9 n. below); on the prime question Carey is non-committal, but his date '1658?' seems to favour Katherine.]

[Honigmann (190–2), after a brief summary of the debate to 1961, favoured the traditional view but thought 'it would be folly to pretend that Mary Powell's claims have been completely disposed of. The sonnet, after all, could have been written before 1658.'

Parker (*Milton*, 475, 1045, n. 145) briefly reaffirms his 'unorthodox conjecture.'

D. R. Fabian ('Milton's "Sonnet 23" and Leviticus xviii. 19,' *Xavier University Studies* 5, 1966, 83–8) would support Parker and Shawcross. His main point is that, according to Leviticus (12. 5; cf. 15. 19–24), the period of purification after a daughter's birth was 80 days (not 66, as Parker has it), and that Mary Milton died within the first two-week time of extreme 'impurity,' while Katherine died 108 days after childbirth. Also, Milton was reluctant to embrace his wife (cf. Lev. 18. 19), having realized in his dream that she had not been purified before she died.

It may be thought that Parker, Pyle, Shawcross, and Fabian all mistake the significance of the allusion to *Purification*. Milton would naturally link Katherine's death in some way with childbirth, and, the churching of women being still a religious practice, he would naturally think of that. But the lines about *Purification* are *not* a statement about his dead wife, they are only a simile, a Hebraic simile corresponding to the preceding classical one and merely explaining her appearance: she is *vested all in white*, the garb of heavenly purity—*as if* she had partaken of a religious ritual of purification. Thus arguments about the Levitical number of days, etc., are simply irrelevant; likewise the date of the Feast of Purification (besides, as Shawcross says, Milton would not appeal to an especially Romanist tradition). His use of *yet once more . . . Full sight* is a quite characteristic example of Miltonic compression: he has now had one sight of her, a partial, visionary one; he may therefore hope for another, a full and actual one. We may conclude that the arguments for Mary evaporate, and that all the evidence there is strongly favours the traditional view.]

It is accepted that the amanuensis who transcribed the sonnet in the MS. was Jeremie Picard, and C. R. Dahlberg (*N&Q* 194, 1949, 321) noted the absence of any proof that Picard was Milton's scribe before 14 January 1657–8. [M. Kelley elaborates the data and inferences (*MP* 54, 1956–7, 23–4). He finds that 'the evidence of the Milton manuscripts militates against Parker's association of Sonnet 23 with Milton's first wife, Mary, and his proposed date of 1655 for the poem.' He notes the beginning of Picard's employment, finds that 'Milton's amanuenses regularly entered his later sonnets at the time when, or soon after, he had composed them.'

Third, Picard's hand also appears in the tenth and last entry in Milton's Bible, which records the death of Milton's second wife, Katherine, and her daughter in 1658. Thus the period at which Picard worked for Milton, Milton's habit of having his later sonnets promptly entered in the Cambridge Manuscript, and the presence of Picard's hand in both the transcript of Sonnet 23 and the record of Katherine's death all combine to indicate that Katherine, rather than Mary, was the 'late espoused saint' of Sonnet 23; that the sonnet was consequently composed after her death on February 3, 1658; and that Picard's transcript of the poem was made not demonstrably later than 1660. Sonnet 23, therefore, should be placed within these terminal dates, 1658 and 1660, with the added observation that nothing in the Milton manuscripts even hints that the traditional date of 1658 is unsatisfactory.

Parker, who thinks (1063, n. 54) that Picard 'was Milton's amanuensis from at least 1655...or even earlier,' regards arguments based on him as irrelevant because the fair copy might have been made years after composition (a view shared by Honigmann and Carey).]

Our knowledge of Katherine Woodcock's character and the deep affection that she inspired in Milton comes entirely from the sonnet (if we accept her as its subject). Smart discovered evidence which permitted the inference that she had an unsettled and not happy childhood. [On her life and relations see also Parker, 1053–5.] Her father, William Woodcock, called (according to Phillips) Captain Woodcock, inherited from his unfortunate father (who died in a debtors' prison) an embarrassed estate, which he himself had helped to embarrass. In Smart's words (123), 'He had no occupation, and led a careless existence....He could not be trusted with money, and had an easy habit of living with his family at free quarters in the houses of his wife's relations.' There seems to be no ground for Warton's assertion that he was 'a rigid sectarist.' His early death was probably no great loss. Katherine seems to have endeared herself to her maternal grandfather's second wife, who left her a legacy. After the death of William Woodcock, his widow and her daughters settled at Hackney, then a pleasant suburb, the dwelling place of her cousin William Humble and his brother-in-law, Thomas Vyner, both men of substance who were created baronets after the Restoration. In Vyner's house the Woodcocks were finally given rooms. Since Vyner had some associations with the government of Cromwell and was moreover one of the treasurers of the fund raised, with Cromwell's active support, for the Waldensians (*Sonnet* 18, headnote), it may well be that he was acquainted with Milton and that Milton met Katherine in his house.

While the deep personal feeling of the sonnet is unmistakable, its theme, not unnaturally, occurs 'in the wide literature of the Italian sonnet,' and Smart prints one by Berardino Rota (already noticed by Hallam), in which is found the incident of the dead wife's appearing to her husband in a dream. The theme occurred too in other poetic forms (see below, 14 n.).

T. B. Stroup ('Aeneas' Vision of Creusa and Milton's Twenty-third Sonnet,' *PQ* 39, 1960, 125–6) notes that the allusion to Alcestis does not fit the end of the sonnet, since Alcestis is restored and Milton's wife is not. He observes further that various sources have been suggested for the end: Ralegh's sonnet (see 1 n. below); Martio Bartolini's *Sogno nel qual vidde la sua donna, che già era morta* and *Apparitione della sua donna morta*; and 'The Vision of Matilda' prefixed to Drayton's *Matilda* (Todd). Stroup would add Virgil, *A.* 2. 789–95, where the shade of Creusa leaves Aeneas just as he is about to embrace her. Stroup lays stress on her plea for care of their child (not hinted at in the sonnet) and claims that, if this is indeed Milton's source, it is evidence for Mary Powell, whose child lived (against Katherine Woodcock, whose child died).

[Honigmann (47–8) adds English analogues, 'to stress the conventionality of Milton's "occasional" poem: B. Griffin's dream of his lady (*Fidessa*, 1596, no. 14: "With that, away she went: and I did wake withal..."), or W. Smith's (*Chloris*, 1596, no. 13: "*Methought I saw* the nymph I would *embrace*...")',' and, as 'even more interesting,' Sidney's *Astrophel* 38: 'This night while sleepe begins with heavy wings.' 'Both Sidney and Milton found that one may see more clearly in a dream than when awake, and in both their dreams the lady *shines*.' Honigmann cites 'some other similar parallels,...Desportes, *Diane*, no. 35, R. Linche, *Diella* (1596), nos. 19, 24, Shakespeare, sonnet 43.' (See *Elizabethan Sonnets*, ed. Sir Sidney Lee, 2 v., London, 1904.)]

II. CRITICISM [D.B.]

George Boas ('The Problem of Meaning in the Arts,' *Meaning and Inter-pretation*, University of California Publications in Philosophy, 25, 1950, 318–19) contrasted the timeless, impersonal universality of Shakespeare's sonnets with such a sonnet as this of Milton, which 'would be as opaque as wood, did we not know something of Milton's biography,' not only of his blindness but of his having never seen his wife. Boas' general and particular ideas were opposed by L. Spitzer ('Understanding Milton,' *Hopkins Review* 4, 4, 1950–1, 16–27; *Essays on English and American Literature*, ed. A. Hatcher, Princeton, 1962). Spitzer argues that biographical knowledge is not necessary, that Milton's poem links itself with others, such as one by Pontano (see below, 14 n.), and with a general tradition. It is a poem 'perfectly understandable without the hypothesis of blindness, indeed one repeating a poetic pattern familiar to other poets of the Renaissance (enjoying unimpaired vision!), but to this he has added a new element, a poignant and perspicacious observation absent from the more intellectualistic poems of his predecessors and truly revelatory of his insight into the nature of dreams. . . . the poet must sharply and painfully perceive the forbidding rigor of the barriers be-tween the dream world and that of reality in which he must live on in irremediable loneliness.' 'Milton presents himself as a Christian Platonist who experiences the harrowing realization that, for all his craving for reunion with the Ideal, in this life there exists no intermediary realm between Earth and Heaven. This was evidently a truth which Milton ratified in his waking hours and if he portrays in the poem his hopes and disillusionment, it is in order to proclaim the harsh necessity for dreams to recede before reality—quite the reverse of the interpretation proposed by Boas (as the only alternative for a reader ignorant of Milton's blind-ness): "that to Milton dreams were more real than waking life."' (Spitzer does not think that *Her face was vail'd* and *without restraint* are allusions to blindness.) The sonnet has a 'tripartite *crescendo* arrangement' reminiscent of *At a solemn Musick*: (1) ancient pagan tradition; (2) ancient Jewish tradition; (3) Christian tradition and hope. Thus 'the main theme and the only problem of the sonnet. . . is not, as Boas would make it appear, the problem of Milton's blindness (nor that of the death of his wife), but the generally human problem of the Ideal in our world (and in this respect. . . our sonnet is as greatly determined by literary tradition—this time the tradition of the *donna angelicata* borrowed from the Italian poets of the *dolce stil nuovo*, from Dante and Petrarch—as are the love sonnets of Shakespeare, who "plucks the same strings as had been plucked by countless Italian poets before him"). And the detail of blindness, which in Milton's personal life was a cruel physical fact, is made to serve in our poem only a "metaphorical" function, suggesting, as it does, our actual world deprived of the Ideal. . . .' 'Boas' thesis is tantamount to repudiation of all classical art which prefers the general to the specific, a repudiation of the greater part of our Western tradition.' Quoting Boas' summary of Milton's actual situation, Spitzer affirms that 'The appreciation of the work of art seems here to be drowned out by the interests of the psychologist interested in the biology of the artist.'

In a rejoinder ('Understanding Spitzer,' ibid. 28–30), Boas notes that, while Spitzer will not allow knowledge of Milton's biography as necessary, he does postulate—for what he calls an 'autonomous and self-sufficient artistic structure'—a knowledge of Euripides, Hebraic Law, Dante, Petrarch, Pontano, and other poets. Boas does not share Spitzer's apparent belief 'that "the grandiose picture of man between two separated worlds" is somehow more important than "the personal detail that Milton was blind."' Boas by no means repudiated all classical art; he only maintained that 'each work of art is an individual thing, dated and located in history.' Boas' forceful answer implies, if it does not expressly say, that Spitzer's interpretation so radically alters the focus and meaning of the poem that it becomes unrecognizable.

Leone Vivante (*English Poetry*, London, 1950, 73–4) remarks that in 9–12 ('Came vested. . . more delight') 'there is not one single thing with distinct outlines—none that the grammarians would call a "concrete noun", except a few which are very indefinite, in the expressions: "her face"—yet "veiled"; "her person", "no face". . . . We find here strikingly the same serenity and spirituality, and perfection of form, as in some of the most beautiful stanzas of Petrarch; yet the use of the essences without place or shape is even more daring and absolute. These are quite radical concepts of the mental synthesis, highly indetermined, yet, in the verse, so much the more alive. Besides, the word "delight", as it is used at the end of the passage..., appears like a jewel in a translucent sea, and satisfies our claim for the finite. The "white", and the "pure", and "love", and "sweetness", and "goodness", and the "clear", all these terms express here the (in tendency) self- and form-transcending value of deep original freedom; that is, of the active principle in its *potential* intensity, and in its primal character. These are obviously moral values....'

Woodhouse (*Milton the Poet*, 1955, 6–8), commenting on poems which bear an evident relation to Milton's experience, notes that they fall into two classes: those which commence with an experience affirmative, improblematic, and productive of no tensions, so that the effect of the poem is merely to clarify and intensify the affirmation (e.g. *El* 5, *Nativity*), and those in which the initial problem and tension are resolved (e.g. *Sonnets* 7, 19). The unique example of the former class which issues in intensified negation (not affirmation) is *Sonnet* 23. It would be surprising to find anyone but Johnson speaking of Milton's having 'honoured' his wife's 'memory with a poor sonnet' [*Lives*, 1, 116]. With the possible exception of one private (19) and one public sonnet (18), it is the most moving he ever wrote—and even these are only *possible* exceptions.

E. M. W. Tillyard (*The Metaphysicals and Milton*, London, 1956, 2–11) compared this sonnet with Donne's 'Since she whom I lov'd hath payd her last debt.' While Donne's is 'a self-centred sonnet' and his dead wife, its 'nominal concern,' 'is not in the least characterised,' 'Milton has his eye on his deceased wife and not on himself' (for though the 'night' of line 14 may be read as referring to his blindness, it need not be [see below, 14 n.]). His sonnet honours her 'as a real woman' and records his deep love for her and his sense of irreparable loss. 'Even so, Milton carefully keeps the public decencies.' The dream of the dead as still living probably recorded Milton's actual experience, but it is a common experience 'and the theme had already occurred among the Italian sonneteers, thus becoming public property' [see the end of 1 above].

Milton raises it to a new dignity by his ascending classical and scriptural allusions. In 'his logical structure, though Milton varies his thought he never turns back on himself, as Donne does.' His ascending images culminate in that of his wife's appearance in 'her resurrected and glorified body. From such height the poet can only descend; and he adds that the virtues which shone in her person, love sweetness goodness,...were yet her attributes on earth. And the descent from Paradise to earth fitly suggests the parallel descent from ecstatic dream to the cruel actuality of present bereavement.' Donne gives the effect of thinking aloud and conveys '"the local excitement of sensation,"' as Milton does not essay to do. This whole effect, including the striking contrast of the last with the first line, 'rests on a rhetoric of emotion, solidly grounded in reason and human nature, publicly ratified, and, in the best sense of the word, conventional.' [This abstract by Woodhouse.]

T. Wheeler ('Milton's Twenty-third Sonnet,' *SP* 58, 1961, 510–15; repr. in A. Barker, *Milton*, 1965) steers between the biographical accounts of Parker and Pyle and the purely literary interpretation of Spitzer. Accepting Milton's dream as a real one, he plays down the question of the veiled figure's identity (though preferring Katherine to Mary), and thinks that Milton, dramatizing the situation, is contemplating an ideal woman, a paradisal companion. He cites Adam's dream of an ideal mate: 'Shee disappeerd, and left me dark, I wak'd / to find her....'(*PL* 8. 478–9).

Honigmann cannot accept the 'ideal' interpretations of Spitzer and Wheeler because both underestimate 'the "occasional" force of the sonnets: *spot of child-bed taint* identifies a particular wife (Katherine, or perhaps Mary), not the *donna angelicata*.' Parker (1045, n. 145) is also unable to accept the views of Spitzer and Wheeler.

T. Stoehr ('Syntax,' *ES* 45, 1964, 294–6) finds that the 'measure is regularly kept, with terminal junctures ending ten of the twelve lines' that describe the dream; and the thought moves in 'syntactic couplets.' These are the two main 'elements of restraint. Several other factors, however, operate to keep the emotional content of the dream close to the surface. Most important of these is another case of disturbed or ambiguous syntax, indicating, as in the sonnet on his blindness, power-ful hidden feeling. The first quatrain is straightforward enough,' but the second 'contains no major structure of predication,' since the verb is delayed to line 9; and the repeated beginnings—'Mine as whom,' 'such, as yet'—suggest the poet's trying to prolong the experience, to cling to the illusion, like a half-awakened sleeper grasping at a vision that is slipping away. 'Other devices bridging the octave–sestet turn are the "accidental" rhymes "sight", "white", and "sight" in lines 8, 9, and 10, and the alliterative–semantic linkage of "Purification" and "pure", "vested" and "vail'd". These patterns, and the general emphasis on light, obscured and revealed, in the first four lines of the sestet ("white", "vail'd", "fancied sight", "shin'd", "clear"), prepare us for the sud-den pathos of the conclusion. Light and dark, fancy and reality, love and loss, life and death are brought together in one final contrast: between the warmth and inclination of line 13, and the sudden, ironic awakening into death and darkness and night. Not the thought of the poem—which has been disciplined, carefully paced, even erudite—but the underlying emotions are now brought to the surface and summarized. This final syntactic couplet bears all the emotional weight that has been accumu-lating, and the shock of resurrection into day and blindness is further intensified by the very structure of the last line. The fact that the serial sequence ("I wak'd, she fled, and day...") is foreshadowed in line 11 ("love, sweetness, goodness") adds to the sense of hopeless inevitability already imbedded in the "*one, two, three*" intonation pattern, which comes down with awful finality on "night"—ironically rhyming to "delight" and "sight". The swift succession of "I wak'd, she fled" hur-ries the inexorable beat of the meter, and thus emphasizes "back", semantic and metrical fulcrum of the dismaying chiastic paradox, "*day* brought *back* my *night*."'

M. Mueller ('The Theme and Imagery of Milton's Last Sonnet,' *Archiv* 201, 1964–5, 267–71) seeks to modify the interpretations of Spit-zer and Parker. He develops Spitzer's idea that the sonnet is based on a 'triptych Greece–Judaism–Christianity' and is arranged in a 'tripartite *crescendo*.' 'The *crescendo* is achieved by a triple relation (or contrast): as

Alcestis is to the purified woman, and as the purified woman is to the veiled saint, so the veiled saint will be to the unveiled saint.' Spitzer is wrong in contrasting Heracles' triumph with the poet's helplessness: Heracles' feat is an illegal act of violence that ultimately fails; it 'suggests the counter-image of the Son of God redeeming mankind through suffering.' 'The violence implicit in the Alcestis image contrasts with the legality of the Old Testament image....But the Old Law can no more defeat eventual death than pagan lawlessness could. The reversal comes with the New Law, for the saint is saved from death forever and the reunion...is a heavenly and eternal reunion in the future.'

After the threefold progression, 'There remains the most powerful contrast in the poem, the contrast between the veiled and the unveiled saint.' The veiled saint for the first time brings light into the poem, and her veiled light 'far outshines the unveiled Alcestis and the purified woman.' Milton is not (as Parker says) contrasting pagan Admetus' failure to recognize Alcestis with his own recognition of his wife, but is comparing the veiled saint with the unveiled Alcestis. 'The ambivalence of the veil-image is supported by the complexity of the sound structure ...a progressive "unveiling" of sound....'

Spitzer and Parker are too one-sided in their conclusions. 'The meaning of the poem is contained in a balance of seemingly contradictory emotions, and this emotional balance is reflected in a balance of two structures, for the sonnet fits both the "Italian"... and the Elizabethan pattern.' After expounding details, Mueller concludes: 'On such a reading the poem turns out to be an expression of both hope and despair, and this agrees with the significance of the veil. The veil contains a promise that makes Milton hope for its eventual fulfilment but despair at the realisation that it is not fulfilled now. The two experiences enhance each other....'

Honigmann (who discounts chronological arrangement) remarks (66) that, while we might expect the two sonnets on Milton's blindness (19 and 22) to be placed together, 22 goes better with 23. 'The affirmation that the blind poet never enjoys the sight of sun, or moon, or star, or man *or woman* (XXII) surely holds our minds "in a certain receptive poise" for the opening of XXIII, "Methought I *saw my late espoused Saint....*"' Further, the switch from the public image of the poet as strong and cheerful (22) 'to the spectacle of his private anguish' (23) 'gives depth to both poems: we see XXII more clearly as an exercise in "cheering oneself up", and the poignancy of Milton's grief for his wife gains in effect coming as it does just after his solemn declaration (in XXII) that he has no regrets.' The critic also sees 'a perhaps quite unconscious association' in the 'absence of *blemish* and *spot*, and of *spot* and *taint*' in 22. 2 and 23. 5. Honigmann (44–5), noting the way in which Milton's thought in the sonnets returns upon itself, finds perhaps 'the neatest reversal' in this one, 'which opens with an emergence from darkness and closes with a return to darkness....'

J. Huntley ('Milton's 23rd Sonnet,' *ELH* 34, 1967, 468–81) reviews recent interpretations and finds none of them satisfactory, whether biographical or abstract. He would take Milton's vision as the occasion, not the subject: 'the dream of a confrontation, something like Admetus', provokes the speaker to conceive and feel metaphysical relationships and spiritual possibilities with unusual vividness' (470). The best part of the discussion, one may think, is the contrast drawn between nature and grace in the experience of the pagan Admetus and the Christian poet: Alcestis was a physical reality, but pale and faint, the poet's wife a dream, but radiantly present; the pagan agent, Heracles, could not give eternal life, but Christ the Redeemer did. 'It is not Milton's claim to heavenly visions or fleshly yearnings that makes his poem interesting, but the deft and poignant contrast between sufficient and insufficient visions of life' (479).

At the same time the poem is 'a partial failure' (476); its design raises problems 'for which the sonnet itself provides no plausible answers' (472). These problems seem to be mainly the critic's creation. For one example of odd reading, he says (475) that in my edition (p. 200) I suspend 'the whole issue of particular determination' between Mary and Katherine Milton—although my notes plainly take the latter as the subject. And I commit the further sin of calling the sonnet a 'very moving expression of devoted love, tenderness, and reverence,' for which there is 'no...warrant.'

III. NOTES

1 *Methought I saw.* Warton cited Ralegh's sonnet on *The Faerie Queene*: 'Methought I saw the grave, where Laura lay.' [Le Comte (*Yet Once More*, 16–17) cites Adam's 'methought I saw' (*PL* 8. 462). See also general analogues to the sonnet mentioned at the end of 1 above.]

late espoused Saint: recently married (Pyle), which one may think the logical and preferable sense; married and now dead (Parker; see the arguments in 1 above). The image of saint and devotee is met in the Petrarchan type of love poetry, as, e.g. in Shakespeare, *Romeo* 1. 5. 95–109. Smart notes that Bembo, having called his dead Lady *santa* in his lament, defended the word by saying that 'All the souls that are in Heaven are saints and may be so called.' It is in this sense, and in this general tradition, that Milton refers to the young Marchioness of Winchester as 'bright Saint' and 'new welcom Saint' (*EpWin* 61, 71). While she was apparently a Roman Catholic, it must be emphasized that, among the Puritans, a 'saint' was a true and devout believer, that the term was in very common use, and that the Milton of the 1650s was much more likely to have been impressed by this fact than the Milton of 1631. [Honigmann cites 'my dead Saint' from Henry King's *The Exequy*.]

2–4 *Brought to me...pale and faint.* As Warton noted, the allusion is to Heracles' rescue of Alcestis from the possession of Death and his returning of her, veiled, to her husband Admetus, as presented in Euripides' *Alcestis*. Heracles is addressed as 'noble son of mighty Zeus' (1136: Verity). The detail *pale and faint* is from line 1127 (Browne). [On Alcestis' need of purification see Pyle (*RES* 25, 1949, 59), summarized near the beginning of 1 above.]

6 *Purification in the old Law did save.* The rules of the Mosaic law or old dispensation are set forth (as Verity noted) in Lev. 12. They included a sacrifice of atonement; hence Milton's *did save*, which takes on an ironic overtone because nothing could save his wife from death, although in a higher sense she is 'saved' and Milton hopes to have *Full sight of her in Heaven.*' [See Parker, Pyle, Shawcross, Fabian, and D.B. in 1 above.]

9 *vested all in white.* Keightley associated the white robe with the old rite of purification but found no authority for it in the Law. Smart recognized the allusion to Rev. 7. 13–14: 'What are these which are arrayed in white robes?

and whence came they?...These are they which came out of great tribulation, and have washed their robes, and made them white in the blood of the Lamb.' To this may be added [cf. Honigmann]: 'And to her ⟨the Lamb's bride, the Church⟩ was granted that she should be arrayed in fine linen, clean and white: for the fine linen is the righteousness of saints' (ibid. 19. 8). This is the true purification under the Gospel, which, depending on Christ's sacrifice and atonement, effectually saves. On *pure as her mind*, Le Comte remarks (*N&Q* 1, 1954, 245–6) that Katherine is 'pure' (Gk. *katharos*), and he notes the emphasis on purity in the sonnet.

10 *Her face was vail'd*: like that of Alcestis when returned to Admetus, who, however, did not recognize her while she was veiled. Smart commented on the significance of Milton's recognition: blind throughout their brief married life, he had never seen her face. This, we may add, lends poignancy to the blind poet's mental picture, his *fancied sight*, of her, in which all her moral qualities *shin'd | So clear*, and likewise to what goes before, the hope for *Full sight of her in Heaven without restraint*. [Le Comte (above, 9 n.) assembles the reasons for her being veiled: in addition to those already suggested here, a veil is suitable for heaven, and it is akin to a shroud.]

11–14 [Le Comte (*Yet Once More*, 15–16) compares the ideas and some words in *PL* 8. 474–80. On line 11, *Love...shin'd*, Honigmann remarks that Milton may have recalled a passage like Gal. 5. 22: 'But the fruit of the Spirit is love, joy, peace, longsuffering, gentleness, goodness, faith.' The Bible, he adds, is 'responsible for the imagery of the shining face, which seems always to reflect heavenly goodness: cf. Ps. lxvii. 1: "God be merciful unto us, and bless us; and cause his face to shine upon us", Eccles. viii. 1, Rev. i. 16.' Cf. Milton, *El* 3. 54.]

13–14 *But O as to embrace...she fled*. Finley (69) compares Homer, *Od.* 11. 204–8; Virgil, *A.* 6. 700–2, where the shade of Anchises, when Aeneas would embrace him, fled 'most like a winged dream'; and Dante, *Purg.* 2. 80–1. See also T. B. Stroup, at the end of 1 above.

14 *I wak'd...my night*. It is almost too obvious for remark that in this, the most poignant line in Milton's poetry, *night* refers at once to his blindness, escaped in the vision of sleep (except for inability to picture the face he had never seen) and now brought back by waking to a new day, and to his desolation at the flight of the vision, at waking to find it all a dream. Ample precedent associates night with sadness and desolation, e.g. in Shakespeare: 'as sad as night' (*John* 4. 1. 15); *Luc.* 764 f.; [Spenser, *F.Q.* 3. 4. 54–61. Cf. Pontano,

Sonnet 23

De Tumulis, bk. 2, no. 60, *Pontanus Uxorem Ariadnam in Somnis Alloquitur* (*Carmina*, 1902, 2, 222): *Nocte quidem, coniux, tecum vagor, et tua mecum | Umbra venit; sic nox luxque diesque mihi est. | Luce autem sine te tenebris obversor, et ipse | Me sine sum; sic lux nox tenebraeque mihi est. | O valeant luces, lateat sol; sic mihi, coniux, | Vives, sic moriar vivus et ipse tibi.* (Spitzer, 11 above). Warton cited Adam's dream: 'Shee disappeerd, and left me dark, I wak'd / To find her, or for ever to deplore / Her loss' (*PL* 8. 478–80).]

The Fifth Ode of Horace. Lib. I.

Quis multa gracilis te puer in Rosa, Rendred almost word for word without Rhyme according to the Latin Measure, as near as the Language will permit.

☙

I. DATE [D.B.]

This translation was first printed in *Poems* (1673), at the end of the numbered sonnets and before the newly printed *Vacation Exercise* (this last being followed by the tailed sonnet *On the new forcers of Conscience*). In the Errata of 1673 a directive says that the *Vacation Exercise* should be placed 'at the end of the Elegie' on p. 21, i.e. after the *Fair Infant* and before *The Passion* (*Facs.* 14, 46). And ambiguous directives in the MS. (ibid. 452, 454) say that the *New forcers* should come in after *Sonn* 11 (there numbered 12), or possibly, Woodhouse suggests, before *Sonn* 15 (Fairfax). Woodhouse suggests further that 'in making the correction the translation of Horace was overlooked, that not one poem but the two should have been moved back (a mistake understandable enough in a correction dictated by a blind man) to give the sequence: *Fair Infant*, translation, *Vacation Exercise*. This suggestion, if correct, would remove the only argument in favour of regarding the translation as a late poem, namely, its position in 1673, and would place it among the Cambridge pieces, done probably in the spring of 1628, or between 1626 and 1628.'

Shawcross ('Of Chronology and the Dates of Milton's Translation from Horace and the *New Forcers of Conscience*,' *SEL* 3, 1963, 77–84) would put the translation after 1636, perhaps in 1646–8. A change of position for the *Vacation Exercise* was indicated in the Errata (see *Vac* headnote), but, since no such note was given for the Horatian piece, the inference is that it was correctly placed; it 'seems to be placed after the sonnets because it was written in 1646 or later, and before *Arcades* because it is not long, it is not pastoral, and it is a single poem.' Early dates have been suggested because it has been thought a schoolboy exercise; but, Shawcross says, 'the first edition [of Horace] showing virtually no differences from Milton's text' is John Bond's of 1636 (Amsterdam). He thus sums up the case (81): 'Because it is omitted from the 1645 edition, because it is placed "late" in 1673, and because its Latin text seems to be dated after 1636, the translation is most reasonably dated in 1646 or later, perhaps lying close to the psalm translations of April 1648, which also emphasize the nature of the rendering.'

These reasons seem dubious. The poem's absence from the Cambridge MS. suggests a date before 1632. There is the fact that two certainly early poems, the *Fair Infant* and *Vacation Exercise*, were omitted from the 1645 edition and first printed in 1673, so that the similar omission of the *Horace* is not an argument for late composition. There is no logical relation between the *Horace* and Milton's translation of the Psalms, which he would approach in an entirely different spirit. Shawcross notes the several variants from modern orthodoxy in Milton's Latin text—the singular *munditie* instead of the plural, *quoties* instead of *quotiens* (line 5), and *Intentata* instead of *Intemptata* (13)—but, he thinks, 'differences in pointing, indentation, and printing practices (e.g., "u" for "v") indicate that these issues [Bond, 1606–37] did not supply Milton with his Latin text. The only difference from the 1636 text...is the use of commas around "Pyrrha" in line 3, but these commas could understandably be additions by Milton, his scribe, or the compositor.' One might suppose this last explanation equally applicable to the other trifles. 'Milton's text of the poem and also the Latin headnote are verbally identical with those in the editions of Horace edited by John Bond in 1620 and 1630. ...While two of the cited variants appear in other men's editions of these and earlier years (so far as I have explored), Bond alone seems to have *munditie* (and his 1614 edition has *munditiis*). Apparently, then, the text Milton used was available from at least 1620 onward' (Bush, *P.W.*, Boston, 1965, 26).

Thus the question of the date remains open, although recent opinion has in the main taken the piece to be early (e.g. Wright, Woodhouse, Hughes, Leishman, Bush, Parker, Carey). Shawcross's latest comment is cited below. E. Saillens, who is rather given to unsupported assertions, says (*Milton*, 1964, 176): 'In August, 1653, his strength being recovered because he had given up his now purposeless barbarous medical treatment, he played, like a beginner, with putting into rhyme eight psalms in eight days in eight different metres, and translated one of Horace's odes —the maestro was practising his scales.' Parker (57, 745–6, n. 4) suggests that the translation was a product of the April mood that inspired *Elegy* 5 in 1629. Carey proposes 'Late 1629?,' suggesting that the subject, 'deliberate rejection of love,' may link the translation with *Elegy* 6. Bush remarks: 'Possibly the piece was an offshoot of Milton's practice with Horatian meters in his elegies on the bishop of Ely and the Vice-Chancellor of Cambridge (although the autumn of 1626 is overcrowded with longer poems, and in style the ode is unlike the youthful Milton).'

Some eulogists of the poem as an inspired translation have been inclined, on that account, to assign it to a later period, the 1640s or 1650s (see I and II, above and below). No one seems to have connected it with Milton's courtship of Mary Powell or the shadowy Miss Davis, and otherwise, we may think, the strenuous libertarian was in those years much too deeply engaged in public questions for even brief dalliance with Pyrrha. Moreover, if the style does not much resemble that of the early Milton, it does not much resemble that of the later poet either; in fact it is unique. Along with—or apart from—the general process of Milton's stylistic evolution, we must take account of the principle of decorum and of the special demands of metre, literal translation, and forced compression. 'The translation has received some high praise, but it may be thought that Milton only partly overcame the combined difficulties of extreme literalness and the original meter (fourth Asclepiadean). Some good phrases stand out from the prevailing stiffness— which in lines 9–11 becomes ambiguous awkwardness' (Bush, 25).

Shawcross ('The Prosody of Milton's Translation of Horace's Fifth Ode,' *Tennessee Studies in Literature* 13, 1968, 81–9) remarks that 'scholars have consistently scanned the translation in English syllabic meter,' although Milton's headnote emphasized his effort to use the quantitative rules and measures of Latin. He then scans the Horatian ode (written in the fourth Asclepiadean metre) and Milton's version, commenting on the variations Milton felt obliged to introduce because of linguistic difficulties. His general conclusion (86) is that 'Milton, in rendering Latin logæodic [*sic*] rhythms in English, frequently replaced two short syllables by one long syllable, and frequently reduced a trochee to a stressed monosyllable. At times, because of the differing natures of the languages and the pitfalls of quantity in English, questionable quantities are introduced, but Milton still comes "as near as the Language will permit."'

Shawcross also gives a quantitative scansion of *SA* 293–306 and says: 'This closer relationship in the prosodic experiments of the *Fifth Ode* and *Samson Agonistes*, frequently felt before by commentators, implies a closeness of composition date.' For the translation he repeats (see above) the date 1646–8, the date Parker proposed for *SA* (*PQ* 28, 1949, 145–66; [see Parker, *Milton*, 903–17]). But the very weak reasons given for thus dating the ode are hardly strengthened by the still more dubious dating of *SA*.

II. CRITICISM [D.B.]

Wright (*Shorter Poems*, 1938, 107): 'This poem (written perhaps during the Cambridge days) comes near perfection in the art of poetic translation. That it is both an exact translation and a characteristic poem illustrates how much the Miltonic style owes to his study and practice of Latin verse.'

G. N. Shuster (*The English Ode*, 1940, 76): 'The translation from Horace might, indeed, be termed the "version of the forty triumphs," because there are at least that many prosodical marvels. The unrhymed lines that lap over like waves of music; the delicate beauty of the half-revealed assonance that takes the place of rhyme; the inverted stresses that afford a faint but perceptible trace of antique choriambic rhythm; the admirable spondees of

and Seas
Rough with black winds and storms;

505

the stanza itself, Horatian and yet seemingly native English; the apt diction of melancholy—these are some of the treasures of this little poem. It is hardly too much to say that if by chance the rest of Milton's work had been lost, this translation would suffice to prove that he had been a great artist. Nowhere else in such brief compass is the evidence concerning what our literature gained from a study of the classic ode so impressively assembled.' In regard to metrical equivalence Shuster remarks that Milton 'achieved almost perfectly the substitution of stresses for the long Latin syllables, though the rhythm is of course not the same. The first foot of each set of trimeter lines has inverted stress.'

J. B. Leishman (*Translating Horace*, Oxford, 1956, 52–3) remarks: 'Perhaps Milton's youthful version of the Pyrrha Ode (I, v) into the unrhymed metre which Collins borrowed for his *Ode to Evening* is the only English translation in which it is really possible to perceive something of what makes the original what it is: that inimitable combination of difficulty and ease, artifice and grace, gravity and lightness. In almost every other translation of an Horatian Ode that I have seen there is too much ease and too little difficulty: the gravity of the original has vanished, and the lightness has been reduced to triviality.'

Sir Ronald Storrs (*Ad Pyrrham: A Polyglot Collection of Translations*, Oxford, 1959, 26) declares that Milton's version 'most readers would find as difficult to praise as to pronounce. Indeed, his rendering of the Latin, "almost word for word" (as he calls it), brings us to the supreme paradox of such attempts: for Milton's might be the best translation, if it were not intelligible only to readers already so steeped in accurate knowledge of the Latin original as to have no need of it; which, as Euclid would remind us, is absurd.'

Davis P. Harding (*The Club of Hercules: Studies in the Classical Background of Paradise Lost*, Urbana, 1962, 128–34) thinks that in Milton's translation, 'making allowance for the different verse forms, we have... the genuine Miltonic music, the music of *Paradise Lost*.' 'The Horatian stanzas do not mark out the organic structure,' which has three parts (lines 1–5; 5 to the middle of 12; conclusion), and Milton preserves the basic structure, difficult though it is to follow. While avoiding as far as

possible the little words required in English, Milton 'still finds it necessary to use one third again as many words as Horace had used, although
he plainly put himself under the most severe kind of restraint.' 'Milton
follows the Latin word order as closely as he dares.' 'Except in two instances, the verbs are located in the same lines.... In the final movement
of the poem, the word order is, in fact, followed so painstakingly that the
meaning is partially obscured. Despite the obscurity, the lines are impressive; syntactically they are exactly right and it is this which gives
them the strength and beauty inhering in the original.' Not even Milton
can compass Horace's concentrated complexities of meaning: 'Plain in
thy neatness' is, like other men's efforts, a quite inadequate rendering of
simplex munditie. However, citing Robert Bridges (*Poems of John Keats*,
London, 1896, lxx–lxxi) and J. H. Finley on the Horatian quality of many
of Milton's sonnets, Harding concludes that 'the translation of the *Fifth
Ode* would seem to be another substantial piece of evidence in their favor,'
and 'that there was a vital connection between Milton's study of the techniques of Horace and Virgil, and the development of his mature epic style.'

Woodhouse remarks: 'Though it is no part of our task to trace the
literary influence of Milton's poems, the translation had so remarkable a
progeny as to warrant notice. It caught the eye of Collins, who used the
metre in the celebrated *Ode to Evening*; hitherto imitations had been few,
but thereafter their name is legion (see the list in R. D. Havens, *The
Influence of Milton on English Poetry*, Cambridge, Mass., 1922, supplemented by Woodhouse, *TLS*, May 30, 1929; cf. D. Cook, *ib.* June 6).'

III. NOTES [D.B.]

1 *odours*: perfumes (*OED* 2). Cf. *Nat* 23 and n.

8 *admire*: wonder greatly at.

12–16 *Me in my vow'd | Picture...God of Sea.* Wright comments: '*Vota*:
(which Milton always renders by *vows* in English) were prayers to the gods to
avert some danger, accompanied by the promise of thank-offerings if the prayers
were answered; the vow was generally accompanied by a votive tablet, which was
placed on the wall of the temple and contained an inscription or picture relating
to the vow (cp. 'Lycidas,' l. 159).' Carey cites Virgil, *A.* 12. 766–9.

On the new forcers of Conscience
under the Long Parliament

Although this poem is separated from the sonnets in 1673 (see the head-note to *Horace*, 1), there is a directive in the MS. to insert the sonnet after *Sonnet* 11 (there numbered 12): *on y* forcers of Conscience to come in heer turn over the leafe* (*Facs*. 452). The poem itself appears in MS. immediately after *Sonnet* 17 (ibid. 454), with a note in the margin: *to come in as is directed in the leafe before* (deleted). However, the MS. directive is so placed that it might mean, not after *Sonnet* 11, but before *Sonnet* 15; in that case, its position in the chronological sequence would be after *Sonnet* 14 (December 1646) and before *Sonnet* 15 (August 1648).

[The sonnet has been commonly dated '1646?' (e.g. Hanford, Hughes). A. Barker sums up the situation thus: 'The events which disposed an exasperated House to pass the ordinance of March 5, 1646, for the establishment of the Presbyterian system, produced the sonnet *On the New Forcers of Conscience* with its complimentary reference to the Independents in the Assembly and its attack on the chief Presbyterian pamphleteers who desired "to force our consciences that Christ set free"' (*Milton and the Puritan Dilemma 1641–1660*, Toronto, 1942, 220).

Some steps in the not wholly successful establishment of Presbyterianism were these: the abolition of Episcopacy (January 1643: S. R. Gardiner, *History of the Great Civil War*, 2nd ed., 4 v., London, 1893, 1, 84; W. K. Jordan, *Development of Religious Toleration...1640–1660*, London and Cambridge, Mass., 1938, 42); 'Ordination of Ministers, *pro Tempore*, according to the Directory for Ordination' (4 October 1644: C. H. Firth and R. S. Rait, *Acts and Ordinances of the*

Interregnum, 3 v., London, 1911, 1, 521); preaching virtually restricted to ministers of Presbyterian ordination (November 1644: Jordan, 57); abolition of the *Book of Common Prayer* and authorization of the Directory (4 January 1645: Firth and Rait, 1, 582; Jordan, 59); Ordinance on the election of elders: all parishes and places to be 'brought under the Government of Congregational, Classical, Provincial, and National Assemblies,' with a list of London *classes* (19 August 1645: Firth and Rait, 1, 749); the *Prayer Book* again banned (26 August: ibid. 1, 755); further Ordinances for the establishment of Presbyterianism (5–14 March 1646: ibid. 1, 833; Jordan, 80); the ordination of ministers by 'the Classicall Presbyteries' (28 August 1646: Firth and Rait, 1, 865); abolition of archbishops and bishops (9 October 1646: ibid. 1, 879).

J. T. Shawcross (*SEL* 3, 1963, 77–84: see above, headnote to Horatian ode) would assign the sonnet to the first months of 1647: his argument is based on the arrangement of sonnets in the MS., on the compositor's possible handling of his copy, and on inferences from Milton's topical allusions. The arguments are somewhat speculative, and no authority is given for some of his dates: e.g. he gives October 1646 for the establishment of Presbyterian synods or *classes* and takes this as the latest event Milton alludes to and hence a *terminus a quo* for the sonnet. This is not in accord with the data cited above from Firth and Rait.

Hanford (*MP* 18, 1920–1, 481) thought the sonnet was written most probably just after the Ordinance of 28 August 1646 (see above), or perhaps 'just before this final realization of the "just fears" of Milton and the Independents.' Carey, citing Hanford, favours 'Aug. 1646?'

Honigmann thinks the most likely date is 'early in 1646, since two of the Presbyterians referred to attacked Milton in print at about this time' (Baillie in November 1645, Edwards in February 1646).

Parker (301–2, 928, n. 33) proposes January 1646, because of Milton's note in the MS. (see first paragraph above), because of his attack on Edwards (whose *Gangraena*, citing Milton as a heretic, was registered on 8 January), and because of the sonnet's similarity in style and tone to *Sonnet* 11 ('A Book was writ'), which he puts in late 1645 or early 1646.]

This sonnet belongs with *Sonnets* 11, 12, 16, and 17, as one of Milton's poetic records of his concern for liberty; it is a comment on a phase of the struggle now being waged within the Puritan camp. When the Long Parliament met in 1640 the only Puritan group sufficiently organized to lead the attack on Laudian episcopacy was the Presbyterian, and other Puritans gave the Presbyterian leaders more or less unqualified support. Milton's earliest controversial tracts, such as *Of Reformation* (1641) and *The Reason of Church Government* (1642), attacked episcopacy and championed a Presbyterian discipline as at once conforming to the church of the apostles and the modern reformed churches. In retrospect (*Def 2, Works* 8, 129–31) Milton chose to view these tracts as primarily concerned with winning freedom from the tyranny of the bishops, and he maintains in them a clear distinction between the spiritual powers of the church and the coercive force of the magistrate that was common among ardent supporters of a Presbyterian reformation. It is likely enough that under the influence of Thomas Young, his former tutor and now one of the champions of Presbytery who adopted the collective pen-name of Smectymnuus, he may have been led temporarily to adopt Presbyterianism on principle rather than from expediency; certainly he came to the defence of the group in his *Apology for Smectymnuus* (1642). It is not always remembered, however, that the lines between English Presbyterianism and the more conservative type of Independency, non-separating Congregationalism, were less clearly drawn before and in 1640–2 than they came to be a few years later, when the destruction of the episcopate and the liturgy was assured and the task of setting up something in their place in the national church became urgent.

Meanwhile, in 1643, Parliament called into being the Westminster Assembly of Divines, made up almost exclusively of English Presbyterians, but with two other elements which were to prove important far beyond their numbers: the Commissioners sent to the Assembly by the Church of Scotland, Alexander Henderson, Samuel Rutherford, Robert Baillie, and George Gillespie; and a group of English Congregationalists, who came to be known as the Dissenting Brethren, Thomas Goodwin, Philip Nye, Jeremiah Burroughs, Sidrach Simpson, and William

Bridges. The Scots regarded the majority of the English Presbyterians as too moderate and, in their subservience to Parliament, tainted with Erastianism, and they bent every effort to establish and exalt a Presbyterian church on the Scottish model. In his letters Baillie quite frankly pinned his hopes of success on the advance of the Scottish army into England and the need of Parliament for its aid. Meanwhile the Dissenting Brethren, hopelessly outnumbered in the Assembly, and as yet with little support in Parliament, played a waiting game, and finally in January 1644 issued *An Apologeticall Narration*; in this they bowed to the inevitability of a Presbyterian national church, but asked for an 'accommodation' for themselves and like-minded orthodox Congregationalists (Milton, *C.P.W.* 2, ed. E. Sirluck, 1959, 65–73). In so doing they brought down on themselves the censure of the Separatist Roger Williams (*Queries of Highest Consideration*, February 1644) for not espousing general toleration.

Now the battle over liberty of conscience was joined in good earnest. It has been analysed, e.g. by William Haller in 'Before *Areopagitica*' (*PMLA* 42, 1927, 875–900) and his several books of 1934–55, and by Jordan and Sirluck (see above). Milton's most famous prose work does not deal directly with toleration, but (as Haller notes) its primary concern is plainly with the free publication of opinion on religious and ethical questions. The year 1644 also saw a number of pleas for thoroughgoing toleration, among them Roger Williams' celebrated *The Bloudy Tenent, of Persecution, for cause of Conscience*. In this and the years following there were many tracts on both sides. On the Presbyterian side, and against any toleration, there were Samuel Rutherford's *Divine Right Of Church-Government And Excommunication* (1646) and (after the time of Milton's sonnet) his *Free Disputation Against pretended Liberty of Conscience* (1649), which (as Smart observes) proposed to set up what amounted to a Protestant Inquisition; the English Presbyterian Thomas Edwards' *Antapologia* (1644), his reply to the *Apologeticall Narration*, and his *The Casting Down of the last and strongest hold of Satan. Or, A Treatise Against Toleration And pretended Liberty of Conscience* (1647).

Milton did not give a full exposition of his views until *A Treatise of*

Civil power in Ecclesiastical causes (1659), but from this sonnet it is clear that he has cast off whatever allegiance he once owed to Presbyterianism and stands with the champions of toleration. At the time of the sonnet, those seeking toleration could look only to Parliament for relief; although the Presbyterians there had a majority, it was not always available to the Westminster Assembly (see below, 15–17 n.), and there were proponents of toleration led by Cromwell and anti-clerical Erastians such as Selden. Very soon the tolerationists would be able to look with more hope to the leaders of the New Model Army, and finally to the Parliament from which the Presbyterians were evicted by Pride's Purge (December 1648). But even after the setting up of the Commonwealth the idea of a national church still held sway; and of Congregationalists who wished to set up a national system, though with a toleration, Milton would presently speak in terms every whit as harsh as those formerly used of the bishops and here of the Presbyterians (see above, *Sonn* 16 and headnote). On the whole matter of Milton and toleration see Barker (headnote, above).

    The best commentary on the sonnet is found in Milton's own words in the suppressed passage of his *History of Britain* (*Works* 10, 321–2):

And if the state were in this plight, religion was not in much better: to reforme which a certaine number of divines were call'd.... The most of them were such as had preach'd and cry'd downe with great show of zeal the avarice & pluralities of bishops and prelates; that one cure of soules was a full imployment for one spiritual pastor how able so ever.... Yet these conscientious men, ere any part of the worke for which they came together, and that on the public salarie, wanted not impudence to the ignominie and scandal of thir pastor-like proffession & especially of thir boasted reformation, to seise into thir hands or not unwillinglie to accept (besides one sometimes two or more of the best Livings) collegiat master-ships in the universitie, rich lectures in the cittie, setting saile to all windes that might blow gaine into thir covetous bosomes.... And yet the main doctrin for which they tooke such pay, and insisted upon with more vehemence then gospel, was but to tell us in effect that thir doctrin was worth nothing and the spiritual power of thir ministrie less availeable then bodilie compulsion; perswading the magistrate to use it as a stronger means to subdue & bring in conscience then evangellic perswasion. But while they taught compulsion without convincement (which not long before they so much complain'd of as executed unchristianlie against themselves) thir intents were cleere to be no other then to have set up a spiritual tyrannie by a secular power to the advancing of thir owne authoritie above the magistrate....

The sonnet is unique in the Miltonic canon in being a *sonetto caudato*, a sonnet with a *coda* or tail. The *coda* consists of a half-line and a couplet and may be repeated not merely once (as here) but as often as the poet chooses. Smart notes further that the form was widely used in Italian by Francesco Berni and others for humorous and satirical effect.

II. NOTES

1-2 *thrown of your Prelate Lord...renounc'd his Liturgie.* [MS. had *off* (*Facs.* 454). For the parliamentary ordinances see the early part of 1 above. Honigmann suggests a pun on *Lord* and Laud (used in 1655 by Milton's nephew John Phillips in his *Satyr Against Hypocrites*, 16); 'the Liturgy was popularly associated with him—indeed, the rather similar Scottish version imposed by Charles I was known as "Laud's Liturgy." ' Milton 'had a weakness for playing with names,' and such a pun would sharpen the allusion to Laud's victim, Prynne (line 17).]

3 *widdow'd whore Pluralitie.* MS. first had *vacant*, deleted, *widow'd* substituted. Milton personifies the practice of holding more than one benefice at a time, a practice Presbyterians had complained of among the Anglican clergy but were now following themselves (see the extract from his *HistBrit* at the end of 1 above). [Le Comte (*Yet Once More*, 137) gives other Miltonic examples of the common use, in a religious context, of the biblical *whore* as noun and verb.]

4 *abhor'd*: [a quibble on *whore* (3); cf. Shakespeare, *Oth.* 4. 2. 161-2: 'I cannot say "whore." / It doth abhor me now I speak the word' (Honigmann).]

5 *for this*: 'for this purpose, i.e. to be pluralists' (Verity).

5-6 *adjure the Civill Sword...Christ set free.* The Presbyterians insisted upon the duty of the magistrate, the civil power (see *Sonn* 17. 12 n.) to enforce conformity to the national church when duly reformed. This now seemed to Milton not only a confusion of civil and religious authority but a negation of Christian liberty. He had spoken in *Areop* of 'crowding free consciences and Christian liberties into canons and precepts of men' (*Works* 4, 341-2). He was to elaborate the idea in *CivP*: 'I have shewn that the civil power hath neither right nor can do right by forcing religious things: I will now shew the wrong it doth; by violating the fundamental privilege of the gospel, the new-birthright of everie true beleever, Christian libertie' (*Works* 6, 28). This is followed by a massing of texts, such as 'where the Spirit of the Lord is, there is liberty' (2 Cor. 3. 17); 'Stand fast therefore in the liberty wherewith Christ hath made us free, and be not entangled again with the yoke of bondage' (Gal. 5. 1); 'ye have been called unto liberty' (Gal. 5. 13). On 'Christian Liberty' as a force in the Puritan Revolution, see Woodhouse, *Puritanism and Liberty* (1938, 1950).

7 *classic Hierarchy*. The reference is to the Presbyterian system of jurisdiction in an ascending order of courts: parochial eldership, presbytery (or *classis*), provincial synod, national assembly; of these the chief disciplinary bodies were the first and second, the eldership referring cases to the presbytery or *classis*. The adjective *classic* here refers to the *classis*; Milton uses it also in *TKM* (*Works* 5, 6) and *classical* in *OAP* (ibid. 6, 257). [Cf. 'Classick Rout' (*Hue and Cry after S^ir John Presbyter* 41, *Poems of John Cleveland*, ed. B. Morris and E. Withington, Oxford, 1967, 46 and 138.] *Hierarchy* refers to the ascending scale of courts. This was the system of church government insisted upon as *jure divino* and by the Scottish Commissioners as further provided for in the Solemn League and Covenant and subject to no compromises. [The word is intended to recall the Puritans' antipathy for the Anglican ecclesiastical hierarchy, whose powers they had not so much abolished as replaced.]

8 *meer A. S.*: Adam Steuart or Stewart, a Scottish divine, not a member of the Westminster Assembly but resident in London for a time in the 1640s and author of anti-Independent pamphlets. Smart suggests that Milton may have known of him only under these initials; hence the word *meer* (mere). *Rutherford*: Samuel Rutherford or Rutherfurd, a much more considerable figure (see 1 above). In secular politics he took a more extreme line than that embodied in the Solemn League and Covenant with its legal fiction of fighting *for* the king. Rutherford wrote *Lex, Rex* (1644), which, insisting on the king's responsibility to the people for the exercise of the power entrusted to him, anticipated Milton's *TKM*. In this he differed from two of his fellow Commissioners: Alexander Henderson, who drew up the form of the Covenant taken by the Westminster Assembly in 1643 and the *Directory of Worship* which replaced the *Book of Common Prayer*, and who subordinated his devout royalism to his chief concern, Presbyterianism; and Robert Baillie, who supported Charles II when he was proclaimed King of Scotland (1649) and lived to triumph in his letters over 'blind Milton' and 'others of that maleficent crew' (quoted in Patterson, *Student's Milton*, l).

9–12 *Men whose Life... Scotch what d'ye call.* Smart thinks the *Men* referred to are the Dissenting Brethren of the *Apologeticall Narration* (1 above) and notes the respect in which their learning and piety were held by their opponents, notably A. S. and Robert Baillie (see 8 n.), even while the latter accused them, in his *Dissuasive from the Errours Of the Time* (1645), of causing and encouraging heresy. But Milton's position may well have already been (as it certainly became) much to the left of moderate Congregationalism, and *Would have been held in high esteem with Paul* certainly suggests that they were not so held by their opponents. Perhaps it was rather more extreme champions of toleration, such as Roger Williams, Henry Robinson, and John Goodwin, that Milton had in mind. [Honigmann gives examples—one of them Thomas Edwards (line 12)—of the Presbyterians who 'cited Paul as a bitter enemy of false teachers and therefore of toleration.']

12 *shallow Edwards.* MS. (*Facs.* 454) first had *haire* (altered to *hare*) *braind*, deleted, and *shallow* substituted. Thomas Edwards, in addition to writing against toleration (see 1 above), produced *Gangraena* (1646), a huge catalogue of heresies collected with a ready and quite uncritical hand. *Scotch what d'ye call* may refer to some minor writer (of the class of *A. S.*) or may be a contemptuous dismissal of one of the Commissioners (Henderson, Baillie, or Gillespie) whose name, Milton suggests, is not worth remembering. Noting that Baillie in his *Dissuasive* attacked Milton's views on divorce, as Edwards did in *Gangraena*, Masson suggested a personal motive in the sonnet; Smart protests against this idea, [though he thinks *Scotch...call* 'may be certainly identified' as Baillie. Honigmann (198) joins Smart 'in seeing Toleration and Persecution as the poet's central interest,' but at the same time is disposed to support Masson.] Verity notes here an echo of the anti-Scottish feeling of *Sonn* 11.

13–14 *your tricks...wors then those of Trent.* Milton compares the Westminster Assembly to the Council of Trent, which met, with large intervals, between 1545 and 1563, in a rapidly changing situation. Precautions were taken by the papacy to ensure its control of deliberations and decisions, and the Protestant delegates (when they consented to attend) were outnumbered and without influence on the decisions reached, as the Dissenting Brethren were in the Assembly, which was packed in the Presbyterian interest. Milton was familiar with the work of Paolo Sarpi, whom he called 'the great unmasker of the Trentine Councel' (*Areop*, *Works* 4, 302), and whose history of the Council, translated into English in 1620, bears on the title page the words: 'In which are declared..., particularly, the practises of the Court of Rome, to hinder the reformation of their errors, and to maintaine their greatnesse.' ['In *A Vindication of the Answer* (1641) by Milton's Smectymnuan friends, a pamphlet in which he himself may have had a small share (Masson, *Life*, ii. 255–6), the same phrase occurs: "such packing...as perhaps worse was not at the Councell of Trent" (p. 82)' (Honigmann). The idea of Milton's participation does not appear in *C.P.W.* 1, 84 f. (cf. 107), nor apparently in Parker.]

15–17 *That so the Parliament...bauk your Ears.* As in *Areop* and *DDD*, Milton still relies on Parliament to be receptive to those who plead the cause of liberty. The original meaning of *phylactery* was a safeguard or amulet. Various commands to the Israelites were interpreted literally as enjoining the wearing of a scroll containing some part of the Law, as a frontlet between the eyes (Exod. 13. 9, 16), or worn there and on the hand (Deut. 6. 8–9, 11. 18–20). Thomas Godwin (*Moses and Aaron*, 1625, 51) wrote: 'there were two sorts, phylacteries for the head, or frontlets,...tied behinde with a thong; and phylacteries for the hand fastened upon the left arme above the elbow on the inside, that it might be neere the heart' [*OED* 1 quotes 1641 ed., 42]. But there was also the injunction to wear, as a remembrance to keep God's commandments, 'fringes in the borders of their garments' and 'a ribband of blue' (Num 15. 38), so that *phylacteries* came to mean also the hem or fringe of a garment, especially those worn by the scribes and Pharisees, as in Matt. 23. 5: 'But all their works they do for to be seen of men: they make broad their phylacteries and enlarge the borders of their garments.' This is the meaning assumed in Milton's image, and the context in Matt. 23 throws additional light on his meaning. The scribes and Pharisees 'bind heavy burdens and grievous to be borne, and lay them on men's shoulders; but they themselves will not move them with one of their fingers' (4); and they 'love...the chief seats in the synagogues,...and to be called of men, Rabbi, Rabbi' (6–7). [Carey notes that the first example in *OED* of phylactery as a symbol of ostentatious piety is from Milton, *Tetr* (*Works* 4, 68; *C.P.W.*, 2, 582).] It is not alone their ostentatious and hypocritical piety that Milton alludes to, but chiefly their desire for power and their imposition of burdens which he calls on Parliament to curb. 'More than once the Parliament had rebuked the over-officiousness of the Westminster Assembly....Especially in April 1646 there had been a case of this kind, when the Commons voted certain proceedings of the Assembly to be a breach of privilege, and intimated to the Divines that a repetition...might subject them individually to heavy punishment' (Masson, *P.W.* 3, 287).

For line 17 (*Clip*...*Ears*) MS. (*Facs.* 454) had *Cropp yee as close as marginall P—s eares*, deleted and replaced by present text. The original reference was to William Prynne (1600–69), who is still in the revised line glanced at in the allusion to *Ears*. Prynne was a prolific writer, learned but notoriously pedantic, who crammed his margins with references to authorities; hence *marginall*. [Honigmann quotes Milton's gibes at Prynne's marginalia in prose of 1645 and 1659 (*Works* 4, 234–5, 6, 66).] He was sentenced to lose his ears for his *Histriomastix* (1632), an attack on stage plays which was condemned as defamatory of the king and queen. In 1637 the remnant of his ears was removed, when he suffered with the Presbyterian Bastwick and the Separatist Burton for attacks on the church (a fact which perhaps suggests a secondary reference in *marginall*). Hailed as a hero and martyr when released from prison by the Long Parliament, along with Bastwick and Burton, Prynne became the ardent champion of Presbyterianism, first against episcopacy, then against Congregationalism and toleration. He also asserted strongly the final control of Parliament, not the clergy, in matters of religion, so that Robert Baillie could accuse him of Erastianism, a fact Milton chooses to overlook. The history of Prynne and his controversies up to the Restoration throws much light on the interplay and conflict of principles in the successive stages of the Puritan Revolution [see Ethyn W. Kirby, *William Prynne*, Cambridge, Mass., 1931; W. M. Lamont, *Marginal Prynne*, London, 1963]. Milton was bitterly opposed to Prynne's rigid Presbyterian and anti-tolerationist principles, but, as Masson suggests, perhaps remembered his sufferings and reduced the directness of the allusion. Patterson (*Student's Milton*) thinks rather that Milton considered Prynne too contemptible to mention. D. C. Dorian (*MLN* 56, 1941, 62–4) argued that Milton recalled the Mosaic law requiring priests to be free from physical blemishes (Lev. 21. 17–23), with the strong implication that the ears must be intact (Exod. 29. 20; Lev. 8. 23–4), a provision indeed made specific in the Talmudic Mishnah, and that thus the hint of danger to the Presbyterians' ears subtly suggests that not only their power but their official ministry stands in some jeopardy. This would square with the attitude of the Independents at the time of the poem; they wished but hardly expected the overthrow of Presbyterianism. The general meaning of *bauk* (balk) was intentionally to pass by or omit and according to context might mean simply to ignore (*OED*: balk $v.^1$ 2 b) or to avoid a duty or responsibility (ibid. 2 d). [As a further possible reason for Milton's softening the allusion to Prynne, Honigmann suggests his recognition of Prynne's opposing his fellow-Presbyterians' 'demands for full powers to excommunicate heretics' because this would mean tyrannical domineering over Christian consciences (*Foure serious Questions*, 1645, sig. A^r).]

18 *succour*: relieve or remedy a state of want, weakness, etc. (*OED* 3); perhaps rather, relieve a besieged place (ibid. 2).

19 *they*: Parliament (cf. *their*, 16). [MS. first had *you*, deleted and replaced by *they*.] *shall read this clearly*: ['The antithesis to *marginall Prynne* and the Presbyterian cast of mind' (Honigmann).] *your charge*: 'the indictment which will be brought against you' (Verity).

20 *New Presbyter...Old Priest writ Large.* Since etymologically *priest* is an abbreviated form of *presbyter* (*OED*: priest) and *writ Large* means written out in full (*OED*: large B4), the literal meaning is accurate. But Milton means of course that the tyranny and vices of the old priesthood now seem to be intensified in the Presbyterian clergy. [Cf. *Areop, Works* 4, 331: '...will soon put it out of controversie that Bishops and Presbyters are the same to us both name and thing.'] *Presbyter* was not commonly used in the Presbyterian system to designate a minister (other than occasionally as a member of a presbytery); the common term was elder ('literal rendering of Gr. *presbuteros*'), with the addition of 'teaching' for distinction from the lay or ruling elders (*OED*: elder 4). [Cf. the Ordinance of 28 August 1646, cited in 1 above, on the ordination of ministers, which begins: 'Whereas the word Presbyter, that is to say Elder and the word Bishop, do in the holy Scripture intend and signifie one and the same function....' (Firth and Rait, 1, 865).]

Arcades

❧

I. DATE AND CIRCUMSTANCES

Arcades was first printed in *Poems* (1645) and reprinted, with no significant changes, in the second edition (1673). It is the first poem in the
MS. preserved at Trinity College, Cambridge, the MS. constantly
quoted throughout this Commentary (*Facs.* 383–455). The question of
the dating and order of composition of the early pieces in the MS. is
discussed above in the headnote to *On Time*. Although the absence of a
poem from the MS. is no certain indication that it was written before
Arcades, it does constitute a strong probability. The latest poem of
certain date that is not in the MS. is the *Epitaph on the Marchioness of
Winchester* (April–May 1631). And 1631 is the one year in which *Arcades*
could not have been performed at a family gathering in honour of the
Dowager Countess of Derby, since on 25 April (Masson) or 14 May
(*DNB*) her son-in-law, the Earl of Castlehaven, was executed (Masson,
Life, 1, 597 and n.; [T. B. Howell, *Collection of State Trials*, London,
1816, 3, 401–26; Parker, 759]). Since we have no concrete knowledge
regarding the composition and first performance of *Arcades*, scholars
have been reduced to more or less plausible conjectures, e.g. Masson
(*Life*, 1, 599; *P.W.* 1, 136), early in 1634 or 1633; Grierson (1, xxi, 99),
1630 or 1632; Parker (*RES* 11, 1935, 283), 1633 [but in 1968 Parker
(80, 755–8) tentatively puts it back in 1630 or possibly 1629 (see below)];
Woodhouse and Hughes, 1632; Hanford (*Poems*, 1953), 1633–4. The
year 1631, as we have seen, is ruled out. The earliest possible year for
Arcades, if the apparent significance of its place in the MS. is to be
given full weight, is 1632. [On the other hand, *Arcades* must precede
Comus, written in the summer of 1634; and Woodhouse ('Notes,' 93,
99–101) urges that the courtly, secular, purely aesthetic *Arcades* must

have preceded *Sonnet 7* ('How soon hath time') of December 1632, since that earnestly religious self-dedication inaugurated a series of religious poems.]

The MS. text of *Arcades*, despite numerous corrections, appears to be, not the first draft, but one used in the later stages of composition. [From an analysis of Milton's changes, Shawcross ('The Manuscript of "Arcades,"' *N&Q* 6, 1959, 359–64) argues (363) 'that the transcription in the Trinity MS. was made some time after the performance... and independently of it. The date of the original writing of *Arcades* is in no way indicated, although it seems likely that it was written before *Comus* and close to it. The date of this transcription is also not indicated.' 'The significance of such dating, indefinite as it may be, is that the first use of the Trinity MS. can be dated after 1633 (?). If the transcription of *Comus* in the MS. was written down before its September 1634 presentation, then the MS. was begun between these dates. If, however, the transcription of *Comus*, like that of *Arcades*, is found to postdate performance (and a similar argument can be advanced for the transcription of *Comus*), then the MS. may have been begun anywhere from 1633 to *c.* 1638 when Milton's handwriting was undergoing change.' A little later (see articles cited in the headnote to *On Time*) Shawcross argued that the first part of the MS. (*Arcades* to *Lycidas*) belongs to 1637, and that *Arcades*, whenever it was first written, was revised in the second half of that year.

Parker (*Milton*, 1968, 755–8), while allowing for a possible span from 1629 to 1631 or later, prefers 1630. In 1645 and 1673 *Arcades* preceded *Lycidas* and *Comus*, evidently as the first of a pastoral group; this does not help. *Arcades* was clearly performed outdoors, in the summer, but if it was prepared for the Countess' birthday (May 4), Milton would surely have referred to that. Parker discounts two arguments for closeness in date to *Comus*: (1) a second commission for the Egertons; (2) the fact of Harefield's being only ten miles from Horton—since we know now that the Miltons were not living at Horton until 1635. His main argument for 1630 is based on the relationship of the order of the poems in the MS. to the order in the printed texts: '*Only an insistence on a late date for*

Arcades *seriously disturbs the otherwise demonstrable chronological order of the English poems in the printed editions.*' This assertion, however, seems less firm than it looks. Parker assumes one continuous sequence and does not recognize what Milton apparently intended, that is, chronology within *two* groups, the first religious, the second secular (see the quotation from Shawcross near the beginning of the Chronological Survey above). Secondly, 'the otherwise demonstrable chronological order' of the printed poems goes well beyond the facts, since we have only conjectural dates for six of them, the May *Song, On Time* and its group, and *L'Allegro* and *Il Penseroso*. Parker goes on to argue, against Grierson (1, xiv), that *Arcades* was composed, not merely transcribed, in the MS.; he does not take account of Shawcross (just above). A further argument for an early date is the Jonsonian influence, apparent in the poems of 1630-1 on Shakespeare and the Marchioness of Winchester.]

The title informs us that *Arcades* was 'Part of an Entertainment presented to the Countess Dowager of Darby at Harefield, by some Noble Persons of her Family.' [Her estate of Harefield was on the river Colne, about four miles from Uxbridge and 'within about ten miles, cross country' (Masson) from Horton—though, as we have seen, the Miltons apparently did not move to Horton until about 1635 (French, *L.R.* 5, 1958, 380).] Masson assumed (*Life* 1, 598), as the text strongly suggests, that the 'Part' Milton was to be responsible for was 'a little open-air pastoral of songs and speeches,' which could have been performed only in the summer. The 'Noble Persons' probably included some of the young Egertons, who stood in a double relation to the Countess, since she was their maternal grandmother and also, by her second marriage, stepmother to their father, the Earl of Bridgewater.

The aged Countess (b. 1559) was a notable figure in her own right and a link with the life and poetry of an earlier day. [A biography is being written by French Fogle.] Born Alice Spencer, the youngest daughter of Sir John Spencer, she married Ferdinando Stanley, Lord Strange, later fifth Earl of Derby, a prominent patron of the drama and letters, who died in 1594; [in 1600 she married Sir Thomas Egerton, Lord

Keeper of the Great Seal, who became Lord Ellesmere, and who died in 1617]. She was celebrated by the poets, notably by Spenser, a distant relative, in *Colin Clouts Come Home Againe* and in the dedication of *The Teares of the Muses*.

Arcades was not the first masque composed and presented in her honour. Todd gave a detailed account [here revised in spelling from *Poems of John Marston*, ed. A. Davenport, 1961, 192–207] of Marston's *The...Lorde & Lady of Huntingdons Entertainement of theire right Noble Mother Alice: Countesse Dowager of Darby the firste nighte of her honors arrivall att the house of Ashby*. She is greeted on her approach by 'Cornetts,' and, at an antique gate, by 'An olde inchauntres attired in Crimeson velvet,' who opposes her entrance, declaring: 'Heere the pale Lorde of saddnes keepes his courte / rough visagd Saturne; on whose bloudles cheekes / dull Melancholy sitts who straightly seekes / to sease on all that enter through this gate.' But Saturn himself enters, his melancholy banished by the sight of the Countess, and welcomes her. The masque proper is presented when the Countess arrives in 'the great Chamber.' Before the discovery of the masquers, '4 knights & 4 Gentlemen,' Cynthia appears on a cloud and meets Ariadne, who ascends on another. Cynthia calls on the music of the spheres: 'Sounde Spheares, spreade yor harmonius breath / when mortalls shine in worth, Gods grace the earth.' At last, after some high-flown compliments, Ariadne summons the masquers: 'Musique, and gentle night / Beauty, youthes cheefe delighte / Pleasures, all full invite / Your due attendance.' Then 'the Travers...sanke downe,' revealing 'the syde of a steepely assending wood: on the topp of wch in a fayre Oake satt a goulden Eagle: under whose wings satt in eight seurall thrones the eight masquers wth visards like Starres, theire helmes like mercuryes with the addition of fayre plumes of Carnation & white, their Antique doubletts and other furniture sutable to those Cullors, the place full of sheilds lights & pages all in blew satten Robes imbrodered wth Starres.' After the masquers have danced their measure, Cynthia invites them, in speech and song, to take their partners, and the revels continue, with 'many measures galliards Carantos, & Levaltos,' till she bids them prepare for their 'departing measure.' After this is danced a shepherd sings 'a passionate ditty' and has some concluding dialogue with a nymph as the Lady departs.

Todd justifies his 'large extracts' as aiding the reader to 'comprehend the nature of these dramatick entertainments,' and this likewise may perhaps justify the briefer summary here given. The masque form is discussed below, in *Comus* II.

Henry Lawes instructed the young Egertons in music. [As a musician attached to the Court in London, he was probably already acquainted with John Milton senior, a composer of some account, and with his son as well.] It is reasonable to infer (though there is no direct evidence) that Lawes was responsible for the whole 'Entertainment' and invited Milton's contribution, and that the happy result led to the invitation to write *Comus*. [This seems more likely than the suggestion of D. C. Dorian that Milton's connection came through the father of his friend Charles Diodati: '...without exception, every member of the aristocratic family group most immediately concerned in presenting the *Arcades* and *Comus* was connected more or less closely with some patron or patient of Dr. Theodore Diodati' (*The English Diodatis*, 145). Parker (759) does not think these data relevant.

J. G. Demaray (*Masque Tradition*, 49–58) observes that, while no one masque has been cited as a parallel or source, *Arcades* has many 'general resemblances' to pastoral works and to other masques, especially Jonson's. Two pieces somewhat similar in structure are 'the first day's segment' of Campion's 'Entertainment Given by Lord Knowles' (1613: cf. below, n. 'After 25') and still more the anonymous 'Entertainment of Queen Elizabeth at Harefield' (1602).]

II. CRITICISM [D.B.]

Tillyard (*Milton*, 1930, 59–60): '*Arcades* shows Milton the master of a new form, the song, and again illustrates an acquiescence in contemporary taste.... It is very simply but very well constructed, and as a masque is quite effective.' After an account of the action, Tillyard goes on: 'The piece is pretty well perfect; the tact with which Milton subordinates his material, not merely to the poem as a whole but to the poem as a masque, is remarkable. The noble passage about the music of the spheres—the one place where Milton allows his imagination to rove from the courtly vein of compliment he had been commissioned to exploit—is not too long to tire the ordinary listener, must have added a pleasing touch of solemnity to the minds even of those who did not understand it, thereby forming an effective climax, and is perfectly linked to the main theme. The sense of powerful imagination joyfully controlled is here as in the *Nightingale* sonnet, and on a larger scale. Milton must have written *Arcades* in a mood of serene and hopeful endeavour, on the whole well contented with his lot and the England he intended some day to glorify with a great poem.'

Woodhouse's comments ('Notes,' 1943-4, 93-5) follow directly upon his last remarks on *L'Allegro* and *Il Penseroso* (q.v.), which link those poems with *Arcades* as displaying a 'purely aesthetic attitude' and entire tranquillity of spirit. '*Arcades*, which on other grounds, also, probably belongs to the spring of 1632, is the most purely aesthetic of all Milton's great poems. Like the Companion Pieces and *Ad Patrem*, it is unvexed by any problem. Like *L'Allegro*, and to a slightly lesser degree *Il Penseroso* and *Ad Patrem*, it is undoctrinal in its utterances. And, unlike these poems, it makes, so far as can be determined, no drafts whatsoever on Milton's extra-aesthetic experience. One thing, and one only, does it tell us of Milton's state of mind at the time of its composition: it was a state of mind which permitted a sustained and joyous act of aesthetic abstraction. The Companion Pieces and, what is more remarkable, *Ad Patrem* approach this condition. *Arcades* securely attains it.' Woodhouse contrasts 'the highly doctrinal *Comus*,' and, for one concrete item, Milton's use of the music of the spheres. In the *Nativity*, *Ad Patrem*, *At a solemn Musick*, and *Comus*, and in *Prolusion* 2, 'the image is doctrinal, employed to convey, of course in aesthetic form, a truth which has come to Milton from his extra-aesthetic, his ethical and religious, experience.' But in *Arcades* (61-78) 'The Genius of the Wood has listened to the ninefold harmony, not now answering the angel choir, but existing in its own right, and holding nature in her course,' and

'The image is divested of all doctrinal significance. . . . It is, quite properly, fitted to the Genius of the Wood, who (unlike the Attendant Spirit in *Comus*) has no moral or religious significance. Like the Genius, the image which he utters is purely aesthetic and has no implications outside the poem. We shall never again see Milton in precisely this mood—"Nymphs and shepherds, dance no more!"'

[One may perhaps query this denial of any extra-aesthetic significance in the lines on the music of the spheres. Even if the allusion is turned to courtly compliment, in itself it may seem to carry a quite serious metaphysical, religious, and ethical meaning, and to be, so far as it goes, in entire accord with Milton's other 'doctrinal' references. A fully serious reading of the whole masque is given by several of the critics summarized in the following pages.]

Brooks and Hardy (1951: 163–8) read *Arcades* allegorically. The inviting of nymphs and shepherds to leave Arcadia for Britain is 'the search for a new homeland for poetry, specifically for *pastoral* poetry.' It 'is not merely the Countess who is being complimented: it is also the spirit of English pastoral poetry, which the Countess represents.' 'The Genius, in his task and in his recreation, typifies the ideal pastoral poet: he lives close to nature, fosters nature, and is able to hear the harmony, which, deeper than nature itself, holds nature to its course. . . .' 'Moreover, he himself sings,' and for him 'to say that the music of the spheres, could he imitate it, would be most fit for her praise. . . is no idle compliment. It defines the status of the Countess as a "rural Queen," and it defines the essence of the pastoral mode, which attains nobility, not by pompous decoration in the heroic fashion, but by revealing essences in their noble purity.' This allegorical reading is carried into further details: even the description of the grass, 'Where no print of step *hath* been,' becomes 'a further reference to new ground for the cultivation of a new art.' In the piece as a whole, the Countess 'is presented dramatically as a gracious patroness, welcoming the Arcadians, giving the true poets a home, and linking the poetry of the ancient world to that of the new.' But here Milton's characteristic fusion of pagan and Christian appears in its simplest form, though a form befitting courtly ceremony.

Daiches (*Milton*, 1957, 61–3): 'Milton's model for this slight affair . . . was the Jonsonian masque, but there is an Elizabethan freshness about the songs, and a controlled grace about the aristocratic compliment which is the purpose of the whole entertainment, that are not quite Jonsonian.' 'This is an aristocratic art, Elizabethan in feeling, courtly in tone (except when it rises momentarily to mystical contemplation), yet essentially simple in manner. These songs give us some basis for speculating about what Milton might have developed into had he been a contemporary of Sidney and Spenser in fact as he was in many ways in spirit.' In *More Literary Essays* (1968) Daiches remarks that the whole point of such a family masque 'was to transplant classical names and references to the present situation, and to do this with a formal grace. . . . The one line which suggests the formalising of an observed English phenomenon rather than the deliberate transformation of an English scene into a classical one is "O're the smooth enameld green." This is surely the well-kept lawn of an English country estate.' [Are there not some other examples in lines 46–60?]

J. M. Wallace ('Milton's *Arcades*,' *JEGP* 58, 1959, 627–36; rev. in A. Barker, *Milton*, 1965, 77–87) interprets the little masque in terms of biblical and mythological allegory and symbolism, and—not perhaps without some overreading—enlarges its dimensions and deepens its resonance. The initial fact for Milton was the virtuous renown of the Countess, who, honoured in her youth by Spenser, had been celebrated by many writers and was now a special embodiment, both venerable and glamorous, of the wisdom of age and the lustre of rank and beneficence. One main clue to Milton's conception is the couplet in the first lyric—'Less then half we find exprest, / Envy bid conceal the rest'—which echoes the speech of the Queen of Sheba to Solomon (see 12 n. below), an echo Milton 'could confidently expect' to be recognized. 'The Countess, old in years and wisdom, was to see herself as the female counterpart of Solomon, and she was likely to remember that the goddess of wisdom, Sapientia, had traditionally been described in the same terms of light and splendor which greeted her ears once more under the elms at Harefield. In the homage of the shepherd poets she would rightly discern their intention of forsaking Arcadian pursuits in order to worship in the presence of divine philosophy.' In 1654 Milton was to link Christina of Sweden with both the Queen and Solomon (*Def 2*, *Works* 8, 107–9).

The allusions to 'the wise Latona' and Cybele are in keeping with the role of female Solomon. Latona, a northern goddess, was personified by N. Comes (*Mythol.* 9. 6: Padua, 1616, 507) and Sandys (*Ovid*, 1632, 223; 1640, 116) as 'that goodness and innocence...which, in a world afflicted by calamity, hopes to arrive at the celestial beauty.' [Apart from the world of calamity, this idea is hard to find in Sandys and is put differently in Comes.] Following Diodorus Siculus, Wallace takes Cybele as 'a goddess especially reverenced by shepherds for her health-giving and protective powers' [of which Milton's allusion gives no hint]. Thus Milton's tribute was in full accord with other writers' praise of the Countess' wisdom and active Christian piety.

The long speech of the Genius of the Wood 'is a kind of verbal tableau in which the visiting shepherds could perceive the benefits which would accrue from their permanent residence in a new land,' a land, though, subject to hazards which must be guarded against. The shepherds are sprung from Alpheus and Arethusa, of whose story Sandys gives two interpretations, 'both...probably fused in this passage. In one, Alpheus "signifies blots or imperfections" and Arethusa "is by interpretation Vertue"; in the other, Fulgentian, version, "Alpheus is the light of Truth, and Arethusa the excellency of equity"' (Sandys, 1632, 198; 1640, 102). 'In the image of Alpheus, therefore, Milton could discern a shepherd (or a poet) who was "divine" by right and yet blotted with the sin which would require his pilgrimage to the goddess Latona.' The parallel between Alpheus' underwater journey and the shepherd-poets' visit to Harefield 'is another example of Milton's skill in transferring the Arcadian myth into a Christianized landscape.'

The Genius, 'of classical or pagan origin' like the shepherds, and a practitioner of his old arts, has yet 'gained the power of listening to the celestial harmony' and understands its meaning. 'The music of the spheres had once before, in Marston's "Entertainment" [see 1 above], pealed in honor of the Dowager, but Milton invoked the heavenly choir with a far deeper understanding than Marston of what his praise would imply.'

'*Arcades* is, or should be, a *locus classicus* in the seventeenth-century pastoral genre, for it epitomizes the growing dissatisfaction with the Arcadian ideal.' 'The general pattern' of pastoral poets' 'compromise with primitivism was a paradise in which the disruptive forces of contention, infamy, or despair had temporarily taken root, and the expulsion of these extraneous elements restored the garden to its pre-lapsarian state. For Milton, however, the conversion of the pagan world, not a compromise with it, was the only legitimate aim of a Christian.' The concluding allusion to Syrinx brings up several other traditional allegories, especially connected with music. 'In *Arcades*, Syrinx operates as a metaphor for the naturally melodious poet who, corrupted by the world, is exhorted to bring his talents to the throne of sapience.

'To read *Arcades* in terms of a pilgrimage from the profane to the religious, from the classical south to the Christian north, from Saba to Solomon, is to make it consonant with all we know about Milton's early life and work, and his twin themes of renunciation and aspiration are nowhere better illustrated than in his first masque. Furthermore, *Arcades* shows how the persons to whom masques were directed may play an integral part in the structure of the entertainments. The central symbol of *Arcades* is the Countess, personifying heavenly wisdom, but in no part of the text is she so described.' Without her, however, 'the journey of the shepherds would have no more point than a picnic, and the masque no existence at all.'

C. L. Barber (Summers, *Lyric and Dramatic Milton*, 1965, 40-2) in his essay on *Comus* speaks briefly of *Arcades*. 'Milton was, fortunately, enough a man of the age to enjoy the virtues of aristocratic courtesy and the courteous art of the masque. But, of course, he also felt responsible to a wider frame.' The Arcadian idealizing of Harefield and its household 'is perfectly conventional and perfectly done.' But in the speech of the Genius Milton's mind transcends Arcadia and 'flies up beyond festive song to a permanent music, sublimely Orphic.' Whereas in *At a solemn*

Musick he can say what he feels, 'Here in *Arcades* all he can do with the music of the spheres is use it in compliment.' Quoting lines 74–8, Barber says: 'If we pause over this transition, we can feel the difficulty involved in the masque form as a vehicle for Milton's full sensibility.... The word "immortal," when we pause over the use of it in compliment, wavers unsteadily under the weight of the previous immense conception.'

In a general analysis of 'Milton's Salvational Aesthetic' (*Journal of Religion* 46, 1966, 282–95), S. D. Blau's thesis is that 'Milton transformed the criticism of his Elizabethan predecessors to his own Puritan purposes. Milton's own Puritan preoccupations and motivations led him to redefine the nature of the artist and his eloquence in such a way as to substitute salvational for courtly values throughout his critical system.' True eloquence 'was derived from and evidence of the poet's own state of grace.' In accordance with this view Blau modifies Brooks' and Hardy's interpretation of *Arcades* as 'on one level, a search for a new home for pastoral poetry.' These critics, preoccupied with Milton's artistic objectives, 'pass over the obviously salvational suggestion in the genius' own attribution of his special powers not so much to his bucolic occupations as to the fact that he is not corrupted by a "human mold" or a "gross unpurged ear." If the genius of the wood is the ideal pastoral poet who is exemplary for the neophyte nymphs and shepherds, his example would urge them not simply to forsake their Arcadian homeland for England, but to acquire that purified or redeemed state by which they, too, can hear and imitate the music of the spheres. "Arcades," then, is not only about finding a new homeland for pastoral poetry, but it is also about finding a new poetic voice, the special Puritan voice of regenerate eloquence.'

J. S. Lawry (*Shadow*, 1968, 51–63) sees the dramatic *Arcades* as insisting 'upon drawing the audience heavily into the action, while at first glance seeming to remove the author entirely.' It anticipates *Comus* by using quasi-classical myth and using it, not to evade reality, but to intimate a higher reality apprehended through religious contemplation. Here 'a myth is partly created (but only partly, because pastoral–Christian allusion stirs even in the first lines), then enacted, then witnessed as a ritualistic mystery. Much as the shepherds in the Nativity Ode were at once the historical shepherds keeping watch over their flocks and also members of the audience in their fallen state awaiting consecration, so here Arcadian shepherds and nymphs are "really" members of the house of Derby, but also in quest of a virtue or realization "All *Arcadia* hath not seen" (l. 95).' 'The light of the transcendent "Queen" shares the glory of that in *Paradise Lost*, which is associated immediately with God.' Music is a link between the human and the divine world. 'The myth has not only enacted a form of natural epiphany and the rapture of those who witness it, but has then joined heavenly and earthly figures within one joyous celebration,' and the author, 'who had seemed to disappear and become only a stage manager, himself places the audience firmly within the mythic action.' We witness 'the momentary restoration of an Eden, the recovery or realization of original harmony, and a form of human redemption.' The myth has brought the Christian author and audience 'at least to the portals of Christian belief,' and the new and perpetual Arcadia adumbrates 'the renewal that is an aspect of eternal creation.'

III. NOTES

Title. *Arcades*: i.e. the Arcadians. Arcadia, in the centre of the Peloponnesus and surrounded by mountains, has been described as the Switzerland of Greece, whose inhabitants, shepherds and hunters, maintained their identity and independence. It was the reputed birthplace of Pan and his special haunt (*Homeric Hymns* 19: *To Pan*), whence his worship spread to the rest of the classical world (Ovid, *F.* 2. 271–82). Arcadia was thus a natural setting for pastoral fiction and song, supporting that tenuous connection with an idealized primitive life which is one feature of the pastoral tradition. Gradually it took its place beside the Sicily of Theocritus and the rural Italy of Virgil. There are significant references to pastoral Arcadia in Virgil himself (*E.* 4. 58–9, 7. 4–5, 10. 31–45). Not less influential, perhaps, though the setting is epic, is Virgil's account of the idyllic kingdom of Evander in *Aeneid* 8, the king and his followers being Arcadians who have established themselves in Italy and brought with them the worship of Pan and the spirit of pastoral life. Virgil is thus a principal source of that

Renaissance Arcadianism in which courtly manners are superimposed on rural simplicity, as in the *Arcadia* of Sannazaro, the *Arcadia* of Sidney, and in *Arcades* and (with varying degrees of emphasis) in other masques. Hughes has noted Milton's care in reminding his auditors of ancient Arcadia, its rivers (30, 97) and mountains (98, 100, 102), and of Pan's pursuit of Syrinx (106). And beyond that we may observe his deliberate linking of Arcadia and Sicily (28–31 and n.).

Part of an Entertainment. MS. (*Facs.* 384) first read *Part of a maske.* No copy of the other parts, or note of their authors or contents, has come to light.

Scene. It is reasonable to suppose that this preliminary part of the Entertainment—the approach to the central episode—may have been set out of doors, like the similar portion of Marston's masque, described above. Here the Countess' *seat of State*, whether itself set indoors or out, must have been visible from without. Though not always specifically mentioned, the seat of state (or simply 'state,' as it was often called; see 14–19 n.) appears to have been a constant feature of the masque setting; it was occupied by the person in whose honour the masque was performed. Verity (*Arcades and Comus*, Cambridge, 1891) quotes a direction from Shirley's *Triumph of Peace*: 'At the lower end of the room, opposite to the State, was raised a stage with a descent of stairs in two branches...' (Evans, *Masques*, 208; Spencer, *Masques*, 285), which, he infers, was the usual arrangement. Be this as it may, the description seems irrelevant to *Arcades* if it was preliminary to the main entertainment, and enacted in the approaches.

The *Pastoral Habit* of the *Noble Persons* would presumably be symbolic of 'Arcadian' shepherd life and consonant with their actual rank, not realistic as would be the assumed disguise of the Attendant Spirit in *Comus*.

1 *Song.* MS. omits heading and numbers the final song as *2 Song*. Does this mean that the first song was originally written to be spoken as a lyric prologue?

Nymphs, and Shepherds: cf. the opening of the final song (96). These are the 'Noble Persons...in Pastoral Habit.' *Nymphs*: Either the term is to be taken literally and we are to think of the girls as representing the buskined nymphs of Diana's train (below, 33 and n.), or we are to regard the costume suggested as appropriate to Arcadian shepherdesses, part, that is, of the 'Pastoral Habit.' For nymphs as a poetic synonym for maidens the earlier examples cited in *OED* 2 seem less than conclusive, since Lodge's 'Nimph of beauties train' suggests, rather than a synonym, a figurative use from nymph of Diana's train; and in Shakespeare, *Dream* 4. 1. 130, Theseus may be intended to mistake, at first, or pretend to mistake, the sleeping girls for nymphs of the forest. In later pastoral and other poetry, swains and nymphs commonly designate youths and maidens; cf. 26–33 below.

2 *What...Majesty.* Warton cited 'in thy face / Shines more awful majesty' (Fletcher, *F. Shep.* 1. 1. 61–2).

5 (and **17**) *This this is she.* Such repetition for emphasis is fairly common in the songs of masques. Milton's or a parallel phrase had occurred in Jonson's *Entertainment at Althrope* 113–14 and *Pleasure reconcild to Vertue* 328, 339 (*Ben Jonson* 7, 124, 491), and in Marston's masque (103) described above; it is repeated by Milton in a very different context in *SA* 115.

6 *vows*: Lat. *vota*, wishes (Browne); also, prayers, promises; see *Hor* 12–16 n.

7 *solemn search*: search performed with due ceremony (*OED* 3; and below, 39 n.).

8–9 *Fame...profuse*: in reference to the poetic tributes paid to the Countess by Spenser and others, [but carrying the Lat. sense, rather frequent in Milton, of common talk, rumour, report, though here and in 41 below 'less definitely *personified*' (Lockwood) than elsewhere]. *raise*: exalt. *erst*: formerly.

10–11 *We may...accuse / Of.* MS. first had *now seemes guiltie of abuse* (*Facs.* 384).

12 *we find exprest.* MS. first had *she hath express't.* [Cf. the Queen of Sheba to Solomon: '...and, behold, the half was not told me' (1 Kings 10. 7); and Wallace in 11 above.]

13 *Envy bid conceal the rest.* [Todd cited: 'For what so Envie good or bad did fynd, / She did conceale, and murder her owne mynd' (Spenser, *F.Q.* 5. 12. 33).] For *conceal* MS. (*Facs.* 384) first had *her hide.*

14–19 *Mark...her light.* Todd cited the canopy of Mercilla: 'Not of rich tissew, nor of cloth of gold, / ...But like a cloud... / Whose skirts were bordred with bright sunny beams, / Glistring like gold..., / And here and there shooting forth silver streames' (Spenser, *F.Q.* 5. 9. 28). Keightley took the lines to refer to the actual canopy under which the Countess was seated. In the court masques the device was sometimes employed of illuminating a seat, so that the light seemed to come from its occupant; cf. the elaborate example in Davenant's *Salmacida Spolia* (*Works*, Edinburgh and London, 2, 1872, 323; Evans, *Masques*, 241; Spencer, *Masques*, 358). Possibly some simpler effect of this kind was provided here, so that *shining throne* would be a literal description. The word state may be used in a general sense of splendour befitting the great (*OED* 17), or of a raised chair with a canopy, a chair of state (ibid. 20), or of the canopy alone (ibid. 20b). Warton (on line 81) insists on the last of these meanings, citing Milton's description of Satan's throne 'under state / Of richest texture spred' (*PL* 10. 445), and Jonson's of Juno, who 'Displayes her glistering state, and chaire, / As she enlightned all the ayre' (*Hymenaei* 234–5, *Ben Jonson* 7, 217). The words of the Genius, 'Whose lustre leads us' (76) and 'her glittering state' (81), seem to support a literal reading.

18 *Sitting.* MS. first had *seated*. Bush (*SP* 28, 1931, 263; *Mythol.*, 1963, 271) compared the song 'Queene and Huntresse' in *Cynthia's Revels* 5. 6. 1–18: 'Seated, in thy silver chaire, / State in wonted manner keepe: / ...Goddesse, excellently bright' (*Ben Jonson* 4, 161). Here, by the way, 'state' has the abstract sense of splendour (cf. 14–19 n.).

20 *the wise Latona*: the Roman name for the Greek Leto, mother by Zeus of the twins, Apollo and Artemis (cf. *Sonn* 12. 6–7). Verity interprets the myth as signifying 'the issuing from darkness to light,' and adds, obscurely, that Latona is 'Perhaps *wise* because the goddess of obscurity.' Osgood (*C.M.*) says she is named here 'as an example of queenly majesty,' being held in reverence by the ancient poets as the mother of the twin divinities; the epithet *wise* 'seems to have no definite classical original.' Hughes (1937) cites Comes, *Mythol.* 9. 6, where Latona is interpreted as the source of that harmony of the soul which men learned from her son Apollo. Another possibility is that Milton is generalizing from Leto's calming down Apollo when he alarmed the gods by appearing among them with his bow (*Homeric Hymns* 3. 2–13). At any rate the primary emphasis here, as with Cybele and Juno, is on the majesty and the venerable character of the Countess, the mother of a noble race now assembled to honour her. [Possibly the Countess' witnessing the performance of her young relatives recalled Homer's and Virgil's pictures (*Od.* 6. 102–9; *A.* 1. 498–502) of Latona's joy in watching her daughter Diana lead the dance of nymphs; the epithet *wise* may be carried over from the allusion to Solomon (12 n.). See Wallace in II above.]

21–2 *towred Cybele...hundred gods.* Like Spenser (*F.Q.* 4. 11. 28), Milton remembers Virgil's allusion to Cybele (a Phrygian goddess identified with Rhea and Ops, the wife of Saturn and mother of Jove, Juno, and other deities), who rides through the Phrygian cities *turrita* (turret-crowned), rejoicing in her off-spring and clasping a hundred of her children's children (*A.* 6. 784–7; cf. 10. 252–3). For Ovid she is *turrita Mater* (*M.* 10. 696); he explains her 'turreted crown' as meaning that she gave towers to cities (*F.* 4. 219–21). Verity cites Spenser, *Ruines of Rome* 71–3: 'the Berecynthian Goddesse bright / In her swift charret with high turrets crownde, / Proud that so manie Gods she brought to light.' [Cf. Milton, *El* 1. 74 n. (*V.C.* 1, 57).]

23 *Juno...odds.* Juno, wife of Jove and queen of the gods, and therefore the type of female majesty, 'durst not meet her ⟨the Countess⟩ on equal terms, by setting aside her own divinity' (Browne). The word *odds* (treated as singular) here means an equalizing allowance given a weaker player (*OED* 4c). Admitting that *give her odds* 'seems no very elegant phrase,' Todd says that 'it was a mode of compliment usual in Milton's time' and quotes: 'Place her, where her forme divine, / Shall to after ages shine: / And without respect of Odds, / Vye renowne with Demy-Gods' (G. Wither, *Faire-Virtue, Juvenilia*, Part 3, Spenser Society, 1871, 733). MS. first had *Juno*, then *Ceres*, finally *Juno*. Ceres would have shifted the emphasis from majesty to bountifulness, a theme possibly present in later lines (101 n., 104 n.).

24 *had thought.* MS. first had *would have thought.*   *clime*: climate in the sense of locality or region [cf. *Sonn* 8. 8], not necessarily with reference to one of the seven 'climates' thought of by the ancients as presided over by the seven planets or (as Wright assumes) to the twenty-four regions into which the area between the equator and the poles was later divided (*OED*: clime 1 and 2; climate 1 a, b). Presumably Milton is comparing the northern region with the Mediterranean home of the goddesses. [While such a contrast belongs to the theme of *Arcades*, Milton alludes at times to the traditional idea that northern climates were unfavourable to creative genius (*Mansus* 28; *RCG, Works* 3, 237; *Areop, Works* 4, 296; *HistBr, Works* 10, 325; *PL* 9. 44–5. See Z. S. Fink, *MLQ* 2, 1941, 67–80, T. B. Stroup, ibid. 4, 1943, 185–9). Cf. *Mansus* 27–8 n., in *V.C.* 1, 272–3.]

After **25**: ⟨Direction⟩. *As they com...speaks.* MS. had *The Genius of yᵉ wood rises*; *rises* deleted; and inserted above, *appeares As they offer to* (*offer to* deleted) *come forward*, etc. (*Facs.* 384). *Genius of the Wood*: the *genius loci* or tutelary spirit of the place, a common use of *genius* in Latin; cf. *Lyc* 183 and especially *IlPen* 154, both of which suggest beneficent activities, as here in 44–60. Warton (on 83) notes that 'A Genius is more than once introduced in Jonson's *Under-woods* and *Masques*,' and cites particularly the *Entertainment at Theobalds* (1607), where 'the dialogue is chiefly supported by a Genius' and he is instructed by the three Fates, 'Daughters of night,' who 'draw out the chayne of Destinie, / Upon whose threds, both lives and times depend' (*Ben Jonson* 7, 155); cf. below, 62–7, and 62–73 n. Verity notes the presence of 'Silvanus, god of these woods' in Campion's *Entertainment Given by Lord Knowles* (*Works* 86). [Demaray (*Masque Tradition*, 51) cites 'the two Keepers of the Wood' in Campion's work 'and the Forester in Jonson's "An Entertainment at the Blackfriars" (1620).' Starnes–Talbert (257) give references in Renaissance works; see especially, for the tradition up to Milton, Starnes's 'The Figure Genius in the Renaissance,' *Studies in the Renaissance* 11 (1964), 234–44. For allegorical interpretations of Milton's Genius see Brooks and Hardy, Wallace, and Blau in 11 above.]

26 *gentle*: of gentle blood, well-born: originally used as a synonym for noble (which suits this context, since the performers are of the Countess' family), later distinguished from it as either a more general term or a lower degree (*OED* A. 1). There is deliberate contrast with *Swains*, which would ordinarily mean rustic servants, labourers, or shepherds (*OED* 4), but passed readily into the stylized diction and rarefied atmosphere of pastoral poetry (cf. 1 n. and 33).

27 *honour*: nobility, the ground in rank or merit of being honoured.

28–31 *Of famous....Arethuse.* These are no ordinary shepherds but Arcadians and sprung of the tradition of pastoral poetry, which is here (as in *Lyc* 132, 85) represented by *Alpheus* and *Arethuse.* Alpheus, famous in song from Homer (*Il.* 11. 725–8) onward, was, appropriately, the god of the river of that name rising in Arcadia. In myth Alpheus, flowing under the sea—by Milton's *secret sluse* or channel (*OED* 2)—pursued the nymph Arethusa to Ortygia, off the Sicilian coast, where she had taken refuge, transformed by Diana to a fountain, and there mingled his Arcadian stream with Sicilian waters (Ovid, *M.* 5. 572–641; Virgil, *A.* 3. 694–6). Thus was effected a joining of Arcadia and Sicily, the home of pastoral poetry (see above, n. on Title).

32 *breathing Roses.* The Nymphs are thus described in metaphor of sight and smell (*OED*: breathe 2: emit odour). [Milton seems to mean 'roses that breathe,' i.e. are human. Cf. Marlowe's picture of the young beauties of Sestos as 'breathing stars' (*H. and L.* 1. 98).]

33 *silver-buskin'd Nymphs.* Browne says that the buskin, a high boot, 'was worn by Diana,' but cites only the 'gilden buskins' of Spenser's Belphoebe (*F.Q.* 2. 3. 27). More apposite would have been: 'Sometimes Diana he her takes to bee, / But misseth bow, and shaftes, and buskins to her knee' (ibid. 1. 6. 16). Wright asserts that the female masquers were 'clad as nymphs of Diana'; this may be so (see above, n. on Title), but evidence is lacking. Virgil refers twice to the purple buskin of Diana (*E.* 7. 32; *A.* 1. 337). But the buskin is so frequent in other contexts that neither classical nor Renaissance precedent seems to establish it as the identifying mark of Diana and her train. [One might add that Drayton's Phoebe, disguised as a nymph, wears buskins (Drayton, 1, 133), and that Marlowe's Hero had 'Buskins of shels al silvered' (*H. and L.* 1. 31).] The *Nymphs* (whatever the word designates) are marked by the same *bright honour* as the *Swains*: they are as *great*, of equally noble descent, and as *good*, of equal personal merit.

34 *quest*: adventure or expedition (*OED*: sb.¹ 5), with the suggestion of chivalry and romance. *free intent*: 'courteous object' (Wright) appears to receive no support from *OED*. Perhaps *free* rather carries the suggestion of noble, generous (*OED* 4) or unconstrained, willing (ibid. 20).

37 *low reverence*: deep bow (*OED* 2), the action no doubt accompanying the words. From this acknowledgment some have inferred that the role of the Genius was taken by one of the Countess' retainers; [but general probability and Lawes' part in *Comus*, would suggest him in this role].

39 *glad solemnity*: joyous and festive ceremony (*OED* 2). Cf. *Comus* 142 and n., and above, 7 and n.; cf. also Lat. *sollemnitas*, solemnity, festival, celebration.

41 *What shallow-searching Fame*. MS. first had *those ve⟨r⟩tues wᶜʰ dull Fame* (*Facs.* 384). In either form the words continue the rebuke to Fame (8–13 above) which has too superficially examined the virtues of the Countess. See 8–9 n.

44–5 *by lot…this fair Wood*: By divinely appointed destiny (*OED*: lot 2 d; and *Comus* 20 and n.), I am the tutelary spirit (*OED*: power sb.¹ 7), the lesser god (below, 79 n.), of this fair wood. MS. (as Todd was able to read it) first had *have the power & charge of this faire wood*, where *power* would mean authority over (*OED*: sb.¹ 5).

45 *Oak'n bowr*: dwelling (*OED* 1) formed by the overarching branches of oak (ibid. 3). In MS. above 46 appears, but is deleted, *live a thousand yeares* (*Facs.* 386). The present state of the MS. makes the intended relation of the phrase difficult to infer (and Todd did not notice its presence). Whether it is related to *live in Oak'n bowr*, is a substitute for it, or is independent and additional, it is clearly something conferred by lot from Jove. In classic myth the Dryads were not immortal but lived only so long as the trees with which they were associated. Possibly Milton thought of transferring this limitation to the Genius and of prophesying at the same time that the oaks of Harefield would survive a thousand years. [Cf. Shawcross, *N&Q* 6, 1959, 361.]

46 *curl the grove*. *Inter alia*, Warton cited: 'Banks crown'd with curled Groves'

(Drayton, *Poly.* 7. 215; cf. 7. 109); 'And trees... / Did nod their curled heads' (Browne, *Brit. Past.* 1. 4. 599–601); 'the curled woods' (*To Sir Robert Wroth* 17, *Ben Jonson* 8, 97); 'When was old Sherewood's head more quaintly curl'd?' (*The Kings Entertainment at Welbeck* (pr. 1640: ibid. 7, 792). Todd quoted a less apposite couplet from Sylvester (*D.W.W.* 1. 2. 545–6, Grosart, 1, 32).

47 *quaint*: ingeniously contrived to produce an effect of beauty, as in Spenser's description of a forest scene: 'Nor hart could wish for any queint device, / But there it present was, and did fraile sense entice' (*F.Q.* 4. 10. 22; cf. *OED* 4). This added suggestion of beauty and attractiveness is absent from Warton's illustration, 'the quaint mazes in the wanton green' (Shakespeare, *Dream* 2. 1. 99), and from the explanations of most later editors, though Verity glosses as 'dainty, pretty.' [Cf. the second item from Jonson in 46 n. above, and *Lyc* 139.] The semicolon after *quaint* (which replaces the comma of MS. and 1645 and is evidently a printer's error) must not conceal the fact that *wove* is a perfect participle.

48–53 *And all my Plants...venom bites.* Warton noted the general similarity to the offices attributed by Comus (266–9) to the goddess of the wood.

49–50 *noisom winds...evil dew.* Here *noisom* means injurious, noxious (*OED* 1) and *blasting* withering (by the action of wind or other element; *OED*: blast 7). Browne compared: 'An Easterne winde, commixt with noisome aires, / Shall blast the plants' (Kyd, *Spanish Tragedy* 4. 2. 17–18). Warton cited Caliban's 'As wicked dew as e'er my mother brush'd / ...from unwholesome fen' (Shakespeare, *Temp.* 1. 2. 321–2). *Boughs.* MS. first had *leaves.*

51 *thwarting thunder blew.* Here *thunder* is used for lightning (*OED* 1 b), whose visual phenomena are noticed in its colour, blue, and in the epithet *thwarting*, cutting across (the sky), perhaps with the secondary suggestion of thwarting, opposing, the purposes of the Genius (*OED*: thwart 1 and 5). Warton compared: 'when the cross blue lightning seem'd to open / The breast of heaven' (Shakespeare, *Caesar* 1. 3. 50–1). Verity added 'quick cross lightning' (*Lear* 4. 7. 35).

52 *cross dire-looking Planet smites.* Editors identify the planet as Saturn; cf. *EpDam* 79–80 and n. For the malign stroke of planets Verity compares Shakespeare, *Ham.* 1. 1. 162, *Cor.* 2. 2. 118; [cf. *PL* 10. 657–64]. Wright explains *dire-looking* as 'of evil aspect, in the astrological sense.' See *IlPen* 23–30 n.

53 *hurtfull Worm...bites.* Milton seems to combine two meanings of canker as affecting plants. The primary reference is to the canker-worm, which feeds on and destroys the foliage or bloom (*OED*: canker 4); cf. 'Some to kill cankers in the musk-rose buds' (Shakespeare, *Dream* 2. 2. 3). He evidently thinks also of its bite as infecting the plant with the disease called canker (*OED* 3). [Cf. *Lyc* 45–6 and notes.]

54 *fetch my round*: make (*OED*: fetch 9) my customary circuit, like a watchman (ibid. round 15). Verity cites: 'I'll fetch a turn about the garden' (Shakespeare, *Cym.* 1. 1. 81).

56 *odorous breath of morn*. Todd cited *PL* 4. 641 and Dante, *Purg.* 24. 145–7: *E quale, annunziatrice degli albori, | l'aura di maggio movesi ed olezza, | tutta impregnata dall'erba e da' fiori.*

57 *Awakes*: stirs (to motion) from a state (of stillness) resembling sleep (*OED* 6). *tasseld horn*. Newton (reported by Todd) compared the 'horne of bugle small, | Which hong adowne his side in twisted gold, | And tassels gay' (Spenser, *F.Q.* 1. 8. 3); in Milton it is a hunting horn that is thus ornamented.

58 *Shakes*: causes to vibrate, agitates, in the literal sense (*OED* 7), or rouses, startles (Lockwood); perhaps with the metaphor of awakening carried on (cf. *L'All* 53–4).

59 *Number my ranks*: count (to be sure that none is missing) my plants in their rows (which carries on the image of the guardian spirit). Verity explains as a military metaphor of an officer inspecting the ranks. [Cf. 'her flow'ry ranks' (Browne, *Brit. Past.* 1. 2. 723).] MS. first had *& number all my rancks*.

60 *puissant words...to bless*: words of magic power and murmured charms to ensure a blessing. For *murmur* meaning muttered incantation (but there malign) see *Comus* 525 and n.

61 *els*: at other times (*OED* 3c).

62 *Hath lock't up mortal sense*: i.e. the sense or consciousness of mortals. MS. had *hath chain'd mortalitie*; *chain'd mortalitie* deleted; *lock't up mortall eyes*; *eyes* replaced by *sense* (*Facs.* 386).

62–73 *then listen I...gross unpurged ear*. This passage, as Warton (followed by later editors) showed, is based in the main on Plato, *Rep.* 10. 616–17. There the universe is depicted as consisting of eight concentric whorls attached to a spindle of adamant. These whorls, it is clear, are the spheres of what was to be the Ptolemaic system, containing the fixed stars and planets: 'And the spindle turned on the knees of Necessity, and up above on each of the rims of the circles a Siren stood, borne around in its revolution and uttering one sound, one note, and from all the eight there was the concord of a single harmony. And there were other three who sat round about at equal intervals, each one on her throne, the Fates, daughters of Necessity..., Lachesis, and Clotho, and Atropos, who sang in unison with the music of the Sirens, Lachesis singing the things that were, Clotho the things that are, and Atropos the things that are to be. And Clotho with the touch of her right hand helped to turn the outer circumference of the spindle, pausing from time to time. Atropos with her left hand in like manner helped to turn the inner circles, and Lachesis alternately with either hand lent a hand to each' (617: L.C.L.). Cf. Warton's citation from Jonson above ('Direction' after 25).

In conformity with a later development of the Ptolemaic system Milton here (as in *PL*) has nine spheres. He also made specific the identity of the song of Plato's Sirens with the music of the spheres, which is, or symbolizes, the power that keeps nature in her course, but which is inaudible to the human ear. The idea fascinated Milton from *Prol* 2 onward: see *Nat* 125-32, *SolMus*, *Patrem* 35-7, *Comus* 1017-22, and notes. Milton was of course not alone in his interest in the music of the spheres. [The most familiar allusion is Shakespeare's, in *Merch.* 5. 1. 60-5, an allusion which, in a popular play, indicates how generally known the idea was.] Hughes (1937) quotes Sir Thomas Browne, *Rel. Med.* 2. 9 (*Works*, ed. Keynes, 1964, 1, 84): '...and thus farre we may maintain the musick of the spheares; for those well ordered motions, and regular paces, though they give no sound unto the eare, yet to the understanding they strike a note most full of harmony...there is something in it of Divinity more than the eare discovers. It is an Hieroglyphicall and shadowed lesson of the whole world, and [the] Creatures of God; such a melody to the eare, as the whole world well understood, would afford the understanding.'

64 *nine enfolded Sphears.* See above, 62-73 n.   *enfolded*: referring to the concentric whorls, one set within another.

65 *those that hold the vital shears.* Actually it was Atropos alone who bore the *shears* (here called *vital* because affecting life, fatal to it: *OED* 6) and cut the thread of life woven by the other two Fates (cf. *Lyc* 75-6 and n.). The shears are given to the 'Sisters Three' in Bottom's play (Shakespeare, *Dream* 5. 1. 343-8). But Milton's purpose is plain: to present the Fates as destructive and brought under control only by the Sirens' music. Spenser had likewise not distinguished their separate functions: 'Let those three fatall Sisters, whose sad hands / Doe weave the direfull threeds of destinie, / And in their wrath breake off the vitall bands, / Approach hereto' (*Daphnaïda* 16-19: quoted by Verity). As illustrating the Fates in a masque setting, Verity cites Jonson's *Entertainment at Theobalds*:

'...the three Parcae,...the one holding the rocke, the other the spindle, and the third the sheeres, with a booke of Adamant lying open before them' (*Ben Jonson* 7, 155).

67 *On which the fate...is wound.* Immediately after the passage quoted above (62–73 n.), Plato tells of the 'lots and patterns of lives' taken from the knees of Lachesis by a prophet and presented to the souls for their choice (*Rep.* 10. 617–18). Perhaps a memory of this, combined with Plato's image of the spindle and the Fates as spinners of the individual's thread of life, led Milton to the inference here stated.

69–72 *lull the daughters...heavenly tune.* [For the Fates as daughters of Necessity see the extract from Plato in 62–73 n., above.] Milton may here be accommodating another reminiscence of Plato to his metaphor of music. In the *Timaeus* [e.g. 30, 42 f., 48 f., 69] Necessity and Chance, forces hostile to order, are said to have dominated the matter from which the God produced the ordered world. Hence Nature is *unsteddy* and the *low world* must be kept in constant conformity to the order the God sought to impose, order symbolized for Milton as *the heavenly tune*, the music of the celestial spheres.

71 *measur'd*: 'rhythmical; regular in movement' (*OED* 3b).

72–3 *which none...unpurged ear.* In *Prol* 2 Milton thus explained the inaudibility of the music of the spheres: 'Nay rather, let us blame our feeble ears which are not able, or are not worthy, to overhear...such sweet tones.' These we shall 'never be permitted to enjoy so long as we remain brutish and overwhelmed by wicked animal desires; for how can those be susceptible of that heavenly sound whose souls...are bent toward the earth and absolutely devoid of celestial matters?' (*Works* 12, 155–7). Warton, who could find no classical source for this idea, quoted Shakespeare's much quoted lines: 'Such harmony is in immortal souls; / But whilst this muddy vesture of decay / Doth grossly close it in, we cannot hear it' (*Merch.* 5. 1. 63–5). The application is consonant with Plato's depreciation of the sensible. Verity explains *human mould* as human form (though he is evidently uncertain, since he cites the passage to support 'material' in *Nat* 138); Hughes (1937) takes it as substance; Wright [on *Comus* 17] as 'the earth of which man is fashioned'—correctly, as the context, and Milton's use elsewhere, confirm (cf. *Nat* 138 n., *Comus* 17 n., 243 n.).

74–80 *And yet such musick...her worth to celebrate.* Milton returns from the world of Plato to the occasion of *Arcades*. Such music would alone be worthy to *blaze*, proclaim (as with a trumpet), make known (*OED*: *v.*² 2) the Countess' virtues. The music of the spheres, which everywhere else in Milton bears a moral and religious significance, is here subordinated to compliment. [But might it not also be said that Milton manages to link compliment with Platonic metaphysics?]

76 *Whose lustre leads us* is metaphorical, but perhaps also literal (see above, 14–19 n.). Wright takes *lustre* as 'splendour of beauty or renown' and *leads* as 'is foremost,' used here perhaps 'in the specific sense of "lead the dance."'

77 *hit*: to come (by good fortune) on something aimed at (*OED* 11). Cf. *IlPen* 14 and n.

79–80 The Genius is one of the *lesser gods*, a tutelary spirit holding his commission from Jove (44–5 above); what such a being can do he will *assay*, attempt (*OED* 16).

81 *glittering state*. See above, 14–19 n.

82 *stemm*: stock, descent (*OED* 3). [Cf. Nashe, 'True Stemme of Nobilitie' (*Terrors of the night*, dedication, *Works* 1, 341).]

83 *Approach*. See below, 96 n.

84 *enamel'd*. Warton had supposed that Milton supplied the 18th century with this bit of poetic diction, but found that it was common among his predecessors: Sylvester (e.g. *D.W.W.* 2. 1. 3. 332, 2. 2. 2. 546; Grosart, 1, 117, 143), Drayton, et al. Todd added Marlowe, Browne, Beaumont and Fletcher, Carew, and *verde smalto* from Dante (*Inf.* 4. 118). Verity quoted Sidney's *Arcadia*: 'medows, enameld with al sorts of ey-pleasing floures' (*Works* 1, 13). Cf. *Lyc* 139 n.

85 *Where no print of step hath been.* [Brooks and Hardy (166–7) not only find in the line 'the smoothness of the greensward' and a suggestion of 'the immortal lightness of the nymphs and classical shepherds,' but utilize it in their allegorical interpretation of the whole (II above, under 1951).]

87 *warbled*. In this context, the verb means manipulating the strings of an instrument (*OED*: *v.*[1] 5 a).

88–9 *Under the shady…Elm Star-proof.* Warton compared Spenser's shady grove, 'Not perceable with power of any starre' (*F.Q.* 1. 1. 7), as based on Statius, *Theb.* 10. 85 (*nulli penetrabilis astro*), and appropriated in Peacham's *Minerva Britanna* (1612), 182. Verity quoted 'This shade, sun-proof' (Peele, *David and Bethsabe* 1. 1. 14: *Works*, ed. A. H. Bullen, 2 v., London, 1888). [Hughes recalls Osgood's suggestion ('Milton's "Elm Star-Proof," *JEGP* 4,

1902, 370–8) that Milton had in mind the avenue of elms which was the scene of masques when Queen Elizabeth visited Harefield in 1602.]

96 *Nymphs and Shepherds dance no more.* See above, 1 and n. In the absence of the narrative or directions that appear in the printed versions of most masques, we may infer from the text that the masquers 'approach' the Countess (83) but pause to execute a dance, invited thereto by the Genius (87–93), and that the dance is halted by the third song, the opening line serving as the signal, though the sentence, when completed, is an exhortation to dance no more in Arcadia but abide in the presence of the Countess. [A. E. Housman's comment on the inexplicable poetry and pathos of this line (*The Name and Nature of Poetry*, New York, 1937, 45) expressed a very personal reaction: while he recognized that 'the sense of the passage is blithe and gay,' he seemed to read the line by itself, as if the nymphs and shepherds were the short-lived lads and lasses of Shropshire.]

97 *sandy Ladons Lillied banks.* The Ladon, a tributary of the Alpheus (the chief river of Arcadia), is described as sandy (*harenosi . . . Ladonis ad amnem*) by Ovid (*M.* 1. 702: [rendered by Sandys, 1626, 18, as 'smooth Ladon's sandy banks'), who applies the same epithet to the Tiber and the Hebrus (*F.* 1. 242, 3. 737)]. Warton also cited Browne: 'The silver Ladon on his sandy shore / Heard my complaints' (*Brit. Past.* 2. 4. 880–1); [and the references in Sidney's *Arcadia* (*Works* 1, 256–7) to the Ladon and its 'sandie banke']. There appears to be no authority for the added lilies, which may be Milton's poetic compensation for the classical but prosaic *sandy*. It was to the Ladon that Syrinx fled from Pan (Ovid, *M.* 1. 702).

98 *Lycaeus* and *Cyllene* are mountains in Arcadia. From the former (mentioned by Virgil, *G.* 1. 16, as the home of Pan) Syrinx was returning when pursued by the god (Ovid, *M.* 1. 698–9); Cyllene was sacred to Hermes and the birthplace of his son Pan (*Homeric Hymns* 19. 31 f.). [With *Cyllene hoar* Carey compares Virgil, *A.* 8. 139: *Cyllenae gelido . . . vertice*.]

100 *Erymanth.* Milton was either thinking of Mount Erymanthus in Arcadia (whose associations, however, are rather savage than pastoral: the Erymanthian boar, slain by Heracles; the nymph Callisto transformed to a she-bear), or was balancing the Ladon by the river Erymanthus, which rises in the mountain but flows into the Alpheus. [A straw in favour of the mountain is that, in the Homeric simile which Milton perhaps remembered in his allusion to Latona (above, 20 n.), both Leto (Latona) and Mount Erymanthus are named in connection with the dancing of nymphs.]

101 *give ye thanks*: prove grateful (by the return it makes).

102 *Maenalus*. In *El* 5. 125 Milton used the phrase *Maenalius Pan*, remembering from Virgil (*G.* 1. 17) that this Arcadian mountain was a favourite haunt. Verity cites Ovid, *F.* 4. 650, and *Pans Anniversarie*, Hymn 4 (*Ben Jonson* 7, 538). [H. C. H. Candy (*N&Q* 158, 1930, 310–12) cited Browne, *Brit. Past.* 2. 4. 897–8: 'That high-brow'd Maenalus... / And stony hills.']

104 *have greater grace*: have more favour (*OED* 6) shown you (perhaps in the returns for your labour: cf. above, 101 n.); or, more probably, achieve greater honour, in serving the Countess, since the nymph Syrinx herself, though beloved by the Arcadian god Pan, would be sufficiently honoured in waiting on her (106–7). The immediate context (105), with the careful preparation by glancing allusions to the myth of Syrinx (97 n., 98 n.), supports the latter interpretation.

106–7 *Though Syrinx...wait on her*. See 104 n. Warton (on line 5) and Todd found here an echo of 'And the dame hath Syrinx grace! / O that Pan were now in place' (*Entertainment at Althrope, Ben Jonson* 7, 121). Todd interpreted it as a deliberate reminder to the Countess of the performance of Jonson's *Entertainment* at the seat of the Spencer family where she had grown up; the occasion had been a visit from Queen Anne and Prince Henry in 1603.

108–9 The repeated final couplet links the third to the second song, as the opening phrase of the third links it to the first; the couplet also returns to and underlines the significance of the title *Arcades* and at the same time brings the piece to a close with renewed homage to the Countess. Verity thinks that this last song may have been sung as a madrigal by the Genius and the masquers (his pupils if the Genius was played by Lawes), in which case the final couplet could first be sung part-wise, then in full chorus.

Lycidas

❧

I. DATE, CIRCUMSTANCES, AND TEXT

[To begin with the immediate subject of *Lycidas*, data concerning the life of Edward King were collected by Masson. His family was English, but he had been born in Ireland, where his father, Sir John King, was Privy Councillor for Ireland and Secretary to the Irish government, and his uncle was a bishop. Edward and his older brother were admitted to Christ's College on 9 June 1626, some sixteen months after Milton's admission; Edward was fourteen. The two boys were assigned to the popular tutor, William Chappell, with whom the freshman Milton had had trouble. Since Christ's College was small—it had about 260 members—Milton and King would have had some degree of acquaintance; there is no evidence of anything beyond that. Edward Phillips, in his life of his uncle (1694), singled out 'one Mr. King, with whom, for his great Learning and Parts, he had contracted a particular Friendship and Intimacy' (*Early Lives*, ed. Darbishire, 54); but Phillips, who was born in 1630, could have no personal knowledge, and his statement sounds like a mere inference from *Lycidas*. In June 1630, when a College fellowship was about to be vacated, King, who had received his B.A., was nominated for the place by royal mandate and was thus given precedence over some of his seniors, including Milton. In Masson's judgment, 'The royal mandate in King's favour was clearly owing to his family connexions and influence; but to so popular a young scholar the preferment does not appear to have been grudged.' Although Milton endows Lycidas with the power of song, the extant specimens of King's verse—

544

Latin contributions to various volumes chiefly celebrating events in the royal family—are wholly undistinguished. King proceeded to qualify himself for the ministry. In the long vacation of 1637, on his way home from Cambridge, he sailed from Chester for Dublin, but the ship, while still near the Welsh coast, struck a rock and sank, with most of those on board. The wreck occurred on 10 August. Plans for a commemorative volume would have gone forward when, if not before, the members of Christ's College reassembled for the Michaelmas term. Such collections usually honoured older or more exalted personages than King; while in this case we may allow something for the status of his family and for the shock of an early and violent death, the preparation of the volume is evidence of general popularity and esteem.

At the time of King's death Milton had been at home for five years, engaged mainly in laying a foundation in humane knowledge and thought for his unknown future. We might say that those years of secluded intellectual toil had been inaugurated by the sonnet 'How soon hath time' and were concluded with the far more difficult affirmation of *Lycidas*.] *Comus* had been presented on 29 September 1634; Milton made important additions to the text between its first composition and its first publication in 1637 (see *Comus* 1). Apart from these additions [and the translation of Psalm 114 into Greek], he would seem, on the evidence of the Cambridge MS., to have written no verse until *Lycidas*, which is dated *Novemb: 1637* in the MS. (*Facs.* 436). [When a memorial volume for King was being planned at Cambridge, Milton, though he had been away for five years, would be remembered as a poet by the older members of the College and invited to contribute.] There seems to be no ground for the suggestion that he may possibly have written *Lycidas* 'without knowledge of the proposed Cambridge volume' (*Justa*, ed. E. C. Mossner, New York, 1939, vii). In his letter to Diodati of 23 September (*Works* 12, 27), Milton says that he is thinking of immortal fame, although as yet he is only letting his wings grow in preparation for flight; obviously he is contemplating no intrusion of less than epic ambition. [This letter should probably be dated 23 November, in the month of *Lycidas* (see Milton, *C.P.W.* 1, 1953, 325; Parker, 812,

n. 73); Milton's deprecating phrase might cover the composition of the poem.] The volume was published at Cambridge in 1638 as *Justa Edouardo King naufrago, ab Amicis moerentibus, amoris & μνείας χάριν* [('Obsequies for Edward King, drowned at sea, written by his friends in love and remembrance'). It carried an appropriate motto from an odd source, Petronius (115: L.C.L., p. 244, reading *recte* for *bene*): *Si bene calculum ponas, ubique naufragium est* ('Make a fair reckoning, and you find shipwreck everywhere').] The Latin and Greek elegies were followed by those in English, with a separate title page, *Obsequies to the memorie of M*^r *Edward King, Anno Dom. 1638.*[1] *Lycidas* came last, signed 'J.M.'

[Among the contributors of Latin, Greek, and English poems were several men destined to be more or less famous: John Pearson, who became a bishop and author of the once renowned *Exposition of the Creed*; Henry More, who was to be one of the two leading exponents of Cambridge Platonism; Thomas Farnaby, the classical scholar; Joseph Beaumont, the religious poet; and John Cleveland, the metaphysical poet and satirist. We may note that the poem signed by Cleveland ('I like not tears in tune,' *Obsequies*, p. 9) was preceded by an unsigned one ('Whiles Phebus shines within our Hemisphere'), the only unsigned English piece, and this also was probably Cleveland's, in the view of his latest editors, Brian Morris and Eleanor Withington (*Poems of John Cleveland*, xxxviii, 65, 155).

There have been discussions of *Lycidas* in relation to the other poems in the *Obsequies*. Sir Charles Oman gave a popular account of those pieces (*Cornhill Magazine*, 156, 1937, 377–87): the authors of this 'rubbish' 'harp on almost every string that Milton touched, but always out of harmony.' R. Wallerstein has a chapter (96–114) on the book, especially on Joseph Beaumont, as one segment of her highly philosophic analysis of the elegiac genre, 'The Laureate Hearse' (pp. 3–148 in her *Studies* cited in III below under 1950). M. Lloyd (*N&Q* 5, 1958, 432–4) sees the elegies as perhaps intended to be 'a unified work within a flexible

---

[1] [J. T. Shawcross ('Division of Labor in *Justa*...(1638),' *Library Chronicle*, University of Pennsylvania, 27, 1961, 176–9) has distinguished between the portions done by the two Cambridge printers.]

comprehensive design.' Henry King's elegy 'is explicitly written as an introduction to the rest.' *Lycidas* is 'a summary and interpretation of themes already stated,' such as resurrection. In citing numerous particular relations Lloyd hardly allows enough for what he recognizes as the inevitable and central themes of Christian elegists.

A more ample and critical discussion is given by G. Williamson ('The Obsequies for Edward King,' *Seventeenth Century Contexts*, London and Chicago, 1960–1, 132–47). He compares Milton with the other elegists in regard to 'these topics: death must be mourned, association with the deceased, his loss to the Muse, the question of providence, cause of disaster, loss to learning, loss to church, pastoral consolation, the intrusion of reality, religious consolation, and pastoral resolution.' Thus considered, the elements of *Lycidas* are of three kinds, common, uncommon, and unique. 'The other elegists share Milton's themes of lamentation. These arise from a sense of threefold loss as poet, scholar, priest.' On the loss to learning, 'a natural theme for the university world,' 'the other elegists are most prolix'; Milton dwells most on the loss to the church. Many differences are comprised in Milton's adoption of the pastoral convention: 'King's drowning is not forgotten in the pastoral machinery, but submerged in the water imagery. There it is a latent discord, not an open contradiction....By his use of the pastoral convention Milton dramatizes his mourning; the other elegists reflected on the death and its meaning; they employed no dramatic vehicle.' 'It is clear that the form of the pastoral elegy enabled Milton to organize and unify common topics in a far more effective way than his rival elegists....But Milton's greatest source of power is the emotional tension generated by discords within his pastoral unity....Milton exploited the basic conflict between pagan and Christian pastoralism, and so developed a new intensity in his use of the convention....Now the Christian interruptions show emotion breaking through the pastoral convention or display tension between Christian and pagan elements then combined in the pastoral convention. Thus they provide alternations of feeling, and give truer resolutions of problems for Milton, until the two strains are harmonized at the end.'

J. B. Leishman (*Milton's Minor Poems*, ed. G. Tillotson, London, 1969, 248–55) shows in detail how, in contrast with the 'old-fashioned' traditionalism of *Lycidas*, the other elegists in the *Obsequies* weave tissues of more or less ingenious 'modern' conceits.

The closest scrutiny of textual and orthographical variants in the MS. and the several printed texts has been made by J. T. Shawcross, 'Establishment of a Text of Milton's Poems Through a Study of *Lycidas*' (*PBSA* 56, 1962, 317–31). Since most of the countless details of spelling do not (except those in MS.) necessarily reflect Milton's own habits, and seldom affect pronunciation, they have not much critical value. Some items were manifest errors. And a few are of critical account; these, along with errors, are recorded in the notes below.

Shawcross says that the text supplied to the 1638 editor 'must have been a copy originating from the Trinity MS, probably in the hand of an amanuensis....Eight errors in 1638 may arise from errors in the transcript, although some could be due to the printer: 10 "well" omitted; 39 "shepherds" rather than "shepherd"; 56 "Ah" rather than "ay"; 67 "do" rather than "use"; 112 "mitred"; the manuscript has "mitre'd", that is, "mitred" > "mitr'd"; 131 "smites" rather than "smite"; 149 "beauty" rather than "beauties"; 177 omitted, a transcribal error since the pointing of line 176 was changed from what would otherwise have been correct. A misreading of handwriting most likely accounts for six additional differences, probably the scribe's misreading of Milton's autograph, although the printer may have misread his copy: 51 "lord" rather than "lov'd"; 53 "the" rather than "your"...; 64 "uncessant" rather than "incessant"; 66 "stridly" rather than "strictly"...; 73 "where" rather than "when"; 151 "Lycid" rather than "Lycid".'

Copy for the 1645 text was a corrected copy of 1638 (Shawcross, 322). Most of the 1638 errors were put right; of actual changes the most important was at 129 (see note below). According to Shawcross, 'Not only the errors previously noted, but the lack of correction to preferred spelling indicates that the preparer of copy for 1645 was not Milton himself' (326), though 'some spellings may have been created by the printer.' 'Thus it would seem that at least much of the punctuation proceeds from the printer of 1645 and that as a guide to a Miltonic text the punctuation of 1645 is poor and unreliable' (328).

The 1673 edition of the minor poems 'was printed from an augmented copy of the 1645 edition' (328). Some errors of 1645 were corrected and the printer introduced some new ones. The text of *Lycidas* tells the same story as the texts of other poems that were in both editions. 'Obviously 1673 was not printed with an eye toward presenting a text which Milton himself would have produced. Rather it is a reprint of 1645 with new material, incidental variations and errors, and probably only a few significant verbal changes—certainly not the more truly Miltonic text.' (329)

Shawcross insists (330) that a reformed text must follow MS. readings, e.g.: 'should give "well" in line 10 (despite its being hypermetric), "in" in line 30, "herdsmans" in line 121, "little" in line 129 (the meaning of which should be signal enough of Milton's wisdom in changing the word), and "beauties" in line 149 (not yet given in any printed text).' But to cling thus to the MS. seems to imply that Milton could not and did not change his mind about anything between that time and 1645; we cannot assume that the words listed were his final decisions.]

II. THE PASTORAL ELEGY

As background for *Lycidas* (and for the *Epitaphium Damonis*) a brief history of pastoral elegy is needed.[1] In *Samson Agonistes* and *Paradise*

---

[1] Our concern is with the history of pastoral elegy and not specifically with Milton's sources, but the examples cited make up in effect a list of analogues and potential sources. The term elegy is not altogether fortunate, in view of its other meanings for Milton and his age. His own term is monody (the heading of *Lycidas* in 1645). Perhaps threnody is the best name for the genre, but 'elegy' has become established and must be accepted.

Histories of pastoral literature and studies of its many phases and subdivisions are too numerous, or too remote from *Lycidas*, to be listed here, but a few items may be: J. H. Hanford's pioneer analysis, 'The Pastoral Elegy and Milton's *Lycidas*,' *PMLA* 25 (1910), 403–47 (repr., with some editorial revisions, in C. A. Patrides, *Milton's Lycidas: The Tradition and the Poem*, New York, 1961; and, with the notes, in Hanford's *John Milton poet and humanist*, Cleveland, 1966; cited here from *PMLA*); *The Pastoral Elegy*, ed. T. P. Harrison and H. J. Leon (Austin, 1939), which contains, with apparatus, texts and translations of

Lost Milton goes back to the great originals of Greek tragedy and Greek and Roman epic, and the intervening histories of the two genres have at most a secondary and occasional relevance. His two pastoral monodies, in contrast, take their places in a tradition still developing in Milton's day, though no longer very vigorously, and they draw on its accumulated stores from Theocritus onward.

The pastoral elegy is a distinct division of pastoral poetry, but its history cannot be isolated from the larger history of pastoral; and in *Lycidas* Milton reaches out beyond the usual confines of elegy. Pastoral poetry originated in the songs of actual shepherds in Sicily, but its first literary exponent was Theocritus (*c.* 310–250 B.C.), of whom Sir E. K. Chambers wrote (*English Pastorals*, London, 1895, xxii):

Upon Theocritus, a lover of the country, trapped in . . . the court life of Ptolemaic Egypt, those bucolic rhythms, remembered so well from his childhood, had all the fascination which the simple exercises over the complex, a fascination wrought out of contrast and reminiscence. He wove them into poems of a delicate artificiality, preserving the main outlines of the actual life from which they sprang, but . . . rendering them with a keener sense of natural beauty, a more subtle music of the Doric speech, than ever yet glorified any oaten pipe at any festival of Artemis.

many of the elegies cited by Hanford and in the present sketch, and others besides; [and *Milton's "Lycidas"*, ed. Scott Elledge (New York, 1966), which includes five ancient and nine Renaissance pastoral elegies (some of the latter abridged), five contemporary elegies and extracts from the *Obsequies* for Edward King, an account of Milton and England in 1637, brief excerpts from mainly pre-modern critics, and (pp. 251–316) annotation of *Lycidas*]. To these may be added G. Norlin, 'The Conventions of the Pastoral Elegy,' *AJP* 32 (1911), 294–312, and Sir J. E. Sandys, 'The Literary Sources of Milton's "Lycidas,"' *Trans. Royal Soc. of Literature*, Ser. 2, 32 (1914), 233–64. [Some studies of elegies of various kinds are those of Ruth Wallerstein (III below, under 1950); A. L. Bennett, 'The Principal Rhetorical Conventions in the Renaissance Personal Elegy,' *SP* 51 (1954), 107–26; sections of O. B. Hardison, *The Enduring Monument: A Study of the Idea of Praise in Renaissance Literary Theory and Practice* (Chapel Hill, 1962), and of W. L. Grant, *Neo-Latin Literature and the Pastoral* (Chapel Hill, 1965). Much material has of course been accumulated by Milton's editors, who, along with other commentators, are drawn upon in the Notes below (IV). The many critiques summarized in III are more or less concerned with Milton's handling of the pastoral conventions.

Watson Kirkconnell is preparing a volume of sources and analogues for *Lycidas, Comus*, and *Paradise Regained*, on the pattern of his *Celestial Cycle* and *That Invincible Samson*. One unfamiliar piece included, in an admirable translation in *canzone* form, is William Gager's *Daphnis* (1586), on Sir Philip Sidney.]

Theocritus, then, was the founder of the literary pastoral in general, and indirectly of that pastoralism which was diffused through many later poems, not strictly definable as pastorals, including Milton's *Nativity*, *L'Allegro*, *Il Penseroso*, and *Comus*—a pastoralism which was to coalesce with the myth of the Golden Age and deepen a note of nostalgia, very evident in Spenser, though not conspicuous in Milton until he came to describe Eden.

Theocritus was likewise the founder of the pastoral elegy with his lament (*Idyl* 1) for Daphnis, smitten by a new love and resisting it to the death. The poem employed what was to be a common pastoral framework, a song sung for some rustic prize;[2] it introduced in germ the question 'Where were ye Nymphs?' and the procession of mourners, and the sympathetic sorrow of nature.[3] Through Virgil's imitation (*E.* 10) as well as directly, it exercised its influence on later pastoral elegies.

Though narrower in range than Theocritus, and inferior in dramatic interest, Bion and Moschus (to use the name long associated with the *Lament for Bion*) contributed to the development of the pastoral elegy. Bion's *Lament for Adonis* (*Idyl* 1), while not strictly a pastoral, helped to build the tradition by its incorporating of classic, indeed what is today called archetypal myth, though the seasonal renewal and destruction of Adonis are only obliquely hinted at the end. It has been said that a similar motif lies behind Theocritus and so behind the pastoral elegy at its very source. W. Y. Sellar wrote long ago:

Under the symbols of Linus, Daphnis, or Adonis, the country people of early times lamented the decay of the fresh beauty of spring, under the burning

---

[2] Here a bowl of ivy wood newly wrought, and alive with carvings, is described in detail. In contrast with this, Milton's description of the two 'cups' given him by Manso (*EpDam* 180–97) symbolizes heavenly love and life in heaven (Woodhouse, 'Milton's Pastoral Monodies,' *Studies in Honour of Gilbert Norwood*, Toronto, 1952, 269–70). *Idyl* 1 also has a refrain, a frequent though not a constant or peculiar feature of the pastoral elegy. [On these and other matters see the commentary on *EpDam* in *V.C.* 1.]

[3] The question appears in Theocritus 1. 66–9; Virgil, *E.* 10. 9–12; *Lyc* 50–5; the procession of mourners in Theocritus 1. 77–81; Moschus 3. 26–31 (*Lament for Bion*); Virgil, *E.* 10. 19–30; *Lyc* 103–31 and Milton's adaptation of the convention in *EpDam* 88–92. The sympathetic sorrow of nature is represented here only by the animals (71–5) and the general confusion of things attendant upon the death of Daphnis (132–6). See F. Kermode, *English Pastoral Poetry* (London, 1952), 21.

midsummer heat...In the Daphnis of Theocritus, the human passion of love produces the blighting influence on the life of the shepherd which in the original myth was produced by the fierce heat of summer on the tender life of the year. A still later development of the myth appears in the lament over the extinction of youthful genius by early death. (*The Roman Poets of the Augustan Age*, 3rd ed., Oxford, 1897, 155: quoted in Harrison–Leon, p. 1.)

This is the theme of the *Lament for Bion*, which inaugurates the long tradition of lament for a particular person, represented as shepherd and singer. In this *Lament*, which draws on Theocritus and echoes Bion's own *Lament for Adonis*, the mourner, says Hanford (414), now regards himself as 'the poetical successor of the dead shepherd,' and thus opens a way for that dwelling on his own concerns and ambitions which is to be so marked a feature of Milton's monodies.[4] The *Lament for Bion* elaborates the mourning of nature[5] and introduces some other recurrent features, such as the allusions to Hyacinthus and Orpheus,[6] and the contrast of nature's renewal and man's mortality.[7]

When Virgil took up the pastoral it had already accumulated themes and conventions which set it at a distance from actual shepherd life, and this distance he greatly increased by his stylistic elaboration, by premonitions of epic grandeur, and by making the pastoral a vehicle for comment on the state of Italy and his own fortunes, thus substituting for

[4] The poet's desire to descend to Hades, even as Orpheus did, and to bring back Bion to the hills (115–26) appears to symbolize the return of Bion in the person of his elegist. The poem established the tradition of the lament of a poet for a poet, which no doubt encouraged Milton to treat Lycidas (Edward King) as poet as well as priest.

[5] 'Wail, let me hear you wail, ye woodland glades, and thou Dorian water; and weep ye rivers, for Bion, the well beloved!...Now redden ye roses in your sorrow,...now thou hyacinth, whisper the letters on thee graven, and add a deeper *ai ai* to thy petals....And Echo in the rocks laments that thou art silent....Not so much did the dolphin mourn beside the seabanks....Nor so much...in the dells of dawn did the bird of Memnon bewail the son of the Morning, fluttering around his tomb, as they lamented for Bion dead' (1–43: *Theocritus, Bion and Moschus*, tr. Andrew Lang, London, 1880). We may note the emphasis on the flowers (cf. *Lyc* 45–9, 134–51) and the reference to Hyacinthus (cf. *Lyc* 106), the mourning of Echo (cf. *Lyc* 41), the dolphin (cf. *Lyc* 164).

[6] See notes 5 and 4 above. For Milton's reference to Orpheus see *Lyc* 58–63 and n.

[7] *Lament for Bion* 99–106. Christianity, as we see below, renders this contrast obsolete when it transforms the pattern of the elegy by insisting on man's immortality, but Milton (*EpDam* 94–111) can introduce a most effective contrast of man and the rest of nature (see Woodhouse, 'Monodies,' 267–8).

the dramatic realism of Theocritus something akin to allegory. This element was destined to be largely developed by Renaissance poets, notably Petrarch, Mantuan, and Spenser. Such wider reference does not belong to the pastoral elegy proper, but to the eclogue in general, a type of which Virgil may be regarded as the founder; and, until *Lycidas*, it will enter the lament only when the subject is a public figure, as in Petrarch's *Argus*, on Robert of Naples, and Ronsard's *Angelot*, on Henry II of France.

One such death of a public figure was celebrated by Virgil, whose Daphnis (*E.* 5) was identified with Julius Caesar by a tradition that goes back to the time of Servius (Hanford, *PMLA* 25, 421, n. 3). Here Virgil extends the pastoral elegy to lament one not a poet; and, building on Theocritus 1, he yet produces an effect startlingly different. For here death and mourning are opposed and submerged by apotheosis and triumph. 'In this joyful motif lies the poem's most important contribution to elegy; for later pastoralists it remained only to substitute the joys of a Christian heaven' (Harrison–Leon, 263). Earlier laments assumed the pagan view of death as the end, or at the most as entry into a dim existence among the shades; the idea of Bion's permitted return is only a conceit or perhaps a veiled claim that his art lives again in his successor (see above, notes 7 and 4), and the implications of revival in seasonal myths find—despite the assertions of some modern critics—little or no overt expression in the pastoral elegy until Christianity gives them a new and personal significance. No doubt the contrast between pagan and Christian in the presence of death can be too sharply drawn. D. C. Allen (*Vision*, 43) reminds us that the Greek rhetoricians, prescribing the topics to be dealt with in memorials of the dead, ended with arguments against mourning and the assurance that the departed had not only escaped from the trammels of earthly existence but were now in Elysium—a pattern which the Fathers could take over and complete. It remains true, however, that in extant pastoral elegies the rhetorical topics of comfort have no place, and that, in any event, only apotheosis could supply a triumph that included consolation. Here the luck that attended Virgil in the Messianic eclogue did not forsake him;

he was able to strike out in advance the basic pattern of the Christian elegy as well as of the Nativity poem. It was not luck alone, however, but some anticipation also of later sensibility.[8] There is, of course, no such note of triumph in *Eclogue* 10, a deliberate imitation of Theocritus' *Idyl* 1, in which Virgil's friend and fellow-poet Gallus takes the place of the mythical Daphnis, and which underlines what is to be a notable feature of the tradition, virtuosity in imitation, combined in the best examples with a degree of originality. Gallus is a soldier as well as a lover and poet, and this permits the introduction of a martial strain; there is also a deliberate contrasting of real sorrows with Arcadian happiness (*E.* 10. 31–6).[9] In a word, Virgil is the second great source, and the dominating one, of the European pastoral in general and the pastoral elegy in particular, though the full harvest was delayed.

Post-Augustan examples of the eclogue are unimpressive, and pastoral elegies rare, though the *Meliboeus* of Nemesian is echoed in a number of later poems (Harrison–Leon, 50–4, 266–7). But the Carolingian renaissance produced one lament of singular interest and some historical importance: the *Egloga duarum sanctimonialium* of the monk Radbertus commemorates the death of St Adalhard, who founded in Saxony a new monastery of his order, the two nuns, Galatea and Phyllis, speaking respectively for the new foundation and the parent house. There are quotations from Virgil's *Eclogue* 5, and the basic progression culminates in the consoling contemplation of reward in heaven; the poem alle-

---

[8] As well as an expression of the best in Virgil's own time and place. Thus it is not imagined that the apotheosis of Daphnis will render him indifferent to the fate of mankind and Rome: he is to be always gracious to his own, and for this due rites are to be paid to him (65–80). Lycidas, though in heaven, is, we remember, to become the Genius of the shore and beneficent to all who traverse the perilous flood (183–5); and there are a number of intervening examples.

[9] Milton is to make uniquely effective use of this contrast between the real and the fictitious in *Lyc* (Woodhouse, 'Monodies,' 264, 274); and there also the progression of Christian elegy, anticipated in Virgil's *E.* 5, underlies the total movement, as Hanford has noticed (420–1), of *E.* 10.

[F. R. B. Godolphin ('Milton, *Lycidas* and Propertius, *Elegies*, III, 7,' *MLN* 49, 1934, 162–6), while allowing for the dominance of the pastoral tradition, found some structural and incidental parallels between *Lyc* and Propertius' non-pastoral elegy *On the drowning of Paetus*; see below, notes on 51, 58–63, 102.]

gorizes the theme of the *Vita* to which it is appended (Harrison–Leon, 268); in the image of shepherd and flock the classical and Christian associations are securely joined, a union obvious but of great significance for later poetry and not least for *Lycidas*; and here, finally, Christianity gives access to the Old Testament, a third and important source of pastoral poetry.[10]

In Petrarch the medieval elaboration of allegory has its full effect in the eclogue, whether turned to the purpose of satiric comment on the state of the church (as in *Eclogues* 6 and 7) or of commemoration of the dead. In *Eclogue* 6, 'Pamphilus, Saint Peter in pastoral guise, rebukes Mitio, Clement V, who was leading a corrupt life at Avignon, for the ill-keeping of his flocks,' while in *Eclogue* 7 'Epy or France conspires with Mitio, whom she has corrupted.'[11] 'In the introduction of ecclesiastical satire into the pastoral, Petrarch led the way for Mantuan and Marot, who were followed in turn by Spenser' (Hanford, 428).

In *Eclogue* 2, *Argus* (Harrison–Leon, 65–71, 270–2), Petrarch mourns the death of his patron, Robert of Naples, and the disorders that followed, thus combining pastoral lament with comment on the contemporary world. A brief summary will suggest his allegorical method and the place of the poem in the history of pastoral elegy:

Ideus (Barili, in Naples) recounts the mourning of Silvius (Petrarch, withdrawn to Avignon) and Pythias (his friend Barbato, also absent) for the dead Argus (Robert). He begins with an allegorical account of the situation. The golden sun (Robert) was drawing to the west and shepherds and their flocks were enjoying unrivalled peace and plenty. A black cloud obscured the sun and night suddenly fell (death of Robert). Then a fearful storm burst, and a tall cypress, the sun's darling, was struck down (the murder of Andrew, Robert's grand-nephew and heir); the terrified shepherds fled. When the storm (political

---

[10] Hanford, 426–8, Harrison–Leon, 6–7, 267–70. On the importance of Hebrew pastoralism cf. Allen, who remarks (*Vision*, 56–7) that Milton 'was certainly aware of the analogue between the shepherd king of Israel and the pastoral kings of Arcadia and knew that the relationship between the poetry of the Bible and that of antiquity had been described by every apologist for poets from Boccaccio to Giles Fletcher.'

[11] Hanford, 428. [For texts of *Eclogues* 6 and 7 see v. 1 of Petrarch's *Poesie Minori*, ed. D. Rossetti (3 v., Milan, 1829–34). Most of 6 and part of 7 are translated and annotated in Elledge, 45–54.]

upheaval) abated for the time, Pythias, weeping, broke silence with a prayer to Jupiter (Christ) for mercy on the goats (mankind) with which he had once deigned to live (27–37). Hearing from his refuge the voice of his friend, Silvius recites the omens that foretold their woes, and they determine to sing the lost Argus as shepherds once sang Daphnis (Virgil, *E.* 5). Pythias praises, under pastoral images, the manifold accomplishments and beneficent acts of Argus, and bewails their loss (69–102). Then Silvius, asked for his promised song, takes up the lament, but not without a consoling thought: Argus is gone, never to return, gone through trackless ways to the mountains (heaven), there to entrust to Jove (God) the care of his earthly flock: 'Argus, farewell! Brief the delay, we shall all follow thee' (103–21). And Ideus concludes his narrative.

Eclogue 11, *Galatea*, is a more purely personal memorial, with no public reference and with fewer pastoral elements. Proceeding to the tomb of Galatea (Laura), the sisters, Niobe (uncontrollable grief) and Fusca (reason confused with passion and earthly thought), encounter Fulgida (reason illuminated by faith), who points on to the regard of heaven, and Niobe, convinced, declares that, while they live on earth, they will treasure Galatea in their hearts as the model of beauty and virtue. (Harrison–Leon, 272, find a prototype in the women met by the angel at the tomb of Christ.)

Boccaccio's *Eclogue* 14, *Olympia* (Harrison–Leon, 77–91, 273–4; Elledge, 54–67), is remarkable in several aspects. The opening, in which Silvius (Boccaccio), his servants and his dog discover what is at first taken for fire in the night woods, restores something of drama to the pastoral. It is no fire, but the light of a heavenly visitation: Olympia (his dead child) surrounded by her brothers and sisters. Silvius welcomes them with a promise of pagan festival and rejoicing. They sing instead the saving merits of Codrus (Christ). Before they leave, Olympia, to comfort her father, tells him of their dwelling in Elysium, of which Minciades (Dante) has sung; and there follows a long description, based in part on the *Divine Comedy* but with mingled pastoral and pagan elements, and allegorical throughout. They depart, and the old man is left weeping; but *surgit | Lucifer et mediis iam sol emittitur umbris.*

During the Renaissance, and stimulated in part by renewed access to the three Greek pastoral poets in the Aldine edition (1495), and by the recovery of the Greek romances of Longus and others, there was a wide diffusion of pastoralism, which spread from the formal eclogue to lyric, drama, and prose romance. At the same time eclogues and pastoral elegies multiplied: we can notice only a few examples.

Most famous and influential were the *Eclogues* of Baptista Mantuanus (ed. W. P. Mustard, 1911), [which were widely read in European schools, as we are reminded by Holofernes' quotation and exclamation, 'Ah, good old Mantuan!' (Shakespeare, *L.L.L.* 4. 2. 95–102)]. *Eclogue* 5 condemned the neglect of poets, a theme as old as Theocritus 16, and was cited by E. K. in relation to Spenser's *October*. *Eclogue* 6 attacked the corruptions of town life; 7 and 8 dealt allegorically with the religious life and its motives [Mantuan was Vicar-General of the Carmelite Order]. *Eclogue* 9, following the precedent of Petrarch, exposed ecclesiastical abuses at Rome; it became in its turn a model for Protestant attacks on clerical corruption, notably in Spenser's *July* and *September*. Though he wrote no pastoral elegies, Mantuan gave authority to the steadily widening range of subjects for pastoral verse, and, through Spenser, prepared the way for the so-called digressions in *Lycidas*.

Second only to Mantuan in fame was Jacopo Sannazaro (Harrison–Leon, 92–111, 274–7; see also *Jacopo Sannazaro: Arcadia & Piscatorial Eclogues*, tr. Ralph Nash, Detroit, 1966), who made various innovations. He wrote pastorals in Italian as well as in Latin; he composed his *Arcadia* in mingled prose and verse, and, 'restoring the Arcadia of Virgil as a setting,' he made it 'the ideal land of escape from reality, a retreat from the turmoil of actual life'; and—taking a hint perhaps from Theocritus 21—he inaugurated the piscatory eclogue, with fishermen and coastal scenes in place of shepherds and pastoral. Despite these innovations, he practised assiduously the humanistic art of close imitation, and his pages are 'a mosaic of paraphrase and reminiscence,' not only of Virgil and of Petrarch and Boccaccio, but of the Greek bucolic poets (Harrison–Leon, 10–11, 275–6). That Sannazaro's classicism tends rather to replace than to clothe Christian sentiment is clear from his three pastoral elegies (all in Harrison–Leon). In the *Arcadia*, the *Androgeo*, in memory of his father, begins with a prose lament in which the departed is said to be happy only in the honour paid to his memory by gods and men, and while the verses (*Eclogue* 5) that follow commence by picturing the pastoral elysium to which he has retired, they end on the note of the prose lament. *Mamillia* (*Eclogue* 11) is a pastoral lament for his mother, ending indeed on a note of hope, but one which strangely mingles hints of immortal life and hopes for the recognition of the poet's genius. And in the *Piscatory Eclogue* 1, Lycidas' lament for his dead love, Phyllis, ends with her gathering everlasting flowers in Elysium, looking down beneficently upon the fishermen and honoured by them as a goddess; but the concluding dialogue returns to the recognition of the poet's song—and incidentally achieves its quiet ending by returning Mycon to his companions and their labours while Lycidas lingers by the tomb.

If the Christian note of consolation is muted in Sannazaro, it is wholly suppressed in the more rigorously classical *Alcon* of Castiglione (in Harrison–Leon and Elledge), one of the finest of Neo-Latin pastorals. This fact is the more striking since in some respects *Alcon* is the closest known analogue to the *Epitaphium Damonis*: in both, grief for an intimate friend and boyhood companion finds moving expression through the pastoral conventions; in both the poet laments his absence from the dying friend, and in both the poignancy is heightened by the thought of reunion which then engaged the singer's mind. But in *Alcon* there is no progression from lament to triumph, which is the structural principle of the *Epitaphium*: the end is an empty tomb, and if the nymphs deck it with amaranth woven with their violets, there is no word of hope in the legend they inscribe (152–4):

> Alconem postquam rapuerunt impia fata,
> Collacrimant duri montes, et consitus atra est
> Nocte dies; sunt candida nigra, et dulcia amara.

[Some suggested parallels between *Alcon* and *Lycidas* are recorded in the notes in IV below.]

From Italy the classical pastoral in the vernacular spread to France and England. Apart from Marot, who is linked with Spenser, there is no need in this sketch to take account of French pastoral elegies: of

these the most important are Ronsard's *Angelot* (on Henry II), an example
of the movement from mourning to triumph over death, and *Adonis*
(both in Harrison–Leon; extracts from *Angelot* in Elledge).

The formal pastoral was naturalized in England by Spenser's *Shepheardes Calender* (1579), that compendium of bucolic themes. The
pastoral elegy is represented by *November*, a lament for 'Dido' (an
unidentified or possibly imaginary woman) modelled on Marot's elegy
for Louise of Savoy (Harrison–Leon; extracts in Elledge). It is a simple
example of the pattern—the transition from lament to triumph—set by
Virgil's *Eclogue* 5 for the Christian elegy:

> The water Nymphs, that wont with her to sing and daunce,
> And for her girlond Olive braunches beare,
> Now balefull boughes of Cypres doen advaunce:
> The Muses, that were wont greene bayes to weare,
> Now bringen bitter Eldre braunches seare:
>> The fatall sisters eke repent,
>> Her vitall threde so soone was spent.
>>> O heavie herse,
> Morne now my Muse, now morne with heavie cheare.
>>> O carefull verse.... (143–52)

> Why wayle we then? why weary we the Gods with playnts,
> As if some evill were to her betight?
> She raignes a goddesse now emong the saintes,
> That whilome was the saynt of shepheards light:
> And is enstalled nowe in heavens hight.
>> I see thee blessed soule, I see,
>> Walke in Elisian fieldes so free.
>>> O happy herse,
> Might I once come to thee (O that I might)
>>> O joyfull verse. (173–82)

This is the traditional pattern that is to be adapted in *Lycidas* and the
Epitaphium Damonis, though in its archaic style and rustic simplicity
November (like the *Shepheardes Calender* in general) is extremely remote
from *Lycidas*, the most elaborate example of the Virgilian tradition. In
Astrophel, his pastoral lament for Sidney, Spenser adheres to the basic

pattern of Christian elegy, and with a new turn reconciles the two ideas of the happiness of the departed and the grief of those who mourn (*Lay of Clorinda* 91–6):

> But live thou there still happie, happie spirit,
> And give us leave thee here thus to lament:
> Not thee that doest thy heavens joy inherit,
> But our owne selves that here in dole are drent.
>> Thus do we weep and waile, and wear our eies,
>> Mourning in others, our own miseries.

It is not in virtue of his elegies alone, however, that Spenser occupies a conspicuous place in the background of *Lycidas*. Besides *November*, the *Shepheardes Calender* has two other points of contact, and significantly with Milton's so-called digressions. *July* and *September*, stemming from Mantuan, anticipate Milton's attack on a corrupt clergy and the wolf of Rome. *October*, partly linked with Mantuan's complaint of the neglect of poets, touches on the true poet's inspiration and reward, and momentarily (79–84) opens a vista toward Milton's passage on the poet and fame:

> O pierlesse Poesye, where is then thy place?
> If nor in Princes pallace thou doe sitt...
> Ne brest of baser birth doth thee embrace.
> Then make thee winges of thine aspyring wit,
> And, whence thou camst, flye backe to heaven apace.

That these are themes of separate eclogues, and traditional themes at that, illustrates the fact that *Lycidas* draws not only upon the tradition of the pastoral elegy but upon that of the eclogue in general as it develops from Virgil down through Spenser.[12]

---

[12] [L. S. Friedland (*MLN* 27, 1912, 246–50) linked Spenser's *Ruines of Time* with the elegiac tradition and found thematic and incidental resemblances to *Lycidas*.

To suggestions made by Hanford and others of Spenserian influence on *Lycidas*, T. B. Stroup ('*Lycidas* and the Marinell Story,' *SAMLA Studies in Milton*, Gainesville, 1953, 100–13) adds what he takes to be unconscious recollections of the fate of a guardian of the shore (chiefly in *F.Q.* 3. 4, 3. 8, 4. 11–12), an episode closely associated with water. He finds 'not so much verbal similarities, though these occur, as similar situations, similar phrasing and tone, and similar images.' These include the picture of Marinell's

Lycidas

In the six or seven decades before Milton wrote, among plenty of pastoral verse there were relatively few pastoral elegies and nothing that adds to the traditions that culminate in *Lycidas*. Two Latin elegies by Giles Fletcher the elder, on Walter Haddon and his son Clere, have been thought to have had some influence on *Lycidas* (W. B. Austin, 'Milton's *Lycidas* and Two Latin Elegies by Giles Fletcher, the Elder,' *SP* 44, 1947, 41–55 [cf. L. E. Berry, 'Five Latin Poems by Giles Fletcher, the Elder,' *Anglia* 79, 1961–2, 338–77]). Clere Haddon, Fletcher's contemporary and friend, was a young man of brilliant promise who was drowned in the Cam—circumstances which might have prompted Milton to turn to the *Poematum...Duo Libri* (1576) of the elder Haddon, where the poems were printed with other memorial verses. In *Adonis*, on Clere Haddon, the speaker is Lycidas (Fletcher). Like Milton, Fletcher recalls, under pastoral images, the common pursuits of himself and his dead friend; both poets dwell on the changed feelings with which they now contemplate the old haunts; both 'at first reproach the Nymphs,' and then recognize 'the futility of such reproaches'; both 'suggest the tragedy of "unfulfilled renown"'; both let their thoughts dally with false surmise; and both poems have an 'apotheosis near the close.' The elegy on the elder Haddon presents fewer similarities in details (as in circumstances), but is described by Austin as a protracted meditation on 'essentially the same theme as Milton's famous passage on Fame.' 'The phrase *quid juvat*, "what boots it," runs like a motif' through the poem. Each poet is preoccupied with his own ambitions and the possibility of their frustration by untimely death; each voices the ideal of self-denying endeavour and contrasts it with a life of carefree self-indulgence; while Milton looks for fame in heaven, Fletcher reflects that 'virtue is not only its own reward but brings also a fame which defies the fates.'

The advent of English pastoral with Spenser did not drive out the Latin. Thomas Watson's *Meliboeus* (1590) he himself immediately

mother and her fellow nymphs, their lament for and ministration to her wounded son, her use of a team of dolphins, 'her complaint on fame and on the seeming fruitlessness of immortal life,' and other items, such as the nymph Panope (Proteus' charwoman).]

translated into English as *An Eglogue Upon the death of...Sir Francis Walsingham* (both Latin and English texts are given in *Thomas Watson. Poems*, ed. E. Arber, London, 1870, 139–75). Here two shepherds, Tityrus (Thomas Walsingham) and Corydon (Watson), mourn Meliboeus (Sir Francis) in alternating dirges until the evening star bids them drive their flocks homeward. As toward the end (169–71) the note changes from lament to triumph, we encounter a startling blend of the Christian, the classical, and the Arcadian, the elements which in *Lycidas* Milton will first contrast and then with subtle art combine:

> Our Meliboeus livs where Seraphins
>   doe praise the Highest in their glorious flames:
> Where flowes the knowledge of wise Cherubins:...
>   where Throans exhibit earthlie deeds and names...
>
>   Let us be joifull after long annoie,
>   Since Meliboeus livs in perfit joie.
> Now Meliboeus in comparelesse place,
>   drinkes Nectar, eates divine Ambrosia;
> And hath fruition of eternall grace,
>   and with his countnance cheeres Arcadia.
> Then while his spirit dwels in heavnlie towres,
>   let us performe what honor dutie willes:
> Let us adorne his sacred tumb with flowres,
>   and sweete it with the riches of our hilles.

Nor is this all: Walsingham was the servant and guardian of the state and the succession will not fail.

We need not linger with the miscellaneous pastoral verse of the Spenserians, but may mention the last notable pastoral elegy before *Lycidas*, William Drummond's *Teares, On the Death of Moeliades*, his lament for Prince Henry (d. 1612).[13] Two bits of pastoralism (89–92, 126–8) may be quoted:

13 [Both *Teares* and *A Pastorall Elegie on the Death of S. A*[ntonye] *A*[lexander] are given in Harrison–Leon, but the former is quoted—like other poems of Drummond's cited in this commentary—from the *Poetical Works*, ed. Kastner, 1, 75–81. The other piece is in 2, 141–5.]

Lycidas

The Shepheards left their Flockes with downe-cast Eyes,
Disdaining to looke up to angrie Skies:
Some broke their Pipes, and some in sweet-sad Layes,
Made senslesse things amazed at thy Praise....

Sweet Rose, a Princes Death in Purple mourne.
O Hyacinthes, for ay your AI keepe still,
Nay, with moe Markes of Woe your Leaves now fill....

The triumphal close (179–82, 189–96) ends with the couplet-refrain:

Rest blessed Spright, rest saciate with the Sight
Of him, whose Beames both dazell and delight,
Life of all Lives, Cause of each other Cause,
The Spheare, and Center, where the Minde doth pause....

For ever rest, thy Praise Fame may enroule
In golden Annalles, whilst about the Pole
The slow Boötes turnes, or Sunne doth rise
With skarlet Scarfe, to cheare the mourning Skies:
The Virgines to thy Tombe may Garlands beare
Of Flowres, and on each Flowre let fall a Teare.
Moeliades sweet courtly Nymphes deplore,
From Thuly to Hydaspes pearlie Shore.

Drummond's pastoral elegy on Sir Anthony Alexander (d. September 1637), the son of his friend and fellow-poet, Sir William Alexander, appeared early in 1638, the year of *Lycidas*. Drummond took the name Alcon from Castiglione and followed closely the structure and themes of that elegy, even to the exclusion of the Christian note of triumph and consolation at the end; but, for all its imitative character, it is not necessarily inferior (as Harrison thinks) to the *Teares*. And it offers some points of interest in comparison and contrast, not with *Lycidas*, but with the *Epitaphium Damonis*.

[Thus at a time when the tradition of the pastoral elegy, if not moribund, had almost ceased to develop, it was crowned by the greatest exemplar in any language.

Several discussions of sources, accepted or proposed, may be added here.

L. G. Kelly ('*Contaminatio* in *Lycidas*: An Example of Vergilian Poetics,' *Revue de l'Université d'Ottawa* 38, 1968, 588–98) seeks to show how Milton carries on the Virgilian 'fusing of material from several sources to produce one harmonious whole.' Thus the first ten lines of *Lycidas* are an expansion of the first two and a half of Virgil's *E.* 10, but that is hardly realized until we reach the distinct echo in line 10 [see 10 n. in Notes below]. Kelly takes up such canonical examples as Orpheus [see Theocritus in 51 n. below], prepared for by lines 42–4; the procession of mourners; Camus, a *contaminatio* of Silvanus and Pan (Virgil, *E.* 10. 24–7); the kinship between Gallus and Edward King; the apotheosis of Daphnis (Virgil, *E.* 5). '*Lycidas* is a poem solidly based on Greek pastoral conventions, but to achieve this end Milton used Roman techniques as exemplified in Vergil.' As Virgil in his fifth and tenth eclogues re-created Theocritus' first Idyl, Milton re-created all three poems: 'the first 131 lines are drawn mainly from Vergil X with heavy overtones of Theocritus; from 132 to 185 is based on key ideas from Vergil V; and the rest of the poem is modelled on the last section of Vergil X,' both poets bidding farewell to pastoral. While familiar particulars are somewhat freshened by this approach, such a summary greatly over-simplifies a very complex poem; and the restricted focus virtually excludes Milton's real theme, which adds other dimensions to his pastoralism.

A non-pastoral source has been proposed by Bayly Turlington ('Milton's Lycidas and Horace's Odes, I. 7,' *Tennessee Philological Bulletin* 6, 1969, 2–12): 'Teucer's misfortune parallels that of Edward King. Both were victims of disordered situations; both upon water came to the end of the kind of lives they were leading; both were saved by divine agency, King achieving heavenly immortality, Teucer achieving peace of mind regarding his earthly future.' Along with this and other thematic suggestions, numerous particulars are cited. While Milton of course would know the ode, one may not be convinced of affinity in either general theme or details; the parallels seem to be strained.

A non-classical influence on *Lycidas* has been suggested by Gretchen L. Finney ('A Musical Background for "Lycidas,"' *HLQ* 15, 1951–2,

325–49; *Musical Backgrounds* [1962], 195–219). She thinks 'that the poem shows definite structural parallels with sung poetry of Milton's day, and that it suggests a definite manner of musical setting which was peculiar to a specific musical form' (198). She finds that various elements in *Lycidas* point to 'a large vocal form, dramatic in character, which has at least three divisions, each made up of a series of solos, both aria and recitative, and probably choruses' (207). Such a form, with prologue and epilogue, and dealing with 'a pastoral subject in which classic and Christian ideas are combined,' suggests Italian musical drama; and the middle section of *Lycidas* is especially akin to the Italian oratorio. Mrs Finney cites a number of Italian operatic works on the theme of Orpheus, in particular *La favola d'Orfeo* (1607) by Alessandro Striggio and Monteverdi, which 'reveals striking similarities to "Lycidas" both in organization and in treatment of subject,' 'many...coincidental with common interest in the pastoral eclogue,' but others, 'for the most part between the first and last parts of each work, that are unexpected' (213).]

III. CRITICISM [D.B.]

In this section Dr Johnson's notorious paragraphs are followed by a brief sketch of criticism up through 1926. Thereafter come summaries of and quotations from the following critics, in chronological order: E. M. W. Tillyard; J. C. Ransom; P. E. More; M. Y. Hughes; W. Haller; G. W. Knight; G. C. Taylor; C. Williams; A. Barker; E. Wagenknecht; R. Graves; D. Daiches; J. Miles; M. M. Ross; R. P. Adams; C. W. Mayerson; H. V. S. Ogden; Rex Warner; M. Mack; R. Wallerstein; C. Brooks and J. E. Hardy (and E. H. Marks); W. Shumaker; A. S. P. Woodhouse; J. M. French; D. C. Allen; F. T. Prince; K. Muir; W. Sypher; R. Tuve; N. Frye; R. L. Brett; G. S. Fraser; M. H. Abrams; R. Beum; M. Lloyd; L. Nelson; G. Williamson; K. Jones; J. S. Lawry; P. Ramsey; R. Daniells; W. G. Madsen; M. Nicolson; I. G. MacCaffrey; J. Frank; C. H. Hinnant; B. Rajan; W. J. Grace; J. S. Lawry; J. H. Raleigh; J. Reesing; C. F. Stone; T. B. Stroup; K. Winter; J. Auffret; J. Carey; J. B. Leishman; J. A. Wittreich; A. Fowler.

Fourteen of the critics named are included, with editorial apparatus, in the useful anthology of C. A. Patrides, *Milton's Lycidas: The Tradition and the Poem* (New York, 1961). Some scholars and critics are cited in I and II above, and many in IV below.

S. Johnson (*Lives*, ed. Hill, I, 163–5): 'One of the poems on which much praise has been bestowed is *Lycidas*; of which the diction is harsh, the rhymes uncertain, and the numbers unpleasing. What beauty there is we must therefore seek in the sentiments and images. It is not to be considered as the effusion of real passion; for passion runs not after remote allusions and obscure opinions. Passion plucks no berries from the myrtle and ivy, nor calls upon Arethuse and Mincius, nor tells of "rough satyrs and fauns with cloven heel." "Where there is leisure for fiction there is little grief."

'In this poem there is no nature, for there is no truth; there is no art, for there is nothing new. Its form is that of a pastoral, easy, vulgar, and therefore disgusting: whatever images it can supply are long ago exhausted; and its inherent improbability always forces dissatisfaction on the mind. When Cowley tells of Hervey that they studied together, it is easy to suppose how much he must miss the companion of his labours and the partner of his discoveries; but what image of tenderness can be excited by these lines! "We drove a field...dews of night." We know that they never drove a field, and that they had no flocks to batten; and though it be allowed that the representation may be allegorical, the true meaning is so uncertain and remote that it is never sought because it cannot be known when it is found.

'Among the flocks and copses and flowers appear the heathen deities, Jove and Phoebus, Neptune and Æolus, with a long train of mythological imagery, such as a College easily supplies. Nothing can less display knowledge or less exercise invention than to tell how a shepherd has lost his companion and must now feed his flocks alone, without any judge of his skill in piping; and how one god asks another god what is become of Lycidas, and how neither god can tell. He who thus grieves will excite no sympathy; he who thus praises will confer no honour.

'This poem has yet a grosser fault. With these trifling fictions are mingled the most awful and sacred truths, such as ought never to be polluted with such irreverent combinations. The shepherd likewise is now a feeder of sheep, and afterwards an ecclesiastical pastor, a super-intendent of a Christian flock. Such equivocations are always unskilful; but here they are indecent, and at least approach to impiety, of which, however, I believe the writer not to have been conscious.

'Such is the power of reputation justly acquired that its blaze drives away the eye from nice examination. Surely no man could have fancied that he read *Lycidas* with pleasure had he not known its author.'

Dr Johnson's blunt censure of *Lycidas*, 'the first critique of the poem by a major English literary critic' (Fleischauer, below), was, we see, directed against pastoral artificiality, the lack of sincere personal grief, the mingling of pagan and sacred allusions, and harsh diction and irregu-lar versification. Such strictures were partly conditioned by Johnson's temperament and by the climate of his age (although they displeased some people), and they are quite understandable, even if no longer shared. That they were based on critical principles is vigorously main-tained by Warren Fleischauer ('Johnson, *Lycidas*, and the Norms of Criticism,' *Johnsonian Studies*, Cairo, 1962, 235–56). Thomas Warton, whose annotations were of permanent value (as these Variorum notes amply indicate), made only incidental critical remarks, but to *Lycidas* and *Comus* he appended short general estimates, defending both against Johnson. Hazlitt's short essay, 'On Milton's Lycidas' (*Examiner*, 6 August, 1815: *Works*, ed. Howe, 4, 31–6), was mainly a defence against Johnson's condemnation of 'pedantry and want of feeling' and the mixture of pagan fiction with Christian truth. Milton was happily at home with both art and nature, with mythological allusions in their imaginative reality and with flowers of everyday observation.

Nearly all the valuable interpretation of *Lycidas* has come in the last forty years, and we can best measure changes in focus and depth if we glance rapidly at orthodox views of the later nineteenth and the early twentieth century. The critics dealt almost wholly in generalities and said much the same things. As James G. Nelson observes (*The Sublime Puritan:*

Milton and the Victorians, Madison, 1963, 102–3), the three periods of Milton's life provided a critical pattern: the young Milton, the cultivated, courtly, sensuous poet of *L'Allegro* and *Il Penseroso*, was submerged and soured in the Puritan polemicist who was strongly present in the late major poems. This view was congenial to the anti-Puritan prejudice so common throughout the nineteenth century and had a notable exemplar in Arnold. In his one elaborate discussion of Milton ('A French Critic on Milton,' *Mixed Essays*, 1879) Arnold only mentioned *Lycidas* (quoting Johnson with a shudder), but he followed Scherer in emphasizing a long conflict in the poet between 'the Renascence and Puritanism' and, still more, the power of style that saved the later works in spite of their ideas. For critics in general, the rigour of Puritanism began to show itself in *Comus*; at the same time it was St Peter's Puritan attack on the clergy that supplied the animating passion, indeed the main theme, of *Lycidas*. Otherwise, apart from comments on pastoral beauties, the critics hardly even attempted to explain why it was the great poem they agreed that it was.

One representative and influential witness was Mark Pattison (*Milton*, 1879, 29–31), for whom *Lycidas* was 'the high-water mark of English Poesy and of Milton's own production'—a phrase that was to be often echoed. With all its exquisite pastoralism *Lycidas* opened up, in St Peter's speech, 'a deeper vein of feeling, a patriot passion' of a dangerous and enigmatic vehemence comparable only to that of Cassandra in *Agamemnon*. Pattison's whole critique is an elaboration of this contrast and conflict in *Lycidas*, in Milton, and in England. 'The fanaticism of the covenanter and the sad grace of Petrarch seem to meet in Milton's monody. Yet these opposites, instead of neutralising each other, are blended into one harmonious whole by the presiding, but invisible, genius of the poet.' In St Peter's invective 'we have the preluding mutterings of the storm which was to sweep away mask and revel and song, to inhibit the drama, and suppress poetry.... In *Lycidas*, for a moment, the tones of both ages, the past and the coming, are combined, and then Milton leaves behind him for ever the golden age, and one half of his poetic genius. He never fulfilled the promise with which *Lycidas* concludes, "To-morrow to fresh woods and pastures new."' Pattison said similar things, more briefly, in Ward's *English Poets* (1880, 2, 298–9). *Lycidas* 'is the touchstone of taste'—a phrase used by Tennyson, apparently earlier (*Alfred Lord Tennyson: A Memoir*, London, 1897, 1, 36). The poem's 'burning heat of passion' is not sorrow for King but concern for the church; in St Peter's speech 'first emerges the Milton of *Paradise Lost* and *Samson*.'

Later critics echoed Pattison's formula (e.g. Oliver Elton in his small edition of *Lycidas*, Oxford, 1893, reprinted 1929; J. H. B. Masterman, *The Age of Milton*, London, 1897), or made vague or incidental comments on style, or did both together. Saintsbury, in a page of his *Short History of English Literature* (London, 1898), a page partly followed in his chapter on Milton in the *Cambridge History of English Literature* (7, 1911, 129–30), managed, as he so often did, to skate around his subject without saying anything; Saintsbury also used *Lycidas*, with similar results, in 'Milton and the Grand Style' (*Milton Memorial Lectures 1908*, ed. P. W. Ames, London, 1909; *Collected Essays and Papers*, London, 3, 1923). W. J. Courthope, in his spacious *History of English Poetry* (3, 1903, 393–5), focused on Milton's echoes of ancient pastorals, but noted ominous signs of religious controversy. Sir Herbert Grierson (*The First Half of the Seventeenth Century*, New York, 1906, 183) affirmed that 'Johnson's criticism of *Lycidas* as an elegy does not altogether miss the mark.' *Lycidas* shows the emergence of the classical artist, 'combatively Puritan in spirit.' There are only a few moving lines or passages in the poem; it commands admiration as a work of art, and one in the grand style. In *Six Essays on Johnson* (Oxford, 1910, 28–9) Sir Walter Raleigh, though almost frightened at his own temerity, was likewise inclined to endorse Johnson's complaints: 'Is the ceremonial procession of Triton, Camus, and St. Peter an example of Milton's imagination at its best?'

No more interpretative light came from such zealous and notable editors of successive generations as Masson and Verity. Masson, whose strength was of course biographical and historical, contented himself as both biographer and editor with little more than paraphrase. Verity, whose edition of *Lycidas* and other poems (Cambridge, 1891) was re-printed up to at least 1924, saw the poem as 'a study in the pastoral style,' in which St Peter's speech was a violent incongruity barely defensible on the ground of pastoral tradition. After this partial catalogue of inadequacy and misplaced emphasis, it is refreshing to read the six full pages in W. V. Moody's edition of Milton (1899). Moody, a poet as well as a scholar, made what seems to be the nearest approach in the period to modern understanding of *Lycidas*. He recognized, more clearly and firmly than others, the powerfully original handling of a traditional mode, the mythic quality of Milton's wide-ranging allusiveness, the dynamic unity of a structure that barely controls surging emotion. And he saw much of the symbolic import of the poem, which others did not see at all: the death of a young cleric and poet was not merely an excuse for blasting the clergy but was 'a type of touching unfulfillment,' of 'the pathos of mortality,' and for Milton 'the poet and the preacher are one voice.'

However, a number of critics continued for decades to play the old tunes. In an often discerning essay of 67 pages, mainly on Milton the classicist, J. W. Mackail only mentioned *Lycidas* a few times, without discussion (*The Springs of Helicon*, London, 1909). Saintsbury's comments of 1908 and 1911 we have noticed. W. Tuckwell, in the critical part of a small monograph on *Lycidas* (London, 1911), repeated Pattison. W. P. Ker, in several pages of his Clark Lectures for 1912 (*Form and Style in Poetry*, ed. R. W. Chambers, London, 1928, 122–5, etc.), answered Johnson's complaint about unreal artifice and said nothing directly about Milton's theme; but he was aware that *Lycidas* 'is magnificent but not simple,' and he may have had a fuller understanding than he expressed. John Bailey (*Milton*, 1915, 123–31), like many others, concerned himself with Dr Johnson and with particular conventions and passages, but he touched the matter of form and stated a part of Milton's theme: 'the death of all who have been or will be loved in all the world, and the sorrow of all the survivors, the tragic destiny of youth and hope and fame, the doom of frailty and transience which has been eternally pronounced on so many of the fairest gifts of Nature and all the noblest works of man.' From this pitch Robert Bridges brings us down or back to the old question of alleged incongruities, which he defended on the ground of 'Keeping,' or what Milton would have called decorum ('Poetic Diction,' 1923; *Collected Essays Papers &c.*, London, 3, 1928); but we hardly recognize *Lycidas* in the phrase 'a dreamy passionate flux.' Still later critics were satisfied with brief and external comments on Milton's art, such as Elton (*The English Muse*, London, 1933, 235) and Grierson and J. C. Smith (*A Critical History of English Poetry*, London, 1944, 162); in both King's death is still an excuse for an attack on the clergy (what Saintsbury had called a regrettable 'outburst of sectarianism'). Thus successive generations of critics, a number of them distinguished, seem to have had more or less dim notions of what *Lycidas* was about, and no disposition to inquire further.

In 1924 E. Legouis declared: 'Ce n'est pas King qu'il faut y chercher, c'est Milton lui-même' (Legouis and L. Cazamian, *Histoire de la Littérature Anglaise*, Paris, 1924, 567). With this remark, says D. C. Allen (*Vision*, 61), 'Legouis put his finger on the central problem' of *Lycidas*: 'No one had ever asked who the true subject of the elegy was,' and Legouis 'introduced a just speculation that brings us far closer to the meaning and the passion of this poem than ever we were before.' In the first edition of his *Milton Handbook* (New York, 1926) Hanford somewhat enlarged this view. Milton is 'primarily taking account of the meaning of the experience to himself.' If promising youth is cut off, what is the value of high endeavour? 'The answer is Milton's first great confession of faith—in himself and his earnest way of life, in God and immortality.' 'At the close he turns toward his own future, chastened and strengthened by the experience.' His intense emotion is partly sincere grief, but he is 'even more profoundly moved by the realization of the fact of death.'

From here on, critical interpretations are often much fuller than before, and these are summarized more fully. Various brief reactions are also recorded. The handling of both is inevitably inadequate, since space is not unlimited. The order is simply chronological, any kind of logical grouping being quite impossible.

571

Perhaps the first analysis that set modern criticism on a new path was Tillyard's (*Milton*, 1930, 79–85). Milton's general state of mind at the time he wrote *Lycidas* was partly revealed in his letter to Diodati [*Works* 12, 23–9; below, 70–84 n.]: he is meditating an immortality of fame, although as yet he is only letting his wings grow; and, feeling restless at Horton, he thinks of moving to London. Most criticism, said Tillyard, had been off the mark because it failed to distinguish between the nominal subject, Edward King, and the real subject, Milton. If the poem is great, 'it must contain deep feeling of some sort. What then is this deep feeling all about?' Whether or not Milton was thinking of the recent plague or of going abroad, he could not miss 'the analogy between King and himself' in life and, possibly, in early death. 'But his fears of premature death, though part of the subject, are not the whole. The real subject is the resolving of those fears (and of his bitter scorn of the clergy) into an exalted state of mental calm.' Thus the poem has a unity of purpose which integrates all its elements.

An outline verifies its depth and unity. The introduction (1–24) 'ends on Milton's possible death.' The first section (25–84) laments the dead Lycidas, questions the value of virtue and toil, and ends with the assertion of heavenly, if not earthly, fame—an assertion, however, which does not yet carry emotional conviction. 'In the second section, lines 85 to 131, . . . he does exactly the same thing.' The procession of mourners ends with St Peter, whose 'denunciation reveals the second great cause of mental pain in Milton' and 'is not an excrescence but strictly parallel with Milton's earlier outburst about the blind Fury.' Indeed the two are connected, since the hungry sheep are ill-fed by bad teachers and good teachers are or may be cut off by death. And 'the second grievance, like the first, is answered at the end of the second movement. Punishment is waiting; the two-handed engine stands ready to smite. But even less than at the end of the first section has mental calm been attained. . . Milton has stated his quarrel with life: we await the conclusion.'

The third section (132–64) is harder to describe, since it comprises the 'sudden change from the terror of the two-handed engine to the incredible beauty of the description of the flowers' and the escapist vision of the guarded Mount; and these surmises bring only minor comfort. The fourth section 'solves the whole poem by describing the resurrection into a new kind of life of Milton's hopes, should they be ruined by premature death or by the moral collapse of his country.' The wrongness of earth is made good by the rightness of heaven. 'But above all the fourth section describes the renunciation of earthly fame, the abnegation of self by the great egotist, and the spiritual purgation of gaining one's life after losing it.' If we object to the flimsy consolations of heaven, 'the question of beliefs is unimportant' and the poem expresses something beyond particular creeds. 'Milton by ridding himself of his inhibiting fears, by subordinating the disturbing ambition to have done a thing to the serene intention of doing it as well as possible, had proved his mettle and issued from the ordeal a great man. *Lycidas* expresses a mind of the keenest sensibility and most powerful grasp acutely aware of a number of most moving sensations, but controlling these sensations so that they do not conflict but rather by contrast reinforce one another: a mind calm after struggle but keyed up to perform heroic deeds, should they need to be done.'

In *Poetry Direct and Oblique* (London, 1934, 208–13; rev. ed., 1945, 81–4) Tillyard amplified his discussion by emphasizing the value of the structure in the total meaning of *Lycidas*: the use of sudden transition and contrast, and in general Milton's oblique expression of his theme, from which 'emerges one of the supreme commonplaces,' not merely the poet's now fearless resolution to go on with his proper work but 'part of the great Christian paradox, "Whosoever will lose his life shall find it."'

In 'Milton and Keats' (*Miltonic Setting*, 1938, 29–42) Tillyard, reacting against Middleton Murry's anti-Miltonism, drew a partial parallel in theme and structure between *Lycidas* and the *Ode to a Nightingale*.

In a very personal and elusive essay, 'A Poem Nearly Anonymous' (*American Review* 4, 1933; *The World's Body*, 1938; quoted here from Patrides), J. C. Ransom, hardly touching Milton's theme, sees a 'young, brilliant, insubordinate poem' in which the individual man breaks through the mask of impersonal convention and formal craftsmanship. *Lycidas* is a prime example of 'the poet and the man, the technique and the personal interest, bound up tightly and contending all but equally; the strain of contraries, the not quite resolvable dualism, that is art' (66). At this point in his career, between minor and major poems, Milton 'is uneasy, sceptical, about the whole foundation of poetry as an art' (71). Evidence for this view of Milton's state of mind Ransom finds in the poem, in the bold liberties the poet takes with the length of stanzas and in the ten unrhymed lines, which register 'the ravage of his modernity; it has bit into him as it never did into Spenser' (71). *Lycidas*, like some modern poems, 'was written smooth and rewritten rough; which was treason.' 'There did not at the time anywhere exist in English, among the poems done by competent technical poets, another poem so wilful and illegal in form as this one' (71). One example is Phoebus' speech on true fame, a lapse from dramatic monologue into narrative, 'an incredible interpolation' by the author (79). 'So *Lycidas*, for the most part a work of great art, is sometimes artful and tricky. We are disturbingly conscious of a man behind the artist. But the critic will always find too many and too perfect beauties in it ever to deal with it very harshly' (81).

Ransom's account of *Lycidas* was severely handled by W. Lynskey (*College English* 5, 1943–4, 239–49) and M. C. Battestin (ibid. 17, 1955–6, 223–8). F. T. Bowers (*Textual and Literary Criticism*, Cambridge, 1949, 3) noted that the idea of Milton's having roughed up the poem is refuted by the MS. See also Abrams (below, under 1961).

P. E. More's 'How to read *Lycidas*' (*American Review* 7, 1936; *On Being Human*, Princeton, 1936; repr. in Patrides), written by the distinguished veteran at a time when analytical criticism was becoming the vogue, was in the older appreciative vein; indeed the author, with reason, denied that any exegesis could expound the final alchemy of such a poem. While sharing and repeating Dr Johnson's harsh view of the man and the pamphleteer, More pronounced *Lycidas* 'the greatest short poem of any author in English, the very criterion and touchstone of poetical taste.' So far as he touched Milton's theme, More followed Tillyard. What he emphasized was the heroic faith and intensity of

Milton's vision of heaven, a vision in which the 'images are borrowed from the simplest commonplaces of faith.' The worthy reader of the poem must recognize its 'intimate marriage of form and matter, expression and substance,' and 'must be equally sensitive to the delicacy of its art and to the sublimity of its ideas.'

In his widely used edition, *Paradise Regained*, etc. (1937), M. Y. Hughes's introduction was naturally descriptive and historical but embodied some essentials of modern interpretation. The theme of *Lycidas* is both public and private. It mourned the death not merely of King but 'of all noble youth—and invested it with tragic quality. England is betrayed by her intellectuals and premature death snatches away the saving remnant among them.' 'From another point of view, Milton himself is the subject,' in 'his fear of the disappointment of death on the threshold of the career for which he had so carefully prepared.' In his *Complete Poems and Major Prose* (1957) Hughes gave a compendious survey of modern scholarship and criticism, maintaining even-handed objectivity.

William Haller (*The Rise of Puritanism*, New York, 1938, 1957, 321–3), in keeping with his main theme, takes *Lycidas* as 'Milton's most perfect expression of faith in his own conception of priesthood and his most memorable polemic against those who had kept him from exercising that priesthood in the English church.' 'The poem is Milton's personal confession of his effectual calling from God to be a poet, as truly such as the testimony of any of the spiritual preachers, the confession of his calling and of his answering to the call by the dedication of his talents to service prompted by faith.' Thus Milton 'immortalized the zeal of the saints here below.' Although the Puritan preachers would not, any more than Laud, be aware of *Lycidas*, 'there could hardly have been given more extraordinary evidence than that poem gave of the depth and sweep to which their influence had attained. . . . The performances of Prynne, Bastwick and Burton and of Lilburne, the dialectics of John Goodwin, and the appearance of *Lycidas* showed that revolution was ready to burst forth and that repressing preachers, cropping the ears of pamphleteers and church-outing idealistic poets could not stop it.'

575

A comment on *Lycidas* by G. W. Knight (*The Burning Oracle*, 1939, 70) is quoted by H. V. S. Ogden, under 1949 below.

G. C. Taylor ('Milton's English,' *N&Q* 178, 1940, 56–7), taking issue with the conventional view of Milton's English as strongly Latinate, examined the language of *Lycidas*, a poem far removed from daily life in content and artistic method. He found that of about 1500 words in the poem (proper names omitted) only 46 entered the language after 1500 (most of these in the latter half of the sixteenth century). Thus only 3 per cent of the words are foreign (5 per cent if proper names are included). Also, 185 words had appeared in Middle English. Thus 'more than 80 per cent. of the total number of words in "Lycidas" are Old English (Anglo-Saxon).' These statistics apparently include conjunctions and prepositions, which are often repeated.

In his notable introduction to the *English Poems* (London, 1940), Charles Williams strangely ignored *Lycidas* altogether. In an earlier and longer essay ('Milton,' *The English Poetic Mind*, Oxford, 1932, 110–52) Williams had dealt mainly with the larger works and with Milton as the poet of war and struggle. He had a few remarks on *Lycidas*, on its structure and prophetic and self-conscious quality (114–16).

By way of setting up a criterion for the *Nativity*, his main subject (*UTQ* 10, 1940–1, 167–81), A. Barker gave a succinct analysis of the structure of *Lycidas*, since he felt that both poems owed much of their effect to Milton's architectonic power. 'As Mr Tillyard has made clear, the elegy is essentially a personal poem, the ostensible subject making possible the resolution of the emotional problems created by Milton's disciplined devotion to poetry. Like his great poems, it performed a cathartic function for the poet himself, was indeed the very process through which a balanced calm was brought out of emotional disquiet. The achievement of this calm is expressed through the poem's achievement of a symmetry of structure which Mr Tillyard might have emphasized more heavily....It is just Milton's balanced manipulation of this [pastoral] convention to throw into relief the resolution of his own problems, which gives the poem its serene power.

'*Lycidas* consists of an introduction and conclusion, both pastoral in tone, and three movements, practically equal in length and precisely parallel in pattern. Each begins with an invocation of pastoral muses (ll. 15, 85, 132), proceeds with conventions drawn from the tradition of the pastoral elegy (the association of the lamented and the poet as shepherds, the mourning of nature, the questioning of the nymphs, the procession of mourners, a flower passage, and the reassurance), and ends with the formulation and resolution of Milton's emotional problem. The first movement laments Lycidas the poet-shepherd; its problem, the possible frustration of disciplined poetic ambition by early death, is resolved by the assurance, "Of so much fame in heaven expect thy meed." The second laments Lycidas as priest-shepherd; its problem, the frustration of a sincere shepherd in a corrupt church, is resolved by St Peter's reference to the "two-handed engine" of divine retribution. The third concludes with the apotheosis, a convention introduced by Virgil in *Eclogue* V but significantly handled by Milton. He sees the poet-priest-shepherd worshipping the Lamb with those saints "in solemn troops" who sing the "unexpressive nuptial song" of the fourteenth chapter of *Revelation*. The apotheosis thus not only provides the final reassurance but unites the themes of the preceding movements in the ultimate reward of the true poet-priest.

'It is the cumulative effect of its three parallel movements which makes *Lycidas* impressive; the return to the pastoral at the beginning of each makes possible three successive and perfectly controlled crescendos. The gathering up of the first two in the last gives the conclusion its calm finality; and the balanced unity of the design appropriately represents the calm achieved through the resolution of emotional conflicts. The problems are solved for Milton by the apotheosis because he regards himself as a poet-priest who can hope that his "destin'd urn" will bring the same reward.'

E. Wagenknecht ('Milton in "Lycidas,"' *College English* 7, 1945–6, 393–7) found Tillyard's 1930 account of *Lycidas* too narrow in its concern with the poet's personal experience. Milton's intensity of feeling came from his seeing in the early death of King a universal as well as a personal problem. 'Here is the old mystery of evil in one of its most acute forms.' There is nothing egoistic in Milton's facing of the great question.

Robert Graves's essay of 1947, 'The Ghost of Milton' (*The Common Asphodel*, London, 1949, 315–25), is so much like his novel, *Wife to Mr. Milton*, that it is hard to find any critical ideas, much less any valid ones. He doubts if Milton's grief for King was any more sincere than his earlier poem on Shakespeare, though the poet does feel emotion in facing the possibility of early death. Along with that goes jealousy over King's having received by royal mandate a fellowship Milton thought he himself should have had—jealousy that turned him into an anti-monarchist. His attack on the bishops in *Lycidas* was apparently aimed at the tutor, William Chappell, who had got King the fellowship. *Lycidas* 'is a poem strangled by art.' The 'sound...is magnificent; only the sense is deficient.' The spell cast by the opening lines is due to music created at the cost of meaning: 'in the extravagantly artful interlacing of alliteration throughout this passage Milton is adapting to English metrical use the device of *cynghanedd*, or recurrent consonantal sequences, used by the Welsh bards whom he mentioned appreciatively early in the poem.'

The first full explication of *Lycidas* appeared in D. Daiches' *A Study of Literature* (Ithaca, 1948, 170–95). That first version is followed here; no radical changes were made in the version in Daiches' *Milton* (1957; repr. in Patrides).

If *Lycidas* is 'the finest nondramatic poem of the seventeenth century and one of the half-dozen finest in the English language,' one reason is that its 'paradoxes are subdued and woven completely into the texture' (164). It uses 'an enormous number of poetic devices...to provide a constant expansion of the meaning, to make each statement include (one might almost say) its opposite'; and every image is enriched by every other (170). *Lycidas* 'is a conventional pastoral elegy,' yet 'a poem in which the whole achievement of Western civilization—classical and biblical, ancient and mediaeval and modern, pagan and Hebrew and Christian—is somehow embraced; which is both impersonal and personal, elegiac and exultant, derivative and original, topical and universal...' (170–1). Its theme is 'essentially the same as that of *Paradise Lost*—man's fate in the universe,' as that is understood by a Christian humanist.

The simply worded opening takes us suddenly and passionately into the poem. The immediate hint of personal concern is immediately enlarged. The theme is not Edward King, nor even John Milton, but 'man in his creative capacity...for achieving something significant in his span on earth.' Lycidas has died young; hence the problem. 'Milton circles round this problem, and with each circling he moves in nearer the center,' and 'he reaches the center only when he has found a solution.' Those first lines, on the disturbance of the seasonal process—'Shatter' and 'mellowing year'—suggest death and rebirth and anticipate the working out of that theme. The first paragraph balances resignation with resolve (174).

The pastoral convention has the artistic value of an impersonal, universal vehicle. Milton's second paragraph, beginning almost as formal routine, turns to the poet himself; his possible early death is linked with that of Lycidas, with the death of all men. The pastoral passage that follows is not an account of student life but of the joint self-dedication of the two men. Classical and pastoral myth keeps the poem rooted in an elevated conception of the nature, scope, and historical significance of the poetic art; and it preserves aesthetic distance between the reader and the poem. Here human activity is seen against a background of changing nature, with all its cosmic implications. But only one of the two men remains alive; poetic promise is no guarantee of immortality. Images of nature which had previously suggested growth and maturity are replaced by images of decay and death. With allusions to the uncertain scene of Lycidas' drowning, and finally to the hideous end of Orpheus, the concept of the poet's subjection to death is universalized (181–2).

Then why strive? This is one of the main questions posed by the poem, and Phoebus' answer is not convincing; it is as yet a copybook lesson that does not meet the complexities of the problem. That the poet himself is not satisfied is indicated by his proceeding to ask, in pastoral terms, what powers had allowed Lycidas to die. The only answer is dark images of superstition and fatalism. This paragraph (lines 85–102) 'moves from cheerful pastoral imagery to the suggestion of man's helplessness against fate' (184).

But with the word 'sacred' (line 102) a new thought emerges. Lycidas, like Milton, was a dedicated man, dedicated even to the church. 'The hero as poet is now enlarged to encompass the hero as Christian champion,' and now the question is not the loss to the poet in dying young but the loss to society of a spiritual leader and singer. St Peter's speech is not a digression; 'Milton has been developing the theme that the good are destroyed while the bad remain.' Not only is the poet-priest no more likely to survive, but even less, and society suffers an unfair loss. The paragraph ends with the affirmation that those who abuse society's trust will be punished, an affirmation that looks backward to Phoebus' assurance of a reward after death and forward to the vision of heaven. The denunciation of bad priests is to be read in the light of the earlier paragraph on self-dedication. The eventual punishment of hireling shepherds prepares for the final resolution, since it implies the obligation of man as poet and moralist to keep on working and striving.

The poet turns back to Lycidas and vainly seeks a little ease by smothering his body with flowers. No sooner has he accepted anew the fact of death than, with deliberate echoes of earlier references to Mona and Deva, he 'exploits geography with tremendous effect,' calling up historical and patriotic associations. Thus Milton associates Lycidas at last with a sense of triumph, and he can now afford to leave the dead and interpose a great cry for the living, a cry to St Michael to look at the state of England. The problem has now moved beyond Lycidas, whose reception into heaven Milton can let himself picture 'with all the triumphant resources of Christian imagery.' He has prepared the way for the emergence of the Christian humanist's answer to death, and the answer now brings acquiescence, as Phoebus' had not. But the theme requires a return to himself, to man as poet and creator who knows that he may die at any time, yet who must do what he can. In the conclusion Milton revives the image of the poet in relation to the pastoral and the Western poetic tradition. The 'last line suggests a determination to proceed to yet greater poetic achievements.'

Whatever modifications later critics have made, Daiches did much to define Milton's true theme and to show the complexity, coherence, and power of the poem.

Josephine Miles ('The Primary Language of *Lycidas*,' *The Primary Language of Poetry in the 1640s*, University of California Publications in English, 19, 1948, 86–90, rev. in Patrides, *Milton's Lycidas*, 95–100) speaks first of various kinds of repetition, for emphasis (line 8), for guidance to main points of view, as in addresses (15, 50, 85, 132), for variations on themes (8 and 166; 102, 167, and 172). As for individual words, most of Milton's repeated ones are traditional and especially Spenserian—*gentle, old, high, sad, come, go, lie, sing, hear, shepherd, flower, muse, power, eye, tear, dead, weep*. Others 'were brought into strong use first by Milton, and these particularly help define the singularities of *Lycidas*: *fresh, new, pure, sacred, green, watry, flood, leaf, morn, hill, shade, shore, stream, star, wind, fame, ask, touch*. . . . They refer primarily to the natural world, in more specific and sensory terms than were usual before Milton's time.'

The poem's movement 'from low to high, paralleled by that from past to future, takes place through the primary characteristic words. . . . The opening words *Yet once more I come* become the completing *At last he rose*. The plucked brown leaves of mourning become the twitched blue mantle of hope. The meed of some melodious tear becomes the nectar pure of the blest kingdoms. . . . *Fresh, high, new, pure, sacred*, are the especial terms of value: *pure* and *sacred* both classical and Christian, *pure* marking the two key passages of height, the classical and Christian heavens. The poem tries twice for what it achieves; first in the words of Phoebus and Jove, that fame is no mortal plant; then after a deeper pitch into despair of waters and of earth, more triumphantly in the natural analogy of the sun and the Christian terms of grace.

'Two passages. . . participate less than the rest in the process of cumulative repetition,' the procession of mourners and the catalogue of flowers. 'These two passages come between the climactic vision of fame in the first mourning section and the final vision of recompense and redemption in the last section. They...explore the counterforms of what the poem has been concerned with, the implications of the pastoral tradition in a world of spirit. Neither false pastors nor surmised flowers redeem the physical pastoral world of the human spirit; only as it looks higher is it redeemed and reconciled.

'These amplifying passages lead us to see another strong characteristic of Milton's language, its richness in adjectival quality.' While most poetry in English uses more verbs than adjectives, the reverse is true of *Lycidas*. 'The quantitative power of adjectives...supports the qualitative powers' already noted. 'By mid-seventeenth century, few poems were so individual in their use of dominant and repeated language as *Lycidas*,' and much of it was adjectival. 'This emotional language was... not in the more active traditions of Chaucer, Jonson, and Donne but in the more artful and aesthetic tradition of Spenser and Sidney, the poets most fond of pastoral.' Yet a comparison of Spenser's *Astrophel* with *Lycidas* shows Milton's widening of the physical and heightening of the spiritual. 'One reason that his individual emphases do not sound idiosyncratic to us today is that the language of *Lycidas* has had a powerful effect on English, especially American, poetry. The poem drew on the concrete references, the verbal harmonies, the interwoven and cumulative structures of classical sources, especially Virgil, and turned them to the intense purposes of Protestantism with its sense of the natural scope and magnificence of the universe as God's creation, encompassing the depth of hell and sea, the height of heaven and sky....To us today, the integration of sense-imagery with sound-pattern and emotional harmonic structure is natural to poetry.' The repeated and varied thematic terms of *Lycidas* 'carry the poem's sense of renewal from old past to new future, from deep waters and sad flowers to high heavens, from Jove's fame to Christ's redemption, from westering to rising star. For *Lycidas*, for Milton, for English poetry, this was a fresh beginning.'

In 'Milton and the Protestant Aesthetic: The Early Poems' (*UTQ* 17, 1947–8, 346–60; *Poetry & Dogma*, 1954, 183–204) Malcolm M. Ross, writing from the Anglo-Catholic standpoint, finds Milton's Protestant aesthetic first fully developed in *Lycidas*. Miltonic rhetoric destroys ritual. 'In *Lycidas*, the Christian and classical symbols confirm rather than confound one another. The exteriorization of the Christian image is completed with a consequent consistency of style' (201). 'With quite a brilliant Protestant audacity, Milton has St. Peter (keys and all) repudiate his apostolic successors, both Anglican and Roman. St. Peter is thereby freed of ecclesiastical associations and becomes the rock of a reformed structure of Christian symbols which henceforth draw their value from a new and wholly untraditional motivation' (202). 'Significantly, both the Christian image of heaven and the pagan image of the "Genius of the shore" move on a single surface. Finally separated from any possibility of traditional Catholic intention, and put to a combative ethical–social purpose, the Christian symbols easily assume new relationships, new dialectical possibilities. Saints and druids, Christ and the river-god, can be conscripted into one regiment now that the regiment has been made to march.

'The artistic consistency of *Lycidas* is a thoroughly Protestant achievement.... The gain is apparent. An almost infinite artistic freedom is made possible. But, as far as the Christian tradition itself is concerned, the dangers are correspondingly great. For the movement of the specifically Christian symbol from the centre to the periphery of a work of art implies a decisive shift of value and anticipates the emergence of a dominantly secular culture. The exteriorization of Christian symbolism opens a vacuum at the centre which must be filled.' (204)

It was inevitable that critics would take up the 'myth-and-symbol' approach and two did so in 1949: R. P. Adams, 'The Archetypal Pattern of Death and Rebirth in Milton's *Lycidas*,' *PMLA* 64, 183–8, and Caroline W. Mayerson (see just below). Adams noted allusions to fertility rituals in the Greek elegists, which Milton would recognize. In *Lycidas* there are two main series of allusions, to vegetation and to water. Symbols of death or immortality or metamorphosis are the evergreens (1 f.), the rose (45), the hyacinth (106), the violet (145), and the amaranth (149). There are naturally abundant allusions to water, a prime ancient symbol of fertility: at lines 24, 29, 132–3, 137, 140; and the figures of the river Cam and St Peter, and the dolphins. Above all, the 'descent into and re-emergence from water' is related to 'the setting and rising of the sun' (165–73). This passage, besides recalling Peter's attempt to walk on the water, 'coordinates two accounts of the sun's journey,' in 25–31 and 186–93. 'The nadir of the movement from life through death to resurrection follows logically by way of the reference to Orpheus, in which death is final,' a reference which has further ramifications.

Miss Mayerson ('The Orpheus Image in *Lycidas*,' *PMLA* 64, 1949, 189–207) sees the figure of Orpheus as the central clue to the whole poem. She thus summarizes the wealth of meanings the myths of the archetypal poet had gathered up in general, pastoral, and allegorical tradition (198):

Orpheus meant a revered musician-poet-prophet-teacher who had sung of God and creation, whose songs had affected man and beast, stock and stone, even the inhabitants of Hades. His music and his teachings had contributed to the establishment of a harmonious and civilized society. His musical skill, his power over nature, and his premature death kept alive his historic association with the pastoral elegy. To the Christian world, his personality and his accomplishments invited comparison with those of other venerated prophets, both heathen (the Druids, among others) and sacred (Christ). Finally, for a society traditionally inclined to allegorical interpretation, Orpheus became a symbol of human wisdom directed to social ends, the civilizing force which renews itself, despite periodic annihilation. In Orpheus thus interpreted we may recognize another expression of the faith incarnated in the tragic hero: a faith in the collective spiritual power of humanity, which survives any individual defeat by man's own anti-social passions, mischance, or death. Death, rebirth, and the corollary affirmation of the content of good that exists even in the limited, actual world is the traditional theme of tragedy. It will be argued here that it is also the theme of *Lycidas* and that Milton found in Orpheus an appropriate symbol to express and develop it.

Milton had already invoked the myth: in *L'Allegro* and *Il Penseroso*; in *Prolusion* 7 (where he is thinking of him 'as a symbol of human reason and art'); and in the invocation to Book 7 of *Paradise Lost* Milton was to identify himself 'with Orpheus at the moment when the singer was destroyed by the forces of barbarism' (197). In *Lycidas*

The Orpheus image reinforces the pastoral machinery and gives it special direction. The allusion implies that the elegiac and tragic theme of death and rebirth is to be realized through a conflict between order and chaos, and we may expect that at the end Milton will find a way to reconcile these in a more comprehensive order which will take both into account. The Christian connotations of pastoral allow the further possibility that this reconciliation may be effected through the use of Christ as a symbol of universal order in which all of the conflicts of mankind are reflected and resolved. (200)

Miss Mayerson proceeds, with acknowledgments to Tillyard and Hardy (q.v.), to 'show how this synthesis is achieved' and to 'demonstrate the rôle of the Orpheus image in defining the terms of the conflict and contributing to its resolution.' The exposition cannot be briefly summarized and only some concluding remarks can be quoted. The apotheosis of Lycidas means that 'Limited man, although he can but partly understand and perhaps never fully explain either his bestiality or his divinity, is restored to confidence in himself and his world through his ability to catch a glimpse of the divine order of which he is a minute yet significant part, an order in which both good and evil, joy and sorrow, exist, but in which good within and good without must inevitably triumph' (205–6).

Examination of the poem has shown it to be permeated by ideas associated with Orpheus, which converge in lines 56–63. Orpheus is identified with Lycidas, not only because of the former's traditional association with the subject of the pastoral elegy, but, more precisely, because of his attributes. Through this identification, Lycidas' importance as the poet-prophet who is the ordering factor in his world is emphasized. The mythographers' interpretations of the death of Orpheus imbue Lycidas' death and rebirth by water with symbolic value. Finally, the personality and powers of Orpheus associate him with Christ, whose cosmic omnipotence is the means of resolving the poem's conflicts. Milton's adaptation of the Orpheus myth in *Lycidas* unquestionably goes beyond the uses made of it by others. But our knowledge of the tradition helps us to understand the extent to which Milton wove the meanings of the myth into the texture of his poem, and, in so doing, made them his own.

H. V. S. Ogden ('The Principles of Variety and Contrast in Seventeenth Century Aesthetics, and Milton's Poetry,' *JHI* 10, 1949, 159–82) traces these two principles from antiquity to their classical–Christian fusion in Renaissance theory and practice, and finds them signally exemplified in Milton. He comments thus on *Lycidas*: 'Throughout the poem Milton delights in abrupt turns in new directions. The principle of variety through multiplicity is at work, notably in the flower passage, but the more basic principle in this poem is that of contrast. Professor G. Wilson Knight passes the following judgment on *Lycidas* [*The Burning Oracle*, 1939, 70]: "Exquisite in parts and most valuable as a whole, *Lycidas* reads rather as an effort to bind and clamp together a universe trying to fly off into separate bits; it is an accumulation of magnificent fragments." It is hard to see why an accumulation of magnificent fragments should be most valuable as a whole, and I think Professor Knight is wrong. *Lycidas* is a disciplined interweaving of contrasting passages into a unified whole, and as such is indeed most valuable. The passage in Milton's writings which best illuminates *Lycidas* is, I think, the passage in *The Reason of Church-Government* on the disciplined dance of the saints in heaven. . . : "The state also of the blessed in Paradise, though never so perfect, is not therefore left without discipline, whose golden surveying reed marks out and measures every quarter and circuit of new Jerusalem. Yet is it not to be conceiv'd that those eternall effluences of sanctity and love in the glorified Saints should by this meanes be confin'd and cloy'd with repetition of that which is prescrib'd, but that our happinesse may orbe it selfe into a thousand vagancies of glory and delight, and with a kinde of eccentricall equation be as it were an invariable Planet of joy and felicity. . ."' (*Works* 3, 185–6).

Rex Warner (*John Milton*, 1949–50, 25): 'There can be, I should say, no poem more perfect than *Lycidas*. By this time Milton is the complete master of a sustained style, combining the utmost delicacy and strength, imbued too with some rare magic that, it seems to me, is found elsewhere only in Shakespeare and in William Blake. Yet still much of the strength and pathos of the poem is due to the strong, though partially concealed, personality of the self-conscious and ambitious author. He is still, he feels, not ready for his final work; he dreads for himself "the blind fury with the abhorred shears"; and he consoles himself against that eventuality by the kind of Protestant integrity which much later will mark *Samson Agonistes*.'

Later (54–8) Warner remarks: 'Every line, every passage, fills one with a glad surprise; an unearthly simplicity flows, as in the music of Mozart, from so much intricacy. Effortlessly, yet through depths of feeling and with the divine conjunction of delicacy and strength, the poem moves in and represents "the hidden soul of harmony". One may well wonder how such a miracle could have proceeded from so antiquated a method and so well-worn a theme....It must be remembered that the theme, however old, is splendid. It is the death of youth, the theme of the mourning for Adonis or of the Good Friday processions still to be seen in the Greek church. It is also the theme of deification or resurrection, differently imagined in Greek myth or in Christian religion. Milton has written something which, with all its pastoral beauty, is bigger than a pastoral' because of his personal response to the grandeur of his theme. The pastoral conventions 'serve him rather as a medium is assumed to serve a spirit, being in themselves almost meaningless, but revealing powers which, without them, would have remained supernatural. Milton...is forced to think of what, if any, is the meaning of life at all.... His solution to doubt, fear and disappointment is partly the consciousness of his own integrity, partly his faith and resignation to a higher power. The feelings and the kind of purification of them are both real and intense....Every transition is both surprising and appropriate. Blended uncannily together are tenderness and majesty, indignation and romance, a Vergilian and a Christian spirit.' Thus the last sixty lines vary 'from mood to mood of beauty'—the Sicilian Muse and 'the fresh blossoms of an English meadow'; the shift from 'false surmise' to the picture of 'the dead lost body'; 'another transition from the delicacies of pity and regret to the softness and certainty of final peace, the vision of Lycidas' in heaven; and finally the poet's withdrawal 'from his tremendous achievement back to the ordinary world.' 'So, quietly as it began, this great poem ends. It is an elegy on youth; but it is also the triumph of youth. It is the finest flower of culture and of sensibility: it is also the record, in supreme art, of a great mind coming to terms with the world.'

M. Mack (*Milton*, 1950, 9–11), noting in the *Nativity* and *Comus* hints of 'the power of the true Christian poet to mediate between nature and grace,' remarks that *Lycidas* 'sets the problem of the true Christian poet squarely in the foreground.' 'Feeling, in works of art, is necessarily formal. It has to be detached from its individual circumstances...and distanced into the larger patterns of thought and sentiment that all men share. Milton effects this necessary depersonalization in *Lycidas*, partly by making King the symbol of all gifted individuals "dead ere their prime," and partly by the pastoral convention. The very fact that this convention has had a long history...is a part of the meaning it contributes to Milton's poem. The convention pays King the compliment of associating him with the poets for whom Theocritus and Virgil mourned. It assimilates his loss to a long tradition of loss, so that the mystery of the individual occasion is taken up into, and softened by, the general mystery of human fate. And it has, further, the advantage of eliminating irrelevant particulars in favor of what is essential and significant.' Thus the depiction of Cambridge life in pastoral terms points to 'a threefold connection between the inspiration of poetry, the sensuous appreciation of the natural world, and the intuition of mysterious forces (fauns and satyrs) linking poetry and man and nature—which is *truer* than would be any of the actual facts of King's and Milton's stay at Cambridge.

'Most important of all, with respect to structure, the pastoral convention affords a framework of established formal elements upon which, as upon the formal elements in a musical composition, can be based the modulations and resolutions which convey the individual artist's theme. Thus in Milton's poem, the conventional grief of nature and the questioning of the nymphs rise into the poet's more passionate questioning of God's providence; why scorn delights and live laborious days, as Milton was doing at Horton, if death comes arbitrarily to frustrate effort? Similarly, the pastoral procession of mourners (which can contain St. Peter because of the Christian comparison of Christ and his clergy to shepherds) expands into Milton's famous denunciation of a corrupt church which a living Lycidas would have helped to purify.

And the formal element of the strewing of the dead man's bier likewise crescendoes, first, into the acknowledgment that there is no way of glozing over the dominion of death in the *natural* order (this meaning reinforced by the loss of Lycidas's body to the casual indignities of the sea), and then, into the intuitive perception that by way of natural death comes spiritual life, "through the dear might of Him that walked the waves."

'Throughout the poem...water is used with a double or even triple significance. There is the sea, impervious, blameless, but destructive—to which Lycidas and all men fall victims. There are the fountain of the Muses and the pastoral rivers, symbolic perhaps of poetry, and especially of its power to invest the brute facts of experience with moral meaning, as demonstrated in *Lycidas* itself. And last, just hinted in the final paragraph before the close, there is the water of grace, won through Christ, who by his mastery of "the sea" has given a new significance to water. In these last lines, where nature has been redeemed by grace—the old pastoral landscape taken up into a new kind with "other groves and other streams"—Lycidas becomes the Genius of the Shore (compare the Attendant Spirit in *Comus*), and is powerful, through the water of grace, over the water of the natural order.'

Ruth Wallerstein, in a long analysis of elegiac verse, gave one chapter to *Lycidas* and the collection in which it appeared, and discussed at some length the poems of Joseph Beaumont and John Cleveland (*Studies in Seventeenth-Century Poetic*, Madison, 1950, 96–114; enlarged from a paper in *English Institute Essays 1948*, New York, 1949). Milton, a Renaissance humanist in the Christian–Platonic tradition of Spenser, combined all the elements of the elegiac tradition, but 'his feeling is simple and organic' (109). His delight in nature is not merely naturalistic but religious. An elegy is in its own nature ritualistic and universal, but 'the grief which Milton expresses is wilder, and the question it asks is of far wider import than any which naturalistic Greece and Rome had expressed. And...it can be stilled by no human ritual.' Thus at the climax of *Lycidas* 'we are swept out of nature into the transcendent consolation' (110). 'The passage...beginning with Orpheus and ending with the rejection of earthly fame has already both realized an inde-finable grief and prepared the way for the transformation. In that passage Milton, as man, has separated himself from nature and raised himself to grace. And in it are most perfectly reconciled the classical impersonality and the personal Christian passion of the poem. But to complete the theme, the idea of a Christian society, one other element is necessary, the attack on the church' (111). There was a general model in the *Shepheardes Calender*, in Spenser's 'blending in pastoral poetry of social consciousness with the unfolding of the interior life.' 'The pattern which is diffused through Spenser, Milton perfects and makes manifest' (112).

'That *Lycidas* should so overflow with personal passion, though not with personal grief, is then no mere mark of Milton's own nature but the impress of a whole age upon a genius. And though *Lycidas* and Donne's elegy on Prince Henry differ in that one is the drama of doubt and faith, the other the story of man's transcendence from nature to grace, both are dramas of the individual soul, each witnessing the terror of death, the personal experience of grace.' Donne's 'emotion still remains primarily an act of devotion, though he turns it into an object of art by the formal delineation of that emotion. Milton imitates the experience of death and Christian acceptance of it not in a religious form but in an artistic form in which, by the completeness with which the entire experience is represented and by the sensuous and representative quality of the imagery, the most personal experience of one man is universalized' (113).

The discussion ends with emphasis on 'the great depth, scope, and complexity of Milton's imagery when compared to that of the early pastorals and on the relation of it to witty imagery. His depth of ex-pression owes most to the whole quality of his mind....But Biblical symbol and emblem imagery also have contributed something to the deepening. Milton has assimilated the emblem to the imagery of sensuous, of classical, poetry.' The great example is the image of the setting and rising sun, which includes, 'in addition to the obvious sense, ...not only...Matthew's symbolic identification of Christ and the sun, but...the part played by the sun in Platonist thought as the symbol and instrument in this world of the divine energy. It is emblematic both in the sharp logic of its statement and in the way in which it serves to draw together and to transvalue all the matter of the poem.... But if to be "metaphysical" be to feel the objective realities and to contemplate their ultimate meaning chiefly as they transform the inner life of one sensibility and make him a part of his universe, then *Lycidas* is a metaphysical poem.'

Brooks and Hardy (1951), who pay their respects to Daiches, Adams, and Miss Mayerson, develop their own—or rather Hardy's—commentary (169–86) from Hardy's essay of 1945 (*Kenyon Review* 7; the 1951 essay is reprinted 'with a few minor changes' in Hardy's *The Critical Frame*, Notre Dame, 1962). They demand close reading of a poem of 'intricate and subtle architecture,' but at first glance, as M. H. Abrams says (his comments are summarized below), 'it might seem that to these explicators the poem is not really about King, nor about Milton, but mainly about water.' However, Milton has a theme, 'the place and meaning of poetry in a world which seems at many points inimical to it' (172). There is also an antagonism between pagan and neutral nature and Christian supernaturalism. Milton is credited with attitudes that suggest rather the young and cynical Swinburne or the despairing Tennyson. All the divine guardians of the classical tradition appear to be ineffectual; the death of Lycidas 'is not a loss to nature, but a numbing of the poet's sensitivity to nature' (174, 176). The sea 'is consistently presented in the poem as unfriendly and alien' [it was, says Milton, signally calm when Lycidas was drowned], while 'The streams and fountains which run throughout the poem flow with life-giving water' [like the Hebrus?].[1] In general, and in spite of perceptive remarks (as on Milton's last paragraph, though they regard it as 'curious'), the two critics, by magnifying small matters and minimizing or misreading large ones, do much to dissolve (one naturally falls into a watery

[1] E. R. Marks (*Explic.* 9, 1950–1, Item 44) noted that for Adams water is a prime symbol of fertility and hence of rebirth, while Miss Mayerson takes pastoral landscape as representing serenity and the ocean disorder. Marks suggested a double view of water as both nourisher and killer.

metaphor) the view of theme and structure and texture which previous critics had built up.

W. Shumaker ('Flowerets and Sounding Seas: A Study in the Affective Structure of *Lycidas*,' *PMLA* 66, 1951, 485–94), starting from Barker's triple division of the poem (see above), shows with what subtle articulation two 'thematic strands. . .help prepare in the first and second movements for the final resolution in the third.' The third movement begins with the catalogue of flowers, which follows St Peter's invective. In this context 'the thought of floral offerings is consciously and deliberately delusive,' and the poet is plunged immediately into profound depression. The catalogue, however, contrasts with references to vegetation in the first 132 lines; these had consistently suggested 'a sympathetic frustration in nature to balance the human frustrations about which the poem is built.' Thus the floral catalogue 'resumes and develops an established theme, which, however, is now partly inverted. Although the emotional connotations set up earlier are not exactly denied, they are subdued,' and the catalogue is rich in colour, so that 'grief, while remaining grief, is lifted and brightened' (488).

The second theme, the description of King's body tossing in the sea, has been even more elaborately prepared for. There have been successive 'muted statements' of the water theme, and lines 12–13, 50, 62, 89–94, 154–8, 167, and 185 carry more overt and resonant reminders of either drowning or the menace of water. The Irish Sea had been described as weltering and as tranquil; in 154–8 it 'has become a resistless, unsympathetic force which deals with the body of the poet-priest-shepherd exactly as the Hebrus has dealt with the severed head of Orpheus. . . .' But the thought of King's tossing body 'generates immediately, by contrast, that of a redeemed and joyous soul. The flower and water themes, in direct juxtaposition, thus lead directly into the apotheosis, in which all the tensions are finally resolved' (492). The image of resurrection is drawn from the very water that had seemed 'coldly and impersonally fearful' (lines 168–71). Shumaker does not feel entirely happy with Lycidas as the Genius of the shore, but he sees a structural function in the clearing of the Irish Sea from threat, in the removal of the last tension.

The two themes, of flowers and sea, are not of equal importance, since the former 'shows a temporary effect of profound grief' and the latter 'is intimately related to the cause.' But both are essential to the impact of the third movement and the whole poem.

A. S. P. Woodhouse ('Milton's Pastoral Monodies,' *Studies in Honour of Gilbert Norwood*, 1952, 261–78) gives more space to the relatively neglected *Epitaphium Damonis* than to *Lycidas*. He distinguishes, among Milton's early poems, those that are more or less aesthetic patterning and those that involve extra-aesthetic experience and embody a problem, an emotional tension, which must 'be either solved or transcended.' In such poems 'the aesthetic pattern has a larger function to discharge.' 'The pastoral monody (as Christian poets had reshaped its pattern) becomes a vehicle for Milton's profoundest emotions and an instrument, not indeed for solving, but for transcending his problems, and thus for achieving such a resolution of emotional tension as only poetry could effect' (263).

In analysing *Lycidas* Woodhouse follows and refines upon Tillyard and uses Barker's account of three movements (see above). Instead of the simple assertion that the real subject is Milton himself, Woodhouse would prefer to say that 'the principal source of the poem's extra-aesthetic emotion is not grief for the loss of Edward King, but an awareness of the hazards of life and of Milton's own situation' (272). There is a clear relation between these two themes. 'Edward King is priest and poet. Milton is poet and priest: that is, he has changed the medium of his service to God, but not its spirit. For the poet also is a priest and prophet: all the sense of vocation is transferred to the new medium, and more' (272). An essential part of the pattern of Christian pastoral monody 'is the idea of immortality and the progression from a pagan view of life and death to the transcendent view of the Christian. And in *Lycidas* this transition is not less essential to the real than to the occasional subject' (273).

Lycidas 'looks beyond the tradition of the pastoral monody to that of the eclogue' to deal, in the two 'digressions,' with the true poet and the nature of his reward and with the state of the church—topics already treated, for example, in Spenser's eclogues. 'Of the three movements that make up the structural pattern of *Lycidas*, the first two culminate in passages which (as Milton observes in the poem) shatter the pastoral tone, while the third does not shatter but rather transcends it. Clearly, the contrast between the unreal Arcadian world of the pastoral and the concerns of real life which break in upon it, is significant at once for the content and the pattern of the poem' (273). 'The Prelude is heavy with the thought of death...The note of the Epilogue is life, not death.'

In the semiallegorical first movement (23–84), particularly in 56–7 ('Ay me...have don?'), 'The Christian poet recognizes the essential unreality of the Arcadian world,' and 'reality is clamouring for admission' ('Alas! What boots it'). 'The reference to the homely shepherd's trade is appropriate to Edward King, whose lifework was the ministry; the reference to poetry finds its full meaning only in relation to Milton,' who had changed his mode of service. 'Because the image of the shepherd is common to pastoral poetry and the Christian tradition, it is a bridge between them.' 'The first movement ends, then, with a question and an answer...The question springs from experience; the answer, from faith. Both lie outside the Arcadian world, and by them its mood is temporarily shattered' (275).

'In the second movement (85–131) this fact is recognized and the mood of the classical pastoral is restored,' to be shattered again by St Peter's speech. 'The condition of the Church is a theme appropriate to Edward King' and, in a more subtle way, to Milton, since it 'had implications for the life of the nation, and the life of the nation had implications for poetry,' especially for 'a national Christian epic,' which required as audience a united nation and which Milton was to plan, postpone, and give up.

'The third movement (132–85) again commences with a recognition of the shattered pastoral tone, and its restoration,' though the floral catalogue 'is a pagan fancy, a fiction of comfort.' 'But now "false surmise" gives place to Christian truth, and with it weeping gives place to hope and consolation.' 'The vision of heaven (as Dr. Tillyard has observed) makes real the promise of fame therein with which the first movement concluded. But it is less intensely imagined than in the *Epi-taphium*. Lycidas hears, he does not join in, "the unexpressive nuptial song." There is consolation, not rapture, in the greeting of "all the saints above...for ever from his eyes." The lower intensity of the feeling has this further result, that the classical images and the Christian are blended, and not, as they are in the *Epitaphium Damonis*, fused.' 'The image of the Genius is not without precedent in pastoral monodies from Virgil's Daphnis onward. The perilous flood is the world. And Lycidas has already commenced to exercise his beneficent influence on those who travel through it,' and first of all on the poet himself, as the Epilogue makes plain. It balances the opening lines of the monody. 'With faith fortified and vision cleared, and with a mind at peace, he is returned to the world of extra-aesthetic experience, of life and labour.'

These comments were condensed and augmented in Woodhouse's lecture *Milton the Poet* (1955, 9–10). Milton treats the death of King 'not as personal loss, but as universal enigma—the tragic enigma of the youthful life, full of high promise, cut short almost before it is begun.' The poet's mind travels back and forth between the particular death and the general enigma, thinking of 'the hazards of time and fortune' in his own career. In the pattern of Christian monody

immortality becomes the example and symbol of a principle of healing and renewal, the effect of God's encompassing providence and power. Around this central idea, structural and dynamic, Milton weaves his complex pattern, which entails the brilliant adaptation, among many details, of two divergent elements from the pastoral tradition: (i) its ability to present, by means of allegory, considerations germane to the poet and his subject, but far removed from pastoral life; and (ii) its tone of idyllicism, emanating from the pastoral vehicle, which enshrines a vanished pagan world remote from the realities of life. Most poets have been content to accept this paradox and work within its terms. Milton chooses rather to expose and exploit the contradiction.

J. M. French ('The Digressions in Milton's "Lycidas,"' *SP* 50, 1953, 485–90) is concerned to show that the two nominal digressions from the pastoral mode—the passage on fame and St Peter's speech—are not really digressions, as some of the older critics thought, but 'are actually passages of increased intensity, and probably the core of the poem.' The main body of *Lycidas* consists of three parallel sections (15–84, 85–131, 132–80): 'Each has the same purpose, that of raising the mind of the reader from the earthly appearance of defeat to the heavenly promise of victory.' A contrast between the earthly and the heavenly scale of values is presented three times, and 'Each time the pastoral description has led naturally into the Christian assurance of immortality.' Such a contrast is in harmony with the main line of Milton's poetry from the *Fair Infant* onward.

D. C. Allen (*Vision*, 1954, 52–70) moves up to *Lycidas* from classical 'consolations' through Milton's early *Fair Infant*. Although externally an occasional poem, *Lycidas* comes 'from the deep heart's core, and it must be regarded in this way or it cannot be understood at all.' The scholarly and religious poet would be led to pastoral by classical and Renaissance literary tradition and by the actual or metaphorical pastoral-ism of the Bible; and pastoral had also assimilated the tradition of ecclesiastical satire. Notwithstanding the complex traditions and precedents, *Lycidas* is unique. Modern recognition of its uniqueness began with the recognition that the subject of the elegy is Milton himself.

'Though the poem is about Milton and the question that lies on the top of his mind, a mythic identification is invented, as in his first English elegy, and pervades the whole of "Lycidas"' (62). The manifold myths and allegories of Orpheus (see C. Mayerson, above) would here be especially present in the analogy 'Christ: Orpheus: Milton.' The so-called digressions 'marshal the conventions of the pastoral eclogue into something totally new.' In facing the fact of death squarely, 'the poet has it out with God'; and *Lycidas* 'is his first attempt to "assert eternal Providence And justify the ways of God to men."' Following Barker's triple division of the poem, Allen sees the particular questions of the first two parts raised in the last to the universal; and the ultimate answer 'comes with an actuality of conviction that has never been attained by any other English poet' (64).

In the slow opening lines it is in a way 'Milton whom Milton mourns, but it is not a selfish type of mourning. It is not the mourning of a man frightened by his own eventual death but that of one who is confused, who has been given a task by God but perhaps not the time in which to complete it' (64). In the first part, through the allusion to Orpheus, 'the governing metaphors are floral,' but not refreshing. This approach to the first 'digression' is gradual: 'plants, animals, the demigod. With Milton we have ascended the ladder of being in a depressing waste.' The poet-metaphysician 'asks the question that is at once subjective and universal'; the answer is that 'He who loses his fame shall find it' (67). The metaphors preparing for the second question are all based on water, and water has its symbolic implications. 'As the flowers of the first passage are colorless, the waters of the second passage are stagnant.' The second question, approached 'through a cumulative metaphor— that of a dying world presided over by birds of prey,' 'is parallel to the first in that it again interrogates the Providence of God,' now in regard to the state of the church. The answer is that 'God will see that his ends are reached.'

The two questions on which the whole structure of this poem turns are answered in terms of man's acceptance of God's will. Philosophy, as it does in all of Milton's poetry, bows to theology; with this gesture one moves from the homocentric to the theocentric world and all things change. The fact of death becomes truly unimportant and the world which had been dead, dry, colorless, and stagnant comes bursting into life....All is color and motion as the brooding melancholy of the poet is swept away by his angelic understanding of the ultimate solution of what he had formerly seen as poignant aspects of the problem of evil, of the unintelligibility of Providence. (68–9)

The vision of heaven is presented, as P. E. More said, through commonplaces. 'This is the Christian alphabet by which all is spelled; to use other letters is to impoverish the imagination. By the clear and fresh ordering of Christian clichés, Milton answers the universal question that is the pre-text of "Lycidas." With it are answered the special questions of the poet-priest.' The poem had begun with reluctance, with bewilderment. 'But the fear is gone now, purgation of doubts is certain and has come with the completion of the elegy. Milton upheld by the arms of Providence has stared Death down.'

The most expert and precise account of the form of *Lycidas* is given by Prince (*Italian Element*, 1954, 71–88). This last and most perfect poem of Milton's youth 'shows him as more conscious than ever before of the possibilities of moulding English verse by Italian methods.' He had no exact precedent but was powerfully original in 'his application of certain first principles to form a new combination of familiar elements.' *Lycidas* is a complex 'development of the disciplined improvisation of. . . *On Time* and *At a Solemn Musick*.' The discipline is that of 'the *canzone*, as it was modified and adapted in lyrics and eclogues of the *Cinquecento*,' but Milton made 'wide deviations from the strict form.'

A *canzone* consisted of a complex, fully rhymed stanza of some length, repeated several times, and followed by a shorter concluding stanza, the *commiato*. *Lycidas* consists of eleven 'verse-paragraphs' of lengths varying from ten to thirty-three lines, closely but irregularly rhymed, and including ten lines, scattered throughout, which do not rhyme at all; the last verse-paragraph is of eight lines, rhymed like an *ottava rima*, and undoubtedly corresponds in its own way to a *commiato*. The six-syllable lines are disposed as irregularly as the rhymes, but are governed nevertheless by certain limitations: they are used somewhat sparingly, and they always rhyme, and always with a ten-syllable line which has gone before. (In making this predominance of longer over shorter lines Milton follows Dante's prescription for a 'tragic' *canzone*.) (72–3)

'Milton's first and clearest impression' of 'the liberation of some Italian lyric verse from stanzaic form' would have come from Tasso's *Aminta* and Guarini's *Pastor Fido*. But while these late pastorals moved away from Virgil, Milton remained in touch with Virgil and Theocritus. In that respect *Lycidas* was closer to such earlier pastorals as those of Sannazaro and B. Rota, whose technique Prince describes. *Lycidas* shows the results of two technical experiments which marked Italian pastoral verse in the sixteenth century: 'the attempts to evolve a poetic diction equivalent to that of Virgil, and the attempt to combine the tradition of the *canzone* with that of the Classical eclogue' (81). These technical advances were not reflected in Spenser's pastorals, although '*Daphnaïda* and *Astrophel* were the finest pastoral elegies written in

English before *Lycidas*, and must be reckoned important features of Milton's poetic background' (83).

The principle of structure relevant to *Lycidas* 'is that the stanza of a *canzone* is most commonly built of two sections, which are linked by a key line or *chiave.*' 'One or the other of the two parts of such a stanza might also be divided, but not usually both.' 'It is the sense of movement, and the habits of rhetoric, deriving from these divisions, which determine the methods of Milton's poem.' 'The divisions in both sonnet and *canzone* made possible a kind of rhetoric of rhyme: lines which rhymed had differing weight and emphasis according to their position and function.' 'The most obvious feature which this method gives the poem is the failure of Milton's sentences to correspond to the pattern of rhymes; the ebb and flow of statement, the pauses and new departures, appear to be independent of any necessity but their own' (85).

Thus in the passage 103–9 there is a strong pause at the end of 105 ('dearest pledge'), 'yet the next line, introducing a new series of rhymes, takes its own rhyme from those of the completed statement' (86). In the passage 165–71 the first strong pause comes at the end of 171 ('morning sky'), 'yet this line introduces a new rhyme. Everywhere in the poem we find such effects, and they are due to the working of a positive principle, not to a mere negative overriding of a casual rhyme-scheme. Milton has in mind the chief principle resulting from the *stanza divisa* of the *canzone*: that each group or series of rhymes must be linked to its predecessor by a key line.' In the first of these passages either line 107 or 108, preferably 108 ('Last...go') may be regarded as such a key, taking up a rhyme from the preceding lines. In the second passage line 169 ('And yet...head') 'is such a key, though again it is followed by a line which also takes up a rhyme from' 165–8. Another such key is 136 ('Ye valleys...use').

The rhetoric of rhyme derived from the *canzone* has thus provided Milton with an invaluable instrument—a type of rhyme which looks both back and forward. His ear had been so trained by the *canzone* as to appreciate this effect not only in the key, or *chiave*, where it is most obvious, but in subtler details. One of these is the use of the six-syllable lines, which are also placed so as to give a sense of expectation: they not only always rhyme with a previous longer line (thus looking back), but they give the impression of a contracted movement which must be compensated by a full movement in the next line (which is always of full length), and they thus look forward. (86–7)

Thus Milton's 'very precise principles' combine close control with a liberty that is functional. 'He has made his own rules for this poem, but made them out of his knowledge and enjoyment of the strictest Italian practice.' He apparently 'decided that his rhymes must not generally be separated by more than two lines. For the scattered un-rhymed lines he had sufficient Renaissance authority. He has also accepted from Dante the preference for a couplet to end his paragraphs.' 'Indeed, the only true couplets in *Lycidas* are those which conclude verse-paragraphs; and one of the best ways to appreciate the articulation of the poem is to analyse the effect of those rhymes coming together elsewhere, which might appear to be couplets, but which are not, because the second rhyming line always looks forward to what comes next' (87–8). Examples are 15–18, 78–82, 100–2.

'To analyse *Lycidas* in the light of the *canzone* and the Italian eclogues is to realize with vividness that only a poet of Milton's intellectual energy could have devised and successfully applied such a formula.... The discipline of *Lycidas* has left little mark on the tradition of the English ode; it has proved to be inimitable.'

K. Muir (*J.M.*, 1955, 1960, 44–9) sees *Lycidas* as an occasional poem turned 'into a soul-searching examination' of Milton's 'poetic ambitions.' In the final section he 'resolves the problems which had obsessed him. He is consoled for his fears of early death by the prospect of immortality; his fears for the future of the Church are compensated by the "solemn troops and sweet Societies" of the saints in heaven; and his agonizing desire for fame is succeeded by trust in God.' Along with such a statement of the theme and a brief summary of the poem, Muir gives the usual defence of Milton's choice and handling of the pastoral mode and touches on a few possible poetic influences, Italian (see G. L. Finney in II above) and Jacobean (the Fletchers and William Browne).

W. Sypher (*Four Stages of Renaissance Style*, New York, 1955, 174–5, etc.) puts *Lycidas* on the pinnacle of mannerist art (as *Paradise Lost* exemplifies baroque). 'The distances between life and art are all uncertain in *Lycidas*, perhaps the greatest mannerist poem, and one where the planes of reality are so interchanging and complex that we shall never be able to "read" it better than we "read" *Hamlet*. In *Lycidas* the young Milton is using in a very personal willful way the traditional elegy, just as Michaelangelo, earlier, used the traditional orders of architecture in a willful personal way in the ante room of the Laurentian Library. Edward King is dead, and Milton, too self-consciously, must exhibit his talent prematurely; this striking self-awareness gives to the elegiac formula with its *mondain* air of sophisticated and vocal grief a very private and expressive accent. Lycidas must not float unwept: but clearly this poetic occasion does not account for Milton's disturbance any more than Gertrude accounts for Hamlet's. First, the ceremonial lament, the backward glance at Old Damoetas, the resumption of the pose of grief with appeals to those bloodless Nymphs, those austere Muses, and the abstract Universal Nature—figurines like the thin, chill, elegant forms painted by the School of Fontainebleau. Then, amid these learned and classic niceties, the hideous roar as the gory visage of Orpheus is borne down the swift Hebrus; and the urgent question whether it were not better to sport with Amaryllis...; and the desperate fear that the blind Fury may slit the thin-spun life—the young Milton's life!' Then comes 'the inexplicably stern outburst of the dread Puritan voice, the onslaught against blind mouths.... This is hot anger and contempt, very private, entirely out of context. Without any transition whatever, Milton again shifts perspective' to the catalogue of flowers. The poet's climactic vision is described as 'the false and formal inflation of the celestial triumph with solemn troops and sweet societies.' The thematic value of the last paragraph vanishes when it is seen as a piece of 'the picturesque.' 'Finally, and possibly most disconcerting of all the shifts, there is Milton's youthful eagerness, this lament done, to turn to fresh woods and pastures new. All this, we remind ourselves, is supposedly about Edward King. What could possibly account for this erratic performance with its frigidity, its discouragement and tenderness, its rage, its callow hope, and its pictorial harmony?' *Lycidas* 'has no adequate objective correlative,' and its tensions are 'unresolved' (192). The term 'mannerist' also takes in Milton's *Nativity* (106) and apparently all of Donne. For comment on Sypher's brilliant if sometimes erratic account of Milton one may cite R. Tuve, 'Baroque and Mannerist Milton?' (*JEGP* 60, 1961, 817–33). A more extended 'mannerist' analysis of *Lycidas* is given by R. Daniells (below, under 1963).

R. Tuve's elaborate study (*Images*, 1957, 73–111) is not the most closely ordered of critiques, but it is full of illuminating and corrective ideas that spring from sensitive insight guided by active learning. For such reasons one cannot provide a summary but only set up a few signposts. Miss Tuve's first paragraph defines Milton's theme, which some critics miss:

Lycidas is the most poignant and controlled statement in English poetry of the acceptance of that in the human condition which seems to man unacceptable. I do not of course refer simply to the calm ending of the elegy, but to its whole poem-long attempt to relate understandably to human life the immutable fact of death—the pain of loss, the tragedy of early death, the arraignment of the entire natural world..., and finally the center and heart of the matter: the questioning of a justice that would take the young and leave the ripe, take the devoted and leave the self-indulgent, so too would take the shepherd and leave the destroyer....

The second paragraph relates the theme to structure and method:

Indictments of the unfathomable total moral order, and answers to them, are matter of tragedy, not of pastoral, and Milton twice recognizes this and twice returns from that higher mode...Each question has its answer before he makes this return...One is in terms of the folly of the poet's devotion (since Death ends it, irrelative of fulfillment), and one in terms of the flat impossibility of the priest's task, when an inscrutable power extinguishes those who alone would do its work here. The answers are not so much cognate as the same, that judgement is the Lord's. In each case the meaning of the answer transcends man's unaided wisdom, and it is properly spoken by an unearthly voice. This last is simply one aspect of the imagery which keeps each answer exactly suited to the nature and philosophical weight of the question.

Lycidas

The first answer was made by Phoebus (lines 76–84). Milton saved for his second great answer the overtly Christian terms of St. Peter's speech, by which time the sudden blaze and clear light of unequivocal terms is wanted. This is not a matter of 'Christian' and 'pagan' but of direction and indirection, of a less or a more figurative functioning in the language. Both are Christian. The question of Milton's pagan imagery in *Lycidas* here comes up in its first form, and we make the first answer to it, that such *terms* do not make images non-Christian. The additional element of indirection in the first question and answer was of a kind endeared to the Renaissance reader by long habit. (75–6)

'Milton never does turn in this poem from a non-Christian sense that death may be the only answer given for the riddle of life to a Christian belief in eternal life. He turns, more than once, from what seems senseless in death to death made tolerable' (78–9). 'There is no single "Christian consolation" in the poem; the whole texture of it is replete with these, and the imagery is the major voice carrying that constant burden' (79).

However, not only is the poem a structure of cumulative, not contrasted, insights into the meaning of life and death, but also there is yet to come the vision of the nuptial union of the soul with the source of love, a third vision of judgement. Moreover, though it is notable that symbols are chosen at these three crucial points to convey great fundamental oppositions like growth and destruction, life and nothingness, union and sundering, fruition and annihilation, there is also the whole continuing web of the poem with its living and tender sense of imperishable sweetness in all moving and growing things. The affirmations of *Lycidas* begin with its first line. (79)

Miss Tuve insists or implies that we cannot understand *Lycidas* without recovering knowledge of traditions, the pastoral in particular, that Milton inherited and transcended. 'His method is not primarily symbolic (differing here from that of the *Nativity Hymn*), and no archetypal symbol such as those of purgation, rebirth, love (water, fire, cave, garden, or the like) pervades or organizes his poem' (87–8).

The opening of the poem is not a revelation of Miltonic egotism. 'It is *Lycidas*' garland which, like his poetic promise, is cut while it is still harsh and unready....I do not read in Milton's first lines the note of apology for his own unripe verses familiarly referred to in commentary and criticism. This poem brings honors, does not constitute them; the garland is a symbol, and Milton does not pluck his *own* unripe honors.' ' *Unripeness*—the flaw is in our entire condition...' (88).

Then the pastoral picture of the two young shepherds (23–36) is not a picture of Cambridge life (90). 'All the adventure and freshness of Milton's morning, all the endless noons when the gray-fly's languorous horn stops only to start over—these all say with one voice *life without time*, man without his mortality, the rose without the thorn and the garden before what happened in it' (92). 'The subject of all this first portion of *Lycidas* is what King's death meant (still means); not "King's death" nor "Milton's fears of death" nor "his poetic aspirations", but the pathos, unnaturalness, disorderliness, and impotence, hidden, and revealed, in the fact of all early death. As Milton pursues the subject, it comes closer to the tragedy than the pathos of the destruction of promise, for the poem almost defines this as the nature of human life' (93).

The ancient figures through which man's death is lamented as a great flaw in the fabric of nature are structurally used by Milton, by his attaching them to the other ancient motif fixing responsibility for a particular death....Milton can... make double structural use of the lamenting natural creatures and powers,

who 'exonerate great Neptune, and exonerate Natura herself.'

Yet it is partly the long history of these and all aspects of the natural world *as mourners*...that rules out here in *Lycidas* any sense of a framework of 'Nature' inimical or indifferent to 'Man' or from which he is separable; a pure gentleness like cool balm breathes through all these passages. (97)

The despairing sense of a whole powerful creation powerless before one ultimate threat is the ground of the final vision of love's conquest of death. Not truly sudden, or new, not opposed by but joined underneath to the image of the strewn flowers, this consolation—the only one Milton finds—has been shadowed throughout the poem. The ebb and flow of love and hostility in the universe is the secret of *Lycidas'* obscure and almost primitive power. (98)

Thus Miss Tuve does not share a common view of the floral catalogue as deliberately factitious and ironical. 'For the sense that there is
such a thing as loving pity in the natural universe (of which evil men and
good are a part), seeping in after the inimical violence which preceded,
becomes a calm strong tide carried by the generous abandon of these
lines' (104). Lines 152–3 ('For so...surmise') are not 'an indication
that Milton repudiates the truth of preceding reflections—because he
finds that his "pagan" and his Christian comforts conflict and therefore
asks us to throw away, as "false surmise", solace we have all felt to be
real as we read' (105).

It is now possible to see with more exactness and force that we disturb and
nullify this entire design of images that discuss meaning and destiny in the
universe when we import into pastoral even subconsciously that special and
quite recent way of thinking which takes 'Man' out of 'Nature'. The very
ground of the imagery in pastoral writing is the integrity of the great fabric of
created nature, and a chief contribution of reading to saturation in Milton's
predecessors and fellows is a posture of the mind, an immediate and unreflecting
readiness to feel this assumption true. (106)

Finally, 'In Milton's anagogical figure for the complete victory of
that principle which he has shadowed forth in all the consolations
throughout his poem, the terms are largely Christian, and one Christian
symbol, a usual one, is basic—the marriage between the human soul
and Heavenly Love' (110). 'There is no incongruity and certainly no
surprise in the classical close of Milton's image' (111).

Northrop Frye has analysed and synthesized *Lycidas* with results that,
as we might expect, in some essentials differ widely from what approximate orthodoxy modern criticism has developed ('Literature as Context:
Milton's *Lycidas*,' *Comparative Literature I: Proceedings of the Second
Congress of the International Comparative Literature Association*, ed. W.
P. Friederich, Chapel Hill, 1959, 44–55; repr. in Patrides, 200–11, the
text cited here, and in Frye's *Fables of Identity*, New York, 1963).

Frye's method is partly apparent in his initial assumption or equation.
'The pastoral elegy seems to have some relation to the ritual of the Adonis
lament,' and Edward King 'is given the pastoral name of Lycidas,

which is equivalent to Adonis, and is associated with the cyclical rhythms of nature,' especially of the sun, the seasons, and water flowing from fountains through rivers to the sea. Lycidas is the 'archetype' or literary symbol of King, and Milton adds 'the conventional archetypes of King as poet and of King as priest,' that is, Orpheus and Peter, whose attributes 'link them in imagery with Lycidas.'

The body of the poem is arranged in the form ABACA, a main theme repeated twice with two intervening episodes, as in the musical rondo. The main theme is the drowning of Lycidas in the prime of his life; the two episodes, presided over by the figures of Orpheus and Peter, deal with the theme of premature death as it relates to poetry and to the priesthood respectively. In both the same type of image appears:...the 'abhorred shears'...and the 'two-handed engine'.... (202)

Milton accomplishes transitions from these episodes back to the main theme by open allusion to the pastoral tradition. And, following that tradition, he associates himself with the dead man.

'Apart from the historical convention of the pastoral,...there is also the conventional framework of ideas or assumptions' which in poetry 'is rather a framework of images.' 'It consists of four levels of existence': that of Christian belief; that of human nature (man fallen but seeking to regain something of Eden and the Golden Age); physical nature, 'which is morally neutral but theologically "fallen"'; and the unnatural disorder of sin and death. 'Lycidas has his connections with all of these orders,' as the critic shows in detail.

Four inter-related principles work together in the composition of *Lycidas*: convention, genre, archetype, and a nameless fourth, 'the fact that the forms of literature are autonomous: that is, that they do not exist outside literature.' Unless we start with the hypothesis that the poem is a unity we may be misled by biographical data or literary sources or the related fallacy which confuses 'personal sincerity and literary sincerity.' Milton 'was even by seventeenth-century standards an unusually professional and impersonal poet,' and *Lycidas* must not be approached primarily as a biographical document (208). One more critical principle, the one Frye's paper is written to enunciate, is a logical

consequence of the others: 'It is literature as an order of words...
which forms the primary context of any given work of literary art. All
other contexts...are secondary and derivative contexts.' 'The short,
simple, and accurate name for this principle is myth. The Adonis myth
is what makes *Lycidas* both distinctive and traditional...The Adonis
myth in *Lycidas* is the structure of *Lycidas*....It is the connecting link
between what makes *Lycidas* the poem it is and what unites it to other
forms of poetic experience.' Thus 'the primary business of the critic
is with myth as the shaping principle of a work of literature.' 'In its
simplest English meaning a myth is a story about a god, and Lycidas is,
poetically speaking, a god or spirit of nature, who eventually becomes a
saint in heaven, which is as near as one can get to godhead in ordinary
Christianity.'

Since 'all problems of criticism are problems of comparative literature,' there must be some standard of comparison, and literary criticism
seems to lack such standards. 'The first step, I think, is to recognize
the dependence of value-judgments on scholarship.' 'The second step
is to recognize the dependence of scholarship on a coordinated view
of literature. A good deal of taxonomy lies ahead of us.'

If we are disturbed, as we may be, by Frye's making Adonis central
in a poem that never alludes to him (see Abrams below, under 1961), we
may recall some corrective and pregnant sentences from his *Anatomy of
Criticism* (Princeton, 1957, 121–2): 'Each aspect of *Lycidas* poses the
question of premature death as it relates to the life of man, of poetry,
and of the Church. But all of these aspects are contained within the
figure of Christ, the young dying god who is eternally alive, the Word
that contains all poetry, the head and body of the Church, the good
Shepherd whose pastoral world sees no winter, the Sun of righteousness
that never sets, whose power can raise Lycidas, like Peter, out of the
waves, as it redeems souls from the lower world, which Orpheus failed
to do. Christ does not enter the poem as a character, but he pervades
every line of it so completely that the poem, so to speak, enters him.'

R. L. Brett ('Milton's *Lycidas*,' *Reason & Imagination*, London,
1960, 21–50) does not give much space to the poem itself. He sketches

the young Milton's inheritance of Christian humanism, the traditional accord between reason and faith, nature and grace, the classics and Scripture, a synthesis threatened by scientific rationalism and Puritanism. *Comus*, though a product of Milton's Christian Platonism, showed signs of tension, and *Lycidas* reveals open conflict, especially at three points: line 50 ('Where were ye Nymphs'); line 76 (the speech of Phoebus, i.e. God); and 108 (St Peter's speech). These conscious disruptions of the pastoral mode indicate that the fact of death has shaken the values of the natural order, which Milton's Christian faith finds quite inadequate. 'What we have in *Lycidas* is not a mingling of the sacred and pagan but an opposition between them' (45). 'The poem is concerned then with the battle between the reason and the senses; between humanism and Puritanism; between the Renaissance and the Reformation conceptions of poetry. Moreover, the battle is a personal one; it is being waged in Milton's own mind as well as in the world.' The last line is a 'farewell to the pastoral tradition and all that it symbolizes' (47).

G. S. Fraser's 'random reflections' ('Approaches to *Lycidas*,' *The Living Milton*, ed. F. Kermode, 1960, 32–54) can hardly be said to advance criticism but have special interest as coming from a poet and critic of modern literature. Fraser stresses a kinship between *Lycidas* and Spenser's *Shepheardes Calender*; opposes Ransom's theory that *Lycidas* was a piece of 'nearly anonymous' pastoralism, a theory refuted by Milton's manuscript revisions; and opposes also the views of two prejudiced critics, Robert Graves (*Lycidas* is a poem 'strangled by art') and Dr Johnson. In countering such aberrations Fraser draws aid from R. Tuve, whose essay (see above) is 'the finest' he knows. Her wholly sympathetic acceptance of Milton's religious beliefs may not, however, be possible for those modern readers who cannot take as 'real' Milton's proclamation 'that not decay and death but life and creativity and love is the universal principle' (*Images*, 103). One answer to such readers 'is simply this: the creation, the existence, the survival, the impact upon ourselves of a poem like *Lycidas* is, surely, a very important part of the evidence we have' for that very principle. 'Art *makes* truth, its own kind of truth.' While repeating the tiresome complaint that it is hard to like

Milton much, Fraser avows enormous admiration. 'He moves in less solitary grandeur, I think, in *Lycidas* than anywhere else. No poem, of that length, in the English language, is more through and through an art-work; yet what other poem of that length touches so vividly, or so deeply, the primal sympathies?'

M. H. Abrams comes in happily at this point with an incisive review of main lines of previous interpretation ('Five Types of *Lycidas*,' Patrides, 212–31, the text here cited; repr. as 'Five Ways of Reading *Lycidas*,' *Varieties of Literary Experience*, ed. S. Burnshaw, New York, 1962). He finds that, 'on the evidence of their own commentaries, critics agree about the excellence of quite different poems.'

(1) The view that prevailed during the period from the first volume of Masson's *Life* (1859) up to the age of Eliot and Richards was epitomized in the first edition of Hanford's *Handbook* (1926): an elegy on King, following the pastoral convention, ending with a Christian consolation; a poem mainly impersonal but, in the two 'digressions,' expressing Milton's own concern about premature death and his abhorrence of clerical corruption. The poem was seen as clear enough, apart from the crux of the 'two-handed engine.'

(2) In 1930 (*Milton*: outlined above) Tillyard 'sounded the new note in criticism' by distinguishing 'between the nominal and the real subject,' King and Milton—a method of splitting meanings 'extraordinarily widespread' in modern criticism of poetry and 'repeatedly applied to *Lycidas*' (a method descended from the old allegorical defences of poetry).

(3) At the opposite pole from Tillyard was Ransom (see above), who took *Lycidas* as 'the public performance of a ritual elegy,' 'an exercise in pure linguistic technique, or metrics,' and also 'an exercise in the technique of what our critics of fiction refer to as "point of view."' 'There is no passion in the poem, and so no problem,' although there are gestures of 'rebellion against the formalism of his art.' Abrams remarks that 'two of the items' Ransom 'decries as arrogant gestures of Milton's originality are exactly those in which he closely follows established conventions,' that is, the adaptation of the *canzone* and the attack on the clergy.

(4) Brooks and Hardy (see above) are preoccupied with images, especially of water. But images are symbols, and 'the early part of the poem presents the despairing theme that nature is neutral, emptied of the old pastoral deities...; and this concept is transcended only by the movement from philosophic naturalism to Christian supernaturalism, in the pastoral imagery of the conclusion in heaven.' Such a theme 'seems to be startlingly anachronistic' and belongs rather to *In Memoriam*. It 'is by a notable sleight of explication' that Brooks and Hardy convert into the sense of nature's neutrality 'the very passage in which Milton explicitly states the contrary' (lines 39 f.).

(5) The archetypal approach is represented by the 'fairly traditional' Adams and the very radical Frye (see above).

Each of these essentially different readings 'claims to have discovered the key element, or structural principle' which governed the composition of the poem and 'establishes for the reader the meaning, unity, and value of the whole' (221). [Abrams' survey leaves out some other critics who might be less vulnerable.] The best hope of remedy 'lies in going back to Milton's text and reading it with a dogged literalness, except when there is clear evidence that some part of it is to be read allegorically or symbolically.' This Abrams proceeds to do (221–31).

A poem is made of speech and entails a particular speaker, and Abrams emphasizes the *persona* of the uncouth swain, whom 'Milton is at considerable pains to identify as someone other than himself.' The feeling in this 'dramatic lyric' 'is experienced and expressed not by Milton,' but by the singer, who sets out 'both to lament and to celebrate Lycidas.' But in a second and important sense the subject 'is a question about the seeming profitlessness of the dedicated life and the seeming deficiency of divine justice raised by that shocking death in the mind of the lyric speaker. That the rise, evolution, and resolution of the troubled thought of the elegist is the key to the structure of *Lycidas*, Milton made as emphatic as he could,' notably in the final picture of the elegist reassured (224). The images are 'less determining than determined'; they do not displace but corroborate the process of feeling and thought.

Lycidas

Lycidas is not about Adonis, to whom it never alludes. As a learned Christian humanist of the Renaissance, Milton well knew the place of pagan myth in relation to the one archetypal body of truth, the Bible. Further, if we take rebirth as a theme revealed in the opening lines and repeated with variations throughout, 'then the denouement of the poem lies in its exordium and its movement is not a progress but an eddy' (226).

'The movement of *Lycidas*, on the contrary, is patently from despair through a series of insights to triumphant joy.'

Milton achieves this reversal by a gradual shift from the natural, pastoral, and pagan viewpoint to the viewpoint of Christian revelation and its promise of another world, the Kingdom of Heaven. He carefully marks for us the stages of this ascent by what, to contemporary readers, was the conspicuous device of grading the levels of his style.

Abrams describes these gradations (227-9). St Peter's speech, a close paraphrase of Christ's parable of sheep, wolf, and good shepherd (John 9. 39-41, 10. 1-18), turns out 'to be nothing less than the climax and turning point of the lyric meditation,' because 'A Christian subject is here for the first time explicit,' and because the allusive parallel between Lycidas and Christ assures the final resolution.

The elegiac singer, however, is momentarily occupied with the specific references rather than the Scriptural overtones of Peter's comment, with the result that the resolution, so skillfully planted in his evolving thought, is delayed until he has tried to interpose a little ease by strewing imaginary flowers on Lycidas' imagined hearse. But this evasion only brings home the horror of the actual condition of the lost and weltering corpse. By extraordinary dramatic management, it is at this point of profoundest depression that the thought of Lycidas' body...releases the full implication of St. Peter's speech, and we make the leap from nature to revelation, in the great lyric peripety: 'Weep no more...that walk'd the waves.' (229)

'This consolation is total, where the two earlier ones were partial.' And while the earlier promises of Apollo and Peter had been hearsay, now a style of biblical and soaring sublimity brings direct vision of ultimate truth, and with that the transfiguration of all that had gone before. The scene and style subside to the solitary piper 'facing with restored confidence the contingencies of a world in which the set and rise of the material sun are only the emblematic promise of another life.' However 'unexciting' the conclusion, '*Lycidas* is really what it seems.'

R. Beum's 'The Pastoral Realism of *Lycidas*' (*Western Humanities Review* 15, 1961, 325–9) is a semipopular appreciation of the pastoral form and rightness of a poem which transcends the tradition and 'achieves realism: a slice of life, cut from the inside.'

M. Lloyd ('The Two Worlds of "Lycidas,"' *Essays in Criticism*, 11, 1961, 390–402) sees the poem's structure as based on the distinction 'between a mortal world self-absorbed, and one seen rather in relation to a supernatural world. The poem shows their interaction; and what in the sole light of the corporal world brought despair, will lead to its contrary when seen in relation to a world beyond the corporal' (390).

Milton deals chiefly 'with the salvation of the shepherd rather than the sheep.' The bad shepherd, absorbed in the corporal world, 'exemplifies that spiritual death, dependent on the Fall, from which man may now be reprieved' (392). 'The good shepherd...will survive corporal death because his understanding is not confined to the corporal world.' 'The good shepherd, poet or cleric, marks the voice that gives knowledge of the supernatural world...' (394). For the basic distinction in the poem, St Peter's speech 'is crucial...it continues the process begun by Phoebus: it separates and defines the merely mortal, and shows what had hitherto been seen in self-contained mortal terms in the light of a transcendent world....Peter leads us to conceive of the Fury's own blind action as limited to the corporal existence' (394). There are contrasted ideas of opening and closing, heaven and hell, golden and iron, sheephook and engine, the protective and the destructive. These ideas of life and death are worked out in images of water, the sun, the Fury's shears and the shearers' feast. The image of Michael touches his double function, earthly and heavenly: 'God and angel are active in saving mortal man from the "perilous flood."' 'The good shepherd Lycidas will also remain active' in the corporal world as the Genius of the shore (398).

Lycidas

'The poem is conceived so as not merely to expound but to dramatise this contrast between the two worlds....Milton has dramatised his theme in terms of the poet-speaker, in whom an initial exclusive awareness of the corporal world is enlightened by divine voices, whose revelation he then publishes to those still within the corporal world and grieving within its limited understanding.' The poem 'is from the first pregnant with substance to be later interpreted; but in its opening phase, its phenomena are either misunderstood by the poet or not suspected to be significant' (398). From poetry as merely the classical Muses, and the poet's death, to the poet's (and good shepherd's) reward, limited earthly ideas are reinterpreted in supernatural terms. At the end 'The poet is replaced in the context of untranscended nature, of which in mortal life he remains a part.' But now, with the reinterpretation of phenomena, 'the poet himself is changed' (401), and nature, which had been the scene and instrument of violent disturbance, is viewed as ordered process; 'but the very landscape of "tomorrow" carries both a memory and a prophecy of the landscape to which the dead poet is translated' (402).

Lowry Nelson ('Milton's "Lycidas,"' *Baroque Lyric Poetry*, 1961, 64–76) pursues his discussion of 'time structure' (see *Nativity* III, under 1954). In the *Nativity* the time perspective is given; in *Lycidas* the poet must construct it. In the opening lines 'two time planes are... firmly established: the speaker's present and the remote past of Lycidas' and the speaker's youth.' The next two paragraphs (37–63) present the times of present loss and of the drowning. In 64 f. ('Alas! What boots it') 'the poem works out of the past...and emerges into a general present. It is actually a return to the first time plane, that of the speaker "performing" his discourse,' and the 'ultimate question' is posed in the present tense. Phoebus' reply (76 f.) is in the past tense, a reply to a question that could be asked at the time of Lycidas' death. The same effect is carried on in 85 f. ('O Fountain Arethuse'), where 'performance' continues in 'proceeds' and 'listens' but Phoebus, Triton, Camus, and St Peter 'are all described in the past,' yet a past more recent than that of Lycidas' youth or death. The flower passage is 'entirely in the present.

It is the first long passage which implies a time plane identical with that of the speaker.' Thus 'there has been a gradual progression from the remote past to the present; and with each stage the sharpness of grief for Lycidas' death has been intensified.' In the climactic paragraph 'sunk low' refers to the past and 'but mounted high' 'to the new present, a present continuing into the future,' 'for ever.' Lines 182-5 are parallel in time and complete 'the whole ceremony of mourning' and the process of reconciliation. The last paragraph, put into the past, gives 'a final impression of the poem as performance....We are left with a rich double sense of finality and continuance.'

Nelson thus summarizes the 'time planes': '(1) present (speaker's performance), (2) remote past (speaker and Lycidas' youth), (3) less remote past (Lycidas' death), (4) recent past (procession of 'mourners'), (5) present (flower passage), and (6) new present (Lycidas risen).' 'Throughout the poem we are not allowed to lose sight of the speaker's present' and the act of performance. 'The space required for working out the poem as performance and for evolving the time scheme is a major source of tension; for it allows the detailed elaboration of the causes for grief, and the gradual intensification of what seems hopelessness.' Nelson objects to premature Christianizing of pagan allusions as damaging to the final Christian solution toward which the whole evolves.

Nelson returns to *Lycidas* (pp. 138-52) to discuss the rhetorical structure and baroque 'dramaticality.' He sees three sections, 1-84, 85-164, 165-85 [the last two are not the orthodox divisions of Barker et al.]. In the first, which establishes the whole rhetorical situation, the speaker addresses a succession of audiences: his immediate hearers, the Muses, a more general audience, Lycidas, the Nymphs, and the hearers or readers again. The first section ends with grief tempered by recognition of 'the benevolence of Nature and the possibility of *some* heavenly reward.' The second section, describing the mourners and invoking the flowers, 'has no one clearly defined audience.' St Peter carries the personal grief of the speaker, the Nymphs, and Camus into 'a public or even a social dimension.' The speaker is now able to continue with formal public obsequies and, as he goes on, 'he more and more identifies himself with others.' Discussion of the third section is concerned chiefly with Christian allusions and symbols and with the change in the speaker's role 'from that of mourner to that of universal comforter.' The last eight lines 'objectify the original speaker' and 'catch up main threads and bind the poem.' And 'the reader is brought in again as final witness to a summary of the whole situation of the poem.' 'Also, the dominant fiction of the poem, the pagan pastoral convention, reasserts itself, having been reconciled with Christianity.'

George Williamson, 'The Obsequies for Edward King,' *Seventeenth Century Contexts* (1961), 132–47. See 1 above and, in IV below, notes on 1–36, 104–6, 132–3, 167–73.

K. Jones's 'A Note on Milton's "Lycidas"' (*American Imago* 19, 1962, 141–55) is an unfortunate piece of popular psychologizing; it stresses Milton's feeling guilty of jealousy over the mediocre Edward King's having received the fellowship that he himself should have had (a notion perhaps taken from Robert Graves).

J. S. Lawry ('"Eager Thought": Dialectic in *Lycidas*,' *PMLA* 77, 1962, 27–32; repr. in A. Barker, *Milton*, 1965) sees lingering complaints about pastoralism (Dr Johnson et al.) and lack of order and unity (G. W. Knight, above, under 1939) largely nullified if we read *Lycidas* 'as in part a dialectical process' of thesis, antithesis, and synthesis. 'Within *Lycidas*, the major subject of this process is poetry itself. The timeless, serene, and objective attitudes of pastoral, impassioned only in formal artistic imitation of loss, are opposed by the skeptical affronts of death, temporal corruption, and several failures of consolation, all of which are impassioned in and through actual experience. However, each of these two modes of awareness or response is found to be incomplete in the course of the work, and a consummate statement, greater than either but partaking of both, gradually evolves. Put another way, the general issue is that of the possibility of poetry and, more particularly, of Christian poetry.' Pastoral attitudes and materials 'are held to be *ideally* poetic. . . . But the "digressions" enforce actuality upon this ideal, threatening to destroy it exactly as actuality had destroyed Edward King.'

This dialectical process is not argumentative, since *Lycidas* 'is triumphantly a poem, not discourse.' 'Not only are potentialities of synthesis lodged in the early stages of the poem, but also pastoral details appear in the digressions and pressures of actuality in the pastoral sections, thereby suggesting in another way the immense reconciliation which is to come.' The poem is not about King nor about Milton: 'it is about poetry and the poet, generally conceived, and of the conditions impelled by existence upon the poet and his works. It is with this concern that the dialectical process begins. On the one hand, King's death (and the death of any person, but especially of any poet) is objective material for poetic expression, the "ideal" form of which is the pastoral elegy.... But on the other hand, the death of the individual poet, King, implies the real death of the poet generally and the consequent death of poetry. Melodious artistic lament...is confronted by the anguished recognition of real physical loss, of defeated promise, and of corrupt society. Lament veers sharply away from the provinces of "pure" art as the vulnerable poet himself and his equally vulnerable creations become its subject.'

The nature of 'pure' poetry is illustrated by *L'Allegro* and *Il Penseroso*, in which the poet is delighted with his world but is, as a man, uninvolved. '*Lycidas* begins within the pastoral mode' of those poems, in which 'objective—"pure"—elegiac lament is possible.' But the initial apology becomes more than pastoral convention because 'King's untimely death *forces* expression'; the real impinges upon the ideal. 'The pastoral convention is maintained in the invocation to the muses, but a dominating point of opposition is again reached in the immediate connection of the lost Lycidas with poetry....Lament for Lycidas will necessitate lament for poetry—by implication, for the very poetry of the present elegist' [lines 19–22]. 'The sense of the loss of Lycidas, partially held off again for a time by conventional pastoral images of desolated nature—which, however, bear their own grim sense of mortality—returns strongly with "Such, *Lycidas*, thy loss to Shepherd's ear": again the threat of reality to poetry overcomes the pastoral attitude.'

'Ensuing conventional appeals to pastoral deities are intersected by the same sense of destruction, and for a time the pastoral convention is nearly surrendered....The materials of "pure" poetry seem useless or unuseable, denied by death. This unwilling but progressive surrender of the pastoral attitude moves directly from the recognition that Orpheus' voice, too, was stopped in death, to the first alleged "digression,"' the passage on fame and the blind Fury; in Phoebus' words 'praise of poetry and of the poet is not so much denied by reality as lodged elsewhere than in the world....For the first time in the poem, synthesis—in the partly disclosed theme of resurrection and right judgment—tentatively reveals itself.'

'However, Phoebus' lofty and not immediately comforting statement is left suspended as the poem returns to pastoral conventions..., which have already shown themselves unequal to the thrust of reality.' The pastoral world is guiltless of Lycidas' death, but could not prevent it. 'Then suddenly St. Peter, a water-figure for the moment alien to the pastoral world, appears, shivering the helpless pastoral scene completely for the time.' He 'speaks not through the imaginative and beautiful pastoral convention but through stern theological "realities," judging the contemporary physical reality.' The 'two-handed engine' 'will somehow restore justice,' but 'little mitigation is offered for the present.' 'However, the second note of synthesis has been lodged, and a transformation of the pastoral attitude now begins. Transferred into Christian application, gradually adopting the Christian iconology of the shepherd as poet-priest, the pastoral materials can move into and beyond formerly antagonistic reality.'

'Such a change within pastoral is distantly figured as the poem returns from the second "digression" to the pastoral mode: the stream of Alpheus, shrunken by the "dread voice" of St. Peter, returns to fullness.' 'The poem proceeds now in a mood of relative serenity, as if both real corruption and the apparent powerlessness of the pastoral were largely overcome. Before the final synthesis is reached, however, there appears the lapidary flower section, in which pastoral impotence, if alleviated, is yet present. As Wayne Shumaker has shown [above, under 1951], these memorial flowers bring color and a lightening of the grimmest sense of death; yet they offer only illusory ease and "false surmise" against the reality of loss. But "false surmise" looks ahead, as well, to the evident physical reality—the terrifying picture of King's body "hurl'd" or hidden in the destructive sea....The two attitudes of the poem here meet: pastoral poetry in and of itself is weak before the onslaught of actuality, but actuality itself gradually has been discovered to rest within a vastly larger aspect, that of eternity. The confrontation of the two modes, each of which has revealed weakness and incompleteness, together with the emergent Christianizing of both, permits the poem to move with certain confidence beyond the last eddy of doubt, in which both attitudes were caught in the suspense of "false surmise" and were thereby made ready for the reconciliation which follows.'

With 'Lycidas your sorrow is not dead' synthesis is fully achieved. 'All the water images, formerly given to sterility, the unbearable reality of drowning, or to the impotence of pastoral beauty...now unite to present resurrection. The seemingly dying Day-Star sinks in order to rise, just as Christ, who also triumphed over the waves and made them benign, "died" to a greater life....Lycidas in his way becomes transformed from victim to saviour, like Christ; he is delivered beyond the lament either of pastoral or of reality. There is a full return to pastoral convention at the end of the elegy, but that convention now has been shot through with Christian illumination....The formerly agonized reception of reality now is altered as a higher vision leads the speaker into "eager thought."' 'Temporal reality is revealed in a far different light as Christian judgment and Christian confidence in resurrection bring corruption to account and death into increased life....Theocritus has assumed the harp of David....The poet may now confront, receive, and finally surmount experience, combining pastoral or "pure" beauty with his expression of experienced realities; for those realities, seen within God's eternally Real purposes, are materials for holy song.'

Paul Ramsey ('Lycidas: A Proper Poem,' *The Lively and the Just,* University of Alabama Studies 15, 1962, 41–61) begins: 'Lycidas is the best shorter poem in the language...it is great because it fits neoclassical (that is, correct) standards,...a propriety to subject, intent, genre, theme; propriety of sound, image, syntax, structure. It obeys the rules.' We may quarrel with 'because,' since there have been many 'correct' dead poems, but Ramsey rises above his text to a perceptive if not notably fresh demonstration of the poem's universality and uniqueness. While we cannot follow his various headings, some comments may be recorded. Milton's subject is not Milton but King; the poem 'exalts him, universalizes and idealizes him, so that he *becomes* a serious figure that the proper emotions really adhere to.' What the poem 'is most importantly about' is 'the problem of justice; he says that our fears and doubts can be resolved by the knowledge that God will judge finally and truly.' The passage on fame 'faces out one major cause of doubt: the brute power and meaninglessness of the physical universe and of death.' St Peter's speech represents 'human corruption *as a cause of metaphysical and religious doubt.*' The answer to both 'needs to be given as vision,' a vision of justice and mercy. The whole subject, then, is (as Daiches said), 'nothing less than man's activity on earth.' In the presentation and resolution of the grand problem all the major and minor proprieties are fulfilled and transcended.

As we may infer from his title, *Milton, Mannerist and Baroque* (University of Toronto, 1963, 37–50), Roy Daniells is concerned, like Wylie Sypher (above, under 1955), to show that *Lycidas* is a Mannerist poem. He accepts Barker's account of three parallel movements with their several climaxes [above, under 1940–1], but within that taut structure he sees the dynamics of Mannerism at work: e.g. in the learned and eclectic handling of traditional convention, the introduction of heterogeneous named or nameless figures, and especially the constant shifts of scene and tone. 'These manipulations of space are of the greatest importance in the identification of Mannerist effects' (40). 'There is no ordered landscape....Each figure tends to bring his own space with him and these neither combine into a totality of perspective nor separate into planes having some relation' (40). The rapid shifts, the refusals to satisfy expectations, appear in the versification as well as in the treatment of ideas and images. 'The effect upon the sensibility is emphatic but mysterious....' 'The vision [of heaven] approaches mystical insight and it has often been wondered why it is in fact so much less satisfying than Dante's heavenly rose and eternal fountain, why it suggests, though it vastly transcends, the heaven of "The Blessed Damosel."' The reason is that Milton's imagery is in part 'dream-like and peripheral,' 'not directed explicitly to or about the presence of God,' and that the nuptial song 'does not unite the soul of the dead shepherd to the love of the Great Shepherd.' 'A complete Christian apotheosis... would shatter the whole poem' and make irrelevant the themes of fame, vengeance on the clergy, and even sorrow for the loss of Lycidas. [One cannot help wondering whether this logic, if it would not shatter Dante, would not make much of him irrelevant?] Milton avoids the difficulty by a swift return to pastoral; the heavenly vision 'is in accordance only with the demands of the poem...' (47). Milton's resolution in his final paragraph is, it 'has often been noted,' out of key with the whole poem. The opening of the poem was also out of key, since the poet's passionate concern with his own fame asserted itself 'with what seems inexcusably indecent haste' (38). Notwithstanding such signal defects, Daniells concludes that '*Lycidas* in achieving its place as the most effective lyric utterance in the English language has relied heavily upon its Mannerist method.' Its 'crowning achievement...lies in the enormously ramified complex of reactions, conscious and unconscious, which it provokes.'

Like Abrams, W. G. Madsen ('The Voice of Michael in *Lycidas*,' *SEL* 3, 1963, 1–7) finds most recent interpretations unsatisfactory because they get too far away from the text: witness the varying accounts of the floral catalogue—by Daiches, Hardy, Shumaker, Allen, and R. Tuve—as ironic and delusive or affirmative and exultant. Abrams' account [see the last long excerpt in the summary of Abrams above] Madsen thinks 'psychologically unconvincing' because the uncouth swain must be assumed to be 'a Christian well versed in the New Testament,' although he sounds so much like a pagan, turning to nature for consolation, questioning the nymphs, accepting pagan superstition about the wrecked ship, calling on the dolphins. Madsen suggests that 'the current confusion about *Lycidas*...has resulted from assuming that the consolation is spoken by the uncouth swain. We have failed to hear the voice of Michael. If we disregard the speeches of Phoebus and the pilot of the Galilean lake and read only those passages in which the uncouth swain speaks in his own person, we will see that up to the consolation he does not progress one iota from the "natural, pastoral, and pagan viewpoint" of the opening.' The Christian revelation 'occurs because the angel does indeed melt with ruth and reveal to the uncouth swain that there are "other groves, and other streams" than those of the pastoral tradition.' *Lycidas* is 'not dealing with metaphors but with typological symbols.' We share the pagan and pastoral experience of the swain, from despair to 'the exaltation he must have felt when he heard the voice of the angel.' But as Christian readers we have another and higher experience, since we, all along, comprehend far more than the singer can. Madsen repeats this view in his small edition, *Milton* (New York, 1964) and in his study of Milton's typology, *From Shadowy Types to Truth* (New Haven and London, 1968), 6–17. It seems to raise difficulties: how can we 'disregard' the passage on heavenly fame and St Peter's speech, which are parts of the evolving poem?

Marjorie Nicolson (*John Milton: A reader's guide to his poetry*, 1963, 87–111), in keeping with the purpose of her book, is concerned with introducing the uninitiated to 'the most perfect long short poem in the English language.' She gives information about the pastoral conventions, explains Milton's adaptation or re-creation of these, and shows how he blends pagan and Christian allusions and ideas (she disagrees with those who see lines 1–84 as pagan and 85–193 as Christian). In the second half of her commentary Miss Nicolson turns from details to their organization in the poem as a whole, to Milton's development of the successive themes of loss and grief, the questioning of divine justice, and the final ecstatic vindication of God's ways to men. She emphasizes the structural principles of both the Italian *canzone* and the Italian *monodia* (the latter defined by G. L. Finney as 'music sung by a solo voice in the new recitative style'), and sees a good deal of structural and emotional significance in Milton's use of 'Myrtle and laurel, sadness and triumph.'

Isabel G. MacCaffrey ('*Lycidas*: The Poet in a Landscape,' *The Lyric and Dramatic Milton*, ed. J. H. Summers, 1965, 65–92) observes that

'*Lycidas*, almost alone among Milton's important poems, does not suggest at the beginning how it will end.' The opening, too, unlike other openings, is direct, personal, 'dramatic, unmediated, unfolding in time and in the space of a recognizable but, at the beginning, incompletely realized pastoral landscape' (69). The theme is 'the loss of innocence,' rendered, not as in *Paradise Lost*, but with a foreshortened temporal development, 'an exposure of the process, known to each one of us, by which innocence *becomes* experience'—the process generated by the impact of Death and Chance and Time (the linked powers which, in Milton's earlier poem, can be conquered only by Eternity).

'The true landscape of *Lycidas* is the speaker's consciousness'; 'the shepherd awakens from the dream of innocence to find himself living in a world of experience, a world of death, injustice, and sick roses, ruled by a blind Fury.' 'Both the temporal and the spatial perspectives of *Lycidas* are designed to convey the implications of this awakening.' 'In shifts of tone, setting, and temporal planes, Milton imitates a basic pattern of consciousness, the emerging sense of loss in all its catastrophic significance' (72). In the first paragraph the theme of loss and disorder appears in the untimely plucking of berries and leaves and in the image of Lycidas weltering in the sea. The 'most complete rendering of landscape' in the poem is the pictured memory of pastoral innocence (lines 23–36), now replaced by 'the fallen world of heavy change'—that is, by the change in the speaker's state of mind, the result of experience. 'Two facts about "nature" become visible: a desolating unconcern with man, implicit in her ability to renew her life; and the fact that the only valid "sympathy" between macrocosm and microcosm must be based on their common corruption as fallen worlds'—though nature, unlike man, cannot be aware of its state. It is only in the mind of man that benign past and harsh reality can co-exist (76). '*Lycidas* reenacts, then, both the immemorial journey of the maturing spirit and the development of one of humanity's most resourceful metaphors for that journey. It is a poem "about" poetry *and* about human life—about the two in conjunction, man's vision of himself and the mirror of art in which he sees the vision. It can be read as a reassessment of the pastoral mode itself. Innocence is exchanged for bleak experience, in turn to be replaced by a wiser innocence' (77–8).

'All four elements play a part in *Lycidas*, and all an ambivalent part, reflecting their divided allegiance in a fallen world where they may either serve as emblems of their Creator or become the playthings of satanic forces.' The speaker 'reaches a point where the demonic aspect of creation dominates his consciousness. Experience has supplanted innocence, and the pastoral metaphor of a nature exactly congruent with man's life, responsive to his hopes and fears, has been revealed as inadequate.' Nature is found not to be responsible for Lycidas' fate, and is excused, but man is not. 'The passages on Fame and the Church move away from the pastoral foreground into the vicissitudes of history and the consequences of our lost innocence' (80). 'The source of contagion in flower and flock is not "innocent nature" but sin-ridden human beings, here monstrously reduced to "blind mouthes"' (83).

'In the final paragraphs of the song, resolution and consolation are achieved and the validity of the pastoral mode is confirmed,' but only at the end of 'this our darke voyage' (*RCG, Works* 3, 186). 'We turn from a minute and loving attention to the details of pastoral landscape in close-up, to the gigantic horizons of distant seascapes, from the bottom of the monstrous world to the heavenly hosts singing in their glory. The sequence...renders metaphorically the fundamental pattern of Christian literature, a movement through the tragic phase to an ultimately comic vision' (83–4). The floral passage brings a measure of consolation, but is a 'false surmise.' 'Pastoral as the dream of an actual earthly paradise is about to be finally abandoned, but pastoral as a holy fiction foreshadowing a heavenly meed is about to be confirmed.' The picture of the helpless, tossing body leads into the sudden vision of St Michael. 'The hinge of the transition from the infernal underworld to the heaven of heavens is the Sun image, the second of the two major similes in *Lycidas*' (86). 'This parallel is profoundly reassuring in its context—chiefly...because it denies the most poignant disparity between man and the nonhuman world.' 'Milton's conclusion reaffirms the congruence between nature's cycle and man's: Lycidas, *like* the daystar, is "sunk low but mounted high."' 'Milton wishes us to hold apart in imagination the various realms of being—natural, human, supernatural—precisely so tnat we can admire the marvelous correspondences between them' (87). 'We are able, owing to the song's last paragraph, to look back to earlier sections, especially the flower passage, and see them in a new light....' 'The force that accomplishes these metamorphoses is the same that translates Lycidas: "the dear might of him that walk'd the waves."' 'In the poem's temporal scheme, however, the redemption of nature is not final, and the speaker, who has descended and reascended in imagination, must be returned to his native element of life in time....The metamorphosis of Lycidas effects this return....As the Genius of the shore, he will mediate between the still fallen world of the perilous flood and the realm of redeemed nature glimpsed by the speaker in vision' (89). When the song is ended, 'Its meaning is confirmed in the receding perspective of the coda which offers us, now more distantly but also more distinctly, a figure in a landscape, long familiar but now transfigured, *because* the song has been sung and the vision realized.' Milton's 'deliberate allusions to literary tradition underline the function of the stanza as a "return": a return to the pastoral landscape and the poetry based on it, now made potent as a vehicle of human meaning because its patterns are seen to be reproduced in the divine plan of the universe.' 'As for "tomorrow," it marks the return of a world where the future once again exists as full of promise, not a long day's dying, but "such a day tomorrow as today," a process endlessly renewed by the covenant of God himself. In this world will flourish, not eternal boyhood, but a wise innocence that has absorbed and transcended experience.' 'The poem's world becomes our world, the song's pattern a paradigm of our experience.'

Some of the leading ideas developed here are touched more briefly in Mrs MacCaffrey's edition, *Samson Agonistes and the Shorter Poems* (New York, 1966).

J. Frank ('The Unharmonious Vision: Milton as a Baroque Artist,' *Comparative Literature Studies* 3, 1966, 95–108) sees Milton, throughout his poetry, exploiting, stretching, and breaking traditions and conventions, in a thoroughly Baroque way. Even within so well-defined a form as the pastoral elegy, Milton seeks 'not to break a trail but to find the most difficult path. One critic[L. Nelson, *Baroque Lyric Poetry*, 67: above, under 1961] has aptly labeled the poem a "performance." As such, it differs from most poems in being at once more subtly and more obviously exhibitionistic. Milton dominates the poem, but sometimes one has to look hard to see him. Thus, for example, the shift to the third person in the concluding lines is the poet's curtain-call following the triumphant climax.' Frank stresses the number of roles Milton plays. 'His poetic voice...suddenly shifts from outraged zeal to quiet regret. More subtle are the modulations between homocentric and theocentric speaker, between subjective and objective observer, between John Milton and a Miltonic Edward King. Lycidas, the central "character," is shepherd, poet, priest, scholar, drowned corpse, heavenly singer of "the unexpressive nuptial Song," and guardian of all sailors crossing the Irish Sea. The range of tone is equally broad. The placement of the action in time changes, as does the scenic background, and both speaker and audience move from the here and now to different timeless worlds—classical, submarine, Christian—and back and forth between an indifferent and a responsive cosmos. In this performance Milton is not only writer and director, but he plays all the parts.

'Line by line the poem can be viewed as a medley of irresolutions, conventions, fragments. Yet the ensemble—the performance—seems resolved, unique, unified. The traditional pastoral elegy served Milton in the same way that the *Ur-Hamlet* served Shakespeare. And *Lycidas*, too, transmits a message that is inherently personal and ambiguous. It dramatizes the story of a young man facing up to the fact of death, bringing to the modern reader the consolation of beauty and honesty, if not of theology. Most seventeenth-century elegies bear bleak testimony to the hollowness and obsolescence of a form made too simple and utilized by poets who have all too willingly followed the rules. Milton as elegist had no understudies.'

C. H. Hinnant ('Freedom and Form in Milton's *Lycidas*,' 1967: *Papers of the Michigan Academy of Science, Arts, and Letters* 53, 1968, 321–8), seeking to explain the 'deliberate roughness' of Milton's 'varying line lengths and irregular stanzaic patterns,' offers two reasons. First is the agitation of grief traditionally associated with pastoral elegies (Spenser, *Daphnaïda* 11–14; L. Bryskett, *Mourning Muse of Thestylis* 124–8; etc.); an example closer to *Lycidas* is Cleveland's elegy in *Justa Edouardo King*, which proclaims his inability to keep sorrow in regular channels. A second reason 'was that the *persona* of pastoral was conceived as an actual shepherd, half-civilized, half-barbarian,' an 'uncouth Swain.' Hinnant cites Milton's *Elegy* 6. 5–8 and *Lycidas* 1–5, especially 'forc'd fingers rude.' The two smoothest passages in the poem are the assured judgment of Phoebus (76–84) and the concluding paragraph in which 'Milton shifts from the *persona* of the shepherd to omniscient narrator.'

B. Rajan ('*Lycidas*: The Shattering of the Leaves,' *SP* 64, 1967, 51–64; repr. in *The Lofty Rhyme*, 1970), while accepting the various lights criticism has thrown upon the poem, seeks to read it with 'educated innocence.' Milton's changes in lines 4–5 [see Notes below] introduce a sudden note of violence 'that opens the lonely road to the blind fury' (53). 'What is being "forced" is ultimately the decorum of the poem'; there is an 'angry challenge' to the tradition the poem inherits. The two passages most heavily revised are that on Orpheus and the catalogue of flowers, the former 'towards ferocious elementality,' the latter 'towards conventionality in the best sense, the pastoral mood wrought to the height of its beauty' (54). Such changes 'can only mean that he wished deliberately to intensify rather than to diminish the oppositions that dominate the poem'; 'the struggle between them is not one for supremacy, but rather for a vision which can include both.'

Each of the three parts [Rajan cites Barker: see above under 1940–1] 'begins with a statement that the pastoral convention has been or is about to be violated.' 'The assault of experience on the convention then develops and chaos beats against the wall of the poem's order, until an equilibrium is restored' (55). Thus 'there is involved...an assault upon the poem's own assumptions, which the poem in the act of making itself recognizes and progressively strengthens' (56). The 'consolations of the pastoral decorum, the coupling of life and death to the rhythm of nature, are designed so that the violence which follows can sweep them aside; but they also remain alive for the eventual restoration' (56). Rajan analyses these conflicts, especially the lines on Orpheus and on fame. The second part, beginning with the procession of mourners, carries on the theme that 'The calamity is no part of the order of life; it emanates from a world of arbitrary destructiveness and the Fury's true function is to slit the thread of design' (58).

The 'first temptation to irresponsibility' is 'the personal questioning of one's vocation,' the second is 'the public abandonment of one's calling' (58–9). The third is 'dalliance not with Amaryllis, or with the spoils of a desecrated office, but with that frail and precious sense of order out of which the poem has no choice but to advance' (59). [For Rajan's further comment on this passage see below, 154–7 n.]

Each of the three parts 'discloses a different face of God or more precisely, a different form of man's recognition of God's nature': the god of justice (the all-judging Jove of 76–84), 'the apocalyptic god of retribution' who crushes the godless, and, thirdly, the one recognition of God 'that can truly answer man's agony,' the God of redemptive love (61). 'In the end, even the shores and sounding seas are joined in a pattern of purpose, not a chaos of nihilism' (63). The conclusion marks a position established, a recognition achieved. 'The subtle shift from first to third person is a beautifully judged manoeuvre, distancing the poem, depersonalizing it and leaving it decidedly behind.' With all its intricate articulation, its 'technical accomplishment of extreme sophistication,' *Lycidas* 'is a voyage towards recognition, a poem that resolutely faces itself, that opens all windows upon the storm of reality and takes all assaults into its ultimate order. What gives the questioning its singular strength and the final resolution its inclusive validity is the complete integration of experience, structure and language.... It is because of this total authenticity that the poem is able to accommodate and eventually to unify a range of dissension that would otherwise tear it apart.'

W. J. Grace (*Ideas in Milton*, 1968, 145): 'The beauty of the poem actually consoles, in a spiritual as well as an aesthetic sense. One is led to feel the presence of a power, however mysterious and undefined, that is truly right, and *right* throughout the universe—and, moreover, communicable to human beings in terms to which they can respond through love to a divine love that is uncensorious, that delights in its own being and in our being. Milton's religious sense in this work far surpasses any intellectual mode; it is instinctive, intuitive, expressing a redemptive image that radiates through and transforms intellection and verbalization, even in the face of outright negation, as in the case of the corrupted clergy. The inner strength of the piece is such as to assimilate and transcend the thoughts and feelings that might threaten its harmony. The harsh and indignant voice is essential to its beauty, just as Dante's Hell is essential to his assertion of Paradise, for such contrasts and oppositions serve to create dynamic rather than flat, unilateral statements. Today the recognized word for this kind of artistic process is *tension*. In the final analysis "Lycidas" is not a poem of several moods but of one mood, one overriding tension, transcending and reconciling opposites.'

To J. S. Lawry's essay of 1962 (above) may be added his later discussion (*Shadow*, 1968, 96–120), which is governed by his general theme of 'matter and stance.' In earlier poems he noted the young Milton's lessening serenity and increasing recognition of sin and evil (see below, *Comus* IV, under 1968), and he remarks that the speaker in *Lycidas* is alone, without the Lady's divine aid. The dynamic structure is produced by 'three stances': first, that of 'an earthly Eden' (in the pastoral sections), now only remembered; that of lamentation and protest in the face of loss and corruption; and that of consolation, the assurance of immortality. The first two are partial and are swallowed up in the final truth of the third. 'The major stance of the prelude...is before the ancient altar of poetry.' But that the suppliant cannot maintain; although poetry is immortal, he is driven to despair by the fact of death. The benign pastoral landscape slides downward into 'a general protesting lament for lost poetry and priesthood' (lines 64 f.). However, through Apollo, the poem now 'retrieves its initial stance—that of immortal faith and poetry,' though it is not yet finally consoling. The poem returns to death and accuses the 'fatal...Bark'; this implies that 'original sin and Satan, not nature, are the causes through which death enters the Edenic world.' Then comes the speech of St Peter, a protest from God's spokesman, not from the doubting poet, and divine justice is guaranteed. In the flower passage the speaker moves from false surmise toward final truth. 'Heaven itself stoops toward mortal grief, in another great bond of reconciliation.' The ultimate assurance joins heaven and earth, and is not merely personal but universal.

J. H. Raleigh ('*Lycidas*: "Yet once more,"' *Prairie Schooner* 42, 1968–9, 303–18) looks at the poem as a document (1) of personal experience, (2) of English Renaissance Christianity, and (3) of timeless concern to readers. (1) The young King's death, shocking in itself, involved such striking facts as a calm sea and his praying while other passengers were fruitlessly busy about their mortal lives (French, *L.R.* 1, 341). Milton's mother and Ben Jonson died during 1637, and the plague of 1636–7 struck Horton. (2) *Lycidas* is concerned with permanence and change in three interconnected worlds, the natural, the human, and the heavenly. While nature on earth can be fatal to man, Heaven, with its groves and streams, is seen as '*a place of nature.*' Human fortunes and life are both transitory and subject to corruption, and felicity is possible only in heaven. The three divisions of the poem are not only dramatic and thematic but historical units as well. The first is almost wholly pagan (up to Apollo and Jove); the second, with its invective against the clergy, is in the spirit of the Old Testament (although, like the whole poem, it echoes the New); and the third ends joyfully with the ascent to the Christian heaven. '"Lycidas" is thus an epitome of Western civilization.' (3) Asking why *Lycidas* makes such an impact upon a modern unbeliever, Raleigh answers that it embodies 'all the outlines, concerns, movements of the psyche, existentially considered. It is about "becoming," the emergence of the ego to its full power.... It faces squarely, and derives its meaning from, the fact of death.'

J. Reesing ('Justice for Lycidas,' *Milton's Poetic Art: A Mask, Lycidas, Paradise Lost*, Cambridge, Mass., 1968, 21–8) comments on the apparent suddenness of the shift from despair to sublime reassurance, a passage which far transcends the elegiac convention in complexity and resonance. The idea of community, explicit or implicit in preceding allusions to shepherds, scholars, and priests, is now expanded to embrace the universe. In 154–64, where 'the very existence of cosmic order is being questioned,' there are latent suggestions—not yet understood by the speaker—of that order: 'a real seeing ("the great vision," "Looks," "Look") and a providential care ("the guarded Mount"). Also his words about Lycidas ("Visit'st," "Sleep'st") interject into this picture of mindless, mechanical force a softening note of humanity.' Thus 'the truth of what he has known all along begins to take possession of him' and inspires the swift 'vision of a greater pastoral order in heaven, and finally of a new harmony between heaven and earth.' Whereas St Peter's prophecy of vengeance had been inadequate, the final consolation is not, and in it 'Christ is everywhere...but always indirectly,' in his several roles as shepherd, judge, and king. 'For the speaker the vision of justice for Lycidas dissolves all the grounds of protest. For the poem itself the painful tensions are resolved through the quiet impersonality of a third-person perspective in the *ottava rima* stanza at the end, for which Milton imagines another, anonymous, voice, with a more predictably regular pattern of rhythm and rhyme. Images of sound and light and gesture recall earlier, agonized, moments, as in line after line they quietly affirm a recovered sense of order and meaning in life.'

C. F. Stone ('Milton's Self-concerns and Manuscript Revisions in *Lycidas*,' *MLN* 83, 1968, 867–81) studies the passages on Orpheus (57–63) and flowers (142–50), in which revision becomes the poet's reinterpretation of his own work and outlook. Whereas in *Arcades* and *Comus* the English pastoral world preserves human virtue and also a link with the divine, Lycidas, the poet and priest, 'the epitome of the pastoral man,' dies without the divine assistance afforded the Arcadians and the Lady. His death calls for a repudiation of the earlier pastoral visions as no longer truly depicting the ways of God to men. The first set of revisions 'arise from Milton's painful sense of identification with Orpheus and his attempts to ease this pain' by reinterpreting the significance of Orpheus' death. Citing *PL* 7. 32–9, on Orpheus, Stone sees Milton assigning 'the cause of fond dreaming to a dependence on classical inspiration.' In *Lycidas* he moves from classical to Christian figures. 'The pastoral now requires divine intervention or compensation to correct its imperfections [did it not in *Comus*?], but each intervention of this higher world into *Lycidas* disrupts it as a pastoral poem.' The tension is resolved only by Milton's vision of Lycidas in heaven. The flower passage grows out of Milton's identification of himself with Lycidas; 'he begins with a false surmise in order to interpose some ease for himself.' The original floral and mythological images (e.g. Narcissus) suggest the poet's frustrated self. By repressing these 'Milton preserves the poem in its public role as an elegy for Edward King. But the self-confrontation negates the poem as a mediation of Milton's self-concerns. The terms of this mediation remain the same; Milton must establish a viable relation between the self and its divine aspirations.'

Thomas B. Stroup (*Religious Rite & Ceremony in Milton's Poetry*, Lexington, Kentucky, 1968), while concerned mainly with the late long poems, speaks of early ones from the *Nativity* to *Comus* and *Lycidas*. In the last 'Milton adapts the classical conventions to suggest a Christian memorial service for the dead or a burial rite. The schema enables us to recognize in the poem the sermon-meditation, the interior ritual, and the memorial.' The stanza at the end puts the whole poem in a dramatic framework. Within the monody proper the sermon-meditation and ritual are interwoven. In the consolation, with its opening image of 'the day-star,' Milton seems to remind the reader of Luke 1. 78–9: '...whereby the dayspring from on high hath visited us, To give light to them that sit in darkness and in the shadow of death, to guide our feet into the way of peace.' 'Both in imagery and import the consolation suggests several passages from the burial services in the several versions of the Book of Common Prayer....' The consolation 'also reminds us of the *consolatio* of the funeral or memorial sermons, itself a formulary,' such as the end of Bishop Buckeridge's funeral sermon on Andrewes: '"From henceforth, saith the Spirit, they rest from their labours;" all tears are wiped from their eyes, and all sighs from their hearts.' Stroup recalls here the conclusion of Milton's *Elegy* 3 [see *El* 3. 64 n. for the echo of Rev. 14. 13]. When in *Lycidas* Milton echoes Rev. 7. 17

and 21. 4 ('And wipe the tears for ever̄from his eyes'), 'he expects the reader to associate the line immediately with rite and formulary, with high ceremony and priestly idiom.' Even the concluding stanza 'serves the purpose of the "*Ite*" at the end of the Mass or one of the many benedictions and dismissals which come at the close of any Christian rite or service. Cleansed by the experience now and reassured of God's providence, the participant is ready to go forth and, as a true, warfaring Christian, carry out God's purposes.'

K. Winter ('A Comprehensive Approach to Lycidas,' *Research Studies*, Washington State University, 36, 1968, 237–44), considering the diversity of modern criticism, summarizes five approaches: the literal (Masson, Hanford), the biographical (Tillyard), the technical (Ransom), the imagistic (Brooks and Hardy), the archetypal (R. Adams, N. Frye). These and their exponents were distinguished in Abrams' 'Five Types of *Lycidas*' (above, under 1961), an essay Winter does not cite, though he takes most of his materials from Patrides' anthology in which it first appeared. He finds all five approaches inadequate because—although he quotes what might seem to be satisfying bits from D. C. Allen and R. Tuve—they do not explain the poem's aesthetic impact and the comprehensive organic unity and originality achieved by a powerful genius working through conventions sanctified by long tradition.

J. Auffret ('Pagano-Christian Syncretism in *Lycidas*,' *Anglia* 87, 1969, 26–38) begins by saying that 'Little attention has been paid so far to Renaissance themes and symbols in *Lycidas*'—an odd assertion, but he mentions no critics except Tillyard and Cleanth Brooks [see above, under 1930 and 1951], whom he respectively opposes and complements.

As a prelude to his argument Auffret comments—with aid from Panofsky—on 'contemporary paintings representing The Shepherds of Arcadia,' Guercino and Poussin in particular.

The critic's first point is that 'The protagonist of *Lycidas* is not a Cambridge student, but a quasi-illiterate Arcadian shepherd,' as the last lines make clear [cf. the much more moderate W. G. Madsen above, under 1963]. This statement, which makes us rub our eyes, is thus supported: 'But throughout the piece, and particularly in the first one hundred lines, the faulty rhetoric and the faulty logic of the character are apparent. Milton believed that ignorant shepherds were greater poets than students and dons'; Greek pastoralists and the writers of Scripture 'convinced him that faulty rhetoric and faulty logic are the concomitants, even the prerequisites of oracular poetry.' [Milton was soon to declare that the scriptural writers surpassed the classics not merely in their divine inspiration but 'in the very critical art of composition': *RCG, Works* 3, 238.] The critic's demonstration, which we may skip, leads to this conclusion (31):

Faulty syntax, animistic fetishism, technical terms conspire to build up the persona of the Mourning Shepherd, a contemporary of the Biblical Prophets, or a primitive after Wordsworth's heart. His religion is paganism, but an early form of Paganism; or the Paganism of the backwoods.

Coming to his second point, 'Pagan–Christian equivalents,' Auffret sees Milton clearly following the tradition that Orpheus was a type of Christ. The poet used only relevant parallels: death at the hands of a crowd, a death lamented by Nature, a gory visage suggesting a crown of thorns, the helplessness of the two victims' mothers. [On Orpheus, cf. C. W. Mayerson above, under 1949.] The Phoebus who addresses the poet 'may be the Holy Ghost' in his reference to the Day of Judgment. These allusions 'the unenlightened shepherd-poet' does not understand.

The strict system of equivalences gives unity and depth to the poem. Pagan half-truths unfold into Christian mysteries. But the most astonishing equivalence is that established between shipwreck in the Irish Seas, and the foundering of the Body in Death. The 'fatal and perfidious bark'…is the Body of Man, built, since the Fall of Adam, in the eclipse of God's Grace, and rigged with the dark curses of *Genesis*…3. 16–19.

[Cf. M. Lloyd above, under 1961, and Lloyd and M. Mack below, in *Lycidas* 100–1 n.] 'This basic Christian allegory of the bark of Passage is maintained throughout the poem; it reappears with "the pilot of the Galilean Lake"' and with the making of Lycidas into 'the Genius of the shore,' i.e. 'Angel of the Good Death….'

Thus, in the poem as a whole, the 'illiterate shepherd' who calls upon the Muses is visited instead by the Holy Ghost.

The Orpheus passage is prophecy; but the unenlightened pagan stumbles again in darkness; then Phoebus (whether he be Christ or the Holy Ghost) dramatically intervenes. Lines 76–84 are not the shepherd's but God's...Finally, I suggest that lines 165–185 must be placed between inverted commas, like 107–131, and attributed to St Michael, who, provoked by the shepherd,...abruptly vindicates himself and the ways of God. [Cf. Madsen, cited above.]

'*Lycidas* is Christian in spirit *throughout*, and just as thoroughly Pagan in form.' Milton was quite in accord with Renaissance syncretism in his Christian use of pagan symbols. 'The parallelism between *Lycidas* and the *Fourth Eclogue* is striking and certainly deliberate. The Roman poet (so thought Milton) reached Christian Truth through pagan idioms and pagan concepts [*did* Milton think that?]. The Christian poet abandons the specific and somewhat trite formulation of Truth in favour of its poetical anticipation.' And, in the spirit of Renaissance humanism, he could share in 'the worship of Nature' which the moderns had lost: the flowers 'testify that Lycidas is not dead, but metamorphosed.'

Even *Lycidas* does not escape the hostility of J. Carey (*Milton*, 1969, 55–62). In contrast with the intimacy of the *Epitaphium Damonis*, 'our appetite for vicarious emotion' suffers; 'Grief cannot keep its sharpness in the classical air.' To the climactic vision the critic responds in this manner: 'Tremulous moments do survive—"Weep no more, woeful shepherds, weep no more" (165) would have the stoniest shepherd reaching for his handkerchief.' Even the passages of 'higher mood' (76–84, 113–31) 'preserve the pastoral mannerisms and do not look squarely at King's death but aside at Milton's anxiety about his own fame and the future of the Church of England.' The poem is evasive, artificial, split between classicism and 'nature-cycles' on the one hand and Christian assertions of eternity on the other. It displays an unclear mixture of present and past tenses. 'In *Lycidas*, as in *Comus*, fertility collides with chastity.' 'The Shakespearean amplitude of the masque's style has ebbed.' Decorativeness 'can jumble the images.' Most of these charges are strangely remote from modern criticism and indeed—like Carey's critiques of the *Nativity* and *Comus* (q.v.)—belong to a bygone age. However, he admits that 'the supernatural figures are sometimes translated into water-pastoral brilliantly,' and that 'Verbal playfulness is left behind by the power-driven lines which speculate on the body's whereabouts... Milton's imagination is at last gripped by King's predicament.' But otherwise *Lycidas* 'keeps itself at a remove from experience'; Milton, as usual, feels bound to renounce earth for heaven.

The discussion by J. B. Leishman (d. 1963: *Minor Poems*, 1969, 247–343) is an almost wholly literary commentary on selected topics and especially on passages, allusions, diction, and possible echoes of earlier poets; a few of the comments are recorded in the Notes below. (The book reached me after my MS. had left my hands.) Leishman had his share of attractive gusto and taste, and his remarks on the details of craftsmanship in *Lycidas* (and other poems) are sometimes fresh and suggestive; but such remarks fall short of an adequate reading of what he, like many other people, regards as 'the most perfect poem of its length in the English language' (271). Indeed, while concerned throughout with *Lycidas* as a pastoral elegy and with its ancestry, he gives no hint of Milton's theme (the nearest approach is the statement that the 'two digressions compose the doctrinal or didactic element of the poem, as distinct from the descriptive'); nor does he give any hint of acquaintance with modern interpretative criticism.

J. A. Wittreich ('Milton's "Destin'd Urn": The Art of *Lycidas*,' *PMLA* 84, 1969, 60–70) argues that the evolution of ideas is paralleled and reinforced by the manipulation of rhymes in the ten verse paragraphs of the monody proper. 'The "spherical" pattern of the perfectly executed madrigal is thus made to adumbrate "the Charm of the Circle of Perfection." In the process, *Lycidas* becomes a sophisticated hieroglyphic poem that, through its rhyme pattern, images forth eternity.... It is not without purpose that Milton takes us precisely *ten* rhymes into a third alphabet or that final consolation comes in the *tenth* verse paragraph. The number ten, through numerological tradition associated with totality and perfection, emphasizes "the poem's completeness, its circularity, its perfection, and its unity" [quoted from J. T. Shawcross on *PL*, *SP* 62, 1965, 708: Wittreich misquotes 'its unity' as 'eternity']. Besides being the numerological symbol for the geometric figure of the circle that the rhyme scheme inscribes and that the imagery supports and helps to define, the number ten possesses a special religious significance that... derives from the book of Revelation and figures prominently in this verse paragraph. In the Apocalypse, *ten* stands for divine control and completeness....'

Alastair Fowler ('"To Shepherd's ear": the form of Milton's *Lycidas*,' *Silent Poetry: Essays in numerological analysis*, ed. Fowler, London, 1970, 170–84) mixes some accepted interpretative ideas with statistics which can only be sampled. The climactic stanza ten (the number ten denoting 'the summed form of the *tetraktus*') is the only stanza not broken by short lines (which indicate grief and re-enact the dismemberment of Orpheus), since it embodies 'the Christian consolation that is to end mourning.' It is somehow significant that, in the poem as a whole, there are 24 couplets, which 'exactly compensate for the 10 unrhymed and 14 short lines.' There is also 'a number symbolism in the central placing of 4 speeches between groups of 7 invocations: 7s of mutability ordered and transformed by the virtuous *tetraktus*, the form-giving *vinculum* or spirit linking earth and heaven.' The 8-line conclusion 'may symbolize either the octave of harmony or the eternal life beyond mortality's 7s.'

Granted of course the tradition of mystical mathematics, an un-regenerate reader may find in such applications about as much relation to Milton as Baconian and Oxfordian ciphers have to Shakespeare.

IV. NOTES

As in the notes to other poems, only variants of some critical interest are noticed. The following texts are referred to: MS.: the full text, much revised, in the Cambridge Manuscript (*Facs.* 436–43), with a separate page containing versions of certain passages (ibid. 434), here designated MS. 1; the text in *Justa Edouardo King*, 1638 (ibid. 346–52; also *Justa*, ed. E. C. Mossner, 1939); the text in *Poems*, 1645 (*Facs.* 185–9). The text here cited is, as usual, that of 1673. The last three texts are cited by their dates.

Title. The name Lycidas, bestowed on Edward King, is fairly common in

Lycidas

pastoral verse, e.g. in Theocritus 7 and 27. 42; Bion, 2 and 6; Virgil, *E.* 7. 67 and 9; Sannazaro, *Pisc. E.* 1; Giles Fletcher the elder, *Adonis*; also, outside pastoral, in Horace, *C.* 1. 4. 19. Milton uses it again in *EpDam* 132. There seems to be no special significance in the choice, as there is perhaps of Damon in *EpDam*. [T. O. Mabbott, in a letter, remarks that the Lycidas of Virgil's *E.* 9. 30 f. is a poet, self-confessedly not a good one, and a shepherd, not a goatherd as in Theocritus 7.] In Theocritus 7, Lycidas is the friend of the speaker and the singer of one song, the speaker supplying the other; Sandys ('Sources,' 238) notes that here and in *Lyc* 'the two principal personages are the poet and his friend, and, in both, the friend is named Lycidas.' In Sannazaro, Lycidas sings the lament for Phyllis, who has met her death by drowning. More striking is the fact (see W. B. Austin in II above) that Lycidas is the singer in the *Adonis* of G. Fletcher, which mourns the death of young Clere Haddon, drowned in the Cam. To these possible instances of association (rather than significance) E. A. Strathmann (*MLN* 52, 1937, 398–400) has added the fact that in Theodore Bathurst's Latin translation of Spenser's *May* eclogue (in MS. when Milton wrote) the Protestant pastor is called Lycidas. And E. E. Duncan-Jones (*N&Q* 3, 1956, 249) has noted, in Lucan 3. 635–46, a Lycidas who perishes in the sea, though not by drowning. There was speculation on a relation between the names Lycidas and Lycaeus by G. McColley, T. C. C., and T. O. Mabbott in *N&Q* 172, 1937, 352, 447, 462, and 173, 159.

Epigraph: 'In this Monody...in their height'; not in 1638. The first sentence is in the MS., but not the second: 'And by occasion...height.' The attack on episcopacy, which began with the meeting of the Long Parliament in 1640, induced and permitted Milton to print the epigraph, adding the second sentence.

[John Crossett communicates a note on 'monody,' as it was anciently understood. The *threnos* (Homer, *Il.* 18. 561–72, 24. 720 f., *Od.* 24. 60 f.) became a usual though not a regular part of tragedy: the *kommos* was a *threnos* sung jointly by chorus and actors (Aristotle, *Poetics* 12. 9); a song done by actors alone was a *monodia* (Suidas; Hesychius). Hellenistic rhetoricians considered the *monodia* a special kind of speech. The form is discussed at length in the *Rhetoric* of Menander (*Rhetores Graeci*, ed. L. Spengel, Leipzig, 1856, 3, 418), where it is a branch of the *logos epitaphios* and allied with the speech of consolation, *logos paramythetikos* (Spengel, 413). The speeches of Andromache, Hecuba, and Helen in *Il.* 24 are called monodies (ibid. 434–7). Menander gives specific instructions for such a speech, including the injunction not to tire the audience by exceeding 150 verses.]

637

1-14 Though the song commences immediately, without narrative introduction, these lines, expressing the singer's reluctance overmastered by his sense of obligation, have something of the effect of a prelude, an effect reinforced by 'Begin then' (15) and utilized at the end of the poem, where they are balanced by a narrative conclusion (186–93 and n.). Most commentators [e.g. Coleridge (Brinkley, 560–1)] agree with Warton that 1–7 are a personal utterance avowing Milton's reluctance to interrupt his preparatory studies and break the silence maintained since *Comus* (1634). J. A. Himes (*Miltonic Enigmas*, Gettysburg, 1921, 19) complained that such an explanation makes Milton an egotist: 'True, he shrank from the duty, not, however, for this reason, but from a proper regret at having to notice so often the incursion of death [this in reference to his Latin elegies].... His grief is increased by the consideration of the youth of this latest death. His friend's years and genius were unripe and not his own. Nothing could well be more detached from his own interests or more in harmony with the occasion.' Some earlier critics (e.g. Richardson, cited by Todd) take the lines to refer, not to Milton's poetry, but to King's premature death (see further 1–2 n. [and R. Tuve in III above]); and this view is necessarily revived by those who reject altogether the idea that *Lycidas* bears any reference to Milton's own situation. Warton's opinion, shared, as we saw, by many, is supported by Milton's letter to Diodati of 23 September 1637 (*Epistol* 7, *Works* 12, 22–9), in which he speaks of not at that time writing verse but letting his wings grow for the major flight he intends. [This letter, as was noted in I above, should probably be dated 23 November. A. Rudrum (*Comus*, 62) thinks 'that the primary meaning of the passage is the assertion of Milton's artistic unripeness; and that he deliberately expresses this in a way which *might* be taken to refer to King's early death in order to suggest the poignancy of the event which constrains his pen, and to suggest that it is ironically appropriate that King's elegist should be unripe since Lycidas himself was "dead ere his prime". This kind of compression...is typical of the rich texture of "Lycidas."' See 1–2 n. below.

K. Rinehart (*N&Q* 198, 1953, 103) sees in 1–14 Milton deliberately approximating the sonnet form in order to emphasize the necessity of singing for Lycidas and the poet's need of forcing his muse.]

1-36 [While Milton has the loss to learning lamented by Camus, and the loss to the church lamented by St Peter, he 'begins his lament on the theme of King's loss to the Muse of poetry...it is significant that he speaks to the first theme in his own person,...because he comes as a poet to mourn King's death, and because it is this aspect of King with which he is now most closely associated. That is why the theme of association ends with the line, *And old Dametas lov'd to heare our song.*' (G. Williamson, *S.C.C.*, 141).]

1 *Yet once more.* Warton compared 'Yet once againe my muse' (*Tottel's Miscellany*, ed. Arber, 203; ed. Rollins, 1, 194)—[and drew a protest from Coleridge (Brinkley, 560) for citing a phrase any poet might think of]. Cf. Sannazaro, *E.* 11. 3: *Ricominciate, o Muse, il vostro pianto* (Harrison–Leon, 98). Peck (*New Memoirs*, 1740, 165) and Newton (both reported by Warton and Todd) saw a reference to Milton's earlier memorial poems, *FInf, EpWin*, etc.; Warton, to the poem last written, *Comus*, observing that the plants mentioned (1–2) are not peculiar to elegy but 'symbolical of general poetry.' Browne noted that critics have taken the phrase as a formula of identification analogous to the fuller one in Spenser, *F.Q.* 1, proem 1 (imitated from Virgil, *A.* 1. 1–4 variant), and, we may add, *Passion* 1–4; but the reference is much too vague to identify anyone. [D. S. Berkeley (*N&Q* 8, 1961, 178) cites the repeated phrase, 'Yet once more,' in Heb. 12. 26–7.]

1–2 *Laurels...Myrtles...Ivy. Laurel* or bay was sacred to Apollo (cf. Theocritus, Inscriptions 1), and was the traditional crown of the poet, but also of the victor, the poet being a victor over his competitors, as Milton well knew (*Patrem* 102, *Mansus* 6). He refers to laurel in association with Apollo (*El* 6. 16), with poetry and the Muses (*Patrem* 16, *EpDam* 180, *Prol* 3 and 6, *Works* 12, 163, 213), with the poet's crown (*Patrem* 102, *Mansus* 6, 92). *Myrtle* was sacred to Venus as a symbol of love and, in its application to poetry, of love poetry (cf. Ovid, *Am.* 1. 1. 29). It might be contrasted with laurel: 'Since then the Baies so well thy forehead knewe / To Venus mirtles yeelded have their place' (*The Countess of Pembroke's Antonie*, ed. A. Luce, Weimar, 1897, 68). Myrtle and laurel come together in Virgil, *E.* 2. 54–5: *et vos, o lauri, carpam et te, proxima myrte, / sic positae quoniam suavis miscetis odores*; and in Ovid, *A.A.* 3. 690. Milton refers to myrtle in association with love (the nuptial bower of Adam and Eve, where myrtle and laurel are combined, *PL* 4. 694), with the poet's crown (again connoting love and combined with laurel, in *Mansus* 92, *aut Paphia myrti aut Parnasside lauri / Fronde*), and perhaps with poetry in *EpDam* 131. [M. H. Nicolson (*John Milton*, 90, 106–11) takes myrtle as a symbol of mourning.] *Ivy* was symbolic of learning. Horace speaks of it as forming the poet's crown—*doctarum...praemia frontium*—to which he aspires (*C.* 1. 1. 29). In Spenser (*October* 109–12) the ivy crown of the poet is closely linked to Bacchus, whose special symbol of course it was, and who was patron of civilization as well as of wine. Milton joins ivy with laurel in the crown of the victorious poet (*Patrem*

102, *Mansus* 6). But laurel and ivy were not necessarily associated with poetry. They shade the empty tomb in Castiglione's *Alcon* (144) and are among the plants scattered on the tomb in Marot's *De Madame Loyse de Savoye* (230: Harrison–Leon, 118, 143), though they may represent the poet's tribute. Ivy, especially, was in Christian art symbolic of immortality; and laurel (bay) and myrtle could also be used as symbols; cf. Drayton, *Egl.* 6. 105–8 (2, 549). Some of the references above are drawn from Warton, Todd, C. S. Jerram (*The Lycidas and Epitaphium Damonis of Milton*, London, 1874; rev. 1881), and Verity (*Comus & Lycidas*, Cambridge, 1919; first pub. 1898; also the volume cited in *Nat* 7 n.).

[J. B. Trapp, in a full discussion of 'The Owl's Ivy and the Poet's Bays: An Enquiry into Poetic Garlands' (*JWCI* 21, 1958, 227–55), links Virgil, *E.* 2. 54–5 (quoted above) with *E.* 8. 12–13: *hanc sine tempora circum | inter victrices hederam tibi serpere laurus*, which Milton had echoed in *Patrem* and was to echo in *Mansus* (see above). Trapp thinks Milton may have known of some poetic crownings, especially that of Petrarch, who was honoured with ivy, laurel, and myrtle.]

Various explanations have been offered: (*a*) that Milton's allusion is to the poet's garland or crown, whose materials he is constrained to gather prematurely (see above, 1–14 n.); (*b*) that it is the poet's crown gathered prematurely for King, cut off before fuller achievement was possible; (*c*) that it is a crown for King symbolizing his qualities and accomplishments: *laurel* (poetry), *myrtle* (of a proper age for love), *ivy* (learning); of this notion, Newton's, Warton was justifiably sceptical; (*d*) that the wreath of evergreens symbolizes personal immortality (Jerram), or the immortality of fame the poem will bestow on King (Verity); (*e*) that it refers to the poem and suggests *inter alia* its 'pastoral or rural turn' (Warton). Of these, (*a*) and (*b*) are alike possible in the context; (*b*) is perfectly consonant with the facts of King's life and death, and (*a*) with Milton's situation. In (*c*) the explanation of myrtle appears in the context incongruous, though it is conceivable that an allusion to some attachment, now unknown, might have been intended. In (*d*) the immediate context, including everything that lends support to (*a*) or (*b*), seems to be ignored; Jerram might, it is true, claim support from the emphasis on immortality with which the poem ends (165–85) and of which this might be thought to be a premonitory suggestion. For Verity's immortal fame to be conferred by the poem there is no supporting evidence. Warton's explanation (*e*), if not very convincing, is innocuous because it does not rule out others (Warton takes the whole passage to indicate Milton's reluctance); it amounts to little more than saying that this is a pastoral elegy from its first lines onward.

2 *brown*: dark (without the notion of the specific colour). It is common in poetry (*OED* 1), e.g.: 'shadows brown' (*IlPen* 134); 'breathes a browner horror on the woods' (Pope, *Eloisa to Abelard* 170). And it is appropriate English for *nigraque myrtus* (Ovid, *A.A.* 3. 690) and *pulla myrto* (Horace, *C.* 1. 25. 18, where dark myrtle is contrasted with green ivy). *never sear*: never dry or withered (*OED* 1). Cf. 'the sere, the yellow leaf' (Shakespeare, *Macb.* 5. 3. 23), and Spenser, *S.C.*, *January* 37.

3–5 Cf. Castiglione, *Alcon* 31–2 (Harrison–Leon, 113): *Immatura rudis non carpit poma colonus:* | *At fera te ante diem mors nigro immersit Averno*, where the reference is to premature death. The *Berries* (of myrtle or ivy) are plucked while yet unripe (Lat. *crudus*), and before time has matured them the *leaves* are scattered (see below, 5 n.) by *fingers* that are ungentle or unskilled (Lat. *rudis*) and *forc'd*, constrained to their action, with perhaps a secondary suggestion of force *in* the action. Dunster (reported by Todd) cited Cicero, *Senec.* 19. 71, 'where the death of young persons is compared to unripe fruit plucked with violence from the tree...': *et quasi poma ex arboribus, cruda si sunt, vix* [traditional reading *vi*] *evelluntur, si matura et cocta, decidunt, sic vitam adulescentibus vis aufert, senibus maturitas*. Judgment of the relevance of this citation will depend on one's interpretation of the whole passage in *Lyc.* Jerram pronounces against it, 'the reference being obviously,' not to King's achievements, but to Milton's 'efforts in verse, which were, in his own opinion, "harsh and crude", but whose time of maturity a pious duty compelled him to forestall.' See above, 1–14 n.

5 *Shatter your*. MS. 1 had *crop yoᵣ young*, deleted, and replaced by present reading (*Facs.* 434). *Shatter* is the same word as *scatter*, and was only gradually differentiated in meaning: 'scatter,...throw about' (*OED* 1), but also 'damage ruinously, destroy by fracture' (ibid. 2b). In *Comus* 798 the word connotes 'destroy'; in *PL* 10. 1066, both 'scatter' and 'destroy.' *mellowing*. Jerram remarks that the word (Lat. *mollis*) would apply to the fruit, not the *leaves*; the association of ideas is that in general, when the fruit ripens, the leaves fall of themselves.

6 *Bitter constraint, and sad occasion dear*. Todd compared 'deare constraint' (Spenser, *F.Q.* 1. 1. 53) and 'Thou [Time] art the father of occasion deare' (Sidney, *Arcadia*, *Works* 2, 33; Ringler, 80–1, line 12). From the original sense of O.E. *deore*, 'precious,' two meanings, among others, developed: 'beloved' (*OED*: a.¹ 2) and 'costly' (ibid. 6). Also, from O.E. *deor* came the meaning 'severe, heavy, grievous' (*OED*: *a*.² 2). This last is the primary meaning here, with perhaps secondary suggestions from the other two.

7 *Compells.* Since the *occasion* constrains, *occasion* and *constraint* are regarded as one, like *pietas* and *Musa* in *dis pietas mea | et Musa cordi est* (Horace, *C*. 1. 17. 13–14); but, 'even without any such connexion of meaning,' it was common in Milton's day to make 'the verb agree in number with the nearest preceding noun' (Jerram).

8 *For.* MS. 1 (*Facs.* 434) had *young*, deleted, and *for* substituted. Evidently *prime* does not here refer to the springtime of life (from about 21 to 28 years of age), as in *Sonn* 9. 1 (*OED*: *sb*.¹ 8), but to the period of greatest vigour or perfection (ibid. 9); King was twenty-five.

8–9 *Lycidas.* See above, **Title**, n. Editors observe that such repetition for an effect of pathos occurs in Spenser (*S.C.*, *November* 58–9, *Astrophel* 7–8, *F.Q.* 3. 6. 45).   *hath not left his peer.* [W. Tuckwell ('*Lycidas*':*A Monograph*, London, 1911, 26) cited Horace, *C*. 1. 24. 8: *quando ullum inveniet parem?*]

10 *Who would not sing for Lycidas?* Editors compare *neget quis carmina Gallo?* (Virgil, *E*. 10. 3). *he knew*: so 1638, 1645, 1673; MS. and MS. 1, *he well knew* (*Facs.* 347, 185, 434, 436). That this was Milton's intention is confirmed by the correction in his copy of *Justa* in the Cambridge University Library. [But we may think that Milton would not have been content with an awkwardly hypermetrical line, and, if he had wished to keep *well*, he could have inserted it in 1645 or 1673. J. S. Diekhoff (*PQ* 16, 1937, 408–10) endorses and strengthens Percy Simpson's view that in his corrected copy of 1638 Milton was preparing a text for a printer and in his final version rejected a metrical audacity and accepted the error of his first printer. He may have been originally betrayed into the audacity by the accidental omission of *not* in *who would ᶰᵒᵗ sing for Lycidas he well knew* (*Facs.* 434). Having written the line, Milton perhaps at once inserted the omitted *not*, without noticing or for the moment caring that it gave him eleven syllables; and so the line was transcribed into the main text. Then Milton, or his copyist preparing copy for 1638, or the printer of that edition, omitted *well*. But in preparing the text for 1645 Milton noticed the discrepancy between the MS. and 1638 and inserted *well* to agree with the MS. Later, perhaps recalling the reason for omitting *well* in 1638, he returned to the 1638 reading. Some editors (e.g. Hanford, H. Darbishire) print *well*, and Shawcross (end of 1 above) insists on it.]

10–11 *he knew...to sing*: knew how to sing. For this Latin idiom Verity cites *reddere qui voces iam scit* (Horace, *A.P.* 158); 'O know to end, as to beginne' (*Hymenaei* 386, Ben Jonson 7, 223); 'Well knows to still the wilde winds when they roar' (*Comus* 87).

11 *build the lofty rhyme*: construct noble verses (not rhymed verse, as *OED*1 mistakenly assumes; King had written only Latin verse). Warton compared 'The wanton Ovid, whose intising rimes' (J.F., *Poems: By Francis Beaumont*, 1640; Chalmers, *English Poets* 6, 179). See further *PL* 1. 16 and n. Todd cited 'To builde with levell of my loftie style' (Spenser, *Ruines of Rome* 349). Editors have compared ἀοιδὰς εὐδαιμονίας ἐπύργωσε (Euripides, *Supp.* 997–8) and πυργώσας ῥήματα σεμνά (Aristophanes, *Frogs* 1004); [and R.Y.Tyrrell (*Classical Review* 9, 1891, 11–12) cited Pindar's use of 'builders' (τέκτονες) of lays (*Pyth.* 3. 113)]. Editors further compare *seu condis amabile carmen* (Horace, *Ep.* 1. 3. 24) and *si carmina condes* (Horace, *A.P.* 436). Jerram saw Milton's model in the Horatian phrases and in Lucretius' *carmen* / *condere* (5. 1–2), though *condere* in itself does not necessarily contain any metaphor from building, since it means simply to put together. [But the chief dictionary senses of *condere* are 'found, build, compose,' and Milton used the Latin verb in the literary sense in *Sals* 22, and that sense seems to be included in the *condita* of *El* 6. 32. Hughes cites (privately) 'The loftie verse of hem was loved aye' (Spenser, *S.C.*, *October* 66) and Kluge's note, quoting Mantuan, in the Variorum Spenser, *Minor Poems*, 1, 385. Hughes favours the Aristophanic parallel, though doubting the relevance of σεμνά ('revered, august, reverend, holy, solemn'). A. H. Gilbert (privately) questions the relevance of the Horatian parallels and likewise favours the phrase from the *Frogs*, adding τέχνην μεγάλην...κἀπύργωσ' οἰκοδομήσας from Aristophanes' *Peace* 749–50.] Masson, who examined the extant specimens of King's verse, found them simply the academic product of a humanist education and little deserving of this eulogy or of other praises in the *Obsequies* (e.g. pp. 2, 8, 14). But in memorial verses a man is not upon oath, [and beyond King Milton sees the ideal poet, the archetypal Orpheus].

12 *watry bear*. The bier was a movable frame on which the body was placed and carried to the grave (*OED* 2); like the word *hearse*, it came to be used more generally and figuratively. Warton cited 'watrie hearse' (Jonson, *Cynthia's Revels* 1. 2. 59) and Todd 'watry herse' (P. Fletcher, *P.I.* 1. 30). See below, 151 n.

13 *welter*: roll to and fro, driven by wave and wind. Cf. *Nat* 124 n. and 'weltring by his side' (*PL* 1. 78). *parching wind*. Jerram remarks that the effect might be produced by cold as well as heat. Cf. 'the parching Air / Burns frore, and cold performs th' effect of Fire' (*PL* 2. 594–5); *Boreae penetrabile frigus adurat* (Virgil, *G.* 1. 93).

14 *meed*. From its initial meaning of something 'bestowed in requital of labour or service, or in consideration of (good or ill) desert' (*OED* 1) the word developed specialized meanings: reward, merited portion of honour or praise, and (though rarely) gift (ibid. 1, 1 e). Here it means a gift betokening recognition of merit and paying of honour. Jerram compared 'honour vertues meed' (Spenser, *F.Q.* 2. 3. 10). For *meed* meaning gift, *OED* cites 'No meed but he repays' (Shakespeare, *Tim.* 1. 1. 288).[Tuckwell cited *debita...lacrima* (Horace, *C.* 2. 6. 23).] *melodious tear*. Explaining that *tear* 'means a funeral elegy,' Todd cited Gabriel Harvey's *Musarum Lachrymae*, Spenser's *Teares of the Muses*, Drummond's *Teares, On the Death of Moeliades*, and John Cleveland's caustic comment: 'I like not tears in tune; nor will I prise / His artificiall grief, that scannes his eyes' (*Obsequies*, 9). Jerram cited Milton's 'Here be tears of perfect moan' (*EpWin* 55). Verity quoted 'Cambridge and Oxford, lend your learned teares' (Sylvester, *Monodia*, Grosart, 2, 330), and remarked: 'Many of the collections of elegiac verse issued by the Universities bore the title *Lacrymae*.' Thus the older scholarship, which was content to prove Milton's phrase a synonym for poetic lament. Brooks and Hardy (171–2), emphasizing 'the water imagery' as one of the most important elements in the poem 'and one of the most startling, once it is seen,' proceed thus: 'The contrast between the salt water of the immensity of the sea and the salt water of the melodious tear...as the poem develops...comes to mean a great deal. The "melodious tear" promises to overwhelm the "sounding Seas."'

15 *Begin*. The word reinforces the impression of the first 14 lines as introduction and of the first movement of the monody proper as beginning here. Editors note parallels in Theocritus 1. 64 ('Begin, ye Muses dear, begin the pastoral song,' which commences the lament proper after the narrative prelude and also serves as refrain); Moschus, *Lament for Bion* (refrain: 'Begin, ye Sicilian Muses, begin the dirge'); Virgil, *E.* 10. 6, where Arethusa is called on to begin; Spenser, *Teares* 53–4: 'Begin thou eldest Sister of the crew ⟨Clio⟩, / And let the rest in order thee ensew.'

15–16 *Sisters of the sacred well...doth spring*. Jerram was undoubtedly right in tracing these lines to Hesiod, *Theog.* 1–4: 'From the Heliconian Muses let us begin to sing, who hold the great and holy mount of Helicon, and dance...about the deep-blue spring and the altar of the almighty son of Cronos' (L.C.L.). As Jerram explained, *the sacred well* is Aganippe on Mount Helicon, and *the seat of*

Jove is the altar to Zeus on the same hill. Cf. *IlPen* 47–8 n.; *PL* 1. 10–12 n.; and *Prol* 2: *Hinc quoque Musarum circa Jovis Altaria dies noctesque saltantium ab ultima rerum origine increbuit fabula* (*Works* 12, 154). Todd cited 'any one sent from the sacred Well' (Browne, *Brit. Past.* 1. 5. 903) and Spenser's *Teares* 1–6, which calls upon the 'sacred Sisters nine' to rehearse the strains they poured forth as they sat 'Beside the silver Springs of Helicone.' Sandys ('Sources,' 233–4) concurred in finding the source in Hesiod, but thought *the sacred well* to be Hippocrene, in which Hesiod (*Theog.* 5–6) describes the Muses as bathing. He noted that the Muses gave Hesiod the gift of song (ibid. 22). The weight of evidence (which includes the parallel to these lines in *PL* 1. 10–12) is against Masson, Browne, Rolfe, Wright, [Harrison–Leon, Patrides, and Prince], who take *the sacred well* as the Pierian spring, the birthplace of the Muses, at the foot of Mount Olympus, for them *the seat of Jove* referred to. Explaining *well* as 'spring,' Verity cites: 'And eke you Virgins, that on Parnasse dwell, / Whence floweth Helicon the learned well' (Spenser, *S.C., April* 41–2); the Gloss explains Helicon as a spring at the foot of Parnassus and also a mountain in Boeotia. [Le Comte (*Yet Once More*, 142–4) thinks no decision can be made between Helicon and Olympus. It may be added that it would be characteristic if Milton had in mind Rev. 22. 1 (quoted below in 174 n.).]

17 *Begin...string.* Harrison compares *Sicelides Musae, paulo maiora canamus* (Virgil, *E.* 4. 1). Jerram's explanation, 'make no uncertain answer to my appeal,' and Rolfe's view that the reference is to the character of the poem, 'no slight elegy, but a longer and loftier strain,' seem equally fanciful. [But *somewhat loudly* must have some meaning, and these several suggestions, combined, seem to approximate it.]

18 *coy* (Fr. *coi*, Lat. *quietus*). Verity notes that it was a stronger word than now and cites Ascham's complaint of the courtier as 'coye, big, and dangerous of looke' (Ascham, *English Works*, 207). *OED* 3 (without citing Milton) defines as 'Of distant or disdainful demeanour' (with further examples, which support Verity). But cf. ibid. 2, 'shyly reserved or retiring' (supported by *PL* 4. 310, 'coy submission, modest pride'), which comes nearest to the meaning here [cf. *Comus* 736]. There is perhaps the suggestion of the poet as wooer, the Muses as wooed.

19 *So may.* For the construction Jerram cited Virgil, *E.* 9. 40 [presumably meaning 9. 30–1, *Sic...sic*] and 10. 4 (*sic tibi*), Horace, *C.* 1. 3. 1 (*Sic te*), etc. [Cf. *Comus* 241.]

19 *Muse*: poet, 'one under the guidance of a Muse,' as in 'that memorable Sea-battle...sung by a crowned Muse ⟨James I⟩' (G. Sandys, *Relation*, 1615, 4; *OED*: *sb.*[1] 2c). Keightley quoted: 'And, o, if ever time create a Muse, / That to th' immortall fame of virgine faith, / Dares once engage his pen' (Marston, *Antonios Revenge*, Malone Society, 1921, 5. 6. 2170–2; *Plays*, ed. H. H. Wood, 3 v., Edinburgh and London, 1938–9, 1, 133); and: 'This sung the sacred Muse, whose notes and words / The dancers' feete kept, as his hands his cords' (Chapman, *Od.* 8. 499–500). Verity added 'Our second Ovid, the most pleasing Muse' (Browne, *Brit. Past.* 2. 2. 287—speaking of Drayton, not of Chapman, as Verity supposes). [Cf. Shakespeare, *Sonn.* 21. 1.]

20 *With lucky words*: words 'presaging...good luck; well-omened' (*OED* 3, which quotes Coverdale's *Paraphrase of Erasmus upon the newe testamente*, 2 v., London, 1548–9, 2 Cor., 2, 44: 'With all good and luckye woordes, blessed... bee God'). But the meaning may be 'felicitous' in a literary sense, happily hit upon (*OED* 1d, whose earliest example, however, is of 1700). [This sense is noted, and favoured, by G. O. Marshall, *Explic.* 17, 1958–9, Item 66.] *favour*: Lat. *faveo*, befriend, countenance, draw favour to. [Jerram cites *favete linguis* (Horace, *C.* 3. 1. 2).] *Urn*: grave (from the practice of urn burial). Cf. 'Or lay these bones in an unworthy urn' (Shakespeare, *H. V* 1. 2. 228).

22 *bid fair peace be to my sable shrowd*: say *requiescat in pace* [cf. *Mansus* 89–93]. *shrowd*: a white winding-sheet, but through its association with death and mourning here pictured as *sable* (black); apparently *shrowd* stands for the body it enwraps, since *peace* is desired for it. The word also meant shelter (*OED* 2; *Nat* 218 n., *Comus* 147 n.), and Dunster took *sable shrowd* to mean the dark shelter of the grave; Todd cited: 'cover'd with a sable Shroud / Hath She kept home' (Sylvester, *Bethulians Rescue* 4. 313–14, Grosart, 2, 193). [This idea may be included in Milton's phrase, but the first explanation seems to give the primary sense. Two implausible suggestions may be recorded. J. A. S. Barrett (*TLS*, 11 Jan., 1934, 28), thinking line 22 halting in rhythm and unsatisfactory in sense, would emend *to* to *too*, thus making *peace* to be the poet's *shrowd*. G. M. Gathorne-Hardy (ibid. 18 Jan., 44) rejected this idea (since the *shrowd* is *sable*), but questioned the usual interpretation of *Muse* as 'poet'; he took *my destin'd Urn* as 'the memorial I am now, under inspiration of the Muses, preparing for Lycidas'; *he* would be Lycidas.]

23 (or **25**)–**36** are reminiscences of life together at Cambridge, rendered in pastoral terms, a feature of pastoral elegy illustrated by Castiglione's *Alcon* and Milton's *EpDam*. Opinions have differed on the degree of realism in details and the degree of intimacy indicated. Masson was strong for both, while Verity deprecated literal interpretation. It is generally agreed that *the self-same hill* (23) means Christ's College, and that *We drove a field*, etc. (27 f.) refers to studies pursued in common. But Masson would have *Rural ditties* (32) stand for college exercises, *Satyrs* and *Fauns* (34) for undergraduates, and *old Damaetas* (36) for William Chappell, King's tutor and Milton's first tutor, or for Thomas Bain-brigge, the Master of the College, or for Joseph Mead (Mede) or some other don. Verity found sufficient reason for *Rural ditties* in the pastoral convention; *Fauns* attracted by pastoral song have their precedent in Virgil (*E.* 6. 27–8); and *old Damaetas* looks on because Meliboeus does so (ibid. 7. 8–17), the name being taken from Virgil, *E.* 3. The two approaches would seem to be not incompatible if we remember that the pastoral tradition carries a strong vein of allegory, that Milton is in control of conventions, not controlled by them, and that the poem was written for an audience of academic contemporaries. [But recent commentators appear, if only in their silence on most details, to incline to Verity's side, and to be content to take the items together as a picture of pastoral innocence, of carefree youth unconscious of the fact of death.]

Damaetas has continued to stir guesses at identification. Jerram suggested that Milton took the name from Sidney's *Arcadia* and had its suspicious and uncouth possessor in mind in glancing at Chappell. [This idea was restated by F. Pyle (*Hermathena* 71, 1948, 83–92).] E. S. de Beer (*N&Q* 194, 1949, 336–7) argued against any personal allusion, but thought a contemporary reader would remember Sidney's loutish clown who oversaw rural sports with ignorant approval and disapproval and who was old, whereas the bearers of the name in Theocritus 6 and Virgil, *E.* 3, were young; in his view Milton used the name generically of the ignorant who were nevertheless pleased with the immature verses of himself and King. A more sympathetic figure than Chappell, Joseph Mead, has been supported by M. H. Nicolson (*MLN* 41, 1926, 293–300). [H. F. Fletcher (*JEGP* 60, 1961, 250–7) reasserted the case for Chappell.]

23–4 In MS., 1645, and 1673 the paragraph ends with 24; 1638 has no break and has a semicolon, instead of a period, after *rill*. Warton (followed by Todd, Masson, Rolfe, Verity, Moody, et al.) breaks after 22 (*shrowd*), commencing the paragraph with 23, thus including 23–4 with the lines descriptive of life at Cambridge. [Coleridge (Brinkley, 562) argued against Warton's arrangement.] Browne followed 1638. Jerram, Bell, Grierson, Columbia, Hughes, Wright, [Hanford, H. Darbishire, Patrides, Shawcross, Bush, I. G. MacCaffrey, Elledge, Prince, Carey] follow 1645 and 1673. Tillyard (*Milton*, 385) argues for this reading, interpreting 23–4 as, 'If...Lycidas is favoured with an elegy, then I, brought up with him, his equal, should be favoured too,' and he connects the lines with 19–22 as *For* suggests; otherwise one must, with Keightley, regard 19–22 as parenthetical and take *For* as referring back to 18.

25–30 Harrison (Harrison–Leon, 290) notes a somewhat similar development of the theme *Together both* by Castiglione: *Nos etenim a teneris simul usque huc viximus annis, | Frigora pertulimusque aestus, noctesque, diesque, | Communique simul sunt pasta armenta labore* (*Alcon* 78–80).

25 *high Lawns*: grassy uplands. *OED*'s most suitable definition (1 b) is 'A stretch of untilled ground; an extent of grass-covered land.' For other examples of Milton's use see *Nat* 85, *L'All* 71, *Comus* 567, 964, *PL* 4. 252.

26 *opening eye-lids of the morn*: *glimmering eye-lids* in 1638; MS. deletes *glimmering*, substitutes *opening* (*Facs.* 436). Warton cited 'Dropt from the opening Eye-lids of the Morne' (T. Middleton, *A Game at Chesse*, ed. R. C. Bald, Cambridge, 1929, I. I. 86). Todd added 'eyelids of the morning' (Job 41. 18; cf. 3. 9, A.V. margin, 'dawning of the day') and similar phrases from Marlowe, Sylvester, et al. [H. Darbishire (*Essays and Studies 1957*, 38–9) links Milton's phrase of 1638 with Spenser's phrase about Pastorella, 'twixt the twinckling of her eye-lids bright' (*F.Q.* 6. 11. 21). She adds that that first phrase carried 'the subtle suggestion of light a little further than Milton wants in his simple statement of the two young shepherds setting out at dawn. So he substitutes an inherited poetic phrase which gives him the vigorous sound he needs—the right broad vowel in *opening*.' Cf. C. L. Wrenn ('Language,' 259).]

28 *What time*: Lat. *quo tempore*. [Verity cited Ps. 56. 3, 'What time I am afraid'; Shakespeare, *Titus* 4. 3. 19. Cf. *Comus* 290; *PL* 1. 36; Browne, *Brit. Past.* 1. 5. 163–4: 'What time the world... | A stage made.'] *Gray-fly... sultry horn*. *OED* (trumpet 7) quotes: 'we call it the grey fly from it's colour, or the trumpet fly from the noise it makes in the heats of summer' (John Hill, *History of Animals*, 1752, 31).

29 *Batt'ning...with the fresh dews*: 'feed to advantage, fatten up' on the grass with the dew still fresh upon it (used transitively, as here, but more commonly intransitive: *OED*: batten 3). Jerram cited: *Luciferi primo cum sidere frigida rura | carpamus, dum mane novum, dum gramina canent, | et ros in tenera pecori gratissimus herba* (Virgil, *G.* 3. 324–6; cf. *E.* 8. 15). [E. F. Daniels (*Explic.* 21, 1962–3, Item 43), saying that wet grass would be bad for sheep, proposes another meaning of *Batt'ning*, 'barring' or 'enclosing,' *with* meaning 'at the same time as.' He recognizes that 30–1 imply prolonged action, but takes the passage as loosely describing all-night labour. That is only one of the difficulties —and Virgil did not think wet grass bad for sheep.]

30–1 *Oft till the Star...westering wheel*: in 1638, *ev'n-starre bright* and *burnisht* for *westering*; MS. deletes these words and substitutes reading of 1645 and 1673, but with *in* for *at* (*Facs.* 348, 436). Keightley objected that Milton 'surely could not mean the evening-star, for it *appears*, not *rises*, and it is never anywhere but *on* "heaven's descent"'; he concludes that the reference cannot be to Hesperus, the evening star, but to some other that fulfilled the condition. Jerram cited Spenser (*F.Q.* 3. 4. 51): 'the golden Hesperus / Was mounted high in top of heaven sheene.' Verity takes *the Star* as Hesperus but notes Milton's mistake. That Hesperus was originally intended the initial reading, *the ev'n starre*, seems to prove. Possibly by the revision Milton intended to remove any necessary association with Hesperus or he may have made it on stylistic grounds alone. The problem of the evening star arises again in *Comus* 93–4, and there Milton did not revise his phrasing for 1645, which argues against any intentional change of meaning here. It would seem that *the Star*, whichever it be, is one with 'The Star that bids the Shepherd fold' (*Comus* 93)—an injunction disregarded by the allegorical 'shepherds' of the present passage (see further, *Comus* 93–4 n.). If the evening star (Hesperus) is meant, then the same luminary is the last to disappear as the morning star, Lucifer (cf. *Nat* 74 and n.). Himes (*Enigmas*, 20–1) argues that Milton is referring not to the evening star but to a star in the 'aggregation including the Wagoner (Bootes) and the Wain (Ursa Major), dominated by Arcturus, the second brightest star in the northern firmament,' which, he says, '*fits* the conditions especially in accounting for the *westering wheel*'; this does not mean passing to the west 'but *rounding* or *circling the west*,' since 'the Wain does not set, but nearing the horizon sweeps around north-westward....' *OED* defines *westering* as declining 'from the meridian towards the west.' In any event, the lines complete the cycle of twenty-four hours begun at 25, and perhaps suggest night-long study like that indulged in by Il Penseroso (*IlPen* 87, where the reference is to Ursa Major).

33 *Temper'd to*: brought into harmony with, attuned to (*OED*: temper *v.* 16). [Tuckwell cites Horace, *C.* 4. 3. 18: *dulcem quae strepitum...temperas.*] Warton compared: 'Temp'ring their sweetest notes unto thy lay' (P. Fletcher, *P.I.* 9. 3).

Oaten Flute: pipes made from oat straw, one of the traditional instruments of pastoral song. Cf. *silvestrem tenui musam meditaris avena* (Virgil, *E.* 1. 2); 'oaten pype' (Spenser, *S.C.*, *January* 72); 'mine Oten reedes' (ibid. *October* 8 and Gloss: 'Oaten reedes) *Avena*'; also cf. *F.Q.* I, proem I. 4); 'When shepherds pipe on oaten straws' (Shakespeare, *L.L.L.* 5. 2. 913); *Comus* 344 and *Lyc* 88. Verity noted that in his Latin verse Milton commonly prefers *cicuta*, the hemlock pipe (e.g. *EpDam* 135, 157). Jerram observed: 'Although the oaten pipe has been chosen by English poets as the representative of pastoral music, the classical authority for such usage is more than doubtful....Perhaps the earliest instance of *avena* in this sense is Virgil, *Ecl.* i. 2 (cf. Ov., *Met.* viii. 191[-192]; Tibull. III. iv. 71); but it is a question whether the word may not there mean any reed or hollow stalk....'

34-5 *Satyrs* in Greek myth were beings human in form, but with pointed ears and a tail, who wore skins of beasts and lived in forest and field; they were followers of Dionysus and represented the vital powers of nature and the unrestrained pleasures of the senses. The Romans tended to identify them with their own *Fauns*, derived from the primitive Italian deity Faunus, himself identified with Pan, and (like Pan) represented with goat's horns, tail, and cloven hoofs. Thus the *Fauns*, and by association the *Satyrs*, became shaggy creatures, half-human, half-goat [cf. *El* 5. 122]; hence *Rough* and *with clov'n heel*. In Virgil, *E.* 6. 27-8, the Fauns are attracted by pastoral song and dance to the music. Newton (reported by Jerram) cited: 'Ye Silvans, Fawnes, and Satyres, that emong / These thickets oft have daunst after his pipe' (L. Bryskett, *Pastorall Aeglogue* 116-17 [in Spenser's *Poetical Works*, ed. J. C. Smith and E. de Selincourt, Oxford, 1912, 555]).

36 *old Damaetas*. See above, 23-36 n.

37-49 This passage—and, in a measure, 133-51—represent the pastoral convention of nature's mourning for the shepherd. In Theocritus I. 71 f. the animals grieve; in Bion's *Lament for Adonis* Aphrodite and Echo, hills and springs, rivers and oak-trees mourn, and flowers turn red for grief; in the *Lament for Bion* that goes under the name of Moschus, all creatures and flowers are called upon to join in sorrowing, the hyacinth to whisper the letters graven on its petals. In Virgil, *E.* 10, the laurels and tamarisks and the Arcadian mountains wept for Gallus. In Sannazaro, *E.* 11, there is an appeal to the shore and to flowers, among them the hyacinth. A specimen of the convention may be taken from Castiglione's *Alcon* (Harrison–Leon, 113-14):

Alas, ill-starred youth! with thee has perished the solace of the fields, with thee Love and the Graces, and our joys. Their tresses have fallen from the trees, the woods are spoiled of their glory and deny to shepherds their accustomed shade. The meadows have lost their splendor...;

dried are the springs, the rivers are dry. The sterile fields deny their promised yield, and evil rust has devoured the growing wheat....Naught but mournful are the sounds of woodlands, pastures, and rivers...Alas, ill-starred youth!

In 39–44 Milton makes a restrained use of the pathetic fallacy, gliding at 45 from statement to simile. [C. A. Patrides (*Milton*, 77) comments: 'Milton's use of the convention of "pathetic fallacy" in *Lycidas* (ll. 39 ff., 134 ff.) may seem to argue against his espousal of the Christian view of nature, but in fact the lamentation of the natural order for the dead poet is not an end in itself; it is rather a step in the progress of the poem from the secular to the sacred, from the non-Christian to the Christian, culminating in the vision of him that walked the waves. In retrospect, this appearance of the Lord of nature in *Lycidas* transforms even the conventional mourning of nature from a mere "pathetic fallacy" to a categorical affirmation of its transcendental significance.' Rudrum (*Comus*, 65) remarks: 'In lines 39–41, for example, the fact that Nature has cause to lament for itself as well as for Lycidas lends added resonance to what might have been a purely conventional "pathetic fallacy". This in turn prepares for the lines which follow. Here we do not merely see Lycidas's death in terms of natural parallels (which might have the effect of reducing its significance); instead our awareness is broadened to take in the inescapability and universality of death.']

38 *never must*: 'art destined never to' (Verity); most simply explained as inverted order, 'must never.'

39 *Thee Shepherd, thee the Woods.* The 1638 text has *Thee shepherds, thee the woods*, the shepherds being made the first mourners. Dunster (reported by Todd) cited Ovid, *M.* 11. 44–6: *Te maestae volucres, Orpheu, te turba ferarum,* / *te rigidi silices, te carmina saepe secutae* / *fleverunt silvae*. Todd compared the similar pattern in Lucretius' address to Venus (1. 6), *te, dea, te fugiunt venti...*, and Spenser's version: 'Thee goddesse, thee the winds, the clouds doe feare' (*F.Q.* 4. 10. 44). Jerram added: *te, dulcis coniunx, te solo in litore secum* (Virgil, *G.* 4. 465). [Sandys ('Sources,' 242) cited Virgil, *E.* 1. 38–9: *ipsae te, Tityre,* *pinus,* / *ipsi te fontes, ipsa haec arbusta vocabant.*]

39–40 *Caves,* / *With wilde Thyme and the gadding Vine o'regrown.* Perhaps Milton remembered 'I know a bank where the wild thyme blows' (Shakespeare, *Dream* 2. 1. 249 f.), though the plants that follow differ. Keightley compared *aspice, ut antrum* / *silvestris raris sparsit labrusca racemis* (Virgil, *E.* 5. 6–7). A. S. Cook (*MLN* 15, 1900, 509–10), taking the vine to be ivy, noticed that thyme and ivy occur together in Virgil, *E.* 7. 37–8, that ivy is associated with a cave in Theocritus 3. 13–14, and that Virgil has the phrase *errantis hederas* in *E.* 4. 19, *errantis* giving the sense of *gadding*, a participial adjective from *gad* (origin uncertain, possibly a back-formation from *gadling*, a wanderer or vagabond: *OED*). Jerram noted the figure in Latin poetry of wedding the vine (here of course the grape) to the supporting tree (Horace, *C.* 4. 5. 30, *Epod.* 2. 10; Catullus 62. 49; [for a full account of the figure see P. Demetz, *PMLA* 73, 1958, 521–32]), and the application in English of *gadding* to errant wives, as in Ecclus. 25. 25, 26. 8. [Daiches (*More Literary Essays*, 97) quotes Virgil, *E.* 3. 38–9: *lenta quibus torno facili superaddita vitis | diffusos hedera vestit pallente corymbos.*]

41 *echoes mourn.* Echo, originally a mountain nymph, mourned her unrequited love for Narcissus (Ovid, *M.* 3. 358 f.). Milton, here as in *Passion* 50–3, follows Ovid in referring to a mountain setting. Tuckwell notes Echo's announcement of the death in Bion's *Adonis* 38. Jerram cites Echo mourning among the rocks that she can no longer repeat Bion's words (Moschus, *Bion* 30). In Ronsard's *Adonis* (252–4) 'Echo is not silent, but within her rocks redoubling her feigned voice, through pity for me is repeating my lament' (Harrison–Leon, 168). In Bryskett's *Pastorall Aeglogue* (see 34–5 n., above), after the rivers mourn Sidney, 'Eke wailfull Eccho, forgetting her deare / Narcissus, their last accents, doth resownd' (109–10).

42 Harrison notes a pastoral association for *Willows* in Virgil, *E.* 10. 40, where the willow appears with the vine, and for *Hazle Copses* (ibid. 5. 3), where hazel appears with the elm, which is a common support for the vine (above, 39–40 n.), and also has its pastoral associations (cf. *EpDam* 49). [Daiches (see above, 39–40 n.) cites *densas corylos* (Virgil, *E.* 1. 14).]

44 *Fanning…soft layes*: moving their leaves like a fan (*OED*: fan v. 3 b) in joyful response to the music. In Virgil, *E.* 6. 28, the oaks respond to pastoral song, but without this image of fan-like motion.

45 *Canker*: canker-worm (*OED* 4); see *Arc* 53 n. Warton and Todd noted Shakespeare's fondness for this image. In addition to *Dream* 2. 2. 3 (quoted in *Arc* 53 n.), cf.: 'as the most forward bud / Is eaten by the canker ere it blow' (*T.G.V.* 1. 1. 45–6); 'The canker galls the infants of the spring / Too oft before their buttons be disclos'd' (*Ham.* 1. 3. 39–40). See 46 n. below.

46 *Taint-worm*: 'A worm or crawling larva supposed to taint or infect cattle'; cf. 'taint wormes…that lurke where ox should eat': Tusser, *Five Hundred Points of Good Husbandrie*, ed. London, 1878, 150 (*OED*). The allusion is no doubt to this and not, as some editors have thought, to a small red spider, supposed by country people (according to Sir Thomas Browne, *Pseudodoxia* 3.

27, *Works*, 1964, 2, 261; *OED*: taint 3) to be fatal to cattle. A note by W. W. S. (*N&Q* 176, 1939, 112–13, 153) revived an old confusion by a quotation from John Crawshey's *Countreyman's Instructor* (1636), which defines the taintworm as 'a spider or a little red creeping thing called a *Ting* or *Taint*, which creeps over the fodder.' Milton parallels one noxious worm or larva (the *Canker*) with another (the *Taint-worm*). The phrase from Tusser explains *Herds that graze*. [F. W. Bateson (*English Poetry*, 159: quoted by Carey) identifies the taint-worm as 'the intestinal worm that the modern farmer calls "husk", which is normally only fatal, as Milton correctly says, to newly weaned calves when they start grazing.'] *weanling*: lately weaned and not full-grown. Jerram explained as a diminutive of *weanel*, a weaned animal (cf. Spenser, *S.C.*, *September* 198); but *OED* derives directly from the verb *wean* and the diminutive *ling*.

47 *their gay wardrop wear*. MS. had *thire gay buttons weare*; *beare* substituted, then deleted, and *wardrope weare* substituted (*Facs.* 436). For *buttons* meaning buds see the quotation from *Hamlet* in 45 n. The spelling *wardrop(e)* was Milton's choice among a number of variants; the 1638 text has *wardrobe* (*Facs.* 348), which suggests the history of the word's meaning, from a room where apparel (robes) was kept (guarded), and hence the apparel so kept.

48 *the White Thorn*: the common hawthorn, so called because of its lighter bark as compared with that of the blackthorn (*OED*). For Milton as for Spenser and Shakespeare the hawthorn has pastoral associations and connotes the coming of spring: cf. *L'All* 68; Spenser, *S.C.*, *March* 13–15; and Shakespeare, *Dream* 1. 1. 184–5: '...tuneable...to shepherd's ear / ...when hawthorn buds appear.' *blows*: blooms (*OED*: *v.²* 1).

49 *to Shepherds ear*. Cf. Shakespeare, *Dream* 1. 1. 184 (48 n., above).

50–5 *Where were ye Nymphs*, etc. The question, which became one of the conventions of pastoral elegy, began with Theocritus 1. 66–9. The question was appropriate, since Daphnis was the son of a nymph, was brought up among the nymphs, and was wedded to one of them, and his fidelity to her was the occasion of his distress and death, so that the nymphs would have a special interest in his fate and, had they been present, the desire to avert it; but they were absent from Sicily, perhaps in distant Thessaly. Virgil (*E.* 10. 9–12) addresses the question to the naiads, who were absent from Parnassus, Pindus, and Aonian Aganippe; in choosing haunts of the Muses, appropriate to the guardians of Gallus the poet, he perhaps implied that he was really addressing the Muses. Two later examples are in Antoine de Baïf (*E.* 2), whose nymphs are the Muses but who adds a reference to the Seine, and Luigi Alamanni (*E.* 1), who addresses the Muses but reproaches them for their absence from the Arno (Harrison–Leon, 147, 122–3). Milton uses appropriate British place names, and probably his *Nymphs* are the Muses. [Cf. Milton, *Idea* 1 n., in *V.C.* 1.]

51 *Clos'd o're the head.* See 58–63, 102, 167–73, and notes. [Hanford (*PMLA* 25, 410–11; 32–3 in Patrides) suggested that Milton's idea of a pastoral elegy might have started from the phrase of Theocritus 1. 140–1 which Andrew Lang rendered 'The whirling wave closed over the man the Muses loved' and which Hanford translated literally as 'the eddy washed away...' F. R. B. Godolphin (*MLN* 49, 1934, 165) cited Propertius 3. 7. 56: *cum moribunda niger clauderet ora liquor.*] *lov'd: lord* in 1638. The evident misprint was corrected in two copies— at Cambridge University and the British Museum—['probably but not certainly' in Milton's hand (*Facs.* 348)].

52–3 *the steep, | Where your old Bards, the famous Druids, ly.* The 1638 text has *the old Bards,* thus omitting the connection with the nymphs; the MS. reading was restored in 1645 (*Facs.* 348, 436, 186). Evidently taking the name Kerig y Druidion (Druid stones) to refer to a place of burial (as Milton might, of course, also have done), Warton said: 'For the Druid-sepulchres...at Kerig y Druidion, in the mountains of Denbighshire, he consulted Camden's *Britannia*'; but Camden (*Britain,* tr. P. Holland, London, 1610, 675) speaks only of stones, not sepulchres, traditionally attributed to the Druids. And the context in *Lyc* would seem to require a place on the coast between the Dee and Anglesey, not an inland scene. Keightley (followed by Verity and others) suggested the mountain Penmaenmawr overhanging the sea opposite Anglesey, but gave no literary source. Jerram, noticing that lack of tradition, preferred Kerig y Druidion. Gilbert (*Geographical Dictionary,* 24) suggests Holyhead on the basis of Holinshed's description: 'Herein...is a promontorie...called Holie head... from whence the readiest passage is...had...into Ireland....The Britons named it...holie Ile, of the number of carcasses of holie men, which they affirm to have beene buried there'; but the 'holie men,' as Gilbert admits, were Christians, not Druids. Himes (*Enigmas,* 21) rejects all search for the steep 'among the unfamiliar mountains of Wales,' since King's ship 'in issuing from the Chester estuary had its prow pointed directly at Fairhead...the most conspicuous promontory of the Irish coast' and 'replete with relics of the Druids.' The locality seems best determined, and the lines, with those that follow, seem most fully explained, by facts recorded in Camden and Ortelius' *Theatrum Orbis Terrarum* (discussed by G. W. Whiting, *Milieu,* 103–7), supplemented by passages in John Selden's Illustrations of Drayton's *Polyolbion*. Humphrey Lhuyd's Epistle to Ortelius, printed as an appendix in the *Theatrum* (Latin, 1570 [repr. Amsterdam, 1964]; English, 1606), refers to an island adjacent to Mona, Lymnos or Enlli, 'which the English men call Bardesey, that is,...*Insula Bardorum*, The Bardes iland' (Whiting, 103–4). Camden refers to this island as 'Enhly,' but in English called 'Berdsey, as one would say the Isle of Birds' (pt. 2, 203). [An anonymous contributor to Woodhouse's notes remarks that Milton would not know that Bardsey is 'fifty miles south of the Chester-Dublin route, and therefore much too far away to overlook the wreck. But Milton...was led to believe that Bardsey was adjacent to Mona not by Ortelius, but by Camden, whose phrase *Proxima hinc Mona* (meaning "The next island on my list is Mona") could be taken to mean "Adjacent to Bardsey is Mona."' (This is how Camden's translator took it: see the second sentence below.)] While Camden divests the island of bardic connection, he provides a burial place of holy men: '...this Iland, which toward the East mounteth aloft with an high promontory,...harboured in old time so many holy men, that...ancient histories record there were twenty thousand Saints buried heere. Next unto this lieth Mona, that is, Anglesey...' (pt. 2, 203). These passages explain *the steep*, the association with the *Bards* and with a burial place (though again of Christian saints, not Druids), and why Milton should next mention Anglesey, calling it *Mona*. (See A. L. Owen, *The Famous Druids*, Oxford, 1962, 52–63, etc., and notes.)

If, as seems unlikely, the word *Nymphs* (50) is to be taken literally, the Druids are called *your old Bards* because the Druidic worship (with the *Bards* participating as members of the Druidic order) was carried on in groves and was associated especially with the oak, and the *Nymphs* were divinities of nature, the class of dryads being divinities of trees. But Milton's almost certain use of *Nymphs* for the Muses (above, 50–5 n.) opens up more interesting associations. Diod. Sic. (5. 31. 2–3) refers to the Gauls' lyric poets 'whom they call Bards,' and who 'sing to the accompaniment of instruments which are like lyres,' and also to 'philosophers' or 'men learned in religious affairs' who are especially honoured and 'called by them Druids' (L.C.L.). Fuller information was assembled by Selden: 'For their [the Druids'] Profession, it was both of learning Profane and Holy....In a multitude of verses they delivered what they taught, not suffering it to be committed to writing' (Drayton, 4, 193); when they did write, they used 'Greeke letters, as Caesars copies have.' And the affinity of their language with the Greek is attested by the name Druid, which is related to δρῦς, an oak (192). In their religion and philosophy they were nearer to monotheism than either the Greeks or Romans; they invoked 'one All-healing or All-saving power,' apparently Apollo, 'whom they worshipt under name of Belin' (193–4). On the Druidic worship of Apollo Selden is emphatic, and he associates Apollo's lyre with the harp of the British bards (121). Nor is he less certain of the priority of ancient Britain to Rome and perhaps Greece in learning and poetry (214–15). Without specifically recognizing the Bards as a Druidic order, Selden assumes their identity with the Druids, and speaks of their 'powerfull enchantments' (122). (Strabo, 4. 4. 4–5, and others recognize the Bards as a subdivision of the Druids: see Owen, *Famous Druids*, 17.) Here then is abundant support for Milton's describing the Druids as *Bards* and for his associating them with the Greek Muses, the guardians of poetry and learning, and followers of Apollo; and that this was his intention is confirmed by *Mansus* 35–48. The writings cited in this and the following note justify his assumption that the Druids were *famous*, at least among the learned. On his later attitude to the Druids, see Owen, 55–8.

54 *the shaggy top of Mona high.* The name Mona, used for both Anglesey and the Isle of Man, Milton, following Camden, uses for Anglesey (*HistBrit, Works* 10, 63), which Camden calls 'that most notable Isle Mona, the ancient seat of the Druides' (*Britain*, 1610, 671). Its wooded hills explain *shaggy top*; this phrase, as Todd noted, had appeared in Sylvester (*D.W.W.* 1. 2. 544, Grosart, 1, 32), and was repeated in *PL* 6. 645. Though not high in comparison with the mainland coast, Mona, as shown on Camden's map, is hilly; but Milton would think also of the nymphs on the heights of Etna (Theocritus 1. 69) and Parnassus and Pindus (Virgil, *E.* 10. 11). As the scene of Druidic rites, Mona would necessarily be thought of as wooded. As noticed by Warton, Drayton (*Poly.* 9. 415–20) had Mona speak: 'Sometimes within my shades, in many an ancient wood, / ...The fearelesse British Priests, under an aged Oake, / ...with an Axe of gold, from that Jove-sacred tree / The Missleto cut downe.' Selden comments (Drayton 4, 197): 'The British Druids took this Isle of Anglesey (then well stored with thicke Woods, and religious Groves, in so much that it was called Inis-Dowil) for their chiefe residence....'

55 *Deva spreads her wisard stream.* The Dee (the river on which stood Chester, whence King's ship sailed) was supposed to possess magic powers of divination. Camden (*Britain*, 1610, 602) says that 'Divinitie' was ascribed to the river because 'now and then it changed the chanell, and thereby foreshewed a sure token of victorie to the inhabitants upon it ⟨i.e. the English and the Welsh⟩... according as it inclined more to this side or to that....' Drayton (*Poly.* 10. 186–

218) recounts substantially the same superstition regarding Dee's 'ominous Flood'; he applies the phrase 'Wisard River' to the Weaver, the rival of the Dee in 'prophetick skill' (11. 71, 77). Milton would remember that Theocritus (1. 68–9) associates the nymphs with the river Anapus and the sacred stream of Acis. [Cf. *Vac* 98 and n.]

56–7 This repudiation is balanced by that of 152–3. Harrison (after Tuckwell) notes that in somewhat similar fashion Virgil checks his imagination in *E.* 10. 58–61; cf. Castiglione in *Alcon* 130–1. [*Ay me*: 1638, *Ah me*.]

56 *fondly*: 'foolishly' (Verity: *OED* 1); but the word seems to involve also 'self-pleasing or affectionate credulity' (*OED* 2: though no example is given before 1762). *For* refers back to *fondly*.

58–63 Orpheus, who received the lyre from Apollo and was instructed by the Muses, was the son of the Muse Calliope (and of Oeagrus, king of Thrace) and the mythical father of pre-Homeric song, the archetypal poet and musician. The story of his death at the hands of the Bacchantes is told by Ovid (*M.* 11. 1–66) and more briefly by Virgil (*G.* 4. 517–27). After his final loss of Eurydice (see *L'All* 145–50 n., *IlPen* 103–8 n.), Orpheus roamed his native Thrace, lamenting his loss and charming with his song all nature animate and inanimate (hence *inchanting*). Enraged by his devotion to his dead wife and his implied scorn of them, the frenzied Maenads attacked him, but, charmed by his music, their missiles fell harmless. Then, with the sound of dissonant instruments and with wild yells (*the rout that made the hideous roar*; cf. *PL* 7. 32–8), they drowned the music and their weapons took effect. They tore the singer limb from limb and cast his head and lyre into the Hebrus, which bore them out to sea until they reached the island of Lesbos, while birds and beasts, rocks and trees, mourned his fate (*Whom Universal nature did lament*). Warton observes that 'Lycidas, as a poet, is here tacitly compared with Orpheus,' and adds (quite in the modern manner): 'They were both victims of the water'—though Orpheus of course was not. Neither Ovid nor Virgil mentions the Muse's inability to save her son, the point Milton emphasizes here and in *PL* 7. 37–9. [But Ovid does, in his elegy on Tibullus (*Am.* 3. 9. 21): *quid pater Ismario, quid mater profuit Orpheo?* Cf. L. P. Wilkinson, *Ovid Recalled*, Cambridge, 1955, 77 n. Godolphin (*MLN* 49, 1934, 166) quoted Propertius 3. 7. 9–10: *et mater non iusta piae dare debita terrae | nec pote cognatos inter humare rogos.*] Milton stops short with the arrival of the head on the Lesbian shore and does not follow the rest of Ovid's tale as foreign to his purpose. Nor does he give any hint of later interpretations of the myth. [See C. W. Mayerson in III above, under 1949; and *IlPen* 103–8 n.] References to

Orpheus are fairly frequent in pastoral elegies, usually, however, not to his death but either to his power of charming all nature or to his journey to Hades in quest of Eurydice.

The lines were much revised in MS. but had reached substantially their final form in 1638. MS. first had (*Facs.* 436): *what could the golden hayrd Calliope* (deleted) | *for her inchaunting son* | *when shee beheld* (*the gods farre sighted bee*) (deleted) | *his goarie scalpe rowle downe the Thracian lee* (deleted). Then the margin adds after the second line: *whome universal nature might lament* | *and heaven and hel deplore* (deleted) | *when his divine head downe* (deleted) *the streame was sent* | *downe the swift Hebrus to the Lesbian shore*. Finally, a sign refers back to MS. 1 (*Facs.* 434), where the lines assume their present form, with the new 1½ lines preceding *for her inchanting son* and with *might lament* altered to *did lament* and *divine visage* to *gorie visage*. It seems possible that when *divine head* was introduced there was some thought of a parallel with the *sacred head* of Lycidas (102). We may observe that in the first version the arrival of the head at Lesbos is not even hinted, and that Milton reverts finally to his original epithet *goarie*. [R. B. Gottfried (*N&Q* 5, 1958, 195–6), noting the sequence of readings and Milton's apparent desire to retain the idea of 'ritual death' through an allusion to blood (unmentioned in Ovid, his main source), suggests that he remembered the emphasis given in Poliziano's *Nutricia*—*divulsum caput a cervice cruenta* and *os...cruentum*. H. Darbishire (*Essays and Studies 1957*, 39–40) and D. S. Berkeley (*N&Q* 5, 1958, 335–6) suggest reasons for the various changes in 58–61; and Leishman (*Minor Poems*, 295–8) examines the revisions in the whole passage on Orpheus.

Rudrum (*Comus*, 65–6) observes that the reference to the Druids 'forms a subtle preparation for the lines describing the end of Orpheus. Like King, the Druids were poets and priests' and are dead; like Orpheus, they were poets who had magical powers over nature. 'The "pastoral detail" of "Lycidas" thus represents no inert acquiescence in convention. It really *is* a poem about Nature, Nature which produces, and destroys, men of genius, as it produces and destroys everything else. One element in the greatness of "Lycidas" is that beneath its "decorum" and conventionality there throbs a sense of primitive power.']

61 *rout*: a disorderly, tumultuous, disreputable crowd (*OED*: *sb.*[1] 5), as usually in Milton (cf. *Comus* 532, *PL* 7. 34, 10. 534).

63 *swift Hebrus*. Warton cited *volucremque fuga praevertitur Hebrum* (Virgil, *A.* 1. 317), but noted that Servius, commenting on the phrase, denied that the

Hebrus was swift, though it rose in the mountain range Rhodope and flowed down to the Aegean. Todd quoted: 'As when Calliopes deere sonne, sweete harmony singing, / …Swift-flowing Hebrus stai'd all his streames in a wonder' (Davison's *Poetical Rhapsody*, ed. Rollins, 1, 194). *Lesbian shore*. The island of Lesbos was the home of the Aeolian school of lyrists, the birthplace of Terpander, Alcaeus, and Sappho; hence an appropriate resting place for the head and lyre of Orpheus.

64 *boots*: profits, avails (*OED* 3a; cf. *SA* 560). [Cf. Spenser, *Teares of the Muses* 445–6: 'What bootes it then to come from glorious / Forefathers, or to have been nobly bredd?'; and the nearby lines quoted below in 70 n.]

65 *tend*: attend to (*OED*: *v.*¹ 2c). *homely*: domestic, hence simple or humble (*OED* 4a). Milton speaks of 'the simplicity, and plainnesse of Christianity which to the gorgeous solemnities of Paganisme…seem'd but a homely and Yeomanly Religion' (*Ref, Works* 3, 25). Todd cited 'And holden scorne of homely shepheards quill' (Spenser, *S.C., June* 67). *slighted*: treated with indifference or disdain (*OED* 1).

Shepherds trade. Masson explains as 'according to the established metaphor of pastoralists, "to practise poetry"'; so also Bell (who notes, however, that in 113–20 'the shepherd's trade is not poetry, but the work of the Church'), Verity, Wright, Hanford, et al. But unless *trade* is taken in the sense of 'regular or habitual course of action' (*OED* 3c), song is not the shepherd's 'trade' even in pastoral poetry. Nowell Smith (*TLS*, 6 Dec., 1928, 965) suggests that the reference is to King's proposed work as a college tutor, which would in itself be consonant with the pastoral allegory of 25–36; but if (as seems probable) trade and song are indeed differentiated, it is more natural to relate *trade* to 113–21 and have it refer to the work of the ministry on which King was entering (and which Milton had earlier proposed to himself). Traditionally, the shepherd image itself is as closely associated with Christ and the church as it is with pastoral poetry, and it is an obvious means of uniting the two in a single poem, as the *Nativity* further illustrates. [But lines 65 and 66 are surely variant expressions of the same idea, and the whole passage (50 f.) is concerned with the role of the poet, with service of the Muse and the fame such service might be expected to bring; it does not fit service in the ministry. Leishman (*Minor Poems*, 280) takes the *Shepherds trade* as 'the office of priest or pastor,' which Milton associates with 'the life of the strict meditator of the thankless muse'— King having been on the way to the priesthood, Milton to heroic poetry.]

66 *strictly meditate the thankless Muse*. *OED* (meditate 1c) explains (after

Keightley) that *meditate the...Muse* is a unique example based on Virgil's *silvestrem...musam meditaris avena* (*E.* 1. 2, which Fairclough, in L.C.L., happily translates as 'wooing the woodland Muse'); cf. also *agrestem tenui meditabor harundine Musam* (ibid. 6. 8). The meaning of course is to compose poetry. The adverb *strictly* carries on the idea of *with uncessant care* (64) and, incidentally, differentiates the tone of Milton's phrase from that of Virgil's: song (as Milton conceives it) is as serious an occupation as the shepherd's trade, and undertaken in a similar spirit [but see comment at the end of the preceding note]. According to Newton (reported by Verity), the *Muse* is *thankless* because poetry earns no thanks from an ungrateful world. Verity prefers to regard the *Muse* herself as *thankless* (i.e. as unresponsive, making no return: *OED* 1) because she cannot, in return, save the poet from death (above, 56–63). [But this seems a less natural and logical interpretation, since Milton assumes that the *Muse*, however *thankless* in the worldly sense, can inspire and reward earnest devotees, even though enjoyment of fame may be cut off by death. Leishman (*Minor Poems*, 279) thinks Milton is making the same distinction he had made in *El* 6, between the austere muse of epic and tragedy and the elegiac muse of love-poetry.]

67   *use*: are wont (*OED* 19). The 1638 text has *do*; 1645 restores MS. reading.

68–9   *Amaryllis...Neaera's hair*. MS. and 1638 (*Facs.* 438, 349) had *hid in*, replaced in MS. by *or with*, the reading of 1645 and 1673. [P. Maas (*RES* 19, 1943, 397–8) thought the change awkward, as involving 'an anticlimax, a zeugma, and a slackness of rhythm'; the earlier version, presenting the odd notion of a man sporting with one girl while hidden in another's hair, may have alluded to some frivolous piece of Cavalier poetry.] The name Amaryllis is very common in pastoral and elegiac verse, especially because of the Virgilian lines known to every schoolboy: *tu, Tityre, lentus in umbra | formosam resonare doces Amaryllida silvas* (*E.* 1. 4–5). See also ibid. 30, 36; 2. 14, 52; 3. 81; 8. 77–8, 101; 9. 22; Theocritus 3; 4. 36, 38; and other examples in Sandys ('Sources,' 238, etc.). The name Neaera was much more common in the Renaissance than in antiquity. It appears in Virgil (*E.* 3. 3); Sandys ('Sources,' 239) notes that among the poems of Tibullus are six elegies addressed by Lygdamus to Neaera (3. 1–6), and that Neaera is Horace's subject in *Epod.* 15 and that her myrrh-scented hair is mentioned in *C.* 3. 14. 21–2. In Prudentius (*C. Or. Sym.* 1. 139; *Perist.* 10. 240) Neaera is a general name for a mistress. Verity cited Mantuan, *Eclogues* (ed. Mustard), 4. 176, 6. 4; and noted that the two names occur in Ariosto, *Orlando Furioso* 11. 12 (ed. S. Debenedetti and C. Segre, Bologna,

1960), and in Spenser, *C.C.C.H.A.* 524–31, 540, 564 f. (but here in a totally different context). Warton (474: reported in Todd, 4, 412) noticed the more important fact that George Buchanan [whom Milton sometimes echoed in his Latin poems] had written amatory pieces on Neaera. In *El.* 9 (*Opera*, 1725, 1, 323) Cupid, seeking to subdue the poet, cuts a golden lock from Neaera's head as she sleeps and with it binds him before presenting him to her—thus entangled with her hair. The same theme is pursued in Buchanan's *Epigrammata* 1. 44 (ibid. 371). [R. J. Schoeck (*N&Q* 3, 1956, 190–1) cited also the many poems to Neaera in Joannes Secundus' very popular *Basia*, some of which include references to tangled hair. Hales cited Lovelace, *To Althea, from Prison* 5, 'When I lye tangled in her haire']; and Sandys ('Sources,' 256) quoted: 'Now comes my lover... / And brings my longings tangled in her hair' (Peele, *David and Bethsabe* 1. 1. 92–3). While 67–9 have been thought (no doubt correctly) to glance at the lives and verses of such Cavalier lyrists as Carew, Suckling, and Randolph, we may remember that the amatory verse of Buchanan [and Secundus] represented precisely the sort of thing that Milton described in *El* 6 and reprobated in the retraction added [we do not know when] to his Elegies and in *Apol* (*Works* 1, 210–12, 222; 3, 302–3). [J. W. Saunders (cf. fuller reference in '*L'Allegro* and *Il Penseroso*' III, under 1955) takes the names as representing not only sex but the world of courtly Renaissance poetry and its patrons—like the Countess Dowager of Derby, Spenser's 'Amaryllis.' Le Comte (*Yet Once More*, 6) objects to the literary and 'oblique' interpretation: 'Amaryllis and Neaera stand for the natural pleasures. They are symbolic, but they are also girls.'

Maas (see beginning of this note) took account of the conjecture that *with* in *with the tangles* should be read, not as the preposition, but as the verb *withe* ('bind with withes, twigs of willow'). This suggestion, perhaps first made by J. S. Phillimore, was supported by R. W. Chapman (*The Portrait of a Scholar*, Oxford, 1920, 74), who thought it avoided an awkward zeugma, and adopted by Quiller-Couch (*Oxford Book of English Verse*, ed. 1939, 347) and L. Untermeyer (*Treasury of Great Poetry*, New York, 1942, 449). Maas points out that the verb was not used of plaiting human hair, and that, if Milton had intended that meaning, he would not, after the *with* in 68, have written *with* in 69. The suggestion of *withe* was revived by G. Beaumont (*TLS*, 16 July 1970, 775) and endorsed by D. Greene (ibid. 14 August, 903). The idea had been recorded by E. Le Comte (ibid. 31 July, 855) in his edition, *Paradise Lost and other poems* (New York, 1961). Le Comte (*Yet Once More*, 6–7) assembles Milton's references to amorous nets.]

70–84 The passionate desire for fame, like that for knowledge and for beauty, was a characteristic of Renaissance man fully shared by Milton. He had glanced at the subject in *Prol* 7, concluding that 'not to value fame when you have done well, that is beyond all glory,' but that we may 'hope for an eternal life, which will never wipe out the memory at least of our good deeds on earth: in which, if we have nobly deserved anything here, we ourselves, being present, shall hear it; in which...those would be exalted...by a unique and supreme knowledge, who, first in this life, spent most temperately, have given all their time to good employments....' (*Works* 12, 279–81). Close to the time of writing *Lycidas*, he told Diodati that he was thinking of an 'immortality' of fame on earth to be achieved by a *magnum opus* (*Epistol* 7, 23 Sept., 1637, *Works* 12, 26–7: [this letter should probably be dated 23 Nov.: see Milton, *C.P.W.* 1, 325]. The question of fame and its relative value—[strongly questioned here in *Lyc* 78–84]—continued to engage his thoughts at times and received final comment in *PR* 3. 22–30, 47–8, 60–4. In his notes on these passages, in the present Variorum Commentary, MacKellar traces the contrast of earthly and heavenly fame from St Paul (1 Cor. 3. 21; Gal. 5. 26) through patristic, medieval, and later examples to Joseph Hall: 'I will not care whether I be knowen, or remembred, or forgotten amongst men, if my name and good actions may live with God in the records of Eternitie' (*Meditations and Vowes*, 1606, 3. 94: *Works*, ed. P. Wynter, 10 v., Oxford, 1863, 7, 518). [Cf. Leishman, *Minor Poems*, 283 f.]

70 *Fame is the spur that the clear spirit doth raise.* Todd cited 'Due praise, that is the spur of dooing well' (Spenser, *Teares* 454). Keightley added: 'Honour, the spur that pricks the princely mind / To follow rule' (Peele, *Battle of Alcazar* 1. 1. 1). [The idea and image were a traditional commonplace, e.g. Cicero (*Arch.* 10. 23): *hoc maximum et periculorum incitamentum est et laborum*; Ovid (*Ex Ponto* 4. 2. 36): *immensum gloria calcar habet* (cf. L. P. Wilkinson, *Ovid Recalled*, 11 n.); Amyot, preface to Plutarch's *Lives*, tr. North (Temple Classics, 1, 10): 'the immortal praise and glory wherewith it rewardeth well doers, is a very lively and sharp spur for men of noble courage...'; Sylvester (*D.W.W.* 1. 6. 869, Grosart, 1, 79): 'Spurr'd with desire of Fames eternall merit.' In his edition of Spenser's *Complaints* (London, 1928, 214) W. L. Renwick quoted North in illustration of *Teares* 451–60, and—along with the lines quoted above in 64 n.—lines 451–6 may be added: 'Or who would ever care to doo brave deed, / Or strive in vertue others to excell; / If none should yeeld him his deserved meed, / Due praise, that is the spur of dooing well? / For if good were not praised more than ill, / None would choose goodnes of his owne freewill.']

clear: noble (Lat. *clarus*), or perhaps free from fault (*OED* 15)—save 'That last infirmity.' Todd quoted: 'Yet had not my cleere spirit in Fortunes scorne, / Me above earth and her afflictions borne' (*To Master George Sandys* 29–30, Drayton, 3, 206). Milton uses 'cleare spirit' in *Animad* (*Works* 3, 162) apparently in the sense of noble, generous or exalted in mind; cf. 'most erected Spirits' (*PR* 3. 27), which Jerram takes to explain the meaning here. [Cf. Shakespeare, *Oth.* 3. 4. 140–3: 'Something sure of state, / ...Hath puddled his clear spirit.' See the chapter on 'The Clear Spirit' (1–56, especially 41 f.) in Gordon W. O'Brien, *Renaissance Poetics and the Problem of Power* (Chicago, 1956), and J. Grundy on the use of 'clear' as a critical term by Drayton et al. (*MLR* 59, 1964, 501–10).]

71 *That last infirmity of Noble mind*: i.e. the weakness left when all others have been eradicated. The word *That* suggests the traditional character of the idea (Bell), and many more or less similar phrases have been cited. Warton (after Bowle) quoted Abbate Angelo Grillo: *Questa sete di fama et gloria, ordinaria infirmità de gli animi generosi* (*Lettere*, Venice, 1604, 2, 210); and Todd cited Sir Henry Wotton as speaking of James I [he was in fact speaking of the Duke of Buckingham] in his *Panegyrick to King Charles*: 'I will not deny his appetite of glory, which generous minds do ever latest part from' (*Reliquiae Wottonianae*, 1651, 147). Todd also referred vaguely to Massinger's *A Very Woman* and Tacitus. The former item is: 'Though the desire of fame be the last weakness / Wise men put off' (5. 4. 9–10). Jerram cited Tacitus, *Hist. 4. 6*: *etiam sapientibus cupido gloriae novissima exuitur*. [The Latin phrase was quoted by Owen Felltham, after his own rendering: 'Desire of Glory, is the last garment, that, even wise men, lay aside' ('Of Fame,' *Resolves*, 3rd ed., 1628, 47). The idea is expressed or approached in Cicero, *Arch.* 11. 26, *Offic.* 1. 8. 26, *Tusc.* 5. 36, Seneca, *Ep.* 21, 102, 113; etc. C. C. J. Webb (*John of Salisbury*, London, 1932, 62: cited by R. J. Schoeck, *N&Q* 2, 1955, 236) quoted John's *Haec est praestantes quae deserit ultima mentes* (*Entheticus* 875; Migne, *Pat. Lat.* 199, 984) as closer to Milton than John's remarks on pride and vainglory in *Polycraticus* 8. 1 (tr. J. B. Pike as *Frivolities of Courtiers and Footprints of Philosophers*, Minneapolis, 1938, 295). H. M. Currie (*N&Q* 5, 1958, 106–7) cited Silius Italicus (6. 332–3) on Regulus: *abripuit traxitque virum fax mentis honestae / gloria et incerti fallax fiducia Martis*. J. L. Coolidge (*PQ* 42, 1963, 176–82) added illustrative passages from Boethius (whom Webb had referred to vaguely), *Consol. Phil.* 2. 7 (L.C.L., 212), 3. 2 (228–32).]

73 *Guerdon*. The word was commoner in the 16th and 17th centuries than

Jerram supposed (see *OED*); he argued in part from its being explained in the Gloss to Spenser's *S.C., November* 45.

74 *sudden blaze.* The noun means splendour, brilliant display (*OED* 5 b). Verity suggests some influence from the verb *blaze*, 'make public' (cf. *Arc* 74). Warton compared 'the blaze of fame' (*PR* 3. 47), but there the sense is derogatory. [Le Comte (*Yet Once More*, 63) cites *sudden blaze* in *Arc* 2.]

75 *blind Fury...abhorred shears.* Milton is not of course confusing Atropos, the third of the Fates, with the Furies, but is saying that Atropos has the character of a Fury. The long history of the Fates is briefly sketched by Osgood, *C.M.* 34–5; [a large philosophical account is W. C. Greene's *Moira: Fate, Good, and Evil in Greek Thought*, Cambridge, Mass., 1944]. In Homer, *Od.* 7. 196 f., the Fates are associated, under the image of spinners, with Fate. In Hesiod, *Theog.* 217–22, the three are personified and named. In *The Shield of Heracles*, 258 f., their implacable fierceness is emphasized, and Atropos is said to be 'superior to the others and the eldest of them.' Their spinning is much elaborated by Plato (*Rep.* 10. 616–17; see above, *Arc* 67–73 n.). The cutting of the thread of life with the shears Osgood finds to be 'of late Roman origin.' This became common later; cf. Spenser, *Daphnaïda* 16–18; Shakespeare, *John* 4. 2. 91, and the burlesque version in *Dream* 5. 1. 290–2, 343–8. In *Arc* 65 the three 'hold the vital shears.'

The Furies likewise have a long history. Their number varies; Apollodorus (1. 1. 4) names three, Alecto, Tisiphone, Megaera. Their function is always the avenging of crime; while the Fates are sometimes depicted as grave and solemn, the Furies are uniformly menacing and repulsive. The Furies and Fates are sometimes associated in tragedy, e.g. Aeschylus, *Prom.* 516, Shakespeare, *Dream* 5. 1. 289–92. Warton noticed the phrase *blind fury* in *Gorboduc* 5. 2. 2 and, followed by 'fell Erynnis,' in Spenser (*Ruines of Rome* 323, 327).

Milton in this context presents Atropos as a veritable Fury, though not of course as an avenger of crime; he adds blindness, not a recognized attribute of either Fate or Fury, because she seems, at this stage in the poem's development, to act without discrimination. [Since, for the Christian poet, nothing can happen without God's will, the phrase is a violent questioning of divine justice and wisdom, even though it is to be answered as the poem proceeds. M. Lloyd (*MLN* 75, 1960, 103–8) sees Milton substituting a Fury for the Fates in order to define the death as a form of God's just revenge for man's original sin; but Milton is surely not thinking of King's death (or his own) in such terms.]

76 *slits*: severs. Of this figurative use *OED* 1 b gives only three other examples;

two of them, including one from Milton (*Colas, Works* 4, 250), seem dubious and the other is a late and obvious imitation of Milton. Possibly he was influenced by Lat. *incido*, which could be used indifferently for 'slit,' 'cut through,' and figuratively 'cut short.' The *thin spun life* is of course the fragile thread spun by the Fates.

76–7 *But not the praise, | Phoebus repli'd.* As god of poetry, Phoebus intervened to assert that Atropos could not cut off the praise by cutting off life. [Hanford quotes Spenser, *S.C., October* 19–20: 'Cuddie, the prayse is better, then the price, | The glory eke much greater then the gayne.']

77 *touch'd my trembling ears.* Todd gives two parallels: *Cynthius aurem | vellit et admonuit* (Virgil, *E.* 6. 3–4), and *Unde, unde sonus trepidas aures | ferit?* (Seneca, *Herc. Oet.* 1944–5). Verity notes that to touch a witness on the ear was in Rome the manner of summoning him to appear, and cites Horace, *S.* 1. 9. 77. The passage has more interest than Verity sees, for it involves not only the touching of the ear but the saving of the poet by Apollo (ibid. 76–8). Suggestive also is Conington's note (reported by Jerram and Verity) on the Virgilian phrase cited above: that the touching of the ear symbolized recalling something to a person's memory; thus Phoebus' reply reminds the poet of what he already knew. The word *trembling* is of course a transferred epithet; it is the poet who trembles at Apollo's touch. We must reject Masson's suggested reference to the popular belief that tingling of your ears is a sign that someone is talking about you.

78–84 Phoebus is saying that fame, as so far conceived, lives, grows, and dies because it is rooted merely in the opinion and report of mortal men, like a jewel that shines only when artificially displayed; but true fame lives in the sight of God and spreads aloft (in heaven), because it depends on God's perfect knowledge and wisdom. Cf. *Prol* 7 (quoted above, 70–84 n.). ['It is a perfect instance of subtle literary judgement that Milton did not phrase this, as he might have done, in the imagery of "And when the chief Shepherd shall appear, ye shall receive a crown of glory that fadeth not away" (1 Peter v. 4). He saved for his second great answer the overtly Christian terms of St. Peter's speech, by which time the sudden blaze and clear light of unequivocal terms is wanted. This is not a matter of "Christian" and "pagan" but of direction and indirection, of a less or a more figurative functioning in the language. Both are Christian. The question of Milton's pagan imagery in *Lycidas* here comes up in its first form, and we make the first answer to it, that such *terms* do not make images non-Christian.' (R. Tuve, *Images*, 75–6).]

79 *glistering foil.* A foil is a thin leaf (Lat. *folium*) of metal placed behind or under a gem to enhance its brightness (*OED*: *sb.*¹ 5). Warton cited Shakespeare, *I H. IV* 1. 2. 236–9, but there the 'foil to set it off' is 'a sullen ground.' For Milton *glister* does not seem to have in itself any more derogatory connotation (as Verity thinks it has) than *glisten* or *glitter*. The context conveys or supports the particular suggestion when it is present, as in 'they think all is gold of pietie that doth but glister with a shew of Zeale' (*Eikon, Works* 5, 147), where he remembers the original form of the proverb (cf. Shakespeare, *Merch.* 2. 7. 65); it may also decisively exclude the suggestion, as in 'he, the Supreme good... / Would send a glistring Guardian if need were' (*Comus* 216–18).

81 *by those pure eyes*: *by* means 'by the operation of.' Warton cited: 'Thou ⟨God⟩ art of purer eyes than to behold evil' (Hab. 1. 13). The phrase *spreds aloft* does not merely continue the metaphor of *plant* (Verity); the vertical or celestial image is contrasted with the earthliness of *broad rumour*.

82 *witnes*: 'Knowledge,...wisdom' (*OED* 1, which notes it as obsolete and gives no example later than 1482), perhaps combined with the meaning 'testimony' (ibid. 2). Jove, seeing, knowing, and judging all, knows and bears witness to the good; he is, as Wright observes, invoked in all oaths. In the language of Christian humanism, Jove stands for God.

84 *meed*: a synonym for *Guerdon* (73), but also recalling the *meed* of 14. Jerram compared: 'Fame is my meed, and glory vertues pray' (Spenser, *F.Q.* 3. 10. 31). [Cf. Spenser's lines quoted above in 70 n.]

85–8 These lines open the second movement of the monody and deliberately restore the pastoral tone, broken by the words of Phoebus [words which, reported by the poet, are as it were outside the elegy proper]. The *Fountain Arethuse*, the famous spring in the island of Ortygia off the Sicilian coast, near Syracuse, the birthplace of Theocritus, stands for Greek pastoral poetry. Sandys ('Sources,' 236) notes that Daphnis (Theocritus 1. 117) bids farewell to this fountain, which thenceforth becomes 'the characteristic fountain of pastoral poetry'; cf. *Lament for Bion* 10 and 77. In his closest imitation of Theocritus, Virgil invokes the nymph (see below, 132–3 n.) or the fountain, as though addressing his Muse: *Arethusa, mihi concede laborem* (E. 10. 1). *Mincius, crown'd with vocal reeds* is a parallel reference to Latin pastoral poetry and Virgil in particular, since Mantua, which he regarded as his birthplace, was on an island in the Mincius (hence *honour'd floud*). Editors cite: *hic viridis tenera praetexit harundine ripas | Mincius* (Virgil, *E.* 7. 12–13); and: *tardis ingens ubi flexibus errat | Mincius* (*G.* 3. 14–15; cf. A. S. Cook, *SP* 16, 1919, 184–5). Thus

Milton has his *crown'd...reeds* and perhaps the germ of *Smooth-sliding* in Virgil's description of the river's slow motion; the actual epithet occurs, as Dunster and Jerram noted, in Sylvester (*D.W.W.* 2. 1. 1. 117, Grosart, 1, 100). Cook (loc. cit.) found a source for the expression in Ovid's *lubricus amnis* (*Am.* 3. 6. 81) and for *crown'd* in Ovid's *silva coronat aquas* (*M.* 5. 388), though he saw a more obvious source in Drayton: 'fountaine...crown'd, with many a upright plant' (*Poly.* 21. 108). Milton's addition of *vocal* to *reeds* probably referred to the poet's pipe, though Jerram evidently took the word as a reference to the wind's playing among them, since he cites Lucretius 5. 1382–3 in explanation.

85   *honour'd*. MS. first had *smooth* (deleted), then *fam'd* (deleted), finally *honour'd* (*Facs.* 438). See 85–8 n.

86   *Smooth-sliding*. MS. first had *soft sliding* (*Facs.* 438). See 85–8 n.

87   *mood*: mode (Lat. *modus*), the scale or set of sounds in which a piece of music was composed, applied both to the Greek modes and to those of medieval plainsong (*OED*: mode 1). Here the image is from music, and the word has no direct reference to *mood* as a state of mind or feeling. The musical image is appropriate, since the whole poem adopts the convention of the pastoral as sung. But while Milton would have the Greek modes in mind, he would be aware of the strong emotional effects the Greeks ascribed to music, so that *mood* as a state of mind may have a secondary role here.

88   *my Oat*: my pastoral music (see above, 33 n.).

89–131   This is Milton's adaptation of the procession of mourners, one of the features of pastoral elegy, as in Theocritus 1. 80 f., Virgil, *E.* 10. 19 f. [Rudrum (*Comus*, 72) remarks on the logical sequence: 'Neptune, Camus and the Pilot of the Galilean lake form a progression: Nature, Culture, Religion'; and St Peter's theme, the survival of the unworthy, 'is the logical corollary of a thought which has been central to the development of the poem up to this point,' the fate that overtakes the worthiest. 'The prosperity of the wicked, and the consequent perplexity of the religious mind, is one of the commonest themes in the Psalms.'

C. R. Baskervill ('Two Parallels to *Lycidas*,' *Nation* 91, 1910, 546–7) cited the series of 'symbolic' abstractions in Greene's elegy on Sir Christopher Hatton, *A Maidens Dreame* (*Plays and Poems of Robert Greene*, ed. J. C. Collins, 2 v., Oxford, 1905, 2, 221–35). But these are remote from *Lycidas*.]

89   *And listens to*. Editors generally (and *OED* and L. Lockwood) neglect this peculiar, if readily intelligible, use of the word. Jerram explains as the poet listening like a pupil, that he may know what to say. This is true, but not quite adequate. It is the song that is said to listen; i.e. really the auditors listen through the instrumentality of the song, as they have just listened to the words of Phoebus. *Herald of the Sea*: Triton, son of Poseidon (Neptune), so called because he bore a trumpet or shell with which, at his father's command, he roused or calmed the waves. Cf. *Oceani Tubicen* (*Naturam* 58).

90 *Neptune's plea*. Keightley took this to mean a case falling within Neptune's exclusive jurisdiction (as in 'plea of the crown,' *OED* 1 d, and in Milton's phrase 'no jurisdiction, no courts of plea,' *RCG*, *Works* 3, 250), which Neptune has delegated Triton to hear: what follows (91-9) would then be regarded as Triton's taking of evidence. But Jerram and others prefer to take *plea* in its commoner sense of a statement made by or for a defendant (*OED* 2 b), so that what follows is the calling of witnesses to exonerate Neptune from blame.

91 *Fellon*: 'Savage, wild' (*OED*: A. 1 b), probably with the added suggestion of felonious, criminal. Verity (after Keightley) takes this to be the primary sense, and Jerram at least 'the additional sense,' the winds being presumed guilty of King's death. Although 'The Air was calm' (98) when the vessel sank, the reference might be to the general character of the winds. T. P. Harrison (University of Texas *Studies in English* 15, 1935, 22) suggested a French pastoral source which avoids the implication: *Ces gros monstres, Neptune, amene avec la mer | Faisant de vents felons les vagues ecumer* (A. de Baïf, *Eclogue* 15: *Euvres*, ed. Ch. Marty-Laveaux, 5 v., Paris, 1881-90, 3, 82).

93-4 *gust of rugged wings | ...beaked Promontory*. Jerram explains as a winged gust made rugged or ragged (see *L'All* 8-9 n.) by the intervening obstacle, the promontory. Warton cited 'the utmost end of Cornwalls furrowing beake' (Drayton, *Poly.* 1. 69).

96 *sage Hippotades*: wise son of Hippotas, i.e. Aeolus, in whose charge Jove placed the winds (Virgil, *A.* 1. 52-63). Noting that Virgil does not use the patronymic of Aeolus, Warton cited a number of classical poets who do, e.g. Homer (*Od.* 10. 2), Apollon. Rhod. (4. 819), Ovid (*M.* 4. 663; 14. 86, 224; etc.). Aeolus' skill in invention and prediction and his reverence for the gods—as Osgood (*C.M.*) and Hughes (1937) note from Diod. Sic. 5. 7. 7—and Virgil's account of his knowing how to control the winds (*A.* 1. 62-3) alike justify the epithet *sage*. [N. Comes (*Mythol.* 8. 10, p. 451 in 1616 ed.) and C. Stephanus (*Dictionarium*), who follows Comes, call Aeolus *vir sapiens* (Starnes–Talbert, 231).]

97-102   In describing the disaster as inexplicable Milton is not in accord with the Latin preface to the *Justa*, which states (though with no hint of a storm) that the ship struck a rock not far from the British coast and sank. Phrases in Henry King's poem (*Obsequies*, 3) may, as Verity observes (but hardly with the certainty he finds in them), indicate that the sea was rough: but that 'the fairest arm' of the tree 'Is torn away by an unluckie storm' is conventional, and 'the treacherous waves and carelesse wind, / Which did conspire to intercept this prize' says little more than that King perished at sea ('treacherous waves' may even suggest a calm) and that his body was not recovered. [In the whole passage the poet is groping for some apparent cause in nature, an effort which indirectly heightens his questioning of God's providence; the wreck seems as arbitrary as the effect of a thunderbolt from Jove.]

97   *dungeon*: the cave in which Jove imprisoned the winds (Virgil, *A*. 1. 52-7).

98   *level*. The word emphasizes the calm. If Verity is right in the added 'impression of the broad expanse of sea,' this is perhaps supported by the name Panope (see 99 n.). [Cf. the literal sense of Lat. *aequor*, 'level surface,' hence 'sea,' e.g. *aequora ponti* (Virgil, *G*. 1. 469).]

99   *Panope*: one of the fifty Nereids or sea nymphs, daughters of Nereus and Doris (Hesiod, *Theog.* 250). They were said to be propitious to sailors, so that there is irony in their presence at the scene of disaster. Jerram notes that the Greek name Panope denotes 'a *wide view* over a calm expanse of water'; he also observes that Panopea is mentioned by Virgil in *G*. 1. 436-7 and *A*. 5. 239-40, 825-6. [Cf. *Panope centumque sorores* (Ovid, *F*. 6. 499).] Panope appears in a context of mourning in Sannazaro, *Pisc. E.* 1. 86-90 (Harrison-Leon, 109). For *Sleek* as applied to smooth water, cf. *Barons Warres* 3. 47 (Drayton, 2, 58): 'And as the soft Winds waft her Sayles along, / Sleeke ev'ry little Dimple of the Lake.' [Sandys (*Ovid*, 1626, 107), translating *M*. 6. 16, adds the epithet to the Latin: 'The sleeke Pactolian Nymphs.']

100-1   See above, 97-102 n. Verity noted the phrase 'The fatall barks dark cabbin' in *Obsequies*, 12; [cf. M. Lloyd, *N&Q* 5, 1958, 432-4]. For idea and phrasing Newton (reported by Warton and Todd) compared, rather remotely, *Ille et nefasto te posuit die* (Horace, *C*. 2. 13. 1) and *Mala soluta navis exit alite* (Horace, *Epod*. 10. 1).

100-1   Eclipses have been widely thought to portend or accompany disaster. Virgil seems to refer obliquely to a solar eclipse at the time of Caesar's assassination (*G*. 1. 464-8: Jerram). Shakespeare supplies several examples, as Rolfe observes: 'These late eclipses in the sun and moon portend no good to us' (*Lear* 1. 2. 112–13); cf. *Ham.* 1. 1. 118–20, *Oth.* 5. 2. 99–101. In *PL* 1. 596–7 Milton uses the idea of an eclipse of the sun as a portent of disaster, and (as Verity adds) speaks of an eclipse as followed by pestilence in *HistBrit* (*Works* 10, 169). From such associations it is an easy inference 'that work done during an eclipse was likely to fail of success; but there seems to be no evidence to show that the ancients actually so regarded it' (Jerram). For a connection of *curses dark* with the moon's *eclipse* Warton cited 'slips of yew / Sliver'd in the moon's eclipse' (Shakespeare, *Macb.* 4. 1. 27–8); also, in listing possible results of the witches' magic, Macbeth says: 'though the yesty waves / Confound and swallow navigation up' (ibid. 53–4). G. G. L. (*N&Q* 179, 1940, 9) suggests that *eclipse* must mean the eight days of the moon's waning or the *interlunium*, the last four of one lunar month and the first four of the next, as no ship could be built in the short time of an eclipse. T. O. Mabbott (ibid. 141–2) replied that the allusion is purely astrological: some part of the work was done in an eclipse and brought ill luck to the vessel. [M. Mack (*Milton*, New York, 1950) says: 'Literally the line suggests that King's ship was foredoomed to sink by malign supernatural influences. Figuratively, there is perhaps an oblique allusion in *bark* to King's natural body, and in *eclipse* and *curses*, to the Fall and its consequences—the chief consequence being the subjection (which King's death illustrates) of the realm of nature to change and death.' M. Lloyd ('The Fatal Bark,' *MLN* 75, 1960, 103–8) takes man as 'the mortal bark' who since Adam's fall has been under the curse of sin and mortality; and he notes this fatal legacy as the opening theme of the *Obsequies*, in Henry King's poem. A similar view is expressed by J. Auffret (III above, under 1969).]

102 *sunk so low that sacred head*. The epithet here means consecrated—not to friendship, and hence inviolable, as Jerram suggests, but in several other senses: (1) to his sacred calling; (2) to death (cf. 'to destruction sacred and devote,' *PL* 3. 208); (3) to ultimate apotheosis, for this line prepares the way for 167–9, 'Sunk...drooping head.' [Godolphin (*MLN* 49, 1934, 165) quoted Propertius 3. 7. 16: *portabat sanctos alveus ille viros*. Cf. Homer, *Od.* 1. 343: 'So dear a head do I ever remember with longing' (L.C.L., translating τοίην κεφαλήν); φίλον κάρα (Aeschylus, *Agam.* 905); *tam cari capitis* (Horace, *C.* 1. 24. 2).]

103 *Camus*: the genius of the river Cam, representing Cambridge University. Jerram notes that the Thames, Humber, and Severn come, with rivers unnamed, to mourn Sidney's death in Bryskett's *Pastorall Aeglogue* 102–10. Verity cites 'Under old Chamus flaggy banks' (G. Fletcher, *C.T.* 2. 50) and references to

Chamus (the spelling of 1638 but not of MS.) [and Chame], as in P. Fletcher's *Piscatory Eclogues*. *Sire*. In this word a number of meanings seem to converge: an aged person of some note (cf. *PL* 11. 719, 'a Reverend Sire,' and *OED*); lord of a particular place (*OED* 4b); male parent (ibid. 6), in 107 the 'father' of members of the University. Jerram notes that some equivalent of *sire* is a 'usual mythological designation of a river,' e.g. *Tiberine pater* (Livy 2. 10. 11).

went footing slow. Todd cited 'slow footing' (Spenser, *F.Q.* 1. 3. 10) and 'an aged Syre farre off he sawe / Come slowely footing' (G. Fletcher, *C.V.* 2. 15). Dunster (reported by Todd) compared Claudian's description of the Mincius, *tardusque meatu / Mincius* (28. 196–7: 2, 88). Whatever the echoes involved, the reference is obviously to the Cam's slow movement through the flats of Cambridgeshire. [J. M. Morse (*N&Q* 5, 1958, 211) suggests a pun in *footing* as 'pedant'; while Milton, especially in prose, could make Joycean puns, this one would seem to be quite out of key.]

104–6 Cf. Virgil's description of Tiber clad in a mantle and crowned with reeds: *huic deus ipse loci fluvio Tiberinus amoeno / populeas inter senior se attollere frondes / visus (eum tenuis glauco velabat amictu / carbasus et crinis umbrosa tegebat harundo)* (*A.* 8. 31–4), and *velatus harundine glauca / Mincius* (ibid. 10. 205–6). These phrases are closer to Milton's picture of Camus than is Sylvester's personification of Jordan cited by Dunster and Verity (*D.W.W.* 2. 3. 4. 112–33; Grosart, 1, 199), in which several remote parallels are lost in a welter of irrelevances. [J. H. Mozley (*Ovid: The Art of Love*, L.C.L. 339) suggested an imitation of Ovid's *Consol.* 221 f.: *Ipse pater flavis Tiberinus adhorruit undis, / ...Tum salice implexum muscoque et arundine crinem*, etc. He also cited Statius, *Theb.* 9. 404 f. One might quote Milton's own early phrases, *arundiferum... Camum* (*El* 1. 11) and *juncosas Cami...paludes* (ibid. 89).] Warburton (reported by Warton and Todd) thought that *figures dim* referred to the fabulous traditions of the high antiquity of Cambridge; Warton, at a loss about the exact meaning, fancied that Milton, in the same state, left it to the reader's imagination. Warburton took *His Mantle hairy* to allude obliquely to the flocks and herds on the river's banks, though these were not peculiar to the Cam. Todd quoted Plumptre's explanation (in the Latin notes to his Greek version of *Lycidas*), which Masson translated: 'The mantle is as if made of the plant "river-sponge" which floats copiously in the Cam; the *bonnet* of the river-sedge, distinguished by vague marks traced somehow over the middle of the leaves, and serrated at the edge of the leaves, after the fashion of the αἲ αἲ of the hyacinth.' The explanation of *sedge* seems to be confirmed by Milton's first writing *scraul'd ore* in MS.

before substituting *inwraught* (*Facs.* 438). [Hunter ('New Words') and Carey note *Inwrought* as the first example of the word in *OED*; the next is in Pope's *Odyssey* 1. 212.]

Milton takes, or rather makes, this opportunity to introduce obliquely a traditional allusion to the death of Hyacinthus, referred to in the *Lament for Bion* 6, Sannazaro's *E.* 11. 31–3, Alamanni's *E.* 2. 11, and Drummond's *Teares* 127 [all these in Harrison–Leon, 37, 100, 127, 196], and doubly significant here since Hyacinthus was struck down accidentally by Apollo. Ovid (*M.* 10. 174–219) tells how Apollo was hurling the discus and Hyacinthus, running eagerly forward, was hit and killed; the god in his grief caused a white flower to spring up and on it, purpled with the youth's blood, he inscribed *AI, AI* (alas, alas). To the references above might be added 'the lettered hyacinth' (Theocritus 10. 28: Sandys, 'Sources,' 237) [and 'O Hiacinthe let Ai be on thee still' (Sidney, *Arcadia, Works* 1, 499; Ringler, 125, line 29); 'Th' immortall Amaranthus, princely Rose, / Sad Violet, and that sweet Flowre that beares, / In Sanguine Spots the Tenor of our Woes' (Drummond, *Epitaph*, Kastner, 1, 83: cited by Leishman, *Minor Poems*, 304). G. Williamson (*S.C.C.* 142) remarks that Milton's allusion 'reminds us of one both favoured and slain by Apollo, and prepares us for the later development by "every flower that sad embroidery wears."'] Tuckwell (44) takes *on the edge* to refer to the bank of the river, with wild hyacinths growing there.

107 *Ah; Who hath reft...my dearest pledge? reft*: perfect participle of *reave*, which usually connotes violent deprivation. Bowle (reported by Warton and Todd) cited 'And reft fro me my sweete companion' (Spenser, *Daphnaïda* 159).

pledge: child, originally as a pledge or token of the mutual love of parents (*OED* 2d). Cf. 'by him had many pledges dere' (Spenser, *F.Q.* 1. 10. 4); Milton, *El* 4. 42, *SolMus* 1, *PL* 2. 818–19; Lat. *pignus* and Ital. *pegno*. King is described as the dearest alumnus of his *alma mater*. ['Camus, though he is a river god like the rest, wears the clothing of grief and stands like the song itself among the mourners who question rather than among the accused who state their innocence, and it is he that asks the forthright "*Who* hath reft him?" which closes the inquiry; we hear no more of second causes, and nature is acquitted' (R. Tuve, *Images*, 76).]

108–31 In Milton's adaptation of the elegiac convention of the procession of mourners, St Peter, the last, is utilized to inject into the poem an element essential to its effect but one that belongs to the non-elegiac strand in the pastoral tradition: namely, allegorical comment on the contemporary scene and especially on the state of the church (see above, II: Pastoral Elegy). The evils St Peter denounces are those of which the Puritans especially complained in the days of Archbishop Laud, but protests against such evils go back well beyond the Reformation, as the eclogues of Petrarch, Boccaccio, and Mantuan attest. Protestantism, and most signally in its Puritan form, intensified the protest. Spenser's ecclesiastical eclogues are a link between pre-Reformation examples and Milton's diatribe. Into the justice of Milton's attack it is needless to go at any length. With the accession of Charles I, Laud exercised a strong influence in ecclesiastical policy and became Strafford's trusted partner in the notorious practice of 'Thorough.' Translated to the see of London in 1628, and in 1633 to the primacy, Laud used every effort to advance Arminian and Catholic (as distinct from Roman) doctrine, to suppress controversy, to enforce uniformity of observance (though he knew that uniformity of belief could not be enforced), and to ensure decorum and beauty in the services of the church. All these efforts were bitterly resented by the Puritans, with whom Laud dealt severely in the ecclesiastical Court of High Commission and in the yet more dreaded Star Chamber, and they loudly accused him of a desire to reinstate Roman Catholicism. That accusation was groundless; Laud did his best to counteract, and was bold enough to protest openly against, the dangerous influence of the queen and the unofficial papal envoy, Conn. Milton, apparently, felt compelled to make a small concession to this fact (see 128–9 n.). The church's difficulties, including the lack of a vigorous and properly educated ministry in many parishes, were due in part to spoliations dating back to the period of the Reformation, which Laud recognized and tried to curb. Nor was he indifferent to questions of morality; he won perhaps as many enemies by his efforts to suppress vice as by his efforts to suppress Puritanism. For the most part Milton presents, no doubt with entire sincerity, the Puritan version of the situation: benefices are filled with the worldly and self-seeking (later he was to inveigh against Presbyterian and Independent ministers for similar faults—witness *On the new forcers of Conscience* and *Sonn* 16); men with a vocation (but not conformable to Anglican orders and practices) are excluded; preaching (the great duty of the ministry) is often omitted or, if performed, perfunctory; the flock is either neglected or fed with false doctrine (Arminianism, for example, which the Puritans especially hated and Milton was later to embrace); and there are ominous conversions to Rome, with no or little protest. It is sometimes forgotten that there is in *Lycidas* no reference to active persecution of the Puritans (other than their exclusion from 'the shearers feast') [—although, we might remember, the notorious punishment of Prynne, Burton, and Bastwick had occurred some months before the writing of the poem; S. Elledge prints a contemporary account (*Milton's 'Lycidas,'* 207–19]. This, then, is the background of St Peter's harsh and eloquent invective. Verity recognizes that it is not aimed at all the clergy, but only against *such* (114) as are guilty. Moreover, we do not find here the wholesale condemnation of the episcopal system that we meet in Milton's tracts of 1641–2 (at which time, or later, the epigraph to *Lycidas* was no doubt written), and we need not be surprised that St Peter is presented as an ideal bishop rebuking all who are at fault. Nor is there any hint of the still more drastic reforms, even the utter dismantling of a national church, to be demanded in Milton's later writings; only those who imagine that the *two-handed engine* is to be used not against *the grim Woolf* or even the unfaithful shepherds, but only against the fold itself, could read any such hint in the passage.

The most famous commentary on these lines is Ruskin's (*Sesame and Lilies, Works,* ed. E. T. Cook and A. Wedderburn, 18, 1905, 69–75). Whatever the reader's verdict, the effect is cumulative and forbids quotation under separate items. Ruskin defends the choice of St Peter and the recognition of his episcopal mitre and office and keys (he avoids direct reference to papal claims): these are no mere poetic devices, but the vehicles of Milton's meaning. He was no lover of false bishops but was of true ones, and of these St Peter is the type. For the 'power of the keys,' Milton could not (simply because it had become 'a weapon of an adverse sect') blot out Matt. 16. 19 ('I will give unto thee the keys of the kingdom of heaven'), which is indeed 'a solemn, universal assertion, deeply to be kept in mind by all sects.' And this insistence on 'the power of the true episcopate is to make us feel more weightily what is to be charged against the false claimants of episcopate,' against the claims of all those in the clergy who 'for their bellies sake, / Creep and intrude, and climb into the fold.' Those who *creep* 'do not care for office, nor name, but for secret influence,...consenting to any servility...so only that they may intimately discern, and unawares direct, the minds of men.' Those who *intrude* '(thrust, that is) themselves into the fold' are they who 'by natural insolence of heart, and stout eloquence of tongue,... obtain hearing and authority with the common crowd.' And those who *climb* are they who 'by labour and learning, both stout and sound, but selfishly exerted in the cause of their own ambition, gain high dignities and authorities, and become "lords over the heritage," though not "ensamples to the flock."' All those negligent of their duty and caring only for their place 'at the shearers feast' are *Blind mouthes*. Ruskin pauses on this 'strange expression,' 'a broken metaphor, one might think'; 'its very audacity and pithiness are intended to make us look close at the phrase and remember it. Those two monosyllables express the precisely accurate contraries of right character, in the two great offices of the Church—those of bishop and pastor. A "Bishop" means "a person who sees." A "Pastor" means one who feeds. The most unbishoply character... is therefore to be Blind. The most unpastoral is, instead of feeding, to want to be fed,—to be a Mouth.' (We may omit the very Ruskinian effort to bring the true bishop into 'that back street' where 'Bill and Nancy' are 'knocking each other's teeth out,' and the more carefully veiled insinuation that pastors should concern themselves with the physical feeding of the flock, than which nothing could be farther from Milton's meaning.) On *swoln with wind*, Ruskin proceeds (after an etymological excursion on *spirit*, *wind*, and *breath*): 'Now, there are two kinds of breath with which the flock may be filled,—God's breath, and man's. The breath of God is health, and life, and peace to them, as the air of heaven is to the flocks on the hills; but man's breath—the word which *he* calls spiritual—is disease and contagion to them, as the fog of the fen. They rot inwardly with it; they are puffed up by it, as a dead body by the vapours of its own decomposition. This is literally true of all false religious teaching; the first and last, and fatalest sign of it, is that "puffing up,"' which he explains as alluding to those of any sect, great or small, who assume that they are right and all others wrong, 'and pre-eminently' to 'those who hold that men can be saved by thinking rightly instead of doing rightly, by word instead of act, and wish instead of work;—these are the true fog children... corrupt, and corrupting....' Returning then to 'the power of the keys,' Ruskin contrasts the treatment of the motif by Milton and by Dante (*Purg.* 9. 115 f.: already briefly noted by Keightley; see below, 110–11 n.), conceding that 'for once the latter is weaker in thought.' Dante 'supposes *both* the keys to be of the gate of heaven; one is of gold, the other of silver...and it is not easy to determine the meaning...of the two keys. But Milton makes one, of gold, the key of heaven; the other, of iron, the key of the prison in which the wicked teachers are to be bound who "have taken away the key of knowledge, yet entered not in themselves"' (Luke 11. 52). Ruskin attempts no interpretation of the 'two-handed engine,' finding, or rather supplying, the idea of retribution in the image of the keys. Of those who fulfil the duties of bishop and pastor, who see and feed, 'it is said, "He that watereth, shall be watered also himself" (Prov. 11. 25). But the reverse is truth also. He that watereth not, shall be *withered* himself; and he that seeth not, shall himself be shut out of sight—shut into the perpetual prison-house. And that prison opens here, as well as hereafter: he who is to be bound in heaven must first be bound on earth. That command to the strong angels, of which the rock-apostle ⟨Peter⟩ is the image, "Take him, and bind him...and cast him out"

(Matt. 22. 13, 13. 49–50; Rev. 5. 2) issues, in its measure, against the teacher, for every help withheld, and for every truth refused, and for every falsehood enforced; so that he is more strictly fettered the more he fetters, and farther outcast as he more and more misleads, till at last..."the golden opes, the iron shuts amain."' Ruskin concludes with some complacency this 'example of the kind of word-by-word examination of your author which is rightly called "reading,"' and with a warning, not altogether superfluous, against mistaking your own thoughts for the author's.

Modern scholars have of course concerned themselves with scriptural and literary influences on the passage. [C. R. Baskervill (see 89–131 n. above) cited lines 75–81 and 125–31 of Skelton's *Colin Clout*: he thought Spenser (in the *S.C.*) was influenced by Skelton and Milton by both, but more clearly by Skelton in this passage—which seems very doubtful.] E. C. Baldwin ('Milton and *Ezekiel*,' *MLN* 33, 1918, 211–15) and E. L. Brooks (*N&Q* 3, 1956, 67–8) have cited Ezek. 34. 2–5, 10, etc.:

Thus saith the Lord God unto the shepherds; Woe be to the shepherds of Israel that do feed themselves! should not the shepherds feed the flocks? Ye eat the fat, and ye clothe you with the wool,...but ye feed not the flock. The diseased have ye not strengthened, neither have ye healed that which was sick...; but with force and with cruelty have ye ruled them. And they were scattered, because there is no shepherd: and they became meat to all the beasts of the field...Thus saith the Lord God; Behold, I am against the shepherds; and I will require my flock at their hand, and cause them to cease from feeding the flock; neither shall the shepherds feed themselves any more....

[Parallels with Dante were noted by P. Toynbee, *Dante in English Literature* (2 v., London and New York, 1909), 1, 123–4. C. H. Herford declared that 'Milton certainly remembered the terrific passage in which St. Peter... denounces Boniface' (*Parad.* 27. 22 f.), and also 'the poet's own stern rebuke of the futile preachers whose ignorant flocks "turn from the pastures full of wind"' (ibid. 29. 103 f.: 'Dante and Milton,' *The Post-War Mind of Germany*, Oxford, 1927, 83 (with Herford's references corrected): see *Comus* IV, under 1924).] K. McKenzie ('Echoes of Dante in Milton's *Lycidas*,' *Italica* 20, 1943, 121–6) would trace the idea of a digression on the corrupt clergy to Dante's similar digressions. Dante puts in the mouth of St Peter the denunciation of his successors (*Parad.* 27. 19–66; cf. ibid. 9. 130–2), who are called rapacious wolves in the garb of shepherds. And Dante condemns the preaching of idle fables from the pulpits of Florence, whereby the flocks return from the pasture 'fed with wind' (*pasciute di vento*: *Parad.* 29. 103–8), a passage commented on in John Foxe's *Actes and Monumentes* (ed. London, 1570, cited by Toynbee, 1,

57–9): 'Dantes an Italian writer...complayneth...verye muche, the preaching of Gods word to be omitted: and in stede ther of, the vayne fables of Monkes and Friers to bee preached and beloved of the people: and so the flock of Christ to be fed not with the foode of the Gospel, but with winde. The Pope saith he, of a pastor is made a woolfe....' Also, in a number of passages Dante predicts retribution, though none suggests Milton's idea or phrasing. [J. M. Steadman (*N&Q* 5, 1958, 141–2) cites Dante and notes that St Peter was established in Italian poetry as a vehicle for ecclesiastical satire. Milton's Commonplace Book includes the note, probably of 1635–8, that Dante openly censures the avarice of the clergy in *Inf.* 7 (*C.P.W.* 1, 366 and n.; *Works* 18, 131; Parker, 813, n. 82).]

Scholars have naturally quoted John 10. 1–2, 7, 11–12:

He that entereth not by the door into the sheepfold, but climbeth up some other way, the same is a thief and a robber. But he that entereth in by the door is the shepherd of the sheep. ...Verily,...I say unto you, I am the door of the sheep....I am the good shepherd: the good shepherd giveth his life for the sheep. But he that is an hireling, and not the shepherd, whose own the sheep are not, seeth the wolf coming, and leaveth the sheep, and fleeth: and the wolf catcheth them, and scattereth the sheep.

E. Le Comte (*SP* 47, 1950, 589–606: below, 130–1 n., I. b. 6), while admitting that this parable of the good shepherd turns rather on the saving work of the shepherd Christ than on the condemnation of false shepherds, still regards the parable as an important influence. So too does G. R. Coffman ('The Parable of the Good Shepherd, *De Contemptu Mundi*, and *Lycidas*,' *ELH* 3, 1936, 101–13), who is concerned mainly to trace the development of the theme; he suggests Bernard of Morlais' poem, *De Contemptu Mundi* (lib. 3), as a possible immediate source, since it is directed against corrupt clergy, the base means they use to obtain benefices, their gluttony, their indifference as pastors, and since the book had no less than four editions by 1626.

H. F. Robins (*RES* 5, 1954, 25–36: below, 130–1 n., I. e. 6), who takes Matt. 24. 31–4, 41–6, as needed to explain the two-handed engine, collects other data in Matthew: Peter as a fisher of men (4. 19), which Robins links with the title *Pilot* (but see 109 n.); the bestowal on him of the keys (16. 19); a parallel to the corrupt clergy in the scribes and Pharisees who 'say, and do not' (23. 3) and love the place of honour 'at feasts' (23. 6); a source for the phrase *worthy bidden guest* in 'but they which were bidden were not worthy' (22. 8); a juxtaposing of blindness and greed (as in *Blind mouthes*) in 'Ye fools and blind: for whether is greater, the gift, or the altar that sanctifieth the gift?' (23. 19); and an intensifying of the accusation *The hungry Sheep look up, and are not fed* in 'For I was an hungred, and ye gave me no meat...Inasmuch as ye did it not to one of the least of these, ye did it not to me' (25. 42, 45).

[E. Tuveson ('"The Pilot of the Galilean Lake,"' *JHI* 27, 1966, 447–58) seeks 'to find the unity and the historical meaning' of St Peter's speech, which he considers 'the central mystery' of *Lycidas*, by examining 'in depth the allusions and images which...are still imperfectly and haphazardly glossed.' In view of the earlier comments and glosses assembled above and below, Tuveson's complaint and implied claim may be thought somewhat exaggerated. 'The central fact about the passage,' he suggests, 'is that Peter is introduced in his office as the great Pastor, and only in this character.' As the nucleus of the whole passage he cites John 21. 15–17, where, as Protestants understood, Christ the Good Shepherd established the church by transferring his own office to the chosen preachers. 'In this sense alone, the reformers maintained, the minister can be described as coming in an apostolic succession to the Founder' (448). In 'the poem of an alumnus, primarily for alumni,' Peter's coming in just after Camus 'would suggest that preparation for the work of a "herdman" is the supreme function of the university.' 'The keys,...the reformers explained, do not refer to any magical power of absolution and cursing, but "to the worde of God, which is the right key; so that where this worde is not purely taught, there is neither key nor authoritie."...So understood, the "massy Keyes" are...the epitome of Peter's message.'

'The language attributed to Peter is in keeping with the decorum associated with his history and office...but, even so, he is a countryman' (Acts 4. 13), and his language is appropriately 'colloquial, direct, "uncouth"' (448).

Tuveson's comments on particulars are cited below in the notes on 118, 119–21, 126, 128–9, 130–1 (I. b. 16). He concludes (457–8) with remarks on Milton's exalted view of true poets, whose function is similar to that of ministers. 'Thus Phoebus and Peter perform analogous functions in the poem: both reassure the doubting young poet that the higher order of values, in literature or in religion, is real and immutable, since it emanates from a divine Mind.' 'Consequently, Phoebus, Jove, and the other gods symbolize man's intuitive confidence that the values which his reason finds in this world are no mere subjective creations—that they are immutable because divine.' But the only guarantee of that is revelation.

Frank L. Huntley (*MiltonN* 1, 1967, 53–5) sees St Peter as 'not concerned with Roman Catholics. The entire stricture against the ignorant and greedy priests is cast in the wolf metaphor: there is only one set of "wolves." The "besides" of line 128 indicates not external as opposed to internal but three more matters: first, the "daily" as opposed to the occasional and liturgical ("When they list", "the shearers' feast"); second, a sin more heinous than *allowing* the sheep to die, i.e. to *kill* them for food; finally and most shocking, the fact of impunity.' He suggests a background for the wolf image in the fable and proverbs about the wolf that wanted to become a monk but could think and speak only of sheep. He cites Acts 20. 29, Matt. 7. 15, and Milton's other uses of 'wolves' for corrupt priests (*TKM, Works* 5, 58–9; *HistBr*, ibid. 10, 134; *PL* 12. 508).]

109 *The Pilot of the Galilean Lake.* This designation of St Peter is based on his sailing on the Sea of Galilee as fisherman when Christ called him (Luke 5. 3–11). Taken literally, *Pilot* would imply that Peter was the steersman (cf. *PL* 1. 204, *SA* 198), but there is enough warrant for the term in Christ's telling Peter to 'Launch out into the deep' (Luke 5. 4) and Peter's answering from the boat (Matt. 14. 28), along with his general leadership among the disciples. No doubt Milton expected readers to recall that other incident on Galilee when Christ walked on the water and Peter, seeking to go to him, failed, and was rebuked for his little faith (Matt. 14. 25–31); they would then be prepared for the full significance of 172–3 (see n.). Otherwise, in the light of what immediately follows, it might have seemed more natural to describe Peter as the shepherd of Christ's flock, specially commanded to feed them (John 21. 15–17). The phrase used also supplies another link between *Lycidas* and the piscatory eclogue (see 99 n., 132–3 n.). [R. E. Hone (*SP* 56, 1959, 55–61) argues that the *Pilot* is Christ himself. His reasons are: the development of Milton's anti-prelatical thought; his specific utterances on the relative positions of Christ and St Peter in the church; the marked pertinence of Rev. 1 to *Lycidas*; the unified coherence of the poem as a poem of immortality, with Christ as its climactic figure. These may not seem persuasive.]

110–31 [F. Berry (*Poetry and the Physical Voice*, 98–100: see '*L'Allegro* and *Il Penseroso*' III, under 1962) remarks that no other poet in English uses the alveolar nasal *n* and the velar nasal *ng* 'so habitually, so pervasively as Milton,' especially when he is angry, as in this passage, but often when he is not. Berry prints 110–31 with *n* and *ng* italicized.]

110–11 The lines start from Christ's commission to Peter: 'And I will give unto thee the keys of the kingdom of heaven: and whatsoever thou shalt bind on earth shall be bound in heaven: and whatsoever thou shalt loose on earth shall be loosed in heaven' (Matt. 16. 19), read perhaps in the light of Isa. 22. 22: 'he shall open, and none shall shut; and he shall shut, and none shall open.'

The power of the keys was a vital issue in Roman Catholic and Protestant exegesis and controversy. The Protestant position was that the power was given generally to the church, though on the mode of its administration there were differing views, whether the power was entrusted to a duly ordained priesthood (as in the Anglican system), or to a ministry with lay elders (as in the Presbyterian), or to the congregation of believers (as in the Independent); but this is a question into which Milton does not and could not go, and on which he may at this time have had no firm opinion. G. W. Whiting (*Milton and This Pendant World*, Austin, 1958, 35–40) assembles examples to show that many Protestant divines from Tyndale to Perkins interpreted the keys as the Word of God and preaching as the mode of its operation (the position necessarily assumed by any who identify the *two-handed engine* with the *Keyes*: see below, 130–1 n., I. e. 1–3). Editors have cited various passages dealing with symbolic keys. Keightley noted that in Matthew Peter is given keys, with no number specified, but that Dante has the Pope claim two, to lock and unlock heaven (*Inf.* 27. 103–4); he also cited Dante, *Purg.* 9. 115–29 (followed by Ruskin, above, 108–31 n.), on the two keys to the gate of Purgatory bestowed on their guardian by St Peter, the golden one more powerful than the silver. Warton cited 'that Golden Key / That ope's the Palace of Eternity' (*Comus* 13–14). Todd reported Warton's comparing, from Jonson, the Angel's description of Truth holding in her hand 'a curious bunch of golden kayes, / With which heaven gates she locketh, and displayes' (*Hymenaei* 897–8, *Ben Jonson* 7, 239). Todd also quoted P. Fletcher, *Apoll.* 3. 16: 'Three mitred crownes the proud Impostor weares, / For he in earth, in hell, in heav'n will raigne: / And in his hand two golden keyes he beares, / To open heav'n and hell, and shut againe.' But here the intent is satirical (as it is not in Milton's depiction of Peter as ideal bishop), and 'golden' is ambivalent, since the pope 'nor heav'n will buy, but sell.' In *P.I.* 7. 62 Fletcher repeats the description, omitting 'golden' but adding an equation of the true keys with the preaching of the Word: 'Not in his lips, but hands, two keyes he bore, / Heav'ns doores and hells to shut, and open wide' (see below, 130–1 n., I. e. 3). Milton's *amain* ('with full force': *OED* 1) suggests finality. [Cf. *Sonn* 18. 10–14 n. and *QNov* 55 n.]

112 *Miter'd*: wearing, adorned with, a mitre, the head-dress that is part of a bishop's insignia in the western church (*OED*: mitre *sb.*[1] 2b). St Peter is presented as the ideal bishop. Apparently Milton had not yet developed his antipathy to episcopacy as such, or conceived of proving that in the apostolic church bishops and presbyters were one and the same—the burden of his anti-episcopal writings of 1641–2. Warburton (reported by Todd) supposed that Milton 'thought it sharpened his satire to have the prelacy condemned by one of their own order.' *bespake*: spoke out 'with some notion of...remonstrance' (*OED* 2), intensified by *stern*.

113 *spar'd for thee*: dispensed with, parted with (*OED*: *v.*¹ 8a); *for*: instead of (*OED*: for A 5). *swain*: pastoral term for young man (cf. *Arc* 26 n.).

114 *Anow*: 'plural of *enough*' and not merely archaic in Milton's day (*OED* 1); persons enough (ibid. 1c). [MS. had *anough*; 1638, *Enough* (*Facs.* 438, 350).] *of such as*: of such a kind as.

114–15 *for their bellies sake...into the fold*. Ruskin's explanation of *Creep and intrude, and climb* is given above, 108–31 n. [where Ezek. 34 and John 10 are quoted]. Verity explains as a reference to 'those who enter the Church in a stealthy, underhand way ("creep"), those who thrust themselves in with self-assertion ("intrude"), and those who are full of ambition to climb into high places.' Verity notes that Milton used all three verbs in his later ecclesiastical writings: 'they [the prelates] use to clime into their Livings and Bishopricks' (*Animad*, *Works* 3, 150); 'they [the clergy] for lucre use to creepe into the Church undiscernably' (*Apol*, ibid. 3, 360); 'intrude into the ministerie' (*Hirelings*, ibid. 6, 77). Warton cited 'into his Church lewd Hirelings climbe' (*PL* 4. 193). Patterson (*Student's Milton*) quoted Richard Baxter for examples of forged credentials.

116–17 *Of other care...shearers feast*. Verity's paraphrase, 'make little account of any other duty,' seems inexact; *care* means rather 'object of attention' (*OED* 3). Jerram quoted Thomas Becon's *Jewel of Joy* (1553: *Catechism*, etc., ed. J. Ayre, Parker Society, 1844, 431): '...our spiritual men...are...led with no care of feeding Christ's flock...: Christ's threefold *Pasce* is turned into the Jews' double *Tolle*. They feed nothing, except themselves; they toll and catch whatsoever catch they may.' The *shearers feast* was the festive supper given to the workers after sheep shearing, the pastoral counterpart of harvest home; here it means the temporal emoluments of the ministerial office.

118 *And shove...guest*. [Verity quotes Matt. 22. 1–9; cf. Robins at the end of 108–31 n. Tuveson (*JHI* 27, 449–50) cites 1 Sam. 25. 11: 'Shall I then take my bread, and my water, and my flesh that I have killed for my shearers, and give it unto men, whom I know not whence they be?' The image, he thinks, gives some indication of Milton's attitude, in 1638, toward the church. He also cites the illustrious Joseph Mede on the maintenance of the clergy as not necessarily supplied from free-will offerings only; and Giovanni Diodati (Charles's uncle), who said that Ezekiel's condemnation of bad shepherds (34. 10) implied 'no "abolishment of either Ecclesiasticall or Politicall government in the Christian Church,..." but a "more effectuall, and renewed presence of God"'—which was probably Milton's own feeling at this time.] The young Milton gave an example of the common Puritan complaint in the early *El* 4, the epistle to his former tutor, Thomas Young, who had received Presbyterian but not Episcopal ordination and was compelled to seek a post abroad; Milton reproaches his country for forcing such a man into exile. [Later Milton may have numbered Young among the Puritan pluralists (A. Barker, *Milton and the Puritan Dilemma*, 1942, 346–7).]

119 *Blind mouthes.* To heighten the contempt, ambition and greed of gain are reduced to an image of gluttony, as if the hireling shepherds were all mouth; their gluttony is a little later contrasted with the hunger of the sheep. See Ruskin under 108–31 above. Jerram took *mouthes* to refer not only to gluttony but to preaching; in the latter capacity they are spiritually blind and ignorant of pastoral duty. Verity cited 'to our Soules a sad and dolefull succession of illiterate and blind guides' (*Ref, Works* 3, 67). J. H. Himes (*MLN* 35, 1920, 441–2; cf. R. J. Kane, ibid. 68, 1953, 239–40) traced Milton's phrase to τυφλό-στομον, 'blind-mouthed,' applied by Strabo (4. 1. 8: L.C.L. 2, 188) to a river mouth choked with silt; thus Milton's idea would be not of greed but of shallowness of thought and utterance—which, so explained, seems forced. Jerram remarked on 'the classical usage of transferring to one bodily sense the functions of another,' citing Sophocles, *O.T.* 371 ('In ear, wit, eye, in every-thing...blind'), Val. Flacc. 2. 461 (*caecus clamor*), Pliny, *N.H.* 37. 18. 67 (*surdus colos*) and 9. 30. 66 (*proceres gulae*). Tuckwell (46) found precedents in 'the classical use of the word "blind" to express ineffective, useless,' citing Sophocles, *O.C.* 183, 1639. [Jerram and Sandys ('Sources,' 234) cited 'Shepherds of the wilderness, wretched things of shame, mere bellies' (Hesiod, *Theog.* 26); cf. N. Frye (*Milton's Lycidas*, ed. Patrides, 205). W. Elton (*N&Q* 192, 1947, 429) quoted *cieca cupidigia* in Dante, *Inf.* 12. 49, *Parad.* 30. 139. D. R. Fabian (*AN&Q* 6, 1967–8, 136–7) makes the rather remote suggestion that Milton recalled the 'explicit correlation between the eyes and mouth of Jonathan' in 1 Sam. 14. 27–30, a chapter he cited in his list of subjects for tragedies (*Works* 18, 236, no. 24).]

119–21 The *Sheep-hook* is perhaps intended to suggest the symbolic crosier or pastoral staff, part of the insignia of a bishop (although, unlike the mitre, not mentioned in the description of Peter). See below, 130–1 n., under I. d. 2–3.

Herdmans art. MS. has *heardsmans*. *Herdman*, the earlier form of herdsman, seems to have been used for the keeper of any domestic animals that went in herds or flocks, and sometimes specifically for a shepherd (as in Coverdale's rendering of Isa. 40. 11: 'He shall fede his flock like an herdman': *OED*), and even figuratively for a spiritual pastor, as in the *Primer* of Edward VI: 'Shepherd, and Herdman of our souls' (*OED*). [Tuveson (*JHI* 27, 450–1) queries Ruskin's distinction between bishop and pastor (see above, 108–31 n.), and insists that Peter's words must embody scriptural authority. He cites the usual Ezek. 34 and John 10, and also Milton, *Apol* (*Works* 3, 345): 'No marvell if the people turne beasts, when their Teachers themselves as *Isaiah* calls them, *Are dumbe and greedy dogs that can never have anough, ignorant, blind, and cannot understand, who while they all look their own way every one for his gaine from his quarter*, how many parts of the land are fed with windy ceremonies instead of sincere milke; and while one Prelat enjoyes the nourishment and light of twenty Ministers, how many waste places are left as darke as *Galile of the Gentiles, sitting in the region and shadow of death*; without preaching Minister, without light.']

122 *What recks...are sped.* What do they care (*OED*: reck *v.* 8: [with a punning jingle on 'reck'ning' (116)?]) What are they in need of? They have got what they wanted (literally, are brought to the condition desired: *OED*: speed *v.* 7).

123–4 Only Jerram seems to be conscious of any problem in these lines; other editors assume without question that they refer to the quality of the preaching. At this conclusion Jerram also arrives, but he sees a difficulty:

That the 'lean and flashy songs' represent unsound oral instruction is plain from the context; but in the pastoral prototype singing and piping are the *recreation*, not the business of shepherds, and the meaning ought simply to be that the spiritual pastors amuse themselves instead of tending their flocks. In that case however there would be no point in the allusion to the wretched quality of the music, which could in no way affect the welfare of the sheep. The confusion of metaphor thus involved needs simply stating to be apparent; the true analogy lies in the unhealthiness of pasture, to which a sudden transition is made in *l.* 126.

This is an admirable statement of the problem, but the conclusion is far from certain. So careful a poet should not hastily be convicted of a blundering mixture of metaphors (as distinct from such a conscious combination of them as in 119–20). It is clear that Milton at least begins by maintaining the distinction 'in the pastoral prototype' between the shepherd's 'trade' (the tending

of the flock) and his recreation (song): it is indeed essential to his dual consideration of Lycidas as poet and priest under the uniting image of shepherd (see
above, 65 n. [and appended query]). Why should it be assumed that he has
abandoned the distinction here? Editors in general take *when they list* to mean
when they choose (*OED v.*[1] 1)—no doubt seldom—to preach; but *list* can just
as well carry a stronger notion of desire and be rendered 'when they wish'
(ibid. 2), which would be much better completed by 'to sing' than 'to preach.'
Nor is it true, in the light of the poem's dual concern with the priestly and the
poetic office, that reference to the quality of the song is irrelevant: Lycidas,
St Peter's choice, is a poet, but would not neglect his flock. But the unfaithful
shepherds sing when they ought to tend their flocks. If we will allow Milton to
maintain the distinction 'in the pastoral prototype,' and perhaps remember his
implied condemnation of songs about Amaryllis and Neaera (68–9), the only
kind the unfaithful shepherds ('Blind mouthes!') would be likely to sing, and if
we take singing here as there to symbolize idle pleasure and general neglect of
duty, there is no need to infer any mixture of metaphors: the shepherds neglect
their duty and the sheep suffer, which is the burden of the whole diatribe. [This
interpretation may seem somewhat strained: one may not see more force in
'wish' than in 'choose'; and the whole context surely implies preaching, not
merely idle pleasure, since otherwise there would appear to be no point in harsh
censure of the quality of the *songs*, which leave the sheep unfed. In 50 f. King is
seen as a poet, here as a priest.] Another possibility (though less consonant with
the trend of the passage and the structure of the poem) is that Milton is contrasting with preaching those liturgical and musical services—to which he had
warmly responded in *IlPen* (161–6 and n.)—which Laud fostered at the expense
of the sermon, to the increasing indignation of Puritans. Milton was later to
refer to the liturgy as 'in conception leane and dry, of affections empty and un-
moving' (*Apol, Works* 3, 352). See also, however, 126 n.

123 *flashy*: destitute of meaning, trifling, trashy (*OED* 2c).

124-31 [G. W. Nitchie (*N&Q* 13, 1966, 377–8) notes that the last 8 lines of
St Peter's speech anticipate the rhyme pattern, *ottava rima*, of the final paragraph, and sees a conscious stratagem of Milton's.]

124 *Grate...straw*. Warton explained *scrannel Pipes of wretched straw* as a
contemptuous replacement of Virgil's *tenui avena* (*E.* 1. 2). Peck (170), and
Newton (reported by Todd) cited *non tu in triviis, indocte, solebas | stridenti
miserum stipula disperdere carmen* (ibid. 3. 26–7). The word *scrannel* has not been
found in English before Milton and later examples—the earliest from Henry

More's *Divine Dialogues* (1667), with the literal sense of 'thin,' 'weakly'—seem for the most part to depend on Milton (*OED*). If he invented the word, he had some support in the Norwegian *skran* (thin, lean, dry); but he may have picked it up from some dialectal use. Skeat (*Concise Etymol. Dict.*) records *scranny* (thin, lean) as provincial English, and *scrannel* (a lean person) as of Lincolnshire. No doubt Milton was attracted by the harsh sound exactly suited to his verb *Grate*. [H. Darbishire (*Essays and Studies 1957*, 37) remarks that 'in fact it is a dialect word, and you can still hear talk in Lancashire of an "owd 'ooman wi' a *scrannel voice*."']

125 See above, notes on 108–31, 123–4.

126 *swoln with wind.* Peck (reported by Todd) noted the parallel with Dante: *sì che le pecorelle, che non sanno, | tornan del pasco pasciute di vento* (*Parad.* 29. 106–7); cf. above, 108–31 n. Dante is describing preaching in Florence; if Milton had these lines (94–108) in mind, it would support the idea that his *flashy songs* are sermons (see 123–4 n.). *rank*: corrupt, foul (*OED* 14b); cf. 'rank vapours' (*Comus* 17). *draw*: breathe, inhale (*OED* 23). The *wind* betokens empty, frivolous words; the *rank mist*, false doctrine. Jerram cites lines spoken by the Priest of Pan in Fletcher's *F. Shep.* 2. 1. 12–18:

> At whose rising mists unsound,
> Damps and vapours fly apace,
> Hovering o'er the wanton face
> Of these pastures, where they come,
> Striking dead both bud and bloom:
> Therefore, from such danger lock
> Every one his lovèd flock.

[Tuveson (*JHI* 27, 450–2) quotes Milton, *Apol* (see above, 119–21 n.) and 2 Pet. 2. 17–18: 'These are wells without water, clouds that are carried with a tempest; to whom the mist of darkness is reserved for ever. For when they speak great swelling words of vanity, they allure through the lusts of the flesh, through much wantonness, those that were clean escaped from them who live in error.']

127 *Rot inwardly.* W. B. Hunter (*MLN* 65, 1950, 544) suggests that Milton had in mind Aristotle, *Parts of Animals* 672a–b, or some Renaissance adaptation of the passage. E. S. Le Comte (ibid. 69, 1954, 402–4) suggests that Aristotle's influence came through Petrarch, *Ecl.* 9: e.g. cf. *Rot inwardly* and *saniem inclusam* (*Poesie Minori*, ed. D. Rossetti, 1, 168).

128–9 *Besides what the grim Woolf…nothing sed.* Although Newton identified the *Woolf* as Laud [but see below, 130–1 n., I. a. 1] and Todd cited Laud's Diary for a 1637 'libel' on the persecuting 'arch-wolf of Canterbury' (quoted in Elledge, *Milton's 'Lycidas*,' 292), the general consensus is that the *Woolf* stands for Roman Catholicism and its depredations for conversions to Rome. This is borne out by Milton's changes in 129: *nothing sed*: MS. deleted *nothing*, substituted *little*; the 1638 text read *little*, that of 1645 *nothing* (*Facs.* 440, 350, 187). George Conn came to the queen's court as papal agent in 1636 and was active in intrigue and conversion; in October 1637 Laud protested against his activities, and as a result a proclamation was issued on 20 December against Roman Catholics (Gardiner, *History of England...1603–42*, 10 v., London, 1893–9, 8, 236–42). Presumably it was in response to this proclamation that Milton changed *nothing* to *little*, but in 1645, when it was all in the past, he felt free to restore *nothing* (E. S. de Beer, *RES* 23, 1947, 61). Jerram recalls that Spenser (*S.C.*, *September* 148–61) describes Roman priests as wolves 'prively prolling too and froe' (160) [see notes on these lines in the Variorum *Spenser* for examples of the use of *wolf* in this context]. Milton's *privy paw* is a more potent phrase, suggesting the secret insertion of a paw to grasp the victim. [G. I. Soden, *Godfrey Goodman* (London, 1953, 225) lists some ten aristocratic converts to Rome, including the Duke of Buckingham's mother, his two brothers, Lords Purbeck and Anglesey, his niece (wife of Endymion Porter), et al. Cf. Gardiner, 8, 238–9. Tuveson (*JHI* 27, 452–3) observes that for Milton the Reformation 'was not simply an important event, but the supreme and crucial fact about the history of Christendom,' and he cites the eloquent paean from *Ref* (*Works* 3, 4–5; also 54, on 'Antichrist' as 'Mammons Son'). The Reformation 'had made possible Christian liberty, which alone makes possible the ideal life'; and 'There was indeed good reason to think the "antichristian tyranny" might return.' Tuveson also quotes 2 Pet. 2. 1, on false prophets and teachers, and Joseph Mede's comment on that text.]

130–1 St Peter's speech ends with what has become the most debated crux in Milton. Where so much has been said we need not be surprised to find a fair proportion of nonsense. There have been numerous partial listings of interpretations; one that has been helpful is in J. R. Hurt's unpublished 'Lycidas: Toward a Variorum Edition' (1957). [The fullest lists in print—prior to that in the Index below—are in Patrides, *Milton's Lycidas* (1961), 241, and Elledge, *Milton's 'Lycidas'* (1966), 293–7.] The preceding lines 113–29, for all their vehement eloquence, set forth the Puritan party line and are relatively clear; but the final couplet raises questions about both its own meaning and its relation to what has gone before. Does the threatened operation of the *two-handed engine* refer to the *Woolf* alone (as the punctuation certainly suggests) or is it a threat of retribution for—and by implication a promise of reform of—all the evils just catalogued (in which case one would have expected different punctuation)? Prior to interpretation is the image formed from the crucial phrase itself. While the word *engine* (with its evident relation to Lat. *ingenium*) carried from the first some suggestion of an ingenious instrument or tool, it came to be applied to almost any kind of instrument (*OED* 4), and especially to weapons, usually of war (ibid. 5), not necessarily to large or complicated machines but to any weapon capable of destruction. This obviously opens a wide range of speculation [although, as some critics have remarked, Milton's use of *that* implies, in spite of some sinister vagueness in his prophecy, that the *engine* is a well-known and recognizable thing].

Milton's other uses of the word are not of much positive help: *PL* 2. 65 (applied to God's 'Engin,' thunder and lightning); 2. 923 (Bellona's 'battering Engines bent to rase / Som Capital City'; cf. 'Engines to batter with': *Eikon*, *Works* 5, 214); 4. 17 ('like a devillish Engine'—probably a cannon which recoils when fired); 6. 484, 518, 586, 650 (all applied to Satan's artillery); and *RCG*, *Works* 3, 265 ('such engines of terror God hath given into the hand of his minister,' applied figuratively to the spiritual means of disciplining the sinner). Since one might expect a scriptural image, it is relevant to note (after Masson) that engines in Ezek. 26. 9 are evidently battering rams, while axes are mentioned separately: 'And he shall set engines of war against thy walls, and with his axes he shall break down thy towers.' The other example (which Masson omits) connotes massive weapons of defence: 'engines, invented by cunning men, to be on the towers and upon the bulwarks, to shoot arrows and great stones withal' (2 Chron. 26. 15). As to *two-handed* and *smite* [*smites* in 1638 text], Milton used them in his poetry only once more (*PL* 6. 251, 324), with reference to Michael's huge sword, which a number of scholars have invoked to explain the crux in *Lycidas*.

We may divide interpreters into two groups: I. The majority, who regard the *engine*, however envisaged, as an instrument of retribution (and sometimes of reform); II. The minority, who take it as the last in a series of dangers menacing the well-being, even the existence, of the church. We may then proceed to a brief summary under the image specified or implied.

The Minor English Poems

I. *An Instrument of Retribution (and Reform)*

I. a. *An Axe*

(1) [Newton in his prefatory Life (*Poetical Works*, 1761–2, 1, xxiii) took the *Woolf* as Laud, but in his notes (3, 492–3) he offered an alternative explanation (supported by Thyer and Richardson): 'Besides what the popish priests privately pervert to their religion.'] Accepting the *engine* as the axe of Reformation, he cited a number of the biblical illustrations appealed to by modern scholars: 'And now also the axe is laid unto the root of the trees: therefore every tree which bringeth not forth good fruit is hewn down, and cast into the fire' (Matt. 3. 10; cf. Luke 3. 9). *at the door*: near at hand. Cf. 'it [the Last Judgment] is near, even at the doors' (Matt. 24. 33); 'behold, the judge standeth before the door' (James 5. 9). *smite no more.* Cf. 'God hath delivered thine enemy into thine hand this day: now therefore let me smite him...even to the earth at once, and I will not smite him the second time' (1 Sam. 26. 8). [All these citations in Newton.]

(2) Rejecting Warburton's suggestion of a sword, Warton (without acknowledgment) followed Newton in taking the *engine* as the axe of Matt. 3. 10 and Luke 3. 9, emphasizing a note of urgency and quoting *Ref* (*Works* 3, 47): 'they ⟨the Jesuits⟩ feeling the Axe of Gods reformation hewing at the old and hollow trunk of Papacie.' Warton further identified the axe as that destined to behead Archbishop Laud, whose 'death would remove all grievances in religion, and complete the reformation of the church.' Todd accepted Warton's view, but Keightley and later editors rejected the idea of a prophetic reference to Laud's execution. [Editors of the later 19th century (e.g. Hales, Browne, Jerram, Rolfe, Bell, Trent, Moody) remained neutral or inclined to the axe. For supporters of the sword see I. b below.]

(3) G. G. Loane (*TLS*, 25 April 1929, 338) insisted on the headsman's axe, acquiesced in the allusion to Laud, and offered a source in Sir Thomas Smith's *Certaigne Psalmes...with other Prayers* (1549: [excerpted in Sir E. Brydges, *Restituta* 4, 1816, 189, and in B. Danielsson, *Sir Thomas Smith*, Stockholm, 1963, 37]):

> This day made new Duke, Marquis, Earle, or Baron,
>   Yet maie the ax stande next the dore;
> Everie thing is not ended as it is begonne,
>   God will have the stroke, either after or before.

Later repeating this (*N&Q* 181, 1941, 320), Loane drops Laud for the general idea of Milton's anticipating that the civil power will intervene to rectify abuses in the church. The second and only essential line in Smith's stanza had been already cited by Mitford (*Poetical Works*, 3 v., London, ed. 1834–5, 3, 130), and was thence advanced as evidence for the axe by G. H. Powell (*Athenaeum*, 5 May 1906, 547). H. Beckett (*TLS*, 3 July 1943, 319) supports the executioner's axe (or sword) but suggests a pictorial source, noting that Rembrandt's *Beheading of John the Baptist* was 'unfortunately' not available in 1638, and offering no interpretation. Tuckwell ('*Lycidas*,' 1911, 47), while regarding the lines as 'purposely enigmatical, the terror...enhanced by their obscurity,' still holds Milton 'to have meant the axe and block, still "at the door" of recent history, and ready to be brought forth again.'

(4) W. H. Ward (*Athenaeum*, 14 April 1906, 451–2) argues for a battle-axe, to be used against the corrupters of God's worship. He finds the source in Ezek. 8, an attack on the abominations practised in the Temple, which are shown to the prophet after he is brought 'to the door of the inner gate' (8. 3), i.e. of the inner court. Threatening dire retribution (8. 18), God orders the summoning of those in charge of the city, 'every man with his destroying weapon ⟨rendered in R.V. margin 'battle axe' in accordance with the Hebrew and Greek texts⟩ in his hand'; they are to slay without pity, sparing only the righteous (9. 1 f.). The *engine*, the battle-axe, is not to batter in the door (as Masson supposed), but to destroy the corrupters and corruptions of religion once for all.

I. b. *A Sword*

(1) Warburton (reported by Warton) explained the *engine* as St Peter's sword (John 18. 10) turned into the two-handed sword of romance. Warton rejected the idea, though he conceded that Michael's sword 'with huge two-handed sway' (*PL* 6. 251) 'is evidently the old Gothic sword of chivalry.' But Warburton has had one follower, W. R. Dunstan (*TLS*, 12 June 1943, 283), who, while apparently going along with Mutschmann (below, I. b. 7), identified the *engine* with the sword of Huanebango in Peele's *Old Wives Tale* (see below, *Comus* III. 1). It might be added that literature provides much better swords, such as Guy of Warwick's two-handed one in Drayton, *Poly.* 12. 272–8. H. L. (*Athenaeum*, 30 June 1900, 815) cited 'A sacred Fencer' with a 'two-hand Sword' sent by God against the Assyrians (Sylvester, *D.W.W.* 1. 1. 812–13, Grosart, 1, 26). Less relevant still is the two-edged sword in Euripides, *Hipp.* 780 (Keightley). [The preceding reference to Sylvester may be thought less irrelevant than Woodhouse implies, at any rate less so than many items in this catalogue, since the biblical incident (2 Kings 19. 35) shows God destroying his

enemies, since Milton had referred to it in *El* 4. 113 f., and since he had at least an early interest in Sylvester.]

(2) Cut loose from romance, the sword has proved a popular explanation. Verity [followed, briefly, by H. F. Fletcher (*Poetical Works*, Boston, 1941), and tentatively by Mack (1950)], took the *engine* as 'the sword of Justice,' which Milton was to declare to be above every ruler, describing 'the tryal of Justice' as 'the Sword of God' (*TKM, Works* 5, 3 and 7). [Saillens (*Milton*, 62) sees this as a possible secondary meaning; cf. below, I. c. 2.]

(3) In relating 113–31 to Ezek. 34. 2–10 (above, 108–31 n.), E. C. Baldwin (*MLN* 33, 1918, 211–15) saw the *engine* as symbolizing generally God's justice and referring to the punishment of the shepherds and the rescuing of the flock by God's action, as promised in Ezek. 34. 10; there no instrument is mentioned, but that a sword is implied is made probable by the famous sword-song of 7. 14 f. [and 21. 1–17]. Assuming then a sword, and the sword of justice, we need read no more in *two-handed* than an indication that, while keen, it is large and heavy like those used in the later Middle Ages. It may be identified with Michael's sword (*PL* 6. 251), which came from 'the Armorie of God' (ibid. 321), and whose 'one stroke' 'not need repeate, / As not of power, at once' (ibid. 317–19). [Wright (1938) remarked: 'Of the innumerable interpretations the best is that the two-handed engine is the sword of justice or vengeance of God, its merit being that it tells us no more than Milton's verse.' So also Prince (1968).]

(4) E. S. de Beer (*RES* 23, 1947, 60–3), assuming the *engine* to be a sword, for the punishment of bad shepherds, suggests a source in a conflation of Zech. 13. 7 and 11. 17: 'Awake, O sword, against my shepherd...smite the shepherd ...,' and 'Woe to the idol shepherd that leaveth the flock! the sword shall be upon his arm, and upon his right eye....'—which entails ignoring the sense and context in which the former is quoted in Matt. 26. 31 and Mark 14. 27. [Leishman (*Minor Poems*, 276) endorses De Beer, citing also Rev. 19. 11–21.]

(5) A number of critics support the sword of St Michael as to be later used in *PL*. C. M. I. (*N&Q*, Ser. 6, 12, 1885, 351) questioned Jerram's use of Matt. 3. 10 in support of the axe and urged the sword of Michael, identifying the *Woolf* as Satan. To *PL* 6. 250–1 and 320–3 M. Kelley (*N&Q* 181, 1941, 273) added Jer. 50. 25: 'The Lord hath opened his armoury, and hath brought forth the weapons of his indignation'; he finds in the fusion of these passages 'the indignation that prompts the whole digression.' [Hanford (*Poems*, 1953) says: 'Perhaps the most likely allusion is to the sword of God's vengeance, the sword which Michael wielded...and which went before the Cherubim in Eden'

Lycidas

(*PL* 6. 251, 12. 632–3). M. C. Treip (*N&Q* 6, 1959, 364–6) supports Kelley and Baldwin in regard to Michael's sword, an image strongly supplemented by Rev. 1. 16 and 2. 12 and 16, and Matt. 3. 10, along with the sword of God's justice in Ezekiel. Masson and others have concentrated too much on allegorical interpretation at the expense of the poem's metaphorical and dramatic consistency. Milton's entire picture demands some personal agent; this cannot be Christ, who has no place in the actual situation of *Lycidas*, nor can it be Peter. The most logical wielder of the sword is Michael, whose role here (as in *PL* 6. 318, 'one stroke'; cf. 6. 321) lends itself to this act, and who can properly stand in Christ's place at the door of the fold. It is no objection that Michael does not enter the poem openly until 161; in 130–1 he is *in potentia*. Later he is logically called upon to look homeward, and perhaps to use that idle sword. This view does not exclude other elements; the door of the fold probably means the door of both the church and heaven (Le Comte, *SP* 47, 1950, 589–90). The various biblical images present different facets of one idea.] R. Daniells (40–1: see above, III, under 1963) also associates the *engine* as Michael's sword with the great vision of the guarded Mount. [Two recent editors, Shawcross (1963) and I. G. MacCaffrey (1966), take a sword as probable and cite St Michael. M. H. Nicolson (*John Milton*, 1963, 99–100) prefers Michael's sword but does not think that Milton visualized his *engine* or intended us to do so.]

(6) Whatever doubts may be left respecting the source proposed, one of the most valuable examinations of the problem and of many previous inquiries is provided by E. S. Le Comte ('"That Two-handed Engine" and Savonarola,' *SP* 47, 1950, 589–606). He sees the theme of the speech in John 10, and applies as a first principle the question what a reader in 1638 would be likely to understand. He argues that the *engine* is not some prophetic axe but more generally the sword of God's justice, to be wielded by the Deity himself. '"The sword of the Lord" is a common expression in the Old Testament, and "smite" is a common verb, either with "sword" or with God as the agent, and sometimes with both (Deut. 28: 22; Zech. 13: 7...).' And if one wants some instantaneous duality of effect in Milton's phrase, what but death and damnation, the fate he predicted for those who seek their own advancement 'by the impairing and diminution of the true Faith,' namely, that they, 'after a shamefull end in this Life (which God grant them) shall be throwne downe eternally into the darkest and deepest Gulfe of Hell' (*Ref, Works* 3, 79)? 'The poem is mainly about... salvation...but here it turns off, to deal, with terrible brevity, with *damnation*, with the iron key instead of the golden.' While admitting that Milton needed no other source for the sword than the Bible, Le Comte argues for his memory of

the phrase repeatedly used by Savonarola in his sermons, *Ecce gladius Domini super terram cito et velociter*, and from that to his having read the preacher's other sermons predicting the fate of a corrupt church which must be smitten before it can be reformed, notably one on Ps. 73. This leads the critic to an actual disaster which overtook a Roman congregation in Blackfriars in 1623 and was celebrated in Latin verse by Milton's friend, the younger Alexander Gill [see *QNov*, headnote, n. 3, in *V.C.* 1]; Protestants took this disaster as a divine judgment. (See also Le Comte's 'Supplement,' *SP* 49, 1952, 548–50.) The writer seems to be most satisfying in his treatment of others' speculations.

(7) A. H. T. Clarke (*TLS*, 11 April 1929, 295–6) suggested the sword of Revolution, an idea rejected by G. M. Trevelyan (ibid. 25 April 1929, 338) because thoughts of revolution were far from the Puritans in 1637. D. A. Stauffer (*MLR* 31, 1936, 57–60), without defining the image, argued for a more precise allusion: the *engine* is two-handed in reference to the future joint action of the English and Scots against the corrupt episcopacy, the prophecy being inspired by Scottish resistance to the imposition of the Anglican liturgy, notably by the riots in Edinburgh in July 1637, and the sympathy of English Puritans. A similar suggestion, of a Scottish 'sword of war,' was made by H. Mutschmann (*TLS*, 25 April 1936, 356). Mutschmann amplified his suggestion (*N&Q* 2, 1955, 515), proposing, as before, a scriptural source for *at the door* in Acts 5. 9–10: 'Behold, the feet of them which have buried thy husband are at the door, and shall carry thee out'—destruction falling in turn on the oppressors of the Scots and of the English. A. F. Pollard (*TLS*, 29 August 1936, 697) opposed the idea: Scottish troubles did not become acute until 1638–9; reference is to the two-handed sword as known to English history; and the prophecy is of an English rising alone.

(8) R. E. Hughes (*N&Q* 2, 1955, 58–9) argues that the *engine*, a sword, is intended to convey no more than 'a general suggestion of Puritan zeal': zeal and the sword are closely united in Ps. 149. 6 ('Let the high praises of God be in their [the saints'] mouth, and a two-edged sword in their hand'), and St Augustine couples righteous anger and the sword (*Conf.* 12. 14). The *door* is an image with multiple reference: to the door of the fold and the doors opened and shut by St Peter's keys. R. J. Schoeck (ibid. 235–7) supported this interpretation of the sword with John of Salisbury's description of a 'duly ordained soldiery' (*Policraticus* 6. 8), which draws on Ps. 149.

(9) In his note on *either sword* (*Sonn* 17. 12) Pattison referred briefly to the two swords, spiritual and temporal, which 'together make up the "two-handed engine at the door" in Lycidas.' H. Van Tromp (*TLS*, 25 April 1929, 338)

repeated this interpretation and sought support in a passage from Dante's *De Monarchia* and in a reference to it in Boccaccio's *Life* of Dante, which do not further elucidation.

(10) Some interpreters, whether or not accepting the image of a sword, have taken the *engine* to be the Bible. C. A. Ward (*N&Q* Ser. 6, 11, 1885, 516), protesting against excessive particularizing, held that the *engine* represents the judgment which is to fall on the church in which the flock is neglected and preyed upon by wolves. He quoted Heb. 4. 12: 'For the word of God is quick, and powerful, and sharper than any two-edged sword...and is a discerner of the thoughts and intents of the heart.'

(11) M. Hussey, urging that the *engine* is the Gospel (*N&Q* 193, 1948, 503), quoted Thomas Adams: 'The Gospell is the power of God to salvation....It is the power of God to confusion. It is a double-edged sword, and gives either instruction, or destruction' (*Workes*, 1629, 1016).

(12) L. Howard ('"That Two-Handed Engine" Once More,' *HLQ* 15, 1951–2, 173–84) takes the *engine* as a sword, specifically as the two-edged sword proceeding out of the mouth of the Lord (Rev. 1. 16), which was often presented in illustrated Bibles as the two-handed broadsword of medieval combat. Howard interprets this sword as the Word of God executing judgment upon the wicked (Rev. 19. 15) and completing the work of reformation, not necessarily the Last Judgment alone (cf. Rev. 2. 12–16). The punishment of the wicked is accompanied by the reward of the just (Rev. 19. 1–9), as it is in *Lycidas* if we look on to 165–81 and Lycidas' hearing 'the unexpressive nuptial Song.' The image of the Word as a sword appears in other passages of scripture to which the mind of poet and reader would naturally turn: 'the sword of the Spirit, which is the word of God' (Eph. 6. 17); 'the word of God is...sharper than any two-edged sword' (Heb. 4. 12); a gloss in the Geneva Bible on Rev. 1. 16 says: 'This sworde signified his worde and the vertue thereof....' Howard concludes: 'The most reasonable gloss for the passage...seems to be that the engine is the Word of God as it was regularly symbolized by the Biblical sword, and that the threat is the threat of the Protestant reformation as it was being continued in the Puritan movement of which Milton was a part.'

(13) Like others, J. M. Steadman (*N&Q* 3, 1956, 249–50) sees the two-edged sword of Rev. 1. 16 as the Word of God. He finds support, and also a close connection with the Reformation, in the device of Calvin's Geneva printer, Jehan Gerard, which represents this sword as a broadsword (sometimes two-handed, sometimes not, so that this feature seems to have no special significance beyond size and weight) and employs as mottoes Heb. 4. 12 (quoted in 10 above),

Joshua 5. 13–14 ('a man...with his sword drawn in his hand' came 'as captain of the host of the Lord'), Isa. 40. 8 ('the word of our God shall stand for ever'), Matt. 10. 34 ('not...peace, but a sword'). In *N&Q* 7 (1960), 237, Steadman added, from Benlowes' *Theophila* (1652): 'And in mystical Divinity His [Christ's] two-handed sword is the Word and Spirit, which wounds and heals' (*Minor Poets of the Caroline Period*, ed. G. Saintsbury, 1, 321).

For Whiting's relating of the *engine* as sword to the *Keyes* (110), and Stroup's supporting quotation, see below, I.e.3.

So far as we have gone, it is plain that, where the *engine* is thought of as a definite weapon, the sword is the favourite image, whether it signify God's justice or his Word. We might add an excerpt from William Browne which, although like some other quotations it has 'two-edged' and not 'two-handed,' may not be irrelevant: 'O ever, ever rest upon that word / Which doth assure thee, though his two-edg'd sword / Be drawn in justice 'gainst thy sinful soul, / To separate the rotten from the whole' (*Brit. Past.* 1. 5. 565–8). In contrast with Milton's immediate context, Browne emphasizes God's mercy, not his justice or wrath; but the significant point is that the sword here is not merely destructive but reforming, as Milton's total context perhaps requires it to be.

[Some later dealings with the idea of a sword must be added.

(14) Michael Fixler (*Milton and the Kingdoms of God*, 1964, 60–1) does not offer a set theory but approaches one, in discussing St Peter's posing of the problem of divine justice, a problem beyond the remedies celebrated in *Comus*. 'Within individual regenerate human nature contemplation can find what grace extends to cope with temptations, but against the rampant corrupting force of evil discharged through fallen human nature into the very instruments intended for salvation, the saints demand and heaven grants a mightier weapon. In Milton's own words: "Truth is properly no more then Contemplation; and her utmost efficiency is but teaching: but Justice in her very essence is all strength and activity; and hath a Sword put into her hand, to use against all violence and oppression on the earth" (*Eikon, Works* 5, 292). As witness that God's ways are just on earth as they are in heaven, against the perversion of his earthly Kingdom *that two handed engine at the door | Stands ready to smite once, and smite no more.* The vindication of God is apocalyptic, for the death of King had raised the question of the perversion of the evangelical vocation Christ had given his Church. Nothing but divine judgment could be set against an evil so radical and universal.' Fixler contrasts the literal prophecy, some years later, of *RCG*, end of 1. 6 (*Works* 3, 222).]

[B. R. Rhodes (*N&Q* 13, 1966, 24) supports the idea of a sword, citing Rev. 1.

16 and 2. 14–18 on the two-edged sword issuing from Christ's mouth and promised as a weapon against corruption. These citations had been used by Masson (below, I. c. 2) and others (above, I. b. 5, 12.]

(15) [D. Stempel (*ELN* 3, 1965–6, 259–63) quotes Knox's *History of the Reformation in Scotland* (*Works*, ed. D. Laing, Edinburgh, 1846–64, 1, 139) on the 'twa handed sweard' accepted by Knox from the martyr George Wishart. The *History*, suppressed by the Stationers' Company in 1587, lacked this item in a reprint of 1644—a deletion evidently in Milton's mind when he referred in *Areopagitica* to the suppressing of a book because of 'one sentence of a ventrous edge,...though it were Knox himself...that spake it' (*Works* 4, 326–7). 'For Milton, Knox's two-handed sword was a symbol of the just vengeance of the Scottish reformers on a "corrupted Clergy then in their height," and it was to Scotland that he looked for support in his crusade against the corrupted clergy of his own country': Stempel cites his Commonplace Book (*C.P.W.* 1, 502: '1639–41?') and Stauffer on England and Scotland (I. b. 7 above). In 1649–51 Milton saw the execution of Mary Stuart as marking the triumph of Knox's revolution (*Works* 5, 29; 6, 266; 7, 47). The phrase in *Lycidas* suggests that when England wielded the sword, 'only one blow would be needed, not the three wavering strokes' of Mary's executioner. This is ingenious, but, even if in 1637 copies of Knox's suppressed *History* were 'not impossible to obtain,' the reference would still be very abstruse, whereas Milton's *that* seems to imply that the *engine* is well known.]

(16) [Tuveson (*JHI* 27, 1966, 453–6), objecting to the idea of deliberate vagueness as incompatible with Peter's previous explicit clarity, supports the image of a sword, though not Michael's. Peter is there to make the speech, he still presides over the shepherds, and the *engine* is ready *at the door*. Tuveson cites Peter's using his sword against the high priest's servant (John 18. 10 f.), and Luke 22. 38, 2 Cor. 10. 4, Heb. 4. 12, Eph. 6. 17, Rev. 1. 16. He connects Peter with the *door* (John 18. 16–17; and 10. 7–9, Col. 4. 3). Tuveson, however, sees 'probably...an immediate, topical significance,' a reference to a 'powerful group known as the "spiritual brotherhood," dedicated to reform of the church from within through preaching,' which 'had for a number of years been quietly but surely making progress,' a group led by William Gouge and Richard Sibbes (Haller, *Rise of Puritanism*, 82). He finds three possible meanings for 'two-handed': (1) 'the pastors who...combine doctrine and example in their teaching'; (2) 'the double sources of doctrine, as the Geneva Bible says, "preached both in the Law and the Gospel"'; (3) 'the sources of religious faith,' the 'twofold Scripture; one external, which is the written word, and the

other internal, which is the Holy Spirit, written in the hearts of believers' (*DocCh* 1. 30, *Works* 16, 273). Tuveson is also tempted (n. 10) by the old idea of English and Scottish allies in reform. He adds: 'The fact that this sword of the spirit is limited to one blow is not merely a detail connecting it with Peter, whom Jesus forbade to strike a second time; it may be, in fact, the most hopeful note in the prophecy,' signifying an inward and final 'transformation of the souls of men.' He observes that the reading *and smite* (which replaced the *and smites* of 1638) 'suggests that there is some kind of destiny inhibiting the engine from smiting more than once. The first one is closer in spirit to the story that Jesus rebuked Peter after one blow. It also seems to reenforce my suggestion that there is an optimism in these lines; perhaps the mutual assistance of the two ministries [i.e. English and Scottish] will insure that this reform, at length, will not have to be repeated.']

I. c. *Axe or Sword (or a conflation of the two)*

(1) Keightley refused to determine as between 'the axe of the Gospel' and 'the two-edged sword of the Apocalypse,' and was followed by Rolfe.

(2) Masson rejected Newton's idea of the axe at the root (a. 1 above), since the *engine* is *at the door*, and also Warton's 'absurd' notion of the axe that was to behead Laud. He begins with the basic image of an axe, a picture of 'a strong man wielding a huge axe..., and ready to batter down the opposing timbers, so as to let the besiegers in.' But, Masson goes on, Milton may also have intended an oblique allusion to Rev. 1–3, especially 1. 16 ('out of his mouth went a sharp two-edged sword') and 2. 12–16 ('the sharp sword with two edges.... Repent; or else I will come unto thee quickly, and will fight against them with the sword of my mouth'). The whole passage, 2. 12–16, is readily applicable to the state of the English church as the Puritans viewed it, reformed in doctrine but containing much corruption. Masson was less fortunate in trying to relate the *door* to 'Behold, I stand at the door, and knock' (Rev. 3. 20), where Christ is the gracious guest, not the stern executant of justice, and 'knock' does not mean *smite*. Returning by implication to the battering axe, Masson suggested the further 'hypothesis that Milton did not take his image from the Bible, but invented one to describe the agency by which...he foresaw the English Church would be reformed,' namely, 'the English Parliament with its two Houses.' This idea has fared better than Warton's fancy about the axe and Laud [though not in recent years]. It was rejected by Elton for the reason Masson urged against Warton, that it involved prophecy impossible in 1638, and by Stauffer (I. b. 7) because the Lords favoured episcopacy. It was reported without

comment by Browne, Rolfe, and others, but was accepted by G. M. Trevelyan (*TLS*, 25 April 1929, 338), who had always taken the *engine* to be a sword meaning Parliament but found 'the two Houses' perhaps 'too fanciful.' This idea was accepted in 1937 by Hughes, who in 1957 was non-committal [and by Saillens (*Milton*, 1964, 62)].

(3) D. C. Dorian (*PMLA* 45, 1930, 204–15), paying little attention to the image but accepting the general reference to Parliament as the agent of reform, suggested that the *engine* is '*liberty* conceived as a *weapon* or *instrument* to be wielded by parliament against the unworthy self-seekers among the clergy.' In a long disquisition on liberty, ranging, without reference to any development in Milton's ideas, from his first tract up to *DocCh*, Dorian emphasized these points: that '"true" or "honest" liberty is an efficient instrument in the hands of "just and virtuous men"'; that for Milton true liberty and religion are indissolubly joined in the doctrine of Christian liberty (*DocCh* 1. 26, 27; etc.); that Milton looks to Parliament for the practice and furtherance of liberty (*Works* 3, 336–7; 4, 293); that the executioner's sword or axe, which needed to smite but once, might in this context remind poet and reader of the 'sharp two-edged sword' of Rev. 1. 16; that the two hands were those of Parliament; that the *engine* was *at the door* because, 'in 1637, "the stern resolve of the people" (as Green calls it) should have been enough to tell the members of parliament that they had then only to seize this weapon, liberty, and "*smite once...more*" in order...to remove not only the corrupt clergy, but whatever was "grievance and unjust" to the people' (215). In regard to this line of argument it must be remembered that Parliament had not met since 1629 and that no meeting was in prospect in 1637, and it is questionable how far one could assume general discontent and 'stern resolve.' [Patterson found Dorian's case plausible. Dorian's suggestion that Milton associated the scriptural swords, i.e. Gospel truth, with liberty led M. M. Ross to remark on Sir John Stradling's use of those swords as the weapons of Heaven and the clergy (*HLQ* 14, 1950–1, 146, n. 21).

Since the supply of swords is inexhaustible, one might add Fuller, *Historie of the Holy Warre*, 1639 (3. 1, p. 109): 'But our Conrade plainly told him, he must use as well the weapons of the left hand as of the right; meaning the sword as well as prayers...']

I. d. *Other Weapons of Offence or Defence*

(1) C. G. Osgood (*RES* 1, 1925, 339–41) suggested the flail of Talus, the henchman—indeed 'The true guide of his way and vertuous government'—of Artegall, Spenser's knight of Justice (*F.Q.* 5), an instrument Milton later

referred to (*Eikon*, *Works* 5, 110). Talus not only used his flail to punish and destroy the unjust, but with it 'thresht out falshood, and did truth unfould' (5. 1. 12). [In spite of the general popularity of Spenser, this would be a relatively obscure allusion.] J. M. Steadman (*N&Q* 3, 1956, 335) offered some support for the *engine* as flail in William Hog's Latin paraphrase of *Lycidas* (1694): *Machina sed gemino ad portae armata flagello | Protinus his uno parat ictu accessere fatum*—though this is so ambiguous as itself to need explanation, and Steadman elsewhere supports the sword (I. b. 13).

(2) E. M. W. Tillyard (*Milton*, 1930, 387) suggested a weapon from Ps. 2. 9: 'Thou shalt break them [the heathen] with a rod of iron; thou shalt dash them in pieces like a potter's vessel.' Milton was to allude to this (*Ref*, *Works* 3, 69), contrasting 'the Pastorly Rod, and Sheep-hooke of Christ' with 'the iron Scepter of his anger.' The sheep-hook gives the pastoral connection; the *engine* (*two-handed* only in reference to its weight) is 'the iron Scepter' of Christ's anger, which will break down the door of the fold and punish the false shepherds. [In their edition of *Comus*, etc. (London, 1952), Tillyard and P. B. Tillyard accept the sword of the Lord, as understood vaguely.]

(3) C. W. Brodribb (*TLS*, 12 June 1930, 496; ibid. 5 June 1943, 271, here citing John 10) suggested one of the large sheep-hooks (shod with iron at the straight end, and capable of being used as a weapon) such as are illustrated in the woodcuts in Spenser's *S.C.* Since this becomes 'the Pastorly Rod, and Sheep-hooke of Christ,' and since it is Christ who is at the door to exercise the function of the true shepherd, replacing the lax and ignorant (119–20), the whole allusion is lifted above contemporary politics. The arguments for a sheep-hook, by Brodribb and others, were discussed by M. H. Studley (*English Journal*, College Edition, 26, 1937, 148–51). L. W. Coolidge (*PQ* 29, 1950, 444–5) supported the sheep-hook, already alluded to in 119–20, and linked both allusions with the pastoral staff, part of the symbolic regalia of a bishop, whose dual function is to pull men back from hell and to put down the wicked (cf. *Piers Plowman* B. 8. 94–7, and Anglican Ordinal, 1549). The *engine*, then, is the pastoral staff wielded as an instrument of discipline: St Peter warns his unworthy successors that, since they are incapable of using the staff aright, it will be turned to their destruction.

[To John Reesing ('The Decorum of St. Peter's Speech in "Lycidas,"' *Milton's Poetic Art*, 1968, 31–49) Milton's strong belief in decorum (*Works* 4, 286) suggests that his almost certainly biblical image is something that can be associated with both shepherds and bishops (Christian shepherds). Starting from the rod and staff of Ps. 23. 4 and other biblical passages, he sketches the symbolism for their derivative, the crosier, and argues that the *engine* is the rod of Christ suggested in the parable of the Last Judgment (Matt. 25. 32). Milton's climactic image denotes Christ's rod and at the same time reminds the reader of the sheep-hook (i.e. crosier) of line 120. Reesing differs from Coolidge (just above), who equates the *engine* with the sheep-hook and identifies both as the crosier. To summarize: since the bad shepherds (the bishops) have not fed their flocks, the chief Shepherd (1 Pet. 5. 4) will smite them down with His rod, which is the archetypal reality behind every bishop's staff. The two-handed engine is the irresistible rod (Matt. 25. 32) of Christ the divine Shepherd, King, and Judge. It is thus the instrument of divine justice by which the sheep-hook of each hireling shepherd will be abased.]

(4) M.D. (*Athenaeum*, 28 April 1906, 515) suggested the scythe of Time (or possibly of Death) as a variant of the 'abhorred shears' (75), perhaps to be associated here with the sickles of angels gathering grapes for the winepress of God's wrath (Rev. 14. 15–20). K. C. Tomlinson (*TLS*, 12 June 1943, 283) urged Time's scythe, *at the door* of 'our earthly house,' the body (2 Cor. 5. 1). But one does not see Milton waiting for Time to set things right. K. A. Esdaile (*TLS*, 19 June 1943, 295) supported the scythe of Death, on the sole ground that many monuments of the period so represent Death.

I. e. *Other Images (or None)*

(1) E. S. Le Comte (I. b. 6) suggested, but only to reject, the idea that the *two-handed engine* represents the two 'massy Keyes' of St Peter. 'The door is the door of the sheepfold, which is the door of the church (which is, in turn, the way to heaven: thus we are back in thought to the beginning of the passage, and a lover of novelty might even proffer a twenty-ninth explanation, that the engine *is* the keys...taking "smite" as wholly figurative)' (*SP* 47, 1950, 590). Precisely this interpretation is argued in detail by J. M. French (*MLN* 68, 1953, 229–31), with scriptural examples of figurative uses of *smite*.

(2) W. A. Turner (*JEGP* 49, 1950, 562–5) [lists ten earlier proposals and sets down nine conditions an ideal interpretation should fulfil. He thinks the last part of the prose epigraph imposes two conditions not required by, and indeed incompatible with, those required by the poem: 'that St. Peter's prophecy was fulfilled by 1645, and consequently that the two-handed engine was an earthly instrument, whether wielded by earthly hands or not.'] He would identify the *engine* with 'the lock on St. Peter's door (or the power of the lock), to which he carries the keys.' This meets the conditions of appropriateness, familiarity,

consistency, etc. The word *two-handed* would mean 'having two purposes,' admission and exclusion. 'It could smite in the figurative sense of rendering judgment, and even literally by slamming ("shuts amain," or with force).' *OED* suggests no such meaning for *smite*.

(3) G. W. Whiting (*This Pendant World*, 1958, 29–58) believes that the image must carry a specific meaning and not rely on vagueness for its effect, and that the meaning must be determined in relation to the whole passage (108–31). He also therefore goes back for a clue to the keys (see his interpretation above, 110–11 n.): the keys, in Protestant exegesis, are the Word of God, the Law and the Gospel, which close or open the gates of heaven, and the due preaching thereof is thus to bind and loose (cf. P. Fletcher as quoted above, 110–11 n.). But, by another image, the Word is also a sharp sword, the spiritual sword (as distinct from the temporal and physical sword wielded by the magistrate), and it too is the Word preached, as figured by the two-edged sword proceeding from the mouth of one like unto the Son of man (Rev. 1. 13–16). Keys and sword, then, are both the Word. But it is also by the Word that false teachers (and notably the papacy and its supporters) are to be exposed and punished, and the church reformed: all of which Whiting illustrates from Protestant commentary. The conclusion is that the *engine* is a sword, to be used not to destroy the church but to extirpate false teachers and thus purify it, but that this spiritual sword figures an aspect of the Word, just as do the keys.

T. B. Stroup (*N&Q* 6, 1959, 366–7) supports this interpretation by quoting P. Fletcher, *Apoll.* 1. 24: 'In midst of peace that sharpe two edged sword / Cuts through our darknes, cleaves the misty night, / Discovers all our snares; that sacred word / (Lockt up by Rome) breakes prison, spreads the light…' But it seems somewhat fanciful to find a hint of the keys in Satan's parenthetical remark about Rome's locking up the Bible in Latin. [Fletcher was briefly cited by Dorian (I. c. 3 above).]

(4) E. L. Marilla ('That "Two-Handed Engine" Finally?' *PMLA* 67, 1952, 1181–4; repr. in Marilla's *Milton and Modern Man*, University of Alabama, 1968), citing especially Le Comte and acquiescing in the image of a sword or an axe, associates the operation of the *engine* with Christ's judgment on episcopal subverters of the church. His whole emphasis falls on the immediacy of the Millenarian hope for the coming of Christ, 'the Eternall and shortly-expected King' (*Ref, Works* 3, 78), a hope sufficiently widespread among Puritans to enable them to interpret the lines. He also cites *Animad* (*Works* 3, 148): 'but thy Kingdome is now at hand, and thou standing at the dore.' This hope, though, was less widespread in the 1630's than Marilla supposes, and

never shared by Puritans within the English Church, as Milton still was, or by the Presbyterians as a group.

(5) H. F. Robins ('Milton's "Two-handed Engine at the Door" and St. Matthew's Gospel,' *RES* 5, 1954, 25–36: see also above, end of 108–31 n.) opposes Le Comte (above, I. b. 6) on several grounds, and would stress Matthew rather than John 10. He argues that *But* is adversative to the whole account of the corrupt clergy (not merely to *nothing sed*) and that *that* betokens something instantly recognized (and does not refer back to an antecedent, be it keys or sheep-hook). Noting that *OED* 10 allows for the figurative use of *engine* to designate a person as agent or instrument, he argues that it means man, a particular man, and, further, that *two-handed* implies two distinct functions. Since preceding lines include the good as well as the bad, the dual function of the *engine*, man, is to reward the good and punish or smite the bad, *smite* being figurative (as often in the Bible). The man who pre-eminently performs this dual action, as is clear from Matt. 25. 31–4, 41–6, is 'the Son of man,' who 'shall come in his glory' and 'shall separate them one from another, as a shepherd divideth his sheep from the goats,' setting 'the sheep on his right hand, but the goats on the left,' and adjudging the former 'into life eternal,' the latter—those who have neglected every Christian duty—to 'everlasting punishment.' The *engine* or instrument of this judgment, then, is Christ, whom Milton ⟨but much later⟩ did not scruple to describe as 'the secondary and instrumental cause' of whatever his Father, the primary cause, ordained (*DocCh* 1. 5, *Works* 14, 205; cf. *PL* 3. 383–91) and who himself, in respect of the Last Judgment, declared: 'I can of mine own self do nothing: as I hear, I judge: and my judgment is just; because I seek not mine own will, but the will of the Father which hath sent me' (John 5. 30). To Christ also the phrase *at the door* 'unequivocally points,' for Christ's description of events leading up to the Judgment concludes: '... when ye shall see all these things, know that it [margin: Or, *he*] is near, even at the doors' (Matt. 24. 33), a passage Milton was to echo in 'but thy Kingdome is now at hand, and thou standing at the dore' (*Animad, Works* 3, 148).

[R. Tuve, though she uses the word 'sword,' sees the image as meaning the day of judgment (*Images*, 1957, 78).

(6) N. Frye (*Paradise Lost*, etc., 1951), listing some of the interpretations, says that 'none...accounts for both "door" and "smite once." It is far more important to notice the link in imagery with 75.']

(7) E. L. Brooks (*N&Q* 3, 1956, 67–8), who refers the whole attack on the corrupt clergy to Ezek. 34 (above, 108–31 n.), here cites specifically, but with no

particular image in view, God's assertions: 'I am against the shepherds; and I will require my flock at their hand' (34. 10); 'Behold, I judge between cattle and cattle, between the rams and the he goats' (17). Reading the latter with reference to Matt. 25. 33 ('And he shall set the sheep on his right hand, but the goats on the left'), he draws the rather startling inference that the *engine* may be the Godhead itself.

(8) Some heterogeneous proposals will round out the record. N. W. Hill (*TLS*, 28 July 1927, 520) suggested that the *engine* represented a warning that an attempt to restore Roman Catholicism would result in war and that Milton coined the phrase with thoughts of the double-faced Janus and the door of his temple in mind. E. S. Fussell (*N&Q* 193, 1948, 338–9) saw an analogy between Milton's lines and Donne's *To the Countesse of Bedford* 43–5 (ed. Grierson, 1, 197): 'In none but us, are such mixt engines found, / As hands of double office: For, the ground / We till with them; and them to heav'n wee raise.' The inference is that the *two-handed engine*, man, in his dual functions of labour and prayer, will terminate clerical corruption. H. R. Williamson (*N&Q* 3, 1956, 89) recalled, with no supporting image or argument, an interpretation given to him of the *engine* as the Statute of Provisors (1351, 1390), forbidding papal appointments of aliens to English benefices, and the Statute of Praemunire (1353, 1393), forbidding appeals from the king's courts to Rome. These statutes would be presumably taken as symbols of opposition to Rome. [C. A. Thompson (*SP* 59, 1962, 184–200) offered a long argument for 'a turret-clock automaton: a figure made in the image of a man, standing in the tower at the door of a church, ready with sword or axe to smite, once for all, the hour of eternal doom —and eternal salvation—and smite no more, for time will have a stop.' J. Auffret (*Anglia* 87, 1969, 34: see *Lyc* 111, under 1969) suggests 'the Club of Hercules, the engine that slays the Hydra of Sin on the walls of the Catacombs.' He finds support in the 'Pilot of the Galilean lake,' who is 'the Christian Charon.']

[(9) Kathleen M. Swaim's 'Retributive Justice in *Lycidas*: The Two-Handed Engine' (*Milton Studies II*, ed. J. D. Simmonds, University of Pittsburgh Press, 1970, 119–29) appeared too late to receive a logical place and number in this catalogue (cf. I. e. 1, 2, 3, 6, above) and must be added here. The author (who refers to many previous discussions) gives this summary of her own: 'In the image of *Lycidas* 130 Milton conflates "th'abhorred shears" of Atropos and St. Peter's two keys. *Two-handed* is ambiguous, held with two hands or composed of two portions. *Engine* covers both keys and shears, and perhaps also sheep-hook. The fateful shears invoke the ritual harvest of "the shearers feast"

(117). "Blind Fury" similarly conflates a Fury and Fate (Atropos). The ambiguity of image and phrasing in "two-handed engine" accommodates a combination of pagan and Christian instruments of final justice, as so much of *Lycidas'* thought and imagery interweaves humanistic and Christian material, especially pastoral, while building toward a new revelation of triumphant Christian truth. Structurally, the engine image concludes the second movement of *Lycidas* with emphasis on punishment imposed from above according to human deserts, as the first movement ends with emphasis on reward ("meed") imposed, and as the third ends with Grace that uplifts beyond human deserts.']

II. *A Culminating Example of Danger to the Church*

(1) G. McL. Harper (*TLS*, 16 June 1927, 424) took the *engine* as representing the ever present danger of an alliance between Spain and France, the two chief Roman Catholic powers, which it had been England's policy to prevent. This danger would be enhanced by any weakening of the English Church such as is implied in the preceding lines 128–9, which glance at conversions to Rome and connivance at growing Papist influence. (If this interpretation were acceptable on other grounds, it might be fortified by the reference in 161–2 to the guardian Michael looking toward Spain.)

(2) K. N. Colvile (*TLS*, 22 Nov. 1928, 909–10) saw in the *engine* the crowning example of ecclesiastical tyranny, as the Puritans declared it to be, the Court of High Commission, an ecclesiastical court which wielded the power of both spiritual and temporal swords. He quoted [not quite accurately] David Calderwood's *Altar of Damascus* (1621, [p. 32]), which condemns a court that 'may strike a man at one strike, in one sentence, for one and the selfe same fault, both with temporall and Ecclesiasticall censures and punishments'; and the expanded Latin version, *Altare Damascenum* (1623), which employed the image of the double sword. (For an answer to this letter which applies to all suggestions in II, see N. Smith at the end of the section.)

[(3) G. N. Shuster (*The English Ode*, 1940, 74) quotes Sylvester's *Funerall Elegie* 110–12 (*Lachrymae Lachrymarum*, 1613; *D.W.W.*, 1621, 1150, Grosart, 2, 278):

> With Two-hand-Sins of Profit and of Pleasure;
> And (th'odious Engin, which doth all include)
> Our many-pointed proud Ingratitude.

'This clearly suggests Milton's "two handed engine." When in addition one notes that Sylvester had introduced into the *Divine Weekes* [2. 3. 4. 1230 f.;

Grosart, 1, 209] a passage, of his own making, to denounce the Gunpowder Plot and warn the ministers of Christ to protect their "Lambs" against Rome, curiosity rises still higher. "Muzzle those [these] Sheep-clad bloudy Wolves of Rome," writes Sylvester; and I believe we may say that the meaning of the famous passage is clearly that the "engine" waiting to smite decisively is the Church of Rome, incarnation of profit and of pleasure.']

(4) W. J. Grace ('Notes on Robert Burton and John Milton,' *SP* 52, 1955, 578–91) sees the *engine* as standing in apposition to the *Woolf* (the Roman Catholic Church): besides those it devours (seduces) without public notice, it is ready to mount one more attack operating through its twin appeals, the *hope* of gain and the *fear* of consequences; but its days are numbered and its defeat imminent, so that it can smite but once and no more. This reading Grace supports from Burton's *Anatomy* (3. 4. 1. 2: 3, 325–6, 336). Burton declares that the Devil, the 'first mover of all superstition' 'with several engines...hath deceived the inhabitants of the earth'; and 'the means...the devil and his infernal ministers take, so to delude and disquiet the world with such idle ceremonies, false doctrines, superstitious fopperies, are...hope and fear, those two battering cannons and principal engines, with their objects, reward and punishment....'

(5) To Colvile (II. 2 above), Nowell Smith (*TLS*, 6 Dec. 1928, 965) offered objections which apply to all views under II: that this interpretation does violence to the syntax (by ignoring the adversative *But*); that it robs the lines of the 'threatening quality which Milton obviously intends' (cf. *stern bespake*, 112, and *dread voice*, 132); and that it contradicts Milton's own prefatory assertion of the impending ruin of the corrupted clergy, a prophecy uttered in the poem only in these lines. [Although Smith's objections seem quite conclusive, one might add two examples of the prevalent view of Romanist 'doubleness': 'But what say wee to Usurpers, Wolves, Tyrants, that call themselves Watch-men? that (*Bi-nominis, bi-linguis*) Double-named, double-tongued, double-sworded; and not single hearted, Demi-god of Rome, calls himselfe sometimes a Watch-man, sometimes a King, the Servant of servants, the King of Kings...' (Thomas Adams, *Workes*, 1629, 11); 'Popery is a double thing to deal with, and claims a twofold Power, Ecclesiastical, and Political, both usurpt, and the one supporting the other' (Milton, *TR*, 1673, *Works* 6, 171–2).]

Lycidas

III. *Editorial Comment*

To dispose first of II (interpretations of the *engine* as a culminating danger to the church), the three objections of N. Smith (II. 5) seem insurmountable, and a fourth would be the structural pattern of the poem. All the interpretations in the much larger group, I. a–e, assume that the *engine* (whatever the image involved) is an instrument of retribution, and almost all assume that it is directed to the punishment of the corrupt clergy and reform of the church— even if this entails something like its destruction (which was approximately what the Puritans effected but few foresaw in 1638). It must be reaffirmed, if only because it has been so consistently ignored, that the punctuation—which remains constant through 1638, 1645, 1673, that is, a colon after *spread* (127) and only a comma after *sed* (129) [not quite correct: in 1638 there was a period, in 1645 and 1673 a comma]—makes strongly against this second assumption, and suggests that lines 130–1 refer back to the depredations of the *Woolf* alone, and that the *engine* (whatever it may be) is to be used against that marauder only. If the reference back included the whole indictment of the unfaithful shepherds, so as to direct the *engine* against them, we should expect the punctuation to be reversed (and Milton was not careless about these lines, since he changed *nothing* to *little* (129) for 1638, and back to *nothing* for 1645, 1673). If these facts were given full (and exclusive) weight, the *engine* would have to be read as some weapon kept at the door of the fold for its defence against the *Woolf*—not as an instrument for punishing the shepherds, much less for battering down the door of the fold. The sheep-hook would plainly not do; for, while it might in an emergency be used for defence, it would not be provided for that purpose: the weapon must be a sword or something of the kind, and it must signify, not perhaps the statutes of Provisors and Praemunire (I. e. 8), but laws already on the statute-book against Roman Catholicism (the *Woolf*) and requiring only to be applied in their full rigour to be effective (*to smite once, and smite no more*).

But this interpretation, perfectly consonant with syntax and punctuation, encounters, in addition to its meagreness, two crippling obstacles: like those listed under II, it ignores Milton's prefatory note, and it almost as effectively destroys the parallel of St Peter's words with those of Phoebus (76–84) and the preparation for the final resolution (165–93). If one decides to ignore the punctuation, reduce the fear of Roman Catholicism (which was certainly widespread) to a minor role, and take *But* as adversative not to 128–9 only but to everything that has gone before (113–29), a large range of possibilities remains. As the basic image represented by the *engine*, the axe at the root of the

705

tree seems merely to result in a mixed metaphor, and the sword (however irritating it is to find commentators unable to distinguish *two-handed* from 'two-edged') seems to hold the field as a common biblical symbol of divine retribution: it works well for the unfaithful shepherds, less well for battering in the door. On any hypothesis, the demonstrative *that* causes difficulty. Does it demand some antecedent and, if so, what? The *Sheep-hook* (120)? But it is not an instrument for punishing. The *Keyes* (110)? But St Peter (as Le Comte observes, *SP* 49, 550) is carrying them, and not *that...engine* but 'this... engine' would be the appropriate phrase. Or does *that* suppose no antecedent but simply denote that the object is universally known? A claim instantly submerged in the flood of conjecture recorded above [but not necessarily so baffling in its own age].

To look before or after for a clue (back to the *Sheep-hook* or the *Keyes*, or on to Michael on guard with his sword but besought to look homeward) would seem to be sound in principle as recognizing Milton's constant attention to structural parallels and patterns, yet the result here is inconclusive. Certainly the reader would have no ground for immediately thinking of Michael on meeting the *engine*, and not much more for recalling it when he came to 'the guarded Mount.' Supporting image, phrase, or idea from later works may help to throw light on Milton's meaning here, but allowance must be made (as it sometimes is not) for rapidly changing conditions and for radical developments in Milton's thought: it is far from certain that what he clearly says in *PL* or *DocCh*, or even in *Ref*, would define his position in *Lycidas*. When we admit the difficulty of one kind or another that seems to confront every detailed explanation, and at the same time feel the potency of the lines, we can understand the retreat of Moody, Elton, Tuckwell, and others to the position that the vagueness is part of the potency; and yet, as Robins (I. e. 5) points out, the description is not deliberately and emphatically vague like that of Sin and Death in *PL* 2. It is an editor's duty to register these caveats; it is the reader's privilege to make his own choice [—or to offer a new one, if that is possible].

132–3 The lines that open the third movement, like those opening the second (85–8), admit a departure from the pastoral strain and deliberately restore it, with a parallel apostrophe. The nymph Arethusa, bathing in the river Alpheus, was pursued by the river god, and, that she might escape his embrace, was transformed by Diana into a stream, which, descending into the ground, rose again as a fountain in the far-off island of Ortygia, on the Sicilian coast (Ovid, *M.* 5. 572–641); cf. Virgil, *A.* 3. 694–6; Moschus 6. Since Alpheus is now united with Arethusa, to summon the one is to summon the other; thus the invocation means exactly the same as that of 85–6. But to reinforce it, Milton adds *Return Sicilian Muse*; cf. *Sicelides Musae* (Virgil, *E.* 4. 1), and the same words in Greek in the refrain of the *Lament for Bion*. Jerram suggests that the phrase here stands for pastoral poetry in general, with no differentiation of Greek and Roman as in 85–6. *The dread voice is past, | That shrunk thy streams* is contrasted with *That strain...was of a higher mood* (87): Phoebus' words introduced a higher hope, something beyond pagan pastoral; St Peter's carry, primarily, the terror of retribution. Todd (after Dunster) compared: 'At thy rebuke they ⟨the waters⟩ fled; at the voice of thy thunder they hasted away' (Ps. 104. 7).

D. C. Allen ('Milton's Alpheus,' *MLN* 71, 1956, 172–3)—conceiving of a somewhat different basic structure in *Lycidas*—notes that an 'allusion to Arethusa begins the St. Peter passage ⟨with of course Triton, Aeolus, and Camus, 88–107, intervening⟩ and an invitation to Alpheus practically concludes it by inaugurating the choral solution of the second problem [the state of religion and the church in England] posed by the young poet.' He further considers 'the possible anagogical implications of Milton's classical and figurative allusions,' noting that allegorical readings of the myth go back to Fulgentius: *Alpheus enim Grece quasi aletiasfos, id est veritatis lux, Arethusa vero quasi areteisa, id est nobilitas aequitatis. Ergo quid amare poterat veritas nisi aequitatem, quid lux nisi nobilitatem. Ideo et in mari ambulans non miscetur, quia lucida veritas omni malorum morum salsidine circumdata pollui aliqua commixtione non novit* (*Myth.* 3. 12, *Opera*, ed. Helm, 80).

Allen also refers to Sandys (*Ovid*, 1632, 199):

By this fable...the ancients expressed the divine affection of the soule, and excellency of vertue. For as the matter seeks after her forme, as her proper and only good, without which she is idle and uselesse; even so is vertue pursued by the Soule. Alpheus which signifies blots or imperfections, is therefore said to follow Arethusa, which is by interpretation Virtue. But Fulgentius more fully, that Alpheus is the light of Truth, and Arethusa the excellency of equity, and what can truth more affect then equity; or light then excellency? Alpheus runs unmixt through the sea: because illustrious truth, although invironed with vices, can never be disseasoned with their bitternesse, but unpolluted falls into the bosome of Arethusa, or noble integrity.

These passages are worth recording in illustration of the attitude toward classical myth, even though we may question their relevance to *Lyc*, where Milton has another use to which to put the story. [G. Williamson (*S.C.C.*, 143) remarks: 'It is interesting that Isaac Olivier [*Obsequies*, 16], who has most pastoral myth in common with Milton, uses this myth in the dual capacity of lover and conqueror of the sea, although he conflates Alpheus and Achelous.']

134–51 The poet imagines the body of Lycidas to have been recovered and summons the flowers to strew on his *Laureat Herse*. The pastoral convention of thus decking the dead body goes back to Bion's *Lament for Adonis* 75–6; this is an elegiac subdivision of the larger pastoral convention of bringing or summoning gifts of flowers for the beloved (Theocritus, 11. 45, 56–7; Virgil, *E.* 2. 45–50; Spenser, *S.C., April* 136–44). It is to be distinguished from the other convention of having the flowers, as a part of nature, mourn for the dead shepherd, which goes back to the *Lament for Bion* 3–7 and which Milton has already tentatively employed (39–49 and n.). The decking of the tomb is illustrated in Castiglione's *Alcon* 142–50 (significantly the empty tomb) and Marot's *Lamentation for Louise of Savoy* 225–40, while Spenser (*Lay of Clorinda* 67–72) introduces a new note by reserving the decking for apotheosis. Milton indeed allows the mourning of nature to colour his catalogue of funeral flowers at several points, 142, 144, and especially 147–50. Like his striking and elaborate use of another convention of pastoral elegy ('Where were ye Nymphs...?' 50–63), this is brought in only to be in effect repudiated (see 152–4 and n., and cf. 56–7 and n.). But on the catalogue of flowers he lavished the greatest care: for his painstaking revisions see 142–51 n. [W. G. Madsen (*From Shadowy Types to Truth*, 1968, 10–12) summarizes the very diverse reactions of half a dozen modern critics to this passage.]

134 *hither*: here where the poet is, and, specifically, to the *Laureat Herse*, which is not mentioned until 151 and which exists only in the poet's imagination.

135 *Bells*: descriptive of some of the flowers (cf. the rejected *buttons* of 47).

136 *use*: habitually resort (*OED* 22). Newton (reported by Todd) cited Spenser: 'where never foote did use' (*F.Q.* 6, proem 2). Verity, more appositely, quoted Sylvester: 'Climb night and day the double-topped Mount, / Where the Pierian learned Maidens use' (*Urania* 26, Grosart, 2, 4).

137 *shades*: 'tree-shaded places' (Wright); *OED* 9. Evidently a wooded valley is envisaged. *wanton*: here applied in its radical meaning of 'unrestrained' to the winds that blow where they list, and not in the sense of 'lustful' as in Shakespeare's 'wanton wind' (*Dream* 2. 1. 129): Verity. [Sandys ('Sources,' 244) cites Horace, *C.* 1. 26. 2–3, *protervis...ventis*.]

138 *lap*: a fold (whether of skin or garment) producing a hollow; hence by transference a hollow among hills (*OED* 5b). This is clearly the meaning here, with a reference back to *valleys low* (136), despite Verity's citation from Shakespeare ('frosts / Fall in the fresh lap of the crimson rose' (*Dream* 2. 1. 107–8), which is wholly inapposite, and the fact that *OED* gives no example before 1745. [Cf. 'the flourie lap / Of som irriguous Valley' (*PL* 4. 254–5).] The *swart Star* is Sirius (commonly called the Dog-star, as part of the constellation Canis); it rose in the hottest season of the year and was thought of as causing or bringing the heat. Cf. Virgil, *G.* 4. 425–6: *Sirius*... / *ardebat caelo*; *A.* 3. 141: *tum sterilis exurere Sirius agros* (cf. 10. 273–4); Horace, *C.* 3. 13. 9–10; Tibullus 1. 7. 21–2: noticed in part by Newton. Warton cited 'Free from [the fervour of] the Sirian star' (Beaumont and Fletcher, *Philaster* 5. 3. 30). The epithet *swart* (dark in colour, blackish: *OED* 1) is transferred, as Warton remarked, from the effect (the scorched vegetation) to the cause (Sirius). Keightley noted *solem* / *tam nigrum* (Horace, *S.* 1. 9. 72–3), but *nigrum* is here figurative, as indeed *swart* may be; it has been questioned whether Milton may not refer to the sun rather than Sirius.

The MS. substituted *faintly* for *sparely*, then restored the latter (*Facs.* 440). Warton suggested that *looks* here bears an astrological sense and compared 'the cross dire-looking Planet' (*Arc* 52) and: 'There's some ill planet reigns. / I must be patient till the heavens look / With an aspect more favourable' (Shakespeare, *W. Tale* 2. 1. 105–7). Though *OED* records no such meaning of *look*, such quotations strongly support the idea, and it seems readily explicable in relation to the astrological meaning of *aspect* (both as substantive and as now obsolete verb), the word being a derivative of Lat. *aspicere*, to look. There may be a further suggestion from the belief that the human eye could carry malign influence. An astrological overtone would be appropriate enough in a poem which deals with a real disaster seemingly inexplicable save as the result of malign influences (cf. 100–1); nor is it any objection that the general effect of the imagery here is not to call up the real world with its calamities but an Arcadian scene, for the point made is negative and by way of contrast: these influences are *not* here.

139 *Throw*: MS. (*Facs.* 440) *bring*, deleted, replaced by *throw*, partly, no doubt, to avoid a repetition of *Bring* at 142, but also perhaps to convey a new suggestion: the flowers in the list that begins at 142 are brought, but all the flowers of the valleys, thought of as eyes, are bidden to turn their gaze toward the *Laureat Herse* (*OED*: throw v.[1] 16; Spenser, *F.Q.* 3. 1. 16: 'Still as she fled, her eye she backward threw'), though of this one cannot be certain; it depends on the sense in which 141 is read (see n.). [One may not discern any suggestion of the flowers as gazing: *Throw...eyes* may seem to mean the same as *cast | Their Bells* and to refer only to their coming together.] *quaint*. Jerram explains as 'in its usual Miltonic sense of "curious" or "fantastic"' and compares *Nat* 194, *Arc* 47, *PL* 9. 35. But in its various uses to the end of the 17th century the precise sense of the word is (as *OED* notes) often uncertain (see notes on the lines cited by Jerram). Because of its ultimate derivation (Lat. *cognitum*) *quaint* often betokened knowledge, skill, ingenuity; from the intermediate Fr. *cointe* came the idea of adornment, elegance (*OED* 1–3 and 5). Even if Jerram is right as to the primary meaning, *quaint* here seems to be coloured by the idea of elegant adornment and perhaps to anticipate the modern meaning, 'unusual... attractive...old-fashioned prettiness or daintiness' (*OED* 8). Also, is *quaint* to be taken as adjectival, modifying *enameld eyes*, or as adverbial (*OED* 11B), or, which amounts to the same thing, as the first component in a coined compound *quaint-enameld* (ibid. c), the force being 'quaintly enamelled,' with the different possibilities of *quaint* still operative?

The word *enameld* likewise carries more than one suggestion: certainly of both smoothness and colour, as in examples collected by Jerram and Bell: 'O're the smooth enamel'd green' (*Arc* 84: see n.); 'Blossoms and Fruits... | Appeerd, with gay enameld colours mixt' (*PL* 4. 148–9); 'Th' enaml'd Bravery of the beauteous spring' (*Muses Elizium* 3. 6, Drayton, 3, 267); 'that sweet plain,...still enamelled with discoloured [i.e. variegated] flowers' (Peele, *David and Bethsabe* 1. 1. 35–6). The total effect is unmistakable: the flowers scattered over *the green terf* seem like eyes looking up from it, the whole having the appearance of something done in enamel. Among objects resembling an eye, and hence so named, is the centre of a flower (*OED* 10c, but its examples are late). [Eyes though, do not *suck the honied Showres*.]

140   *terf*: obsolete form of 'turf' (*OED*).   *honied*: Lat. *mellitus* (cf. Horace, *Ep.* 1. 10. 11). Peck (108) thought the word a coinage of Milton's, but Jerram cited examples from Shakespeare (*H. V* 1. 1. 50) and P. Fletcher (*Pisc. Ecl.* 3. 14). [Cf. *IlPen* 142, which Peck had in mind.]

141   *And purple...vernal flowres*. Like Lat. *purpureus*, the verb *purple* (empurple) connotes any bright colour from a dazzling white (Horace, *C.* 4. 1. 10) to a deep red (Virgil, *A.* 9. 349; cf. *PL* 7. 30 (Jerram). It is evidently possible to take the line as indicative and coordinate with 139: in the latter case *Throw... eyes* could not be interpreted as 'turn your gaze' (see 139 n.). [D.B. I do not understand the preceding sentence: at any rate it seems natural to take *purple* as imperative and not coordinate with 140, *That...showres*, but with 139, *Throw*

Lycidas

...*eyes.*] The majority, though not all, of the flowers to be mentioned are *vernal*; but those that are have a special significance, a secondary suggestion of resurrection or renewal—hence perhaps the calling of attention to them here.

142–51 The MS. has a first draft of these lines: the first (MS. 1) of twelve lines, unaltered, but the whole deleted (*Works* 1, 470; *Facs.* 434); the second (MS. 2) of ten lines, somewhat altered (ibid.). The original draft and subsequent changes deserve careful study [cf. Leishman, *Minor Poems*, 299–313]. All substantive variants are recorded below: lines, phrases, and words common to MS. 1 and MS. 2 are in ordinary type; those found in MS. 1 but discarded or changed, in italics and designated by the numeral (1); those found in MS. 2 only, in small capitals and designated by the numeral (2). Numbered footnotes are attached to eight of the lines.

Bring the rathe primrose that (1) *unwedded*[1] (2) FORSAKEN dies
(1) *colouring the pale cheeke of uninjoyd love*[2]
(1) *and that sad floure that strove*[3]
(1) *to write his owne woes on the vermeil graine*[4]
(1) *next adde Narcissus*[5] *yᵗ still weeps in vaine*

[1] Evidently revision was later, but the next line was already removed.

[2] This line, though discarded, puts beyond doubt the Shakespearian derivation of Milton's primrose: 'pale primeroses, / That die unmarried ere they can behold / Bright Phoebus in his strength (a malady / Most incident to maids)...' (*W. Tale* 4.4.122–5). Warton saw here (as in Shakespeare) a reference to the idea that the sun was in love with some sorts of flower, but could instance only the marigold: Drayton, 2, 523, 566 (*Egl.* 2. 58 and 9. 93–6) and Shakespeare, *Sonn.* 25; and the pansy (Drayton, *Egl.* 9, loc. cit.). Milton's revision removes any such specific suggestion and leaves the primrose to bloom modestly in the shade, forsaken (by the sun?) or perhaps (as Jerram suggests) merely unnoticed by any. [Hughes (1937) quotes *Prol* 1 (*Works* 12, 137–9).]

[3] The sad flower is the hyacinth, which occurs in several pastoral elegies (see below, and 106 n.). Besides the more familiar myth of Hyacinth and Apollo (106 n.), there was another (Ovid, *M.* 13. 394–8): that the flower sprang from the blood of Ajax when he took his own life, the marking (not made by a god but produced by the flower itself) now standing both for the words of woe and for the first two letters of his name. To this tale Milton apparently here refers. The two lines, unexceptionable in themselves, were presumably rejected in favour of the oblique allusion of 106.

[4] Normally *vermeil* means of a bright red colour (so defined and illustrated with this example in *OED* A; [cf. 'vermeil-tinctur'd lip,' *Comus* 751]); but, as with 'sanguine' (106), it is the colour of the blood rather than of the flower that Milton must be thinking of. The word *graine* meant dye, originally applied to scarlet dye (*OED* 10, 11; see *IlPen* 33 n.).

[5] *Narcissus* fell in love with his own image in a pool, wept because he could not embrace it, and pined away, leaving instead of his body the flower that bears his name (Ovid, *M.* 3. 402–510). The narcissus figures with the hyacinth in Castiglione's *Alcon* (see below). No doubt Milton cancelled the lines because the allusion seemed incongruous. The result of his

(2) THE TUFTED CROWTOE AND PALE GESSAMIN

(1) *the woodbine* (2) THE WHITE PINKE, and yᵉ pansie freakt wᵗʰ jet
    the glowing violet

(2) THE MUSKE ROSE AND THE GARISH COLUMBINE⁶ (deleted)
        WELL-ATTIR'D WOODBINE (substituted)

(1) *the cowslip* wan that (2) wᵗʰ COWSLIPS wan that (1) *hangs his*
        (2) HANG THE pensive head

and every (1) *bud* (2) FLOWER that (1) *sorrows liverie*
        (2) SAD ESCUTCHEON BEARES (deleted) IMBROIDRIE⁷
        weares (substituted)

let Daffadillies fill thire cups with teares

bid Amaranthus all his (1) beautie (2) BEAUTIES shed

(MS. 2 indicates reversal of order of last two lines and substitutes & for *let*
before *daffadillies*.⁸)

Milton's catalogue of flowers has many analogues and possible sources. We
have already noticed (134–51 n.) the place of such catalogues in the tradition of
the pastoral elegy, distinguishing there between two contexts, the mourning of
nature for the dead shepherd and the decking of the bier. This distinction we
may now ignore and consider first the flowers introduced in the pastoral elegy,
then in pastoral or quasi-pastoral poetry outside the elegy, italicizing whatever is found also in this passage in *Lycidas*. [Theocritus 1. 132–3 names
violets and narcissus.] In the *Lament for Bion* (5–7) *rose*, wind-flower, and
hyacinth occur; in Castiglione's *Alcon* (142–9), narcissus, *rose*, *hyacinth*, *violet*,
and *amaranth*, along with ivy, laurel, cassia, and cinnamon; in Marot's *Louise
of Savoy* (225–40), lily, rosemary, *rose*, marigold, crowfoot, coxcomb, lavender,
carnation, *hawthorn* (white and blue), and laurel, ivy, and olive; in Spenser's
Lay of Clorinda (70–2), lily, *rose*, *violet*. Other examples could be collected [and

---

removing this and the foregoing lines is (as Jerram said) to reduce the whole to 'A simple
enumeration of the flowers' in place of 'the learned description originally introduced,' and
flowers were added to the catalogue.

⁶ *columbine*: any of a number of flowering spring plants of the crowfoot family. Spenser had
the 'purple Cullambine' coupled with the 'Pinke' (*S.C.*, *April* 136). Milton deleted it to
make way for the displaced *woodbine*, and in any case *garish* needed to be removed as
destructive of the tone of the passage.

⁷ *sorrows liverie*: the garb of mourning. Jerram compares 'nights sad liverie' (P. Fletcher,
P.I. 8. 5); *escutcheon* is a shield with armorial bearings, here a funeral hatchment (*OED* 1, 2);
imbroidrie returns to the image of garb, but, suggesting the markings on the flower, is a less
palpable conceit (see 148 n.).

⁸ The effect of the changed order is to give less prominence to *Amaranthus* and hence to
whatever suggestion of immortality it may carry (see 149 n.).

species and names are not always certain]. Sir John Beaumont's elegy on Edward Stafford, quoted by Jerram, is interesting in assigning (as Milton does not) specific significance to the flowers thrown on the hearse (*Bosworth-field*, 1629, 169):

> Here fresh *Roses* lie,
> Whose ruddy blushes modest thoughts descry....
> The spotlesse Lillies shew his pure intent,
> The flaming Marigold his zeale present;
> The purple *Violets* his Noble minde....
> And last of all the *Hyacinths* we throw,
> In which are writ the letters of our woe.

[L. B. Marshall ('William Lathum, a Seventeenth-Century Poet,' *RES* 8, 1932, 37–43) described Lathum's volume of 1634, *Phyala Lachrymarum, or a Few Friendly Teares, shed over the dead Body of Mr Nathaniel Weld*. Marshall found in *Lycidas* 'few verbal reminiscences' of Lathum, and 'no passages of deep resemblance,' but thought it 'almost certain that Milton read the Elegy.' Milton may have done so, though the evidence is less than persuasive. Lathum's long floral catalogue includes some of Milton's flowers, such as the primrose, pink, and violet, along with many others. Perhaps our most judicious conclusion is that catalogues of flowers were a favoured elegiac device.]

Among catalogues outside the elegiac context the most relevant are those of Spenser (*S.C.*, *April* 60–3, 136–44) and Shakespeare (*W. Tale* 4. 4. 118–27). Spenser has *roses*, '*Daffadillies*,' '*Primroses* greene,' 'the sweete *Violet*'; 'the *Pincke* and...*Cullambine*,' *Cowslips*, the 'pretie *Pawnce*' (pansy), and various other flowers. In Shakespeare, Perdita lists 'some flowers o' th' spring' (113) that she wishes she had 'To strew him o'er and o'er' ('What, like a corse? / No,... / Not like a corse': 129–31). She names *daffodils*, *violets*, 'pale *primeroses*, / That die unmarried ere they can behold / Bright Phoebus in his strength,' 'bold oxlips and / The Crown imperial, lilies of all kinds, / The flow'r-de-luce being one.' Items from these passages were noted by Bowle and Warton. [H. H. Adams (*MLN* 65, 1950, 468–72) has argued that Milton's catalogue was a late interpolation, a presumably unconscious imitation of Shakespeare, and that he revised it in order to remove both any apparent plagiarism and the erotic associations of some flowers and to reinforce the funereal theme.] Other precedents have been cited: e.g. Ovid, *F.* 4. 435 f.; Quarles, *Emblemes* (1635), 5. 2. 4 (Grosart, 3, 90), where, along with the *violet*, lily, *pansy*, *columbine*, thyme, *daffadilly*, *pink*, eglantine, and *rose*, the *jessamine* makes its solitary appearance, but concealed under a false etymology (Jerram); Browne, *Brit. Past.* 2. 3. 351–84, cited by Masson but of little relevance; *Pans Anniversarie*

7-45 (*Ben Jonson* 7, 529-30), cited by Verity. W. L. Thompson (*N&Q* 197, 1952, 97-9), opposing Adams (above), claims this last as Milton's main source, since it names eight of his flowers.

Precisians have complained that Milton neither keeps his promise (141) in regard to vernal flowers nor confines himself to autumnal ones as suited to the season of King's death; but why should he, since the decking of the hearse is purely imaginary and so timeless? More impressive, but perhaps equally mistaken, is Ruskin's objection (*Modern Painters* 3. 2. 3, ed. Cook and Wedder-burn, 4, 255-6): Milton's passage exemplifies 'imagination...mixed and broken with fancy,' while Shakespeare's is pure imagination, which penetrates from outward appearance to inward meaning. Ruskin is here assuming his favourite theory, that imagination is always concerned with truth, and mere creativeness, which inevitably entails fiction, belongs solely to fancy. Even if Milton's lines, in their revised form, depend less for their effect on the observation of nature than Shakespeare's do (which may be doubted), Ruskin altogether ignores the difference in the two genres and their demands. His charge of fancifulness would have been more cogent if directed against the unrevised version.

[Daiches (see 39-40 n. above), dealing with pastoral imagery, remarks that Milton's catalogue 'includes English flowers not to be found in Theocritus or Virgil.' More interesting than classical precedents for a list 'is the choice of flowers and the way each is given an adjective or a descriptive phrase as flowers so often are in the classical pastoral even though the actual description may be original.']

142 *rathe*: early, especially of flowers and fruit that bloom or ripen early (*OED*: *a.*¹ 2b). Warton cited 'And made the rathe and timely Primrose grow' (E. B., *Palinode*, *England's Helicon*, 1, 14). [C. L. Wrenn ('Language,' 258) remarks that '*rathe* was a technical gardening-term applied to plants that ripened too quickly, which were sometimes described as *rathe-ripe*: and Milton had seen this hitherto essentially practical and prosaic word used' in E. B.'s poem; 'the difference in impression between the two uses is a measure of his achievement in the use of words.' Verity cited *rathe* in Spenser, *S.C.*, *July* 78 and *December* 98. In 1638 the line ended with a comma; the period of 1645 was not corrected in 1673 (*Facs.* 351, 188, 55).]

142 *forsaken*. MS. 1 had *unwedded* (see above, 142-51 n.).

143 *Crow-toe*. It seems impossible to be certain what flower Milton meant. In support of the hyacinth Verity cited Henry Lyte's translation of R. Dodoens,

A New Herball (ed. 1586, 234) and John Gerard's *Herball* (1597, index). But the names crow-toe, crowfoot, and crowflower were used of plants ranging from the hyacinth or wild hyacinth to the buttercup (*OED* on these names). Milton's cancelling of the lines on the hyacinth (if it was to avoid repetition) seems to rule out hyacinth here. *pale Gessamine*: the common or white jasmine.

144 *Pink*: the name (of obscure origin) given to various forms of dianthus (*OED*: A. I. I). In *Comus* 847–50 shepherds offer Sabrina wreaths of 'pancies, pinks, and gaudy Daffadils.' *freakt*: flecked or streaked capriciously: 'the word [in this sense] seems to have been formed by Milton' (*OED*). [C. E. H. and others had some notes on the flower and the phrase in *N&Q* 177 (1939), 98, 139, 175. J. F. Killeen (*N&Q* 9, 1962, 70) suggests that Milton coined the word on analogy with the past participle passive of Lat. *ludere*, used in the sense of 'adorned.'] *jeat*. MSS. 1 and 2 spell *jet*, which reveals, instead of obscuring, the rhyme with *violet* (*Facs.* 434).

145 *The glowing Violet*. [The correct comma of 1638 (*Facs.* 351) became a period in 1645 and was not corrected in 1673 (ibid. 188, 55).]

146 *Musk-rose*: so called from its smell; a late-blooming variety, *rosa autumnalis*, according to Lyte's *Herball* (760), cited by Verity. Cf. Bacon: 'In May and June come...roses of all kinds, except the musk, which comes later' (*Of Gardens*). *attir'd*. Verity noted that the word may refer to dress generally (attire) or the head-dress specifically (tire). *Woodbine*: a name for various climbing plants (*OED* 1), especially for the honeysuckle (ibid. 2), with which (as Verity noted) Lyte (454) and Gerard (743) and apparently Shakespeare (*Much* 3. 1. 8, 30) identify it. Roses are common in pastoral catalogues (above, 142–51 n.), but neither *Woodbine* nor *Musk-rose*; it is worth while, then, to compare: 'I know a bank where the wild thyme blows, / Where oxlips and the nodding *violet* grows; / Quite over-canopied with luscious *woodbine*, / With sweet *musk-roses*...' (Shakespeare, *Dream* 2. 1. 249–52: italics ours, as above).

147 *Cowslips wan...pensive head*. Verity contrasted 'The yellow Cowslip, and the pale Primrose' (*May* 4), but the contrast may be less marked than it appears: *wan* when used of colour seems to have meant pale or light, as in 'the wan and yellow colour of Golde' (John Maplet, *A Greene Forest*, 1567; repr. London, 1930, 15: cited in *OED* 4e), though there is a secondary suggestion from the stock phrase 'pale and wan' and from *pensive head*, which recalls 'the pale cast of thought.' Verity quoted 'hung downe his pensive head' (G. Fletcher, *C.T.* 1. 39).

148 *sad embroidery wears.* For revisions, see above, 142–51 n. The word *sad* refers primarily to colour, dark, subdued, or sober (*OED* 8), but implies the emotions associated with mourning (ibid. 5). The primary reference in *embroidery* is to the markings on the flowers (cf. 104–6 n., and 144), but Jerram recalls the idea of the flowers forming embroidery on a green field or other ground (cf. Chaucer, *C.T.*, *Prol.* 89–90), the sense also in *Comus* 232 and *PL* 4. 700–2, and perhaps carried as a secondary suggestion here; cf. 'A faire hearse curiouslie embrothered' (J. Dickenson, *Shepheardes Complaint*, 1596, quoted in *OED*: embroider 1).

149 *Amarantus* (Gr. 'unfading'). *Amaranthus* [so MS., 1638, 1645] is the name both of a genus of ornamental plants with coloured foliage, of which Love-lies-bleeding is one species (*OED* 2 cites Spenser, *F.Q.* 3. 6. 45: 'Sad Amaranthus, in whose purple gore / Me seemes I see Amintas wretched fate'), and of an imaginary flower, reputed never to fade (*OED* 1). Editorial comment has been sparse. Wright records both meanings briefly, expressing no preference. The second meaning—as Hughes (1937) implies—is supported by *PL* 3. 353–61: Amarant, before the Fall, grew in Eden by the Tree of Life, but thereafter was removed to heaven, where it blooms and shades the Fount of Life and is inwoven in the angels' crowns. There certainly it reflects 1 Pet. 1. 4, on the believer's heavenly inheritance 'that fadeth not away.' Taken in this sense, *Amarantus* would be a symbol of immortality. Todd quoted the list of flowers in Drummond's *Epitaph* (1, 83), which includes 'Th'immortall Amaranthus,' but there, despite the epithet, the primary sense is uncertain, as it is in *Lycidas*. The other flowers in Milton's list are all real and native to (or naturalized in) Great Britain. Nor is it easy to see how an immortal flower could *all his beauty shed*, in the sense of lose, cast off (*OED* 10b), though it might do so in the sense of give forth, pour out (ibid. 9c). Perhaps we should recognize both meanings, the primary one literal, with a secondary but potent suggestion—unique in this list—of immortality. This would be in harmony with the intermittent hints of Christian truths lurking beneath the surface of the pagan pastoral imagery. [D. C. Allen (*MLN* 72, 1957, 256–8), noting some of the ideas and data given above, suggests, with special reference to *PL* 3. 353–61, that Milton's conception was indebted to two authors he knew: Clement of Alexandria, *Paedagogus* 2. 8. 78 (Migne, *Pat. Gr.* 8, 485), who speaks of the crown of amaranthus awarded the righteous in heaven; and Claudian, *Laus Serenae* 1–10 (30: 2, 238), where amaranth is not named but other flowers are made immortal.]

150 *Daffadillies*: a common variant of daffodil (cf. Spenser, *S.C.*, *April* 60), itself ultimately a corruption of asphodel. In the process the flower seems to have lost whatever suggestion of immortality the field of asphodel (Homer, *Od.* 11. 539, 24. 13) may have carried, and to have become instead the type of the quickly fading bloom, as in Herrick's *To Daffadills*.

151 *To strew...Herse.* Jerram (on 142) cited: 'And strew'd with dainty flowers the lowly herse' (P. Fletcher, *P.I.* 9. 46); in that line *herse* clearly means bier (*OED*: hearse 5). Since the obsequies of Lycidas are purely imaginary, the precise meaning is less certain. Jerram quotes A. P. Stanley's *Historical Memorials of Westminster Abbey* (London, 1868, 341): '"the herse"' was 'a platform...decorated with black hangings, and containing a waxen effigy of the deceased person....Laudatory verses were attached to it...' (cf. *OED* 2c). Jerram also cites Henry King's elegy on Donne: 'Each quill can drop his tributary verse / And pin it, like the Hatchments, to the Hearse' (*Poems*, ed. Grierson, 1, 371). This is perhaps supported by *Laureat* (see below). Masson, followed by Verity, Hughes (1937), Wright, et al., defines *Herse* as a bier (a word applied variously but here presumably to the wooden stand on which the body was placed before burial, or perhaps carried to burial); and Masson and Hughes seem to regard the meaning as identical in *Lyc* 151 and *EpWin* 58 (but see n.). Jerram's explanation seems the more likely.   *Laureat* (Lat. *laureatus*, decked with laurel), by association with the poet's crown of laurel, signifies that the *Herse* is a poet's; it may refer obliquely to the custom of attaching memorial verses (see above), and that in turn might be thought to symbolize the collection of which *Lyc* was the last poem.   *Lycid.* Verity noted this contracted form in Spenser, *C.C.C.H.A.* 907, but actually the word there is *Lucid*—[for 'Lucida,' line 456].

152–62 [T. S. Eliot ('Note on the Verse of John Milton,' *Essays and Studies* 21, 1936; *On Poetry and Poets*, 1957, 164) quoted lines 156–62 and remarked that, 'for the single effect of grandeur of sound, there is nothing finer in poetry.' F. R. Leavis (*Revaluation*, ed. 1963, 55–6) quoted Donne's lines on the hill of Truth (*Satyre* 3. 79–84) and then *Lyc* 152–62, and said: 'The contrast is sharp; the use of the medium, the attitude towards it in both writer and reader, is as different as possible. Though the words are doing so much less work than in Donne, they seem to value themselves more highly—they seem, comparatively, to be occupied with valuing themselves rather than with doing anything.' So much for Milton's overwhelming picture, intensified by the volume of sound, of the frailty of mortal life, here symbolized by Lycidas' dead body tossed about in the sea.]

152-3 As Hanford noticed in his study of the pastoral elegy, the imagined decking of the empty hearse, *to interpose a little ease*, is reminiscent of the promised building and decking of the empty tomb, *nostri solatia luctus*, in Castiglione's *Alcon* (139-40). For Milton this indulgence is *frail thought* dallying with *false surmise*; it is *frail* because unable or unwilling to face the fact that the body, not decorously prepared for burial, is still the prey of the sea, with all that this implies of the hazards of life and the special horror of death by water. [In MS. (*Facs.* 440) *fraile* replaced *sad*; cf. 148.] *dally*: converse lightly; hence, play with a subject (*OED* 2b), but with ideas of trifling and delaying (ibid. 3, 4, 5). *surmise*: the act of imagining, or the image formed of, something unsupported by evidence (*OED* 4); the adjective *false* converts the unsupported to the purely fictitious. Milton's comment plainly parallels his earlier dismissal of another pastoral convention (after indulging it) in 56-7. [Cf. Sandys, *Ovid*, 1626, 147, 'false surmises' (*M.* 7. 824, *criminis...ficti*.] Warton noted that the semicolon after *surmise* in 1638 became a period in 1645, which he took to be a printer's error. The change does not destroy, though it possibly somewhat weakens, the contrast between the imagined scene and the reality described in 154-62. Its chief importance, as Warton saw, is for the syntax of 153-4: if *Whilst* introduces a clause dependent on *Let...dally*, *Look homeward* is an interjection; if, on the contrary, *Whilst* introduces a new sentence, *Look* is the main verb, necessary to complete it (see 163 n.). [Shawcross (*PBSA* 56, 1962, 322, n. 6) comments (in part): 'The punctuation—whether that of 1638 or that of 1645—requires an independent element to support the dependent clause beginning with "whilst" and ending with "hold" in line 162. Line 163, however, cannot be that element for the "thou" referred to in lines 154-60 is Lycidas, and the one entreated to "Look homeward..." is the Archangel Michael.' The MS. 'uses no punctuation here and capitalizes only "Ay", but it thus subordinates the dependent elements "whilst...hold" correctly to "Let our frail thoughts...surmise" and shows poignantly why the notion of a flower-bestrewn hearse is false. The interjection, which is an aside, is a pathetic introduction to the subsequent musing on the whereabouts of Lycidas' corpse.']

154-8 ['The false surmise is not only that there is no laureate hearse; it is also the assumption that absorption in a ritual, however ardent, can serve to protect one against the assault of reality. This is the third irresponsibility: the dalliance not with Amaryllis, or with the spoils of a desecrated office, but with that frail and precious sense of order out of which the poem has no choice but to advance.

The forces of chaos muster for their assault and Milton, in three daring revisions, makes clear not only his uncompromising sense of direction but the imaginative risks he knows he can negotiate. The "floods and sounding seas" become the "shoars and sounding seas" as if to destroy any residual sense of security and to suggest inexorably that, for those who ask ultimate questions, neither land nor ocean can provide a place of refuge. "Sad thoughts" become "frail thoughts," to stress the precariousness of the defense against chaos; and the "humming tide" becomes the "whelming tide," giving additional strength to the attacking forces. Even nature, which mourned Lycidas and lamented Orpheus, now seems committed to the "monstrous world" of the enemy.... What is at stake in the inner world of the poem is nothing less than that sense of order and design in reality without which no man can survive in this perilous flood.' (B. Rajan, *SP* 64, 1967, 59–60).]

154 *Ay me*. This parallels the same exclamation at 56 and recalls what preceded that line; it also, less obviously, parallels the *Alas* of 64, which heralds the return to harsh reality. Here, however, the Arcadian dream (which implies the sympathy of nature) and the harsh reality (which underscores nature's ruthless and apparently undirected menace) are compressed into a single paragraph. For *shores* MS. first had *floods*, which at first glance might seem more appropriate [but was virtually repeated in *sounding Seas*]. Jerram argued that *shores* includes beaches covered at high tide, visited by the body in its wanderings, though not cast up and left as in Virgil's *nunc me fluctus habet versantque in litore venti* (*A*. 6. 362, cited by Newton). To Verity the revised phrasing suggests the helpless body 'dashed from coast to coast, as though land and sea were leagued against it.' [Carey takes a similar view. Richardson (reported by Newton) cited Statius, *Theb*. 9. 358–9: *iacet ipse procul, qua mixta supremum / Ismenon primi mutant confinia ponti*.]

156 The *Hebrides*, exposed to Atlantic storms, mark almost the northern extremity of Britain, as Land's End (160) marks its southern extremity, the scene of King's drowning lying roughly midway between them.

157 *whelming*: MS. and 1638, *humming* (*Facs.* 440, 351; *Works* 1, 471). This word was changed to *whelming* in copies of the *Justa* in the Cambridge University Library [and the British Museum 'in the same handwriting as before' (i.e. 'probably but not certainly' in Milton's hand): *Facs.* 351, 348]. With the original reading Warton and Todd compared 'humming water must o'erwhelm thy corpse' (Shakespeare, *Per.* 3. 1. 64). T. H. Banks (*MLN* 62, 1947, 39–40), interpreting *humming* as murmuring (*OED* 1), suggested that Milton changed the phrase, from the same source (as Verity had noticed), because it was a weaker variation of *sounding Seas* (154). It seems just as likely that he saw its weakness in relation to *stormy Hebrides*.

158 *Visit'st the bottom of the monstrous world*: the sea-bottom, a world of monsters. Warton cited: *qui siccis oculis monstra natantia, | qui vidit mare turbidum....?* (Horace, *C.* 1. 3. 18–19); and *quae marmoreo fert monstra sub aequore pontus* (Virgil, *A.* 6. 729). Jerram remarks that Lat. *monstruosus* is never used in this sense; and *OED* 3b gives only one other example, Pope's *Odyssey* 4. 658, an obvious echo of *Lyc.* Milton himself affords another (noted by Verity), Comus' 'monstrous rout' (532); elsewhere he uses the word in its normal sense (*Comus* 604; *PL* 2. 625). [R. Tuve remarks that 'the irony of the intimate communication in *visit'st* is less grim than piteous' (*Images*, 96).]

159 *moist vows*: tearful prayers (Lat. *votum*). 'But there may be a quaint allusion to the *water*' (Warton). [The phrase may carry a remote echo of the Horatian ode (1. 5) that Milton translated: *me tabula sacer | votiva paries indicat uvida | suspendisse potenti | vestimenta maris deo.*]

160 *Sleep'st by the fable of Bellerus old.* Though the general meaning is plain, the phrasing is curious and perhaps unique. Jerram explains 'fabled abode of Bellerus' and cites *fabulae Manes* (Horace, *C.* 1. 4. 16) for *Manes fabulosi*, but this is not a real precedent; and *OED* reports no such use of *fable*. Verity interprets as 'fabled Bellerus' (which is a degree closer to Horace) and compares 'by them stood | Orcus and Ades, and the dreaded name | Of Demogorgon' (*PL* 2. 963–5), where the final phrase stands for the presence of the personage himself. Here, as in *Lyc*, the effect is to shroud in mystery, to suggest that little or nothing is known beyond the name or the fable; and even this would be an understatement, since Milton seems to have invented *Bellerus* from Bellerium, the Roman name for Land's End (Diod. Sic. 5. 21. 3). Warton inferred that Bellerus was to be taken for one of the giants who (as Milton recounts in *HistBr*, *Works* 10, 12–14) still inhabited the region when Brutus reached England; Cornwall was assigned to his follower Corineus, who liked to deal with giants (ibid. 14). The MS. first had *Corineus*, which was replaced by *Bellerus*. It is not certain of course that Milton thought of Bellerus as one of the giants Corineus fought against (since he invented the figure, he might conceivably have intended an ally or subordinate of Corineus), but, if he did, one can find reasons for his substituting the giant for the giant-killer: to suggest, not Cornwall in general, but Land's End, and to carry on the idea of menace, of *the monstrous world*. We may remember that Corineus slew another giant, Goëmagog, by throwing him 'headlong all shatter'd into the Sea,' which Milton reports as part of 'a grand Fable, though dignify'd by our best Poets' (ibid.).

161–2 The archangel Michael is seen (in vision) standing guard on the Mount that bears his name and looking out toward Spain, England's traditional enemy, represented here by the district of Namancos and the castle of Bayona. Warton collected most of the scanty evidence to be found concerning St Michael's Mount, in Mount Bay, not far from Land's End. It was anciently the site of a monastery, with a church dedicated to St Michael, and a fortified castle. Warton quoted from Richard Carew's *Survey of Cornwall* (1602, 154ᵛ) on a part of the rock 'called S. Michaels Chaire,' which he in turn explains by a reference in William of Worcester's *Itinerarium* (Cambridge, 1778, 102) to an apparition of St Michael there, though Carew says nothing of this. Warton further reports a tradition still alive in his day, to the effect that a vision of St Michael on this crag had appeared to some hermits, which occasioned the founding of the monastery, gave the place a reputation for sanctity, and made it the object of frequent pilgrimages. Finally, Warton quotes from Carew (155ᵛ) the 'old rhymes': 'Who knowes not Mighels mount and chaire, / The Pilgrims holy vaunt...?'; and adds that the monastery was a cell of one on Mont-Saint-Michel in Normandy, 'where was also a Vision of saint Michael.' Todd (3, 341) noted that Carew did not in fact describe the verses quoted as 'old rhymes,' and suspected that he wrote them himself. Later editors have not added anything substantial.

Camden refers briefly to the vision (*Britain*, 1610, 188):

This Rocke is of a good height and craggy....It is land and Iland twice a day....In the very top heereof within the Fortresse, there was a Chapell consecrated to S. Michael, the Arch-angel, where William Earle of Cornwall and Moriton...built a Cell for one or two monks; who avouched that S. Michael appeered in that mount: which apparition, or the like, the Italians challenge to their hill Garganus, and the Frenchmen likewise to their Michaels mount in Normandie.

We can only infer Milton's acquaintance with this passage in Camden or with the tradition Warton reported as still current, and with the 'old rhymes,' either in Carew's version or from some other source. Todd cited Spenser (*S.C.*, *July* 41–2): 'S. Michels mount who does not know, / That wardes the Westerne coste?'; but the Gloss on this, 'a promontorie in the West part of England,' suggests no knowledge of the specific tradition. Warton took *guarded Mount* to refer to the remains of the fortified castle, but Verity suggests, as the more likely meaning, 'protected by the presence of the angel,' which Milton evidently takes to be constant. Warton noted that *Mount* was the name by which this promontory was known, citing Daniel's *Panegyrike Congratulatorie* (st. 19: *Works*, ed. Grosart, 5 v., 1885–96, 1, 149); and he might have added Drayton, *Poly.* 1. 80–116. Finally, he cited Camden's notice of the fact that this region is the only part of England that looks directly toward Spain, and quoted: 'Then Cornwall creepeth out into the westerne Maine, / As (lying in her eye) shee poynted still at Spaine' (Drayton, *Poly.* 23. 75–6). We may add that Milton might have been led to look for a corresponding point in Spain, a tower, by a remark in Carew's *Survey* immediately preceding his description of the Mount in his account of Penwith Hundred (1602, 154; ed. F. E. Halliday, London, 1953, 231–2):

M. Camden observeth, that neere hereunto, stood the watch-towre, mencioned by Orosius, and oppositely placed to such another in Galitia.

Stepping over to the South sea, (for the distaunce is in comparison, but a step) S. Michaels mount looketh so aloft, as it brooketh no concurrent, for the highest place....The same is sundred from the mayne land, by a sandy playne, of a flight shoot in breadth, passable, at the ebbe, on foote; with boat, on the flood. Your arrivall on the farther side, is entertayned by an open greene, of some largenesse, which finishing where the hill beginneth, leaves you to the conduction of a winding and craggy path; and that at the top, delivereth you into a little plaine, occupied, for the greatest part, by a fort of the olde making....A little without the Castle, there is a bad seat in a craggy place, called S. Michaels Chaire, somewhat daungerous for accesse, and therefore holy for the adventure.

On *Namancos and Bayona's hold* Warton had nothing to say. Dunster (reported by Todd) took Namancos to be the ancient Numantia and identified Bayona with 'the French Bayonne' rather than the Spanish Bayona. The right explanation came from Todd, who in Mercator's *Atlas* (Amsterdam, 1623, 1636) found the two names in the map of Galicia: 'Namancos T' near the point of Cape Finisterre and the castle of Bayona making 'a very conspicuous figure.' This was clearly Milton's source. A. S. Cook ('Two Notes on Milton,' *MLR* 2, 1906–7, 124–8) explained Namancos as the name of a district, the 'T' standing for *Tierra* in Ojea's map of Galicia (published in Ortelius' *Theatrum Orbis Terrarum*, 1606) and copied therefrom by Mercator, along with the spelling *Namancos* for Nemancos, which thus found its way into *Lycidas*.

163 *Look homeward Angel now, and melt with ruth*. Against Thyer (who 'seems to suppose' the *Angel* to be Lycidas, adjured to look down from heaven), Warton argued cogently that the *Angel* is St Michael. (This entails returning to the punctuation, in 153, of 1638: see above, 152–3 n.) Michael is asked to turn his gaze away from Spain and *Look homeward*. The sudden shift in attention from Lycidas (which will in any case occur in 164) need not trouble us, since he is still present as the immediate object of the Angel's *ruth*, as of the dolphins' aid. Warton has been followed by most editors: Keightley, Masson (who, strangely, thought the line 'the worst in the poem, and the most like a "conceit"'), [Hales, Jerram (in his second edition), Bell], Browne, Rolfe, Verity (though with some concern regarding the syntax and the supposedly abrupt shift from Lycidas), [Trent, Elton], Wright, [Hanford, et al.]. Jerram [in his first edition of 1874] took the *Angel* as the spirit of Lycidas, citing instances in pastoral elegy of the invoking of the spirit of the departed, as in Bryskett's *Pastorall Aeglogue* (135 f.) and especially Sannazaro's *Pisc. E.* 1. 91–8 (which he described as 'Milton's original'). [In his second edition (1881) Jerram shifted to Warton's view (without changing the punctuation of 153).] His [earlier] interpretation was accepted by Hughes in 1937, but Hughes in 1957 reverted to Warton; and he added that St Michael is the patron of seafarers and so recognized in the church of Mont-Saint-Michel (hence his concern for the lost Lycidas). The idea of the *Angel* as Lycidas is upheld by Harrison (293), who cites Virgil, *E.* 5. 56–7, and the lines cited above in Sannazaro (translated in Harrison-Leon, 110). Thus almost all commentators agree that Michael is to look down from *the guarded Mount* at the body of Lycidas and *melt with ruth* (pity) at the sight. (L. H. Kendall, *N&Q* 198, 1953, 145, cites the collocation of *melt* and *ruth* in Chaucer, *Tr.* 1. 582, and Spenser, *F.Q.* 3. 7. 9.) It is tempting to find a secondary suggestion which would link the line with St Peter's attack on the clergy: that St Michael is to turn his attention away from the foreign threat to danger at home [so, e.g., M. C. Treip (above, 130–1 n., I. b. 5) and Saillens, *Milton*, 1964, 63]. This is suggested by Himes (*Enigmas*, 23), but as the primary meaning and as part of an elaborately symbolic reading of 154–63.

164 The *Angel* has been called to pity, not to act, so the *Dolphins* are summoned to convey Lycidas' body to land (*OED*: waft *v.*[1] 2; cf. Shakespeare, *2 H. VI* 4. 1. 114, cited by Verity). Verity quoted from *Obsequies* (15): 'Why did not some officious dolphine hie / To be his ship and pilot...?' Milton's line has been commonly referred to the most famous story of rescue by a dolphin, that of Arion (Herodotus 1. 24; Ovid, *F.* 2. 79–118; etc.): leaping into the sea to escape his pirate captors, and bearing his lyre with him, Arion so charmed a dolphin by his music that the fish carried him safe to shore, whence he returned to Corinth and his friend Periander. This would seem appropriate enough, since Arion was a poet like Lycidas, since the dolphin restored him (though living of course) to his friend, and since the whole incident may be read as an example of saving one's life through losing it. This is not, then, as it might at first appear, another relapse into *false surmise* like lines 50–63. But Richardson (reported by Newton and Jerram) saw a possible allusion to the story (for which he cited Pausanias) of a dolphin's conveying to shore the drowned body of the infant Melicertes (the story is summarized below, *Comus* 874 n.). The tale as told by Ovid (*M.* 4. 481–542; *F.* 6. 485–550) and Apollodorus (3. 4. 3) has no mention of a dolphin; nor does Virgil's allusion (*G.* 1. 436–7); the dolphin appears in Pausanias 1. 44. 7–8 and 2. 3. 5. Philostratus (*Imagines* 1. 19; see *Comus* 46–9 n.) brackets together the stories of Palaemon (Melicertes) and Arion, both being carried by dolphins. T. O. Mabbott (*Explic.* 5, 1946–7, Item 26) urges the inappropriateness of Arion, who, quite unlike Lycidas, was not a hapless youth but a lucky one, and the appropriateness of Melicertes, whose dead body was returned to shore by a dolphin and who became the guardian of the place where he perished and was indeed identified with the Roman god of harbours (Ovid, *F.* 6. 541–50; *Lyc* 183–5). Thus, if taken to allude to Melicertes, the reference to the dolphins, though lacking the implied allusion to Lycidas as poet, seems to fortify, and not conflict with, the structural pattern of the poem. May not Milton, in his own way, have coupled the two myths [cf. R. Tuve, *Images*, 96; E. C. Schweitzer, *Explic.* 28, 1969–70, Item 18], taking from each the suggestions appropriate to Lycidas: from that of Arion the dolphins' love of song (and thence of Lycidas as singer) and the return of the singer (though now but of his body) to the waiting friend, and from that of Palaemon the bearing of the dead body to land and the deifying of the spirit as the beneficent genius or god? [M. Lloyd (*MLN* 75, 1960, 107; *Essays in Criticism* 11, 1961, 397–8) suggests a less familiar myth, from Servius on Virgil, *A.* 3. 332: '...Phoebus Apollo himself in the guise of a dolphin rescued his drowning son Icadius, and carried him to Mount Parnassus. That must be seen as the mortal poet's translation to immortality, the source of poetry and the home of the divine Muses' (see Lloyd in III above, under 1961). Eunice B. Stebbins (*The Dolphin in the Literature and Art of Greece and Rome*, Menasha, 1929) gives, with full references to ancient sources, these three stories of Palaemon (63–5), Arion (66–70), and Icadius (77–80). Among analogous tales she includes (71–2) that of the poet Hesiod, whose murdered body was carried ashore by dolphins (Hesiod, L.C.L., 587–9). G. Sandys has similar tales of dolphins (*Ovid*, 1632, 221). Mrs Stebbins (81 f.) discusses the tradition 'that the dolphin is the conveyor of the living and of the dead in the legends and folk-tales which have sprung from the myth of Dionysus, and that Apollo is also a conveyor either as a god or in the form of a dolphin.' Cf. Eugenie Strong, *Apotheosis and After Life:...Certain Phases of Art and Religion in the Roman Empire* (New York: Dutton, n.d.), 215: 'The dolphins and marine monsters, another frequent [sepulchral] decoration, form a mystic escort of the dead to the Islands of the Blest, and at the same time carry with them an allusion to the purifying power of water and to the part assigned to the watery element in Mithraic and other cults.' Mrs Strong's book is cited by some critics of Yeats, e.g. F. A. C. Wilson, *W. B. Yeats and Tradition* (London, 1958), 220–1; Richard Ellmann, *The Identity of Yeats* (New York, 1954, 1964), 220, 284.]

165–85 form the conclusion of the third movement, and of the monody proper, in a pattern set by Virgil, *E.* 5. 56–80, and widely adopted by Christian elegists, namely, the apotheosis of the departed. Jerram contrasts the conclusion of the *Lament for Bion*, observes that 'Milton, as a Christian, claims for all pious souls' the glory Virgil reserved for an extraordinary hero, and compares Spenser, *November* (*S.C.*), Thomas Watson, *Meliboeus* (on the death of Walsingham), and Milton, *EpDam.* Verity adds two elegies on Sidney, Bryskett's *Mourning Muse of Thestylis* [in Spenser's *Poetical Works*, Oxford, 1912, 550–3] and Spenser's *Lay of Clorinda*. For fuller discussion see above, II: The Pastoral Elegy. Thyer (reported by Todd) remarked on the sudden transition at 165 and compared Spenser's *November* 163 f.

166 *your sorrow*: the object of your sorrow, as in the phrase 'my love'; Jerram notes analogies in Latin, e.g. Propertius 1. 14. 18: *illa etiam duris mentibus esse dolor.* With the triumphant *is not dead* Warton compared: 'Ah no: it is not dead, ne can it die, / But lives for aie, in blisfull Paradise' (Spenser, *Lay of Clorinda* 67–8). [The most obvious citation is the 'He is not here' of Matt. 28. 6, Mark 16. 6, and Luke 24. 6.]

167–73 Characteristically, since it is classical rather than Christian throughout, Castiglione's *Alcon* (57–64) contrasts the sun which sets to rise again with the dying who sink to rise no more (Harrison–Leon, 114):

> Adspice, decedens jam Sol declivis Olympo
> Occidit, et moriens accendit sidera coelo;
> Sed tamen occiduo cum laverit aequore currus,
> Idem iterum terras orienti luce reviset.
> Ast ubi nigra semel durae nos flumina mortis
> Lavere, et clausa est immitis janua regni;
> Nulla unquam ad Superos ducit via, lumina somnus
> Urget perpetuus, tenebrisque involvit amaris.

[The sinking and rising of the sun was a symbol of death and resurrection among the church fathers, e.g.: Jerome, *Commentarius in Ecclesiasten* (Migne, *Pat. Lat.* 23, 1015–16); Ambrose, *Hexaemeron* 4. 2. 7 (*Pat. Lat.* 14, 190); Athanasius, *Expositio in Psalmum 67. 34* (Migne, *Pat. Gr.* 27, 304D); Augustine, *Enarratio in Psalmum 103, Sermo 3. 21* (*Pat. Lat.* 37, 1374). These references are from Hugo Rahner, *Greek Myths and Christian Mystery*, tr. B.

Battershaw, London, 1963, 113–15; his reference for Jerome, *Pat. Lat.* 23, 1067, seems to be a mistake and is altered above.

G. Williamson (*S.C.C.*, 145) comments: 'Then the real consolation parallels the Alpheus myth, for he too sank "beneath the watry floore" before he rose in the fountain of Arethusa. And the resurrection theme passes through the natural level in the figure of the setting and rising sun to the supernatural level through the figure of Christ walking on the water. This passage is explicitly marked from the natural parallel, "So sinks the day-starre," to the supernatural parallel, "So Lycidas sunk low."' Williamson seems to be less carried away by these lines than most readers and critics are. Quoting 168–71, at which 'we may boggle,' he says (147): 'This again is not a style inspired by the pastoral classics, but rather by Sylvester or some minor Spenserian. It belongs with the "Sun in bed" passage of the *Nativity Ode*. It is a style which ended in Benlowes and Butler's "Character of a Small Poet."']

167 *floar*: floor, the extended level surface (*OED* 7). [Cf. above, 98 n.]

168 *the day-star*: the sun, 'this diurnall Starr' of *PL* 10. 1069, as most editors and *OED* 2 (following Newton) agree. Jerram, however, while admitting the force of this example and even citing classical instances of the sun's being called a star and of its dipping its rays in the waves, takes the *day-star* as Lucifer, the morning star (*OED*: day-star 1), which had set as Hesperus and now rises as Lucifer *mutato nomine* (Catullus 62. 35). His best evidence is the lines from Virgil that Milton seems to be recalling: *qualis ubi Oceani perfusus Lucifer unda,* / *...extulit os sacrum caelo tenebrasque resolvit* (*A.* 8. 589–91); and he adds: 'So fairest Phosphor the bright Morning starre, / But neewely washt in the greene element, / ...Shooting his flaming locks with deaw besprent, / Springs lively up into the orient' (G. Fletcher, *C.T.* 2. 12). Verity, granting that morning star is the commoner meaning, and adding Isa. 14. 12 (A.V. margin) and 2 Pet. 1. 19 to Jerram's examples, nevertheless takes *day-star* as the sun. He cites (after *OED*): 'While the bright day-star rides his glorious Round' (Sylvester, *D.W.W.* 2. 2. 2. 577, Grosart, 1, 143); and (after Keightley) the parallel image in W. Hall's poem in *Obsequies* (13):

> Thus doth the setting sunne his evening light
> Hide in the Ocean, when he makes it night;
> The world benighted knows not where he lies,
> Till with new beams from seas he seems to rise:
> So did thy light, fair soul, it self withdraw
> To no dark tombe by natures common law,
> But set in waves, when yet we thought it noon,
> And thence shall rise more glorious then the sunne.

[One might add a figurative use from Drayton's *Shep. Garl.* 2. 112–14 (1, 53): 'Oh cleerest day-starre... / Bright morning sunne.']

169 *anon*: literally, '*in one* (moment), immediately'; cf. Shakespeare, *1 H. IV* 2. 4, *passim* (Jerram); 'Gradually misused (like *presently...*) to express: Soon, in a short time' (*OED* 5). *repairs*: renews, restores to a sound condition by making good some loss (*OED*: *v.²* 3). Jerram compares *damna tamen celeres reparant caelestia lunae* (Horace, *C.* 4. 7. 13). [Cf. Milton, *El* 1. 54: *Quae possit senium vel reparare Jovis.*] Significantly, in the light of what follows, *repair* could also mean 'adorn, ornament' (*OED* 1).

170 *tricks*: dress, adorn (*OED* 11. 5 and *IlPen* 123); also, arrange, trim (*OED* 11. 6). It seems unlikely that Milton intends a further suggestion of the specialized meaning in heraldry, to draw the figures in a coat of arms (ibid. 111. 7; a meaning noted by Jerram), though it is just possible (see end of note). *spangled*: made to glitter as if adorned with spangles (*OED* 1 b). *Ore*: gold. The usual meaning was and is a mineral containing a workable deposit of some precious or useful metal (*OED* 1), but it might, especially in poetry, stand for the metal itself (*OED* 2, which cites no example before 1639). For ore as gold Jerram cites 'like some ore / Among a mineral of metals base, / Shows itself pure' (Shakespeare, *Ham.* 4. 1. 25–7), and 'the golden ore' (*Comus* 932). If (as seems certain from the context) the meaning here is gold, it is presumably by association with the heraldic *or* (Lat. *aurum*).

 [E. F. Daniels (*AN&Q* 6, 1967–8, 100–1) notes parallel rhythm uniting 'the two climactic moments of Christian revelation,' lines 81–2 and 170–1, the movement of 82 and 170 being exactly parallel.]

171 *forehead of the morning sky*: forefront (*OED* 3). Verity cited 'forehead of the morning' (Shakespeare, *Cor.* 2. 1. 57).

173 'A designation of our Saviour, by a miracle which bears an immediate reference to the subject of the poem' (Warton). The allusion to Matt. 14. 25–31 is intended to remind the reader of the whole incident, including the role of Peter, already associated with the Sea of Galilee (109 and n.), and carries more than one suggestion. The *dear might* is Christ's power to save those who have faith in him; thus Christ is contrasted with the St Peter of the poem, who can only threaten retribution, not himself save. Also, in the present context, Peter symbolizes in one aspect Lycidas, who is raised from the engulfing sea, and in another the mourner who has had to this point too 'little faith.' In the MS. a colon follows *waves*, in 1638 a semicolon (*Facs.* 442, 352). Since *Where* (174) depends on *high*, and introduces a complex of non-restrictive relative clauses, either of these punctuations is possible, as a comma would be also. The lack of punctuation in 1645 is clearly a printer's error which escaped detection and was repeated in 1673 [see, however, *Facs.* 188 n.].

174 'For the emphatic *other...other*, implying *better*, cf. *Com.* 611' (Verity). [Richardson (reported by Newton) compared Ariosto, *O.F.* 34. 72: *Altri fiumi, altri laghi, altre campagne | sono là su, che non son qui tra noi; | altri piani, altre valli, altre montagne...*] Todd cited: 'Other Hilles and Forrests, other sumptuous Towres, | Amaz'd thou find'st, excelling our poor Bowres' (Drummond, I, 80, *Teares* 171–2). Harrison [Harrison–Leon, 96, 156] cites: *Altri monti, altri piani, | Altri boschetti et rivi | Vedi nel cielo...* (Sannazaro, *Arcadia, Ecl.* 5. 14–16); and *Tu vois autres forests, tu vois autres rivages, | ...autres plus verds bocages, | Autres prez plus herbus, & ton troupeau tu pais | D'autres plus belles fleurs qui ne meurent jamais* (Ronsard, *Angelot* 61–4). *Groves* and *streams* of heaven are perhaps intended (as Verity suggests) to recall the Apocalypse: 'And he shewed me a pure river of water of life, clear as crystal, proceeding out of the throne of God and of the Lamb...and on either side of the river, was there the tree of life, which bare twelve manner of fruits, and yielded her fruit every month: and the leaves of the tree were for the healing of the nations'; 'For the Lamb...shall lead them unto living fountains of waters: and God shall wipe away all tears from their eyes' (Rev. 22. 1–2; 7. 17). Jerram takes *along* as 'beside, amidst, without the usual idea of *motion*'; but motion is implied in Rev. 7. 17 (above) and in Ps. 23. 2: 'he leadeth me beside the still waters.' Jerram cites 'So sweetly sung your Joy the Clouds along' (*Circum* 4), but there Milton alludes to the angels' singing at the Nativity, and it is plain, from *Nat* 93–116, that he did not think of them as motionless.

175 *Nectar.* Cf. Spenser, *S.C., November* 194–5: 'There lives shee with the blessed Gods in blisse, | There drincks she Nectar with Ambrosia mixt'; and the Gloss: 'Nectar and Ambrosia be feigned to be the drink and foode of the gods.' [Cf. Plato, *Phaedrus* 247E; Edgar Wind, *Pagan Mysteries in the Renaissance* (New Haven, 1958), 63.] In Eden 'the crisped Brooks, | ...With mazie error under pendant shades / Ran Nectar' (*PL* 4. 237–40); and, since Eden is a reflection of heaven, we may (with Verity) associate *Nectar* here with the *other streams* (174). For bathing in nectar, Jerram compares Homer, *Il.* 14. 170, 19. 38–9, and *Comus* 836–7 (see n.), and, for nectar as anointing the heads of the immortals, 'thou some goddess fled | Amongst us here below to hide thy nectar'd head' (*FInf* 48–9). [Newton cited Horace (*C.* 3. 4. 61–2): *qui rore puro Castaliae lavit | crines solutos*.] Although *Nectar* carries primarily a pagan suggestion, it does not seem to have evoked the same sort of objections as the Genius (183). We may observe that *Lycidas* has no such complete fusion of pagan and Christian imagery as there is in *EpDam* 215–19. *oozy*: 'because still moist with sea-slime' (Verity); see *Nat* 124 n. [T. H. Banks (above, 157 n.) suggests that Milton still has in mind the passage in *Pericles* (3. 1. 61): 'scarcely coffin'd, in the ooze.'] *Lock's*: *locks* in MS. and 1638 (*Facs.* 442, 352).

176 *And hears*: MS. *listening*, deleted, replaced by *& heares* (*Facs.* 442). *unexpressive*: inexpressible; cf. *Nat* 116 n. and *inenarrabile carmen* (*Patrem* 37). [Ruby Nemser (*MiltonN* 2, 1, 1968, 1–2) thinks that 'inexpressible,' the common editorial gloss, is weak in both sense and authority (*OED* cites only one early example, Shakespeare's 'unexpressive she,' *A.Y.L.* 3. 2. 10). Miss Nemser argues that Milton is thinking of celestial music as beyond mortal perception: she cites *Prol 2* (*Works* 12, 156–7), *Arc* 72–3, *SolMus* 3–8, *PL* 4. 680–4, and the reference in *Apol* (*Works* 3, 306) to 'those celestiall songs to others inapprehensible.' Thus Lycidas, now a spirit in heaven, '"hears" what man on earth cannot hear'; Miss Nemser cites the 'unexpressive notes' of *Nat* 116. This is an attractive idea, though one could wish for more support of 'inapprehensible' as a meaning of *unexpressive*.]

nuptial Song. On account of the adjective, Jerram takes this to refer to the song at the marriage of the Lamb (Rev. 19. 6–7), not to the song of 'the hundred and forty and four thousand' who 'were redeemed from among men, being the first-fruits unto God and to the Lamb' (Rev. 14. 1–4). But the second reference alone seems appropriate in the present context, though Lycidas merely hears and does not, like Damon (*EpDam* 215 f.), participate as one of the band. Much turns on the sense in which one takes *Saints* and *entertain* (178: see 178–80 n.). But perhaps Milton is remembering without much distinction both allusions in Revelation to joyful song. [Rev. 14. 1–4 may well have been in Milton's mind, but it does not explain *nuptial*; and Rev. 19. 6–9 has been cited by almost all editors who have a note on the line: Jerram (above), Bell, Elton, Trent, Rolfe, Verity, Moody, Hughes, Mack, Frye, Hanford, Le Comte, Patrides, M. Nicolson, Bush, I. G. MacCaffrey, Prince, Carey. Hales cites Rev. 22. 17.]

177 This line was not in the 1638 text. It was written in the margin of the Cambridge University copy [and of a copy in the British Museum; the word *meek* is lacking, probably because of badly worn margins (*Facs.* 352)].

178–80 Reasons can be found for taking *Saints* as 'the blessed dead in Heaven' (*OED* B. 1), as those who now *entertain* Lycidas, i.e. receive him into their company (ibid.: entertain 12). If this is the true meaning, the *Saints* might indeed signify those who were 'redeemed from the earth' and 'sung as it were a new song before the throne' (Rev. 14. 3; see 176 n.). This, the most obvious interpretation of *entertain*, would rule out the other possible meaning of *Saints*, namely, angels (*OED*: saint B. 3b, and Deut. 33. 2), apparently a rather rare meaning save in Milton, where it abounds. But if *entertain* means 'receive as a guest' (*OED* 13), 'angels' would be preferable. Jerram's view that there is no allusion here to the angelic orders must be dismissed in the light of *PL* 6. 47, 398, 742, 767, 801, 882, 7. 136, 10. 614, in all of which cases *Saints* means angels and in the last is coupled with a reference to the orders. That *Saints* stands for angels and that there is a reference to the angelic orders is suggested by the verb *move*, if, as seems almost certain, the meaning is to move in solemn dance (*OED* 17c). The dance accompanying the angelic song is described in *PL* 5. 618–27 as resembling that of the stellar bodies as 'they move / Thir Starry dance' (ibid. 3. 579 f.). [But does not Milton's phrase *all the Saints above* necessarily include both the blessed dead and the angels?]

181 Cf. Isa. 25. 8; Rev. 21. 4: 'And God shall wipe away all tears from their eyes; and there shall be no more death, neither sorrow, nor crying, neither shall there be any more pain....'; and Rev. 7. 17 (quoted above, 174 n.).

183–5 Thyer (reported by Todd) cited: *deus, deus ille... / sis bonus o felixque tuis* (Virgil, *E.* 5. 64–5). Browne added: *Aspice nos mitisque veni; tu numen aquarum / Semper eris, semper laetum piscantibus omen* (Sannazaro, *Pisc. E.* 1. 97–8). Among various meanings, the Roman term *Genius* designated the divinity or guardian spirit of a particular locality (*Nat* 186 and n.). Newton (reported by Jerram) suggested an allusion to the story of Melicertes–Palaemon as told by Ovid, *F.* 6. 541–50. [If, as seems probable, this story was glanced at in the reference to *Dolphins* (see 164 n.), there is a further appropriateness here, since Palaemon was identified by the Romans with Portunus or Portumnus, the god of harbours.] Jerram and Verity were very severe upon the introduction of the pagan and pastoral *Genius*, but modern critics have better understood the symbolic value of the allusion and the role and function of pastoral imagery in the total pattern. ['The "perilous flood" is this world of chance and change, and Lycidas has already commenced to exercise his beneficent influence on those who travel through it. Of that influence (as the Epilogue makes clear), the poet himself is the first recipient. For his poetic contemplation of Lycidas and his fate has wrought in him a transformation. With faith fortified and vision cleared, and with a mind at peace, he again takes up his lifework...' (Woodhouse, *The Poet and his Faith*, 1965, 102); cf. various critics in III above.]

184 *In thy large recompense*: ['the generous recompense made to you (by God)' (Prince).]

186–93 These lines, which (as critics observe) make a stanza of *ottava rima*, furnish a narrative epilogue. Though *Lyc* has no prologue (as there is, e.g., in Theocritus 1 and Virgil, *E.* 5), the epilogue balances 1–14, which are a sort of prelude to the monody proper. In answer to an absurd suggestion that these lines assert Milton's having written the poem in a single day, P. Michael (*TLS*, 12 July 1947, 351) noted that he is using a conventional pastoral ending: Theocritus 1 closes with farewell and the promise to sing a sweeter song another day; Virgil, *E.* 1, closes with a reference to lengthening shadows and the on-coming evening, and *E.* 2 likewise refers to the parting sun doubling the shadows; *E.* 6 refers to the star that bids the shepherds fold, and, with different embellishments, *E.* 10 dwells on the close of day. [The conclusion approximates the conventional ending of a *canzone*, the poet's address to his own poem (cf. Petrarch, *passim*, and Spenser's *Epithalamion*; and Prince, *Italian Element*, 72–3, and Prince's *Comus*, 147). Also, along with pastoral and formal decorum, these lines describe the peaceful regularity of nature and recall the parallel picture (23–36) of nature as it was before violent death struck one of the carefree pair. Thus the ending is the poet's quiet reassertion of order achieved after his inward struggles.]

186 *uncouth*. The various meanings attached to the word all developed from the initial sense, 'unknown.' *OED* (which is of little help here) remarks on the difficulty of fixing the precise shade of meaning in many seventeenth-century examples. In this case one alternative is 'unknown,' in reference to Milton's state in 1637, and especially in a poem signed only with initials. The word was glossed in J. Minsheu's *Guide to the tongues* (1617) as 'Incognitus, unknowen' (Verity), but was perhaps already somewhat archaic and 'Doric' in this sense (cf. Spenser, *S.C., September* 60 [and the first phrase of E. K.'s dedication, 'Uncouthe unkiste,' from Chaucer]). The second alternative is 'rustic, un-tutored,' in deference to the tradition of the shepherd singer. This seems the more probable meaning in the context of the shepherd's pipe and *Dorick lay*. [T. K. Sidney (*MLN* 23, 1908, 92), rejecting 'unknown,' explained as 'un-taught, unskilled,' citing *indocte* from Virgil, *E.* 3. 26 (lines 26–7 are quoted above in 124 n., since 124 probably echoed Virgil's line 27). Daiches (see 39–40 n., above) remarks that the very English word 'helps, as it were, to de-classicise' the learned singer. This effect—that Milton 'leaves us with a feeling of an English landscape'—is furthered by 'th'Okes and rills' and by the next line, which evokes 'a grey English dawn'—even though line 190 is Virgilian (190–1 n.).] *Okes and rills*: of the earthly setting, in contrast with heavenly groves and streams.

187 *While the still morn...Sandals gray*. The song, which began in the quiet dawn, continued until near the also quiet sunset (190–1); for the reason see 189. Milton applies the word *gray* to dawn in *PL* 7. 373 and *PR* 4. 426–7.

188 *tender*: either frail (*OED* A. I) in reference to the pipes themselves, or sensitive, responsive (ibid. IV). *stops*: Warton quoted *Hamlet* 3. 2. 366–76: 'Will you play upon this pipe?...Govern these ventages with your fingers and thumbs...Look you, these are the stops.' Cf. *Comus* 344 and n. *various*: taken by Jerram 'in allusion to the varied strains of the elegy (at *ll.* 76, 88, 113, 132, 165). This almost amounts to a recognition on the part of the poet of the irregularity of style, the mixture of different and even opposing themes, which some have censured as a defect.' *Quills*: pastoral pipes (*OED*: *sb.*¹ I c: 'homely shepheards quill,' Spenser, *S.C., June* 67; 'Who now shall teach to change my oaten quill / For trumpet 'larms...?' P. Fletcher, *P.I.* 11. 2). [Cf. Browne, *Brit. Past.* 2. 3. 1007–10: 'What music is there in a shepherd's quill / ... / If but a stop or two thereon we spy? / Music is best in her variety.']

189 *With eager thought*: in pointed contrast with the reluctant beginning (1–14). *Dorick lay*: pastoral song, so called because Theocritus and the other Greek pastoralists wrote in the Doric dialect. The Greek phrase 'Doric song' occurs in the *Lament for Bion* 12; and Bion is called (18) the Dorian Orpheus (Jerram, Verity). *OED*: A. I b makes Milton's phrase refer here to the expression, defined as 'not refined; rustic'; but this is misleading unless we remember that the rusticity of the pastoral tended to disappear in practice as the tradition developed (and is conspicuously absent in *Lycidas*), and remained only as a conventional association.

190–1 The stages of the declining day are noted. Jerram remarked upon Milton's improvement on Virgil's *maioresque cadunt altis de montibus umbrae* (*E.* 1. 83). The idea of 191 is a traditional commonplace. Todd compared L. Bryskett's *Pastorall Aeglogue* 159–60: 'The Sun (lo) hastned hath his face to steep / In western waves.' [Cf. Milton, *El* 5. 79–84.]

192 *twitch'd*: pulled up around his shoulders, as he prepared to turn homeward from the scene of his song. [Along with this primary sense, J. A. Wittreich (*Explic.* 26, 1967–8, Item 17) suggests that the word recalls 'the movement of the fingers across the strings of a musical instrument' (*OED* 1), an idea appropriate at the end of the song, and renews the image of 'forc'd fingers rude' at the beginning.]

Mantle blew. [Jerram took blue as 'the colour of a shepherd's dress' and rejected more fanciful explanations.] Verity argued that the shepherd's garb was traditionally gray (Spenser, *S.C.*, Gloss on *May* 5, 'gray coates'; and examples in Robert Greene), though he admitted the occurrence of blue (Spenser, *November*, below; and green in *May* 4), and referred to W. Browne's *Shepherd's Pipe* 2. 37–8: 'Two suits he hath, the one of blue, / The other home-spun grey.' This last item implies that both colours were traditional, blue for festal occasions. Spenser's 'The blew in black, the greene in gray is tinct' (*S.C., November* 107) would seem to mean that with Dido's death the shepherds' blue coats must be changed to black and the green (of their garlands) be abandoned for the gray of their more sober garb. Thus, if Milton remembered this line, gray would be associated with shepherds' mourning, blue with the happiness on which death had intruded; but, like Colin's, the song of *the uncouth Swain* carries him from mourning to rejoicing; hence the *Mantle blew* is appropriate. Another and not incompatible suggestion is that blue is the colour of hope: R. C. Fox (*Explic.* 9, 1950–1, Item 54) cites Spenser's Speranza 'clad in blew' (*F.Q.* 1. 10. 14) and P. Fletcher's Elpinus (Hope) 'clad in skie-like blue' (*P.I.* 9. 30), both examples of religious or heavenly hope, being the colour of the sky. [E. Saillens (*Milton*, 1964, 62) writes: 'If the mantle is blue, it is certainly not because "blew" rhymed with "pastures new". Milton was not that kind of writer. The Covenanters had adopted blue, whereas the Royalists' colour was red. The tribe of the predestinate applied to itself the order given by God to Moses (*Numbers* 15. 38–9): "Speak unto the children of Israel, and bid them that they make them fringes in the borders of their garments...and that they put upon the fringe of the borders a ribband of blue...that ye may look upon it and remember all the commandments of the Lord."' Students of the symbolism of colour do not seem to be very helpful here. D. C. Allen ('Symbolic Color in the Literature of the English Renaissance,' *PQ* 15, 1936, 81–92) says (84) that 'Blue was used regularly in the Middle Ages as a sign of truth, hope and fidelity in love; and it preserves this meaning for the most part in the six-teenth century.' He cites Spenser's Speranza (*F.Q.* 1. 10. 14) as symbolizing hope. But blue was 'more uniformly used as a token of truth or fidelity in love' (e.g. Spenser, *Epith.* 44). It 'became in actuality the color of infidelity' and of the professional fool. Arnold Whittick (*Symbols, Signs and their meaning*, London, 1960, 152, 193) says that blue was 'Sometimes regarded in Christianity as a symbol of heaven'; that the contemplative Cherubim are represented as blue;

and that the colour sometimes was a symbol of monarchy. 'In religious symbolism the colour green was sometimes regarded as symbolic of hope as it betokens the coming of spring.']

193 Warton, followed by later editors, compared: 'To morrow shall ye feast in pastures new' (P. Fletcher, *P.I.* 6. 77). [Mustard, in his edition of Mantuan's *Eclogues* (p. 52), cited the last line of *E.* 9: *Candide, coge pecus melioraque pascere quaere.* S. R. Watson cited both this and Fletcher in *N&Q* 180 (1941), 258. For the idea, not the image, and in keeping with his argument for Horace, *C.* 1. 7, as a source for *Lycidas*, B. Turlington (see end of II above) cites the last line of the ode: *cras ingens iterabimus aequor.*]

Verity could say in 1891, and repeat up through 1924, that 'It is usual to find here an allusion to Milton's tour in Italy'; this has been favoured by Jerram and others, and was accepted by Verity himself, though he noted that there is no hint of travel in Milton's letter to Diodati of [November?] 1637. Jerram and Verity were both sceptical of the notion that Milton was covertly indicating his separation from 'the Anglican and Court party.' Along with the idea of Italy, Verity welcomed a view reported to him, that the singer seeks new haunts because 'the old ones are associated with Lycidas, and so he cannot bear to feed his sheep there alone. . . .' [Some commentators have seen in the line a farewell to pastoral poetry. Recent critics seem in general to set the implications of the line on a higher and less specific level than their predecessors did, and, in various ways, to see the poet, who has come through conflict and vision to acceptance of the conditions of life, facing the future with a new access of illumination and strength. For W. G. Madsen, in accordance with his interpretation of *Lycidas* (above, III, under 1963), the line means a Christian view of life, which has replaced the pagan view of the 'uncouth Swain.']

DATE DUE

GAYLORD			PRINTED IN U.S.A.